PROCEEDINGS OF THE SECOND INTERNATIONAL CONFERENCE ON CREATIONISM
HELD JULY 30 - AUGUST 4, 1990

PITTSBURGH, PENNSYLVANIA
USA

VOLUME II

TECHNICAL SYMPOSIUM SESSIONS AND ADDITIONAL TOPICS

Edited by

Robert E. Walsh, Editor-in-Chief
Christopher L. Brooks

Sponsored By

CREATION SCIENCE FELLOWSHIP, INC.

362 ASHLAND AVE.
PITTSBURGH, PA. 15228

The Proceedings of the Second International Conference on Creationism,
Volumes I and II
Copyright 1990 by Creation Science Fellowship, Inc., Pittsburgh, PA

Library of Congress Catalog Card Number 90-081265

ISBN Cloth: 0-9617068-5-6

Printed in the U.S.A.

Library of Congress Cataloging in Publication Data

International Conference on Creationism (2nd: 1990: Pittsburgh, PA)
    Proceedings of the Second International Conference on Creationism:
Held July 29 - August 04, 1990, Pittsburgh, Pennsylvania, USA

"Sponsored by the Creation Science Fellowship, Inc."
Includes bibliographies.
Contents: Vol. I. General Sessions -- Vol. II. Technical Symposium Sessions and Additional Topics. / Edited by Robert E. Walsh, Christopher L. Brooks.

    1. Creationism--Congresses. I. Walsh, Robert E., 1954-, II. Brooks, Christopher L., III. Creation Science Fellowship, Inc. (Pittsburgh, PA, USA) V. Title.

ISBN 0-9617068-4-8 (Volume I : Cloth)
ISBN 0-9617068-5-6 (Volume II : Cloth)
ISBN 0-9617068-6-4 (Set - Vols. I & II : Cloth)

PREFACE

The Creation Science Fellowship, Inc. (CSF), present these Volumes as the written record of the Second International Conference on Creationism (ICC). This Volume contains the papers presented in the Technical Symposium Sessions and other additional topics.

The Technical Symposium presentations contain three sections. First, the paper itself. Secondly, comments and criticisms (called discussions) by individuals who where felt to be knowledgeable on the author's topic. These individuals were selected by the Technical Review Committee (TRC) of the ICC in the spirit of attempting to build upon and further the creation model. Lastly, the author's closure. Here the author was given the opportunity to respond to his discussors and offer additional information or data not included in his paper. The CSF believe this open forum of critique and response will aid creationists build a coherent model of earth and universal history.

The "additional topics" section includes Dr. Eidsmoe's paper which was not available at the time of the printing of Volume I and an update on research of the carbon dating of dinosaur bones by several researchers.

Regrettably what is not included are the Evening Addresses as well as the Poster Session Abstracts. These items unfortunately had to be excluded from the written Proceedings because of available space. However, these items as well as all of the presentations are available on audio and video cassette. One may write to the CSF address on the first page to obtain information about ICC materials. Moreover, at the Evening Sessions two awards were presented to two creationists of the past generation in recognition of their untiring efforts presenting the creation model of origins to the community at large. Dr. Henry M. Morris, was presented the **Byron C. Nelson Award** for his contribution to the initial systemization of the creation model, and Dr. Duane T. Gish was given the **Luther D. Sunderland Award** in recognition of his lifelong service presenting the evidence of creation on the "front lines".

Each paper in the Technical Symposium was judged by the Symposium participants. Criteria included, scientific merit, how the paper added to the knowledge of the creation model, did the paper offer a systemization of some aspect of the creation model?, etc. The paper receiving the "Best Technical Paper Award" was, "3-D Simulation of the Global Tectonic Changes Accompanying Noah's Flood", by Dr. John R. Baumgardner. Two other papers received honorable mention, "The Sea's Missing Salt: A Dilemma for Evolutionists", by Drs. Steven A. Austin & D. Russell Humphreys, and "Physical Mechanism for Reversals of the Earth's Magnetic Field", by Dr. D. Russell Humphreys. These authors were recognized at the final evening address for their outstanding contribution to the creation model of origins.

Within the Technical Symposium several important topics were addressed and are worthy of note. First, the ideas of Cavitation and Resonance were discussed in the Symposium. These ideas will no doubt be very important in describing the "goings-on" of the Deluge. Secondly, the further systemization of the Earth's Magnetic Field can not go unmentioned. The implications of greater field strength in the past along with a model for its apparent reversals are crucial to a proper model of creation. Finally, the topics of "Discontinuity Systematics" and "Baraminology" were introduced at this ICC. These "avant garde" topics promise an extremely powerful and objective methodology for classification, and could very well have a significant effect on the current understanding of systematics.

As creationists continue to develop a coherent model of earth and universal history, it will no doubt become apparent that nature contains an infinite amount of diversity, yet is a totally unified entity. This notion of diversity within unity is the classic idea of, *trinity*. Therefore, the universe can be thought of as, **"a** fundamental diversity within a fundamental unity".(1) In this light it can be stated that the nature of the universe must also reflect the Nature of its Creator. We can say then that the Nature of the Creator is, **"The** Fundamental Diversity within **The** Fundamental Unity". This means that the creation model of origins must include as a fundamental element, the notion of *trinity*. In touching upon this idea of diversity within unity, we offer the following words from Sir Isaac Newton's, *Principia*:

> ... This most beautiful system of the sun, planets, and comets, could only proceed from the Counsel and Dominion of an Intelligent and Powerful Being. And if the fixed stars are the centres of other like systems, these, being formed by the like Wise Counsel, must be all subject to the Dominion of One; especially since the light of the fixed stars is of the same nature with the light of the sun, and from every system light passes into all the other systems; and lest the systems of the fixed stars should, by their gravity, fall on each other, He hath placed those systems at immense distances from one another.
>
> This Being governs all things, not as the soul of the world, but as Lord over all; and on account of His dominion He is wont to be called, *Lord God*...(2)

The context of the above quotation is Sir Isaac addressing the idea of the complexity (our term, diversity) of the solar system, yet its perfect behavior (our term, unity). He concludes that the solar system must be the design of the Designer.

The ICC's continue to provide a forum for creation scientists to further the creation model of earth and universal history. Neither the CSF nor the authors themselves claim absolute truth about the ideas and models contained within. Rather, it is hoped that these Volumes will aid the creation community in systematizing their model of origins.

In the hope of free and open investigation, we offer these Volumes as the permanent record of the Second International Conference on Creationism, held July 29 - August 4, 1990.

To God be the Glory!

Robert E. Walsh
March 1991

REFERENCES:

1. From the Council of Calcedon

2. Newton, Sir Isaac, <u>Principia Mathematica</u>, University of California Press, Berkeley, CA, 94720, 1934, 1962, Vol. 2, Book 3, p. 544. (Motte's Translation, Revised by Cajori)

ACKNOWLEDGMENTS

The Board of Directors of the Creation Science Fellowship, Inc., (CSF) extends its thanks to all the people who made the Second International Conference on Creationism such a successful Conference of creation scientists. There is not enough space to thank everyone individually for the work that went into the Conference itself and the review and preparation of this technical volume. However, special thanks have been earned by Robert Walsh, Chairman of the Technical Review Committee, for his hours -and hours- of work in the preparation and final review of these proceedings.

The Conference itself could not have happened without the work of our ICC Coordinator, Christopher Brooks as well as the support of Russell Bixler of Cornerstone Television and his clerical personnel, especially Ruth Coles for her administrative skills. The CSF Board also thanks the ICC Executive Committee for their oversight and untiring assistance in making the Conference a success that committee included: Dennis Blackburn, Christopher Brooks (Coordinator), David Doty, Henry Jackson, Anthony Piccirilli, and Robert Walsh. These committee members attended to a myriad of tasks both small and great in order for this landmark, week long Conference to occur.

The task of reviewing, editing, and refining the technical track papers was shared by myself and the very able fellow members of the Technical Review Committee: Richard Crowell, Robert Harsh, Stephen Rodabaugh, Donald Schell, William Stillman, and Robert Walsh (Chairman).

Dennis E. Wert, Chairman
Creation Science Fellowship, Inc.
Pittsburgh, Pennsylvania
April 1991

TABLE OF CONTENTS

Section 2

Technical Symposium

Sessions

RADIOCARBON, DENDROCHRONOLOGY, AND THE DATE OF THE FLOOD

Gerald E. Aardsma, Ph.D.[1]
Institute for Creation Research
San Diego, California

ABSTRACT

Radiocarbon and tree-ring data are evaluated in light of current creationist understanding of the impact of the Flood on global geophysical systems to deduce a most probable date for the Flood. A date within a few thousand years of 12,000 B.C. is found. This date is tentatively accepted, and a creationist model for the increase in global ^{14}C specific activity following the Flood is derived using it. The model readily explains the long-term past behavior of atmospheric ^{14}C recorded by approximately 9000 year continuous tree-ring sequences in Europe and America. This seems to provide strong support for the validity of the model (and, hence, the approximate date for the Flood upon which it is based) as well as the legitimacy of these long dendrochronologies. The model implies that conventional radiocarbon dates in excess of about 11,000 B.P. greatly exceed the true dates. It provides a rational basis for calibrating conventional ^{14}C dates, thus providing creationists with an objective and universal radiometric chronometer for determining the chronology of earth history from the Flood to the present.

INTRODUCTION

For purposes of scientific investigation, the Biblical account of earth history conveniently and naturally divides into two distinct periods. These are the pre-Flood and post-Flood worlds; the historical event which divides them is the Genesis Flood. These two periods are not equally amenable to scientific analysis. The pre-Flood world was brought into being by supernatural activity during the initial creation week. It was totally destroyed by the Flood so that the geophysical systems which were in operation during this period are nowhere preserved today. These two facts — the supernatural character of creation week, coupled with the paucity of empirical data from the pre-Flood period — conspire to render any effort to model pre-Flood geophysical processes and systems highly speculative at the present time. In contrast to this, the post-Flood world was brought about by the catastrophic processes accompanying the Flood and the natural consequences of that cataclysm. The resulting geophysical processes and systems are operative today, and extensive records of their past behavior have been left in sediments, tree growth-rings, ice cores, etc. Consequently, there is an abundance of data available for empirically based scientific investigation of this period. The overwhelmingly (though not exclusively) naturalistic character of the post-Flood period, coupled with the plethora of available data conspire to render it ideal for study and analysis using the usual methods of scientific investigation. Thus, it has seemed prudent to me to focus attention on the Flood itself and the post-Flood world in seeking to further develop the creationist model of the past.

There are two problems which must be solved before substantial progress can be made in the quantitative development of this most important portion of the model. The first and most obvious problem is that of ascertaining the *date* of the Flood. This date fixes the time scale within

---

[1]Though this work has been supported in part by the Institute for Creation Research, the opinions and interpretations which are expressed, together with the conclusions which are reached, are strictly those of the author alone and do not represent any officially endorsed ICR position.

1

which the geophysical aftermath of the Flood develops and post-Flood history unfolds. The second problem is the elucidation of a suitable, objective scientific chronometer. In the absence of an objective scientific chronometer, the scientific and archaeological data bearing on the past can be assembled in a nearly infinite number of permutations, greatly impeding discovery of the correct arrangement. Radiocarbon may provide a very nearly ideal tool for the solution of both of these problems.

About a dozen creation scientists (too many to be reviewed here) have grappled with various aspects of radiocarbon dating in the past. Several different models for the past global behavior of radiocarbon, displaying a wide range of quantitative rigor and geophysical plausibility, have been proposed by these researchers. The earliest work which I have been able to find was published in 1961 by Whitcomb and Morris in *The Genesis Flood* (1). This analysis was perspicuous and contained what still stands as an essentially correct analysis of the probable effect of the Flood on radiocarbon. It effectively predicted the imbalance between the global production and decay of ^{14}C, while being apparently unaware that Libby (2) had already observed this imbalance and that Cook (3) had been arguing for the geophysical reality of Libby's observations since 1956. It failed to consider the effect of the Flood on the active terrestrial reservoirs of stable carbon (a necessary consideration, since it is the *specific* activity of ^{14}C which is of interest for radiocarbon dating purposes, and this is the ^{14}C activity per unit weight of stable carbon in the sample being dated), so wrongly predicted that radiocarbon dates would appear uniformly too old beyond about 2000 B.C. (Dendrochronology has subsequently suggested that radiocarbon dates are uniformly too *young* from about 1000 B.C. to the maximum tree-ring range of about 7000 B.C. See Figure 1.) Subsequent mainstream creationist efforts directed toward understanding radiocarbon have attempted to build upon this fine foundation, though there has been surprisingly little progress. The impediment, in my opinion, has been the almost unanimous a priori commitment of creationist researchers working on this problem to an Ussher-like date for Creation and the Flood. The work described in this paper breaks with these earlier attempts in this regard.

DATING THE FLOOD

The date of the Flood should not be very difficult to determine scientifically. A cataclysm of the magnitude of the Flood would necessarily profoundly perturb most of the geophysical systems operative on the globe. These systems would then inevitably go through a period of transition to new steady state conditions following the Flood. A good example is the "ice age" which is generally perceived by creationists as being a transient artifact of these sorts of post-Flood transition phenomena (4). Some of these transitions would require thousands of years to reach steady state and should still be evident today, unless the date of the Flood is exceedingly remote. By determining the probable initial state of these geophysical systems immediately following the Flood as well as their current rate of change and distance from steady state, it should be possible to deduce the probable elapsed time from the Flood to the present. Several independent analyses of this sort should make the date of the Flood quite conspicuous. Two such analyses follow.

Date of the Flood Using Global ^{14}C Build Up

Of the possible geophysical systems with potential application to dating the Flood, the global radiocarbon system is probably the most elegant. The global inventory of ^{14}C is governed by the equation:

$$\frac{d^{14}C^g(t)}{dt} = \overline{Q}(t) - \lambda^{14}C^g(t) \qquad (1)$$

where $^{14}C^g$ is the total number of ^{14}C atoms in the active radiocarbon reservoirs (i.e. atmosphere, oceans, and biosphere), $\overline{Q}(t)$ is the rate of production of ^{14}C by cosmic rays in the atmosphere, and λ is the decay constant for ^{14}C (1.21×10^{-4} per year). Careful analysis of the function $\overline{Q}(t)$ (5) indicates that for the purpose of ascertaining the date of the Flood it can be reasonably approximated by the time independent quantity $\overline{Q}$, the value of which has been determined to be

$$\overline{Q} = (3.5 \pm 0.6) \times 10^{26} \ ^{14}C/\text{year} \qquad (2)$$

by modern-day measurement (6). Given this substitution for $\overline{Q}(t)$, equation 1 can be solved

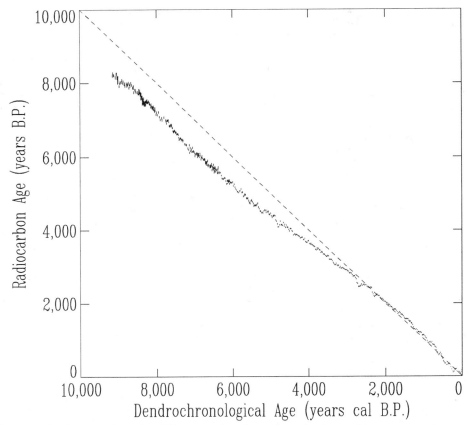

Figure 1: Dendrochronological calibration of radiocarbon. The dashed line corresponds to the prediction of the conventional steady state model.

uniquely once an initial condition is specified. Because of the apparent massive loss of carbon from the active global carbon reservoirs by burial in sediments at the time of the Flood (7), the global ^{14}C inventory in the atmosphere, oceans, and biosphere was probably reduced to near zero following the Flood. Hence, the appropriate initial condition is:

$$^{14}C^g(t_F) = 0 \qquad (3)$$

where t_F corresponds to the year following the Flood. The solution of equation 1 for constant ^{14}C production and the initial condition specified by equation 3 is

$$^{14}C^g(t) = \frac{\overline{Q}}{\lambda}[1 - exp(-\lambda(t - t_F))] \quad \text{for all } t > t_F. \qquad (4)$$

To use this equation to determine the elapsed time from the Flood, t_F, to the present, t_p, it is necessary to substitute t_p for t and rearrange as follows:

$$t_p - t_F = -\frac{1}{\lambda} ln(1 - \frac{\lambda^{14}C^g(t_p)}{\overline{Q}}). \qquad (5)$$

It only remains to determine the value of $^{14}C^g(t_p)$ to obtain the desired elapsed time. From Grey (8) this quantity can be determined to be:

$$^{14}C^g(t_p) = (2.4^{+0.20}_{-0.05}) \times 10^{30} \ ^{14}C \text{ atoms}. \qquad (6)$$

When the values for $\overline{Q}$ and $^{14}C^g(t_p)$ together with their associated error estimates given above are used in equation 5, an elapsed time between the Flood and the present of $14,000 \pm 7,000$ years is obtained. The large uncertainty in this quantity results principally from the uncertainty in the determination of $\overline{Q}$. The uncertainty in this parameter may not be as large as that which has been given by Lingenfelter and Ramaty (6) (which I have used); estimates of $\overline{Q}$ taken from a fairly comprehensive survey of the literature in the years between 1950 and 1980 yield a standard deviation of 0.26 (from seven determinations) compared to Lingenfelter's error estimate of 0.4. This reduces the uncertainty in the elapsed time from 7,000 to about 5,000 years. In any event, the most probable date for the Flood which is calculated by the build up of radiocarbon is 12,000 B.C.

Date of the Flood Using Dendrochronology

It is also possible to obtain an estimate of the date of the Flood from dendrochronology. This method is outstanding for its simplicity of application. In recent decades very long tree-ring chronologies have been constructed for use in calibrating the conventional steady state radiocarbon time scale which Libby (9) initially proposed. The most recent such calibration is shown in Figure 1. As can be seen, the dendrochronologies upon which this calibration is based (10) currently extend to about 7000 B.C. Since it is most unlikely that any trees survived the Flood in their place of growth, and since it seems quite impossible that any trees could do so without considerable indication of trauma in their growth-rings, the Flood seems to pre-date 7000 B.C. on the basis of the extent of these dendrochronologies alone.

Some creationists have been skeptical of dendrochronology in the past [see (11) for example]. I have scrutinized the methodology of dating using tree growth-rings over the course of a number of years and can no longer find any adequate scientific grounds for rejecting the results of this technology. Though it is not my purpose to attempt to answer all of the questions which might be raised about the tree-ring dating methodology here, the reader needs to be aware that considerable progress has been made in this field in recent decades so that many of the old objections are no longer valid. The hypothesis of multiple growth-rings per year as a significant source of error in these dendrochronologies currently has very substantial empirical evidence against it (12). In the initial phase of the application of dendrochronology to radiocarbon only one long tree-ring chronology existed. In recent years a second, independent, long chronology has been constructed (13). This dendrochronology uses an entirely different species of tree (oak as opposed to bristlecone pine) with entirely different growth characteristics. The two types of trees grew on different continents under different environmental conditions, and the dendrochronologies have been constructed by separate groups of researchers. Yet, the two long dendrochronologies agree in essential detail when compared via ^{14}C analysis of decade or bi-decade samples (10). This seems to exclude the possibility of significant error in these dendrochronologies.

Researchers continue to extend these dendrochronologies and are "cautiously optimistic" that they may eventually reach beyond 8,000 B.C. (14). The maximum extent of these dendrochronologies is not expected to coincide with the termination of the Flood, however, but with the termination of extensive glaciation of the regions from which the living and dead trees which comprise these dendrochronologies have been obtained (15). Oard (4) has proposed that the ice age was a post-Flood phenomenon driven by the cooling of the oceans following the Flood. Using global heat balance considerations he concluded that it is not inconceivable that the post-Flood ice age might have transpired in as little as 600 years. I am not aware of any geophysical argument which shows that the post-Flood ice age *must* have been limited to this brief period of time, however. It seems to me from other geophysical considerations, such as the time required to remove excess heat from the oceans, that the post-Flood ice age may have lasted one to two millennia. Such considerations lead to an estimated date for the Flood within a few thousand years of 10,000 B.C., and seem to exclude dates more recent than about 8000 B.C.

The date of the Flood which is implied by the extent of the long dendrochronologies is thus found to be concordant — within the current limits of uncertainty — with that which is determined from ^{14}C build up. I will tentatively adopt the 12,000 B.C. date for the following analysis. The reader should bear in mind, however, that other dates within as much as about four thousand years of 12,000 B.C. would still be consistent with the analysis to this point.

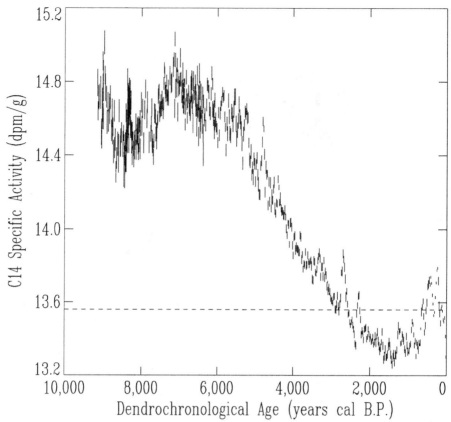

Figure 2: Atmospheric specific activity of radiocarbon (in units of ^{14}C disintegrations per minute per gram of stable carbon) versus time. The dashed line corresponds to the constant initial radiocarbon specific activity assumed by the conventional steady state model.

A CREATIONIST MODEL FOR PAST GLOBAL ^{14}C SPECIFIC ACTIVITY

The principal goal of my radiocarbon research has been to determine how the Flood affected radiocarbon, for the purpose of constructing a reasonably accurate quantitative model for the behavior of terrestrial ^{14}C inventories following the Flood. A knowledge of this behavior is necessary to correct conventional radiocarbon dates and thereby render radiocarbon dating of service to creationists. Detailed analysis of this problem (5) results in the conceptually very simple, analytic, two parameter model for the global behavior of the specific activity of ^{14}C from the Flood to the present given below.

$$\frac{\lambda^{14}C^g(t)}{C} = \frac{\overline{Q}[1 - exp(-\lambda(t - t_F))]}{C^g(t_F) + \alpha \times (t - t_F)} \quad \text{for all } t > t_F. \tag{7}$$

The numerator on either side of this equation is simply the global decay rate of ^{14}C in the active radiocarbon reservoirs at time t. It derives directly from equation 4. The denominator is the global *stable* carbon inventory in the active radiocarbon reservoirs following the Flood. The actual behavior of the global stable carbon inventory in the post-Flood period has never previously been determined that I am aware of, and does not appear to be derivable from independent geophysical considerations. Thus, it was necessary to determine this behavior from the model itself in the usual trial and error fashion. Accordingly, I chose a linear equation

5

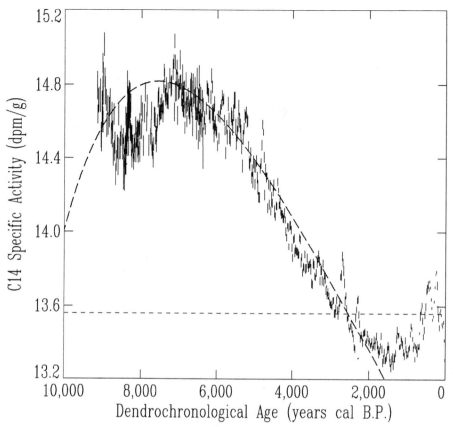

Figure 3: Demonstration of the match between the tree-ring data and our simple transition model. The heavy dashed line is the result of the transition model with $C^g(t_F) = 8.25 \times 10^{18}$ grams and $\alpha = 2.49 \times 10^{15}$ grams per year. The horizontal dashed line is the result of the conventional steady state model.

---

to describe its behavior since this is the simplest function consistent with the knowledge that it is most unlikely that this inventory came out already in steady state following the Flood. This gave rise to the two parameters of the model which are the initial quantity of stable carbon remaining in the active reservoirs following the Flood, $C^g(t_F)$, and the constant rate at which stable carbon atoms are assumed to have been added to or lost from these reservoirs, α.

The Model Confirmed

It is possible to use the radiocarbon calibration data shown in Figure 1 to obtain a record of the atmospheric specific activity of radiocarbon in the past as shown in Figure 2. Since radiocarbon mixes fairly rapidly between the various active carbon reservoirs, these data should provide a very good approximation to the average global specific activity of ^{14}C in the past. The model derived above (equation 7) should show at least some similarity to the actual long-term behavior of the global specific activity of ^{14}C shown in Figure 2 if it is correct. I have found it impossible to apply this model successfully to these data when constrained by the assumption of an Ussher-like date for the Flood. In sharp contrast to this, I found immediate and substantial progress resulted when the date of the Flood deduced above was tentatively adopted.

When I fit the model to the tree-ring data using standard non-linear least squares techniques and assuming a 12,000 B.C. date for the Flood the remarkably good fit shown in Figure 3 was obtained. The ability of this creationist model to fit these data so closely is especially significant since no adequate explanation of these data has, so far, been found within the conventional non-Flood view of the past (16).

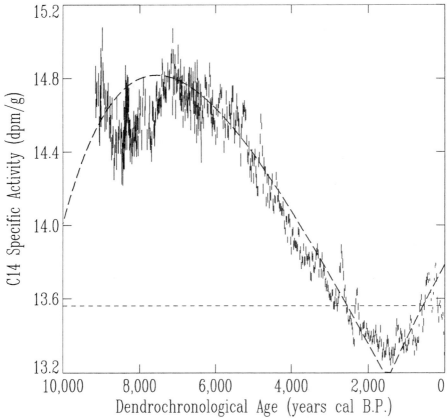

Figure 4: Demonstration of the match between the tree-ring data and our simple transition model when saturation of the oceans with respect to calcium carbonate is allowed for.

The values of the two parameters obtained from the least squares analysis indicate that stable carbon was being added fairly rapidly to the active reservoirs for many millennia following the Flood. This implies a large net uptake of $CaCO_3$ by the oceans from carbonate Flood sediments on the sea floor following the Flood. Modern measurements of $CaCO_3$ concentrations in the oceans (17) show them to be in steady state at present. This implies that the constant rate of uptake of $CaCO_3$ by the oceans following the Flood which the model implies must have ceased at some point in the past. This prediction is also confirmed by the model, which begins to diverge significantly from the tree-ring data at about 1500 years ago suggesting that this was when steady state was achieved. When the model was upgraded to take these additional data and insights into account (by the simple expedient of holding the stable carbon inventory constant from about A.D. 500 to the present time), harmony between the model and the tree-ring data was obtained for the past 1500 years as well (see Figure 4).

The prediction that the dissolved carbonate in the oceans may have increased rapidly following

7

the Flood, only achieving steady state about 1500 years ago is novel. It has important implications for the pH of the oceans and CO_2 concentration in the atmosphere which remain to be fully explored.

CORRECTING CONVENTIONAL RADIOCARBON DATES

These results indicate that radiocarbon can be used by creationists as an objective scientific chronometer suitable for determining the chronology of earth history from the Flood to the present. To do this it is necessary to correct conventional radiocarbon dates, which are derived without proper regard for the impact of the Flood. Figure 5 provides a convenient graph for this purpose. Since the date of the Flood is still uncertain within a few thousand years,

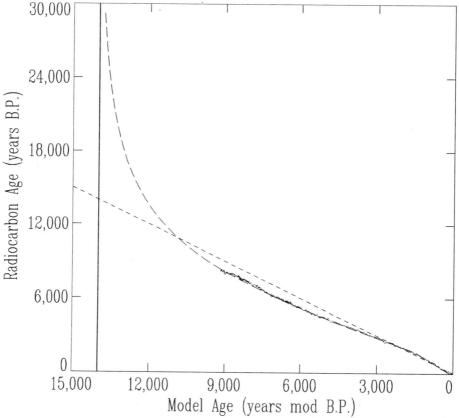

Figure 5: Curve for converting between conventional radiocarbon dates and dates predicted by the transition model (long dashes). The heavy vertical line marks the date for the Flood (14,000 years ago) which was used in constructing the model. The straight line drawn with short dashes is the prediction of the conventional steady state model. The tree-ring calibration data is also shown.

an absolute dating error near this magnitude will necessarily apply to dates approaching that of the Flood. This does not detract significantly from radiocarbon's usefulness as an objective chronometer in this remote period as relative dates should still be correct. It is anticipated that the date of the Flood will be refined considerably in the near future from independent considerations. If so, the absolute dating error for artifacts which derive from the first few millennia following the Flood may be reduced from several thousand to several hundred years.

It is clear from Figure 5 that conventional ^{14}C dates are much too old for samples derived from the early millennia following the Flood. This helps explain the inordinate duration of the Pleistocene which the conventional geologic time scale exhibits (18).

CONCLUSIONS

In summary, four important conclusions result from this work:

1. The date of the Flood is indicated to be within a few thousand years of 12,000 B.C.

2. The integrity and validity of the long dendrochronologies used to calibrate conventional radiocarbon dates is affirmed by their ability to be explained within a Flood framework.

3. The concentration of dissolved carbonate in the oceans may have increased rapidly following the Flood, not achieving steady state until about 1500 years ago.

4. Radiocarbon can be used by creationists to date historical and archaeological artifacts by correcting conventional published dates using Figure 5.

REFERENCES

1. Whitcomb, J.C., and Morris, H.M., THE GENESIS FLOOD, Presbyterian and Reformed Publishing, Philadelphia, 1961, 374-377.

2. Libby, W.F., RADIOCARBON DATING, The University of Chicago Press, Chicago, second edition, 1955, 7.

3. Cook, M.A., PREHISTORY AND EARTH MODELS, Max Parrish, London, 1966, 1-10.

4. Oard, M.J., "An Ice Age Within the Biblical Time Frame", in PROCEEDINGS OF THE FIRST INTERNATIONAL CONFERENCE ON CREATIONISM, R.E. Walsh, C.L. Brooks, and R.S. Crowell, Ed., Vol. II, Creation Science Fellowship, Pittsburgh, 1986, 157-163.

5. Aardsma, G.E., RADIOCARBON AND THE GENESIS FLOOD, ICR Technical Monograph Series, (in press), 1990.

6. Lingenfelter, R.E. and Ramaty, R., "Astrophysical and Geophysical Variations in C14 Production", in RADIOCARBON VARIATIONS AND ABSOLUTE CHRONOLOGY: PROCEEDINGS OF THE TWELFTH NOBEL SYMPOSIUM, I.U. Olsson, Ed., Wiley Interscience Division, New York, 1970, 518.

7. Brown, R.H., "Radiometric Dating from the Perspective of Biblical Chronology", in PROCEEDINGS OF THE FIRST INTERNATIONAL CONFERENCE ON CREATIONISM, R.E. Walsh, C.L. Brooks, and R.S. Crowell, Ed., Vol. II, Creation Science Fellowship, Pittsburgh, 1986, 46-48, 1986.

8. Grey, D.C., FLUCTUATIONS OF ATMOSPHERIC RADIOCARBON, Ph.D. Thesis, University of Arizona, 1972, 60.

9. Libby, W.F., RADIOCARBON DATING, The University of Chicago Press, Chicago, second edition, 1955, 1-33.

10. Stuiver, M. and Kra, R.S. (editors), "12th International Radiocarbon Conference: Calibration Issue", RADIOCARBON, Vol. 28, No. 2B, 1986.

11. Sorensen, H.C., "Bristlecone Pines and Tree-ring Dating: A Critique", CREATION RESEARCH SOCIETY QUARTERLY, Vol. 13, No. 1, 1976, 5.

12. LaMarche, V.C. Jr. and Harlan, T.P., "Accuracy of Tree Ring Dating of Bristlecone Pine for Calibration of the Radiocarbon Time Scale", JOURNAL OF GEOPHYSICAL RESEARCH, Vol. 78, No. 36, 1973, 8849-8858.

13. Pilcher, J.R., "Radiocarbon Calibration and Dendrochronology — An Introduction", in ARCHAEOLOGY DENDROCHRONOLOGY AND THE RADIOCARBON CALIBRATION CURVE, B.S. Ottaway, Ed., 1983, 5-14.

14.   Ferguson, C.W. and Graybill, D.A., "Dendrochronology of Bristlecone Pine: a Progress Report", RADIOCARBON, Vol. 25, No. 2, 1983, 287.

15. Michael, H.N., personal communication, 1988.

16. Aardsma, G.E., "The Tree-ring Calibration", RADIOCARBON AND THE GENESIS FLOOD, ICR Technical Monograph Series, (in press), 1990.

17. Li, Y., Takahashi, T., and Broecker, W.S., "Degree of Saturation of $CaCO_3$ in the Oceans", JOURNAL OF GEOPHYSICAL RESEARCH, Vol. 74, No. 23, 1969, 5507-5525.

18. Harland, W.B., Cox, A.V., Llewellyn, P.G., Pickton, C.A.G., Smith, A.G., and Walters, R., A GEOLOGIC TIME SCALE, Cambridge University Press, 1982.

DISCUSSION

For a first approximation in an effort to obtain a ^{14}C age for the Flood it is appropriate to assume a constant ^{14}C generation rate equal to that determined by modern-day measurement (Equation 2), but the author has not established limits for the range of uncertainty concerning this rate between the end of the flood and the formation of the oldest ^{14}C datable artifacts that can be given precise and unquestioned historical age assignments. The validity of his conclusions depend critically on the magnitude of this uncertainty. There is paleomagnetic data which indicates that ^{14}C production during this period may have reached 40% greater than its modern level. (Bard, et al., *Nature*, May 31, 1990, pp. 405-410.)

The appropriateness of the $14_C g\,(t_F)=0$ (Equation 3) assumption depends on the nature of the subsequent analysis and on the additional assumptions that are taken into consideration. From some considerations it may be just as appropriate to assume a date for the Flood and proceed to a determination of $14_C g\,(t_F)$.

From the data given the equilibrium, or infinite age, ^{14}C concentration may be determined to be $\overline{Q}/\lambda = (2.9 \pm 0.5) * 10^{30}$ ^{14}C atoms. According to Equation 6 the present concentration is probably within the range 2.4 to 2.6 x 10^{30}, or totally within the range of uncertainty for the infinite age value. From my viewpoint the best that can be said from a comparison of these values is that the contemporary ^{14}C concentration is probably less than the infinite age value, but $14_C g\,(t_P)$ and the appropriate $\overline{Q}$ are not known with sufficient precision or accuracy to allow specification to t_p with any confidence.

The dendrochronological calibration scale given in Figure 1 was developed by individuals who did their best to harmonize prehistoric time scale concepts from anthropology, archaeology, dendrochronology, and radiochronology that were developed independent of the chronological data in the Pentateuch. The disagreement between such time scale constructs and a time scale based directly on the chronological data in the Pentateuch indicates a possibility that such constructs are characterized by error that can become apparent only as indicated by historical data such as has been preserved in the Pentateuch. Each individual should evaluate for himself the evidence for the reliability of the affirmations in the Pentateuch.

The Biblical chronological data place the end of the Flood somewhere between about 4250 and about 5350 years before the AD 1950 zero reference point for the radiocarbon time scale. (4800 +/- 550 years.) [The uncertainty range is due to differences of interpretation regarding the Hebrew sojourn in Egypt, and to differences between Masoretic and Septuagint source material.]

If the ^{14}C age is greater than the true age, the characteristic biosphere ^{14}C level was less than it has been over the past 3000 years. If the ^{14}C age is less than the true age, as specified in Figure 1 for ages exceeding 3000, the characteristic biosphere ^{14}C level was greater than it has been over the past 3000 years, as indicated in Figure 2.

The validity of Dr. Aardsma's CREATIONIST MODEL FOR PAST GLOBAL ^{14}C SPECIFIC ACTIVITY depends on which is the most accurate representation of past events and conditions, the dendrochronological model represented in Figure 1, or a straight forward interpretation of the chronological data in the Pentateuch. If the chronological data is fictional, or requires indirect interpretation, how much else of the historical assertions contained there (a **universal** flood, e.g.) are subject to the same classification?

Robert H. Brown, Ph.D.
Loma Linda, California

Concerning this paper, Dr. Aardsma:

1) Does not appear to know that the case for the Biblical Flood, as to both scope and date, rests wholly upon Scripture.

2) Seems to forget that dendrochronology, at best, is a secondary dating method that demands confirmation at one point in any chosen sequence from some primary source, e.g. reliably recorded or otherwise proven (e.g. by radiocarbon), such as Libby used in dating cathedral trusses and Hatshepsut's Nile barge, etc.

3) Fails to employ (and reconcile) the well-established Biblical date of the Flood (very close to 3,000 years before Christ.

4) Ignores, or overlooks, some nine important published references by this reviewer pertaining to radiocarbon-dating of the Flood spanning over 20 years, as well as by other creationists. and

5) By arbitrarily endorsing a Flood-date of ca. 12,000 B.C., and without any showing of adequate grounds on which to so totally reject Biblical chronology, brings discredit upon Bible-science in this area and "gives the ball-game" to evolutionary thinking.

It should be obvious that when we abandon Biblical chronology as the 'benchmark' with which a Flood-date must agree we open the gate to human conjecture rather than Scripture! An unfortunate precedent for this is found in App. II of Morris & Whitcomb's *Genesis Flood* as early as 1961 where the authors dismiss Genesis 11 as chronology (for faulty reasons) and then proceed to speculate that to set the period between the Flood and Abraham at 5,000 years would be "stretching" it, while assuming 100,000 years (to accommodate some "evangelical scholars") would be "very hazardous" (pp.486-489).

Robert L. Whitelaw, M.S.
Blacksburg, Virginia

On the wall of Dr. Aardsma's office at the Institute for Creation Research, I once saw a quotation: "That which has been is remote and exceedingly mysterious. Who can discover it?" (Ecclesiastes 7:24, NASB.) It reminds me that unraveling the past is a tricky business, full of pitfalls for even the best of researchers. Dr. Aardsma is certainly one of the best of researchers, and he does a good job here of summarizing and explaining many things which we need to know about this complex topic. However, I think he has fallen into a pit concerning his very early date for the flood, 12000 B.C. It needs to be taken with a grain of salt, because two of the paper's key assumptions are, in my opinion, very questionable.

The first questionable assumption is that **the rate of production of ^{14}C, $Q(t)$, has been constant since the flood** [eq. (2)]. Dr. Aardsma cites [his ref. 5] an ICR monograph he is working on as giving the reason why he makes this assumption. In the April 1990 draft copy he sent me [pp. 41,42] he acknowledges that (A) a lower strength of the earth's magnetic field in the past could have caused a large increase in Q, and (B) archaeomagnetic data show just such a lower field strength for several millennia after the flood. He points out that the data show that the field was twice as high as the time of Christ as it is now, and apparently felt that this would cancel out the effect of the earlier low field. However, as I will show below, the effect of the low earlier fields would have been considerably greater. Further on, Dr. Aardsma appears to discount the archaeomagnetic data altogether because of one study of ^{10}Be in ice cores from Greenland [1]. The study suggests that the earth's magnetic field has remained constant for the past 5000 years.

But the ^{10}Be paper has a serious flaw: it assumes, with very little explanation, that snow "accumulation rates in Greenland probably did not vary by more than a few percent during the last 5000 years" [Ref. 1, p.383]. This assumption, as the authors acknowledge, has a strong effect on their conclusions. the authors did not specify any direct evidence in their ice cores which would justify their assumption, and I doubt that there was any. If snow accumulation rates were higher in the past, as one would expect in an ice age four to five thousand years ago [2], then the ^{10}Be data would be entirely consistent with the archaeomagnetic data. In fact it could mean that ^{14}C production rates were as much higher in the past as ice-age snowfall rates in Greenland exceeded present-day rates. A recent comment in *Nature* [3] agrees: "... it is extremely difficult to separate the climate signal and the cosmogenic-production signal imbedded in the ice cores."

The same paper [3] shows as archaeomagnetic field strength of less than 50% of today's value at a date which a corrected radiocarbon scale would probably put right after the flood. If the earth's field at that time had been dipolar, the ^{14}C production rate would have been 40% greater than now, assuming a constant flux of cosmic rays. However, my theory [4] of the post flood field fluctuations, and some data, suggests that the field then would not have been nearly as dipolar as it now is, but instead it would have had strong quadrupole and higher-order components. This would mean that $Q(t)$ would have been more than 40% greater.

There are also some creationist reasons to doubt the constancy of cosmic-ray flux. Nobody knows what the source of extra-solar cosmic rays is. What if they are connected to the flood events somehow? Then it is possible that cosmic-ray fluxes were higher after the flood. Solar flares also have a measurable effect on ^{14}C production. If the sun were more active during and after the flood (possibly relating to the speedup of radioactive decay I have suggested in previous papers), then ^{14}C production would again be higher after the flood (possibly relating to the speedup of radioactive decay I have suggested in previous papers), then ^{14}C production would again be higher after the flood than it now is. In summary, there are many good reasons to suspect that ^{14}C production might have been much higher in the past.

What would be the effect of a variable $Q(t)$? Assuming a constant λ (perhaps good for the post-flood period), zero ^{14}C at time $t = 0$ right after the flood, and $Q(t) = Q_o \exp(-\alpha t) + Q_1$, I get the following equation for the number $C(t)$ of ^{14}C atoms:

$$C(t) = \frac{Q_O}{\alpha - \lambda}(1 - e^{-\alpha t}) + \frac{Q_1}{\lambda}(1 - e^{-\lambda t})$$

Taking Q_1 as today's value and α as 0.001 yr $^{-1}$, I find that we would get today's inventory of ^{14}C in only 4300 years with a Q_o of 3.2 times today's rate, it is quite easy to have the flood occurring 4300 years ago instead of 14,000 years ago.

In the denominator of eq. (7) Dr. Aardsma introduces a two-parameter time decrease of the amount of stable carbon C^g in the global biosphere. He feels that the resulting fit to tree-ring specific activity of ^{14}C supports his model. However, it seems to me that a similar variability of $Q(t)$ with constant could easily produce the same degree of fit. Another thing to notice is that the specific activities shown in Figures 2 and 3 are *adjusted* on the basis of the assumed tree-ring age, not measured directly. For example, modern laboratory measurements of the bits of tree ring shown at 5700 years B.P. in Fig. 2 did not really give an average activity of 14.6 disintegrations per minute per gram. Instead, the measured activity was about 7.3 d.p.m./g, and some researcher multiplied that number by 2 to compensate for the amount of decay over the assumed 5700 years. Thus the shape of the specific activity curves are closely tied to the timescale one uses. If some correction were to shorten the timescale by a few thousand years, the left part of the curve would take a nosedive toward zero. So the curve that Dr. Aardsma produced a fit to is not necessarily the correct one.

The second questionable assumption in this paper is that **the tree-ring time scale is correct.** I do not yet feel competent in this field to fully judge it, but I have looked up the references Dr. Aardsma cited. I notice that most dendrochronologists appear to discount the possibility of more than one growth ring per year. They do so on the basis of a uniformitarian assumption: that worldwide climates over the past 10,000 years have not changed enough to significantly influence tree growth. But this assumption does not reckon with the possible effects of an ice-age climate, the details of which are not known. Scripture frequently refers to a seasonal "early and late rain" in ancient times (e.g., Deut. 11:14, Joel 2:23). Commentators try to relate this to present climatic conditions in Palestine, but perhaps it really refers to conditions which do not exist today. For example, suppose that during the ice age the general weather sequence in the temperate zones was this: spring rains; a hot, dry June; a cool, cloudy, wet July; and finally another hot, dry spell in August. This could produce two growth spurts and two rings per year. An experiment by Dr. Walter Lammerts [5] shows that more than one ring per year can be produced in young bristlecone pines by a two-week drought. If two or three rings formed routinely every ice age year, the tree-ring time scale would be shortened by nearly a factor of two.

I certainly don't want to reject *a priori* the possibility that the tree-ring chronologies are correct, especially in the light of my own experience about the reality of geomagnetic reversals [6]. However, what I found in that field was that uniformitarian biases had grossly stretched the paleomagnetic timescale, from one year to 500 million years. Can similar things happen in counting tree rings? I think what is needed is a detailed (tutorial) creationist review of dendrochronology, preferably by someone who has had hands-on experience in the field.

If the tree-ring chronologies are correct, then the flood probably does need to go much further back into time than young-earth creationists have thought. However, there are other data to be reckoned with. For example, my own paper at this conference [7] shows that the data strongly imply that the maximum age of the earth's magnetic field is 8700 years, implying a maximum date for the flood of about 5000 B.C. As another example, if we put the flood at 12,000 B.C., how do we explain the sudden appearance (or decrease of vagueness) of written human history [8] sometime around 3000 B.C.? What were we doing for the previous 9000 years?

Finally, there is the big question on everybody's mind: How can we fit a date for the flood of 12,000 B.C. into the Biblical chronology? One could conceivably squeeze an additional thousand years or so into the Septuagint (less credible but 1000 years longer than the Masoretic) chronology. But eight or nine thousand additional years beyond that just stretches my credibility to the limits. If tree-ring chronologies are correct, it looks as if either the Bible or the straightforward (Prov. 8:9) way young-earth creationists have interpreted it is incorrect (unless someone can find some plausible gaps in the scriptural chronologies). And yet a straightforward view of scripture has paid off handsomely in other areas of science. Which should we take at face value — tree rings, or scripture and the other scientific data? There is a lot at stake in the questions posed by Dr. Aardsma's paper, and the questions deserve to be examined much more rigorously.

1.Beer, J., et al., "The Camp Century ^{10}Be record: implications for long-term variations of the geomagnetic dipole moment," NUCLEAR INSTRUMENTS AND METHODS IN PHYSICS RESEARCH, Vol. B5, 1984, pp. 380-384.

2.Oard, M.J., "An ice age within the biblical time frame," PROCEEDINGS OF THE FIRST INTER-NATIONAL CONFERENCE ON CREATIONISM, Vol. 2, 1986, Creation Science Fellowship, Pittsburgh, PA, pp. 157-166.

3.Bard, E., et al., "Calibration of the ^{14}C timescale over the past 30,000 years using mass spectrometric U-Th ages from Barbados corals," NATURE, Vol. 345, 31 May 1990, pp. 405-410.

4.Humphreys, D.R., "Reversals of the earth's magnetic field during the Genesis flood,; PROCEED-INGS OF THE FIRST INTERNATIONAL CONFERENCE ON CREATIONISM, Creation Science Fellowship, Pittsburgh, PA 1986, pp. 113-126.

5.Lammerts, W.E., "Are the bristle-cone pine trees really so old?" CREATION RESEARCH SOCIETY QUARTERLY, Vol. 20, No. 2, Sept. 1983, pp. 108-115.

6.Humphreys, D.R., "Has the earth's magnetic field ever flipped?" CREATION RESEARCH SOCIETY QUARTERLY, Vol. 25, No. 3, Dec. 1988, pp. 130-137.

7.Humphreys, D.R., "Physical mechanism for reversals of the earth's magnetic field during the flood," PROCEEDINGS OF THE SECOND INTERNATIONAL CONFERENCE ON CREATIONISM, 1990, Creation Science Fellowship, Pittsburgh, PA, in press.

8.Dritt, J.O., "Man's earliest beginnings: discrepancies in evolutionary timetables," PROCEEDINGS OF THE SECOND INTERNATIONAL CONFERENCE ON CREATIONISM, 1990, Creation Science Fellowship, Pittsburgh, PA, in press.

D. Russell Humphreys, Ph.D.
Albuquerque, New Mexico

CLOSURE

The bottom line of each of the reviewer's comments seems to be a feeling that a date for the Flood within a few thousand years of 12,000 B.C. violates a straight forward interpretation of Scripture. It is obvious that this issue must be resolved before serious consideration of the science can really begin.

I am in full accord with the assertion that we must maintain a commitment to a straight forward interpretation of Scripture and refuse to compromise its plain sense. It is for this reason that we understand that the world was supernaturally created and did not get here through any series of natural processes. It is for this same reason that we agree that the earth really was covered by water in the great cataclysm of Noah's day. The Bible is very explicit regarding these things so that they cannot be denied without doing violence to the plain sense of the divinely inspired record, in my opinion.

But Biblical chronology, unfortunately, does not resolve itself in such a simple fashion. Nowhere in Scripture, either in the Old or New Testament, is the date of the Flood ever explicitly given. Nowhere are we told that 2500 years would or did elapse between the Flood and the Messiah, for example. Dates such as these can only be obtained from Scripture by a process of deduction from numerous Bible references. And this process is not at all free from pitfalls of assumption and human finiteness in the unavoidable interpretive process.

When one studies the history of chronologies derived by various Bible scholars from the early centuries after Christ to the present, one is immediately struck by the fact that their results are by no means identical. In fact, they sometimes differ by more than 1,000 years. This does not result from addition errors or sloppy research, but from the fact that it is not always clear how the numeric information in a given reference is to be properly applied for chronological reckoning, compounded with the fact that different Old Testament manuscripts contain different readings at many of the key Biblical chronology passages.

The majority of discussion devoted to any study of post-Flood chronology has been, and always will be, necessarily focused on understanding the full intent of the genealogical list given in Genesis 11. As Dr. Whitelaw has pointed out, Drs. Whitcomb and Morris, both well-known and respected conservative creationist scholars, in Appendix II of *The Genesis Flood* — the book which revitalized the modern creationist movement—present eight cogent reasons why one should not force a strict (i.e. no gaps) interpretation of Genesis 11. They conclude:

> In Summarizing the arguments of this entire discussion, we may say that the lack of an overall total of years for the period from the Flood to Abraham, the absence of Cainan's name and years in the Hebrew text, the symmetrical form of the genealogies of Genesis 5 and 11, the inclusion of data that are irrelevant to a strict chronology, the impossibility of all the postdiluvian patriarchs being contemporaries of Abraham, the Biblical indications of a great antiquity for the judgment of Babel, the fact that the Messianic links were seldom firstborn sons, and the analogy of "begat" being used in the ancestral sense allow the existence of gaps of an undetermined length in the patriarchal genealogy of Genesis 11. (p. 483)

Please note that this conclusion was reached by men whose commitment to a straight forward interpretation of Scripture cannot be denied.

Deducing correct dates from Biblical chronology is not a "straight forward" exercise in Biblical exposition. For this reason there has historically been, and will continue to be, a plurality of viewpoints on the date of the Flood within the recent creation camp. The date for the Flood which I have proposed is simply one more expression of this plurality.

The thrust of the comments relevant to the scientific content of the paper seems to be an assertion that alternate assumptions might produce a different model for radiocarbon which would keep the date of the Flood close to 2500 B.C. and still make good sense of the relevant radiocarbon, dendrochronological and other data from geophysics and archaeology. My own experience in modelling radiocarbon leads me to reject this claim. Though I have contemplated and attempted to quantify several possible post-Flood scenarios, constrained by various different dates for the Flood, the radiocarbon model which I have presented in this paper is the only means of integrating and harmonizing all of the pertinent data within a Biblical creationist, Flood model of earth history which I have been able to discover.

The fundamental difficulty is that there is just too much data to be squeezed into a time frame constrained by a 2500 B.C. date for the Flood. Consider the tree-rings for example. We are presented with a data set comprised of over 9000 tree-rings, each section of which is replicated by numerous physical sections (or cores) from real trees whose ring patterns match and overlap from sample to sample. Now, all creationists that I know of would grant the general validity of secular chronology (including tree-rings and radiocarbon dates) back to 1000 B.C.; this section of chronology harmonizes very nicely with the relevant Biblical data. Thus, we are all agreed on the most recent 3000 years of the tree-ring chronology, leaving the remaining 6000 tree-rings to be explained in the remaining 1500 years required to achieve a date for the Flood of 2500 B.C. This necessitates four growth rings per year on average! I maintain that this is an unreasonable requirement. Any post-Flood climatic scenario which one might imagine to bring about such extreme behavior in these trees would almost certainly not bring about four growth rings per year on average; rather it would almost certainly bring about replacement of these trees by other types of plants more suited to such peculiar conditions.

As one further example, consider the following archaeological data from Jericho. At one location in the ancient mound 26 buildings stages were excavated all belonging to the PPNB period. This data implies that a succession of 26 consecutive house building programs was undertaken at this site during the PPNB. Conventional radiocarbon dates imply that the PPNB lasted a little more than one millennium, roughly coinciding with the seventh millennium B.C. This leads to the conclusion that houses had to be rebuilt at Jericho about once every forty years—a conclusion which seems entirely reasonable. My model does not alter this conclusion. Now let us suppose that these radiocarbon dates are wrong and need to be rescaled to fit within a 2500 B.C. date for the Flood (this to be accomplished by assuming a markedly increased production rate of radiocarbon for some length of time after the Flood, for example.) Obviously, we will have to compress these 1000 radiocarbon years of the PPNB period into a much shorter number of "real" years. In fact, a rough graphical analysis of this problem suggests that it will be necessary to compress this time span into something on the order of 100 years. But this immediately leads to the seemingly unreasonable conclusion that houses had to be completely rebuilt during the PPNB at Jericho once ever four years! Even modern houses last longer than this!

In conclusion, the possibility that the Flood was significantly earlier than 2500 B.C. does not seem to be able to be ruled out Biblically and seems to be strongly implied by presently available radiocarbon, tree-ring, and archaeological data.

Gerald E. Aardsma, Ph.D.

THE SEA'S MISSING SALT:
A DILEMMA FOR EVOLUTIONISTS

Steven A. Austin, Ph.D
D. Russell Humphreys, Ph.D.[1]
Institute for Creation Research
Santee, California 92071

ABSTRACT

The known and conjectured processes which deliver and remove dissolved sodium (Na^+) to and from the ocean are inventoried. Only 27% of the present Na^+ delivered to the ocean can be accounted for by known removal processes. This indicates that the Na^+ concentration of the ocean is not today in "steady state" as supposed by evolutionists, but is increasing with time. The present rate of increase (about 3×10^{11} kg/yr) cannot be accomodated into evolutionary models assuming cyclic or episodic removal of input Na^+ and a 3-billion-year-old ocean. The enormous imbalance shows that the sea should contain much more salt than it does today if the evolutionary model were true. A differential equation containing minimum input rates and maximum output rates allows a maximum age of the ocean of 62 million years to be calculated. The data can be accomodated well into a creationist model.

INTRODUCTION

Sodium is the most common dissolved metal in the ocean. It exists in seawater as a positively charged ion. Sodium ions (Na^+) form the primary salt of the sea along with negatively charged chloride ions (Cl^-). The extreme solubility is caused by the cation's small size (ionic radius is 0.97 Å) and small charge (single positive charge), which allows Na^+ ions to escape most geochemical processes which remove larger ions with the same or greater charge.

The worldwide delivery of Na^+ to the ocean by rivers has been recognized by scientists for hundreds of years. Almost three hundred years ago Edmund Halley [1] recognized that salt cannot easily leave the ocean and suggested that the age of the ocean might be established from knowledge of how much salt enters it year by year from rivers. Nearly one hundred years ago John Joly [2] measured the amount of Na^+ dissolved in river water and estimated with extraordinary accuracy the global yearly input of Na^+ to the ocean. Joly said it would take 80 to 90 million years for the sea to accumulate its present amount of Na^+, if it did so at a constant rate and had none in the beginning. That calculation was accepted by many scientists as giving the age of the earth.

By 1930 radioactive dating methods had been developed which indicated that the age of the earth was longer than anyone had anticipated. Many scientists became convinced that the earth and the ocean are billions of years old. These scientists could no longer endorse Joly's method which they recognized "...leads to the spuriously low geochemical age"[3]. F. W. Clarke, V. M. Goldschmidt, and W. W. Rubey [4] were among many who conjectured that Na^+ is removed from the ocean about as fast as it enters, causing the amount of Na^+ in the ocean to remain roughly constant with time. C. B. Gregor reaffirmed their belief recently: "If magma kept the crust built up against the ravages of erosion and the waste products accumulated in the sea, at present rates of influx the ocean basins should long ago have been choked with sediment and salt....salt must somehow leave the ocean."[5] Those who endorse a 4.5 billion year old earth agree that Joly's 80 to 90 million years is not the age, but the "residence time" for Na^+, that is, the average length of time the ion would survive in the ocean before being removed.

---

[1]Dr. Humphreys is Adjunct Professor at ICR and a physicist at Sandia National Laboratories, Box 5800, Div. 1261, Albuquerque, NM 87185. The Laboratories have not supported this work.

The interpretation that the ocean is in "steady state" with respect to Na^+ was brought to creationists' attention again by Howard J. Van Till, Davis A. Young and Clarence Menninga in *Science Held Hostage*[6]. They endorse radioactive isotope dating and insist that evolutionists are correct when they suppose that the rate of addition of Na^+ to the ocean is balanced by removal processes of equal magnitude. The "residence time" for Na^+, they assert, provides no means for establishing an age for the ocean. They affirm, "The 4.5 billion year chronology of earth history is in no way weakened or disqualified by an appeal to the salt content of the terrestrial oceans."[7] But where is the empirical evidence supporting the "steady state" model? Is there sufficient reason, apart from evolutionary assumption, to dismiss Joly's geochemical age for the ocean? Van Till, Young and Menninga do not present the evidence, but simply endorse the model supposed by earlier evolutionists.

The steady-state hypothesis cannot be tested directly, because, even if the ocean is not in steady state, the change in Na^+ concentration of seawater during recent times would be too small to be measurable. But there is an indirect test for the hypothesis; we can compare measured input rates with all known or conjectured output rates. If outputs are considerably lower than inputs at present, then the sea cannot be be in steady state. If that condition is likely to have persisted for the history of the ocean, there is strong reason to doubt that the sea is billions of years old. Thus, we will examine input and output rates carefully.

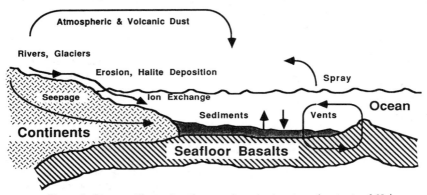

Figure 1: Diagram illustrating the ocean's major inputs and outputs of Na^+.

Figure 1 illustrates inputs and outputs. We define the system in question as being the seawater in the ocean basins, not including water trapped in sea-floor sediments. First, we list all the known or conjectured inputs and outputs and try to quantify them with the latest data from the scientific literature. Then, we specify their past behavior in the evolutionary model. Next, we calculate the maximum possible age of the ocean on the basis of the evolutionary model, in order to show the inconsistency of that model. Last, we indicate the concordance of the data with a creation model, and offer a challenge to evolutionists and old-earth creationists.

PRESENT INPUTS OF Na^+ TO THE OCEAN

Let us define A_i as the mass per unit time of Na^+ delivered to the ocean by the ith source. What follows is a compilation of eleven major natural Na^+ inputs to the ocean. Most considerations of the Na^+ cycle for the oceans only take account of the first three inputs listed (rivers), but we list in Table 1 and below eight additional sources which cannot be neglected.

The most thoroughly investigated process delivering Na^+ to the ocean is rivers. The most recent global survey by the French geochemist Michel Meybeck gives both the total discharge and average Na^+ concentration of rivers. The total river discharge to the ocean is 3.74×10^{16} L/yr, and the globally averaged Na^+ concentration of rivers after man-made pollution is removed is 5.15 mg/L [8]. These numbers allow the global river input of natural dissolved Na^+ to the ocean to be calculated as 1.92×10^{11} kg/yr [9]. According to Meybeck, there are three major sources for Na^+ in river water: (1) sea spray, (2) chemical weathering of silicate minerals, and (3) solution of chloride minerals.

Table 1: Inputs of Na^+ to the world ocean. Units are in 10^{10} kg/yr. Present inputs are listed in column headed A_i. Minimum past inputs are listed in column headed A_{imin}. Models for estimating A_{imin} are denoted "M" for "Modern Earth Model" and "C" for "Cretaceous Earth Model".

i	Na^+ INPUT PROCESS	A_i	A_{imin}	MODEL
1.	Rivers: Sea Spray	5.5	5.0	C
2.	Rivers: Silicate Weathering	6.2	6.2	M
3.	Rivers: Chloride Solution	7.5	7.5	M
4.	Ocean Floor Sediments	11.5	6.21	C
5.	Glacial Silicates	3.9	0.0	C
6.	Atmospheric and Volcanic Dust	0.14	0.14	M
7.	Marine Coastal Erosion	0.077	0.074	C
8.	Glacier Ice	0.12	0.0	C
9.	Volcanic Aerosols	0.093	0.093	M
10.	Ground Water of continents	9.6	9.3	C
11.	Hydrothermal Vents	1.1	1.1	M
		$A_p = 45.7$	$A_{min} = 35.6$	

A_1. Rivers: Sea Spray Component. Spray from ocean waves causes droplets of seawater to evaporate leaving halite aerosol in the atmosphere. A large part of the aerosol is deposited by rain and snow on the continents. The component of Na^+ in river water derived from sea spray was estimated by study of the Na^+ concentrations of numerous rain samples and the total discharge of rivers to the ocean. According to Meybeck [9], sea-spray-derived Na^+ in river water is 5.5×10^{10} kg/yr, which is 29% of the total yearly river flux of Na^+. Thus, $A_1 = 5.5 \times 10^{10}$ kg/yr.

A_2. Rivers: Silicate Weathering Component. Chemical weathering of the continents releases Na^+ from silicate minerals (especially feldspars and clays) the major part of which finds its way to rivers and enters the ocean. Analysis of the mineral breakdown of dissolved ions in river water by Meybeck [10] indicates that 32% of the total Na^+ is derived from weathering of continental silicate minerals. Thus, $A_2 = 6.2 \times 10^{10}$ kg/yr.

A_3. Rivers: Chloride Solution Component. A small area of the continents (approx. 1.3% of area) has outcrops of chloride and sulfate minerals the principal mineral of which is halite ($NaCl$). These are extremely soluble in water. Using the mineral breakdown analysis of dissolved ions in river water, Meybeck [10] calculated that 39% of modern river Na^+ is derived from solution of chlorides. Thus, $A_3 = 7.5 \times 10^{10}$ kg/yr. The sum $A_1 + A_2 + A_3 = 1.92 \times 10^{11}$ kg/yr, which is the total global river flux of Na^+.

A_4. Ocean Floor Sediments. Detailed studies of the Na^+ concentrations of pore waters of ocean floor sediments by Sayles [11] show that their pore waters are enriched in Na^+ relative to sea water. The increase in Na^+ of pore waters with depth within ocean sediments describes a concentration gradient which requires diffusion of Na^+ from ocean sediments into the ocean. Pore waters of ocean sediments show decreasing concentrations of K^+ and Mg^{+2} with depth. This data requires sediments to absorb K^+ and Mg^{+2} from seawater [11].

A good explanation offered for this data is that most Na^+ is released from clays during prolonged burial as K^+ or Mg^{+2} is absorbed in its place. K^+ would be absorbed during prolonged burial of clays because it has larger ionic radius than Na^+. Similarly, Mg^{+2} would be absorbed by clays during prolonged burial because of its divalent charge, twice that of Na^+.

The ocean sediment pore water data for the Atlantic Ocean assembled by Sayles is representative of other oceans allowing the global Na^+ flux out of ocean sediments to be calculated. The estimate of Sayles [11] is slightly adjusted for charge balance and yields $A_4 = 1.15 \times 10^{11}$ kg/yr [12]. This large input to the ocean is 60% of the total river input.

A_5. Finely Pulverized Glacial Silicates. Glaciers produce very finely ground rock flour and, as illustrated by Antarctica and Greenland, add the minutely pulverized material directly to the ocean. This fine rock flour is dominated by silicate minerals which weather rapidly when added to the ocean. Schultz and Turekian [13] describe the silica enriched deep ocean waters

19

surrounding Antarctica and the evidence that about 1.4×10^{12} kg (64%) of the continent's glacial-marine sediments dissolve in sea water before being buried on the sea floor. If we assume that the glacial-marine sediment of Antarctica has 2.4% by weight Na^+ (the composition of the "average igneous rock"), the dissolved silicates add 3.4×10^{10} kg of Na^+ to the ocean each year. The continent of Antarctica comprises 86% of our planet's continentally glaciated area and indicates that the global glacial-marine Na^+ flux is $A_5 = 3.9 \times 10^{10}$ kg/yr. This is 20% of the total river input.

A_6. __Atmospheric and Volcanic Dust.__ A considerable quantity of the dust removed from the continents by wind is added to the ocean. The fine dust is largely silicate minerals, a major part of which dissolve in the sea. According to Garrels and Mackenzie [14], 5×10^{10} kg of atmospheric dust are added yearly to the ocean basins. This is equivalent to an average of 140 kg of dust per km^2 of ocean each year, and agrees with dust fluxes collected over the ocean [15]. Mackenzie and Wollast [16] add to this total 4×10^{10} kg of volcanic dust each year. Assuming that atmospheric and volcanic dust is 2.4% by weight Na^+ and that 64% of it dissolves, $A_6 = 1.4 \times 10^9$ kg/yr. This is 1% of the total river input.

A_7. __Marine Coastal Erosion.__ The direct attack of ocean waves along the coast erodes considerable amounts of sand, silt and clay. Most of the finest particles produced are silicates which have not been rinsed by the fresh water of rivers and remain very reactive with the ocean. According to Garrels and Mackenzie [14], 2.3×10^{11} kg of material is added to the ocean yearly by marine erosion. Assuming that this debris is 0.67% by weight Na^+ (the concentration in the "average sedimentary rock") and that 50% of it dissolves in the ocean, $A_7 = 7.7 \times 10^8$ kg/yr of Na^+ from marine erosion. This is less than 1% of the total river input.

A_8. __Glacier Ice.__ Snow has small quantities of Na^+ derived from halite aerosols of the atmosphere. Melting of glacier ice directly in the sea adds small quantities of Na^+ to the sea. Meybeck [17] lists this value, $A_8 = 1.2 \times 10^9$ kg/yr. This is less than 1% of the total river input.

A_9. __Volcanic Aerosols.__ Dissolved in the steam that continental volcanoes deliver to the earth's surface are small quantities of Na^+. Meybeck [17] calculated the mass delivered from airborne volcanic aerosols to the ocean. He obtained $A_9 = 9.3 \times 10^8$. This is less than 1% of the total river input.

A_{10}. __Ground Water Seepage.__ Geologists have suspected for more than 100 years that water seeps through the continents and issues forth on the floor of the ocean. This was not proven until recently when drilling of sediments of the continental shelves revealed fresh water moving seaward through the sedimentary layers. The dissolved solids of ground waters can be measured in parts per thousand (ppt) and vary significantly from as fresh as rain water (0.0001 ppt) to extremely saline brine (over 250 ppt). For this reason we have great difficulty in estimating their average Na^+ content.

Most near surface ground waters have more dissolved solids than river waters (rivers average 0.13 ppt). Deep ground waters often are saline brines as an example from the southeastern United States illustrates. Strata at depth within the Florida-Bahama Platform are filled with dense brine (over 200 ppt) that seeps from the platform onto the floors of the Atlantic Ocean and the Gulf of Mexico [18]. According to Paull and Neumann [18], major brine seepage causes significant solution of limestone and is believed to be a major cause of the steep slopes at the margins of the platform. The salty brine has actually been sampled in locations where it issues onto the sea floor, and appears to be derived from solution of rock salt (halite) and gypsum within strata under Florida.

The quantity of ground water seepage into the ocean on a global scale can be estimated from the quantity of global yearly rainfall minus global evaporation as compared to global river runoff. Global river runoff is about 10% less than global rainfall minus evaporation [19]. This missing water from the continents (approximately 3.7×10^{15} L/yr) is believed to be the total ground water seepage from the continents. An average Na^+ concentration for this seepage would allow the Na^+ flux to the ocean to be calculated. However, we know this average imperfectly. If we assume that the average ground water has 26 mg/L of Na^+ (5 times the concentration of average river water), the global Na^+ flux is $A_{10} = 9.6 \times 10^{10}$ kg/yr from ground water seepage. This rough estimate represents 50% of the total river input. If further research should increase the global average Na^+ content of ground water, the flux of this very significant source would increase.

A_{11}. Sea-floor Hydrothermal Vents. Fifteen years of intense investigations of hot springs on the deep ocean floor have led geochemists to the understanding that large quantities of ocean water are circulated through a significant fracture system in hot sea-floor rocks. Some of the springs have water hotter than $350°C$ containing significantly more total dissolved solids than seawater. This indicates seawater alters sea-floor basalt by a complex series of metamorphic reactions. According to Seyfried [20], metasomatism dissolves Na^+ from basalt below $350°C$ but fixes Na^+ in mineral phases above $350°C$.

Two classes of sea-floor hydrothermal vents are recognized by Wolery and Sleep [21]: axial and off-axial hydrothermal vents. The axial hydrothermal vents occur along the axes of mid-ocean ridges where active rift faulting has brought the hottest basalts near the ocean floor. These springs are dominated by water hotter than $250°C$. The off-axial vents are located on the flanks of the mid-ocean ridges away from the recent rift faulting. These springs are dominated by water from 80 to $250°C$, which is cooler than the axial springs. Using data on latent heat and heat flow from mid-ocean ridges, Wolery and Sleep [22] estimate the upper limit of water flux on a global scale through mid-ocean ridges: 2.3×10^{13} kg/yr. They believe that 17% of the water flows through axial vents and 83% flows through off-axial vents. Chemical compositions of vent waters allowed Wolery and Sleep [23] to estimate that the off-axial vents add 1.1×10^{10} kg of Na^+ each year to the ocean.

Estimation of the global contribution of Na^+ by way of the axial vents is complicated by the difficulty in measuring the actual vent temperature and calculating the rock to water ratio in these springs. Furthermore, two dozen measurements of axial springs may not be representative of the global flow. Twenty axial springs from the Pacific Ocean have an average Na^+ concentration of 502 mmol/kg, showing an enrichment of 38 mmol/kg above normal seawater [24]. Three axial springs from the Atlantic Ocean have an average Na^+ concentration of 534 mmol/kg, showing an enrichment of 70 mmol/kg above normal seawater [25]. Therefore, the axial spring data indicate that axial hot springs in the Pacific and Atlantic Oceans are enriched by 42 mmol/kg in Na^+. Using the global water flux for axial vents of 3.8×10^{12} kg [22], the global Na^+ flux from axial vents is 3.7×10^9 kg of Na^+ added to the ocean each year.

Addition of the calculated Na^+ inputs from off-axial and axial hydrothermal springs gives the global hydrothermal vent flux: $A_{11} = 1.5 \times 10^{10}$ kg/yr. This is 8% of the total river input.

PRESENT OUTPUTS OF Na^+ FROM THE OCEAN

Let us define B_i as the mass per unit time of Na^+ taken out of the ocean by the ith sink. What follows below and in Table 2 is a compilation of the seven known or conjectured natural Na^+ outputs from the ocean. These outputs are those from the exhaustive list of Holland [26].

Table 2: Outputs of Na^+ from the ocean. Units are in 10^{10} kg/yr. Present outputs are listed in column headed B_i. Maximum past outputs are listed in column headed B_{imax}. Models for estimating B_{imax} are denoted "M" for "Modern Earth Model", "P" for "Pleistocene Earth Model", "C" for "Cretaceous Earth Model", and "S" for time averaged salt deposits of the Permian System.

i	Na^+ OUTPUT PROCESS	B_i	B_{imax}	MODEL
1.	Sea Spray	6.0	6.7	P
2.	Cation Exchange	3.5	5.2	P
3.	Burial of Pore Water	2.2	3.9	P
4.	Halite Deposition	< 0.004	4.0	S
5.	Alteration of Basalt	0.44	0.62	C
6.	Albite Formation	0.0	0.0	M
7.	Zeolite Formation	0.08	0.2	P
		$B_p = 12.2$	$B_{max} = 20.6$	

B_1. **Sea Spray.** Waves of the sea, especially breaking waves along the shore, produce air bubbles in the water. Collapse of these bubbles shoots into the air droplets of seawater which evaporate to form microscopic crystals of halite. Crystals of halite are carried with other aerosols by the winds from the ocean to the continents. A major quantity of these aerosols form condensation nuclei for clouds, some are scrubbed from the atmosphere by rain, and a small fraction falls out dry onto the earth. Analyses of numerous rain water samples from five continents by Meybeck [27] indicate that average rainwater has 0.55 mg/L of Na^+. This average rain value is probably in excess of the actual average because recent studies show that Asia, the continent with the greatest rainfall, averages less than 0.4 mg/L [28]. Furthermore, 2000 m of ice core from Antarctica, the earth's longest duration aerosol record, averages less than 0.1 mg/L [29]. Using the value for global precipitation over the continents of 1.10×10^{17} L/yr [30] and Meybeck's generous value of 0.55 mg/L of Na^+ in average rainfall, we obtain the mass of sea spray deposits of Na^+ on the continents: $B_1 = 6.0 \times 10^{10}$ kg/yr. This output is 31% of the total river input.

B_2. **Ion Exchange.** Clays exhibit significant cation exchange ability especially in response to changes in the chemical environment. River-borne clays have their cation exchange sites dominated by Ca^{+2} because of the relatively high proportion of Ca^{+2} to Na^+ in river water. However, at the mouth of rivers upon entering the ocean these clays encounter seawater which has a significantly higher proportion of Na^+ relative to Ca^{+2}. As a result river-borne clays release Ca^{+2} from their cation exchange sites and absorb Na^+. The ability of river-borne clays to absorb seawater Na^+ is limited by the concentration of Ca^{+2} on the cation exchange sites.

Sayles and Mangelsdorf [31] have studied the cation exchange characteristics of clays of the Amazon River, the world's largest river. Analysis of the river-borne clay of the Amazon showed that the cation exchange process occurs very rapidly as the clays enter the ocean. At the most frequently encountered discharge and sediment levels of the Amazon, Sayles and Mangelsdorf estimate that 20% of the river-born Na^+ is absorbed as clays enter the ocean. This was confirmed by laboratory experiments on the cation exchange abilities of river-borne clay [32]. Using this data, Drever, Li and Maynard [33] estimated the global uptake of Na^+ by river-borne clays at $B_2 = 3.5 \times 10^{10}$ kg/yr. This output is 18% of the total river input.

B_3. **Burial of Pore Water.** Sediments contain open spaces between their grains which in the ocean are filled with pore fluids. Thus, there is some seawater lost each year from the ocean simply by the permanent burial of pore water with the accumulation of sediments. Drever, Li and Maynard [34] used the mass of ocean sediment added to the ocean and accumulated on the sea floor annually (2×10^{13} kg/yr) and the average final porosity (30%) to estimate the quantity of seawater removed. From the quantity of seawater removed they calculate the flux of Na^+ removed yearly by burial of pore water: $B_3 = 2.2 \times 10^{10}$ kg/yr. This output is 11% of the total river input.

B_4. **Halite Deposition.** Many have assumed that the major pathway for Na^+ removal from today's ocean is the deposition of the mineral halite. However, the major halite deposits accumulate currently from concentrated river water on the continents, not from the ocean. Modern marine sedimentary deposits are nearly devoid of halite. Recent marine salt flats and coastal lagoons occur along the Persian Gulf, along the Gulf of California, and on the west coast of Australia, but they have very meager deposits of halite. When halite is deposited in marine salt flats and coastal lagoons, freshening of the brine after deposition often redissolves the halite. Solution of halite in seawater occurs because seawater is very undersaturated in both Na^+ and Cl^-. In fact seawater could contain 20 times its present concentration of Na^+ before deposition of halite would occur. Thus, modern sedimentary conditions seem to prevent large, permanent accumulation of halite in marine environments. The world inventory of modern marine halite deposits must be accumulating today at a rate of less than 1×10^8 kg/yr. Thus, the flux of Na^+ in modern marine halite deposition is: $B_4 < 4 \times 10^7$ kg/yr. Today's oceanic output of Na^+ as halite is trivial when compared to the modern river input.

B_5. **Low Temperature Alteration of Sea Floor Basalt.** The coolest basalts which form the uppermost rock of the ocean floor also circulate seawater but the temperatures of these fluids usually remain below $60°C$. At this lower temperature the basalt is weathered to form clay minerals. Drilling of the upper 600 meters of oceanic basalt showed 5 to 15% weathering of basalt to form very pervasive clays [35]. The primary clay is saponite, a Na^+-containing mineral of the smectite (montmorillonite) group. Therefore, Na^+ from low-temperature seawater reactions with the basalt must remove Na^+ from seawater. The quantity of clays in basalt was reported by Wolery and Sleep [36] to require removal of about 4.4×10^9 kg/yr of Na^+. Thus, removal of Na^+ by low temperature alteration of basalt is $B_5 = 4.4 \times 10^9$ kg/yr. This output is 2% of the total river input.

B_6. <u>Albite Formation</u>. Sea floor basalts above 350°C contain fluids which exchange Na^+ for Ca^{+2} [20]. This metasomatic process, which occurs beneath the ocean, transforms calcium-rich feldspars (anorthite) to Na^+-rich feldspars (albite). Evidence of the process is seen in chlorite-grade metamorphism from basalts dredged from the sea floor. However, as discussed earlier in the input section, the axial hydrothermal vents, even many of those which emit water over 350°C, generally show enrichment, not depletion, of Na^+ [37]. The suggestion by Holland [38] that albite formation is an effective sink for oceanic Na^+ is not supported by the most recent data. It appears that the seawater as it is heated from ocean temperature to 350°C gains as much or more Na^+ from low temperature solution of Na^+ in basalt as is removed above 350°C. Thus, there does not appear to be any significant removal of Na^+ from the seawater by the formation of albite. The Na^+ used in albite formation appears to come from within the ocean crust. It is concluded that albite formation removes essentially no Na^+ from the ocean. Therefore, $B_6 = 0$ kg/yr.

B_7. <u>Zeolite Formation</u>. Minerals of the zeolite group are strong absorbers of alkalies (Na^+, K^+) from seawater and are found in small amounts in ocean sediments. Phillipsite and clinoptilolite, Na^+-rich members of the zeolite group, form from alteration of volcanic ash. According to Mackenzie and Wollast [39] about 4×10^{10} kg of volcanic ash are added to the ocean yearly. If fully one-half of this volcanic ash (averaging 3% by weight Na^+) is converted to phillipsite (averaging 7% by weight Na^+), 8×10^8 kg/yr of Na^+ would be removed from seawater. Thus, a generous allowance for zeolite formation suggests $B_7 = 8 \times 10^8$ kg/yr of Na^+ removal. Holland [40] recognizes the removal of seawater Na^+ by zeolites, but admits the quantity is minor. The output of Na^+ calculated for zeolites is less than 1% of the total river input.

EVOLUTIONARY EARTH MODELS

Constraints on the minimum inputs and maximum outputs for Na^+ can be established by examining three different earth models. These are (1) the Pleistocene Earth Model, (2) the Cretaceous Earth Model, and (3) the Modern Earth Model. These models have been elaborated by evolutionists and are employed here to evaluate the limits of Na^+ variation in the history of earth's dynamic systems.

The Pleistocene Earth Model (abbreviated "Model P") was generated by geologic evidences of widespread continental glaciation. It supposes that the earth experienced an "ice age" [41]. A large area of northern Europe, Asia and North America was covered by continental glaciers when global mean temperature was about 10°C. Compared to today's earth, sea level was lower, about 5% greater area of continents was exposed, and there was greater length of coastline. Total global rainfall was greater than today, and, because of higher river discharge, more elevated continents, and much reduced desert areas, global erosion was more rapid than today [41]. Volcanism was extensive judging from the size and abundance of Pleistocene calderas, but rift faulting at mid-ocean ridges was occurring near today's rate [42].

The Cretaceous Earth Model (abbreviated "Model C") is based on fossil flora and fauna from Cretaceous strata indicating that warm climate extended into polar latitudes [43]. There are supposed to have been no glaciers and global mean temperature may have exceeded 20°C [42]. Higher sea level would have caused the area of Cretaceous continents to be 95% of today's continents [44]. Global rainfall and global continental drainage by rivers may have been 25% greater than today's [44], but because of the reduced elevation of the continents, less continental area, and more extensive soil development, the rate of erosion and sedimentation was about 54% of today's [44]. Cretaceous sea-floor spreading has been supposed to have occurred at 1.4 times today's rate [42]. Perhaps, because of more volatiles released by accelerated tectonics on the sea floor, there was four times the present level of atmospheric CO_2 [42]. Chemical weathering would have been greater than today because of increased soil humidity and acidity [42].

The Modern Earth Model (abbreviated "Model M") is based on our recent earth which is available for our direct study. Today's earth has $15°C$ global mean temperature and, because of modern continental glaciers, more closely resembles Model P than Model C. An important distinctive of our modern earth is its aridity. Desert areas characterize large portions of our continents which have reduced river discharge.

MINIMUM PAST Na^+ INPUTS ACCORDING TO EVOLUTIONARY MODELS

We seek to determine minimum past input rates, A_{imin}, for each of the eleven processes delivering Na^+ to the ocean. We can use our earth models to make this evaluation for the purpose of discerning whether evolutionary explanations for the earth's ocean allow the ocean's Na^+ content to remain in steady state. Minimum values for eleven Na^+ input processes (A_{imin}) are listed in Table 1. For the sake of calculation, we assume the "steady state" condition where the ocean's Na^+ concentration does not change with time.

The flux of river Na^+ from wash out of sea spray aerosol depends on the length of shoreline, area of continents, energy of waves, and concentration of Na^+ in seawater. Assuming the steady-state model (past Na^+ concentration of seawater equivalent to today's), we obtain the minimum sea spray river flux using Model C. Because Cretaceous coastlines would be 97% of today's length and continental area for aerosol to wash out would be 95% of today's, $A_{1min} = 0.97 \times 0.95 \times A_1$.

In a similar fashion past minimum global fluxes can be estimated for inputs A_2 through A_{11}. The rate of release of Na^+ to rivers by silicate weathering (input A_2) is primarily dependent on soil acidity and soil humidity [45]. Soil acid, which is produced primarily from CO_2 generated by organic decay, is the most effective agent for release of Na^+ from silicate minerals. High soil humidity is the factor which increases organic activity in soils, and, in addition, makes possible the leaching of Na^+ from soils to rivers. Thus, it can be argued that Model M with modern, more arid and alkaline soils would produce the minimum global flux of silicate-derived Na^+ to the oceans through rivers. Models P and C have more humid and acidic soils than Model M. The area of modern deserts (where low Na^+ solution from silicates occurs) in Model M more than offsets the increased area covered by glaciers (where low solution of Na^+ occurred) in Model P. Indeed, it is difficult to imagine an earth model where less Na^+ is delivered by rivers to the ocean from weathering of silicates. Therefore, $A_{2min} = A_2$.

The flux of Na^+ through rivers from solution of chlorides on the continent is related to global precipitation and to area of exposed chloride deposits on the continents. All earth models suppose about the same area of exposed continental chlorides, so Model M, the model with the most arid climate, would have the lowest solution rate. Thus, $A_{3min} = A_3$.

The expulsion of Na^+ from ocean sediments (A_4) is directly related to the rate of sedimentation, the lowest sedimentation rate producing the lowest input of Na^+ from buried sea-floor clays. The lowest sedimentation rate is for Model C, evaluated at 54% of Model M by Tardy et al. [44]. Thus, $A_{4min} = 0.54 \times A_4$. For inputs of Na^+ by marine erosion (A_7) and ground water (A_{10}), Model C gives the minimum Na^+ inputs because marine erosion and ground water fluxes are related most strongly to the length of shorelines. Length of Cretaceous shorelines would be about 97% that of modern shorelines. Thus, $A_{7min} = 0.97 \times A_7$ and $A_{10min} = 0.97 \times A_{10}$. Sea-floor spreading has been regarded by evolutionists to be slowing down with time [42]. Therefore, the lowest output of Na^+ from sea-floor hydrothermal vents is today's: $A_{11min} = A_{11}$.

MAXIMUM PAST Na^+ OUTPUTS ACCORDING TO EVOLUTIONARY MODELS

We can also evaluate the past outputs of Na^+ from the ocean and estimate each B_{imax}, the maximum output values for each output process. These are listed in Table 2. The quantity of Na^+ removed from the ocean by the sea spray process (B_1) is, as stated before, related to length of shoreline, area of the continents, energy of waves, and concentration of Na^+ in seawater as each sea spray droplet formed. Evolutionists have supposed the Na^+ concentration of seawater and salt spray droplets have remained roughly constant over hundreds of millions of years. Thus, Model P with the most shoreline, the greatest continental area, and the greatest wave energy produces the greatest sea spray flux. A 2000 m deep ice core from Antarctica

[29] contains old ice left over from the Pleistocene. That ice, however, does not contain a significantly higher Na^+ aerosol content than recent ice deposited on Antarctica. Thus, past maximum rates of removal of Na^+ by sea spray are only slightly greater than modern rates. A generous allowance gives a good value, $B_{1max} = 6.7 \times 10^{10}$ kg/yr.

Approximately 1.5 times the present river sediment load would be carried to the oceans with Model P [44]. This largest global load of sediment in an evolutionary model would allow the largest Na^+ exchange from seawater to river sediments and bury the most pore water within ocean sediments. Thus, it can be estimated that $B_{2max} = 5.2 \times 10^{10}$ kg/yr and $B_{3max} = 3.9 \times 10^{10}$ kg/yr. The most Na^+ removal by alteration of ocean floor basalt would occur in Model C where sea floor is supposed to form 1.4 times faster than today. The value of $B_{5max} = 0.62 \times 10^{10}$ is estimated.

Evolutionists have claimed that the process of halite deposition (B_4) is much different today than in the past. They admit that modern marine halite deposits are of trivial volume, but attribute ancient massive halite deposits to short, irregularly occurring episodes. Drever, Li and Maynard speak for many evolutionists who believe: "...such events appear to be well able to absorb the river excess over long periods of time...."[46].

Na^+ in earth's halite deposits is a relatively small sink for Na^+, as can be appreciated by "time averaging" it over the supposed duration of the deposits. The present inventory of rock salt in the earth's strata contains about 4.4×10^{18} kg of Na^+ [47] which is 30% of the mass of Na^+ in the ocean. Dividing the present mass of Na^+ in global rock salt (4.4×10^{18} kg) by the supposed duration of the Phanerozoic deposits (6×10^8 yr) gives an average rate of Na^+ removal for the Phanerozoic of 7.3×10^9 kg/yr. This flux is an order of magnitude less than the sea spray output process (B_{1max}) and cannot serve to balance during long time intervals any of the major input processes (A_{1min}, A_{2min}, A_{3min} or A_{10min}). Furthermore, it is extremely unlikely that the "time averaged" halite output contains a significant error. No major quantity of halite in the earth's crust could have escaped our detection. Because halite is dominantly a basinal deposit on continents, it is unlikely that any major quantity has been extracted by subduction from the crust into the mantle.

We can estimate B_{4max} by an analysis of halite deposits of the Permian System. The Permian contains the world's thickest and most extensive marine halite deposits. Of the 4.4×10^{18} kg of Na^+ in the earth's rock salt, 1.0×10^{18} kg (23%) resides in Permian rock salt [48]. Assuming that 50% of the Permian halite strata have survived erosion (a good estimate based on the continental exposure of Permian basinal deposits), the original Permian Na^+ mass would be 2×10^{18} kg. The "time averaged" maximum rate of removal of Na^+ by halite deposition is estimated in reference to the supposed 50 million year duration of the Permian Period. The maximum rate of Na^+ removal by marine halite deposition (B_{4max}) is 4.0×10^{10} kg/yr [49]. The rate is only 67% of the present river input of Na^+ derived weathering of silicates (A_2). Even more interesting is the observation that B_{4max} is about half the present river flux derived from solution of continental chloride minerals (A_3).

Past halite deposition (B_{4max}) is not the major process that has been supposed: it ranks third behind past sea spray (B_{1max}) and cation exchange (B_{2max}). Halite in the earth has not been the major sink for Na^+ generated by supposed hundreds of millions of years of continental weathering.

SIGNIFICANCE OF THE IMBALANCE

Data that have been assembled in summary form in Tables 1 and 2 show the enormous imbalance of Na^+ inputs compared to outputs. A_p, the total of the eleven present Na^+ inputs, is 4.57×10^{11} kg/yr, whereas B_p, the total of the seven present outputs, is only 1.22×10^{11} kg/yr. The present output to input ratio ($x_p = 0.27$) shows that only 27% of Na^+ going into today's ocean can be accounted for by known output processes. If the "steady state" model is correct, x_p should be equal to 1.0, not 0.27! It is extremely unlikely that one major or several minor Na^+ output processes, comprising 3.35×10^{11} kg/yr of Na^+, have eluded our detection. That the Na^+ imbalance exists in the ocean is further corroborated by consideration of Cl^-, the primary anion which balances the charge of input Na^+. According to Drever, Li and Maynard [50], Cl^- is also being added to the ocean at a much faster rate than it is being removed. Thus, we have strong evidence that the ocean is not presently in "steady state" condition.

25

If the inputs of Na^+ were constant in time and there were no outputs, the time τ it would take to bring the mass of Na^+ in the ocean from zero to today's amount M_p would be:

$$\tau = \frac{M_p}{\Sigma A_i} = \frac{M_p}{A_p} \tag{1}$$

In a similar fashion the maximum time required to bring the ocean to its present Na^+ level can be calculated assuming the slowest possible Na^+ input processes:

$$\tau_{max} = \frac{M_p}{\Sigma A_{imin}} = \frac{M_p}{A_{min}} \tag{2}$$

Evolutionists call τ the "residence time" of Na^+, implying that τ is the average time a Na^+ ion spends in the ocean. However, as already demonstrated, the present oceans are not in steady state, so τ cannot be the "residence time" for Na^+. For clarity of concepts, we call τ the "filling time". Estimates of the Na^+ filling time ("residence time") in the literature over the last century have varied between 260 Myr [3] and 26 Myr [51], generally getting smaller with time as more Na^+ inputs have been identified and measured more accurately.

Before a filling time (τ) can be calculated, M_p, the present mass of Na^+ in the ocean needs to be determined. The ocean's concentration of Na^+ today is $10,760$ mg/kg [52]. The mass of the oceans is 1.37×10^{21} kg [30], allowing the Na^+ mass in the ocean to be calculated: $M_p = 1.47 \times 10^{19}$ kg. The total of the eleven A_i's listed in the "present inputs" section is $A_p = 4.57 \times 10^{11}$ kg/yr. Substituting the last two values in equation 1 gives a filling time of 32.2 Myr. Because the input fluxes were estimated conservatively, we can say: $\tau < 32.2$ Myr. The maximum filling time calculated using equation 2 gives $\tau_{max} = 41.3$ Myr. Because the minimum input fluxes were estimated very conservatively, we can say $\tau_{max} < 41.3$ Myr.

ESTIMATING THE OCEAN'S AGE

It is important to understand that τ is not the age of the ocean. To get an age estimate, we need to account for three other factors: (1) the output rates, (2) the past behavior of inputs and outputs, and (3) the initial amount of Na^+. Let us consider first the effect of output rates. The three major outputs are aerosol removal by sea spray (B_1), cation exchange with river clays (B_2), and burial of pore water in ocean sediments (B_3). Together these three removal paths account for 96% of the present Na^+ removal from the ocean (see Table 2). However, the rates of Na^+ removal by each of these three processes are dependent on the concentration of Na^+ in seawater. Lower rates of removal for the three processes would be expected in the past when seawater had a lower concentration of Na^+. Thus, these output rates cannot be constant through time, but must be proportional to $[Na^+](t)$, the Na^+ concentration of the ocean at some past time t, and also proportional to $M(t)$, the mass of Na^+ in the ocean at time t. We can express the rates as $B_i(t) = b_i M(t)$, where each coefficient b_i is a proportionality constant.

Next, let us consider outputs. If the sea has been increasing its Na^+ content continually, then today's three major outputs (B_1, B_2 and B_3) must have been smaller in the past. Thus, one cannot simply subtract today's output rates from the input rates and use a form of equation 1 to get the age. Instead, we must solve a differential equation giving the rate of change of $M(t)$ in terms of the input rates A_i and the output rates $B_i(t)$ [53]:

$$\frac{dM}{dt} = \Sigma A_i - \Sigma B_i = A_t - \beta M(t), \tag{3}$$

where we have defined $\beta = \Sigma b_i$ and $A_t = \Sigma A_i$. If A_t and β are constant with time, the solution of equation 3 is:

$$M(t) = \frac{A_t}{\beta} - \left(\frac{A_t}{\beta} - M_o\right)\exp(-\beta t), \tag{4}$$

as one can verify by substitution. Here M_o is the initial mass of Na^+ in the sea. We can solve this equation for the time T it would take the mass of Na^+ in the ocean to reach the present level, M_p:

$$T = \frac{1}{\beta}\ln\left(\frac{A_t - \beta M_o}{A_t - \beta M_p}\right) = \frac{\tau}{x}\ln\left[\frac{1 - (M_o x/M_p)}{1 - x}\right], \tag{5}$$

26

where τ is the fillup time of equation 1 and x is the output-to-input ratio:

$$x = \frac{\Sigma B_i}{\Sigma A_i} = \frac{B_t}{A_t} \qquad 0 < x < 1. \tag{6}$$

Equation 5 would give the age of the ocean if A_t and β had been constant, conditions which undoubtedly do not apply. However, we will use equation 5 in the following discussion to establish a *maximum* age for the ocean. We can say by the evolutionary models discussed previously that A_t, the sum of the Na^+ inputs at any time t in the past, has always been greater than or equal to $A_{min} = 3.56 \times 10^{11}$ kg/yr, the sum of the eleven past minimum input rates for the processes in Table 1. Similarly, we can say that B_t, the sum of the Na^+ outputs at any time t in the past, has always been less than or equal to $B_{max} = 2.06 \times 10^{11}$ kg/yr, the sum of the seven past maximum output rates for the processes in Table 2. The ratio of these two values, B_{max}/A_{min}, gives us a maximum value, x_{max}, for the output-to-input ratio:

$$x = \frac{B_t}{A_t} \leq \frac{B_{max}}{A_{min}} = \frac{2.06 \times 10^{11}}{3.56 \times 10^{11}} = 0.58 = x_{max}. \tag{7}$$

To make our age estimate as large as possible for the benefit of the evolutionary model, we set the initial Na^+ mass $M_o = 0$, even though the creationist model would suggest otherwise. Then, we insert x_{max} from equation 7 and τ_{max} from equation 2 into equation 5 to get an expression for the absolute upper limit for the age of the ocean:

$$T \leq -\frac{\tau_{max}}{x_{max}} \ln\left(1 - x_{max}\right) = \tau_{max}\left(1 + \frac{x_{max}}{2} + \frac{x_{max}^2}{3} + \ldots\right). \tag{8}$$

Using $\tau_{max} = 41.3$ Myr and $x_{max} = 0.58$ in equation 8 gives $T \leq 62$ Myr.

OUTLINE OF A CREATIONIST MODEL

To get a maximum age for the ocean according to an evolutionary model, we had to assume zero initial Na^+ in the sea, but there is no reason for the creationist model to make such an assumption. On the contrary, there may be good biological reasons to expect God to have created the original ocean with significant salinity. In the maximum age calculation we also assumed an evolutionary model with no catastrophic additions of Na^+ to the ocean. The Genesis Flood, however, would have added highly saline subterranean waters to the oceans (the "fountains of the great deep", Genesis 7:11). Furthermore, Na^+ would have been released by reactions with hot basalt spreading out from the resulting mid-ocean ridges, reactions with volcanic ash and basalt, and the massive runoff of waters from the continents (Genesis 8:3-5). For thousands of years after the Flood, the climate would have been hotter and wetter than today, causing enhanced amounts of Na^+ solution. Extensive post-Flood volcanoes would have deposited enormous quantities of volcanic ash which would have weathered and delivered Na^+ to the oceans at a much higher rate than today. Thus, the creationist model implies (1) that the initial level of Na^+ in the ocean was a substantial fraction of today's level, (2) that there was a significant burst of input Na^+ during the Genesis Flood, and (3) the Na^+ input rate was at higher levels than today for thousands of years.

CONCLUSION

Equation 8 reduces the entire controversy down to one question: what is the value of x_{max}? Evolutionists and old-earth creationists must assert that the ocean is in a steady state condition, meaning that input and output rates have been about equal throughout geologic time, on the average. By that view, they assert that $x_{max} = 1$. This means that T would be infinite, and we could say nothing about the age of the ocean from its Na^+ content.

However, data we have been able to compile from our knowledge of the earth, indicate that the present output of Na^+ from the sea is only one-quarter the present rate of input ($x_p = 0.27$). Furthermore, taking into account plausible evolutionary earth models with maximum outputs and minimum inputs we still cannot solve the dilemma. Our most generous output and input models give $x_{max} = 0.58$. This means (1) that the evolutionary steady-state model is inconsistent with the data, and (2) that the ocean is much younger than the 3-billion year age evolutionists commonly suppose. The data and equation 8 limit the ocean's age to less than 62 million years.

The significance of this result is: (1) the evolutionary timescale of geologic events associated with the ocean is grossly wrong in an absolute sense (though not necessarily in a relative sense), (2) the corresponding radiometric dating methods are grossly wrong (probably because of assumptions implicit in the methods), and (3) biologic evolution, which is alleged to have started in the ocean and had most of its history there, has not had time to occur.

Our result is an upper limit on the age of the ocean. It does not mean that the true age is anywhere near 62 Myr. According to the creationist model, most of the Na^+ in the ocean is there as a result of Creation and the Genesis Flood, not as a result of Na^+ input due to geologic processes sustained over a billion years. This leaves room for the possibility that the sea is less than ten thousand years old. Our conclusion from the Na^+ data is that the sea is less than 62 million years old. This is at least fifty times younger than the age evolutionists require it to be.

We challenge evolutionists and old-earth creationists to report quantitative data supporting a steady state ocean. Those who propose that continental weathering and rivers have been delivering Na^+ to the ocean for 3 billion years need to explain the sea's missing salt. We urge Van Till, Young and Menninga to justify their assertion: "The 4.5 billion year chronology of earth history is in no way weakened or disqualified by an appeal to the salt content of the terrestrial oceans" [7].

REFERENCES

[1] Halley, E., "A short account of the cause of the saltness of the ocean, and of the several lakes that emit no rivers; with a proposal, by help thereof, to discover the age of the world," PHILOSOPHICAL TRANS. ROYAL SOC. LONDON, Vol. 29, 1715, pp. 296-300.

[2] Joly, J., "An estimate of the geological age of the earth," SCIENTIFIC TRANS. ROYAL DUBLIN SOC., New Series, Vol. 7, Part 3, 1899. Reprinted in ANNUAL REPORT SMITHSONIAN INSTITUTION, June 30, 1899, pp. 247-288.

[3] Livingstone, D. A. "The sodium cycle and the age of the ocean," GEOCHIM. COSMOCHIM. ACTA, Vol. 27, 1963, p. 1055.

[4] Clarke, F. W. "The data of geochemistry, 5th ed.," U. S. GEOLOGICAL SURVEY BULL., Vol. 70, 1924, 841 pp. Goldschmidt, V. M., "Grundlagen der quantitativen geochemie", FORTSCHR. MINERAL. KRISTALLOGR. PETROGR., Vol. 17, 1933, pp. 1-112. Rubey, W. W., "Geologic history of sea water. An attempt to state the problem", GEOL. SOC. AMER. BULL., Vol. 62, 1951, pp. 1111-1148.

[5] Gregor, C. B., "Prologue: cyclic processes in geology, a historical sketch", in Gregor, C. B., Garrels, R. M., Mackenzie, F. T., and Maynard, J. B., eds. GEOCHEMICAL CYCLES IN THE EVOLUTION OF THE EARTH, John Wiley, New York, 1988, pp. 5-16. Quote from p. 13.

[6] Van Till, H. J., Young, D. A., and Menninga, C., SCIENCE HELD HOSTAGE, Intervarsity Press, Downers Grove, IL., 1988, 189 pp. Chapter 5, "Timeless Tales from the Salty Sea", critiques creationist views of ocean salinity and affirms the steady state model.

[7] Van Till, Young and Menninga, op. cit., p. 91.

[8] Meybeck, M., "Concentrations des eaux fluviales en elements majeurs et apports en solution aux oceans," REV. DE GEOL. DYN. GEOGR. PHYS., Vol. 21, 1979, pp. 215-246. See tabulation of data in Tables 1 and 5.

[9] Meybeck, op. cit., Table 6.

[10] Meybeck, M., "Global chemical weathering of surficial rocks estimated from river dissolved loads", AMER. JOUR. SCI., Vol. 287, 1987, pp. 401-428.

[11] Sayles, F. L., "The composition and diagenesis of interstitial solutions; I. Fluxes across the seawater-sediment interface in the Atlantic Ocean", GEOCHIM. COSMOCHIM. ACTA, Vol. 43, 1979, pp. 527-546. Table 7, column 6 gives the fluxes of ions out of and into ocean sediments.

[12] Drever, J. I., Li, Y. H., and Maynard, J. B., "Geochemical cycles: the continental crust and the oceans", in Gregor, C. B., Garrels, R. M., Mackenzie, F. T., and Maynard, J. B., eds., CHEMICAL CYCLES IN THE EVOLUTION OF THE EARTH, John Wiley, New York, 1988, pp. 17-53. See Table 1.4, column 3.

[13] Schultz, D. F., and Turekian, K. K., "The investigation of the geographical and vertical distribution of several trace elements in sea water using neutron activation analysis", GEOCHIM. COSMOCHIM. ACTA, Vol. 29, 1965, pp. 259-313.

[14] Garrels, R. M., and Mackenzie, F. T., EVOLUTION OF SEDIMENTARY ROCKS, W. W. Norton, New York, 1971, Table 4.11.

[15] Pye, K., AEOLIAN DUST, Academic Press, New York, 1987, p. 90.

[16] Mackenzie, F. T., and Wollast, R., "Sedimentary cycling models of global processes", in Goldberg, E. D., ed., THE SEA, John Wiley, New York, Vol. 6, 1977, p. 742.

[17] Meybeck, "Concentrations des eaux fluviales...", Table 6.

[18] Paull, C. K., and Neumann, A. C., "Continental margin brine seeps: Their geological consequences," GEOLOGY, Vol. 15, June 1987, pp. 545-548.

[19] Garrels and Mackenzie, EVOLUTION OF SEDIMENTARY ROCKS, p. 104.

[20] Seyfried, W. E., Jr., "Experimental and theoretical constraints on hydrothermal alteration processes at mid-ocean ridges", ANN. REV. EARTH PLANET. SCI., Vol. 15, 1987, p. 324.

[21] Wolery, T. J., and Sleep, N. H., "Interactions of geochemical cycles with the mantle," in Gregor, C. B., Garrels, R. M., Mackenzie, F. T., and Maynard, J. B., eds., CHEMICAL CYCLES IN THE EVOLUTION OF THE EARTH, John Wiley, New York, 1988, pp. 77-103.

[22] Wolery and Sleep, op. cit., p. 91.

[23] Wolery and Sleep, op. cit., table 3.5.

[24] Von Damm, K. L., "Systematics of and postulated controls on submarine hydrothermal solution chemistry", JOUR. GEOPHYS. RES., Vol. 93, 1988, pp. 4551-4561. See Table 1 for Na^+ concentrations of 20 Pacific hydrothermal solutions.

[25] Campbell, A. C., et al., "Chemistry of hot springs on the Mid-Atlantic Ridge," NATURE, Vol. 335, (6 Oct. 1988), pp. 514-519.

[26] Holland, H. D., THE CHEMISTRY OF THE ATMOSPHERE AND OCEANS, John Wiley, New York, 1978, 351 pp. See table 5.14.

[27] Meybeck, "Concentrations des eaux fluviales...", p. 242.

[28] Petrenchuk, O. P., "On the budget of sea salts and sulfur in the atmosphere", JOUR. GEOPHYS. RES., Vol. 85, 1980, pp. 7439-7444. Petrenchuk, O. P., and Selezneva, E. S., "Chemical composition of precipitation in regions of the Soviet Union", JOUR. GEOPHYS. RES., Vol. 75, 1970, pp. 3629-3634.

[29] De Andelis, M., Barkov, N. I., and Petrov, V. N., "Aerosol concentrations over the last climatic cycle (160 kyr) from an Antarctic ice core", NATURE, Vol. 325, 1987, pp. 318-321.

[30] Berner, E. K., and Berner, R. A., THE GLOBAL WATER CYCLE: GEOCHEMISTRY AND ENVIRONMENT, Prentice-Hall, Englewood Cliffs, New Jersey, 1987, 387 pp.

[31] Sayles, F. T., and Mangelsdorf, P. C., "Cation- exchange characteristics of Amazon River suspended sediment and its reaction with seawater", GEOCHIM. COSMOCHIM. ACTA, Vol. 43, 1979, pp. 767-779.

[32] Sayles, F. T., and Mangelsdorf, P. C., "The equilibration of clay minerals with seawater: exchange reactions", GEOCHIM. COSMOCHIM. ACTA, Vol. 41, 1977, pp. 951-960.

[33] Drever, Li and Maynard, op. cit., Table 1.3, column 3.

[34] Drever, Li and Maynard, op. cit., p. 27.

[35] Muehlenbachs, K., "The alteration and aging of the basaltic layer of sea floor, oxygen isotopic evidence from DSPDP/IPOD legs 51, 52, and 53", INITIAL REP. DEEP-SEA DRILL. PROJ., Vol. 51, 1980, pp. 1159-1167.

[36] Wolery and Sleep, op. cit., Table 3.2.

[37] Von Damm, op. cit.; Campbell et al., op. cit.

[38] Holland, op. cit., Table 5.14, p. 232.

[39] Mackenzie and Wollast, op. cit.

[40] Holland, op. cit., p. 186.

[41] Flint, R. F., GLACIAL AND QUATERNARY GEOLOGY, John Wiley, New York, 1971, 982 pp.

[42] Berner, R. A., Lasaga, A. C., and Garrels, R. M., "The carbonate-silicate geochemical cycle and its effect on atmospheric carbon dioxide over the past 100 million years", AMER. JOUR. SCI., Vol. 283, 1983, pp. 641-683.

[43] Barron, E. J., Thompson, S. L., and Schneider, S. H., "An ice-free Cretaceous? Results from climate model simulations", SCIENCE, Vol. 212, 1981, pp. 501-508.

[44] Tardy, Y., N'Kounkou, R., and Probst, J., "The global water cycle and continental erosion during Phanerozoic time (570 my)", AMER. JOUR. SCI., Vol. 289, 1989, pp. 455-483. See Table 7.

[45] Berner, R. A., and Barron, E. J., "Factors affecting atmospheric CO_2 and temperature over the past 100 million years", AMER. JOUR. SCI., Vol. 284, 1984, pp. 1183-1192.

[46] Drever, Li and Maynard, op. cit., p. 51.

[47] Estimate of global salt inventory by W. T. Hosler is cited by Holland, H. D., THE CHEMICAL EVOLUTION OF THE ATMOSPHERE AND THE OCEANS, Princeton Univ. Press, Princeton, N.J., 1984, p. 461.

[48] Zharkov, M. A., HISTORY OF PALEOZOIC SALT ACCUMULATION, Springer-Verlag, New York, 1981, 308 pp. Tables 7 and 8 contain data on volume of evaporites.

[49] A greater value for B_{4max} can be obtained if the very unusual Messinian (Late Miocene) evaporites of the Mediterranean region are assumed to be of marine origin. W. T. Hosler et al. ("A census of evaporites and its implications for oceanic geochemistry", GEOL. SOC. AMER., ABSTR. PROGRAMS, Vol. 12, 1980, p. 449) estimate the Messinian rock salt mass, which allows the Na^+ mass to be estimated at 5.8×10^{17} kg. This mass is about 13% of the world's rock salt Na^+ and 4% of the Na^+ in the present ocean. If the "Messinian salinity crisis" is assumed to have had a duration of one million years, B_{4max} would be 5.8×10^{11} kg/yr, a value slightly greater than all the combined inputs. The "Messinian salinity crisis", however, is admitted by many to be a truly extraordinary event. It cannot be used to estimate the long term removal rate of Na^+ in halite.

[50] Drever, Li and Maynard, op. cit., p. 37.

[51] Billo, S. M., "Residence times of chemical elements in geochemistry", AMER. ASSOC. PETROL. GEOL. BULL., Vol. 73, 1989, p. 1147.

[52] Holland, THE CHEMISTRY OF THE ATMOSPHERE AND OCEANS, op. cit., Table 5.1.

[53] Lasaga, A.C., "The kinetic treatment of geochemical cycles", GEOCHIM. COSMOCHIM. ACTA, Vol. 44, 1980, pp. 815-828.

DISCUSSION

The world that we live in is God's world. We are reminded by many passages of Scripture, and especially by Psalm 19:1 that "The heavens are telling the glory of God; the skies proclaim the work of his hands." Therefore, we must give serious consideration to what we learn about God's world through scientific study of that world. From within that perspective, I submit the following comments:

1) Our knowledge and understanding of God's world is less than perfect and less than complete. We have not yet learned in detail all of the processes involving sodium in the ocean environment. Any improvements in our understanding are welcome.

2) The authors speak of the inability to account for all of the factors which affect sodium concentration in the oceans as a "dilemma" for those who think that the Earth is old. However, even if the residence time of sodium in the oceans is less than the 260 million years reported in much of the recent literature, we must remember that the residence time of sodium in the oceans is not the same as the age of the Earth. After all, the residence time of aluminum in the oceans is only 100 years, and that is not viewed as a dilemma.

3) While short residence times for various elements in ocean water are no dilemma for those who think the Earth is old, long residence times for some elements in ocean water decidedly presents a dilemma to those who think that the Earth is young.

4) Sodium is not the only element with a residence time in the oceans which is longer that several thousand years. The residence time for potassium is 11 million years, for magnesium is 45 million years, for silver is 2 million years, and for uranium is 500,000 years. Are all of those long residence times in error? Can all of them be reduced to several thousand years by good data and proper calculations?

5) According to their own calculations, the authors have determined a "filling time" of the oceans of 32.2 million years. Are the authors willing to accept that number as a minimum age of the Earth?

6) After gathering a considerable amount of data, and after performing several calculations and logical analyses, the authors suggest that the scientific study they have done isn't worth anything, after all. They suggest that God might have made the oceans recently, with a great deal of sodium (and other elements) already dissolved in the water. If that is the attitude one wishes to adopt, what is the justification for doing the scientific study? A paper which is only one or two sentences in length would suffice to reach the same result.

7) It is God's world that we are studying by scientific methods. It is God's handiwork that we are learning about through those studies. God deserves to be praised and honored--and believed--for what we have been able to learn about his world. If our careful study of God's world brings us false or unreliable information, then what can it mean for the Psalmist to sing, "The heavens are telling the glory of God; the skies proclaim the work of his hands."?

Clarence Menninga, Ph.D.
Grand Rapids, Michigan

CLOSURE

We had hoped Dr. Menninga would respond to our challenge "to report quantitative data supporting a steady state ocean," but his review contains no such data. An erroneous assumption underlies all of his remarks. It appears implicitly in his points 2 through 4, and explicitly in point 5: he assumes that residence times are minimum ages for the ocean, i.e., that the ocean must be older than any given residence time. He does not explain his reasoning, but it must be something like this: (1) If there were no initial sodium (for example) in the ocean, and (2) if the input of sodium has always been no greater than the present rate, then it would take more than 32 million years (our residence time for sodium) to get the present amount of sodium in the ocean. In other words, Dr. Menninga assumes a uniformitarian view of the origin of sodium in the ocean; he feels that all the sodium in the sea got there by today's processes at essentially today's rates.

The flaw in Dr. Menninga's reasoning is in his two uniformitarian "if" conditions; he has no logical basis for assuming either is true. The creationist model we described provides a specific counter-example; Menninga cannot logically exclude the possibilities that (1) God created the ocean with some initial sodium, and (2) the sodium input during the Flood was much higher than it is today, a very natural consequence of such an event. (See Fig. A.) This shows that Menninga's assumptions are not generally valid, so residence times are not minimum ages. Our specific replies follow:

1. "Our knowledge ... is less than perfect." This is basically an appeal to unknown factors to support his view. "Improvements in our understanding are welcome." Since our paper is the only one which has collected all the diverse data on sodium inputs (including seven previously unrecognized ones) and outputs, it should have improved Dr. Menninga's understanding.

2a. "Inability to account for all of the factors." It is not we who profess such an inability; we wrote that we have accounted for all of the major factors. For over half a century, many evolutionists have been diligently searching for sodium outputs, so we think it likely that all of the major ones have been found. The dilemma for evolutionists is not in accounting, but in facing up to the bottom line of the ledger: the sea is young.

2b. "Residence time ... is not the same as the age." We agree; we never said otherwise. Dr. Menninga evidently overlooked our statement stressing that point: "It is important to understand that t [the residence time] is not the age of the ocean." Apparently he also overlooked our main point, which we emphasized numerous times in the paper: we have determined a maximum limit on the age, not the age itself. Equation (8) specifies this limit, which depends not only on the residence time but also on the maximum output-to-input ratio, x_{max}.

2c. Aluminum's small residence time is not a dilemma for old-earthers. Hence, he implies, sodium's residence time should not present a dilemma, either. But it is not the residence time which makes the dilemma; it is the imbalance between sodium inputs and outputs. We can see this by contrasting what eq. (8) says about aluminum and sodium. The data for aluminum gives x_{max} = 1; using this in eq. (8) tells us that the age of the ocean is equal to or less than infinity. For the data we report concerning sodium, eq. (8) tells us that the ocean is less than 62 million years old. Both statements are true, but the one based on sodium is more stringent, and that is the one which places evolutionists in a dilemma.

3. "Long residence times ... present a dilemma to [young-earthers]."
This would be true only if residence times were minimum ages, an idea we disproved in our introductory remarks above.

4. Can [various large residence times] be reduced to thousands of years? Since residence times are not minimum ages, we are under no obligation to perform such a shrinkage.

5. "Are the authors willing to accept [their 32 million year sodium residence time] as a minimum age?" No. We can be persuaded by valid reasoning, but not by mere repetition of the same error which underlies the previous points.

6. "The authors suggest [their analysis] isn't worth anything." This suggestion comes from Dr. Menninga, not from us. "What is the justification for the study?" The reason for our study is the pursuit of truth.   In the best tradition of science, the study rigorously tests a hypothesis (the evolutionary view of the ocean), and it outlines a testable alternative hypothesis, our creationist model. For reasons he does not specify, Menninga disdains our model, but if he had paid close attention to its implications, he might have recognized the flaws in his own argument.

7. "God's world brings us false or unreliable information." Dr. Menninga's reaction to our paper suggests that it is he who regards information from the natural world as unreliable. He is avoiding a straightforward understanding of the sodium data, because it does not fit into his preconceptions of an old earth. "God's world ... deserves to be ... believed." So why doesn't Dr. Menninga believe it?

CONCLUSION

Dr. Menninga has staked a great deal upon his assumption that residence times represent minimum ages; it is probably one reason he does not respond to our challenge. He failed to see that our analysis and alternative model expose the logical fallacies behind his assumptions and collapse his case. He also misunderstood the thrust of the paper. Our main purpose was not to reduce the residence time of sodium, but to quantify the gross imbalance between sodium inputs and outputs and to clarify its implications. His response fails to make crucial distinctions between four different concepts: residence time, maximum age, minimum age, and true age. His decided preference for the term "residence time" instead of the more neutral term "filling time" clouds the central issue: Is ocean sodium in a steady state?

Dr. Menninga's repeated references to God and the Bible seem inconsistent with his aversion to our creationist model. After all, the two main features of the model came directly from scripture: (1) a recent creation, and (2) a worldwide flood whose natural consequence would be a massive influx of sodium into the ocean. We were aware that Menninga and his colleagues resist a straightforward understanding of the Bible with regard to the youth of the earth. Evidently, they similarly resist the biblical account of the Flood.

We are genuinely disappointed that Dr. Menninga did not overcome his uniformitarian presuppositions enough to follow our reasoning clearly. We did not expect agreement, but we did expect understanding. Therefore we call upon Dr. Clarence Menninga and his colleagues, Drs. Davis Young and Howard Van Till, to re-examine their presuppositions, read our paper more carefully, and respond to our challenge: report quantitative data supporting a steady-state ocean. If they cannot provide such data, then they should cease denying what we are asserting: that all present knowledge about sodium in the sea indicates that the ocean is young.

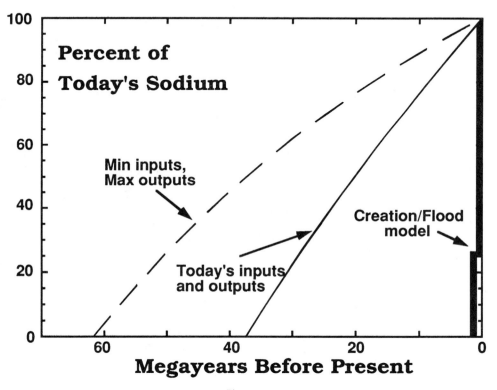

Figure A

Steven A. Austin, Ph.D.
D. Russell Humphreys, Ph.D.

3-D FINITE ELEMENT SIMULATION OF THE GLOBAL TECTONIC
CHANGES ACCOMPANYING NOAH'S FLOOD

JOHN R. BAUMGARDNER, PH.D.
1965 CAMINO REDONDO
LOS ALAMOS, NM 87544

ABSTRACT

This paper presents a mechanism for the large-scale tectonic change that accompanied Noah's Flood. It assumes that the onset of the Flood only a few thousand years ago correlates with the notable stratigraphical and paleontological discontinuity of the Precambrian-Cambrian boundary. This implies that the geological history recorded in the rocks usually classified as Paleozoic and Mesozoic unfolded in a catastrophic manner within a few months time. It also suggests that the primary energy source for the catastrophe was the gravitational potential energy of the pre-Flood ocean lithosphere relative to the base of the mantle. The geological and geophysical data suggest that subduction of the pre-Flood ocean lithosphere began around the margin of a pre-Flood supercontinent. It is proposed that the mantle's viscosity at that time was lower than at present to permit rapid sinking of the lithosphere into the mantle and that the sinking rate was enhanced by a thermal runaway effect associated with a temperature- dependent rheology and localized shear heating near the slabs. Rapid replacement of the cold, dense pre-Flood oceanic lithosphere with hot, less dense mantle material from below resulted in significant elevation of the ocean floors relative to the continental surfaces causing a temporary rise in the world sea level by as much as 1500 meters. Huge volumes of sea water were converted to pressurized steam where the ocean floors rifted apart to produce intense global rain. The deformations induced in the mantle pulled the supercontinent apart, opened the present Atlantic and Indian oceans, and caused large vertical tectonic motions that strongly influenced sedimentation patterns on the continents. A 3-D spherical finite element simulation of the dynamics of this catastrophe is described.

INTRODUCTION

Straightforward reading of the Bible allows no place for large-scale destruction of life on earth prior to the Flood of Noah. The scarcity of multicellular fossils in Precambrian rocks and the abrupt initial appearance in Lower Cambrian rocks of a wide diversity of complex multicelled lifeforms, frequently in high concentrations, seems therefore logically to demand that the onset of the Flood catastrophe correspond to this striking feature in the paleontological record.

If the earliest Cambrian rocks mark the beginning stage of Noah's Flood just a few thousand years ago, then most of the subsequent geological record, from Cambrian to recent, must be the product of a global catastrophe of a magnitude beyond the ability of the human mind to imagine. This catastrophe must involve, for example, deposition of more than a mile of sediment on the average on top of the normally high-standing continents, uplift and erosion of mountain belts like the Appalachians, uplift of all the young mountain belts like the Andes, Alps, and Himalayas, formation of all the coal and oil deposits, formation of all the present day ocean floor, and separation of continents by several thousands of kilometers. The time scale for the most intense phase of the catastrophe is constrained by the Biblical description to be months, although it likely required centuries for the earth to return to what one would consider a state of reasonable tectonic and climatic stability.

The primary objective of this paper is to present a physical explanation for this catastrophe. I shall assume the pre-Flood earth had essentially the same mass and radius as the present earth (i.e., no expansion of the earth will be invoked), a very similar internal constitution and temperature profile as at present, and a distribution of continental crust similar to published reconstructions of Pangea (Fig. 3). The assumption of a single pre-Flood supercontinent is suggested by Gen. 1:9, "Then God said, 'Let the waters below the heavens be gathered into one place, and let the dry land appear'; and it was so."

For the benefit of those readers with limited background in the earth sciences, let me attempt to define at least a few of the most critical terms. One of the most important is lithosphere. The earth's lithosphere is its outer skin, the layer of rock extending from the surface down to a depth of about 50 miles where the rock is sufficiently cool to behave over long periods of time more or less as an elastic solid. At greater depths temperatures are high enough that silicate rock responds more like a plastic solid when slowly deformed. In the present earth,

35

the lithosphere is divided into a dozen or so patches, or plates, that behave more or less as rigid units. Along certain portions of the plate boundaries, the plates are converging, with one of the plates sinking into the earth beneath the other plate. This process is referred to as subduction. Some plates have part of their area covered with a 20 mile thick layer of lower density rock. These areas with this lighter rock layer represent the continents. Areas without this layer comprise the ocean basins. The buoyancy of the continental areas prevents these portions of the lithosphere from sinking or subducting. In contrast, oceanic lithosphere, which has an average chemical composition similar to the warmer rock beneath it, has a natural tendency to sink because of its lower temperature and higher density relative to the rock below. Hence it is the oceanic lithosphere that subducts. Along other portions of the plate boundaries, the plates are diverging and new plate area is formed as magma rises from below and cools to fill the gap. This process is referred to as sea-floor spreading. It is now taking place along the 40,000 mile long mid-ocean ridge system. Currently the plates are moving relative to one another with velocities on the order of a few centimeters per year. Seismological data indicate that silicate rock extends to a depth of about 1800 miles or 2900 km, which is slightly less that half the earth's radius. This silicate portion of the earth is known as the mantle. The ideas of lithospheric subduction, sea-floor spreading, and solid-state flow of mantle rock are abundantly supported by objective geological and geophysical observation.

What events and processes could possibly be responsible for transforming a pre-Flood earth, that supported all the living organisms that now form the planet's coal and oil deposits, to an earth similar to that of today in a matter of months or even centuries? In summary, I argue that the central process was the rapid sinking of the pre-Flood ocean lithosphere into the deeper mantle. It was the stored gravitational potential energy of this cold, dense layer of rock relative to the base of the mantle that served as the primary energy source for the catastrophe. What triggered this event? One possibility is that processes internal to the earth caused stresses in the lithosphere sufficient to produce rupture and initiate its sinking. Another possibility is that impact of an extraterrestrial body disrupted the lithosphere and started the sinking. Once begun, however, the sinking instability was sufficiently strong to lead to catastrophic transformation of the earth within a few weeks time, including the destruction of almost all the air-breathing life on the planet.

What are some of the consequences at the earth's surface of such a sinking event? Subduction of the pre-Flood ocean lithosphere within a period of a few weeks implies plate velocities measured in meters per second instead of centimeters per year. If plate motions today generate magnitude 8 earthquakes and large volcanic eruptions at plate boundaries, it boggles the imagination to contemplate the intensity of tectonic upheaval that accompanied plate velocities more than ten million times higher. One can be sure that the level of seismic energy release was sufficient to generate chaotically violent tidal wave activity along every coastline on the planet. With magma rising to fill gaps some 50 miles deep and tens of thousands of miles long and widening at rates of meters per second as oceanic plates pulled apart, the level of volcanic violence is even more difficult to imagine. Staggering quantities of volcanic ash, water vapor, and CO_2 would be ejected into the atmosphere. The volume of water converted to pressurized steam along belts of rapid sea-floor spreading is easily enough to produce rain over the entire surface of the earth at a rate of a meter per hour continuously for the 40 days and nights mentioned in Genesis 7.

Another notable consequence of the rapid sinking of the pre-Flood ocean lithosphere is a quickly altered sea level. New sea floor formed at spreading ridges has a much higher average temperature and lower density than old sea floor that is subducted. This is the reason that on today's earth the mid-ocean ridges display an elevation some 2000 meters higher than that of the abyssal plains where the lithosphere is relatively much colder. Applied to the Flood model, this observation implies that rapid subduction of the old ocean lithosphere would lead to a reduction in the mean depth of the ocean basins of between 2000 and 3000 meters, depending on the thickness of the pre-Flood ocean lithosphere, and produce a rise in the world sea level of between 1200 and 1800 meters. Such an increase in sea level would of course inundate most of the continental areas. As the newly formed ocean floor cooled, the result would be a deepening of the ocean basins and a runoff of the flood waters from the continents.

In summary we note that rapid subduction of the ocean lithosphere produces several consequences consistent with the Biblical account of the Flood. It generates a huge amount of rainfall, it causes a major but temporary rise in the world sea level, and it leads to a level of tectonic violence sufficient to destroy almost every ecological habitat on the planet. Furthermore, rapid subduction of the pre-Flood ocean lithosphere is a logical requirement of the correlation of the onset of the Flood with the Precambrian- Cambrian boundary, because no ocean floor older than Mesozoic can be found on today's earth. No pre-Flood (i.e., Precambrian) ocean floor, which presumably covered some 60% of the earth's surface area, can be identified anywhere (except possibly as rare ophiolite formations in continental environments). It is therefore logical to conclude that essentially all the pre-Flood ocean lithosphere has sunk into the mantle since the onset of the Flood just a few tens of centuries ago (1).

PHYSICS OF SINKING LITHOSPHERIC SLABS

Most people are aware that most materials are less dense when they are hot than when they are cold. Most know, for example, that hot air rises and cold air sinks. This behavior is also characteristic of the silicate material that forms the earth's mantle. Ocean lithosphere, with an average chemical composition close to that of the underlying mantle but an average temperature that is hundreds of degrees lower, has a resulting higher density and thus a tendency to sink. The style of sinking is for a patch or slab of this thin layer to peel away from the surface and quickly to assume a near vertical orientation as it sinks into the viscous deeper mantle.

Because the ocean lithosphere has a higher density than the underlying material, it possesses gravitational potential energy relative to the mantle below. The amount of this energy per unit volume is given by the product of the density difference, the gravitational acceleration, and the depth it can sink. The density difference is the product of the density, the temperature difference, and the volume coefficient of thermal expansion. If we use representative values for these quantities of 3400 kg/m^3 for the density, 600 K for the temperature difference, 2.5 x 10^{-5} K^{-1} for the volume coefficient of thermal expansion, 10 m/s^2 for the gravitational acceleration, and 2800 km for the effective depth of the mantle, we obtain a value of 1.4 x 10^9 J/m^3 for the gravitational potential energy density. This may be compared with the energy per unit volume required to melt silicate rock, 5.6 x 10^9 J/m^3, and with the energy per unit volume needed to boil cold water at atmospheric pressure, 2.7 x 10^9 J/m^3. Considering the volume of oceanic lithosphere to be a layer 80 km thick covering 60% of the earth's surface, we obtain a value of 3.4 x 10^{28} J for the amount of associated gravitational potential energy. If released near the earth's surface, this amount of energy is sufficient to melt a layer of silicate rock 12 km thick or the boil away a layer of water 25 km deep over the entire earth. It is equivalent to the kinetic energy of 170,000 asteroids, each 10 km in diameter and traveling at 15 km/s. If even a tiny fraction is released near the earth's surface in the span of just a few months, massive catastrophe is implied. Certainly this energy source is easily sufficient to produce the surface tectonic upheaval associated with the Flood.

At this point the reader may be wondering why, since subduction of oceanic lithosphere is presumably occurring now and the gravitational potential energy of the oceanic lithosphere is approximately equal to that just calculated, we are not undergoing a major catastrophe at this present moment? In other terms, one could be asking what was different about the earth at the time of the Flood compared with today that allowed this catastrophe to unfold? The answer to this fundamental question almost certainly involves the issue of the mantle's rheology, that is, its deformational behavior.

Experimental investigations of the rheological properties of silicate minerals have demonstrated that they undergo plastic deformations under stress through the migration of minute defects or dislocations. These studies show that the deformation rate is strongly dependent on the temperature. The rate has an exponential temperature dependence of the form exp(E*/RT), where E* is an activation energy per mole, R is the universal gas constant, and T is the absolute temperature. As an example, the mineral olivine has a value for E* of about 5.0 x 10^5 J/mole (2), which implies the deformation rate increases by more than a factor of 36,000 as the temperature changes from 1200 K to 1500 K. This illustrates the crucial role temperature plays on the rates silicate rock deform and flow.

Another important observation is that mechanical work is converted to heat when materials undergo plastic deformation. Coupled to the strong dependence of the deformation rate on temperature, this deformational heating leads to the possibility of a mechanical instability. As a conceptual aid in understanding this instability, let us consider the idealized problem of a rigid sphere sinking under the influence of gravity in a fluid which has a strong temperature dependence of viscosity. Assume that both are initially at a single uniform temperature. As the sphere begins to sink, a volume of fluid surrounding the sphere undergoes significant deformation and is therefore heated. The heating in this volume in turn leads to an increased temperature and diminished viscosity. The lower viscosity in the vicinity of the sphere leads to a concentration of the deformation in the volume with elevated temperature, which in turn leads to more concentrated heating, higher temperature, yet lower viscosity, and higher sinking velocity. There is a competing process that acts to moderate or even inhibit this situation, however. Diffusion or conduction of heat from warmer regions to cooler ones operates to reduce nonuniformity of temperature. In order for the instability to be expressed, the time involved in heating the strongly deforming volume must be short compared with the time required for cooling the volume by thermal diffusion.

It is instructive to view the instability from an energy balance standpoint. In the regime in which the instability is not expressed and the sphere sinks at constant velocity, the gravitational potential energy of the sphere is being converted to mechanical work to deform the fluid, and this work done on the fluid appears as heat. In this case, all the gravitational potential energy is converted to heat. On the other hand, if heating reduces the viscosity, less energy is needed to deform the fluid, and the remaining gravitational energy is converted to kinetic energy of the sphere, i.e., the sphere is accelerated to a higher velocity. So long as there continues to be more gravitational energy available than needed to deform the surrounding medium, the velocity of the sphere will increase. If increasing the velocity continues to keep the deformational energy less than the available gravitational energy, the velocity will increase without limit in a runaway fashion.

At what point does thermal diffusion cease to be a restraining influence and allow this instability to be expressed? It is when the time interval the sphere resides in a local region of fluid, given roughly by D/v, where D is the diameter of the sphere and v is its velocity, is much less than the characteristic thermal diffusion time, given by L^2/κ, where L is the diffusion length and κ is the thermal diffusivity of the medium. For our purposes, we can take the radius R of the sphere as the characteristic length L. The sinking velocity of a sphere in a constant viscosity medium is given by $0.22R^2\Delta\rho g/\eta$, where $\Delta\rho$ is the density difference between the sphere and the fluid, g is the gravitational acceleration, and η is the dynamic shear viscosity. The condition that the time interval D/v be much less than L^2/κ is then equivalent to the requirement that h be much less than $0.11R^3\Delta\rho g/\kappa$. If we choose R = 100 km, $\Delta\rho = \rho\alpha\Delta T = (3400\ kg/m^3)(2.5 \times 10^{-5}\ K^{-1})(600\ K) = 51\ kg/m^3$, g = 10 m/s^2, and $\kappa = 1 \times 10^{-6}$ m^2/s and assume 'much less than' is a factor of 0.01, we find that the dynamic shear viscosity needs to be on the order of 5×10^{20} Pa-s or less for the instability to be expressed.

A set of numerical experiments were performed using a two-dimensional finite element code to explore the conditions under which this instability occurred for a slab-like body. The problem domain consisted of a rectangular box 1280 km wide by 2560 km high with reflective side boundaries and free-slip top and bottom boundaries. The cells in the 128 x 128 mesh had a 10 km width and 20 km height. The slab was 80 km wide and 500 km high. Other parameters were slab temperature 900 K, background temperature 1500 K, background density 3400 kg/m^3, volume coefficient of thermal expansion 2.5×10^{-5} K^{-1}, thermal diffusivity 1.0×10^{-6}, gravitational acceleration 10 m/s^2, and an activation temperature (E*/R) of 60,000 K. These experiments show that for values of dynamic shear viscosity of 1.0×10^{21} Pa-s and larger there is no instability. However, for values of 5.0×10^{20} Pa-s and smaller, the instability is clearly evident. Figure 2 displays the distribution of shear heating and viscosity just before the onset of the instability for the case of $\eta = 3.0 \times 10^{20}$ Pa-s. As expected, a zone of intense shear heating and reduced viscosity envelopes the slab. In these experiments, once the instability begins, the sinking velocity increases without limit. However, in the real earth it is almost certain that additional physics such as melting would serve to limit the sinking velocity to a finite value.

This type of thermal runaway instability in a viscous fluid with temperature-dependent viscosity was studied over 25 years ago by Gruntfest (3) who approached the problem using an energy balance analysis and a simplified form for the exponential temperature term, $\exp[-a(T - To)]$, where To is a reference temperature and a is equivalent to $E*/RTo^2$. He found that for values larger than a critical number for a dimensionless parameter $G = a\sigma^2L^2/k\eta$, the temperature of a viscous fluid subject to constant shear stress increases without limit. Here s is shear stress, L the thermal diffusion length, k the thermal conductivity, and η the fluid's intrinsic dynamic shear viscosity apart from shear heating. For a planar slab the critical value for G is 0.88. The parameter G represents the ratio t_c/t_v of two characteristic times; t_c is the thermal diffusion time given by cL^2/k and t_v is the time constant associated with the viscous heating of a fluid under constant shear stress without any conductive heat loss, given by $c\eta/a\sigma^2$, where c is the specific heat. Gruntfest's analysis demonstrates clearly that whether or not the runaway instability occurs depends on the relative strengths of viscous heat production and the heat loss due to thermal diffusion. This conclusion is the same as the preceding analysis which made use of the knowledge of the amount of gravitational energy available for viscous heating instead of assuming the shear stress to be constant.

The idea that thermal runaway could occur in the earth's mantle has been addressed by several workers since Gruntfest. Anderson and Perkins (4), for example, proposed that thermal runaway of chunks of lithosphere in the low viscosity regions of the upper mantle might produce surges of hot material that rise and pond against the base of the lithosphere and cause dramatic episodes of igneous activity at the surface. They speculated that the widespread and complex pattern of Cenozoic volcanism in the southwestern United States might be a consequence of such thermal runaway events. With the estimate of 5×10^{20} Pa-s for the threshold of the instability obtained from the numerical experiments described above, however, not only is it plausible that it can operate in the upper mantle, but it is also conceivable that the instability could occur the entire depth of the mantle, were mantle temperatures just a few hundred degrees warmer. Estimates for the lower mantle viscosity are on the order of 10^{22} -10^{23} Pa-s, or only about a factor of 100 larger than the threshold. It appears that the earth at present is just a little bit too cool for the instability to occur on a mantle wide basis. On the other hand, this instability appears just what is required to account for the catastrophic tectonic changes that accompanied the Flood.

A NUMERICAL EXPERIMENT

A global numerical model for the mantle including its cold upper boundary layer, the lithosphere, will now be described. This model is embodied in the 3-D spherical finite element code named TERRA, first developed as part of the author's dissertation research. The code uses a special spherical mesh constructed from the regular icosahedron and employs a multigrid method for solving the momentum conservation equations for the velocity field at each time step. The mesh consists of 17 radial layers each with 10242 cells (Fig. 2). For each of the cells the code solves the conservation equations for momentum, mass, and energy in terms of the variables velocity, density, and temperature using a Newtonian rheological law and general equation of state. The details are described elsewhere (5,6,7).

In the case model, the mantle is treated as a nearly incompressible, constant viscosity fluid with uniform properties except in the surface layer. The portion of the surface layer designated as continent is given a density 150 kg/m^3 less than the remainder of the volume. In addition, the continental area is given an elastic/plastic rheology and divided into nine blocks corresponding to the present continents mapped to their Pangean locations. The lower density prevents the volume representing continental material from sinking into the mantle, and the elastic/plastic rheology causes the continental blocks to behave as more or less rigid units and thus preserve their shape approximately as they move in response to the velocity field in the mantle below. The remainder of the surface layer is treated just like the interior volume. The inner and outer boundaries of the spherical shell corresponding to the core-mantle boundary and the earth's surface, respectively, are treated as isothermal and traction free.

For a better perspective on the meaning of the calculations it is useful to note some of the model's main limitations. One its most prominent is its restriction to constant viscosity, since the thermal runaway depends on a strongly temperature-dependent rheology. In the 3-D model, the higher velocities implied by thermal runaway of sinking lithospheric slabs are obtained in a crude manner by reducing the viscosity everywhere by nine orders of magnitude. This, of course, mostly eliminates the large gradients in velocity, temperature, and shear heating that otherwise would appear if the strongly temperature-dependent rheology were used. On the other hand, very much higher spatial resolution would be necessary to capture these extreme gradients. Such increased resolution makes such 3-D global calculations beyond the capabilities of even the largest supercomputers currently available. One must therefore for now be content to perform the highly resolved variable viscosity calculations in two dimensions and to apply more approximate treatments in 3-D investigations.

In a manner similar to the simple scaling of viscosity, two other physical parameters were also adjusted by large factors from their nominal values for the present earth. These two parameters are the radiogenic heating rate and the thermal conductivity, which were both increased by a factor of 108. Such scaling of the radiogenic heating rate is reasonable, it would seem, given the diverse evidence that a huge amount of radioactive decay occurred during the Paleozoic and Mesozoic portion of the geological record, which unfolds in a matter of months in the computer simulation. Scaling of the thermal conductivity by this factor is done mainly to smooth temperature gradients that otherwise would not be resolved by the mesh. However, an increased value for the thermal conductivity is consistent with the hydrothermal enhancement of heat transport in zones of rapid seafloor spreading. It is just in these zones that diffusion- like transport of heat plays the greatest role in the calculation.

The limitations of incompressibility and spatially constant parameters mean that physics such as mineral phase transitions which occur between depths of 400 and 700 km in the mantle is not included. Although phase transitions are almost certainly important in mantle dynamics, most numerical investigations presently do not include them. Finally, the treatment of the lithosphere, although sophisticated by current standards, is still rather crude compared with the real earth.

These limitations and approximations notwithstanding, a 3-D calculation was performed to explore the response of a Pangean distribution of buoyant continental lithosphere to the sinking of the ocean lithosphere surrounding it in the framework of a Flood timescale. The reconstruction for Pangea is that of Smith, Hurley, and Briden (8) shown in Fig. 3. The black band in the figure represents the zone of initial subduction. The calculation uses a density of 4500 kg/m^3, a dynamic shear viscosity of 2 x 10^{13} Pa-s, a coefficient of thermal expansion of 2.5 x 10^{-5} K^{-1}, a thermal conductivity of 4 x 10^8 W m^{-1}K^{-1}, a specific heat of 1000 J kg^{-1}K^{-1}, a radiogenic heat production rate of 4 x 10^{-4} W/kg, a gravitational acceleration of 10 m/s^2, an inner boundary temperature of 2300 K, and an outer boundary temperature of 300 K. This case required approximately 900 time steps to reach a problem time of 100 days.

Fig. 4(a) shows the initial temperature distribution at a depth of 74 km together with the outlines of the continental blocks mapped to their Pangean locations. Cold temperatures occur inside the tightly concentrated contour lines and correspond to the initial distribution of subducting lithosphere. Fig. 4(b) - (d) are snapshots of the computed solution at 20, 40, and

60 days, respectively, at the same depth of 74 km. Arrows denote the material velocity field, the finer contours represent the temperature distribution, and the coarser lines are the 80% of initial continental thickness contour. Because of the asymmetrical sinking of surface material into the mantle at the continental margins due to the buoyancy of the continental areas, there exists the tendency of the zones of subduction to drift backward, in the direction away from the continent. The resulting pattern of flow acts to pull the supercontinent apart. Including the elastic/plastic treatment of the pre-defined blocks concentrates the strain into the zones between the blocks. The pattern of motion that develops resembles in a qualitative sense the motions of the continents on the earth since the time of Pangea. A noteworthy and unexpected feature in this calculation is the rapid movement of the Indian block to the northeast.

This experiment provides a general sense of the consequences of most of the ocean lithosphere sinking around the perimeter of a supercontinent resembling Pangea. Seismic tomography studies (9) indicate the existence of a band of material near the base of the mantle with high seismic velocity, presumably indicating cooler temperature, forming a ring around the present Pacific Ocean. These data argue strongly that a substantial amount of material has indeed been subducted around what was once Pangea and that a process similar to that evident in the numerical experiment has indeed taken place in the earth. Together, the geophysical observations and the computer results argue that such a pattern of subduction of the ocean lithosphere must have occurred in a Flood catastrophe that generated most of the Phanerozoic geologic record. Coupled with the potential of thermal runaway of lithospheric slabs and the huge source of energy in these slabs available to perform tectonic work, the case that this is the primary physical mechanism responsible for the large scale tectonic changes associated with the Flood seems to be a reasonable one.

CONCLUSIONS

Because no ocean floor on the present earth is older than Mesozoic, a Flood whose beginning correlates with the Precambrian-Cambrian boundary that produces the geological change associated with the Paleozoic and Mesozoic portions of geologic history must necessarily involve the subduction of all the pre-Flood ocean lithosphere. This appears to be a logical imperative, assuming there has been little or no differential expansion of the earth. If this subduction occurs within the several month time frame of the Flood, it seems likely that it involved a thermal runaway instability that can occur in a viscous material with a temperature-sensitive rheology in a gravitational field. The threshold for this instability is not far removed from mantle conditions in the present earth. The gravitational potential energy available to drive the instability and to perform the Flood's tectonic work at the earth's surface is easily sufficient. Rapid sinking of the ocean lithosphere during the Flood was shown to produce an intense period of rainfall, a major but temporary rise in sea level, and tectonic activity sufficient to accomplish the dramatic geological change recorded in the Paleozoic and Mesozoic rocks. Numerical simulation of this process in 3-D spherical shell geometry suggests that subduction of the pre-Flood ocean lithosphere around a pre-Flood supercontinent resembling Pangea leads to a distribution of continents similar to today's earth. It is concluded that rapid sinking of the pre-Flood ocean lithosphere played a central role in the tectonic aspects of Noah's Flood.

REFERENCES

1. Baumgardner, J. R., "Numerical Simulation of the Large-Scale Tectonic Changes Accompanying the Flood", Proceedings of the First International Conference on Creationism, Vol. II, 1986, pp. 17-28.

2. Weertman, J., "The Creep Strength of the Earth's Mantle," Rev. Geophys. and Space Phys., Vol. 8, 1970, pp. 145-168.

3. Gruntfest, I. J., "Thermal Feedback in Liquid Flow; Plane Shear at Constant Stress," Trans. Soc. Rheology, Vol. 8, 1963, pp.195-207.

4. Anderson, O. L. and Perkins, P. C., "Runaway Temperatures in the Athenosphere Resulting from Viscous Heating," J. Geophys. Res., Vol. 79, 1974, pp. 2136-2138.

5. Baumgardner, J. R., "A Three-Dimensional Finite Element Model for Mantle Convection," unpublished Ph.D. thesis, UCLA, 1983.

6. Baumgardner, J. R. and Frederickson, P. O., "Icosahedral Discretization of the Two-Sphere," SIAM J. Num. Anal., Vol. 22, 1985, pp.1107-1115.

7. Baumgardner, J. R., "Three-Dimensional Treatment of Convective Flow in the Earth's Mantle," J. Stat. Phys., Vol. 39, 1985, pp. 501-511.

8. Smith, A. G., Hurley, A. M., and Briden, J. C., Phanerozoic Paleocontinental World Maps, Cambridge University Press, 1981, pp. 52-55.

9. Dziewonski, A. M. and Woodhouse, J. H., "Global Images of the Earth's Interior," Science, Vol. 236, 1987, pp. 37-48.

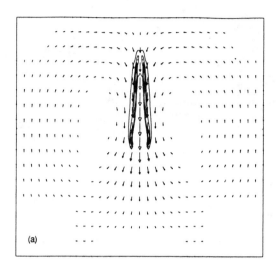

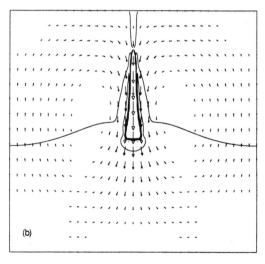

Figure 1. Snapshot from a calculation of the sinking of a vertical slab in a temperature--dependent viscous fluid just prior to thermal runaway. (a) Contours of shear heating rate show heating is strongly localized in zone next to slab. (b) Contours of the logarithm of viscosity show contour of minimum viscosity enclosing bottom of slab. Arrows denote the velocity field.

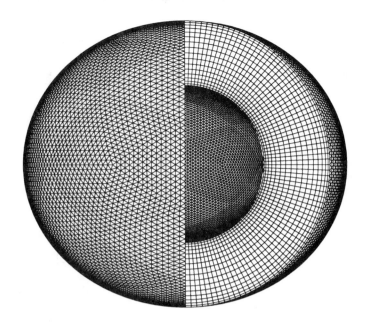

Figure 2. Cutaway view of the computational mesh for spherical shell used in 3-D finite element calculation. Mesh has seventeen layers of cells with 10242 cells in each layer.

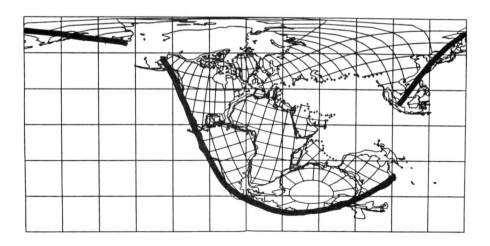

Figure 3. Reconstruction of Pangea published by Smith, Hurley, and Briden (8). The dark band indicates the distribution of initially subducting ocean lithosphere in the 3-D calculation.

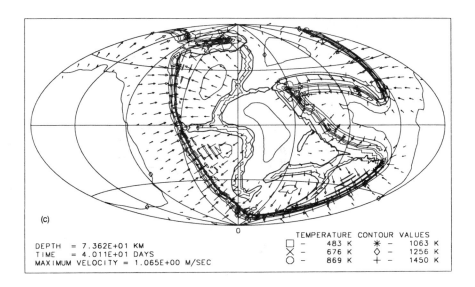

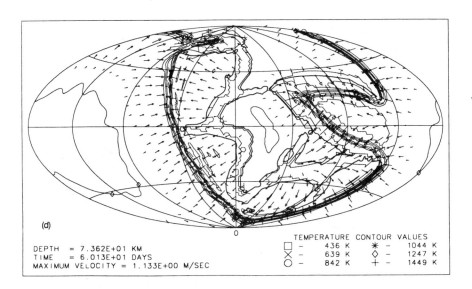

Figure 4. Snapshots from a 3-D calculation to investigate the consequences of initial subduction about a Pangean supercontinent. (a) Initial temperature contours and outlines of continental units that are treated as separate elastic/plastic blocks. (b)-(d) Solution after 20, 40, and 60 days, respectively, at a depth of 74 km. Finer lines are temperature contours, coarser lines are the 80% of initial continental thickness contour, and arrows represent the velocity field.

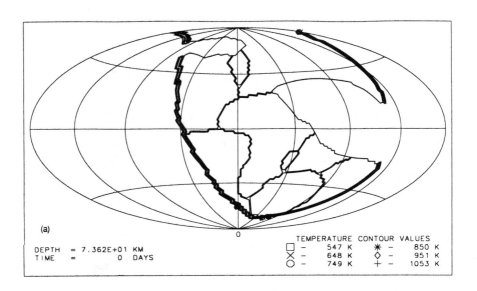

(a)

DEPTH = 7.362E+01 KM
TIME   =   0 DAYS

TEMPERATURE CONTOUR VALUES
□ —   547 K   ＊ —   850 K
✕ —   648 K   ◇ —   951 K
○ —   749 K   + —   1053 K

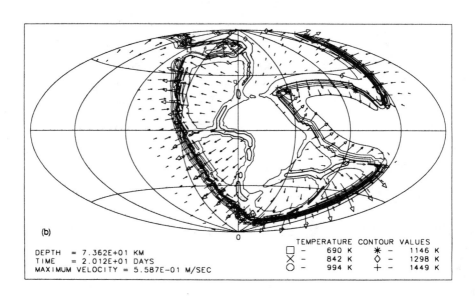

(b)

DEPTH = 7.362E+01 KM
TIME   = 2.012E+01 DAYS
MAXIMUM VELOCITY = 5.587E-01 M/SEC

TEMPERATURE CONTOUR VALUES
□ —   690 K   ＊ —   1146 K
✕ —   842 K   ◇ —   1298 K
○ —   994 K   + —   1449 K

DISCUSSION

Models for subduction of pre-Flood oceanic crust continue to be explored by Dr. Baumgardner. These models offer an excellent mechanism explaining the tectonics and sedimentation associated with Noah's Flood. The gravitational potential energy possessed by the pre-Flood oceanic crust does appear to have been large enough to accomplish the colossal tectonics of the Flood. Furthermore, the mechanism of catastrophic subduction of oceanic crust is shown to be possible if values of mantle viscosity and thermal conductivity are assumed.

Details of the model will, no doubt, be debated. For the most part the framework of assumption within which the model is constructed is representative of current creationist thinking. The assignment of the primary tectonics of the Flood to Paleozoic and Mesozoic, for example, is consistent with what I believe to be correct.

The assumption concerning the configuration of Pangea in early Paleozoic time will need to be substantiated by further research. Are there evidences for Cambrian rifting of Pangea?

Steven A. Austin, Ph.D.
Santee, California

CLOSURE

I appreciate the positive comments from Dr. Steve Austin. In regard to his question about the configuration of the continents before and during early Paleozoic time, I would say that there is a wide diversity of opinion among secular geologists on this matter. For example, in a recent issue of *Science News* (April 27, 1991, Vol. 139, pp. 266-267), there is an article reviewing the work of two geologists who are proposing a late Precambrian supercontinent in which Antarctica is joined to what is today southwestern North America. In setting the context for such a startling notion, the author points out that "At present, reliable paleomagnetic evidence from the Precambrian period is scant, leaving geologists free to propose almost any conceivable orientation during that period.

My own view is that the pre-Flood continental configuration was likely similar to reconstructions of Pangea as indeed I suggest in my paper. This conviction is based on geological considerations as well as geophysical ones. Geological observations indicate the Paleozoic Caledonian orogeny indisputably involved North America and northern Europe. This Caledonian upheaval involves the opening and closing of a proto-Atlantic, but the spatial relationship between North America and Europe prior to this event does not seem to be significantly different from what it was afterward. I suspect a similar sort of early Paleozoic tectonic upheaval occurred among the five southern continents (Africa, South America, Antarctica, Australia, and India) that formed Gondwanaland. Although their late Precambrian spatial relationships are a matter of debate and speculation as the *Science News* article indicates, since they display so many common geological features and a distinctive Paleozoic flora and fauna, it is almost certain that the five blocks were in close proximity in the late Precambrian, i.e. at the onset of the Flood. My view is that the Pangean configuration for their arrangement is the most likely choice.

Furthermore, geophysical evidence concerning the existence of a band of cold, dense material in the present-day lower mantle coincides with the notion that vast areas of lithosphere subducted around the margins of Pangea and sank into the lower mantle to produce the observed density distribution. The simplicity of this pattern obtained by seismic tomography is suggestive that the subduction occurring Paleozoic time was similar to what has occurred since. Nevertheless, I freely concede that the pre-Flood continent configuration may have had differences from the Mesozoic on, and that the tectonic dynamics may have been more complex that I indicate in my paper. Hopefully, more observation data and more detailed modeling in the future will help to resolve these uncertainties.

John R. Baumgardner, Ph.D.

A STUDY OF ROEMER'S METHOD FOR DETERMINING
THE VELOCITY OF LIGHT

EUGENE F. CHAFFIN
BLUEFIELD COLLEGE
BLUEFIELD, VA 24605

ABSTRACT

Data taken by the author during August to December 1988 on eclipses of the first major satellite of Jupiter are compared with data taken by Roemer and Picard 300 years ago. Both sets of data are analyzed by the same method, or as nearly the same as possible, to determine whether the speed of light has changed. The conclusion depends on, and is rather sensitive to, whether or not Io's mean daily motion has changed in the 300 years.

INTRODUCTION

In the late 1600's Cassini, Roemer, Picard and other astronomers at the Paris observatory accurately recorded times of ingresses and egresses of Io (the first major satellite of Jupiter) into and out of Jupiter's shadow. Since Cassini and other prominent European scientists held that the speed of light was infinite, Roemer's use of these eclipse data to find the time required for light to cross an astronomical unit caused great controversy. In Roemer's day the astronomical unit was not known accurately, hence Roemer avoided giving a value for the speed of light, instead announcing a value of 11 minutes for the time for light to cross an astronomical unit. By today's standards, this value is too large, mainly because Roemer did not have an accurate value for the mean daily motion, n_1, of Io, and because Newton's Principia was not yet published and an accurate theory of the perturbations of Io caused by Europa (the second major Jovian moon) did not yet exist.

Study has shown that Io's mean daily motion differs from twice the mean daily motion of Europa by a value of only 0.8 degrees per day (Greenberg, Goldstein, and Jacobs, 1986). Europa forces Io to have different speeds at different points in its nearly circular orbit. The equatorial bulge of Io nods back and forth due to competition between Jupiter's gravitational pull and this resonance with Europa. Tremendous tidal friction and heating are produced inside Io. The Voyager spacecraft discovered active volcanoes on Io. The Io-Europa resonance also involves Ganymede (the third major Jovian moon), but the effect of Ganymede on Io is smaller than that of Europa. A perturbation of Io's longitude is produced by Europa, whose amplitude is approximately half a degree and whose angular frequency is approximately twice the difference between the mean daily motions of Io and Europa (Goldstein 1975).

There are two major reasons why a creationist might extract useful information from a study of Roemer's data. One is the possibility that the speed of light has changed. Setterfield 1987 and Troitskii 1987 discuss this possibility. Another is the fact that the data could reveal a value for the change in Io's orbital period for the last 300 years, and that coupled with theory can be used to estimate the amount of energy loss caused by tidal heating inside Io. If the tidal heating is significantly less than the measured infrared heat flux (which seems to be the case according to studies by Lieske 1987), then that would speak in favor of a young solar system which has not had time to cool.

MODERN DATA COMPARED TO ROEMER'S DATA

To provide a group of control data, the author personally observed ingresses and egresses of Io into Jupiter's shadow from August 1988 to the present. A six inch Newtonian reflector telescope was used to observe Jupiter, and the audible tones from National Bureau of Standards radio station WWV were used (counted) as a clock. The WWV tones have an accuracy of better than one second over the years it has operated, broadcasting universal coordinated time (UTC). For ingresses of Io into Jupiter's shadow, Io was watched until it disappeared (and also the area was observed for a half minute or so afterwards, to be certain that it was really gone). For egresses, observation was made from a few minutes before the expected egress until well after Io appeared. The WWV tones were simultaneously noted in order to determine the exact time of these events. My data are given in Table I.

TABLE I. 1988 DATA ON ECLIPSES OF IO

Coordinated Universal Time of Event (UTC)		Ingress (i) or Egress (e)
August 12	9:46:06	i
September 20	8:14:40	i
September 27	10:08:33	i
September 29	4:37:21	i
October 6	6:31:40	i
October 13	8:25:25	i
October 15	2:54:30	i
October 29	6:43:33	i
December 7	7:23:35	e
December 25	0:11:19	e

A computer program was written to evaluate the parameters L_0, L_2, and L_3 of the perturbation in longitude of Io caused by Europa. These are essentially the same parameters as defined by Goldstein 1975. The results of the program for both the 1988 data (ten points) and the Roemer-Picard data (using 19 of the best points recorded in Goldstein et al. 1973) are presented in Table II. The mean daily motion parameter L_1 was held constant at the value reported by Goldstein 1975 by slightly adjusting the perturbation frequency ω. Following Goldstein 1975, I took into account the 48.6 degrees/year precession of Io's orbit (which is inclined by only 2 arc minutes to Jupiter's equator) by slightly adjusting the inclination angle i of Io's orbit to the plane of Jupiter's orbit. The Roemer-Picard data were relatively insensitive to this inclination angle i, hence I adopted Goldstein's value of 3.06752 degrees. The 1988 data were more sensitive to this parameter, since they are only spread over some five months, and Jupiter's equator was inclined during this period by the maximum amount possible relative to Earth. The value of 3.12 degrees gave the best fit for the 1988 data.

TABLE II. PARAMETERS FOR THE PERTURBATION IN IO'S LONGITUDE CAUSED BY EUROPA

Data	L_0(deg.)	L_1(deg./day)	L_2(deg.)	L_3(deg.)	(rad/day)
Roemer-Picard	-.11934	203.488959	-.11263	.47268	3.56462
1988	.25698	203.488959	-.24090	.43715	3.56410

The data for the longitude and distances of Jupiter were taken from the Astronomical Almanac for 1988 (Washington, W.S. Government Printing Office). Figure 1 illustrates the angular relations between Io's orbit and Jupiter's orbit. Figure 2 illustrates the spherical triangle formed by w = the true anomaly of the Jupiter, i = the inclination of Io's orbit to the plane of Jupiter's orbit, l = longitude of Io from its ascending node, and λ = the latitude of the antisolar point. The following equation follows from the spherical trigonometry:

$$ l = \tan^{-1}\left[\frac{\tan(w - w_0)}{\cos(i)} \right] \qquad (1) $$

Having determined L_0, L_2, and L_3, a second computer program was written to accept as input the speed of light and use it to calculate the time of ten successive eclipses. Then the program calculated the sum of the squares of the differences between theoretical and observed times, in seconds. Then I ran the program for several values of the speed of light. The results are in Table II. As can be seen from the values in the table, the 1988 data are consistent with the modern value of the speed of light, 2.99792458×10^8 meters/second, the sum of the squares of the residuals being smallest in that case. This provides a control, indicating that the methodology is most consistent with a value of 3.2×10^8 meters/second, which is 6.7% larger than the modern value. For various reasons, I expected this work to prove that the speed of light was the same in the 1670's as today, but this is apparently not the outcome.

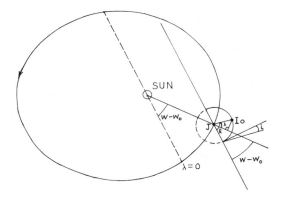

Figure 1. The orbits of Jupiter and Io, showing the angles involved. W is the true anomaly of Jupiter, while W_0 is the true anomaly of the position in jupiter's orbit where the latitude λ, of the antisolar point is zero. l is the longitude of Io in its orbit, measured from its ascending node. i is the inclination of Io's orbit to the plane of Jupiter's orbit.

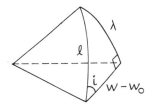

Figure 2. The spherical triangle formed by the angles defined in Figure 1.

TABLE III. RESULTS SHOWING THE SUM OF THE SQUARES OF THE RESIDUALS
IN SECONDS VERSUS THE ASSUMED SPEED OF LIGHT

Speed of Light (m/sec)	Data	Sum of the Squares of the Residuals
2.8×10^8	1988	10001.050
2.9979×10^8	1988	1603.279
3.05×10^8	1988	1974.113
3.1×10^8	1988	3154.281
3.2×10^8	1988	7633.448
2.8×10^8	Roemer-Picard	32736.34
2.9979×10^8	Roemer-Picard	27680.10
3.05×10^8	Roemer-Picard	27020.43
3.1×10^8	Roemer-Picard	26603.55
3.2×10^8	Roemer-Picard	26330.78
3.3×10^8	Roemer-Picard	26698.16
3.5×10^8	Roemer-Picard	28932.33

IS IO'S PERIOD CONSTANT?

It should be noted that Goldstein 1975 and Jacobs 1986 concluded that Io's mean daily motion increased from 203.48892 degrees/day in the 1670's to 203.488959 degrees/day in the twentieth century. However, this is controversial since Lieske 1987, on the basis of extensive modelling of Voyager data, Lunar Ranging Laser Data, as well as modern and medieval eclipse data of Jovian satellites concluded that Io's mean daily motion decreased rather than increased. The result is strongly dependent on the theory adopted for the correction between universal time and ephemeris time. Universal time essentially uses the Earth's rotation rate as a clock, whereas it is known that the Earth's rotation rate is variable. Ephemeris time is based on planetary orbital motion, and is expected to give a uniform rate. These differences are not so important in comparing time changes over, say, the 10 or so years of the Roemer-Picard observations, but they are important over the 300 year gap between then and now. In particular, they effect the value of the mean daily motion that emerges from the Roemer-Picard data.

Because of the above mentioned controversy, I felt free to adopt the present value, n_1, of the mean daily motion of Io, rather than Goldstein's value for the 1670 epoch, which is 1.9×10^{-5} per cent smaller. This would seem to be proper methodology, since differences in the data ascribed by Goldstein et al. to changes in the period of Io might really be due to changes in the speed of light. However, when Goldstein's value n_1 = 203.48892 degrees per day is used, the situation actually got worse, the data giving the best results for a speed of light equal to 3.5 $\times 10^8$ meters per second.

One might adopt the viewpoint that Lieske is right, and the value of n_1 in the past was larger rather than smaller. However, Lieske 1987 gave $\dot{n}_1/n_1$ = $-0.74 \pm .87 \times 10^{11}$ per year, and although the sign is now correct, the amount is now too small. The 1670's data still support a value for the speed of light larger than at present, about 3.2×10^8 meters/sec.

But suppose that Lieske was too conservative, and the value of $\dot{n}_1/n_1$ was larger in absolute value than he concluded. Then it would be possible to conclude that the speed of light 300 years ago was the same as today. The model must then allow tides raised on Jupiter by Io to be significant, in order to provide the torque, (Jupiter's reaction back on Io) necessary for this change. The long term average tidal dissipation rate inside Io must then be relatively small, too small to account for the measured high heat flux coming from Io. The conventional literature could not accept this situation without an abnormally high amount of radioactive material inside Io, to generate the extra decay heat needed to balance the energy equation. But young Earth creationism could readily accept this situation, since in a 6000 year old solar system there would not have been much time for crustal heat loss rates on Io to have dropped. This alternative thus also seems to support the young Earth position, as does the variable speed of light alternative.

CONCLUSION

The possibility of the speed of light changing with time has interesting implications with regard to the age of the universe. Goldstein, Trasco, and Ogburn 1973 analyzed data taken by Roemer and Picard in the late 1600's and concluded that the speed of light had not changed by more than 0.5% if at all. But later work--Goldstein 1975--increased the margin of error to 2.6% The purpose of this work was to analyze the sources of error to understand and present the results from a creationist's standpoint. For this purpose, the author personally took data on the times of ingress and egress of Io (the first major satellite of Jupiter) into the shadow of Jupiter. The data were taken during August to December 1988, using National Bureau of Standards radio station WWV as a clock, and were analyzed for comparison with the data of 300 years ago. The analysis included important geometric effects such as the change in the length of the part of the shadow that Io traverses. The results show that if the period and other parameters of Io's orbit have been constant, then the speed of light must have been greater in the past. However, there are tidal forces operating on Io which could well have changed Io's mean daily motion over 300 years. The future analysis of these tidal actions may well lead to the conclusion that Roemer's data do not support the idea of a variable speed of light.

REFERENCES

Goldstein, S.J., Trasco, J.D., and Ogburn, T.J. III 1973, On the velocity of light three centuries ago, The Astronomical Journal 78(1):122-125.

Goldstein, S.J. 1975, On the secular change in the period of Io, The Astronomical Journal 80(1):532-539.

Goldstein, S.J. and Jacobs, K.C. 1986, The contraction of Io's orbit, The Astronomical Journal 92(1):199-202.

Greenberg, R., Goldstein, S.J., and Jacobs, K.C. 1986, Orbital accelerations and the energy budget in the galilean satellite system. Nature 320:789-790.

Lieske, J.H. 1987, Galilean satellite evolution: observational evidence for secular changes in mean motions, Astronomy and Astrophysics 176:146-158.

Setterfield, B. and Norman, T. 1987, The Atomic Constants, Light, and Time, available from Lambert T. Dolphin, 2111 Grenola Drive, Cupertino, CA 95014, 90 pages.

Troitskii, V.S. 1987, Physical constants and the age of the universe, Astrophysics and Space Science 139(2):389-411.

DISCUSSION

Dr. Chaffin has done a good job of helping to clarify the numerous complexities which surround attempts to measure the speed of light with high precision using Roemer's method. It is very refreshing to see some modern experimental input into the question of the constancy of the speed of light by a creationist.

Why are the sum of the squares of the residuals so much larger for the Roemer-Picard data in Table III than for the 1988 data?

The main conclusion I draw from this paper is that it is probably hopeless to try to disentangle hypothesized changing speed of light effects from other plausible yet unrelated phenomena affecting Roemer type measurements of the speed of light over the past 300 years at the required precision. Does Dr. Chaffin agree with this conclusion?

Gerald E. Aardsma, Ph.D.
San Diego, California

The measurements by Roemer give us some of our best early data on the velocity of light. The author has carefully repeated Roemer's method in our time in order to better understand his data and associated error factors. Dr. Chaffin also considers possible changes in the motion of Jupiter's moon Io which could account for Roemer's value for "c" being significantly higher than the present value. This is an outstanding and careful paper. It is clear, very well written and appropriate for the current discussion that the velocity of light might not be a true constant of nature. I recommend this paper without hesitation, it is excellent.

Lambert T. Dolphin, Ph.D.
California

I like Dr. Chaffin's approach of doing both observation and analysis for himself in this study; it is a refreshing change from the secondhand science which unfortunately has obscured some previous creationist studies of the speed of light. In addition, the paper is valuable because it reveals the complexities involved in the analysis of Roemer's data. It appears that Roemer's choice of Io as the Jovian satellite to observe was unfortunate, since Io interacts so strongly with Europa and Jupiter. I had not known that astronomers do not agree on whether Io is accelerating or decelerating in its orbit at present. Until that basic question is settled, it looks like we cannot say from Roemer's data whether or not the speed of light was different in the seventeenth century. Another important contribution of the paper is its clarification of the young solar system implications of the observed high heat flow from Io.

D. Russell Humphreys, Ph.D.
Albuquerque, New Mexico

The exact procedure followed by Roemer, and by Dr. Chaffin could be made more clear. Dr. Chaffin's general conclusion is that Roemer's data, which had great influence on Setterfield's "c-decay" theory, may not be used to support it. More important to this reviewer is the fact that this entire debate on "c-decay" for the past 10 years has failed to address the fundamental question, "What does one exactly mean by the speed of light?", and it was hoped that Dr. Chaffin would be the one to do so. Let me illustrate. If one assumes that light is a stream of particles called, photons, like water droplets from a nozzle, then the "speed of light" (as usually measured) is simply the statistical average of the various photon speeds, including those that suffer an absorption and re-emission along their path. Hence one must carefully distinguish between the speed of uncollided photons (which we define in vacuo) and remainder whose speed is really (distance travelled divided by transit time plus residence time during each absorption by a nucleon in its path). Nor may one assume that the path used by Roemer (from the earth to the moon of Jupiter) is anything close to a perfect vacuum now that we know how much "trash" fills outer space, most is invisible. If on the other hand, one assumes that light is a wave phenomenon, in harmony with the divine pattern used elasticity, sound and water waves, then we have the problem expressed in the old quatrain: "If sound waves wave air, and water waves wave water, what is it that waves when a lightwave waves?"

Robert L. Whitelaw, M.S.
Blacksburg, Virginia

CLOSURE

I appreciate the positive comments of Drs. Aardsma, Dolphin, Humphreys, and Mr. Whitelaw. In answer to Dr. Aardsma's questions, Goldstein 1975 gave the standard deviation as 31.5 seconds for the fifty points included in his final solution. However, that was <u>after</u> the period of Io had been adjusted to give the best fit. Before the adjustment the residuals are larger. These residuals are larger than for the 1988 data since Roemer did not have radio station WWV or atomic clocks. Time zones did not exist in Roemer's day. Roemer evidently recorded his eclipses in <u>apparent solar time</u>, which must be corrected to a "true" time scale. The equation of time corrections are discussed in the Goldstein 1975 reference.

Can hypothesized changing speed of light effects be disentangled from other plausible yet unrelated phenomena? I think that independent study of tidal friction on Io and Jupiter may eventually provide an answer to the question of how much energy is being removed from Io's orbit via these dissipative effects. Parameters of tidal friction, including the constants called the Love numbers by geophysicists, are poorly defined for Jupiter at present. Analysis of space probe data may soon define the parameters more accurately, however.

Since the conference I have found that the results of my computer programs depend more on which points are analyzed than I thought at the time. The 6.7% faster value for the speed of light reported here thus should not be taken as a precise prediction resulting from a body of theory but merely as an indicator of the realm of possibility that is consistent with the data. The fact that Goldstein and Lieske did not agree on whether Io's period increased or decreased appears to be linked to this variability of the results with the choice of data set.

I thank Professor Whitelaw for his questions. I found that there were others at the conference who had similar questions which they expressed verbally. In my opinion, experiments have shown that the speed of light does not depend on the velocity of the source. Also, the velocity of the Earth in its orbit is 30 kilometers per second, while that of Jupiter is 13 kilometers per second. Hence, the relative velocity of Earth and Jupiter is negligible compared to the speed of light. Even if one were to assume some sort of dependence of the speed of light on the speed of the source, the results of my computer programs would not be significantly changed. With regard to extinction of the light due to dust, cosmic rays, protons, electrons, hydrogen atoms, etc. in interplanetary space, the densities of these types of matter can be found in various sources. At the distance of the Earth from the sun, there are about 8 electrons per cubic centimeter of space, and the extinction length can be calculated to be about 400 to 500 astronomical units. The theory behind these calculations can be found in the following:

Brecher, K. 1977. "Is the speed of light independent of the velocity of its source?" Physical Review Letters 39(17):1051-1054.

Filippas, T.A. and J.G. Fox 1964. "Velocity of Gamma Rays from a Moving Source." Physical Review 135(4b):1071-1075.

Hamilton, J. 1959. <u>The Theory of Elementary Particles</u> Clarendon Press: Oxford, pages 16-19.

As to Prof. Whitelaw's final question about what the medium for light waves is, I will say that this question seems to be an important one, and that the final form for the answer will be very important for our understanding of physics, but that it will not affect the operational questions addressed in this paper.

Eugene F. Chaffin, Ph.D.

RESONANCE AND SEDIMENTARY LAYERING
IN THE CONTEXT OF A GLOBAL FLOOD

M.E. Clark and H.D. Voss
Genesis Research Laboratory
2020 Zuppke Drive
Urbana, IL 61801

ABSTRACT

Much of the layering in the sedimentary column demands a cyclic mechanism for its development. Newton's gravitational attraction principle as manifested in the tides provides such a mechanism. The Resonance phenomenon, produced by tides and other excitation sources, are invoked to provide the global ocean tides with the ability to transport and deposit the required amount of sediment. Computer simulations are used to develop an understanding of the events.

INTRODUCTION

Sedimentary structures cover the earth in profusion. While some of these structures are due to deposition by the wind, the vast majority have been deposited by water. Many of these structures are characterized by their enormous lateral extent, reaching over vast areas of the earth's surface, requiring the label "persistent facies". Another distinct characteristic is the parallelism (if not the horizontality) of the sedimentary layers. Logic requires that the watery depositional medium was as extensive as the facies and that it was an active agent in the sedimentary layering process. The thought vector points to a global flood and to a flood geology. Such was the prevalent view prior to the Darwin revolution and it was held by the vast majority of the scientists of the day, some of whom were responsible for the invention of the so-called geologic column. With gradualism a firm requirement in the evolutionary process, it was necessary to have a concomitant uniformitarian interpretation of the geologic record. But this interpretation, that the sedimentary structures were developed slowly with ancient sea-floor subsidence equalling the "gentle rain" of sediment from above, proved to be no more satisfactory than was Darwin's interpretation in the biological sphere. Accordingly, non-creationists are presently espousing saltational advances in biology and catastrophic mechanisms in geology. The latter explanations, however, do not involve the one vehicle which lends credence to the catastrophic viewpoint, the global flood. To attempt to explain the development of the layered column of sedimentary structures without a body of water as extensive as the persistent facies is illogical. Of necessity, a body of water that large would undoubtedly extend by hydromechanic principles to the ends of the earth. Thus, the global ocean had to be a reality in the history of the earth. The sedimentary layers on top of all the principle mountain ranges today witness to the conclusion as well.

The need exists among young-earth creationists to explain the events associated with the rapid formation of the sedimentary column on top of the basement rocks of the original creation and above the sedimentary layers of the original runoff associated with the uplifts of Genesis 1. Once the concept of a global ocean is accepted, it is possible to develop rational fluid--mechanic mechanisms capable of producing sequences of sedimentary layers. The amount of sedimentary material is huge but an ample source of mineral material can be postulated as coming from the opening of "the fountains of the great deep"(Gen.7), if these events can be interpreted as tectonic activity similar to that occurring today with the eruption of volcanoes. If one Mt.St.Helens can scatter millions of tons of debris over the northwest United States, what would be the case of a thousand such occurrences in a few months of time? The lush antediluvian vegetative and animal environments would have provided sufficient material for the coal and oil deposits found in the column. What remains to be explained are the mechanisms which can take these materials and lay them down in horizontal (or nearly-horizontal parallel) layers of great lateral extent in a relatively short period of time, in a minuscule amount of geologic time. Many evolutionary geologists are now ready to invoke catastrophism as the prominent mechanism for generating sedimentary structures, however, they want nothing to do with the young-earth concepts of limiting this generation to one catastrophe with its limited time-span of one year. So there is still a dichotomy between evolutionary and creationary explanations of the geologic record even though both use the catastrophic approach.

The thrust of this paper is to offer a modern interpretation of a mechanism of long standing, dating back possibly as far as Sir Isaac Newton, for the development of a major part of the whole sequence of conformable layers. Newton is, at the least, responsible for the development of the basic principle involved, that is his law of gravitational attraction. Whether the impetus for this development was inspired by the Scriptural account of Noah's flood has not been confirmed in the literature. Since he was a firm believer in the exactitude of the Bible, his work on the tides could have been fostered by his Biblical studies. This gravitational attraction principle as manifested in the lunar and solar tides is the one fluid-mechanic mechanism possessing sufficient power and world-wide scope that could accomplish the buildup of the sedimentary column in the allotted time. Present-day tides have amplitudes too small to produce velocity fields sufficiently large so as to be able to move the required amount of sediments at the bottom boundaries of a global ocean. However, present-day tides move in oceans of limited extent where the tidal mechanism is frequently interrupted in its development by land masses. Hence, the build-up of amplitude of these tidal waves is hindered. During the flood year, when the waters completely covered the globe, these hinderences would have vanished and then the repetitive cyclic activity of the tides would have had the possibility of moving towards resonance with the accompanying build-up of tidal amplitude and the accompanying ability of the tidal waves to move the sediment at the bottom of the ocean. Since no incontrovertible time marks are stamped on the geologic record and since the biblical record speaks directly in terms of days, we feel justified in seeking out a method that would rapidly manufacture the sedimentary column.

TIME AND SEDIMENTARY LAYERING

Since the evolutionary and creationary catastrophic explanations of the build-up of the geologic column differ primarily on the matter of the time necessary to do the building, the following points of discussion deal with the characteristics of the column that require or demand rapid build-up.

1. The fact that the layers are conformable and follow in unbroken sequence one on top of the other requires a rapid (within hours) deposition rate. Conformable means that the layer above lies directly on top of the layer below with only a fine line of demarcation between. Because of the water deposition, undisturbed layers would be horizontal; if tilted, at least they would be parallel. If the lower layer was not quickly covered and weeks, months, or years passed instead, the top surface would have been cut by erosional features, especially since the watery medium which laid the material down would still be present to cut it up. With long periods between layers, root systems of plants and trees would also have been developed. Since the demarcation line is fine, it means that none of these events occurred because there was not enough time for them to eventuate.

2. Since there are no world-wide unconformities, each of the conformable layers can be traced around the intruding features. Since each of the conformable layers was produced rapidly, the sequence of layers must have been also.

3. The fact that so many fossils are found in the layers requires their rapid deposition. The fossilization process requires rapid burial, otherwise, the animal remains will decay, will be taken by predators, or will be mechanically destroyed by the elements. The fossilized tracks of animals are all the more susceptible to destruction unless covered almost immediately by a subsequent layer.

4. The presence of cyclothems in many parts of the stratigraphic record, where coal seams are seen as just another layer in the overall sequence of rock layers, indicates that coal formation was a rapid event as well. This event came about when the lush vegetative material from the antediluvial world (uprooted, ground into pulp by the water agitation, and left floating on top of the flood waters) became waterlogged or heavy due to accumulation of debris from the atmosphere and sank periodically to the ocean bottom there to form the coal layer. The great lateral extent of these coal layers also calls for a global ocean. The fact that there are no root systems growing into the layers below the coal seam argues against a grown-in-place theory and for a come-from-elsewhere theory.

5. The fact that there are such huge oil deposits throughout the world, the ingredients of which had to come from living sea and land animals and plants, necessitates that these deposits are the sites of vast graveyards of these living things. The remains have been transformed into their present form by heat and pressure. Only catastrophic motion within a global ocean could have moved all this mass into such extensive accumulations.

6. The mass graveyards of animal remains which have not been so transformed to oil also agree well with the rapid layering scenario. Animals of different types who are normal enemies do not congregate together for their last rites. They must have been caught up in flood waters and transported to the place of burial, there to be covered rapidly for fossilization and preservation by the subsequent layers of sediment.

7. Polystrate fossils argue persuasively for a rapid layering rate. How could a tree remain intact and vertical for such extended periods of time as to have 10 to 12 distinct layers of the column built up around it if each layer took centuries to make? Contrariwise, the tidal layering mechanism could place those 10 to 12 layers in less than a week.

8. The fact that no meteorites have ever been found buried in the geologic column but rather are concentrated near the earth's surface is further evidence that each layer was not on the surface very long before being covered over and that the whole column was placed within a short time span. Meteoritic activity was probably greater in the past when the universe was younger and so more not less meteor deposits should be found in the column if it is geologically old.

WAVE PHENOMENA

Two types of wave phenomena can be associated with the formation of the sedimentary column. The tsunami is a wave motion associated in some way with sudden shifts in crustal position, either the subterranean sub-aquatic earthquake or the slippage of a great earth mass down a slope into a large body of water. Early during the flood year, when the "fountains of the great deep" were building up the water depths on the earth and before the gravitational attraction principle could have significantly affected the waters, large tsunami waves could have moved much sediment from place to place. Such depositions would, however, have lacked order and the layers thus deposited would have been haphazard and without pattern. Once anything near a global ocean was present, the tsunami would have lost its major role. It could have persisted in conjunction with the tidal wave mechanism for a while but would have been relegated to a minor role as the waters gained in depth or as the eruptions of the fountains ceased.

The dominant mechanism in the rapid formation of the sedimentary column must have been the gravitational attraction phenomenon created by the presence of the moon (and to a lesser degree the sun). A global ocean in the presence of such a large earth satellite would have had to react to it with the formation of semi-diurnal bulges of water which touched every point of the earth's surface. These bulges would have had wavelengths equal to half the earth's circumference. The parameters yet to be determined are their amplitudes. As mentioned previously, present day tides range from 2 to 5 meters in amplitude at most places on the earth. Where they are larger than this, the phenomenon of resonance is the cause of the increase. The Bay of Fundy in Nova Scotia has tidal amplitudes of 17 meters but it has an appropriate bottom slope and geometric planform and length so that the reflections of the tidal waves from the end of the Bay reinforce the incident waves coming in at the mouth in just the right way so that resonant buildup of amplitude occurs.

There is little doubt that much larger tides would occur today if the tidal action was not interrupted by the large continental land masses. The amplitude buildup that could occur without such interruptions would be of a different kind than that which occurs in the Bay of Fundy. There the wave reflection phenomenon is dominant. Reflected waves, carrying their own sediment load, could have played a secondary role in the buildup of the column. Reflection sites could be attributable to uneven terrain on the ocean bottom or land masses not yet covered by the flood waters or land masses uncovered as the flood waned. Resonance on a global ocean of uniform depth would occur when the forced wave speed equals the free wave speed. The forced wave speed, due to the gravitational attraction of the moon, is known since the period of the moon is known to be 24 hours and 50 minutes. For a semi-diurnal wave length of half the earth's circumference at the equator (20,000 km), the forced wave speed is 1614 km/hr (1003 mph). The free wave speed is the speed of travel of a disturbance imposed on the ocean, say by some giant drumstick hitting the ocean or by a sub-aquatic earthquake which causes a surface disturbance to emanate therefrom. Since tidal waves can be classified as shallow water waves because of their large wavelength, the speed of a disturbance is given by the square root of gH where H is the ocean depth. The depth to obtain the 1614 km/hr value would be 20 km. For a global ocean of this depth, the resonance condition would be met at the equator. Since the mean depth of today's oceans is about 3.14 km, the 20 km depth would represent a huge increase in the amount of water needed to fill the global ocean. However, if a latitude of 60 degrees rather than the equator is considered, the forced wave speed is halved since the circumference at 60 degrees is halved. The depth to obtain a free wave speed of 807 km/hr is only 5.12 km, a much more reasonable answer.

The resonant condition, with its extremely large amplitudes, can be thought to develop as follows: The moon attracts the waters of the global ocean pulling them up to form a tidal bulge. Due to its rotation on its own axis, the earth moves underneath the moon. The bulge then takes on the characteristics of a wave moving over the ocean as the moon seemingly moves over the earth. At each instant, the moon is essentially creating a new wave much the same way as the great drumstick would create a wave. After each new wave is created, it moves over the ocean at a speed equal to the free wave speed. If the ocean depth is 20 km, the free and forced waves travel at the same speed at the equator and each new wave created by the moon would travel at that speed as well. The accumulation of these waves all moving at the same speed would be manifested by a buildup of amplitude to enormous heights.

CANAL THEORY AND COMPUTER SIMULATION

The availability of present-day digital computers allows many large-scale and small-scale real-world events to be simulated. An event as large as a global flood is no exception. As long as the governing equations, the boundary conditions, and the forcing functions are known and can be programmed, information regarding the event can be generated. The amount and applicability of the information is determined by the complexity built in to the simulation. The most appropriate model of a global ocean would be constructed using spherical coordinates and governing equations. Many such models have been constructed for the present-day ocean topographies. No references have been found that pertain to a global ocean using the spherical constructs. There are, however, many references to simpler modes of analysis, primarily canal theory. This theory postulates a two-dimensional analysis with a canal running circumferentially at the equator (or any other latitude) with the moon travelling directly overhead. The semidiurnal tide is expected to be the major mode of oscillation on this global canal since it is forced by the earth's rotation rate. The magnitude of the amplitude of the wave response to these forces is very much dependent on whether the frequency of the forcing function is near the natural frequency of the system. Observations (1,2) suggest that the earth's oceans have natural modes with frequencies about 12 hours.

To investigate some aspects of the global ocean problem, it is useful to consider the semidiurnal tide using a simple zonal canal, shown without curvature in Figure 1, that extends about the circumference of the earth (3). The rotational dynamics are considered to be of second order for such a two-dimensional canal and the governing equations are considerably simpler. Cancellation of the rotational ($\omega \times V$) and viscous ($\nu \nabla^2 V$) terms in the generalized momentum equation reduces it to an Euler equation which can be written as:

$$\frac{\partial u}{\partial t} = -g \frac{\partial (S - S_e)}{\partial x} \tag{1}$$

where S_e is the surface height of the equilibrium tide (the tide that the global ocean would adopt if there were no dynamic effects due to the rotation of the earth). This equation shows that the time-varying currents in the global ocean are independent of depth. Equation 1 can be used to simplify the generalized continuity equation so that it can be integrated with respect to depth. Using the boundary conditions at the bottom (w=0 at z=-H) and at the surface (w= $\partial S/\partial t$ at z=S), the continuity equation becomes:

$$\frac{\partial S}{\partial t} + H \frac{\partial u}{\partial t} = 0 \tag{2}$$

In a zonal canal, the equilibrium tide may be approximated(3) by:

$$S_e = A \sin(2kx - 2\omega_1 t) \tag{3}$$

where $2\omega_1$ is the frequency of the semidiurnal tide ($2\pi/\omega_1$ = a lunar day of 24 hours and 50 minutes), and k = $2\pi/\omega_1$ where l is the semi-circumference of the earth at the latitude of the canal. Differentiating Equation 3 with respect to t and combining the result with Equation 2 yields an equation for the dependent variable S as follows:

$$\frac{\partial^2 S}{\partial t^2} = -H \frac{\partial^2 u}{\partial x \partial t} = gH \frac{\partial^2 (S - S_e)}{\partial x^2} \tag{4}$$

This result is in the form of the wave equation with wave speed c equal to the square root of gH. Using a sinusoidal response as a solution to the wave equation, the result is of the form:

$$S = S_0 \sin(2kx - 2\omega_1 t) \qquad (5)$$

Substitution of Equations 4, 6, and 7 into Equation 5 gives an expression for S_0, the wave amplitude, as follows:

$$S_0 = A/(1 - (\omega_1/ck)^2) \qquad (6)$$

Near resonance, the long-wave speed $c=(gH)^{1/2}$ approaches the equilibrium tide speed ω_1/k, and the amplitude S_0 approaches the resonant value of infinity. Calculations of free modes in the present-day oceans have shown frequencies near the semidiurnal frequency (4). The viscous term, eliminated from the momentum equation, acts to limit the resonant amplitude of infinity and to produce large but reasonable values. These terms which have been eliminated from the foregoing analysis can be reinstated in the governing equations when numerical methods are used in the solution of the equations.

In a previous paper (5) concerned primarily with establishing the validity of a canal theory computer code developed from a SOLASURF code (6), many model and a few prototype situations were computed. The equilibrium tide at the equator was determined as a function of viscosity. Since those results are pertinent to the present discussion, they are presented in Figure 2. All calculations were started at a canal depth of 20 km, the depth at which resonance was expected to occur with the lunar force field. As is seen in the figure, for inviscid motion ($v = 0$) the tidal amplitude oscillated freely at what one would expect to be the natural frequency of the system. The period of this oscillation is seen to be about 48,000 sec (13.33 hr), somewhat greater than the 12.42 hr corresponding to the lunar semidiurnal tide. Since there is no dissipation, this oscillation would continue indefinitely. When increasing amounts of viscosity were added to the fluid, the oscillation amplitudes decreased. For $v = 0.0004$ and 0.004 km²/sec, the motion appeared as an underdamped approach to the equilibrium tide height of 20.047 km. For $v = 0.04$ km²/sec, the free surface did not oscillate but made an overdamped approach to the equilibrium tide height.

The canal theory code was used to investigate the variation of tidal height with the angular velocity associated with the rotation of the earth on its own axis. In the left most frame of Figure 3, the equilibrium tidal height at the equator is compared with the solution for an angular velocity of 0.00007 rad/sec (the value corresponding to the lunar day). Both calculations were made with the same amount of damping, $v = 0.004$ km²/sec. Whereas the equilibrium tidal height peaks at about 20.075 km, the tide on the rotating earth peaks above a value of 20.10 km. The curve shows a decreasing slope at the end of the calculational period so it seems evident that this calculation (if continued) will not lead to an excessively large tidal amplitude (although an amplitude of 100 meters is not small). It is possible that, with more calculational effort, this curve could experience some oscillations and each successive oscillation could range higher in amplitude. These calculations were quite CPU intensive so they were terminated at 44,000 sec. Another treatment of these same data is presented in the bottom frame of Figure 4. Here, the temporal development of the tidal free surface over the complete equatorial circumference is shown. Two rates of advance of the tidal bulge are evident with the second (and greater) advance rate starting after the dwell between 20 and 25,000 sec seen in Figure 3. The cause of the change in advance rate is not obvious but could be due to some complex interaction between the components of the lunar gravity forces(5).

Returning to the right most frame in Figure 3, the corresponding 60 deg latitude calculation is shown. As indicated previously, the depth associated with resonance (on the basis of equality of the two wave speeds) was calculated to be 5.12 km. The curve represents the computer results for the earth angular velocity of 0.00007 rad/sec and a viscosity of 0.004 km²/sec. The initial peak occurs at 5.132 km after which the tidal height demises, rises again slightly, and seemingly settles at a depth of 5.129 km where the calculations were terminated at 68,000 sec. The temporal development of the free surface is also depicted in the upper frame of Figure 4. Again, two rates of advance of the tidal bulge are seen. Not much evidence of resonance at this latitude is apparent in either figure. For the equatorial canal, it was noted that the period of the natural mode of oscillation for the 20 km depth was greater than half the lunar day. There is the distinct possibility that some other depth in the neighborhood of 20 km would produce a tide height greater than 20.100 km even one that would develop excessive heights moving towards infinity as indicated by Equation 6. It would take a cut and try process to locate such an initial depth at the expense of a great amount of CPU time. Since there would undoubtedly be a gradual build-up to resonance, each trial would have to be given an extended calculational effort before deciding it was not the resonant depth. Such a process is being contemplated for future work.

Hough(7) solved Laplace's spherical tidal equations using some semi-analytical methods and calculated the ratios of the tidal height to the equilibrium tidal height for various ocean depths. He says "We see, then, that though, when the period of forced oscillation differs from that of one of the types of free oscillation by as little as a minute, the forced tide may be nearly 250 times as great as the corresponding equilibrium tide. . . . The critical depths for which the lunar tides become infinite are found to be 26,044 feet and 6,448 feet. Consequently, this phenomenon will occur if the depth of the ocean be between 29,182 and 26,044 feet or between 7,375 and 6,448 feet." Here then Hough, with spherical governing equations, was able to show resonant conditions at reasonable ocean depths. It would seem prudent to repeat Hough's calculations using present-day numerical methods. Such work is also contemplated in the future.

CONCLUSIONS

A survey of the literature showed ample evidence that tidal resonance is a phenomenon that can occur in today's oceans. When, in a global ocean, the disruptive barriers are removed, the resonance activity would be considerably greater. Accordingly, the cyclic action of the tides is put forth as a viable method for the rapid building of the sedimentary column during the year of Noah's flood. Computer simulations of the tidal event based on canal theory are capable of duplicating the buildup of the tidal amplitude. Parameter studies help to explicate this complicated event.

REFERENCES

1. Garrett, C.J. and Greenberg, D.A., "Predicting Changes in Tidal Regimes", J.Phys. Oceanography, Vol.7, pp. 175-181, 1977.

2. Heath, R.A., "Estimates of the Resonant Period and Q in the Semi-dirunal Tidal Band in the North Atlantic and Pacific Oceans", Deep-Sea Res. Vol.28, pp. 481-493, 1981.

3. Gill, A.E., "Atmosphere-Ocean Dynamics", Intern. Geophys. Series, Vol.30, Academic Press, 1982.

4. Platzman, G.W., Curtis, G.A., Hansen, K.S. and Slater, R.D. "Normal Modes of the World Ocean", J. Phys. Oceanography, Vol.11, pp. 579-603, 1981.

5. Clark, M.E. and Voss, H.D. "Gravitational Attraction, Noah's Flood, and Sedimentary Layering", Science at the Crossroads, Onesimus Pub.MN, pp. 42-56, 1985.

6. Hirt, C.W., Nichols, B.D. and Romero, N.C. "SOLA-A Numerical Solution Algorithm for Transient Fluid Flows", Los Alamos Sci.Lab., Rept. LA-5852, 1975.

7. Hough, S.S. "On the Application of Harmonic Analysis to the Dynamical Theory of the Tides", Phil. Trans. Royal Soc. Vol. CXIX, pp. 139-185, 1897.

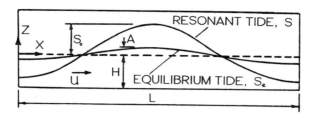

FIGURE 1 CANAL THEORY DEFINITION SKETCH

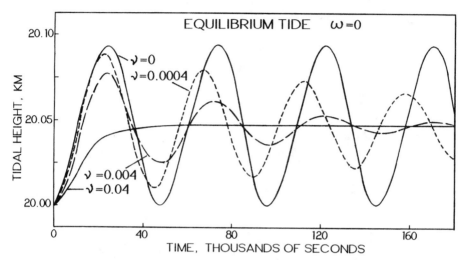

FIGURE 2 EQUILIBRIUM TIDE WITH VARIOUS AMOUNTS OF DAMPING

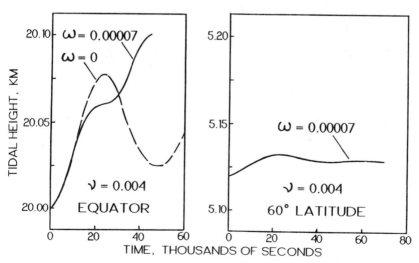

FIGURE 3 TIDAL HEIGHT VARIATION WITH ANGULAR VELOCITY

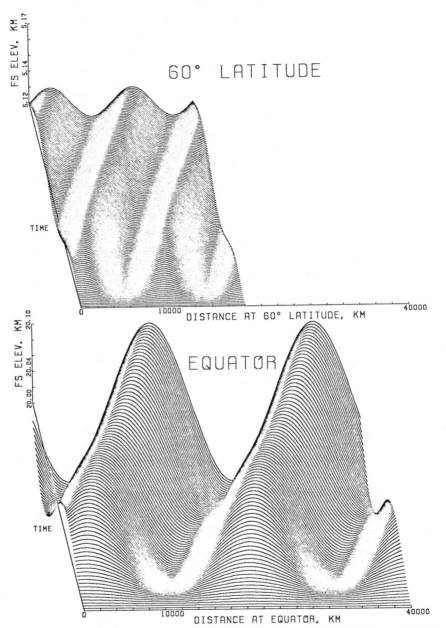

FIGURE 4 TIDAL FREE SURFACE VARIATION WITH TIME

This paper exhibits a fine effort to apply theoretical modeling to geology. It may very well be that the authors have identified a primary mechanism for Deluge sedimentation.

As an observation, however, (rather than a criticism) the endeavor suffers from necessary simplification. If the earth's sedimentary deposits were of an "onion skin" nature with beds typically continental in scope, then the tidal mechanism would certainly play a dominant role.

Unfortunately, the deluge deposited things unevenly. The geologic record does not, in my opinion "demand a cyclic mechanism," as much as it does a continually recurring suite of mechanisms. Nonetheless, the need to simplify for analysis is beyond question. In this, the authors have done an admirable job!

I would favor greater weight placed on tsunamis due to the "fountains" which continued pulsating for 150 days (Gen 7:11 - 7:24 - 8:2). Such processes do produce (contrary to the author's assertion) bedded deposits. The author's simplifying assumption of a constant water depth worldwide cannot be true, (and they would not claim it to be) but does not the tidal model depend on the lack of shallow areas which would inhibit resonance?

John D. Morris, Ph.D.
San Diego, California

1. The authors need to identify geologically that which they call, "the basement rocks of the original creation". I have not been able to recognize any formations in the bottom of the geological column which could qualify.

2. The theoretical presentation of the paper is excellent. It undoubtedly points to a major depositional factor in that section of the geological column which represents the Noahic Flood in its near global or at its global stage. However the paper fails to face the question: "Where are the Noahic Flood layers in the geological record today. The paper also fails to consider the great variety found in the actual deposit series in the geological column in the field. These are far too diverse simply to represent oscillating marine disturbances of the Noahic ocean bottom. Regrettably the theory does not approach nor consider the vast scope of field evidence.

3. In turning to "...the lush antediluvian vegetative and animal environments.." for the source of coal deposits, the authors need to raise the question: "Where is the Noahic Flood and deposit of antediluvian debris recorded in the geological column?" Coal is found in several sections of the geological record, obviously recording diverse stages of Biblical history. Are all of these Noahic tidal deposits?

4. The paper largely ignores violent submarine crustal movement in the deepening of ocean basins after the Noahic Flood and in the rapid separation of the continents well after the Flood as an instrument generating high velocity, erosive, and depositional waves.

5. I propose that the great bluffs of Mesozoic beds exposed at the juncture of the Green and Yampa Rivers at Echo Park near the Colorado/Utah border as a specific location for oscillation study. I interpret these bluffs as evidence of alternating wind deposits interrupted by tidal intrusions. However, I long have "oscillated" between a tidal and a tsunami explanation of these interruptions.

6. In the discussion of page 4, a third cause of serious wave phenomena depositing major sedimentary beds, not mentioned by the authors, is horizontal plate movement. See the Franciscan Assemblage of Northern California (Bul. 183, California Division of Mines and Geology) and my comments in the Creation Research Society Quarterly, March, 1970. This assemblage of formations appears to be the violently ground, rapidly deposited deep submarine deposits ground by the continental plate overriding the eastern margin of the vast Pacific Ocean. Estimates of this deposit have run to 50,000 feet thick, hardly a minor depositional role that can be ignored. Neither can it be explained by cyclic Noahic Flood tidal erosion and deposition. It is an unrelated, catastrophic deposit from centuries later.

Bernard E. Northrup, Th.D.
Redding, California

After a useful and descriptive introduction establishing a physical model (pages 1-5), the rest of the paper appears to be essentially the computer output of a simplified mathematical model based on the physical model. Within the limits imposed by such mathematical simplification of the worldwide convulsion of sea, air, and land which we blithely call, "The Genesis Flood", the authors' paper may well give some useful answers that match the real world after the Flood in some places.   I recommend that the authors research earlier attempts at portraying the comprehensive total Flood catastrophe (i.e. mechanics, sequence of events, tectonic, thermodynamic, geologic, and hydraulic effects, etc.), done by biblical creationists, such as in, The Fountains of the Great Deep, and the Windows of Heaven, Proceedings of the 1983 National Creation Conference, Minneapolis, MN, pp. 98-104.

Robert L. Whitelaw, M.S.
Blacksburg, Virginia

CLOSURE

As shown in this paper, it is the resonance condition that can transform a weakly disturbed global ocean into a strongly pulsating ocean. The tidal force between the moon and a one kilogram mass located on the surface of the earth is only about 5E-5 Newtons (about 2.3E-5 pounds).   Yet, the periodic application of this small forcing function has been shown to be capable of producing enormous periodic tidal waves. Various mechanisms may have contributed to the excitation of the global ocean. These mechanisms may have been random impulses like earthquakes, tsunamis, or "fountain of the deep" motions. Those mechanisms which were periodic, however, would have been the only ones which would have been responsible for the development of the resonance condition.

In this paper, we have suggested that tides were the important fluid dynamic force because the tidal period of about 12 hours is near the global ocean resonance period of about 12 hours. Just like in a swing, every little push increases the swing's amplitude but only if the push is in synchrony with the natural frequency of the system. This analogy is similar to tidal resonance in that the rotation of the earth-moon system would "push" the global ocean every 12 hours, building up large tidal waves (equation 6) which would have included in them the fluid dynamics to cause massive sedimentary layering.

An ocean near resonance could also be subjected to impulsive excitations. In the swing analogy, such an occurrence would be similar to creating a large swing amplitude by a single push.   In such an underdamped case, the swing will oscillate many times near resonance before slowing down and coming to rest. For a global ocean, the effect of a large wavelength impulsive force would be to cause significant ringing near the ocean's natural frequency.

Because the sedimentary record, from the Cambrian to the Mesozoic, shows massive parallel sequences of layered rock, the inference is that a massive and pulsating fluid mechanism must have been responsible. In addition to the many technical references to these massive sorted facies in the geologic record, we have studied in detail much of the geology of the Illinois basin and have built experimental equipment to further model sedimentation associated with various dynamic fluid fields. It is beyond the scope of this paper, however, to discuss either geology or sedimentation. The causes and construction of the actual geologic column as it appears in various regions on the earth is a complicated problem that will require many and various techniques to obtain even some partial solutions. Computer simulations, using the basic underlying fluid-mechanical governing equations, is one of those techniques. We have attempted to underscore the importance of resonance in explaining flood dynamics. By using sophisticated numerical computer programs, velocity fields (associated with resonance) near bottom relief can be simulated, placing us a step closer to explaining the sedimentary process in the building of the geologic column.

Dr. John Morris notes in his discussion that constant water depth, as postulated in the numerical calculations, is not a plausible assumption for a global ocean. Again, it was not the purpose of this paper to investigate all flood ramifications. An idea regarding the effects of uneven bottom relief and even shallow water regions on tidal resonance can be gathered from our previous calculations as given in Reference (5). The main tidal waves seem to be built up as they are with uniform depth, however, additional wave reflection from the bottom relief are superimposed on them (cp. Figure 4, Reference (5)).

Dr. Bernard Northrup would like for us to relate our results to the actual sedimentary column as seen at various places on the earth. We are not in a position to do so. Our goal, at present at least, is to show that a flooded planet will inexorably be subjected to certain periodic excitations which, in turn, will cause a predictable periodic response in accord with the laws of fluid mechanics. Other investigators will hopefully extend the concepts to specific situations as he has started to do in his discussion.

Prof. Robert Whitelaw also expects more than was intended from the study. A comprehensive explanation of all facets of The Genesis Flood can be speculated about and computer simulations and other techniques can increase our understanding about some facets, but firm knowledge is an impossible desideratum.

One closing admission will help clarify the results shown in Figures 2 and 3: Since the co-authors conducted this research when widely separated from each other, a misunderstanding arose in the viscosity values to be used in the computer calculations. The kinematic viscosity units required (sq km/sec) are not common in engineering practice. As it turned out, the value selected (v = 0.004 km^2/sec) represents an extremely viscous fluid. It is little wonder that the tidal amplitudes calculated were much less than one would expect from a resonant condition. Recent calculations, using a kinematic viscosity corresponding to water (v = 10E-13 km^2/sec), resulted in a maximum tidal amplitude for a 60-degree latitude canal of some 300 meters (nearly 1000 ft) after some 225,000 sec. of real time. These calculations were started with a constant depth of water (5.12 km). Although the amplitude was still increasing when the calculations were stopped, a secondary wave was superimposing itself on the front side of the tidal bulge. Whether this occurrence signaled a true tidal wave action which developed at this large amplitude or was the beginning of a numerical instability has not been determined, The superimposed wave looked very similar to the secondary wave shown in Figure 10 of Reference (5). This further work will be reported at a later time.

M.E. Clark, Ph.D.
H.D. Voss, Ph.D.

EIGENVALUE ANALYSIS OF THE MAGNETIC FIELD OF THE EARTH AND ITS IMPLICATIONS ON AGE AND FIELD REVERSALS

Kent R. Davey
School of Electrical Engineering
Georgia Institute of Technology
Atlanta, GA 30332-0250

ABSTRACT

The temporal evolution of the geomagnetic field is analyzed using classical electromagnetics via an eigenvalue approach. The analysis points out the error of thinking of the Earth's field decay as a simple exponential decay, the decay constant being the equivalent inductance / resistance ratio of the Earth's core. In reality the field is characterized by a continuum of characteristic decay times (or eigenvalues). Each eigenvalue is associated with a unique shape. The total field is the sum of each eigenshape (or eigenvector) each decaying at a different rate. Since the weighting factors on each of these shapes is dictated by the initial field penetration of the core, it is likely that higher order eigenvectors will have larger weighting factors than the fundamental, more slowly decaying eigenshapes. Field reversals are an expected consequence of correctly analyzing the field transient.

The conclusions of this work are as follows. First, the age of the Earth's field, accounting for the whole continuum of characteristic eigenvalues, cannot be much more than 10,000 years old. Second, one or more field reversals can be expected in the first 1000 years of the field's existence. These reversals are caused by two sources. The first originates in the weighting of the individual eigenvectors as dictated by the initial core field. The second source is through eddy current induction in the ionosphere and/or vapor canopy.

The third conclusion is that motion effects in the core will not give added longevity to the field; the primary motion of the Earth is in the wrong direction to alter the eigenvalues. Secondary motion, i.e. precession, will only perturb the eigenvalues, and these perturbations have the wrong angular dependence around the globe to collectively couple to the main field.

INTRODUCTION

Geochronology is a difficult game to play since the experiment cannot be repeated. The magnetic field of the Earth is an enigma to both creationists and evolutionists. The evolutionist must appeal to dynamo theories [1] and motion effects [2] to support the long age he is committed to believe. The creationist must deal with apparent evidence for magnetic field reversals [3-5]; these explanations include turbulent movements in the core during the Noahic flood [6] and magnetostrictive effects. The intent of this article is to address from a theoretical perspective the following questions:
(1) When and how does fluid core motion affect the characteristic decay of the geomagnetic field?
(2) Are global field reversals predicted by classical field theory independent of fluid core motion?
(3) How can an upper limit be placed on the age of the Earth if there are an infinite number of eigenvalues characterizing the decay of the field?

THEORY

This analysis springboards from the work of Thomas Barnes[7], which found its motivation from that of Horace Lamb[8]. The objective is to predict the temporal evolution of the magnetic field of a conducting sphere stressed by a magnetic field at time t=0. The geometry is shown in Fig. 1. .

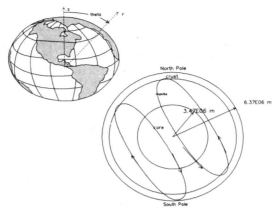

Fig. 1. Geometry of the problem to predict the field in and around the core of the Earth.

The core is thought to be primarily molten iron with a conductivity of 33,000 to 40,000 mho/m [9,10]. Because the temperature is well above the Curie point, we are quite safe in setting the permeability to $4\pi \cdot 10^{-7}$ Henry's/m. For this analysis we shall assume the currents in the core azimuthal or ϕ directed. As a first starting assumption we also assume the core is immersed in a uniform z directed field having a strength equal to that of a magnetic star, i.e., 100 Gauss. By uniformitarian geology, this would set an upper limit to the field, since the dust cloud (soon to be Earth) would have to be coalescing and cooling in close proximity to a large magnetic star to realize these conditions.

The analysis proceeds by solving Ampere and Faraday's equations for the magnetic (B) and electric fields (E),

$$\vec{\nabla} \times \vec{H} = \sigma \vec{E} \tag{1}$$

$$\vec{\nabla} \times \vec{E} = -\frac{\partial \vec{B}}{\partial t} \tag{2}$$

subject to the requirement that the B field be divergence free, $\vec{\nabla} \cdot \vec{B} = 0$. In this magneto-quasistatic regime, it is convenient to represent the B field as the curl of a vector potential A, i.e.,

$$\vec{B} = \vec{\nabla} \times \vec{A}. \tag{3}$$

Combining equations (1-3) yields the result

$$\nabla^2 \vec{A} = \mu\sigma \frac{\partial \vec{A}}{\partial t} \tag{4}$$

Because the currents are assumed to be in the ϕ direction, the vector A has only a ϕ component. Following the lead of Barnes or Smythe [7,11], we can expand A as

$$A_\phi = A(\theta) \cdot A(r) \cdot \exp\left(-\frac{t}{\tau}\right) \tag{5}$$

In spherical coordinates, (4) becomes

$$\frac{1}{r^2}\frac{\partial}{\partial r}\left(r^2\frac{\partial A_\phi}{\partial r}\right)+\frac{1}{r^2\sin(\theta)}\frac{\partial}{\partial\theta}\left(\sin(\theta)\frac{\partial A_\phi}{\partial\theta}\right)+\left(\frac{1}{L^2}-\frac{1}{r^2\sin^2(\theta)}\right)A_\phi=0. \tag{6}$$

where

$$L=\sqrt{\left(\frac{\tau}{\mu\sigma}\right)}.$$

The θ component of the field satisfies Legendre's equation and has the solution

$$A(\theta)=P_l^1(\cos(\theta)). \tag{7}$$

The only solution that is consistent with a dipole field such as we observe occurs when $l = 1$ yielding a θ field dependence of $\sin(\theta)$. With the substitution $r=zL$, the equation for the r component of A becomes

$$z^2\frac{dA}{dz^2}+2z\frac{dA}{dz}+(z^2-2)A=0. \tag{8}$$

The solutions for this equation are spherical Bessel functions

$$j_1(z)=\sqrt{\left(\frac{\pi}{2z}\right)}J_{\frac{3}{2}}(z) \tag{9}$$

$$y_1(z)=\sqrt{\left(\frac{\pi}{2z}\right)}Y_{\frac{3}{2}}(z) \tag{10}$$

At this point, we make an important departure from previous developments in this area. The solution both inside and outside the core will be expressed as an infinite spectrum of eigenvalues L_s each with its own decay constant τ_s.

$$A_\phi(r<r_{core})=\sum_s C_s j_1(z_s)\sin\theta\ e^{-\frac{t}{\tau_s}} \tag{11}$$

$$A_\phi(r>r_{core})=\sum_s \frac{D_s}{r^2}\sin\theta\ e^{-\frac{t}{\tau_s}} \tag{12}$$

The boundary conditions that the normal and tangential components of the magnetic field be continuous pin down the allowable eigenvalues; these yield the two additional equations

$$\frac{D_s}{a^2}=C_s j_1\left(\frac{a}{L_s}\right) \tag{13}$$

$$C_s j_1\left(\frac{a}{L_s}\right)+C_s r\frac{\partial J_1\left(\frac{a}{L_s}\right)}{\partial r}=-\frac{D_s}{r^2}. \tag{14}$$

Note the variable a will be used henceforth for the core radius. These equations can be combined to give the requirement

$$j_0\left(\frac{a}{L_s}\right)=0 \tag{15}$$

or

$$\frac{a}{L_s}=n\pi.$$

The solution for the total field follows by employing the orthogonality condition

$$\int_0^a\left\{\frac{r}{a}j_1\left(\frac{r}{L_s}\right)\right\}dr=\frac{1}{2}a\left\{j_1\left(\frac{a}{L_s}\right)\right\}^2. \tag{16}$$

If the initial core field is constant over the core having the value B_0, then for any position r in the core at t=0 the following relationship must hold

67

$$\sum_s C_s j_1\left(\frac{r}{L_s}\right) = \frac{1}{2} \cdot B_0 \cdot r, \tag{17}$$

since

$$A_\phi = \frac{1}{2} \cdot r \sin \theta$$

corresponds to a uniform z directed B field. Carrying out the mathematics reveals the result

$$C_s = B_0 L_s \frac{j_2\left(\frac{a}{L_s}\right)}{j_1^2\left(\frac{a}{L_s}\right)} \tag{18}$$

$$D_s = a^2 C_s j_1\left(\frac{a}{L_s}\right) \tag{19}$$

where

$$\vec{B}_{out}(r > a) = \frac{2}{r^3}\sum_s \cos\theta \ e^{-\frac{t}{\tau_s}}\hat{a}_r \ + \ \frac{1}{r^3}\sum_s D_s \sin\theta \ e^{-\frac{t}{\tau_s}}\hat{a}_\theta \tag{20}$$

RESULTS - UNIFORM INITIAL FIELD

Fig. 2. shows the θ directed surface field is predicted from (20) using 100 eigenvalues.

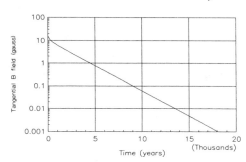

Fig. 2. Primary θ directed field on the surface of the Earth versus time in years.

These results are plotted keeping 100 eigenvalues; this number is adequate to represent the initial field to 4 decimal places. Upon close examination, the reader will note that the initial decay is not exponential (linear on a log scale). The initial decay is actually dictated by the higher order eigenvalues and decays more rapidly. A enlargement of the initial decay is shown in Fig. 3. .

The magnitude of the effect is determined by the weighting of the higher order eigenvalues, which follows from the initial conditions. Fig. 4. shows both the eigenvalue decay constants τ_s and the weighting constants D_s.

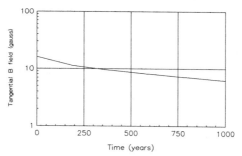

Fig. 3. *Initial Field decay showing the more rapid decay influence of the higher order eigenvalues.*

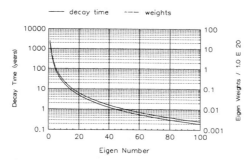

Fig. 4. *Primary θ directed field on the surface of the Earth versus time in years.*

With a core conductivity $\sigma = 4.04 \cdot 10^4$ mho/m the slowest (primary) time constant is $6.204 \cdot 10^{10}$ seconds or 1966.6 years; all other eigenvalues decay faster.

RESULTS FOR A VARIANT INITIAL FIELD

The fact that the weighting values monotonically decrease for the above case is happenstance. It is more likely that the initial field was not uniform. The original vector potential was specified in (17). Suppose this field is altered so the vector potential has a sinusoidal character in the core,

$$A_\phi = \frac{B_0}{2} r \cos\left(\frac{\pi r}{2a}\right) \sin\theta \tag{21}$$

Using the vector potential insures preservation of a divergence free B field. This vector potential and commensurate B field are shown in Fig. 5. .

To allow for any initial condition the weighting constants were performed numerically using Gauss Quadrature integration routines. The formula for finding the weighting constants of any vector potential having radial field dependence is

Variant Initial Field

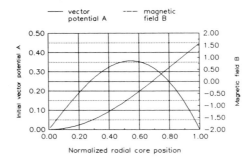

Fig. 5. Vector potential and commensurate tangential B field consistent with equation (21).

$$C_s \frac{a}{2} j_1^2\left(\frac{a}{L_s}\right) = \int_0^a g(r)\left(\frac{r}{a}\right)^2 j_1\left(\frac{r}{L_s}\right) dr \qquad (22)$$

The new decay constants and their weighting values are shown in Fig. 6. .

Eigenvalues and their Weights

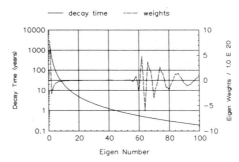

Fig. 6. Decay constants and eigenvector weightings for the variant field shape.

The resulting field decay is quite distinct from the constant field shape (Fig. 7.).

As shown more clearly in the blowup shown in Fig. 8. , the initial field actually reverses in the first 200 years.

Surface Field Decay

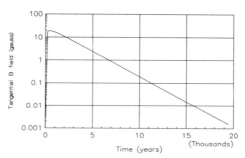

Fig. 7. *Field decay with time for the variant field starting condition.*

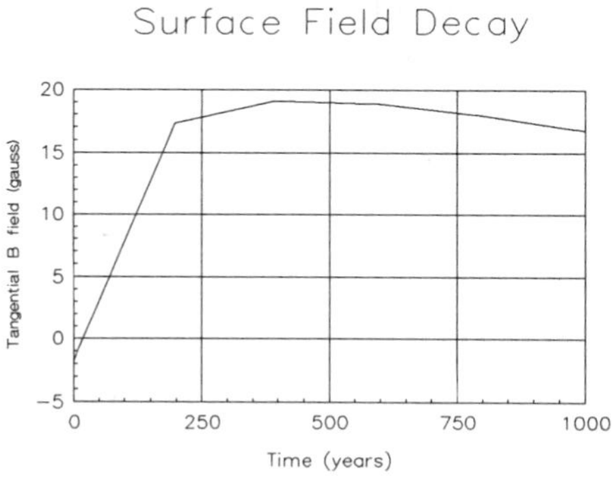

Surface Field Decay

Fig. 8. *Initial field decay shows a reversal of the field in the first 200 years.*

RELEVANCE TO FIELD REVERSALS

It is impossible to know exactly what shape the initial field had. The important issue is there are numerous possibilities which produce higher order eigenvector weightings with magnitudes larger, and signs opposite to the more dominant earlier eigenvalues. When this happens, field reversals will occur. These reversals are in no way tied to core fluid motion.

A second mechanism by which the reversals can take place is through induction. About 10% of the Earth's field is external in origin [1,2], mostly through ionospheric currents. When the internal field decays it induces current in the atmosphere which attempts to oppose the decay. The amount of current is proportional to the rate of decay of the primary field. It is clear from Fig. 5 that some eigenvectors of the field are decaying hundreds of times faster than the fundamental present day decay during the initial period, but their weight factors C_s, D_s are not proportionally smaller. They will induce very large currents both in the ionosphere and in the preflood canopy which will yield large perturbation fields in multiple directions.

MOTION EFFECTS

A recent article in <u>Earth Science</u> [12] suggests that we may be due for another reversal of the Earth's field. The article revolves around the popular notion that fluid motion in the core has a profound affect both on the field decay and its orientation at any time in geological history. The mechanism of possible interaction as revealed in an eigenvalue analysis discloses serious flaws with these notions. In a moving frame the electric field E' is related to that when no motion is present as

$$\vec{E}' = \vec{E} + \vec{V} \times \vec{B} \tag{23}$$

where

$\vec{v}$ = the velocity describing movement of the medium in the presence of an external field $\vec{B}$

Incorporating this into the equation describing A gives

$$\nabla^2 \vec{A} = \mu\sigma \frac{\partial \vec{A}}{\partial t} - \vec{v} \times \vec{\nabla} \times \vec{A} \tag{24}$$

The last term on the right of (24) must be ϕ directed to have any influence at all. This immediately rules out any effect the predominant rotation (also ϕ directed) of the Earth might have. The fact that the Earth's axis is offset from the magnetic axis is no help; since the internal field is essentially homogeneous in the core, the $\vec{V} \times \vec{B}$ field will yield radially directed currents which will cancel side to side.

The precession of the Earth offers some hope at first. The precession is a θ directed movement; the last term of (24) would be

$$\omega_\theta r \frac{1}{r\sin(\theta)} \frac{\partial}{\partial \theta} (\sin\theta A) \tag{25}$$

where

$$\vec{v} = \omega_\theta r$$

It would be tempting to write (24) as

$$\nabla^2 A + \left(\frac{\mu\sigma}{\tau} + 2\omega_\theta \right) A = 0 \tag{26}$$

and then to asses the effects of on the rate of decay by noting that the quantity in parentheses would be the same (i.e., same eigenvalues). If the precession frequency were 200,000 years, the affect would be sizable were it not for one mistake. All but the last term in (24) have a $\sin(\theta)$ dependence; the $\cos(\theta)$ of the last term balances out over the globe. The only type of motion that will have a lasting affect on the dipole field of the Earth, yielding both a ϕ component for the last term in (24) and the appropriate θ dependence in space, is a radial velocity motion. It is hardly necessary to point out that Bernard induced thermal motion will be quite small indeed.

This analysis does not rule out transitory fluid effects as suggested by Humphreys [6], which have a $\cos(m\phi)$ dependence with m not equal to 0. These affects will definitely decay more quickly than those eigenvalues shown in Figs. 4 and 6. A localized turbulent eddy will surely give rise to a current eddy (the two eddy loops will interlink in fact), but the field will decay very rapidly because of the dissipatory nature of each. Unless the turbulence is very large these effects could be safely ignored.

CONCLUSIONS

The complete eigenvalue analysis offers new insight into how the Earth's field decays with time. Field reversals are expected not from complex internal core fluid motion, but initial field conditions. Regardless of these initial conditions, the eigenvalue decay times are known and set; the longest of these is only 1966 years. Because the decay constants τ_s are identical regardless of the initial field, it is difficult to even imagine how the Earth's field can last more than 20,000 years. Complex core turbulence may be responsible for perturbations in the field, but no long term field - fluid coupling appears plausible.

REFERENCES

1. H. Jeffreys,<u>The Earth</u>, 4th Ed.,Cambridge Univ. Press, Cambridge, 1959.
2. J. Jacobs,R.D. Russel and W.J. Tuzo, <u>Physics and Geology</u>, McGraw Hill , New York, 1959.
3. J.G. Neigi and R.K. Tiwari,"Magnetic Field of the Earth involving its Dipole Field Aspect",<u>Sci. AM</u>, vol 250,p.70, March 1984.
4. D.R. Humphreys, "Has the Earth's Field ever flipped?",<u>CRSQ</u>,25 (Dec. 1988).
5. D. Strangway, <u>History of the Earth's Magnetic Field</u>, New York, McGraw Hill,168 pp,1970.
6. D.R. Humphreys, "Reversals of the Earth's Magnetic Field During the Genesis Flood",

Proceedings of the First Int'l Conference on Creationism, vol II, Pittsburgh, pp 113-126, 1986.

7. T.G. Barnes, Origin and Destiny of the Earth's Magnetic Field, ICR, El Cahon, CA 1973.

8. H. Lamb,Phil. Trans, London,174:519,1813.

9. T.G. Barnes, "Decay of the Earth's Magnetic Moment and the geochronological implications",CRSQ, 9, pp 222-230, Mar 1973.

10. F.D. Stacey, "Electrical Resistivity of the Earth's Core", Earth and Planetary Science Letters, 3,pp 204-206, 1967.

11. Smythe, Static and Dynamic Electricity, McGraw Hill,pp 378-380, 1967.

12. S. Bannergy, "Is Reversal of Earth's Magnetic Poles Due?",Earth Science, vol 37,p 10, spring 1984.

DISCUSSION

This is an excellent theoretical paper on the decay of the earth's magnetic field. Of particular importance is Davey's solution in which he deduces, from an initial variant "magnetization" in the core of the earth, reversals of the earth's magnetic field in the early stage of the decay. It is the first rigorous theoretical solution of reversals which this reviewer has seen.

He accomplished his stated mission. It led to the following conclusions: "Field reversals are expected not from complex internal core fluid motion, but from initial conditions" (at creation). "Regardless of these initial conditions, the eigenvalue decay times are known and set: the longest is only 1966 years." That is strong support for a very young age. "Complex core turbulence may be responsible for perturbations in the field, but no long term field-coupling appears plausible."

Thomas G. Barnes, D.Sc.
El Paso, Texas

The eigenvalue approach Dr. Davey presents is a good start toward clarifying creationist analyses of the earth's magnetic field. There must be a factor missing from the first term of his final result in eq. 20 — the first term has no dependence on the initial field B_o. I think the missing factor is D_s. If so, then eq. 20 is simply a superposition of dipole fields of various decay times. A more general solution of the Maxwell equations for this situation, including higher-order spherical harmonic terms such as the quadrupole and octopole moments, would have been useful, because 10% of the present field is non-dipolar, and the past field even more so.

One good contribution of this paper is its clear demonstration that classical field theory can account for several global reversals. That was implicit in eq. 9 of my previous ICC paper, but I never spelled it out. Another important contribution is that the shape of the initial field at creation could excite enough of the higher decay modes (or in his terms, "eigenvector weightings") to produce some global reversals shortly after creation. I had not realized this was a possibility. It could explain some evidence for reversals in Precambrian strata. (Data in those strata are difficult to interpret because even though most Precambrian rocks were probably formed before the Flood, they may have been globally re-heated during the flood, thus acquiring their magnetizations during the reversals of the flood period.) However, Dr. Davey apparently does not realize that the disturbances I hypothesize in the core during the flood would strongly excite *all* the decay modes, not just the modes with non-zero values of m [last paragraph of second-to-last section]. This sets up a new set of initial conditions for the period after the flood, making his analysis even more relevant to the post-flood period than it is to the post-creation period.

It is also important to note that this paper's classical mechanism cannot account for the fifty or more rapid reversals which the evidence clearly indicates occurred during the Flood [Davey's ref. 4]. By the way, I think many (and perhaps most) of those reversals were *global*, a point I have not emphasized before this.

The second-to-last section of the paper attempts to analyze the effect of fluid motions. Unfortunately, the analysis falls far short of Dr. Davey's goals, for two reasons:

1) It ignores magnetohydrodynamic effects, in particular, that magnetic flux lines move with the fluid. This means that the vector potential **A** in eq. 24 interacts with the velocity **v**, with the result that eventually the magnetic flux looks like spaghetti instead of the simple poloidal (azimuthal **A**) field considered by the author.

2) While acknowledging that radial (up and down) fluid motions can induce the necessary azimuthal electric currents, the author dismisses the possibility of such motions with one assertion: "... Bernard [Benard?] induced thermal motion will be quite small indeed." I think he means by this that convection flows of the fluid are negligible, but he produces no justification for this opinion. One of my papers at this conference (1) shows that convection flows, far from being negligible, could have easily been the major cause of the rapid reversals during the flood. However, my paper does support the main point Dr. Davey intended to make in this section: "... motion effects in the core will not give added longevity to the field."

74

REFERENCES:

1) Humphreys, D.R., "Physical Mechanism for Reversals of the Earth's Magnetic Field During the Flood", SECOND INTERNATIONAL CONFERENCE ON CREATIONISM, Creation Science Fellowship, Pittsburgh, PA, 1990, in press.

D. Russell Humphreys, Ph.D.
Albuquerque, New Mexico

The work presented by Dr. Davey is a straightforward and insightful analysis of the behavior of the earth's geomagnetic field in the absence of source terms. A plausible argument based on the presence of higher-order, rapidly decaying eigenmodes, is presented to explain early-time reversal of this field, a phenomenon that is often attributed to fluctuations in the earth's dynamo with a characteristic timescale of millions of years. I can find no fault with Dr. Davey's analysis nor with the implication that field-reversal does not demand an old-earth hypothesis. Nevertheless, Dr. Davey alleges to have proven what he has merely (though, perhaps correctly) assumed, namely the absence of source term. In his section entitled "Motion Effects," he dismisses the coupling of rotational energy to magnetic energy based on the assumption that the currents are always predominantly 0-directed. This assumption, though intuitive, hardly leads to the proof implied in the conclusions. I would urge the author to restate his conclusion to more accurately reflect the assumptions as well as the insights of the paper.

Thomas W. Hussey, Ph.D.
Albuquerque, New Mexico

CLOSURE

The purpose of this paper was to establish an upper limit age index on the primary portion of the Earth' field which is dipolar in shape and show that classical field theory addresses multiple field reversals. This was the reason for not analyzing the higher order field components.

The statement about the analysis not being able to handle multiple reversals is quite erroneous. Depending on the initial shape of the field, the weighting constants for each and every multipole field is established at time t=0.

The reader may argue that if you carry out the calculations, you'll not be able to see any more reversals. It must be stressed that it is not a matter of carrying out the calculations further in time. The key issue is the shape of the field at the start of the transient. The reader is referred to the classical work of Smythe [10] if further clarification is needed. To amplify the point however, consider the initial field shape shown in Fig. 9:

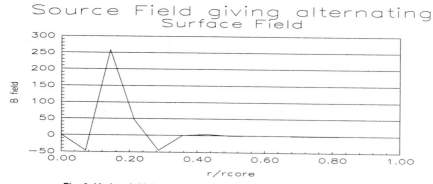

Fig. 9. Variant Initial core field shape emphasizing multiple reversals.

The amplitude is not as important as the decomposition of the shape into each of the eigenvector components. Because of the assumed azimuthal dependence (m=1) all components must be dipolar in nature, but all components decay at a different rate. Fig. 9 happens to be a shape that weights the higher order components more heavily than the dominant decay components. The commensurate field decay is shown in Fig. 10. Little emphasis should be given to the magnitude of the initial field or the magnitude of the variations of the decay field; the initial field was set up arbitrarily to yield unity variation reversals in Fig. 10:

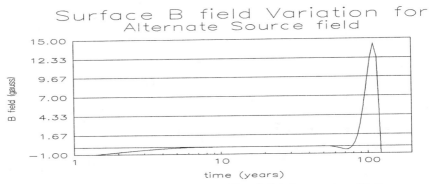

Fig. 10. Field decay commensurate with an initial shape such as Fig. 9.

This is not all that is impressive in terms of the number of reversals until one looks more closely at the "quiet zone" between 10 and 50 years. Fig. 11 shows a blowup of this region with the multiple reversals clearly displayed.

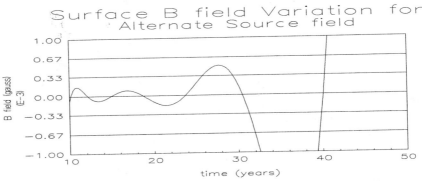

Fig. 11. Field decay commensurate with an initial shape such as Fig. 9 showing a blow up of the faster field reversal region.

By including shapes that encourage higher order eigenvalues, the reversal period can be made very small. In fact there is no theoretical limit to how close these reversals can be in time or to how many there can be. The longest time period is of course fixed by geometry and composition and cannot be altered; it is the long time constant that sets an upper limit to the age of the Earth.

Time t=0 is not necessarily the origin of the Earth as Dr. Humphreys points out. In this conference there was a paper discussing the breakup and sinking of the Earth's lithosphere near the event of the flood. Suggest an event, were it to occur, would constitute a sizable perturbation of the core conductivity. This is one mechanism for exciting all eigenmodes, and setting up a global reversal field such as Fig. 11.

Comments on Motion Effects of Drs. Humphreys and Hussey

I've added additional comments to the section on fluid motion in the paper itself which clear up some of the confusion. The real issue is whether there are (v X B) terms having a ϕ

component and a $\sin(\theta)$. Granted there is radial fluid motion of the core, but del(v) must be essentially zero (to the extent of density variations). For radial motion to couple long term to the dipole field of the Earth, the radial velocity must have no θ dependence. The radial motion one expects to have will have a $\sin(m\theta)$ or $\cos(m\theta)$ dependence, which will not couple long term to the dipole field of the Earth.

Kent R. Davey, Ph.D.

THE EARTH-MOON SYSTEM

Don B. DeYoung
Professor of Physics
Grace College
200 Seminary Drive
Winona Lake, IN 46590

ABSTRACT

The origin of the moon continues to be a lively area of discussion. A collision between a young, molten earth and a large planetesimal has become a popular explanation. After reviewing the traditional origin theories, the likelihood of lunar origin by collision will be examined. An upper limit on the age of the dynamical earth-moon system is also calculated. The result reveals a fundamental time conflict with secular views of the moon's history.

INTRODUCTION

The moon is earth's nearest neighbor in space. As a consequence, its age and history are connected closely with that of the earth. Theories for the moon's origin have proliferated over the years, especially since the Apollo moon landings. However, none of the origin theories have been very convincing, either to secular or creation scientists. Table I summarizes the four most popular lunar origin theories, together with their major problems. The problems fall into three major categories: **dynamical** - usually a conflict with the observed angular momentum of the earth-moon system; **chemical** - both differences and similarities between the compositions of the earth and moon; **probability** - an extremely low chance of occurrence. These three constraints on lunar formation have doomed every attempt to fit the moon into a self-generating, evolutionary history (1).

Origin Theory	Description	Major Problems
Fission	Moon tore loose from a rapidly spinning earth.	c, d
Capture	Moon formed elsewhere in the solar system, and later entered earth orbit.	c, d, p
Nebula Accretion	Moon formed close to the earth, from dust and rocky material.	c, d
Collision	A large object collided with the earth; fragments formed the moon.	p

Table I. Summary of four lunar origin theories. Major problems fall into three categories: chemical differences (c), dynamical conflicts (d), low probability (p).

Recently the collision theory of lunar origin has received wide publicity (2-5). Computer modeling has been used to describe an impact of a large object, called a planetesimal, with a molten proto-earth. Further speculation results in the reformation of the earth with its present tilt, and subsequent moon formation from orbiting collision debris. The collision concept has not become popular because of any inherent ability to solve all of the basic lunar origin problems. Instead, the failure of other theories simply has caused lunar collision to fill the gap as an ad hoc idea, at least until a better origin scenario is developed. Two technical problems with the collision theory will be discussed here. Each problem in itself is sufficient to cast serious doubt on the collision theory.

MEAN FREE PATH AND TIME

The concept of mean free path is usually applied to gas molecules. However, it equally well can describe macroscopic planetary objects. The mean free path of a group of objects is the average distance traveled between individual collisions. This length (ℓ) is given by

$$\ell = \frac{1}{n\,\sigma} \qquad (1)$$

where n is the density of objects (number per cubic kilometer), and σ is the collision cross section (km^2). The mean free time between collisions, τ, is expressed by

$$\tau = \frac{\ell}{v} \qquad (2)$$

where v is the average speed of the objects. Parameter values can be chosen to estimate the likelihood of moon formation by a collision. A reasonable density n is based on 100 Mars-size objects moving randomly in a spherical region three billion miles in radius, the size of Neptune's orbit. In the evolutionary assumption of a chaotic, early solar system, a planar mass distribution has not yet developed. Ignoring gravitational effects, σ is just twice the cross sectional area of Mars, $2\pi r^2$, where r is the planet's radius. The speed v is taken from the orbital motion of Jupiter, a good average value for the solar system. The results follow:

$$n = 2.63 \times 10^{-28} \text{ km}^{-3}$$

$$\sigma = 7.26 \times 10^7 \text{ km}^2$$

$$v = 13.1 \text{ km/sec}$$

$$\ell = 5.24 \times 10^{19} \text{ km}$$

$$\tau = 4 \times 10^{18} \text{ sec} = 127 \text{ billion years}$$

With one hundred planetary objects in random motion, one would thus expect **less** than a **single** collision per billion years. However, the lunar collision origin theory requires a violent interaction within the first few million years of solar system history, a one-in-a thousand chance. Clearly, the collision explanation for the moon's formation is no more credible than the previous failed theories. The improbability is compounded greatly by similar collision explanations for many other moons and planets in the solar system. The high density of Mercury, the backspin of Venus, the severe tilt of Uranus - all conveniently are explained by catastrophic collisions of early solar system objects.

MOON - EARTH SEPARATION

The gravity attraction between the earth and moon at their present separation distance is a stupendous force, 7×10^{19} pounds. There is also a large force differential between the earth's near and far sides from the moon, resulting in the daily tides. The earth's tidal distortion is illustrated in Figure 1. Note that earth's tidal bulges actually occur somewhat East of the moon's location, since the land and seas do not respond instantly to the gravity force. The result of this delay is a continuous, slight forward pull on the moon. Consequently the moon slowly spirals outward from the earth, increasing its

Figure 1. The moon's gravitational attraction results
in tidal bulges a, b on the earth. The angle between
the tidal bulges and the moon, actually 3°, is exaggerated
for clarity. Arrows indicate earth's rotation and the
moon's revolution.

distance at a present measured rate of about 4 centimeters per year. However
this separation rate, dr/dt, is strongly dependent on the total earth-moon
distance r,

$$\frac{dr}{dt} = \frac{k}{r^6} \qquad (3)$$

where k is a constant (6). The effect of this differential equation is shown in
Figure 2.

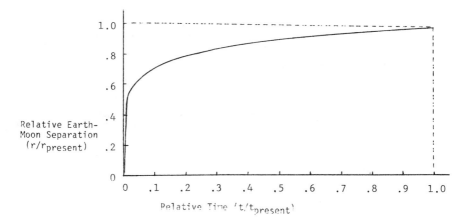

Figure 2. The relative earth-moon separation as a function
of time. The steep curve in the past results from an r^{-6}
dependency of the moon separation rate. Extrapolation shows
that the moon would have physically contacted the earth
about 1.4 billion years ago.

Assuming an original earth-moon contact by either collision or fission. There is
a very rapid initial separation of the earth and moon. Such a close encounter,
with resultant strong tidal heating, should have caused large-scale melting of

81

the earth and moon (7). Early lunar craters would also have been permanently distorted by the large lunar tide effects, since the largest impact basins on the moon are thought to have formed 4 billion years ago. However, evidence for such a close encounter is totally lacking. The earth and moon appear to have been widely separated from the beginning, in agreement with the creation view.

Solution of Equation (3) gives the backward extrapolated time t at which the moon would be in physical contact with the earth,

$$t = \frac{r_{e-m}}{7 \frac{dr}{dt}} \qquad (4)$$

where r_{e-m} is the present earth-moon distance. Substitution gives

$$t = 1.37 \times 10^9 \text{ years}$$

This apparent time of moon origin is 70% less than the moon's assumed age of 4.6 billion years! Clearly, a large scale time problem exists for all secular moon origin theories. In contrast, Figure 1 shows that the earth-moon distance has not changed significantly over the past 10,000 years, only about one-half mile. On a recent creation time scale the earth-moon system shows great stability, and the close-approach problems are avoided.

FURTHER STUDY

If the moon was once close to us, angular momentum considerations require an initial rapidly spinning earth. Data which allegedly supports a shorter rotation period for the early earth need to be critically analyzed (8). Other solar system moons should also be moving outward from their planets due to tidal effects. If future measurements show this motion, especially for the Pluto-Chiron pair, then evolutionary time-scale problems abound throughout the solar system. If moons have indeed spiraled slowly outward from their planets, all intervening matter should have been gravitationally "swept up" and deposited on the moon surfaces. In particular, the observed rings of four planets (Saturn, Jupiter, Uranus, and Neptune) should not exist, since they all have orbiting moons well beyond their rings. Accretion of collision fragments into objects like the moon is an assumption that also needs critical study. For example, the asteroid belt is outside the sun's Roche Limit, yet has not coalesced into a planet. Our own moon and other planetary satellites within the solar system have much to tell us about solar system history.

CONCLUSION

Having given up on traditional lunar origin theories, many scientists now are promoting a collision between the early earth and a Mars-size object. However, fundamental problems remain, including the small probability of collision and also the short upper-limit on earth-moon history, approximately 1.4 billion years. The origin of our beautiful natural satellite, the moon, remains unexplained by contemporary science.

REFERENCES

1.   Whitcomb, J. C., and D. DeYoung, The Moon: Its Creation, Form, and Significance, BMH Books, Winona Lake, IN, 1978.

2.   Bass, A. P., "The Origin of the Moon," Science, 231:4736, January 24, 1986, pp. 341-345.

3.   Taylor, S. R., "The Origin of the Moon," American Scientist, 75:5, September-October, 1987, pp. 468-477.

4.   Hartmann, W. K., "Birth of the Moon," Natural History, 98:11, November, 1989, pp. 68-76.

5.   Kerr, R. A., "Making the Moon, Remaking Earth," Science 243:4897, March 17, 1989, pp. 1433-5.

6.   MacDonald, G. J. F., "Origin of the Moon: Dynamical Considerations," in The Earth-Moon System, Ed. by B. G. Marsden and A. G. W. Cameron, Plenum Press, N. Y., 1966, p. 181.

7.   MacDonald, p. 175.

8.   Horgan, J., "Blame It on the Moon," Scientific American, 260:2, February, 1989, p. 18.

DISCUSSION

Dr. DeYoung focuses upon two continuing problems with lunar formation theories. The first applies only to the relatively recent collision theory -- the probability of such a collision is too low. Unfortunately, his mean-free-path treatment is not convincing for three reasons. He ignores gravity, which would increase the impact parameter and make a better case for collisions, his assumption of 100 Mars-sized objects with in Neptune's orbit seems somewhat arbitrary, and the assumption of chaotic motion is not in accord with current solar system formation theories. When such an analysis still allows a one in a thousand chance of collision, we cannot say that the collision theory has been falsified. The second problem facing evolutionary theories is the lack of evidence for lunar recession over the last 4.5 billion years, a criticism not yet satisfactorily answered by astronomers.

Paul M. Steidl, M.S.
Snohomish, Washington

CLOSURE

I thank Mr. Paul Steidl for his interaction. Gravity has not been fully ignored in the discussion: the planetesimals are gravitationally bound within a Neptune-sized orbit. Gravity between particles is neglected, and is justified in view of the speeds involved. The 100 Mars-sized objects are certainly arbitrary. However, it is a generous concession, since planets are already assumed to have formed. Any refinements will surely lower the probability of lunar origin by collision. Early chaotic motion is a part of current solar system views. This arises from the many extreme dynamical properties of the planets.

Donald B. DeYoung, Ph.D.

A RECONSIDERATION OF THE PHOTOELECTRIC EFFECT AND ALPHA DECAY

Bernard Daly Dusenbury, Jr.
112 North East Street
Raleigh, North Carolina 27601

ABSTRACT

The photoelectric effect is considered as a resonant response of atomic electrons. The periodic nature of the electron is established by the work of Louis de Broglie unifying optical and dynamical path integrals. Finally, the atomic electron response to electromagnetic radiation is modeled using the solution of the damped oscillator. This concept is extended to nuclear phenomena by considering decay rates of alpha emitting nuclides. The implications for determinations of the age of the earth are then discussed.

INTRODUCTION

Resonance and the Photoelectric Effect

In his 1983 book, Physics of the Future, Thomas G. Barnes argues that a revised interpretation of the photoelectric effect is needed. The work of Herbert Ives is cited in describing the photoelectric effect as "due to an internal resonance in the atom, not in the incident light." It is this concept of resonance in the atom (or more properly at this point) the atomic electrons which this paper will initially address. The "photon" concept of light may then be reconsidered and the wave concept of light restored. Finally, a first conceptual attempt at extending this model to nuclear phenomena will be made. This will be done by considering alpha decay rates.

To study the atomic electron as a resonant system will require that the electron be considered as having wavelike properties. There are three reasons to do so.

- The Davisson-Germer experiment in which electrons were passed through crystals shows that electrons exhibit interference effects. This established that they possess wavelike properties.
- In Physics of the Future, Herbert Ives was quoted in his discussion of the photoelectric effect as saying "other attempts of explanation . . . have almost uniformly neglected or ignored the optical factors. These, instead of being secondary or negligible, really dominate." Wavelike properties in ejection of electrons are involved that resemble those of light.
- A unification of the optical and particle aspects of electron phenomena has already been done by Louis de Broglie.

PIONEERING

The Role of De Broglie's Wave Mechanics

Before considering the photoelectric effect as a resonant response by atomic electrons, a brief review of de Broglie's work is in order. To begin with, de Broglie wrote an expression for the momentum, J, of a particle in a potential A. (See Equation #1)

Equation #2 is the resulting Hamiltonian if the path integral for the particle motion is set up. That is, by the principle of Fermat, the derivative of the path integral (for the Lagrangian in generalized coordinates) is a minimum. The rewritten integral was then used to describe only the spatial coordinates, as noted in Equation #3.

Next, de Broglie considered the case in optical theory of a ray of light moving through a medium having a constant index of refraction. First, the phase of this wave is defined by $\emptyset$ and the wave unit vector by n. The "principle of the shortest path" is then written in integral form as demonstrated in Equations #4 and #5.

The relationship between energy E and frequency of light, U, was postulated by Planck to be $E = h\nu$. de Broglie then postulated that Planck's principle was applicable to both cases just considered and allowed a relationship to be derived between them. Recall, at this point, that Planck's Principle was derived to solve the black-body radiation. It was derived under classical assumptions though its results went beyond them. de Broglie then considered the four-dimensional wave vector as previously referenced in Equations #4 and #5. Equation #6 gives the four-dimensional momentum of a particle.

The relativistic expression for momentum is easily recognized above. While Einstein receives the credit, the actual ground work was laid by Lorentz, again working under classical assumptions. de Broglie assumed relativistic invariance. Consider the case for i=4 for both cases and compare, substituting in $W=h\nu$(Planck's principle) and setting them equal:

$$P_{i=4} = \frac{h\nu}{c}$$

Expand this relationship to the complete vectors:

$$\vec{P} = \frac{M_0 V_i}{(1-\frac{V^2}{c^2})^{1/2}} = \frac{h\nu}{V}$$

upon simplification, this result is:

$$P = \frac{h}{\lambda}$$

This is the famous de Broglie equation. Having derived this relationship, the stage is set to consider the electron as a resonant system and how this may give rise to the photo-electric effect. For resonance to occur in a mechanical system (whether that of a mass on a spring or the nucleus) energy must be added to the system as some characteristic frequency which could, presumably, be the frequency of the electromagnetic radiation.

Next, de Broglie considered the electron as having periodic properties as part of its nature, not unlike a "clock" as it were. The electron, by virtue of its wavelike properties, could be represented by being associated with a stationary wave. This wave may be represented in the form:

$$e^{i\nu_0 t_0}$$

where ν_0 is the internal frequency of the electron, V is the electron "velocity", t_0 is time and C is the speed of light. The "clock associated with the electron has a phase $\emptyset$. This phase may be calculated using the following two relations:

$$M_0 C^2 = h\nu_0$$

where h is Planck's constant and m is mass. In addition, the following expression holds:

$$Vv = c^2$$

where V is the velocity of the phase wave of the electron and v is the velocity of the electron on its path. The quantity $\emptyset$ is important in that energy must be supplied by electromagnetic radiation in phase with this internal wave for the photoelectric effect to occur. Equation #7 gives de Broglie's expression for $\emptyset$.

The velocity of the particle in its orbit can be different than that of the phase wave. If the particle wave itself moves at a velocity, V, the phase of this wave (after using the classical Lorentz relations) is given in Equation #8.

The two phases are, in fact, equal. This provides the basis for viewing the electron as a resonant system. When this condition was applied to the orbit of electrons an important result emerges. Consider that an electron starts from a point, 0, at velocity, v, and describes a Bohr orbit. The wave associated with the electron begins to move simultaneously with velocity, $V = v/c^2$. Let us say that the wave overtakes the particle at a point, 0', at some time τ. The wave will have traveled the distance from 0 to 0' and an entire orbit in time $(\tau + T)$ where T is the classical period of the electron. At the instant this overtaking occurs, the following relationship described in Equation #9 holds. Requiring that the phases be the same gives the condition:

$$2\pi\nu_1\tau = 2n\pi$$

where n is the number of Bohr orbits. This was the Bohr condition that allowed the prediction of the hydrogen spectra.

The Electron's Resonance with Varying Fields

Having established that the electron can profitably be viewed as a resonant system, let us consider the electron in its orbit. As it moves around the nucleus, let it have a characteristic frequency in the orbit of w. Upon bombardment by electromagnetic energy of some energy w', some photoelectrons may be given off. To consider this as a resonance condition, let us use the classical expression for a damped oscillator. For a steady state solution, the result is exemplified in Equation #10.

If the force is applied as maximized because $w = w_0$, the amplitude will also achieve a maximum.

In the photoelectric effect, an electromagnetic wave with frequency w' bombards an atom. The maximum energy, E, for electrons given off is given by:

$$E_{max} = (h\nu - w)$$

where h is Planck's constant divided by 2π and W is the work function or binding energy of the lattice. If the E is used as the forcing function, the result is Equation #12.

Thus, the quantity $h\nu$ becomes a unit of resonant response of the electron itself, rather than a discrete unit of electromagnetic radiation that leads to ejection from the atom. This view may help resolve some difficulties with the current view of the electron as a basically inert charged point. This can explain why some electron orbitals seem to preferentially emit photoelectrons. This would be expected when the "clock" frequency of the electron must match that of the incident wave. Although, this phenomena does present difficulties for the strictest point charge view of the electron.

Extension of the Oscillator Concept to Nuclei

It is to be hoped that this treatment could be extended to the nucleus. Many phenomena already are partially viewed in this light, such as nuclear magnetic resonance and photo-fission. The still unexplained production of muons produced by 1 TeV electromagnetic radiation from high-energy galactic sources may also have a resonance explanation. In short, this concept offers fruitful possibilities for a model of nuclear and atomic phenomena with real explanatory power.

Any attempt to formulate a model of nuclear phenomena using this concept will require the insights provided by quantum mechanics. As the derivation by de Broglie illustrates, the predictions of quantum mechanics are based on fundamental physical principles and logical deductions. This is not to say that many of the current philosophical conclusions supposedly drawn from quantum mechanics are either logical or correct.

In attempting to apply the concept of a damped oscillator to nuclear phenomena, alpha decay will be the starting point. Since the early research by Rutherford, Soddy and others, alpha emitting nuclides have been of great interest to nuclear scientists.

The significance of alpha decay for this discussion is that the radioactive elements used to calculate long ages for the earth tend to be alpha emitters such as uranium, thorium, etc. The purpose of this paper is not an in depth critique of current age estimates. On the other hand, a new model of nuclear phenomena will be shown to be consistent with varying alpha decay rates. This would allow for a younger age of the earth when present data is re-examined.

Experimental History of Alpha Decay Studies Using Haloes

Another property of alpha particles is that they tend to produce visible tracks in certain solids. This is due to their massive nature and charged state which induces a large amount of ionization. In fact, many commercial companies use these tracks formed by alphas tracking through plastic to detect radon.

In the early twentieth century, John Joly of the University of Dublin discovered that alpha emitting nuclides such as uranium can leave visible tracks in rocks. These take the form of tracks called "pleochroic haloes." Actually, as alphas leave bits of uranium and bombard the surrounding rock, a spherical pattern of defects is created. When the rock is cut in half, this track may be studied using a microscope. The size of these haloes can be used to determine the energy of the emitted alphas if their range in the substance is known. John Joly made extensive study of these plechroic haloes in rocks such as mica and biotite. As a result of his studies, he became convinced that the rate of radioactive decay for the alpha emitting nuclides had changed in time. Later, Professor G. H. Henderson at Dalhausie University continued these studies. The conventional scientific view became the rates of decay do not change over time but are constant. Any recognition of a change in decay rates would raise some fundamental questions about using radioactivity in dating the earth.

Questions about Varying Alpha Decay

In March 1972, however, Richard Spector re-examined the work of Joly and Henderson. Their data had previously been used to argue for an invariant alpha decay rate. Spector noted that both Henderson and Joly attempted to compare present day alpha ranges with the ranges in Precambrian rocks. These rocks were considered to be the oldest ones according to evolutionary time scales.

The fundamental issue raised in Spector's paper is as follows. Far from being evidence for invariance of decay rates, Henderson's work especially may indicate that alpha decay rates have changed. Henderson and Joly both compared the ranges of the alpha particles in rocks to those in air. The agreement they found was to within 3 percent. Today, however, with improved technology with which to examine the specimens, comparisons between ranges among rock samples is now possible, and to a much higher precision. The range, R, of an alpha particle with mass m in a material of atomic number Z, and ionization energy, I, is given in Equation #13 with the function of f given in Equation #14.

The whole assumption underlying Henderson's work was that the ratio of ranges for two energies would be the same in mica as in air. Mathematically, if we calculate an expression for ranges in air and mica for energies E_1 and E_2, then set them equal (as Henderson believed) the result will be Equation #15.

In Spector's paper, a comparison is made using E_1 = 4.5 MeV and E_2 = 7.5 MeV. The ratio on the left is found to be 0.442. The one on the right is found to be 0.474, an increase of more than 7 percent. From this, Spector has argued for a re-evaluation of plechroic haloes. The most notable recent attempt was by Robert Gentry during his stay at the Oak Ridge National Laboratory. Mr. Gentry concluded from his study of these haloes found in the basement granites that no uranium was initially present. Therefore, he believed the short lived polonium was primordial. For the haloes to provide a record of this polonium, the rock must have crystallized quickly. Though the plechroic halo research by Gentry is better known, there have also been important contributions made to age of the earth questions by his research on zircons. Zircons are crystals often found in granitic rocks having the chemical formula $ZrSiO_4$. As early as 1952, Vinogradov and his co-workers used isotopic dating to determine the ages of materials associated with well known rock types. The advantages to using zircons for dating is that common, non-radiogenic lead does not greatly effect the result. Equation #16 is the basic equation used to date zircons given in Lead Isotopes by B. R. Doe.

Zircons and Age Determinations

The paper by Gentry, et. al. on zircons entitled "Differential Lead Retention in Zircons: Implications for Nuclear Waste Containment" (Science, Vol 216, pp 296-298, 16 April 1982) provides important information regarding age of the earth questions. This paper presents data which calls into question some accepted views of earth history. Zircons pose a problem for evolutionary geology because they often give young ages for the geological formations where they occur. In a survey of the relevant work done in zircons, B. R. Doe notes that zircons are suspected of having low lead retention. This is believed to have caused the low age determinations associated with zircons. In fact, geologists were even willing to allow the possibility of leaching by water action to explain the low lead content. In his paper, Gentry analyzed zircons from a site in New Mexico being considered for a high level radioacitve waste depository. The resulting analysis showed the Pb-206/Pb-207 ratio was the same even at greater and greater depths. This deposit did not seem to have the lead loss noted in other zircons.

With the evidence of lead retention in the zircons presented by Gentry, the argument used by evolutionists against a younger earth is made open to question. In the book, Lead Isotopes by B. R. Doe, several anomalous ages calculated from zircons are given. For example, zircons from the La Sal Mountains of Utah were reported by Stern et. al., in 1965 to have an age of 494 million years. Also a Pb-determination of the age of zircons in the Leadville district of Colorado was made by Pearson et. al. in 1962. All of these results are significantly less than the billions of years assigned to many formations by the evolutionary times scale.

Theory of Alpha Decay

If there is a real variation in alpha decay rates as suggested in Spector's paper, then both the deposits with old ages and young apparent ages can be accounted for. Higher decay rates would cause relatively recent deposits to appear old while some deposits could be expected to appear much younger. The much younger ages would be a result of a lower decay rate in recent geological history. Evolutionists have suggested time dependent diffusion as one mechanism to explain the anomalous zircon data. Gentry's evidence for high retention of lead in the zircons indicate that another mechanism should be considered. As Spector has noted there are experimental considerations that point toward variation in alpha decay rates. There are certain theoretical considerations that point in this direction as well. First, let us consider the background to our current theoretical understanding of alpha decay. This was brought about by the work of George Gamow along with R. W. Gurney and E. U. Condon working independently. The problem was to find a way to predict λ, the decay constant for an alpha to be emitted from a nucleus in a given state. This was done by considering the alpha as a charged particle bouncing back and forth between the walls of a potential well. This potential well was of course the attractive potential of the nucleus. The new understanding quantum mechanics brought to the problem was that it was possible for the alpha to escape the nucleus even though it might not possess the energy to go over the wall. The results of the Gamow-Gurney-Condon theory were calculated as follows. Let λ be the decay constant for alpha emission and may be calculated using:

$$\lambda = fp$$

where f is the frequency of the alpha particles motion inside the nucleus and p is the probability of an alpha particle with mass M escaping the nucleus. The probability p was calculated using Equation #17.

When the following expression for U(r) is used, the integral assumes a new form. The potential is:

$$U = \frac{Zze^2}{r}$$

where Z is the nuclear atomic number and z is 2. The final result for λ appears in Equation #18.

When this integral is evaluated analytically after certain substitutions, predictions for λ can be made. The calculated and actual values for λ are given in Appendix B for selected even A nuclides (taken from Friedlander & Kennedy).

89

There are some differences for these nuclei between the calculated and actual values but also some striking agreements. These agreements were mainly for nuclides with even atomic weights. For nuclides with even Z, or atomic number and odd A or atomic weight, the calculated values were very disparate. In Friedlander and Kennedy it is noted that λ for the transition from U-235 to the ground state of Th-231 is approximately 1000 times greater than the experimental value.

Since Th-231 has a half-life of approximately 25 hours, very little Th-231 should remain on earth. Well, Th-231 is found still, Friedlander and Kennedy resolve this problem by simply stating the fact of the "hindrance factor" or delay by a factor of 1000 for the decay rate. This could be explained as well by a varying alpha decay rate and a much younger earth. Next, let us consider how this might be done in the context of the current theory of alpha decay.

Possible Basis for Varying Decay Rates in Current Theory

In the paper "Alpha Decay", by H. J. Mang, the current state of alpha decay theory is explained. The decay constant λ is given by the following expression:

$$\lambda = \frac{1}{\hbar} \sum_{jl} P\gamma(\varepsilon)^2$$

Where P is the barrier penetration probability and γ (ε) which is determined by properties in the nucleus. The quantity γ (ε) is referred to as the "reduced width" and refers to the probability of alpha particle production. The indices e and j refer to angular momentum states of the daughter nucleus and the alpha particle. The quantity γ is further defined in Equation #19.

This time dependent probability will be considered in more detail here. The g is considered to be a function of space and time variable, and can be described by quantum mechanical wave functions. The most important expression for this probability in our case is given in Equation #20.

The indices j, l, and J have been previously defined, while Γ is defined by the expression:

$$\Gamma = \frac{\lambda \hbar}{4\pi}$$

for the system.

In his paper on alpha decay, Mang notes that the above expression applies only in a very limited space time region. This region's size is less than R = vt where v is the alpha's velocity and t is the travel time since decay. There must be a region of space time for the nucleus where there is time dependent exponential decay of the alpha generation probability. This condition may well be the source of a variable rate of alpha decay. This is the importance of this condition for the study of decay rates. This condition also can be conceptually assigned the role of a damping mechanism to a resonant oscillator as discussed in earlier considerations of the photoelectric effect.

Indeed this time dependent exponential decay may not be the only damping system for this phenomena. Mang notes that the dispersion of a wave packet will produce a time dependence of the form $t^{-3/2}$. If the optical analogy holds for this system, as it does for the electron, this might also produce a damping effect.

In conclusion, there exists experimental evidence that has re-opened the question of variable decay rates for alpha emitters. Some of this evidence has come with increasing precision of instrumentation as noted by Spector. Also as has been noted by Gentry and others studying radionuclide retention in zircons, there are evidences for a much more restricted timescale for earth history. Previous mechanisms for lead diffusion from the zircons were invoked to account for the discrepancies with current age of the earth estimates. With Gentry's determination of low diffusion rates there anomalous values must be reconsidered. A variable alpha decay rate then becomes more plausible. Finally, alpha decay can provide another application for the damped resonant oscillator concept to atomic and nuclear systems. This is certainly worthy of further investigation.

TECHNICAL SUMMARY

In this paper, the photoelectric effect is re-examined with the ejection of photoelectrons considered by viewing the electron as a resonant system. This view is derived from de Broglie's work to unify optical and dynamical formulations for light waves and particles, which resulted in the principle of phase harmony. This allows emission of photoelectrons to be viewed as the resonant response of a damped oscillator. The quantity "$h\nu$" becomes a characteristic quantity of resonant response in the atomic electron rather than a discrete unit of electromagnetic energy. This concept of a damped resonant oscillator is then applied to the nuclei of alpha emitting elements in nature. This was done by examining possible variations in decay rates. Evidence of possible variations in even Z, odd A, nuclides will be considered along with implications for age of the earth determinations.

Thank you for your consideration. The opinions and conclusions expressed in this paper are those of the author alone. No other endorsements by any authors cited here are implied.

REFERENCES

1. Diner, Simon; Fargue, D.; Lochak, Georges and Selleri, F., Editors, "De Broglie's Initial Conception of De Broglie Waves", THE WAVE-PARTICLE DUALISM: A TRIBUTE TO LOUIS DE BROGLIE ON HIS 90th BIRTHDAY, D. Reidel Publishing Company, Dordrecht, Holland, 1984, pp. 1-8.

2. Boyce, William E., and DiPrima, Richard C., "Second Order Linear Equations", ELEMENTARY DIFFERENTIAL EQUATIONS, Third Edition, John Wiley and Sons, New York, New York, p. 137.

3. Friedlander, Gerhart, Kennedy, Joseph W., Macias, Edward S., and Miller, Julian Malcolm, "Radioactive Decay Processes", NUCLEAR AND RADIOCHEMISTRY, John Wiley and Sons, New York, New York, pp. 61-63.

4. Doe, Bruce R., "U-Th-Pb Dating", LEAD ISOTOPES, Springer-Verlag, Berlin, 1970, pp. 11-18.

5. Burchfield, Joe D., "Radioactivity and the Age of the Earth", LORD KELVIN AND THE AGE OF THE EARTH, Science History Publications, New York, New York, 1975, pp. 188-190.

6. R. M. Spector. "Physical Review A, 5", pp. 1323-1327, (1971).

7. H. J. Mang. "Alpha Decay", Ann. Rev. Nucl. Sci. 14, pp. 4-9, (1964).

8. R. V. Gentry. "Radioactive Haloes", Ann. Rev. Nucl. Sci. 23, pp. 349-362, (1973).

9. R. V. Gentry. "Differential Lead Retention in Zircons: Implications for Nuclear Waste Containment", Science, pp. 269-298, (1982).

10. I. Perlman, A. Ghiorso and G. T. Seaborg. "Systematics of Alpha Radioactivity", Physical Review 77, pp. 40-45, (1950).

COMPARISON OF DECAY CONSTANTS CALCULATED FROM (3-6) WITH EXPERIMENTAL DATA

Alpha Emitter	T (MeV)	R_1 X E+13 cm[a]	λ_{calc} (s^{-1})[c]	λ_{exp} (s^{-1})[b]
Nd-144	1.9	7.950	2.7 X E-24	1.0 X E-23
Gd-148	3.27	8.014	2.6 X E-10	2.2 X E-10
Po-210	5.408	8.878	1.0 X E-6	5.80 X E-8
Po-214	7.835	8.927	4.9 X E+3	4.23 X E+3
Th-226	6.448	9.072	2.6 X E-4	2.95 X E-4
Th-228	5.521	9.095	8.0 X E-9	8.35 X E-9
Th-230	4.767	9.118	1.7 X E-13	2.09 X E-13
Th-232	4.080	9.142	7.8 X E-19	1.20 X E-18
Fm-254	7.310	9.390	1.3 X E-4	5.1 X E-5

Nuclear and Radiochemistry, 3rd Edition, Friedlander & Kennedy.

Zircon depth (m)	Filaments analyzed	Average zircons per filament	Total Pb counts	Counts of Pb-204	Pb-204 / total Pb	Average Pb-206/ Pb-207	Range Pb-206/ Pb-208
960	4	~ 10	1.2 X E+6	235	2.0 X E-4	9.6 ± 0.3	6.5- 9.2
960	4	1	1.3 X E+5	35	2.7 X E-4	9.9 ± 0.4	5.8-14
2170	3	~ 5	8.9 X E+5	269	3.0 X E-4	10.0 ± 0.4	6.4-12.4
2900	3	~ 4	4.1 X E+5	114	2.8 X E-4	11.2 ± 0.3	0.4-11.4
3930	2	~ 10	6.5 X E+5	132	2.0 X E-4	11.0 ± 0.4	5.9- 8.7
3930	2	1	8.0 X E+4	46	5.8 X E-4	10.4 ± 0.1	3.1- 6.9
4310	7	~ 10	5.6 X E+6	1400	2.5 X E-4	9.7 ± 0.6	3.4- 9.8
4310	2	1	1.6 X E+5	100	6.0 X E-4	9.8 ± 0.4	4.5-10.7

Results of thermal ionization mass measurements for zircons with a Pb-205/Pb ratio of less than 2 X E-3. The background correction was taken from 208.5 mass position; it was applied to the raw data to obtain the isotopic abundances, which were used to compute the isotopic ratios. Standard deviations are listed with the Pb isotopic ratios.

From Gentry et. al., Science, Vol. 216, pp. 296-298.

a - radius values calculated using $R_1 = (1.30 \times A^{1/3} + 1.20) \times 10^{-13}$ cm
b - λ is the partial decay constant for ground state transitions

$$J_\alpha = M_0 c U_\alpha + e A_\alpha \tag{1}$$

where: M_0 = rest mass
C_0 = speed of light
U = velocity as a relativistic function
α = three space variables and time

$$\delta \int_P^Q J_\alpha dx^\alpha = 0 \tag{2}$$

$$\delta \int_P^Q Ji dx^i = 0 \tag{3}$$

where: P = path endpoint
Q = path endpoint

$$\delta \int_P^Q d\phi = \delta \int 2\pi 0_\alpha dx^\alpha \quad (\alpha = 1,2,3,4) \tag{4}$$

where: O = a four dimensional wave vector given by:

$$\vec{0}_i = \frac{\nu}{V} \vec{n}_i \ (i = 1,2,3) \ \vec{0}_4 = \frac{\nu}{c} \tag{5}$$

where: ν = wave frequency
V = phase velocity
P = spatial endpoint
Q = spatial endpoint

$$J_\alpha = M_0 C U_i = \frac{M_0 V_i}{(1-\frac{v^2}{c^2})^{1/2}} = P_i \ (i = 1,2,3) \ J_4 = \frac{W}{c} \tag{6}$$

where: V = velocity
P = momentum
W = energy
C = speed of light

$$\phi \ clock = \nu_1 t = \frac{m_0 c^2}{h} (1-\frac{v^2}{c^2})^{1/2} \frac{X}{V} \tag{7}$$

where: X = the location of the particle as viewed by an observer
in a non-accelerating frame of reference
t = time

$$\phi = \nu(t-\frac{vx}{c^2}) = \frac{m_0 c^2}{h} \frac{1}{(1-\frac{v^2}{c^2})^{1/2}} (\frac{x}{V} - \frac{vx}{c^2}) = \frac{m_0 c^2}{h} (1-\frac{v^2}{c^2})^{1/2} \frac{x}{V} \tag{8}$$

$$2\pi\nu_1\tau = \frac{2\pi m_0 c^2}{h} (1-\frac{v^2}{c^2})^{1/2} X \frac{v^2}{c^2-v^2} X \ T \tag{9}$$

$$u = \frac{F_o \cos(wt - \delta)}{(m^2(w_o^2 - w^2)^2 + c^2 w^2)^{1/2}}$$ (10)

where: u = the amplitude of the vibration
w_o = the characteristic angular frequency
c = a constant and can be calculated from Equation #11

$$\delta = \cos^{-1} \frac{m(w_o^2 - w^2)}{(m^2(w_o^2 - w^2)^2 + c^2 w^2)^{1/2}}$$ (11)

where: w = the angular frequency of application of the force F_o

$$E = \frac{(h\nu - W) |\cos wt| (wc)}{(m^2(w_o^2 - w^2) + c^2 w^2)^{1/2}}$$ (12)

$$R = \frac{1}{128\pi} \frac{m_\alpha}{m_e} I^2 \frac{1}{NZe^4} \left(\frac{4m_e}{m_\alpha} \cdot \frac{E}{I}\right)$$ (13)

where: N = atomic density
E = alpha energy
m_α = alpha mass
m_e = electron mass
e = charge of the electron

$$F^{-1} = \left[-\frac{EdE}{(\ln \frac{4m_e}{m_\alpha} \frac{E}{I})}\right]_o^E$$ (14)

where: F^{-1} = antiderivative of function between limits 0 and E

$$\frac{f(\frac{4m_e}{m_\alpha} \frac{E_1}{I_{air}})}{f(\frac{4m_e}{m_\alpha} \frac{E_2}{I_{air}})} = \frac{f(\frac{4m_e}{m_\alpha} \frac{E_1}{I_{mica}})}{f(\frac{4m_e}{m_\alpha} \frac{E_2}{I_{mica}})}$$ (15)

$$\frac{(\frac{Pb_{207}^{obs} - Pb_{207}^{init}}{Pb_{204}^{obs} - Pb_{204}^{init}})}{(\frac{Pb_{206}^{obs} - Pb_{206}^{init}}{Pb_{204}^{obs} - Pb_{204}^{init}})} = \frac{(\frac{U_{235}}{U_{238}})(e^{\lambda_5 t} - 1)}{(e^{\lambda_8 T} - 1)^{obs}}$$ (16)

95

where: "obs" = superscript presently observed isotopic ratios for radiogenic lead

"init" = superscript for ratios at crystallization

λ_5 = decay constant for U-235 (equal to 9.71×10^{-10} yr^{-1})

λ_8 = decay constant for U-238 (equal to 1.54×10^{-10} yr^{-1})

T = elapsed time

$$P = \exp\left(\frac{-4\pi}{\left(\frac{h}{2\pi}\right)}(2\mu)^{1/2} F^{-1}[(U(r)-T)dR]_{R_1}^{R_2}\right)$$

(17)

where: μ = the reduced mass of the nucleus

U(r) = the attractive potential as a function of nuclear radius r

T = the total kinetic energy of the alpha particle and recoil nucleus

$$\lambda = f \exp\left(\frac{-4\pi}{\left(\frac{h}{2\pi}\right)}(2\mu)^{1/2} F^{-1}\left[\left(\frac{Zze^2-Tr}{r^{1/2}}\right)^{1/2} dr\right]_{R_1}^{R_2}\right)$$

(18)

$$\gamma^2_{Jj1} = \frac{h}{8\pi^2 m} R_o |g_{j1J}(R_o)|^2$$

(19)

where: γ^2_{Jj1} = the square of the reduced width of the system containing an alpha particle of angular momentum state 1, and a daughter nucleus having an angular momentum state, j, with a total angular momentum J

R_o = the radius of the parent nucleus

g = time dependent probability amplitude for the generation of alpha decay

$$g_{j1}^{J}(R,t) = \exp\left(\frac{-2\pi i}{h}(E-i\Gamma)t\right)g_{j1}^{J}(R)$$

(20)

where: E = the α energy

i = the complex quantity

R = the relative distance between the α particle and the nucleus

t = time

DISCUSSION

This paper begins by referring to Barnes' book, *Physics of the Future*, in which it is argued that it is impossible for anything to exhibit both wave and particle properties. However, this paper presents some of the convincing evidence indicating the wave nature of electrons and other particles. Indeed, the alpha particle decay of nuclei seems to be predicted correctly through the theories of quantum mechanics and seems to be impossible to explain through any classical theory that denies that an alpha particle might exhibit any wave-like properties. However, it is not clear whether this paper rejects any or all of the particle-like aspects of electromagnetic radiation that have been used to explain the photoelectric effect. Specifically, the equation $E_{max} = (hn - W)$ is quoted and then modified. The derivation of this equation is usually based on the photon or particle-like behavior or electromagnetic radiation. The modification of this equation is given as equation (12) in this paper, but the notation is not clear. Care must be taken to distinguish between two experimental quantities: (1) E_{max}, which is the energy of the most energetic photoelectron, and (2) the number of photoelectrons emitted at some energy. The equation $E_{max} = (hn - W)$ makes no reference to the number of photoelectrons. Understanding the number of emitted photoelectrons may indeed require an analysis which involves resonance, as the author notes, "This can explain why some electron orbitals seem to preferentially emit photoelectrons." However, equation (12) must be clarified before its validity can be discussed. Specifically, a dimensional analysis indicates that the equation must be modified if E stands or energy. If E does not stand for energy, what does it stand for? If E does stand for energy, is it the energy E_{max} or is it the energy of some of the less energetic photoelectrons? Since cos(wt) can be both positive and negative, can E be both positive and negative? If the cos(wt) term is ignored, this equation predicts that E will decrease as w increases, as long as w is greater than w_o. While this decrease may be true for the number of photoelectrons observed at some energy, this is not true for the energy of the photoelectrons themselves. Thus, the author's analysis of the photoelectric effect may be correct, but clarification is needed.

Mr. Dusenbury then mentions some experimental evidence indicating that the present quantum mechanical treatment of alpha decay may be inadequate in explaining all the features of alpha decay, especially when examining haloes and/or zircons, and he suggests that a damped resonance effect may explain some of these discrepancies. The mathematical application of damped resonance to alpha decay does not seem to be presented, and the present reader does not see how the concept of damped resonance can be applied to alpha decay for two reasons:

1. As the author mentions, "For resonance to occur in a mechanical system (whether that of a mass on a spring or the nucleus) energy must be added to the system at some characteristic frequency . . . ." However, in alpha decay, there is no source of energy that is adding energy. There is no outside frequency at which energy is being added and which can establish resonance with the internal system of the nucleus.

2. The author indicates that a damped resonance would predict a changing decay rate for the alpha decay of a given isotope. Thus, the decay rate should be different if the time at which the decay is measured is greater. However, what is the starting point for this time that is greater or less when the decay rates are being compared? Perhaps the author was referring to the elapsed time since the isotope had been formed. If so, this would seem to predict that a quantity of a radioisotope that was newly formed would have a different decay rate from the same quantity of that same isotope, if all the latter isotopes had existed for some time. While it is difficult to check the accuracy of this experimental prediction with isotopes whose half-lives are millions of years, this prediction can be checked with great accuracy with short-lived alpha emitters, such as Rn-222, Rn-218, Po-210, Rn-220, Po-216, etc. I know of no evidence of changing decay rates even for nuclei whose ages are hundreds of half-lives. Thus, it seems that the author would have to refine his theory if he is predicting that the decay rate will change in several half-lives for long-lived radioisotopes but will not change in hundreds of half-lives for short-lived radioisotopes.

William F. Junkin, Ph.D.
Due West, South Carolina

Herbert Ives argued that the optical data is compatible with an atomic model with finite size electrons in some sort of resonant states and not with quantum mechanics of point-like electrons and quanta. De Broglie continued this idea when he equated Einstein's mass $m_o c^2$ with Planck's energy hv_o, i.e. $m_o c^2 = hv_o$. This identified the frequency v_o of the resonant state with the particle and not the wave or quantum. Dr. Thomas Barnes has given qualitative arguments indicating that such a model is feasible. However, Dr. Barnes left the development of explicit models to future scientists. Such models will need to predict the energy levels of the known atoms, at least as well as the Dirac equation, including such effects as spin-orbit coupling and the Lamb shift. No such models yet exist.

It may be somewhat presumptuous at this point in the development of theory to assume that the processes going on in the interior of the nucleus are the same as those involving the atomic electrons. However, those scientists willing to work on these problems leading to truth should be commended.

In this paper the use of quantum mechanics to derive a formula for alpha decay to test the idea of the nucleon being a finite size particle in a resonant state is inconsistent. Quantum mechanics is based on Hamiltonian mechanics for point-like particles only!. A finite size nucleon or electron in a resonant state is incompatible with point-like particles. One needs to use a classical type derivation for alpha decay if one wants to be consistent.

Charles W. Lucas, Jr., Ph.D.
Temple Hills, Maryland

CLOSURE

The discussion by Dr. Junkin indicates several areas that may need clarification in my paper. I will do this on the conceptual level primarily. The wave characteristics of subatomic particles are experimentally well established. The point of the paper was to seek an understanding of these properties using an oscillator model. Two separate phenomena were considered, namely the photoelectric effect and alpha decay. There were two different approaches put forth as models, but both utilized the concept of a damped oscillator. In the case of the photoelectric effect, the electromagnetic radiation falling on the metal acts like a forcing function on the electron, while the binding energy of the metal acts like a damping force. It's as if a weight were attached to the end of a spring. If the top of the spring was moved up and down the weight would be set in motion. Under the proper conditions, the weight could even break the spring, and fly off into space. This breaking of the spring is similar to the ejection of an electron in the oscillator model of the photoelectric effect. The energy of the ejected electron depends on the frequency of the impinging light being in phase with an internal frequency of the electron. This internal frequency was first discussed by Louis de Broglie, and I believe it has been demonstrated by Hans Dehmelt. The mathematical expression of this concept is found in equation 12. The reviewer is correct to note that this is only an expression for the maximum energy of the ejected electron. Ejected electrons of lesser energy would result when the light frequency does not approximate the internal electron frequency.

In regard to alpha decay, when a damped oscillator model is used, there is an important difference. There is no forcing function for one thing. The damping force would possibly cause a reduction of the rate of decay in time. This case is similar to a spring with one end hooked to a beam and a weight on the other. If the weight is pulled down and released, the weight will move up and down. The damping force of friction will bring it to a stop however. No attempt was made to quantify this in the paper, but merely to suggest it as one approach for understanding experimental results that may indicate changing decay rates. To detect change in decay rates for short lived nuclides may be possible using the tracks produced in solids by the decay of the nuclides. For example, the decay of radon-222 produces tracks in solids such as glass or plastics. This process is described in *Nuclear Tracks in Solids* by Fleischer, et al. If objects with such tracks are available they might be used to check known to make such a determination, however. The decay rate for different periods of historical time might be compared between objects of different ages.

The comments by Dr. Lucas raised an important point. It is true that the Schrodinger formulation of quantum mechanics was only for point particles. The experiments carried out by Hans Dehmelt indicating that the electron has real structure creates real problems for the point particle approach. However, this does not indicate to me that there is no role for other tools that quantum mechanics might possibly provide. There are several possible options that may be pursued in the study of the electron as a resonant system.

First, a classical solution may be possible if the electron is considered to be made up of constituent particles. The stability of the particle orbits in the electron must be demonstrated in such a treatment.

The next possible option does involve using the tools of quantum mechanics by constructing wave functions to model an electron of finite radius. This approach has been used to generate nuclear wave functions and may be useable in this case. The wave functions would of course have to meet certain mathematical conditions such as orthogonality and being single valued. There is a greater ease of physical understanding using a classical methodology that this approach might lack, however.

Finally, a nonlinear approach might be used. Optical phenomena can sometimes be understood using such an approach. In the case of the electron, it may be that scattering, and resonance conditions could be predicted using a non-linear Schrodinger equation. The principle of superposition is not always obeyed under such a treatment. For this reason, the greater depth of physical understanding may result from the semi-classical approach. Until this is demonstrated there is still a use for quantum mechanical tools as they can be brought to bear on the problem.

Bernard, D. Dusenbury, B.S.

CAVITATION PROCESSES DURING CATASTROPHIC FLOODS

Edmond W. Holroyd, III, Ph.D.
8905 W. 63rd Avenue
Arvada, CO 80004-3103

ABSTRACT

The destruction of rock by cavitation processes will be examined using a monograph and accompanying software written for evaluating man-made structures. Starting with actual damaging conditions in eight dam structures, the software will be stretched towards examining cavitation potential in simulated natural stream channels during catastrophic flood conditions.

INTRODUCTION

The geologic processes thought to have occurred both during and after the Flood at the time of Noah must have involved the rapid destruction of rock of numerous hardnesses. The erosion processes normally observed today seem too gentle to be the required mechanism. The process of cavitation is examined and found to be a suitably destructive mechanism for flows of shallow, high speed water.

The process of cavitation has been reviewed by Falvey (1) and Holroyd (2,3). Cavitation is the creation of gaseous phase bubbles in a liquid as a result of a decrease in pressure. The creation of bubbles themselves is relatively harmless. If they choke the flow in confined conduits, like tubes, then the blockage is more of a nuisance. It is the collapse of bubbles that can cause structural damage to surfaces that are in contact with the liquid. It will cause powerful shockwaves and possibly minute jets of water that impact the solid surfaces. Though the collapse of bubbles is actually the opposite of the creation of vapor cavities, the term cavitation tends to be used to refer to the entire process.

Cavitation has been involved in the damage of many types of man-made structures. Shock waves and water jets caused by the collapse of cavitation bubbles can clean, dent, or pulverize materials of many types, including concrete and metals. Flow speeds greater than 30 m/s appear necessary for cavitation damage, but thereafter the damage potential can increase rapidly, perhaps at rates proportional to the sixth power of velocity. Major damage can occur with flow depths of only a few meters. Damage initiated by cavitation can provide opportunities to accelerate the rates for normal erosion processes as water plunges into the holes created by cavitation.

Damage potential decreases with flow depth because increasing pressures make it less likely that internal water pressures can be dynamically forced to become less than the water vapor pressure. Cavitation damage is greatly reduced as the air content of the water is increased, suggesting that cavitation damage is unlikely to be found in "white water" rapids. The roughening of water channel surfaces also decreases cavitation damage by slowing the flow speeds and thereby increasing flow depths for constant flow discharge.

A computer model by Falvey (1) predicting damage potential, calibrated qualitatively with actual damages to dam spillways, is used in this study to indicate the locations and relative intensity of damage for several spillway profiles. Those described below include the actual Glen Canyon Dam left spillway, a nearly flat and level surface, and a wide surface having the profile of a small side channel of the Grand Canyon. These studies indicate that the process of cavitation appears to be a likely mechanism for rapid removal of rock in channels having catastrophic flows of high speed shallow water with little air bubble content.

The importance of cavitation in the rapid erosion of rock was physically illustrated during the floods within the Colorado River basin in 1983. After a winter of near-normal snowfall in the basin the snowpack was rapidly increased by spring storms. The record snow pack was then subjected to very warm conditions, causing a rapid melt. In response to the unusual flow of water into the system of dams and reservoirs, water had to be released rapidly from reservoirs to make room for the new water that was soon to arrive. In addition, the height of the Glen Canyon Dam spillway gates, near Page in northern Arizona, was increased by over two meters to create additional storage capacity. These measures were sufficient to limit the damage by the flood waters to the spillway tunnels at that dam.

Water was released past the Glen Canyon Dam through four by-pass tubes, then through the left spillway, and sometimes through the right spillway as well. Flows through the left tunnel began on 2 June, at rates of up to 571 m^3/s (20176 cfs). After about 24 hours at the high rate rumblings were heard from the tunnel. An inspection showed that damage characteristic of cavitation was occurring in the 12.5 meter diameter spillway tunnels. Flows were reduced for about a week, but the coming flood waters necessitated a resumption of high water flows, peaking briefly during a test at 906 m^3/s. Concrete and rocks torn from the tunnel walls could be seen being ejected by the high flows. In late July flows were reduced below 100 m^3/s. Lesser flows were released through the right tunnel during that period.

Later inspection of the tunnels revealed large caverns excavated through the one-meter thick reinforced concrete liner and up to 9 more meters into the sandstone rock. Figure 1 shows a view looking downstream into the largest cavity (10 m deep, 12 m wide, 37 m long). The men and the ladder help provide a scale. Boulders as big as automobiles were excavated by the water from the bedrock and some of them remained in the tunnel downstream of the damage. The largest, which had to have been lifted out of the 10 m deep hole, blocked part of the 12.5 m diameter tunnel. Others are seen in Figure 2, captured from a video (4), at the exit of the tunnel. More illustrations of the dam and damage are given in Holroyd (2).

STUDIES OF CAVITATION PROCESSES

The U.S. Bureau of Reclamation conducted extensive studies to be able to understand the conditions under which cavitation damage might occur, to predict the location and severity of damage, and to design corrections to prevent future damage to water conveyance structures. The studies were then summarized in a monograph by Falvey (1). It thoroughly explores the state of knowledge of cavitation as it relates to the structures typically built and managed by Reclamation. Over 200 references are cited, including work from many foreign countries.

The monograph, giving all relevant equations and some field calibrations, includes a set of 5.25 inch floppy disks of executable programs, source code in FORTRAN, and sample data for use on an IBM compatible microcomputer. One of the programs receives as input a nominated initial flow condition and structural profile. The output is a table of cavitation and flow conditions throughout the structure, and some optional graphs of a few parameters. Other programs provide guidance for profiles having a constant cavitation index, for design of aerator slots for injecting air bubbles into the flow, and for estimating the damage index from a record of historical flow conditions.

Falvey suggests that water heads (indicating the energy available from elevation changes) in excess of about 45 meters and flows in excess of 30 m/s are suspect for the potential for producing damage to structures by cavitation. It was found possible to control the curvature of spillways in the design process so as to minimize the possibility of cavitation damage. But redesigning and modifying structures that were already constructed was potentially too expensive.

The ingestion of air bubbles was found to lower the speed of sound in the water from about 1400 m/s to at or below the speed of sound in air (about 340 m/s). This effect significantly decreases the shock pressure intensities at the solid surface. At about 0.07 moles of air per mole of water, cavitation damage is completely eliminated. Reclamation's solution at the Glen Canyon Dam was to create an air slot part way down the spillway tunnel. After the air slot was made the spillway was tested at water flows greatly exceeding those which caused the damage of 1983. There were no traces of any damage after these tests nor since then.

This effect of air bubbles is of vital importance in dealing with natural water channels. Any channel irregular enough (boulders, ledges, sharp turns) to create "white water" by its turbulence will be unlikely to be damaging its channel bed by cavitation. There will be too much air mixed into the water. It is the high speed clear turbulent flow that is damaging.

UNDERSTANDING THE PROCESS OF CAVITATION

Water boils at that temperature at which the vapor pressure equals the total atmospheric pressure. As the atmospheric pressure is decreased, as at higher elevations, water boils at lower temperatures. Water is usually made to boil by the addition of heat to the liquid. In the process of cavitation water is made to vaporize, like boiling, by instead reducing the atmospheric pressure to below the vapor pressure of water at the temperature of that water.

Bubbles need not be of pure water vapor; other gasses may be present. Gaseous cavitation occurs when cold water is warmed, forcing dissolved air to come out of solution and form bubbles. Gaseous cavitation is also observable when the pressure is reduced by opening a container of a carbonated beverage and bubbles of mostly carbon dioxide are formed. The reduction of pressure as a diver rises from deep water causes the formation of bubbles of nitrogen gas in his blood, leading to the bends.

The pressure at any point within a fluid is the sum of static and dynamic pressures. Static pressure is generally from the weight of all of the fluid above that point, including the atmosphere. Dynamic pressure is the additional contribution, positive or negative, that results from the movement of the fluid. Positive dynamic pressure is like the pressure of the wind or of water flow against a stationary object. Negative dynamic pressure occurs, for example, in the air above the curved wing surface of an aircraft and causes it to fly. Ship propellers are subject to damage by cavitation on the fore side because of decreased dynamic pressures there. Dynamic pressure decreases resulting in cavitation damage also occur in water valves, pumps, and gates that regulate the flow of high speed water.

DAMAGE FROM CAVITATION

The bubble formation itself does not create the damage of cavitation. It is the downstream collapse of those bubbles, where pressures are restored in excess of the vapor pressure, that can subject solid surfaces to shock waves and water jet impacts. Falvey summarizes two methods that may be involved. Bubbles that collapse within the water send out shock waves. As these shock waves encounter another bubble, they subject it to a pressure increase that is likely to cause the collapse of that bubble as well. The newly collapsed bubble adds its energy to the shock wave. In this manner the bubbles collapse in phase and together create a shock wave of large amplitude. When the shock wave produced by the collapsing bubbles reaches a solid surface, even if there are no bubbles there, they strike the surface with a considerable force. The present theory suggests that the magnitude of the pressures that are generated can exceed 200 times ambient pressure.

The other mechanism for damage is for bubbles in contact with a solid surface when they collapse. The contact gives the bubbles a slight to major asymmetry. The dynamics and wave mechanics of the collapse cause a water jet to be initiated on the bubble surface opposite the solid surface. That tiny jet then strikes the side of the bubble in contact with the solid surface. Such jets have pitted aluminum with a yield strength in excess of 300 MPa, or 3000 times normal atmospheric pressure.

Falvey gives some preliminary indications of the relative strengths of some materials in terms of the amount of time to achieve the same amount of damage from cavitation. The relative scale gives concrete--1, polymer concrete--42, aluminum or copper--80, carbon steel--286, stainless steel--2000. Some values for granite, sandstone, shale, and limestone would have been desired, but the concrete value might approximate that for limestone.

There are three numbers among the equations of Falvey that are used to describe several aspects of the cavitation process: the cavitation index, the cavitation damage potential, and the damage index. Only the damage potential will be discussed here. It addresses the question, given that cavitation is likely to occur at a location, of how strong the damaging forces will be. The damage potential was crudely calibrated by Falvey by comparing actual damage at several dams with the theoretical damage potential numbers. He gives values of damage potential for "incipient", "major", and "catastrophic" damage as 500, 1000, and 2000, respectively. The damage at Glen Canyon Dam was considered to be "catastrophic".

LOCATING THE CAUSES FOR CAVITATION

The Falvey monograph summarizes theoretical cavitational characteristics for a variety of general flat and curved profiles of water channels. Concrete structures do not remain smooth, even if so constructed. There may be displacements along joints, calcite deposits, and craters changing the surface by a variety of mechanisms. While bumps in a smooth surface are likely origins for cavitation, it was found that uniform roughness could create a thicker boundary layer and decreased flow speed at the bumps that would ordinarily initiate damage.

Cavitation damage can be recognized by its texture, locational symmetry, and origin, as described by Falvey. Cavitation damage always occurs downstream of its cause and never propagates upstream. Surface irregularities that cause cavitation are left intact and can be inspected upstream of the damaged area. Cavitation damage created by longitudinal vortices will not have exact origins, like surface bumps, to identify them.

A bump (it can also be an offset into or away from the water stream) initiates cavitation damage by creating a flow disturbance that results in a dynamic pressure decrease sufficient to create bubbles, as illustrated in Figure 3. These bubbles collapse downstream and damage the nearby surface. Prolonged damage produces another flow disturbance, more bubbles, and more damage. The surface downstream of a bump can thereby develop a chain of craters. A series of holes about 3 meters deep and 6 meters wide was the form of the damage upstream of the largest hole in the Glen Canyon Dam left spillway.

Once a hole is started by cavitation, the flow of water begins to be diverted into the hole. High velocity water will impinge on the downstream end of the hole, creating higher pressures there compared to the ambient pressures. The high pressure water typically finds minute cracks and forces them to enlarge. The destructive process then changes from cavitation to normal erosion as large chunks of material are ripped out of the surface of the water channel. Whereas pitting from cavitation tends to be at random locations, erosion tends to be more organized and striated.

COMPUTER SIMULATIONS

The Falvey software presents theoretical cavitation characteristics for a variety of flat and curved profiles of water channels, surface rugosities, flow depths and speeds, and several sizes and shapes of flow disrupters. Some of the programs describe and graph the flow and cavitation conditions for any nominated profile and initial flow conditions. The software has been run for over twenty Reclamation-designed dams and others throughout the world. The software is currently able to predict locations of cavitation damage with high reliability. Though more research and calibration is probably in order, the present computer model can be considered to be approximately calibrated for real flow conditions. Its outputs are in good agreement with observations. The limitations of the software are reviewed by Holroyd (3).

The "catastrophic" flows through the Glen Canyon Dam drainage tubes were small compared to flows that those interested in catastrophic geological processes would like to consider. Therefore the software was used to explore greater magnitudes of flows. The Glen Canyon left tunnel model was subjected to flows from so low that the software complained of analysis difficulties up to the limit of the design capacity of the tubes. Then the left tube profile was retained but the cross section, width, approach and exit characteristics were changed and the flows were varied again from the lowest to the highest that the software would accept. Such variations on the Glen Canyon profile showed that the model could be extrapolated into conditions unlikely to be experienced today. The integrity of the results during such changes gave confidence that the next modifications to artificial and natural profiles would give reasonable results. In this way there was an orderly progression from known cavitation conditions to those far beyond present day experiences.

THE GLEN CANYON LEFT SPILLWAY SIMULATIONS

The program was stepped through an orderly series of initial depths with the flow rate carefully adjusted to produce initial speeds of 5, 10, and 20 m/s at the top of the spillway. The water rapidly accelerates as it falls down the spillway. After passing the 700 m mark (from an upstream reference point) the tube bends to the horizontal (starting about 800 m). The sudden transition between the centrifugal pressures of the curved profile and the sudden static pressures of the horizontal flow produces a forward acceleration and suddenly higher velocities there. It is also the location of the shallowest flow and deepest damage.

The damage potential over the length of the spillway is graphed in Figure 4 as a function of initial flow depth. In this and following figures the surface perturbation consists of a 10 mm (1/2 inch) circular arc. At that size the damage potential is nearly proportional to the size of the bump. The rugosity value was that for very smooth concrete. For this and the other figures the damage potential contours are given number labels, n, on a logarithmic scale, where the damage potential is 1000×2^n. With this coding a -1 is for "incipient" cavitation, 0 for "major" and 1 for "catastrophic". A number of 11, to be seen in the next figure, would then indicate a damage potential 1024 times larger than that of the 1983 Glen Canyon Dam flows.

At the top of the graph for the 5 m/s initial speed the actual cavitation damage, in terms of relative depth, is shown by the shading. At the left of all three parts of the figure are shown indicators for the initial flow depths corresponding to 300 (strong), 600 (high), and 900 (peak) m³/s flow rates. The Falvey monograph does not give the initial flow speeds for the historic flow rates. The failure of the computer program to model the higher flow rates at the 5 m/s speed suggests that the actual speeds might have been between 10 and 20 m/s.

For later comparisons the 10 m/s initial speed was selected as a reasonable value.

Cavitation damage is not the same as damage potential. Though there was only one major peak of damage near the 800 m location, the curves of Figure 4 indicate two peaks for damage potential, at the start and end of the circular transition from near vertical flow to near horizontal flow. Damage potential is greatly reduced in the circular bend because the centrifugal forces produce larger pressures, making cavitation less likely. Of all of the dam profiles tested by the Bureau of Reclamation with this program, only the upper peak in damage potential in the Glen Canyon Dam spillway failed to be actualized. Furthermore, while there is less damage potential in the circular bend than in the transitions on either end, damage still occurred there. A change in the simulations from smooth concrete to a rough concrete surface (not shown) decreased the calculated damage potential.

Figure 4 also illustrates some of the theoretical behaviors discussed in Falvey (1) and reviewed in Holroyd (2). The shallow initial flow depths produce even shallower depths downstream. Friction limits the speeds of the shallow depths of water and therefore causes the steep gradient of damage potential with depth for initial depths of less than 2 meters. The 20 m/s diagram shows that increasing initial depth actually decreases the damage potential because increasing depth increases static pressure and makes it more difficult for dynamic pressure reductions to reach values at which water will vaporize. The effect of increasing initial depth on decreasing cavitation damage potential is especially strong in the circular curvature section between 700 and 800 meters, where centrifugal forces add to the static pressure. This is a strong reminder that great depths of water will not cavitate. An ocean of water traveling across land at high speeds may be quite destructive, but it will not be by cavitation.

THE SEMI-HORIZONTAL SIMULATIONS

The possibilities of cavitation over nearly flat terrain were then examined. Input width was changed to 1 km and a simple profile was designed which consisted of 5 km of nearly flat terrain having a constant slope of only 0.004. Then, to drain the water away from the semi-flat region, the terrain was given a parabolic profile matching the free fall arch of an object traveling horizontally at 500 m/s. Initial flow speeds of up to 100 m/s were used in the simulations and the conditions in the parabolic section were ignored. The water was always decreasing its speed over the semi-flat portion and therefore increasing its depth to maintain a constant flow.

Numerous computer runs were made in order to map out the damage potential in Figure 5. In this figure it is the actual water depth that is the ordinate and the actual flow speed for the abscissa rather than the initial conditions. The logarithmic coding of the damage potential is again used. The solid lines give the locations of the calibrated "incipient, major, and catastrophic" conditions and the dotted lines the extrapolated values.

It is seen that significant damage potential begins with shallow flows of about 30 m/s. It increases rapidly with flow speed, remembering that the contour lines differ by a factor of 2. It is also seen that the damage potential decreases with increasing flow depth. This is because the increased ambient pressure caused by greater depths makes it harder for dynamic pressure fluctuations to reduce to the vapor pressure of the water.

In creating this figure, no consideration was made as to how such speeds might be achieved. The rapid reduction of speed with downstream distance that appeared in the simulations indicates that viscosity and friction will prevent high speeds from being sustained at a slope of 0.004. Yet Figure 5 indicates that if there is some cause for water to exceed a speed in excess of about 30 m/s, then cavitation damage potential exists for even semi-flat terrain. The nearly flat terrain of this simulation was especially designed to produce a simplified diagram in which the speed threshold of cavitation damage potential and the normally inverse relationship of flow depth to damage potential were readily evident.

THE PAPAGO CREEK (GRAND CANYON) SIMULATIONS

A natural channel was then chosen to see if there were any conditions under which cavitation would occur if various flows of water were allowed to follow such a profile. In order to get depth and variety, a steep and generally straight side channel of the Grand Canyon of Arizona was chosen. The profile was along a line parallel to Papago Creek (about 36° 2'N, 111° 54'W), from the highway towards Solomon Temple, at an azimuth of 333°. The horizontal distance was the distance of the contours from the highway, not the integrated distance along the twisting channel. The resulting profile of the cross section is shown in the upper part of Figure 6. The elevations were taken from a 1:62500 scale topographic map of 80 foot contour interval. Though nearly 60 contours were available, only 40 could be used in the model. So 160 foot contours were used initially and then supplemented by 80 foot contours in sections (generally flat) recommended by the software.

Though the coded contours of damage potential are not always resolvable in this reproduction, what is important is their density and location. The middle drawing has rugosity and initial conditions comparable to those in Figures 4 (middle) and 5. Yet in many locations the damage potential equals or greatly exceeds that for the Glen Canyon Dam spillway profiles. The curve labeled 8 indicates a damage potential exceeding 100 times the conditions observed in the 1983 floods. The lower part of Figure 6 is probably more realistic for a natural channel roughness. Yet it also indicates the possibility of equal or greater damage from cavitation than observed in 1983 at the Glen Canyon Dam.

The water depths were not increased to the level beyond which the cavitation potential would decrease. The cliff-like portions of the profile made the software issue complaints for depths greater than those illustrated.

Comparing the upper and lower parts of Figure 6 gives an indication of which parts of the profile are likely to cause cavitation damage. The highest damage potential occurs where water would encounter a negative radius of curvature for the surface. This condition reduces the ambient pressure (weight of the water above a point) much like a vehicle traveling over the same profile experiences a tendency towards weightlessness. But such locations can also inject air into the water stream if they are cliff-like, such as the Redwall limestone near the 1 km location.

Other locations for enhanced damage potential are where the water has a great speed from a recently rapid drop in altitude. On the other hand, the reduced damage potential from 2 to 3 km results from reduced speeds and increased flow depths caused by the more level terrain. In general, the damage potential is greatest where there are steep drops in the stream profile. This suggests that the heads of canyons can experience rapid removal of rock as a result of cavitation processes if such large flows of water spill into them without much ingestion of air.

The choice of Papago Creek was made to find out what a variety of rock strata would do, as represented by present profiles. Hard rocks will have semi-horizontal top surfaces and cliff-like edges. Softer shales will have intermediate slopes. If a large flow of water was to pass over the cliff edge in such an environment without ingesting much air, then damage initiated by cavitation is likely to occur. The choice of Papago Creek was for convenience. It does not indicate any suggestion that a large flow actually occurred in that location. There is presently no way such a flow of water could arrive at the cliff edge and the size of the headwaters is trivial. However, the hardnesses of the rocks during the carving of the Grand Canyon might have been similar to those observed today and reflected in the present erosion profile. A catastrophic flow of water, such as might result during the capture of the Colorado River through the Kaibab uplift, might encounter similar profiles. This computer simulation shows that there are indeed locations for cavitation processes to greatly accelerate the removal of rock.

DISCUSSION AND CONCLUSIONS

As considered in this paper, cavitation is the creation of water vapor bubbles within liquid water by the reduction of pressure to the vapor pressure of water at the temperature of that water. The term cavitation has been erroneously extended to include the damaging processes associated by the collapse of those bubbles.

The process of cavitation damage relating to water conveyance structures was explored with the help of a monograph on cavitation and the accompanying software packages. Variables of particular importance during the process of cavitation are the head of water (available energy from elevation changes), water depth and speed (affecting the static and dynamic pressures), water temperature (affecting the vapor pressure), surface roughness, material strength, and especially air bubble content. The software, qualitatively calibrated by assessments of historical damage to existing spillways, was used to map flow and cavitation conditions for the Glen Canyon Dam left spillway tunnel. After documenting the software behavior for known damage, the programs were used for other simulations. That for wide, nearly flat, terrain illustrated the effects of water speed and depth on the cavitation process. It indicated that cavitation damage should be suspected for flow speeds greater than 30 m/s in shallow water. The simulated spill of water over the rim of the Grand Canyon indicated a potential for greater cavitation damage to the rock than the greatest damage observed in the 1983 floods.

The purpose of these initial simulations was to examine the cavitation process for a few profiles during conditions of water flow much greater than modern science has measured.

Though the monograph labeled the 1983 Glen Canyon Dam spillway damage as "catastrophic", the software was pushed to damage potentials over 100 and 1000 times as great. The software cannot be calibrated for those conditions, but it still gives guidance for such extremes. As expected, flows in excess of those observed in 1983 can be expected to produce damage much more severe than that which created automobile-sized boulders out of sandstone bedrock during a several-week period. It suggests that greater flows of water might have the potential for carving canyons even in hard rocks in several weeks rather than the slower thousands-of-years rates observed with normal erosion processes. Yet the simulations also showed that damage potential eventually decreases with increasing water depth. Water depths cannot exceed a few tens of meters or else cavitation will cease.

This has been only an initial exploration of cavitation with software simulations. The variety of possible input conditions is practically infinite. There is much opportunity for further research into numerous phenomena related to the process of cavitation. The software can be run on many natural profiles for water channels to explore the range of profiles and water flows that might lead to cavitation conditions. Of particular interest might be scenarios of catastrophic drainage of post-glacial lakes. There are several canyons which, if plugged, would support vast lakes upstream of them. A breaching of the dam, a natural ridge holding back the lake waters, could involve water speeds sufficient to initiate cavitation damage.

But even with the present knowledge and actual experience it appears that the rapid destruction of rock by the process of cavitation can greatly assist the process of normal erosion in removing rock from water channels during truly catastrophic flows of water. Thousands or millions of years are not necessarily needed for the carving of some valleys and canyons if the process of cavitation becomes involved.

ACKNOWLEDGMENTS

Parts of this study were funded by the Creation Research Society Laboratory Project, 1306 Fairview Road, Clarks Summit, PA 18411.

Figure 1. A view of the greatest cavitation-initiated damage in the left spillway tunnel of the Glen Canyon Dam, near Page, Arizona. The tunnel diameter is 12.5 meters; the ladder into the 10 m deep hole and the workmen provide additional scales. (Bureau of Reclamation photo)

REFERENCES

(1) Falvey, Henry T., CAVITATION IN CHUTES AND SPILLWAYS. Bureau of Reclamation, Denver, Colorado. 1990 (in press).

(2) Holroyd, Edmond W., III., "An Introduction to the Possible Role of Cavitation in the Erosion of Water Channels", CREATION RESEARCH SOCIETY QUARTERLY, Vol. 27, 1990, (accepted).

(3) Holroyd, Edmond W., III., "Some Simulations of the Possible Role of Cavitation in Catastrophic Floods", CREATION RESEARCH SOCIETY QUARTERLY, Vol. 27, 1990 (accepted).

(4) "Challenge at Glen Canyon", 27-min video, Bureau of Reclamation, Denver, Colorado, 1984

Figure 2. Large boulders were excavated by the water and deposited at the end of the left spillway tunnel. The 12.5 meter diameter of the tunnel and the workmen provide a scale. (from Bureau of Reclamation video)

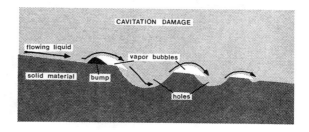

Figure 3. Cavitation damage can occur to a solid surface by the formation and collapse of vapor bubbles downstream of a bump. Large holes can cause more downstream cavitation and damage.

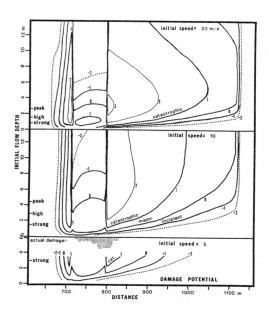

Figure 4. The damage potential for the Glen Canyon Dam left spillway tunnel as a function of initial depth. The damage potential is labeled in terms of powers of 2 times "major" cavitation damage potential.

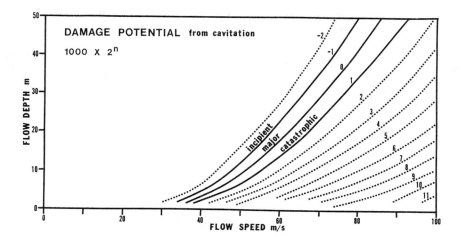

Figure 5. The damage potential for nearly flat terrain for actual, rather than initial, flow depths and speeds.

109

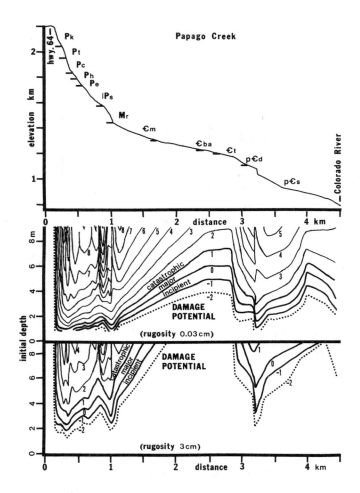

Figure 6. (Top) The vertical profile of Papago Creek and the geological strata exposed. (Middle and Bottom) The damage potential as a function of initial depth for a 1000 ft wide Papago Creek profile for 10 m/s initial flow speed. The middle curves, coded as in previous Figures, are for a smooth surface and the bottom curves are for a rough surface.

DISCUSSION

Dr. Holroyd is helping perpetuate the vision of the vast potential that cavitation related damage has for explaining a vast restructuring of much of the crust of the earth during and after his Historical Flood. I believe the use of the title Historical Flood is justified because of the 200+ widely separated flood records, legends, oral traditions, myths, etc., that are obviously referring to the same event recorded most thoroughly and accurately in genesis 6-9. It is also referred to by Christ in matthew 24, and elsewhere by Christ and many other recorders of history in the Bible and other sources. Also that term should blunt the anti-Biblical bias so pervasive and unfortunately growing in our culture.

Dr. Holroyd makes very good use of the Bureau of Reclamation accumulated history of cavitation damage collected, summarized and computerized by Dr. Henry T. Falvey. Fortunately the Bureau and others have learned how to preclude cavitation damage to many man made structures. The short time duration of their tests prove that they know from experience how rapidly cavitation bubble collapse can erode strong materials. the fact that potentially catastrophic floods can be caused at dams does focus attention on the continuing studies at dams where constant monitoring and exact dimensions are available.

The availability of a computer model provides means for widespread efficient study of cavitation potential. The realistic possibility of the Grand Canyon having been formed in a short time is greatly enhanced by the Papago Creek Model suggested by Dr. Holroyd.

I would like to see studies of flow velocities from unrestrained tides for nearly a year over much of the submerged land forms combined with the resultant cavitation and erosion forces and have the magnitude for erosion estimated. Along with that I ask the question: Where was the material that makes up the upper 95% of the mile thick sedimentary layer when the lower 5% was being deposited? Another related question: What would result from a broad spectrum of fluid specific gravities causes by intense cavitation and erosion activity over a year and how would it settle out as flow velocities gradually decreased?

Dr. Holroyd has made a major contribution in adjusting the focus knob and improving our viewing of the potential from cavitation and related forces for a quick restructuring of much of the crust of the earth during and after the Historical Flood.

The likelihood that the Chernobyl disaster was caused by inadequate knowledge about cavitation should certainly cause a quantum leap in the search for all possible information about cavitation.

Paul M. MacKinney
Carlsbad, California

As ambient fluid hydrodynamic pressure increases, hydrostatic pressure decreases; if hydrostatic fluid pressure falls below fluid vapor pressure (at a given temperature), bubbles may form at the point of minimum hydrostatic (maximum hydrodynamic) pressure.

P_o = Fluid Static Pressure

P_V = Fluid Vapor Pressure

C = Fluid Density

V_T = Fluid Total Velocity

V_I = Initial Velocity

$$\frac{(P_o - P_V)}{\frac{1}{2} C V_T^2}$$

$$V_T = V_I \sin \theta$$
$$@ \ G = 90°$$

V_T = Maximum Dynamic Pressure, minimum static pressure

Dr. Holroyd seems to indicate that *decreased* dynamic pressure results in cavitation (pg.3 Para 2); this is only correct if by "cavitation damage" he is not referring to "initiation" of cavitation (formation of bubbles), since this phenomenon occurs in regions of maximum dynamic pressure. It is true that in regions of <u>least</u> dynamic pressure and max static pressure, the bubbles will <u>implode</u>. Cavitation damage will occur if a rock surface is in close proximity to implosion-generated spherical shock waves. Damage proximity is in accordance with $\left(\dfrac{1}{r^2}\right)$ from spherical shock front origin.

Critical to any discussion of cavitation are the parameters of
*   <u>Cavitation initiation zone</u>
          — max dynamic pressure
          — minimum static pressure
*   <u>Cavitation surface reduction zone</u>
          — minimum dynamic pressure
          — max static pressure

1- Note that the pressures (static and dynamic) are exactly opposite for cavitation initiation and reduction (damage). In my opinion Dr. Holroyd does not present this adequately, the differentiation of the two unique environments are very vague in his paper.

2- He should definitely include the cavitation number:

$$\sigma = \left[\frac{\left(P_{\text{Ambient}} - P_{\text{Vapor}}\right)_{\text{Static}}}{\frac{1}{2} C^{V^2_{\text{Total}}}} \right]$$

The probability of cavitation *initiation* varies inversely proportional to sigma.

Clifford A. Paiva, M.S.
Edwards AFB, California

CLOSURE

Reply to Mr. Paul MacKinney

When pondering possible scenarios in which cavitation might be a mechanism for the rapid removal of rock, several factors must be remembered. An energy source must be available to accelerate the water to speeds in excess of 30 m/s. This can be provided by a water head in excess of 45 m. The water must be shallow because depths greater than 10 m cause static pressures greater than 2 atmospheres against which dynamic forces must operate to vaporize the water. Hot water will cavitate at higher pressures than cold water. Air bubbles in the water, ingested by stream turbulence, greatly reduce the possibility of cavitation. Cavitation will not be a significant mechanism in rough mountain streams and in deep bodies of water.

Further research needs to be done on the relative strengths of various rocks against the forces of cavitation. Perhaps there is someone with mountain stream property that will support a penstock about 50 m (150 ft) tall, from which water can be directed to flow across large rock samples. Such an outdoor laboratory would need to be properly engineered to withstand the forces involved.

Computer simulations can be performed on a variety of natural channels. The sudden drainage of the glacial waters of Lake Missoula across the channeled scablands of central Washington provides a possible simulation scenario. A mountain river flood possibility is the 1976 Big Thompson Canyon flood. If the simulations indicate that cavitation was a possibility, then the river channel can be examined for evidence of rapid destruction of rock. Similarly, tall waterfall regions can be examined to see if cavitation is not operating where water heads and speeds are sufficient for the process.

Those individuals who have already taken up the study of the cavitation mechanism should not be relied on for all future research. Additional workers are needed to bring new insights and clarifications on the rapid destruction of rocks during catastrophic floods. Perhaps some readers will be inspired to study the physics and join the research.

Reply to Mr. Clifford Paiva

This paper is a brief summary of the two CRSQ references, of 10 and 7 pages each, which themselves contain brief summaries of the 145 page Falvey monograph. Mr. Paiva did not have access to any of these at the time of his review. The misunderstandings partly result from the summarization process which lead to the intentional absence of equations in this ICC version. The rest appears to come from style and notation differences.

Mr. Paiva's initial expression is of the same form as his final equation for the cavitation number. Falvey and I give this equation in our referenced works, but we name it the cavitation index instead. We differ from Paiva in that his "total velocity" term is a reference velocity in our expressions, measured at the same up-stream point as the reference pressure term in the Bernoulli equation.

Neither Dr. Falvey nor I make any sinusoidal assumptions for the form of the velocity term. In the equivalent expressions, ours are reference velocities at an upstream point and are therefore understood to be constant for a given flow. Though Mr. Paiva makes no explanation for his sinusoidal expression, it would seem to allow counterflows, moving upstream against the current with speeds up to the maximum downstream speed.

My understanding of Dr. Falvey's use of pressure is that it is the same as the pressure term in the Bernoulli equation and therefore distinct from the velocity term. For constant elevation (no total energy changes) the Bernoulli equation shows pressure changes to be of opposite sign to changes in the square of the velocity. Furthermore, my understanding is that the pressure term is the sum of static and dynamic pressure components. The static pressure is simply that resulting from the weight of all fluid and atmosphere above the level of measurement. The dynamic pressure is caused by changes in velocity and can reduce or add to the total pressure, as measured by a gauge. Both Dr. Falvey and I use an absolute pressure scale.

Mr. Paiva's P is an ambient static pressure only. He appears to call his velocity term the dynamic pressure, such that the greater the velocity, the greater the dynamic pressure. This results in an opposite sign from ours. Our sense follows the Bernoulli equation, whereby an increase in speed results in a decrease in pressure, as over an airplane wing.

A better understanding of the theory of cavitation processes can be obtained from a study of the Falvey monograph rather than from my summaries.

Edmond W. Holroyd, III, Ph.D.

MISSING TALUS ON THE COLORADO PLATEAU

Edmond W. Holroyd, III, Ph.D.
8905 W. 63rd Avenue
Arvada, CO 80004-3103

ABSTRACT

A photogrammetric examination of the size distributions and degrees of aging of talus boulders at several locations in western Colorado, northwestern New Mexico and northern Arizona indicates that steady-state cliff erosion and talus formation has not been continuous. The recent removal of earlier talus by the shoreline waves of large extinct lakes is suggested.

INTRODUCTION

The erosion patterns of the Colorado Plateau, including the Grand Canyon, the mesas and buttes of Monument Valley, and the arches in the national monuments, are commonly thought to be indicative of many tens of thousands to millions of years of natural sculpturing processes. However, the lack of aged talus beyond the bases of numerous cliffs in the area appears to be testimony of the removal of previous rocks by wave action at the shorelines of extinct lakes. The angular nature of the present talus indicates a relatively recent demise of those lakes, which could not have coexisted with the Grand Canyon. This is an indication that the Grand Canyon is post-Flood and was carved recently.

Such a scenario was mentioned in a short note by Holroyd (1) along with a photograph of talus falling from the western cliffs of Mesa Verde. The note pointed out the lack of aged talus on the flat plains (pediments) away from the cliffs. At similar locations, previous rock strata continuity for hard rocks over soft rocks can be assumed across the valleys of dissected plateaus; the valley is the vacated volume caused by previous erosion. One would therefore expect to find a trail of decaying talus left on the pediments by the receding cliffs. But such a trail is not always present.

Several explanations for such "missing talus" were offered. A more rapid decomposition of the hard sandstone talus than the soft shale and mud on which the talus fell seems unlikely; hard rocks should last longer than soft rocks. Rock removal by a river is not appropriate at that location because of the lack of a river in the region. A general regional scouring of the landscape by some unknown broad sheet of flowing water might have caused the widespread removal of the softer strata and the gross carving of the cliff edges. But a lake shore erosion scenario appeared to be the simplest solution for cleaning the cliff bases of old talus. The note recommended that careful field observations be made to refine hypotheses about possible missing talus.

A preliminary photographic survey was made on 35 mm film of talus at the several locations in the Colorado Plateau listed in Table 1. Cliffs with basalt and similar igneous rock caps were excluded from consideration because prior existence of extensive beds of such hard strata above the present pediments could not be assured. Some photogrammetric analyses have been completed to characterize the size, location, and shape characteristics of the talus at some of the sites. The resulting distributions at one site were "aged" to examine what a steady state distribution of talus away from the cliff might look like. The Bangs Canyon site was photographed, but not yet analyzed, to serve as an counterexample of a broad valley in which talus can be found strewn across its entire 0.8 km width.

The existence of large glacial and post-glacial lakes is generally accepted in geological literature. Lake Bonneville is named as such a predecessor for the Great Salt Lake on the basis of raised beaches throughout the basin, as summarized by Hintze (2). Many other lakes are named by Whitcomb and Morris (3). Numerous biblical creationists, such as Oard (4) and Northrup (5), recognize a glacial period, giving it a setting well after Noah and probably during the lifetime of Job. Burdick (6) and Northrup (7) point to the rapid draining of such a post-glacial lake as the mechanism for the carving of the Grand Canyon.

To examine the lake shore hypothesis, digital elevation data for the Colorado River basin were examined. The Grand Canyon was "plugged" up to the level at which the water would flow through a different spillway around the Kaibab uplift. The extent of the resulting "lake" was thereby mapped. A more recent lake, created by the damming of the Colorado River by lava from Vulcan's Throne, was mapped in a similar manner. The shorelines of these "lakes" were nearly coincident with the "missing talus" sites under examination.

Table 1. The locations and rock strata of sites photographed for this study.

Site no., name	approx. location			base elev. m	hard strata	soft strata	period
near Towaoc, Colorado:							
1. Mesa Verde	37° 12.5'N	108°	40'E	1770	Mesa Verde ss.	Mancos shale	Cretaceous
2. Flat Top Rock	36 58.5	108	44	1610	Mesa Verde ss.	Mancos shale	Cretaceous
near Grand Junction, Colorado:							
3. Book Cliffs	39 7.5	108	22	1460	Mesa Verde ss.	Mancos shale	Cretaceous
4. Bangs Canyon	38 57.5	108	31	1580	Dakota ss.	Morrison shale	Cret./Juras.
near Marble Canyon, Arizona:							
5. Marble Canyon	36 49	111	38.5	1120	Shinarump cong.	Moenkopi silts.	Triassic
6. rd. to Lees Ferry	36 50.5	111	38	1070	Shinarump cong.	Moenkopi silts.	Triassic
in Monument Valley, Arizona:							
7. Rain God Mesa	36 57	110	5	1580	De Chelly ss.	Cutler shale	Permian
8. Spearhead Mesa	36 56.5	110	3.5	1580	De Chelly ss.	Cutler shale	Permian

THE TALUS OF FLAT TOP ROCK

Several kilometers to the south of the photo of Holroyd (1), just across the border into New Mexico, the road passes about 550 m to the west of a mesa named Flat Top Rock. It is a smaller cliff with the same strata of hard Mesa Verde sandstone lying on soft Mancos shale. Its top is about 100 m above the immediately surrounding plains. Most talus traveled no farther than the 100 m horizontally to the base of the shale slopes, though a few rolling boulders made it to almost 150 m from the cliff edge.

A pair of photos were exposed from the road according to the geometry illustrated in Figure 1. Thin vertical and horizontal lines form squares of 1 km in the Universal Transverse Mercator grid system. The northernmost, part of which is shown in Figure 2, was taken from a range of about 1070 m from the facing slopes. The other photo was taken at a range of about 550 m from the facing slopes and is shown in Figure 3.

The focal length of the nominal 50 mm lens was calculated from photographs of stars to be actually 51.3 mm. The base line between the photos was about 990 m based on the positions of other mesas in the backgrounds. The photo in Figure 2 was aimed at azimuth 126.6° with an elevation angle of 7.0°. The photo in Figure 3 was aimed at azimuth 70.5° with an elevation angle of 10.9°. The large angle of about 56° between the two photos made it relatively easy to determine the 3-dimensional position of any point visible in both photos.

The original slide photos were scanned in color at 2000 pixels per inch for use in an image processing microcomputer system. The software used for the analysis was the Map and Image Processing System (MIPS) from MicroImages, Inc. (8). Equations were derived relating pixel positions (lines and columns) to angles and then to distances. Horizontal locations were measured in the photo of Figure 2. Both horizontal and vertical locations were measured in the photo of Figure 3. These three numbers (pixel positions) were entered into an HP-67 programmable calculator to derive the horizontal coordinates (meters east and south of photo site for Figure 2), range from photo site of Figure 3, and elevation (meters above sea level).

A map was thereby derived which showed the locations of the largest rocks seen in both photos and the approximate elevation contours. At the north and south ends of the map the rocks in the drainage channels were hidden from view of one camera by adjacent ridges. Contours away from major rocks were not analyzed. It had been hoped to accurately locate the positions of all rocks at the base of the cliff. But the leveling of the terrain of the foreground pediment caused many rocks to be behind foreground rocks in at least one of the photos and thus impossible to correctly identify as being the same rock in both photos. Aerial photography from a low enough altitude to resolve the rocks would greatly improve future studies of talus locations.

The analysis provided the measurement that beyond about 100 m from the cliff edge there were almost no boulders of any size. There were only a few of similar aging that happened to have

116

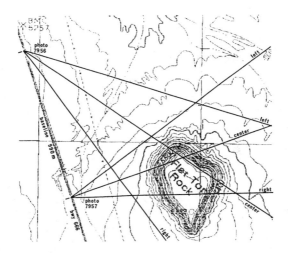

Figure 1. A topographic map of the vicinity of Flat Top Rock showing the fields of view of the two photos analyzed.

Figure 2. Flat Top Rock as seen from the northwest.

Figure 3. The northwest side of Flat Top Rock.

rolled farther. It also showed that the slopes of the shale surface ranged from about 36° at the north to about 30° at the south end of the study area.

The photo of Figure 2 was used for a size spectrum. All rocks analyzed were assumed to be at a range of 1070 m. This created size errors of up to 5 percent. Using a constant range for talus in the photo of Figure 3 would have created errors of up to 27 percent or else laborious corrections.

The rock sizes were measured with the MIPS software. It was assumed that the rock orientation with respect to the plane of the photo was mostly random and so the maximum extent of the rock, as viewed, was a sufficient measurement for a size distribution of many rocks. The cursor was therefore placed at the maximum extremities of each rock. The software automatically converted that distance into meters. A label indicating the pixel coordinates of the bottom of each rock was typed into the computer and then stored in a file with the rock size. Rocks smaller than 1.5 m were often measured but were ignored in compiling the size spectra.

Using the coded labels, the rocks were then sorted by altitude and partitioned into distance groups at 10 m intervals from the cliff edge, and into size groups at 0.5 m resolution. The number of rocks in each distance bin is shown as the lower line in Figure 4a. It is seen that the number of rocks increases with distance from the cliff and then drops abruptly beyond the 100 m position marking the approximate bottom of the slope. The size spectrum is shown in Figure 4b in terms of cumulative percent of all rocks in the distance interval. Though the size spectrum is noisy for this number of rocks, the general trend is for larger sizes to be near the base of the slope. There is no transition back to small, decaying sizes for increasing distances from the cliff across the pediment.

This should be an expected result for a fresh fall of rocks from the cliff. The largest rocks would have the largest momentum and energy and should travel the farthest. However, at the base of the cliff the terrain flattens and provides little further gravitational assistance to the movement of the rocks. They therefore quickly come to a stop. Rain and frost heaves will not provide much more horizontal movement of the larger rocks thereafter. Their geographic location should remain close to where they fell from the cliff until they decay to a more mobile sand.

ESTIMATES OF SPECTRA OF AGING TALUS

This irregular size and location spectrum was then used as a basis for estimating what a spectrum of decaying rock might look like. The present spectrum, by its abrupt cutoff at the base of the slope, appears to be similar to a relatively fresh fall of talus with little aging. The rocks at the bottom are still angular with limited rounding due to decay. It is therefore assumed that talus falls in the past would produce the same size and location distributions, with respect to the cliff edge, as the present data set.

An "aged" spectrum was assembled in each location bin of 10 m horizontal width. Into each bin went all of the present rocks for that location. Then the additions were the present spectrum offset at successive 10 m intervals (to represent contributions from each step in the recession of the cliff edge) but successively shrunk as well by moving all rocks a set number, n, of 0.5 m size bins to a smaller size. The process was repeated, shifting 10 more meters and shrinking the previously shrunk spectrum n more size bins, until no more rocks remained. Rocks becoming smaller than the 1.5 m limit of the original spectrum vanished from consideration.

Four shrinkage rates were considered for this simulation. The rocks were decreased in size at 5, 2.5, 1, and 0.5 m for each 10 m shift in horizontal location. These rates represent a loss of material from each end of a rock of half of those numbers. The shale, however, presents only one surface for erosion. It is therefore more appropriate to compare the 10 m recession rate of the shale and cliff with the one-sided talus shrinkage rates of 2.5, 1.25, 0.5, and 0.25 m. The ratio of such rates are then 4, 8, 20, and 40 meters of shale per meter of sandstone. The simulations are labeled with these latter numbers representing the relative erosion rates of the two rock types.

Figure 4a shows total rock counts in each distance bin for the original count and those for three of the four aging rates. The 4:1 rate is so fast as to hardly change the rock counts. The rates of 20:1 and 40:1 have appreciable tails of decaying talus on the pediment.

The size spectrum for the relative decay rate ratio of 40:1 is presented in Figure 4c for comparison with the original spectrum in Figure 4b. The spectrum on the shale slope is similar to the original, but the shrinking effects of the decay are obvious farther out. The spectra for the faster decay rates are intermediate.

TALUS ON PEDESTALS

In some locations the boulders have shielded the underlying shale from erosion, resulting in the boulders sitting on pedestals of shale. Figure 5, taken along the road from Marble Canyon to Lees Ferry, Arizona, illustrates an extreme example of such pedestals. The ages of my children at the time ranged from 5 to 13; their presence under the rock provides a scale. Such pedestals confirm that there is a great difference in erosion rates for the two rock types.

The pedestal thickness can be used together with the slope of the surrounding surface to compute a horizontal recession distance of the softer strata since the boulder arrived at the site. Photos at the same site taken parallel to the surface elevation contours suggest a slope of about 1:10 where most of the large talus is located. The pedestal in Figure 5 is about 3 m tall, giving a horizontal shale recession distance of about 30 m. If the boulder has lost 2 to 3 m of material from all sides since landing, then a relative decay rate ratio of 15:1 to 10:1 can be roughly estimated.

Most of the adjacent boulders do not sit on tall pedestals, so such a decay rate ratio calculation should not be considered final. Yet it is in the range by which Figure 4a suggests that there should be some detectable trail of decaying talus remnants across the pediment. Photos to the right and left of Figure 5 show an abrupt cessation of talus at large sizes, just like at Flat Top Rock.

AN AGING TALUS INDICATOR NUMBER

An index, designed for images made up of pixels, is introduced by Holroyd (9) for classifying the shapes of snow particles. It is calculated as $F = P*D/A$, where P is the perimeter of the image (including internal perimeter for interlocking branches), D the maximum dimension, and A the cross sectional area (holes subtracted). The smallest this index can be is 4.0 for a solid circle. It is 6.55 for a semicircle, 5.66 for a square, and 6.71 for a rectangle of sides with a ratio of 1:2. For needles and stellar shaped ice crystals the ratio can approach about 50. It is a good classifier for the amount of fine structure in the image. It is also independent of particle size.

This number could be highly useful for giving a relative index for rock aging. Fresh talus should be highly angular, giving a relatively large number. As the rock ages, its corners should round and the shape should tend towards spherical or hemispherical, thereby achieving a lower index number. MicroImages, Inc. (8), added this index to their MIPS software for use in this project, calling the index "roughness".

The rocks at the far lower left and the lower right of center of Figure 3 were analyzed for roughness. Using the MIPS software the boulders were carefully outlined. Because the ratio is independent of scale, the range of the rocks did not matter. The outlines of the rocks were then extracted from the image and the roughness was calculated for each. The results for 60 of the rocks in Figure 3 are presented in Figure 4d as the dotted line in a cumulative percentage curve. In this particular sample of rocks there was a slight tendency for an increase in the roughness with size, but the correlation coefficient was small.

For comparison the "roughness" ratio was calculated for talus in Monument Valley, Arizona. One site, No. 7, of relatively old talus was photographed at the northwestern corner of Rain God Mesa. An aerial view of the same location, but from farther away, is given by Baars (10), with the site being the near corner of the mesa in the center of the view. The talus ends abruptly at the base of the shale slope, as confirmed by that aerial photo.

The other site, No. 8, was the southwest corner of Spearhead Mesa, which lies east of Rain God Mesa. The talus here is more angular and presumably fresher than at the other sites examined, but some of the boulders are on short pedestals. Four photos were combined for a large sample of the rocks at this mesa corner. Those photos which included a view of the pediment showed the typical abrupt cessation of the talus and at large sizes.

The cumulative distributions of the roughness index for the two Monument Valley sites are shown in Figure 4d as solid lines. The Rain God Mesa distribution, 7, shows smaller numbers and therefore more rounding than the Flat Top Rock distribution. The Spearhead Mesa distribution, 8, shows larger numbers, in keeping with the angular nature of those rocks.

In general, roughness distributions for differing geologic formations should not be compared for the purposes of determining relative age. While the Rain God Mesa talus can be judged to have been aged longer than the talus examined at Spearhead Mesa (both are of De Chelly sandstone), it is not appropriate to conclude that the Flat Top Rock talus is intermediate in age. The Mesa Verde sandstone most likely has a different rate of decomposition from the De

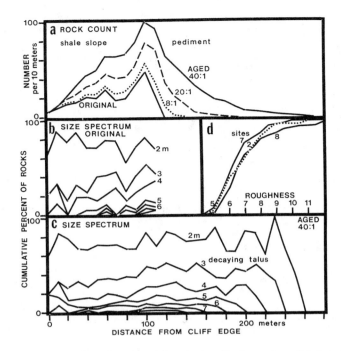

Figure 4. The original and "aged" number (a) and size (b,c) spectra of talus with distance from the cliff edge. The ratio of the relative single direction decay rates for the shale and sandstone are 8, 20, and 40:1 as labeled for the "aged" distributions. In (d) is the cumulative percent distribution of the "roughness" index for talus at three locations identified by number from Table 1.

Figure 5. Conglomerate talus sitting on siltstone pedestals along the road from Marble Canyon to Lees Ferry, Arizona. The children provide a scale for this extreme example, suggesting a pedestal height of about 3 meters.

Chelly sandstone. Talus at the site of Figure 5 appears more rounded, but the roughness distribution has not yet been measured.

POTENTIAL POST-GLACIAL LAKES

One of the explanations offered for the "missing talus" was wave destruction of previous talus at the shorelines of recently extinct lakes. To examine this hypothesis digital elevation data for the Colorado River Basin were examined to determine the extent of possible lakes that might have been present if the Colorado drainage was blocked. The data have a horizontal resolution of 30 seconds of latitude and longitude and 20 ft elevation. They were derived from 1:250,000 scale topographic maps of typically 200 ft elevation resolution. The numbers in this data set tend to cluster near the even 200 ft elevations.

As indicated in Holroyd (1), plugging the Grand Canyon at about 1700 m elevation (5600 ft) would cause the Colorado River to be diverted to the north of the Kaibab uplift, near the Arizona-Utah border. It would also cause the formation of a series of large lakes. Those possible lakes for a 1700 m surface are shaded with the MIPS software in Figure 6 using present topography. It is recognized that surface topography is always changing by erosion and deposition, by uplift and subsidence, and by igneous activity. In this study the topography of the recent past is assumed to be nearly the same as that of today, but only to get a general idea of the possible locations, areas, and volumes of recently extinct lakes.

The southern basin of that series of possible lakes fills the present Painted Desert of Arizona. Geologists (11-14) recognize the recent (Pliocene) presence of a Lake Bidahochi in that location on the basis of the lacustrine Bidahochi formation in northeastern Arizona. The top of that formation is above 1850 m (6070 ft), indicating a lake surface higher than that considered in Figure 6. But none of the references illustrate a possible extent of Lake Bidahochi. It would have been larger than that shown here.

Geologists (13-16) also point out that lava has plugged the Grand Canyon several times at Vulcan's Throne. The much smaller lake that would be formed if the lava from Vulcan's Throne plugged the river to the top of the canyon at that location (1160 m, 3800 ft) is shown as an inner solid black in Figure 6. Nations and Stump (15) indicate that the oldest remnant of lava in the canyon has a top elevation of about 925 m (3035 ft). Baars (16) mentions a plug whose top would be at about 670 m (2200 ft) for the most recent flows of lava.

The talus site numbers from Table 1 are plotted in Figure 6. It is seen that the Kaibab plug produces a "lake" whose shores would be near most of those sites. The Vulcan's Throne plug produces a possible shoreline at the Marble Canyon site. This provides circumstantial evidence that shoreline cleansing of the slopes of previous talus might have been possible.

The software of Jenson and Domingue (17) was used to determine the basin upstream from the junction of the Colorado River and Bright Angel Creek in the Grand Canyon. A program was then written to convert the elevation data within that basin outline to a table of areas and cumulative "lake" volumes within each elevation contour. The calculated areas and volumes behind the Kaibab plug would be about 69,000 km^2 and 12,600 km^3. For comparison, Hutchinson (18) gives the area and volume of Lake Superior as 83,300 km^2 and 12,000 km^3. So the series of lakes that might have existed behind a Kaibab plug would sum to a lesser surface area but a similar volume to the world's largest fresh water lake.

SUMMARY AND DISCUSSION

This study has amplified on a previous note that raised the question of possible "missing talus" on the Colorado Plateau. Photogrammetry was used to examine the talus at several widely separated locations as a part of a continuing analysis. Size, location, and roughness distributions were measured for the talus at Flat Top Rock. They showed that the largest boulders tend to be found at the base of the shale slopes, where there also are the greatest numbers of rocks. But the presence of talus abruptly ceases a short distance away across the flatter surfaces of the pediment. There is no trail of decaying talus beyond the large talus boulders. This pattern is repeated at Monument Valley, Marble Canyon, and presumably at many more sites not yet examined.

The present talus size and distance spectrum was "aged" in a numerical experiment. Size and distance spectra were calculated for four different relative rates of decay for the shale and sandstone rocks. If the rates do not differ by more than about 10:1, then it will be difficult to detect the trail of decaying talus because it would be hidden amongst the more recently fallen boulders. But if the rates of decay differ by more than 20:1, then there should be a very obvious distribution of shrinking talus with distance out onto the pediment. Those decaying rocks are not present at most of the sites, indicating that previous talus has

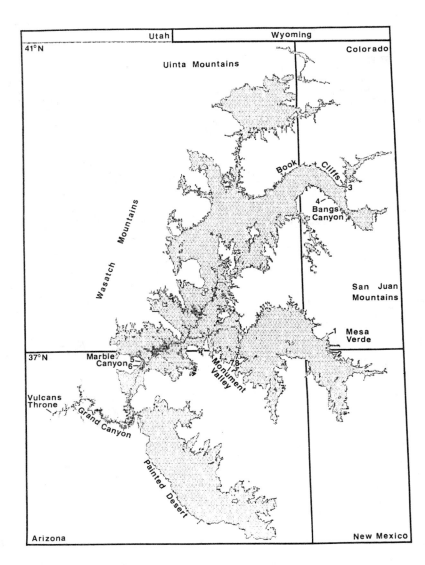

Figure 6. The outlines of "lakes" formed on present topography if the Colorado River was plugged at the Kaibab Uplift (shaded) and at Vulcan's Throne (inner black). The talus study sites listed in Table 1 are identified by number.

been removed by some process and that the elapsed time since the cessation of that process has only been sufficient to erode the cliffs back several tens of meters.

A crude estimate of relative decay rate was made on the basis of a pedestal under a giant boulder near Marble Canyon. The result was in the range that would require expectation of a short trail of decaying talus. But there is a need for a large number of measurements of the relative decay rates for different rock formations. This is a critical number for determining that talus might be missing.

The presence of large lake bodies which have since become extinct is a reasonable concept in terms of post-glacial lakes. Many other former lakes are already recognized by geologists. The outline was derived for a lake that might have existed before the carving of the Grand Canyon. It had an area and volume comparable to Lake Superior. Also sketched was a much smaller and more recent lake caused by the plugging of the Colorado River at Vulcan's Throne by lava pouring into the canyon. All or parts of both lakes are recognized by many geologists. The shorelines of those lakes are near the sites of the talus studies.

These studies are preliminary and there is much more that can be done. Additional cliffs could be examined by low level aerial photography or video to better map the extent of the talus with respect to the cliff edges. Other studies need to establish the relative rates of decay of the hard and soft rocks. Numerous small cliffs on the Colorado Plateau might be examined for possible shoreline etchings.

To date these preliminary studies suggest a link between "missing talus" and extinct shorelines. The present talus is decaying and the cliffs are receding. The "missing talus" phenomena indicate that the demise of those lakes was relatively recent. The cliffs have receded only tens of meters since then. In fact, perhaps half of the shale slopes at Monument Valley have not yet had a subsequent fall of talus. Yet the lakes that would have washed the slopes of Monument Valley and Mesa Verde could not have coexisted with the Grand Canyon. Therefore, because the demise of those lakes appears to have been recent, the carving of the Grand Canyon must also have been recent.

ACKNOWLEDGMENTS

Parts of this study were funded by the interest of the Creation Research Society Laboratory Fund. MicroImages, Inc., of Lincoln, Nebr., provided the Map and Image Processing System software and the scanning of the 35 mm slides. Dr. Tom Huber of the University of Colorado-Colorado Springs provided the scanning of the topographic maps.

REFERENCES

(1) Holroyd, Edmond W., III, "Missing Talus", CREATION RESEARCH SOCIETY QUARTERLY, 24, June 1987, pp. 15-16.

(2) Hintze, Lehi F., GEOLOGIC HISTORY OF UTAH, BYU Geology Studies, Vol. 20, Pt. 3, pp. 85-94.

(3) Whitcomb, John C., and Morris, Henry M., THE GENESIS FLOOD, Baker, Grand Rapids, 1961, pp. 313-317.

(4) Oard, Michael J., "An Ice Age Within the Biblical Time Frame", PROCEEDINGS OF THE FIRST INTERNATIONAL CONFERENCE ON CREATIONISM, Vol. II, Pittsburgh, PA, Aug. 4-9, 1986, pp. 157-166.

(5) Northrup, Bernard E., "There Really Was an Ice Age", PROCEEDINGS OF THE FIRST INTERNATIONAL CONFERENCE ON CREATIONISM, Vol. I, Pittsburgh, PA, Aug. 4-9, 1986, pp. 93-100.

(6) Burdick, Clifford L., "The Canyon of Canyons", PROCEEDINGS OF THE FIRST INTERNATIONAL CONFERENCE ON CREATIONISM, Vol. I, Pittsburgh, PA, Aug. 4-9, 1986, pp. 39-41.

(7) Northrup, Bernard E., "A Walk Through Time, A Study in Harmonization", PROCEEDINGS OF THE FIRST INTERNATIONAL CONFERENCE ON CREATIONISM, Vol. II, Pittsburgh, PA, Aug. 4-9, 1986, pp. 147-156.

(8) MicroImages, Inc., "Map and Image Processing System", 201 N. 8th Ave., Suite #15, Lincoln, Nebraska 68508-1347, Versions 2.1 and 2.2, 1989.

(9) Holroyd, Edmond W. III, "Some Techniques and Uses of 2D-C Habit Classification Software for Snow Particles", JOURNAL OF ATMOSPHERIC AND OCEANIC TECHNOLOGY, American Meteorological Society, Boston, Massachusetts, Vol. 4, No. 3, September 1987, 498-511.

(10) Baars, Donald L., THE COLORADO PLATEAU, A GEOLOGIC HISTORY, University of New Mexico Press, Albuquerque, New Mexico, 1983, pp. 100-101.

(11) Ibid., p. 225.

(12) Nations, Dale, and Stump, Edmund, GEOLOGY OF ARIZONA, Kendall/Hunt Publishing Co., Dubuque, Iowa, 1981, p. 90.

(13) Chronic, Halka, ROADSIDE GEOLOGY OF ARIZONA, Mountain Press Publishing Co., Missoula, Montana, 1983, pp. 186-189.

(14) National Geographic Society, "The Grand Canyon of the Colorado", NATIONAL GEOGRAPHIC, Washington, D.C., July 1978, map insert.

(15) Nations and Stump, op. cit., pp. 171-172.

(16) Baars, op. cit., p. 231.

(17) Jenson, S. K., and J. O. Domingue, "Extracting Topographic Structure from Digital Elevation Data for Geographic Information System Analysis", PHOTOGRAMMETRIC ENGINEERING AND REMOTE SENSING, Vol. 54, No. 11, November 1988, pp. 15931600.

(18) Hutchinson, G. Evelyn, A TREATISE ON LIMNOLOGY, Vol. 1, John Wiley & Sons, New York, 1957, p. 169.

NOTE

Flat Top Rock (Site 2) and Monument Valley (Sites 7, 8) are within the Navajo Reservation. Therefore a Field Investigation Permit was required for the research reported in this paper. Individuals or organizations desiring to conduct geological, paleontological or other related scientific investigations on the Navajo Reservation must first apply for and receive a permit from the Navajo nation Minerals Department, P.O. Box 146, Window Rock, Arizona, 86515. The permit application fee of $100.00, a map detailing the area of the proposed investigations, and a complete description of all proposed activities are required for processing the application.

The Navajo Nation Minerals Department in no way condones or supports this research. The issuance of a permit does not indicate approval or disapproval of the conclusions of the report by the Navajo Nation.

Dr. Holroyd has provided valuable observations concerning the deficiency of expected talus deposits in an important geologic area. Uniformitarian geologists would suppose significant foot-slope deposits if landscapes of the Colorado Plateau have been backwearing slowly during millions of years. These, as the author points out, are not found. I have personally inspected the slope near Lees Ferry (Figure 15) and can attest to the fact that it is a remarkable contradiction to uniformitarian orthodoxy.

Dr. Holroyd proposes that many slopes on the Colorado Plateau have been affected by shoreline wave erosion from high elevation lakes. I agree. Not mentioned by the author are important recent studies on the Colorado Plateau showing the importance of sapping, the failure of foot-slopes by outflow of water from the strata. Sapping process would be an extremely important cause of slope failure following catastrophic drainage of lakes. Catastrophist geomorphology is alive and well on the Colorado Plateau!

Steven A. Austin, Ph.D.
Santee, California

If as Dr. Holroyd states in this paper that there are practically no boulders more than 100 meters from the base of the cliffs, then this is truly a remarkable piece of information.

1) Is it possible that including boulders smaller than 1.5 meters would alter his conclusions?

2) Is it possible that many of the older boulders have been buried by clay washed down from higher on the slope and are thus hidden from view? Did Dr. Holroyd investigate this possibility?

Glenn R. Morton, M.S.
Dallas, Texas

Dr. Holroyd misunderstands Burdick's explanation of the carving of the Grand Canyon. Burdick had explained it by means of dammed up Noahic flood waters during the retreat of the Noahic flood. In no way does Burdick's explanation relate to an erosion of the canyon by trapped glacial melt waters from a post Noahic flood ice age several centuries after the flood as I had first proposed in 1968.

Dr. Holroyd's idea of mapping the beaches of the ice age lakes which I had proposed as the instrument that abruptly eroded the Grand Canyon was excellent. Nevertheless, it is handicapped by the uniformitarian assumption that the Kaibab/Coconino plateaus and the 5,600 ft. level imposed by his computer simulation based upon present elevation configurations. Of course these fossil beaches also may be testimonies of the uneasy profile of the continent during the centuries of major continental division in the post-flood era. Indeed, they probably are just that.

The order of events at the Canyon can be reconstructed from the present scene.

1) The Mesozoic Navajo, Kayenta, Chinie, Shinarump and Moenkopi Formations (which survive in the Vermillion and Echo cliffs) overlaid the area of the Colorado Plateau.

2) These, clearly preserved in the Vermillion and Echo Cliffs, were removed, almost without trace, from the Kaibab formation in the Kaibab/Coconino Plateaus by moving waters that carried them into the great estuary of the sea which then lay to the west. The erosion of the Grand Canyon had begun.

3) Powerfully moving ice age melt waters from the north now found the great crisscross faults which had fractured the well indurated Noahic flood formations of the upper Grand Canyon layers were now exposed. these had resulted from major continental movement and the resulting uplifts several centuries after the flood. The racing glacial melt waters ripped blocks as large as a football stadium from the formation, using them as erosive tools as the Canyon and its abrupt, fault-structured side canyons abruptly were carved. (The Colorado Rover today meekly follows the course of its violent, catastrophic path through the resulting canyon).

4) The present surface of the plateau, the Kaibab formation, then was upwarped between 7,000 and 8,000 ft. along the Kaibab Plateau.

5)   Probably it was the same violent adjustment that downwarped other parts of the Kaibab formation to lie at less than 5,000 ft. near Fredonia, east of the Grand View fault toward Cameron and also near the Mesa Butte fault near the San Francisco Peaks. Careful study will demonstrate that the original Paleozoic deposits in the Canyon's walls strongly suggest repeated major sea intrusion and retreat during their deposition at near sea level. The continuation of this crustal disturbance conceivable be preserved for us in the continued elevation of fossil lake bed beaches to the north, east and northeast of the Canyon.

As a result, it is highly probable that we cannot estimate the original elevation of the present 5,600 ft. saddle north of the Kaibab uplift at the time of the Canyon's erosion. Neither can we know for certain the elevation of the upper layers of the near 2,000 feet of Post-Flood Mesozoic alluvial sand deposits which initially were stripped off of the Kaibab/Coconino Plateaus before the waters carved their way through the massive crisscross fault structures in indurated Kaibab and underlying structures to form the Grand Canyon. Only by comparison of the present fossil beach levels in different parts of the great lake system which once existed above the Grand Canyon can we even estimate the elevation of the Kaibab/Coconino plateau when that erosion began. The actual erosion took place when the trapped post-flood ice age waters broke through the dam which had impounded them, allowing the catastrophically abrupt erosion of the Grand Canyon. I originally had proposed that the Kaibab/Coconino uplift itself had been that temporary dam. However, presently I think that Walter Brown is correct in proposing that the Vermilion Cliff/Echo Cliff uplift was the barrier behind which the ice waters impounded.

Whether it is true that the Kaibab/Coconino Plateau has continued elevation after erosion or the proposed depression of the saddle to the north is the problem or perhaps both remains for researchers to discover. The question needs far more careful study by creationists who are physical geologists who also recognize a valid working model for the catastrophic post-Noahic flood centuries. My own discovery of man's firepits on the ancient shores of fossil Lake Uinta east of the Vernal, Utah, (a lake that contributed to the erosion of the Grand Canyon), is suggestive of the kind of a time frame needed to establish the approximate time when these glacial waters from Wyoming, Montana, Colorado, Arizona and New Mexico carved the Grand Canyon. This indicates that it was well after the tower of Babel which forced man to flee onto that which became major continental blocks in the following centuries.

Dr. Holroyd also would do well to examine the giant deltas found at the mouths of deep canyons in the Roan and Book cliffs to the northeast of Arches National Monument. These appear to have been deposited while Fossil Lake Kapirowitz had backed up the present Green River Drainage to the very foot of the Uinta Mountains into Fossil Lake Uinta. Apparently the great Green River Basin of southern Wyoming succeeded in working its way across the eastern end of the young Uintas to form the great Green River Gorge and join the Fossil Lake Uinta extension of Fossil Lake Kapirowitz even as the Uintas were still rising. It was geologically a very unstable period of Biblical history, a factor which the author has neglected in his computer mapping of the fossil lakes which carved the great Grand Canyon Gorge.

Bernard E. Northrup, Th.D.
Redding, California

CLOSURE

Reply to Dr. Steven Austin

I have not yet addressed the sapping process in this "missing talus" study. Sapping does not appear to be a present process at most of the sites used in this study. Site 4, Bangs Canyon, is the exception. At all the other sites the strata are nearly perfectly horizontal or else such that water would drain inwardly, from the cliff edge towards the interior of the mesa. There are no springs at the bases of these cliffs.

At Bangs Canyon, to be addressed in a subsequent study, the talus formation appears to be the result of sapping. A photograph of talus strewn across its entire 0.8 km width was shown in the oral presentation at the ICC. A local water well driller has frequently found a layer of very soft mudstone separating the water-bearing Dakota sandstone above and the more impervious Morrison shales below. The highlands of the Uncompahgre Plateau capture more precipitation than the neighboring lowlands. That water drains downhill through the Dakota strata, sometimes resulting in artesian wells at lower elevations. Where erosion has cut through the sandstone there appears to be a rapid widening of the resulting valleys. It is hypothesized that at such exposures of the strata the mudstone, above which the water had been flowing, was rapidly flushed out, undermining the sandstone blocks. Surface waters then poured into the resulting depressions and were able to erode the Morrison shales as well. The durable sandstone blocks were left littering the surface.

The rocks in Bangs Canyon were photographed from the air several years ago. Similar rocks in the neighboring and more accessible Unaweep Valley were visited and photographed to aid in the analyses.

Dr. Austin makes an important point about possible sapping following the catastrophic drainage of lakes. He has documented the rapid formation of a canyon system north of Mt. St. Helens following the major eruption. Part of the water-saturated new strata turned into a mud flow and left cliffs similar to those in this study. (See his paper in Volume 1 of the 1986 ICC Proceedings, p.5.) Though sapping does not appear to be presently happening at most of the "missing talus" study sites, sapping associated with the catastrophic demise of large lakes could have been the agent to form the cliff edges in the first place. Sapping would have been even more effective in the early years following the Flood because the strata would still have been water saturated and poorly consolidated. This is certainly a good topic for further research.

Reply to Mr. Glenn Morton:

During the past year I have obtained a copy of NAPP aerial photograph number 1106-66 to refine my analyses of Flat Top Rock. The 1:44420 measured scale of the image permits only resolution of large talus, about 4 m and larger, depending on illumination. Matching individual boulders from Figure 2 with those visible in the aerial photograph allowed a better definition of the slope at the base of the mesa. The range of the farthest boulder was revised from 150 m to 175 m. Yet 63 percent of the boulders were still within 100 m from the cliff edge. On the far side of the mesa the farthest boulder was found at a range of 220 m. Such a revision of distances, however, does not change the conclusions.

Including boulders smaller than 1.5 meters also would not alter the conclusions. Such smaller sizes were visible in the roadside photographs, especially Figure 3. Any that might have been farther away from the cliff edge would have been closer to the camera and therefore even more visible. The median size of the farthest-out boulders was about 4 m, with none smaller than 2 m. It is the total absence of the smallest sizes at the farthest ranges that is so remarkable at all of the study sites. Small decayed talus remnants are definitely missing.

Some talus boulders right at the change in slopes at the cliff base can be found to be partly buried in clay and smaller fragments. However, farther out on the pediment there have been no indications of significant burial. The tendency there is more towards pedestal formation, as in Figure 5, than burial. The pediment is often of undisturbed shale strata with only a thin layer of dirt and clay on top, removing the need for excavations to find buried boulders.

This is a preliminary study, to introduce a new topic for research. A next logical step would be to measure sizes, roughnesses, burials, and pedestals more precisely at these and other sites. The findings of this present research hopefully justify such confirmatory studies.

Reply to Dr. Bernard Northrup

I included references to the works of Burdick and Northrup because I was influenced by their writings more than a decade ago, perhaps in the Bible-Science Newsletter. I could not, however, identify the source of that influence for this paper, nor correctly summarize the contents. I am therefore highly pleased with Dr. Northrup's explanation presented here. It is the best that I have seen.

I recognize the limitations of my uniformitarian assumption of former surface elevations similar to those of today. I state this in my text and did so even more in my oral presentation. The latter presented new analyses of the elevations of cliffs throughout part of the region, particularly the Defiance Plateau-Chuska Mountain area. The cliff bases were at varying altitudes, possibly requiring a Defiance uplift after the demise of the shoreline-cutting lake. I therefore do not require any elevations to have remained constant during and after the proposed processes. This study has used modern elevations to show the reasonableness of a scenario. I am sure that further investigations will give evidence to define the shorelines better.

Dr. Northrup has nominated additional locations for study. It would be helpful to receive a more precise listing of all suspected shoreline locations, giving latitude, longitude, and elevation coordinates, as I have in Table 1, both from Northrup and from any others who think they may have found something. The Colorado Plateau is a large area, and I do not expect to visit even most of it personally. I can, however, use remote sensing techniques, satellite images, aerial photography, geological maps, and elevation data to examine pro-posed shoreline locations. The many shorelines of former Lake Bonneville are slightly tilted because of the subsequent rebound of the land. I would expect similarly varying shoreline elevations for the proposed lakes in my study.   A finding of consistent tiltings could be of benefit to the scenario.

Suggestions of other sites should not just be limited to positive evidence of shoreline action. The absence of such etchings may also be informative. The slopes of Navajo Mountain should certainly be examined. I have yet to notice any shoreline etchings in my remote views of the mountain, the photographs of others, or in topo-graphic maps.   If there are no shoreline etchings in strata capable of preserving them, then perhaps my hypothesis fails, or else the Navajo Mountain laccolith was formed after the demise of the lake.

Travelers through the Colorado Plateau region should remain alert to phenomena related to this issue. I am highlighting the testimony of "missing talus" and possible shorelines. It is highly likely that further contributions from other observers will refine or refute this scenario. The rocks have a story to tell us.

Edmond W. Holroyd, III, Ph.D.

PHYSICAL MECHANISM FOR REVERSALS
OF THE EARTH'S MAGNETIC FIELD DURING THE FLOOD

D. Russell Humphreys, Ph.D. *

ABSTRACT

Recent paleomagnetic data [1] strongly supports my hypothesis [2] that the Earth's magnetic field reversed itself rapidly during the Genesis flood. This paper shows specifically how convection upflows of the electrically conductive fluid in the earth's core would produce such rapid reversals. The analysis shows that (1) the upflows had to have been faster than 3 meters per second and larger than 5 kilometers in diameter, and (2) each reversal would decrease the strength of the field slightly. All the evidence indicates that the earth's magnetic field has continuously lost energy since its creation, implying that the field is less than 9000 years old.

INTRODUCTION

The earth's magnetic field has reversed its polarity many times in the past, according to a massive body of data [3]. These reversals were not changes in the earth's rotation or gravity, but were simply 180° changes in the direction a compass needle would point. At least fifty such polarity changes are recorded in geologic strata worldwide. Evolutionists [4] and old-earth creationists [5] assume that millions of years elapsed between reversals, so they use the large number of reversals as evidence for a great age for the earth. However, the assumption of million-year reversal periods rests on the validity of radiometric dating methods, which young-earth creationists question [6]. In 1986, at the First International Conference on Creationism, I suggested that most of the reversals occurred during the Genesis flood [7]. Such a short time scale -- approximately one year -- implies that the average time between reversals was a few weeks, not millions of years. I showed how this hypothesis explains the paleomagnetic (magnetism of ancient rocks) data better than the evolutionary model does. In the conclusion, I suggested that a good test of my hypothesis would be to "look for strata which clearly formed within a few weeks and yet contain a full reversal." In particular, I proposed examining "distinct lava flows thin enough that they would have to cool below the Curie temperature [at which cooling rock "freezes" magnetic information] within a few weeks." A polarity transition recorded in such a thin layer would be strong evidence for rapid reversals.

Recently, to my great delight, two respected paleomagnetists, Robert Coe and Michel Prévot, have found such evidence and published it in *Earth and Planetary Science Letters* [8]. They found a Pliocene basalt flow, number B51, at Steens Mountain, Oregon which apparently recorded a polarity transition which took place in about a fortnight:

> ... even this conservative figure of 15 days corresponds to an astonishingly rapid rate of variation of the geomagnetic field direction of 3° per day ... The rapidity and large amplitude of geomagnetic variation that we infer from the remanence directions in flow B51, even when regarded as an impulse during a polarity transition, truly strains the imagination ... We think that the most probable explanation of the anomalous remanence directions of flow B51 is the occurrence of a large and extremely rapid change in the geomagnetic field during cooling of the flow, and that this change likely originated in the [earth's] core.

A commentary in *Nature* [9] is cautiously favorable to this interpretation. Hitherto, most scientists have thought (1) that the earth's core requires more than a few thousand years

*Dr. Humphreys is a physicist at Sandia National Laboratories, Division 1271, Albuquerque, NM 87185. The Laboratories have not supported this work, and they neither affirm nor deny its scientific validity.

to make such large magnetic field changes, and (2) that the earth's mantle was too conductive (at the time of the reversals) to allow a 15-day change to pass though to the earth's surface. Both assumptions appear to be wrong. This data implies that, somehow, the earth managed to reverse its magnetic field very rapidly in the past. But how did it do so?

PURPOSE AND OUTLINE OF PAPER

My 1986 ICC paper was not specific about the physical mechanism which caused the reversals. I merely showed that fast reversals were physically possible and suggested that strong convection (upflows and downflows) in the earth's fluid core might cause them. I suggested that a powerful event in the earth's core at the beginning of the Genesis flood produced the convection. I do not know what that event was. It could have been, for example, heating of the core due to a sudden increase of radioactive decay [10] or cooling of the mantle above the core [11]. It is not my purpose here to specify that event further. Instead, I want to develop a theory of how the resulting convection flows would produce magnetic reversals.

I will assume that the reader is familiar with basic electricity and magnetism, for which Barnes' textbook [12] is an excellent introduction. In the following section I will explain some very important background concepts from some more specialized areas of study. After that I will introduce the main idea of this paper, reversed flux generation, listing some characteristics of the new flux and the type of convection flows needed to generate it. Then I will show the history of a magnetic flux line step by step, estimate the period of the reversals, and comment briefly on my theory. Finally, I will discuss the earth's magnetic field today and how this theory implies that the field is young. In all of this I will not try to be mathematically rigorous, but instead emphasize basic concepts. From time to time, I will refer to the Sun, which like the earth's core is a sphere of hot, electrically conducting fluid. Astronomers have observed the Sun reversing its general magnetic field every eleven years [13].

BACKGROUND CONCEPTS

To understand my theory, the reader needs to understand some important results from geophysics and *magnetohydrodynamics* (MHD), the study of magnetic fields in electrically conducting fluids. These results are well-understood by specialists, and well-verified experimentally. Shercliffe's textbook [14] is a concise introduction to MHD. Moffet's [15] and Parker's [16] books are more advanced, but quite helpful.

Earth's Interior Structure. The earth's core is a sphere of hot, dense material 3500 km in radius at the center of the earth (Figure 1). Some of it (the very center) is solid, but most of the core is an electrically conductive fluid, an abyss more than 2000 km deep. Above this great deep is the earth's mantle, 3000 km of dense rock foundation supporting the granite crust beneath our feet. The mantle is much less electrically conductive than the core.

Heat and Convection. When the lower parts of a body of fluid are sufficiently hotter than the upper parts, the fluid begins to circulate in the following way: Imagine a small parcel of fluid deep in the earth's core which becomes hotter than the fluid around it. The parcel expands and becomes less dense. Buoyancy then pushes the parcel upward, as if it were a bubble. As the parcel moves up, the pressure on it from the surrounding fluid decreases because the amount of material above it has decreased. Because the pressure decreases, the parcel expands further. The expansion decreases the temperature in the parcel slightly. But the parcel has moved to a higher altitude, where the surrounding fluid is

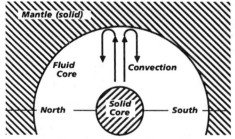

Figure 1. Convection flow in the earth's core.

cooler. If the fluid within the parcel always remains hotter than the surrounding fluid, the parcel will continue to rise all the way to the surface of the core. The extra heat in the parcel will be transferred by conduction to the cooler mantle, and the fluid in the parcel will move to one side away from still-rising hotter fluid and begin to sink. This circulation of hot fluid rising from the interior and cool fluid sinking down, shown in Figure 1, is what we mean by convection. Evidence of small- and large-scale convection has been seen on the Sun, causing the patterns called "granulation" and "supergranulation" [17]. More familiar examples are the rise of bubbles in a boiling pot of oatmeal, or the turbulent upwelling of a thunderhead as it rises into the stratosphere.

Frozen Flux. Now let us consider what our rising parcel of hot fluid does to a magnetic field. One of the most fundamental results of MHD is *Alfven's theorem:* conductive fluids moving perpendicularly to magnetic lines of force tend to carry the lines along with them, as if the magnetic field were "frozen" into the fluid [18]. This means that if the parcel of fluid contains some horizontal magnetic lines of force before it begins to rise,

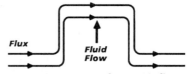

Figure 2. Transport of magnetic flux

it will carry those lines upward as it rises. The portions of the same lines of force in non-rising fluid will stay below, and the lines of force at the boundary will be stretched out like rubber bands between non-moving and rising portions of the fluid as Figure 2 shows. This transporting and stretching of magnetic flux has been observed in the laboratory [19] and on the Sun [20]. Thus convection flows carry magnetic flux upward from the interior to the surface.

Reconnection. When an upward convection flow reaches the surface of the core, it spreads out to the side and then sinks down again. This pattern of flow distorts a flux line into the shape shown in Figure 3(a). Notice the regions where several parts of the line of force are next to one another, but in opposite directions. If such line segments are close enough together, another MHD phenomenon will occur, the rapid reconnection of adjacent but opposite flux lines [21], resulting in the more simplified structure of Figure 3(b).

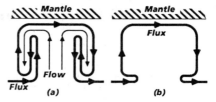

**Figure 3. Effects on a magnetic line of force.
(a) After convection. (b) After reconnection.**

Magnetic Buoyancy. Lines of force in the same direction in turbulent fluid tend to cluster, forming tubes of flux in which the magnetic field is stronger than in the surrounding fluid. The stronger field expels some of the fluid in the tubes, making the tubes less dense than the surrounding material, and thus buoyant [22]. The buoyancy of the flux tubes makes them resist being carried downward with the sinking cooler fluid. It is easier for the fluid to carry magnetic flux upward than downward. Thus convection flows carry more flux up than down, and flux accumulates at the surface.

Diffusion and Flux Transport. *Magnetic diffusion* causes concentrations of flux to spread out into areas having less flux, whether fluid or solid [23]. Diffusion is a slow process, very much like heat conduction. The higher the electrical conductivity of the medium, the slower the diffusion. This means that flux diffuses slowly through the core but rapidly through the mantle. For example, the effect of a sudden change in the magnetic field deep in the interior of the core would take thousands of years to diffuse up through the highly conductive core fluid to the core surface. Convective fluid flow, on the other hand can carry flux upward much faster. Flux accumulated within the topmost few kilometers of the core will diffuse up into the mantle within a few weeks. Thus the combined effect of convection, magnetic buoyancy, and diffusion is to carry magnetic flux up from the deep interior, as shown in Figure 3(b), and push it outward into the mantle. Related concepts in MHD literature are "flux exclusion" and "topological pumping" [24], both of which also move flux out of the interior. Once flux is out of the core, it can diffuse rapidly up through the much less conductive mantle, reaching the earth's surface within days.

REVERSED FLUX GENERATION

This section describes an effect which is crucial to the theory I am developing: *Magnetic flux being moved rapidly generates new magnetic flux of the opposite polarity.* I have not been able to find this effect described anywhere in the literature, but it follows straightforwardly from basic electromagnetic phenomena and the reasoning described below.

For the following discussion, it is very important to clearly visualize the various directions (see Figure 4). Imagine yourself standing within the earth's core near its equator. "Down" is toward the center of the earth, beneath your feet, and "up" is toward the core-mantle interface, above your head. Define "up" to be the x-direction. Now face toward sunrise (if you could

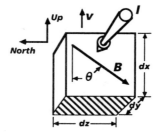

**Figure 4. Fluid parcel moving up.
Current I is eastward, into paper.**

see through the mantle), just as if you were on the earth's surface. That direction is "east," which we define as the y-direction. Keep on facing east for the next two sections of this paper. To your left is "north," which we define as the z-direction. Your frame of reference is at rest with respect to the center of the earth; it does not move during our discussion.

Imagine a rectangular parcel of fluid in front of you. It has dimensions dx, dy, and dz. Suddenly, at time $t = 0$, the parcel begins moving upward in the x-direction at velocity $\mathbf{v}$ (bold type denotes vectors) with respect to your frame of reference. The parcel contains a southward (toward your right) magnetic field $\mathbf{B}$ making an angle θ with the (vertical) x-axis. As mentioned in the previous section, this magnetic field is "frozen" into the parcel and moves upward with it. The Lorentz force, $\mathbf{F}$, on an ion of charge q moving with the parcel is:

$$\mathbf{F} = q\,(\mathbf{E} + \mathbf{v} \times \mathbf{B}) \tag{1}$$

where $\mathbf{E}$ is the electric field in the parcel, initially zero. According to the familiar right-hand rule for vector products, the $\mathbf{v} \times \mathbf{B}$ force pushes positive ions eastward (the direction you are facing) in the y-direction, producing an eastward electric current I through the parcel. Imagine, for now, an instant when the parcel has not moved up very far compared to its dimension dx. Since current is conserved in an electrical conductor, this current must leave the east side (away from you) of the parcel, circle back around you, and return from the west (behind you). Most of the current will be in your vicinity. The resulting loops of current constitute an electric circuit whose self-inductance is L and resistance is R (Figure 5). Since

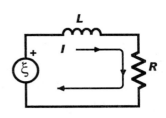

Figure 5. Equivalent electric circuit for current induced by v x B force.

the rest of the fluid in your vicinity is not moving, this circuit is motionless in your frame of reference. The voltage source in this circuit is the electromotive force (e.m.f) ξ produced by the $\mathbf{v} \times \mathbf{B}$ force over the length dy of the moving parcel:

$$\xi = |\mathbf{v} \times \mathbf{B}|\,dy = v\,\sin\theta\,B\,dy \tag{2}$$

where $v = |\mathbf{v}|$ and $B = |\mathbf{B}|$. Some readers may think the parcel will produce no e.m.f. because the source of the field is moving along with the conductor, but it turns out that this is not so [25]. The induced e.m.f. of the inductance L and the voltage drop across the resistance R produce an electric field $\mathbf{E}$ in the parcel which exactly balances the $\mathbf{V} \times \mathbf{B}$ force. That is, the current I and its rate of change dI/dt will be such that:

$$\xi = L\frac{dI}{dt} + I\,R \tag{3}$$

Since the parcel began moving at time zero and maintains a constant velocity thereafter, the electromotive force of eqs. (2) and (3) will be a step function of time. Then the solution of eq. (3) is:

$$I(t) = I_{max}\,(1 - e^{-t/\tau}) \tag{4}$$

where $I_m = (\xi/R)$ is the maximum current, and $\tau = (L/R)$ is the time constant of the circuit. If the velocity v greatly exceeds a critical velocity v_{crit} such that:

$$v \gg v_{crit} \equiv \frac{dx}{\tau} \tag{5}$$

then the parcel will move a distance equal to its own x-dimension dx in a time dt which is much less than the time constant τ. During that time, the second term of eq. (3) is much smaller than the first term, and we have:

$$\xi \approx L\frac{dI}{dt} \tag{6}$$

The current I moving through inductance L produces magnetic flux, Φ_{new}, which did not exist previously. The next section discusses the location and orientation of this new flux (Figure 7). Since by the definition of inductance, $\Phi_{new} = LI$, the rate of increase of the new flux is:

$$\frac{d\Phi_{new}}{dt} = L\frac{dI}{dt} \tag{7}$$

132

Using eqs. (2) and (7) in eq. (6) gives:

$$\frac{d\Phi_{new}}{dt} \approx v \ sin \ \theta \ B \ dy \tag{8}$$

The magnetic field intensity B in the moving parcel is simply the old flux, $d\Phi_{old}$, in the parcel divided by the area normal to the field lines:

$$B = \frac{d\Phi_{old}}{sin \ \theta \ dx \ dy} \tag{9}$$

Using this equation and the fact that $v = (dx/dt)$ in eq. (8) gives us:

$$\frac{d\Phi_{new}}{dt} \approx \frac{dx}{dt} \ sin \ \theta \ \frac{d\Phi_{old}}{sin \ \theta \ dx \ dy} \ dy = \frac{d\Phi_{old}}{dt} \tag{10}$$

Integrating eq. (10) shows that the amount of new flux generated in the circuit is approximately equal to the amount of old flux moving through it:

$$\boxed{\Phi_{new} \approx \Phi_{old}} \tag{11}$$

After the old flux in the rising parcel moves out of your vicinity, the electromotive force in the circuit of Figure 5 will drop to zero, but the magnetic energy stored in the inductance L will keep the current I circulating around the circuit [26]. This means that the new flux will continue to exist in your vicinity, even though the old flux which produced it has moved away from you. The current and the new flux will then decay with time constant τ as power is dissipated in the circuit resistance R.

CHARACTERISTICS OF THE NEW FLUX

Figure 6(a) shows a new loop of flux generated by a brief upward motion of a line of old flux. The crossed-circle symbol (arrow going into the paper) shows the newly-generated electric current going eastward (away from you). As I mentioned above, this current circles back around all sides of the new flux loop and re-enters the parcel from its west side. Most of this current will be within a radius several times the dimensions of the parcel. The upper side of the new flux loop is next to the old flux, and it points in the same direction, south (to your right). The lower side of the new flux remains right in front of you at the location where the old flux started its journey upward, and it points in the opposite direction, north (to your left). Figure 6(b) shows a second loop of new flux created by a second brief motion of the old flux. Notice that in the region where the two new loops are next to one another, the two new lines are in opposite directions, and reconnection can occur. The two loops cancel where they oppose one another and combine to form the larger loop shown in Figure 6(c). If the motion had been continuous, the flux loop of Figure 6(c) would have been produced immediately.

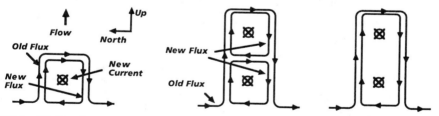

Figure 6.   (a) New flux generated
by brief upward motion of the fluid.
　　　　(b) Additional new flux made
　　　　by a second upward motion.
　　　　(c) After new flux reconnects.
　　　　Currents eastward, into paper.

In Figure 6(c) there is twice as much current as there was in Figure 6(a). But the flux lines circle a perimeter which is twice as long, so by Ampere's law the field B along the perimeter remains the same. Thus the total number of flux lines in the loop remains the same from 6(a) to 6(c). The flux lines now occupy a greater volume, which means that the energy stored in the new flux has increased. In other words, it requires energy to increase the area of a flux loop. This energy comes from the rising parcel, and ultimately from the heat which creates the buoyancy of the parcel. The buoyant force works against a retarding force produced by the action of the old flux on the new current. You can feel the same retarding force in a hand-cranked electrical generator whose output has been shorted with a loop of wire. In a similar way, the buoyant parcel performs work to produce the new currents and flux. Some of this energy is dissipated immediately in ohmic heating, but much of it is stored in the new magnetic flux. Regardless of the energy losses, the amount of new flux will be nearly the same as the amount of old flux, if the fluid is moving fast enough to generate the new flux in a time which is short compared to the decay time τ of the loop. However, because the fluid cannot move infinitely fast, the amount of new flux will always be less than the amount of old flux:

$$\Phi_{new} < \Phi_{old} \tag{12}$$

CRITICAL SIZE AND VELOCITY OF FLOWS

Figure 7 shows the electrical currents around the new flux in the case that $dx \approx dz$. By approximating the current configuration as a section of coaxial cable, one can show that the time constant τ of the circuit is of the order of

$$\tau \approx \mu_o\,\sigma\,(dx)^2 \tag{13}$$

where μ_0 is the magnetic permeability of free space and σ is the electrical conductivity of the fluid. Solving this for the critical linear dimension dx_{crit} necessary to get a certain value of τ gives:

$$dx_{crit} \approx \sqrt{\frac{\tau}{\mu_o\,\sigma}} \tag{14}$$

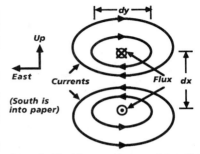

Figure 7. Electric currents around new flux.

The conductivity of the earth's core as estimated from the observed decay rate is about 40,000 mho/m [27], which agrees with Stacey's rough estimate based on material properties [28]. To get a decay time greater than two weeks, eq. (14) requires that the rising parcel of fluid must have linear dimensions greater than about 5 km. Convection of parcels much smaller than this will not have any effect on reversals having a period of several weeks. Eq. (14) also shows that the flux generation process which I describe could not be used to support the idea of very slow reversals, because periods greater than twenty thousand years would require convection flows whose scale is larger than the earth's core.

Now we can determine the critical fluid velocity v_{crit} referred to in the previous section, the velocity which the fluid must exceed to generate a significant amount of new flux. Using eq. (14) in eq. (5) gives:

$$v_{crit} \approx \frac{1}{\sqrt{\mu_o\,\sigma\,\tau}} \tag{15}$$

For the conductivity of the earth's core fluid given above and a time constant of two weeks, $v_{crit} = 0.4$ cm/s. Even at the critical velocity, the amount of new flux generated would be less than half the old flux. For efficient new flux generation, the fluid velocity would have to be more than an order of magnitude greater than the critical velocity, say roughly 10 cm/s. Below we shall see that another condition raises the required velocity to several meters per second.

HISTORY OF A MAGNETIC FLUX LINE

Figure 8 shows, in a simplified way, how the above process eventually results in reversed flux outside the core. In Figure 8(a) we see an original, first-generation line of force which points southward in the core and northward outside it. By Ampere's law, the electric current which maintains this line must be within it. Since the core is a much better conductor than the mantle, most of the maintaining current will be in the core. This current circulates westward around the whole core, as shown by the circle-and-dot symbols (arrows coming out of the paper).

Figure 8(b) shows what happens as a parcel of heated fluid carries a segment of the flux line to the surface of the core. A second-generation loop of flux has been created. The electric current maintaining the new flux moves eastward though it and circles back westward around it on all sides. Part of the first-generation line has popped out into the mantle, along with some of the westward current maintaining it.

In Figure 8(c) we see the result of many parcels having risen to the surface. Now the first-generation line has been pushed almost completely out of the core, and its maintaining current is circulating westward through the mantle around the core. There are many loops of second-generation flux left behind in the core, each with their own maintaining currents.

134

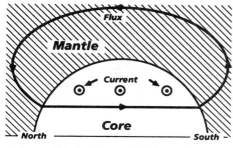

Figure 8(a). First-generation flux and current.

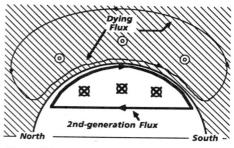

Figure 8(d). Second-generation flux reconnects.

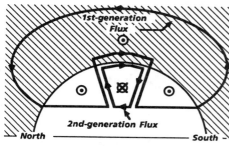

Figure 8(b). New flux is generated.

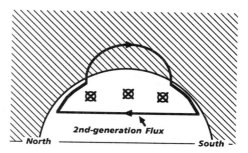

Figure 8(e). Flux begins emerging from core.

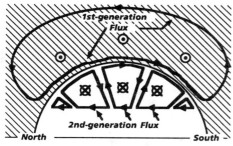

Figure 8(c). First-generation flux out of core.

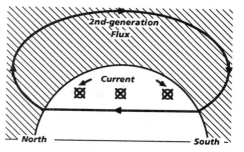

Figure 8(f). Reversed flux and current.

Figure 8(d) shows what happens after the second-generation loops of flux reconnect, forming a single large loop within the core. Similarly, the maintaining currents link up with currents from other second-generation lines to the east and west, becoming larger in diameter until the currents go all the way around the core eastward. In the meantime, the first-generation flux is dying away, because its westward maintaining currents have been dissipating themselves in the higher-resistance material of the mantle.

Figure 8(e) shows the second-generation flux after it has partly diffused out of the core surface. Once free of the core, it moves rapidly up to its full extent, as shown in Figure 8(f). It is very similar to the first-generation flux, except that its direction is reversed. In the meantime, convection flows continue, beginning to produce third-generation flux. This cycle of reversals will continue as long as convection flows greater than the critical size and velocity persist. When the upflows become smaller or slower, the reversals cease.

PERIOD OF THE REVERSALS

In actuality, convection flows are much more turbulent than Figure 8 would suggest, and Figure 8(c) should probably look more like Figure 9, a large number of small second-

135

generation flux loops. These loops will not reconnect until the the core becomes crowded enough with them to bring them close enough together to cause reconnections. During this complex stage, no net third-generation flux is created, because the effect of fluid parcels containing northward flux is cancelled by an equal number of parcels containing southward flux. Eventually, however, the interior becomes crowded with second-generation loops, and reconnections begin. When the reconnected second-generation loops become comparable in size to the core, as in Figure 8(d), then creation of third-generation flux begins.

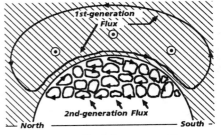

Figure 9. New flux before reconnection.

The time required to go from Figure 8(a) to Figure 8(f), i.e. the half-period of a reversal cycle, is partly, and perhaps mainly, determined by the time it takes the convection flows to push most of the first-generation flux up to the surface out of the core. Thus the reversal period is roughly related to the effective velocity of flux transport, v_{eff}:

$$\tau \approx \frac{R}{v_{eff}} \tag{16}$$

where R is the radius of the core. This effective velocity depends on what fraction k of core fluid is moving at any given time, the average velocity v_{ave} of the flows, and the efficiency ε with which the flows manage to deposit flux at the surface without taking it back down again:

$$v_{eff} = \varepsilon k v_{ave} \tag{17}$$

From eq. (16) we find that to get flux from near the center out to the 3500-km radius of the core in two weeks would require an effective velocity of 3 m/s.

COMMENTS

This theory hinges on the validity of the mechanism for generating reversed flux outlined in eqs. (1) through (11). This mechanism is a new effect, not discussed in any of the MHD literature as far as I know. Thus I invite careful scrutiny of that section. If it is a valid effect, then we must ask ourselves why it has not been noticed before. Two of the reasons could be that: (1) Most MHD discussions of similar situations center on steady-state effects instead of time-dependent, transient effects, and (2) the external circuit is rarely considered. For example, textbooks often discuss Hartmann flows [29], which have the same orientation of magnetic field, fluid velocity, and induced current as in Figure 4. However, the textbooks only consider the steady-state solution and do not say where the current goes, thus neglecting transient effects and inductance in the external circuit.

The process I have outlined above is simple compared to the evolutionary "dynamo" theories. It differs fundamentally from the dynamo theories in that it is not intended to maintain the earth's magnetic field for billions of years. Rather, it inverts a previously-existing field over and over again. Far from maintaining a field indefinitely, this process accelerates the decay of a planetary field. The field strength at the peak of each cycle is less than the peak of the previous cycle, because the inverting process does not completely reproduce the flux, according to eq. (12). New flux rises, phoenix-like, from the ashes of the old flux, but the new is always less than the old. This means that the energy contained in the post-flood magnetic field would be considerably less than that of the pre-flood field.

Paleomagnetic (during-flood) data could support this view, but analysis is complicated because the attenuation of the earth's mantle [30] would decrease as convection velocities and reversal periods slowed down during the flood. Archaeomagnetic (post-flood) data show a much lower field energy than the estimated pre-flood level [31], just as we would expect. The core disturbances during the flood would excite non-dipole (four or more poles) components of the field. After the flood such components would die away, causing the field at any given point on the earth's surface to fluctuate up and down for several thousand years [32]. During that time the total energy in the field would continue to decrease [33]. Slowing convection flows persisting after the flood probably also contributed to these fluctuations. According to archaeomagnetic data, magnetic fluctuations stopped about 1500 years ago and the field began decaying steadily.

THE EARTH'S MAGNETIC FIELD TODAY

There is evidence that slow convection flows are occurring in the earth's core at present. Contour charts of the field's strength and direction show a pattern of "hills" and "valleys" which change shape over decades, like isobars on a weather chart. The whole pattern drifts westward at about 0.18° per year [34]. The simplest explanation for this behavior would be the existence of convection flows. If there are convection flows at present, then there is a chance that the reversal process could still be going on today. Let us consider this possibility.

According to the magnetic contour data, the average upflow velocity is v_{ave} = 0.04 cm/s [35], and the fraction of core affected appears from the charts to be roughly $k \approx 0.1$. If the upflows were 100% efficient in carrying flux to the surface, we would have ε = 1.0. Using these values in eq. (17) gives an effective velocity of about 0.004 cm/s. Using this value in eq. (16) gives a period of roughly 3000 years, not much different from the observed decay time of 2000 years. Using the period above in eq. (14) tells us that the diameter of the upflows must be of the order of 1000 km to be effective, roughly the same size as the contour plots indicate. In the absence of more detailed information about the flux-carrying efficiency of the convection flows, we cannot exclude (on the basis of this theory) the possibility that a reversal process is at work in the earth's core today.

There is some evidence for the feeble stirrings of such a process. Most of the energy of the earth's magnetic field today is in its dipole (two poles, north and south) component, and that energy is decreasing steadily [36]. However, a small part of the field energy is in non-dipole components (quadrupole, octopole, etc.), and that energy is presently increasing [37], showing that the core still has some magnetic activity. Some dynamo theorists interpret this activity as evidence that the present decay of the dipole field is part of a full-fledged reversal cycle in progress. If that were so, the non-dipole components at this stage of the alleged cycle would be strong, according to solar and paleomagnetic reversal data [38]. However, the non-dipole components are relatively weak. Another consideration is that there are no known polarity reversals in the archeomagnetic data, even though those data include a period after the flood when the core convection would have been more vigorous than it is today. Thus it appears that the reversal process today is making only a minor contribution to the decrease of the field. But even if the reversal process were dominant today, the mechanism I depict in this paper would still, in the long run, dissipate field energy, not add to it.

CONCLUSION

Even though creationist explanations of planetary magnetic fields are still in their infancy, they appear to be more complete and successful than the forty-year old dynamo theories. Recent magnetic measurements by Voyager at Uranus and Neptune have confirmed the predictions of a creationist theory on the origin of planetary magnetic fields [39], a theory which had already explained magnetic data in the rest of the solar system better than dynamo theories. Recent measurements cast doubt on a dynamo operating in the earth's core at present [40]. As yet there is no dynamo theory which accounts for the extremely rapid variations reported by Coe and Prévot. Dynamo theorists acknowledge that their theories are incomplete, very complex, and not very successful at making predictions [41].

Early forms of the creationist free-decay theory were straightforward and mathematically complete [42]. They showed that if the earth's core had no internal motions (as if it were solid), the earth's magnetic field should always decrease. However, the real world is not as simple as that. The core is a fluid which has internal motions, and there is clear evidence that the field has gone through reversal cycles. Dynamo theorists have tried to use this evidence to support their view that the earth's field has persisted for billions of years. Until a few years ago they could claim this ground by default, but now my theory of reversals provides an alternative and (I think) better explanation. The theory accounts for fluid motions and explains the reversal data well, particularly the Coe and Prévot data. According to this theory, the energy (or during reversals, peak energy) in the earth's magnetic field has been decreasing rapidly ever since creation.

Such a decrease implies that the earth's magnetic field is not eternal, but is relatively recent. If we extrapolate today's energy decay rate back to the the theoretical maximum energy at creation [43], we get an upper limit for the age of the field: 8700 years. However, the rate of energy loss would have been greater during and after the flood, as I mentioned above. Figure 10 shows one scenario with about 90% of the field energy being lost during the flood or shortly thereafter. This would make the age of the field about 6000 years, thus allowing the tight-chronology Masoretic text age for the earth [44]. In summary, all the theoretical and observational information we have about the earth's magnetic field supports the Biblical record of a recent creation.

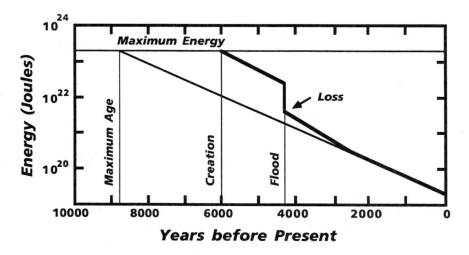

Figure 10. Energy in the earth's magnetic field.

REFERENCES

1. Coe, R. S. and Prévot, M., "Evidence suggesting extremely rapid field variation during a geomagnetic reversal," EARTH AND PLANETARY SCIENCE LETTERS, Vol. 92, No. 3/4, April 1989, pp. 292-98. Humphreys, D.R., "New evidence for rapid reversals of the earth's magnetic field," CREATION RESEARCH SOCIETY QUARTERLY, Vol. 26, No. 4, March 1990, in press.

2. Humphreys, D. R., "Reversals of the earth's magnetic field during the Genesis flood," PROCEEDINGS OF THE FIRST INTERNATIONAL CONFERENCE ON CREATIONISM, Vol. 2, Creation Science Fellowship, Pittsburgh, Pennsylvania, 1986, pp. 113-26.

3. Humphreys, D. R., "Has the earth's magnetic field ever flipped?" CREATION RESEARCH SOCIETY QUARTERLY, Vol. 25, No. 3, December 1988, pp. 130-37.

4. Dalrymple, G. B., "Can the earth be dated from decay of its magnetic field?" JOURNAL OF GEOLOGICAL EDUCATION, Vol. 31, No. 2, March 1983, pp. 124-32.

5. Young, D. A., CHRISTIANITY AND THE AGE OF THE EARTH, Zondervan, Grand Rapids, Michigan, 1982, pp. 117-24.

6. Gentry, R. V., CREATION'S TINY MYSTERY, 2nd Ed., Earth Science Associates, Knoxville, Tennessee, 1988.

7. Humphreys, 1986, *op. cit.*

8. Coe and Prévot, *op. cit.*

9. Fuller, M., "Fast changes in geomagnetism," NATURE, Vol. 339, 22 June 1989, pp. 582-83.

10. Humphreys, 1986, *op. cit.*, pp. 117, 125.

11. Baumgardner, J. R., "Numerical simulation of the large-scale tectonic changes accompanying the flood," PROCEEDINGS OF THE FIRST INTERNATIONAL CONFERENCE ON CREATIONISM, Vol. 2, Pittsburgh, Pennsylvania, 1986, pp. 17-30. See esp. p. 29.

12. Barnes, T. G., FOUNDATIONS OF ELECTRICITY AND MAGNETISM, 2nd Ed., D.C. Heath & Co., 1965, New York. 3rd Ed., Thomas G. Barnes, 1977, El Paso, Texas.

13. Montie, M., "More study needed on magnetic fields," CREATION RESEARCH SOCIETY QUARTERLY, Vol. 19, No. 3, December 1982, p. 196. Sheeley, N. R., Jr., "The influence of differential rotation on the equatorial component of the Sun's magnetic dipole field," ASTROPHYSICAL JOURNAL, Vol. 243, 1 February 1981, pp. 1040-8. Newkirk, G. and Frazier, K., "The solar cycle," PHYSICS TODAY, Vol. 35, No. 4, April 1982, pp. 25-34.

14. Shercliff, J. A., A TEXTBOOK OF MAGNETOHYDRODYNAMICS, Pergamon Press, 1965, London.

15. Moffatt, H. K., MAGNETIC FIELD GENERATION IN ELECTRICALLY CONDUCTING FLUIDS, Cambridge University Press, 1978, Cambridge.

16. Parker, E. N., COSMICAL MAGNETIC FIELDS, Clarendon Press, 1979, Oxford.

17. Noyes, R. W., THE SUN, OUR STAR, Harvard University Press, 1982, Cambridge, Massachusetts, pp. 22-25, 136-40.

18. Moffatt, op. cit., p. 43.

19. Kolm, H. H. and Mawardi, O. K., "Hydromagnet: a self-generating liquid conductor electromagnet," JOURNAL OF APPLIED PHYSICS, Vol. 32, No. 7, July 1961, pp. 1296-304.

20. Wang, Y. M., Nash, A. G., and Sheeley, N. R., Jr., "Magnetic flux transport on the Sun," SCIENCE, Vol. 245, 18 August 1989, pp. 712-18. The fluid of the Sun rotates around its axis at different rates at various latitudes and depths. This "differential rotation" causes the north-south ("poloidal") flux lines to be stretched out in the direction of rotation, thus adding an east-west ('toroidal") component to the field. However, the existence of this part of the flux depends on the existence of the north-south flux, whereas the converse is not necessarily true. In the case of the earth's core, there is observational evidence [40] that the east-west component is not very strong. In this paper I show a mechanism which reverses the north-south component without any dependence on an east-west component.

21. Parker, op. cit., pp. 392-439.

22. Parker, op. cit., pp. 205-73, 314-58.

23. Shercliff, op. cit., pp. 32-34.

24. Moffatt, op. cit., pp. 59, 70. Parker, op. cit., pp. 314-58, 440-63.

25. Panofsky, W. K. H. and Phillips, M., CLASSICAL ELECTRICITY AND MAGNETISM, Addison-Wesley, 1955, Reading, Massachusetts, p. 150: "the force which acts on a moving electron within a moving [conductor] is independent of whether the magnetic field is external or due to the magnetic moment of the [conductor] itself."

26. Nayfeh, M. H. and Brussel, M. K., ELECTRICITY AND MAGNETISM, John Wiley & Sons, 1985, New York, pp. 395-96.

27. Barnes, T. G., "Electromagnetics of the earth's field and evaluation of electric conductivity, current, and Joule heating in the earth's core," CREATION RESEARCH SOCIETY QUARTERLY, Vol. 9, No. 4, March 1973, pp. 222-30. Barnes, T. G., ORIGIN AND DESTINY OF THE EARTH'S MAGNETIC FIELD, 2nd. Ed., Institute for Creation Research, 1983, El Cajon, California, pp. 81-99.

28. Stacey, F. D., "Electrical resistivity of the earth's core," EARTH AND PLANETARY SCIENCE LETTERS, Vol. 3, 1967, pp. 204-206.

29. Shercliff, op. cit., pp. 143-49.

30. Humphreys, 1986, op. cit., pp. 114-15.

31. Extrapolating today's decay rate forward 1656 years from the theoretical maximum created field [43] gives a field strength before the flood 30 times today's level, corresponding to a field energy of about 2×10^{22} Joules.

32. Humphreys, 1986, op. cit., pp.119-20.

33. The field at a particular point fluctuates because of the different rates of decay of multipole components having different polarities, but in a free decay each component would steadily dissipate its energy into heat.

34. Vorhees, C. V., "Steady flows at the top of the earth's core derived from geomagnetic field models," JOURNAL OF GEOPHYSICAL RESEARCH, Vol. 91, No. B12, 10 November 1986, pp. 12,444-66. Bloxham, J. and Gubbins, D., "The secular variation of Earth's magnetic field," NATURE, Vol. 317, 31 October 1985, pp.777-81.

35. Moffatt, op. cit., p. 89. Bloxham, op. cit., p. 781.

36. Barnes, T. G., "Decay of the earth's magnetic moment and the geochronological implications," CREATION RESEARCH SOCIETY QUARTERLY, Vol. 8, No. 1, June 1971, pp. 24-29.

37. McDonald, K. L. and Gunst, R. L., "Recent trends in the earth's magnetic field," JOURNAL OF GEOPHYSICAL RESEARCH, Vol. 73, No. 6, 15 March 1968, pp. 2057-67.

38. Schneider, D. A. and Kent, D. V., "The paleomagnetic field from equatorial deep-sea sediments: axial symmetry and polarity asymmetry," SCIENCE, Vol. 242, 14 October 1988, pp. 252-56. Jacobs, J. A., REVERSALS OF THE EARTH'S MAGNETIC FIELD, Adam Hilger Ltd., 1984, Bristol, pp. 65-72. Moffatt, *op. cit.*, pp. 101-105.

39. Humphreys, D. R., "The creation of planetary magnetic fields," CREATION RESEARCH SOCIETY QUARTERLY, Vol. 21, No. 3, December 1984, pp. 140-49. Humphreys, D. R., "Good news from Neptune: the Voyager 2 magnetic measurements," CREATION RESEARCH SOCIETY QUARTERLY, 1990, in press.

40. Lanzerotti, L. J., *et al.*, "Measurements of the large-scale direct-current earth potential and possible implications for the geomagnetic dynamo," SCIENCE, Vol. 229, 5 July 1985, pp. 47-49, reports measurements implying that the toroidal component of the earth's magnetic field within the core is relatively weak. Most, and perhaps all, dynamo theories depend on the existence of a strong toroidal component. Hence these data imply that there is no such dynamo in the earth's core today.

41. Dessler, A. J., "Does Uranus have a magnetic field?" NATURE, Vol. 319, 16 January 1986, pp. 174-75. Bagenal, F., "The emptiest magnetosphere," PHYSICS WORLD, October 1989, pp. 18-19, says: "... you would have thought we would have given up guessing about planetary magnetic fields after being wrong at nearly every planet in the solar system ..."

42. Barnes, 1973, *op. cit.*

43. Humphreys, D. R., "The creation of the earth's magnetic field," CREATION RESEARCH SOCIETY QUARTERLY, Vol. 20, No. 2, September 1983, pp. 89-94, gives a field at creation 70.35 times greater than today's. Barnes, T. G., "Earth's magnetic energy provides confirmation of its young age," CREATION RESEARCH SOCIETY QUARTERLY, Vol. 12, No. 1, June 1975, pp. 11-13, shows that the energy presently in the dipole part of the earth's magnetic field is 2.52×10^{19} Joules. The higher field at creation would have an energy of 1.25×10^{23} Joules.

44. Niessen, R., "A biblical approach to dating the earth: a case for the use of Genesis 5 and 11 as an exact chronology," CREATION RESEARCH SOCIETY QUARTERLY, Vol. 19, No. 1, June 1982, pp. 60-66.

DISCUSSION

Dr. Humphreys has, once again, demonstrated the fertility of creation science in his novel explanation of the magnetic field reversal data. The detailed theory presented in this paper warrants further, careful consideration by specialists in magnetohydrodynamics and geomagnetism.

For my own part, I am primarily concerned with the relationship of Dr. Humphreys' work to the age of the earth question -- a very minor portion of the present paper. Dr. Humphreys states that his theory implies an age for the earth's magnetic field of less than 9,000 years. This obviously conflicts with other geophysical data which strongly suggest a date for the Flood prior to 10,000 years ago [Aardsma, this conference]. I am of the opinion that there is no real conflict of substance here, however, since the magnetic field data are not now, and have never been, definitive regarding the age of the earth. There is, of course, the obvious precariousness of such a large extrapolation of the relatively small amount of modern data into the distant past (to a starting value which can not be determined experimentally) which is required to determine the age of the earth (actually the age of the magnetic field) in this way. But more fundamentally, there is nothing either implicit or explicit in the recent creation framework which disallows the possibility that the earth's magnetic field might be dynamo driven after all. Though an old earth framework must reject a free decay theory because of the time factors involved, there is nothing about a recent creation framework which rules out a dynamo theory. Thus, the recent-creationist has two possible theories for explaining the earth's magnetic field data -- free decay *and* dynamo. Since these two theories do not share identical implications for the age of the magnetic field all conclusions about the age of the earth which are drawn from magnetic field data must be viewed as tentative.

Quite apart from the existence of an alternate theory for the origin and sustenance of the earth's magnetic field is the question of the actual boundary on the age of the earth within which a free decay theory can function. Dr. Humphreys has shown one possible scenario (Figure 10) for the decay of the field energy, consistent with a 4000 B.C. date for creation. It would be very helpful if he would discuss other possible scenarios and the consequent range over which the date of creation might ultimately be found without falsifying his free decay theory. Specifically, does he feel that free decay would be ruled out if the true date of creation were found to be say 12,000 B.C.?

Gerald E. Aardsma, Ph.D.
Santee, California

This review will be restricted to the physical mechanism for reversals of the earth's magnetic field. Dr. Humphreys has come up with a novel and physically sound approach to reversals of the magnetic field. He correctly employs the principles of magnetohydrodynamics, to the electrically conductive fluid in the molten core of the earth, in connection with heat and convection there.

One of the phenomenon in magnetohydrodynamics is magnetic diffusion. It is not dependent on fluid flow. The rapidity with which magnetic diffusion takes place is inversely proportional to the electrical conductivity. The author makes use of the fact that the mantle has a much lower conductivity than the core.

Making use of that great increase in rapidity of magnetic diffusion, along with some of his original development, yields a very plausible mechanism for rapid magnetic field reversals outside of the core. Dr. Humphreys is to be commended for this ingenious approach to magnetic field reversals during the flood.

Thomas G. Barnes, D.Sc.
El Paso, Texas

I can find no fault with the magnetohydrodynamic mechanism proposed by Dr. Humphreys to explain the earth's magnetic field reversal, nor do I dispute the timescale inferred for this field reversal, given the sudden onset of worldwide turbulent flow described by Figures 8a-f. Dr. Humphreys correctly points out, however that the onset of this supposed turbulent flow requires a postulated "powerful event." This postulated core temperature inversion, which must be both very intense and very uniform, seems to me to be a suspect as the steady-state dynamo theories. I recognize that Dr. Humphreys' theory is remarkably successful at explaining existing paleomagnetic data and should be taken seriously. I also accept his assertion that existing data on field reversal obviates steady-state dynamo theories. It seems intuitive that heating mechanisms such as tidal forces, radioactive decay, and Joule heating would be non-uniform and not steady-state, so that a successful dynamo theory, if it is ever developed, would have to accommodate the physics that Dr. Humphreys has described in this paper.

Thomas W. Hussey, Ph.D.
Albuquerque, New Mexico

CLOSURE

Dr. Aardsma brings up some good points in regard to using the earth's magnetic field to estimate the age of the earth. I agree with him that in principle, self-sustaining dynamo theories are available to the young-earth creationist as a possible option. However, I don't think they are a very good option, because (a) no complete or even plausible dynamo theory exists, and (b) recent observations weigh against a working dynamo in the earth's core today [Ref. 40]. So it is my judgement (which could be wrong) that a self-sustaining geodynamo is unlikely.

On the basis of the magnetic field data alone, I cannot completely exclude Dr. Aardsma's possibility of a creation in 12,000 B.C., and free decay would not be ruled out by such a timescale. The problem is that we have no direct measurements of the core's electrical conductivity. So I cannot say that all of the present decrease is due to free decay; some of the decrease might be caused by a residual form of my dissipative reversal mechanism, as I pointed out in the second-to-last section of my paper. That would reduce the slope of the line in my Fig. 10 and push the dates of the Flood and creation backward. However, as my comments on Dr. Aardsma's article show, I do not find the case for a Flood earlier than 5,000 years ago very compelling.

Several years ago Dr. Barnes was justifiably concerned about the idea of rapid reversals, because at that time I had proposed no physical mechanism showing how such reversals could take place. I wrote this paper to relieve such concerns. Therefore I am very glad that he has found no fault with the mechanism I have presented, and I am quite grateful for his commendation.

I'm glad that Dr. Hussey found nothing wrong with the mechanism I proposed, because much of his professional experience has been closely related to magnetohydrodynamics. Upon further discussion with him since the time he submitted his comments, he has decided that the temperature distribution required for my mechanism would not have to be uniform. As for the intensity required, I offer the following rough calculations:

The temperature gradient required for convection to occur in the core has been estimated at about 14 degrees K per km [F. D. Stacey, Physics of the Earth, 1st ed., 1969, p. 255]. The gradient could have been at or near that value before the events of the Flood. To overcome magnetic forces (viscous forces turn out to be negligible), a parcel 5 km in diameter only needs to be one or two degrees K hotter than its surroundings. This means that to power 50 reversals, the average core temperature does not need to change by more than 100 degrees K during the course of the Flood. The corresponding amount of energy is consistent with either the radioactive heating or lower-mantle cooling models (Ref. 2, p. 126). Thus the reversal mechanism I propose fits in quite reasonably with other events associated with the Flood.

D. Russell Humphreys, Ph.D.

A COMPUTER MODEL OF THE PRE-FLOOD ATMOSPHERE

Greg S. Jorgensen, P. Eng.
Creation Engineering
234 Enfield Cres.
Winnipeg, Manitoba
Canada R2H 1B4

ABSTRACT

The existence of a pre-flood water vapor canopy on top of the existing atmosphere is strongly implied in the Scriptures (Genesis 1:7, 7:11-12, Proverbs 3:20)[1]. This paper studies the properties and characteristics of such a canopy by the development of a computer model. The model accurately predicts the vertical temperature profile of the U.S. Standard Atmosphere, thereby gaining credibility in its use on the pre-flood atmosphere.

The model reveals a pre-flood utopia over the entire face of the planet. The average ground temperature would have been a moderate 15 to 25 degrees Celsius and the base of the canopy, at 5 to 6 kilometers, would have been 70 to 90 degrees Celsius. This temperature inversion created a very calm stable atmosphere, with no clouds, no storm systems (just gentle breezes), no rain (Genesis 2:5). This condition allowed the base of the canopy to exist in a state of supersaturation (below dew point), due to the lack of precipitating nuclei. When the great deep broke up (Genesis 7:11), believed here to be volcanic eruptions, the hot dusty gases rose up despite the inversion and provided condensing nuclei for the supersaturated canopy, which then rained out. The extensive volcanic activity caused the continents to sink, and this, along with the water held in the canopy (5 to 10 meters), created a world-wide flood. As the canopy condensed a world-wide cloud cover would have developed, decreasing the amount of solar radiation on the earth, which in turn caused a great ice age after the flood. The canopy would also prevent the formation of carbon 14, and therefore, anything which existed under the canopy would contain no carbon 14 and when examined today would yield a false old age. The collapse of the canopy explains the extinction of many of the life forms on the planet, and the formation of fossils, coal, oil, and gas.

INTRODUCTION

The existence of the pre-flood canopy is a powerful tool in explaining the earth's young age and much of today's sedimentary geology. The canopy would create a world-wide utopia perfect for lush plant and animal life, even at the poles. This is collaborated by the evidence seen today. But is a pure water vapor canopy technically feasible? Would it not mix and precipitate out? What about the winter season, especially at the poles, how could the canopy survive there? To answer these and other valid questions, a model will have to be developed. A model is a mathematical prototype which attempts to simulate some real process. Models can be simple or very complex. The simpler the model, the easier it is to understand and manipulate. It also takes much less time and effort to develop. Once a simple model is made and well understood, a more complex and accurate model can be developed. This paper develops a simple model and attempts to achieve an intuitive understanding of the earth's atmospheric radiation balance. The computer program, written in Basic, is provided and it is hoped that interested parties will use this program to develop a more complex model.

UNDERSTANDING THE ATMOSPHERIC RADIATION BALANCE

Figure 1 shows the details in calculating the average energy striking the earth as one quarter of the incoming solar flux.

During the winter season, the pole receives very little sunlight and it is difficult to imagine the canopy not precipitating out. For this reason, it will be argued that the pre-flood earth had a declination angle close to zero. It is a widely accepted theory that a large meteorite hit the earth and perhaps this is what caused the 23 1/2 degree declination we observe today.

Figure 2 illustrates that the surface area of a sphere, for a uniform width of incident solar radiation, is the same at 60 or 80 degrees latitude as it is at the equator [2]. At 80 degrees the incident radiation strikes the surface at an angle (greater unit area) but the circumference is less. This means that the poles would receive the same average amount of solar radiation per unit area as would the equator (some thought will prove this out). The poles would be cooler, however, due to greater reflection of solar rays. This can also be understood by realizing that the equator only receives 12 hours of sunlight per day and the polar regions receive continuous sunlight. It is the 23.5 degree angle of declination which is mostly responsible for today's cold polar regions.

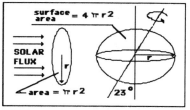

FIG 1 AVG. INTENSITY = SOLAR FLUX /4

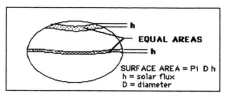

FIG 2 WITH NO DECLINATION THE POLE RECEIVES THE SAME SOLAR ENERGY AS THE EQUATOR

Radiation

Every object in the universe above absolute zero (-273 degrees Celsius) radiates energy due to atomic vibrations. The hotter an object is, the faster its atoms vibrate, causing shorter wavelengths and a higher energy output. When a body becomes increasingly hot it begins to radiate waves so short they enter the region of visible light (approximately .5 microns). An extremely hot body such as the sun emits a range of short wave radiation as shown in Figure 3. It is interesting that God designed the sun to emit a significant part of its energy in the visible region.

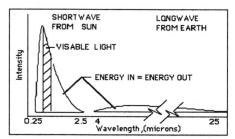

FIG 3 SUN-EARTH RADIATION EQUILIBRIUM

Atmospheric Absorption

As solar radiation strikes the earth's atmosphere, it can be reflected back into space, scattered, absorbed by the atmosphere, or transmitted to the ground were the remaining energy can be absorbed or reflected back to space. All the energy absorbed by the atmosphere and the ground must be radiated back to space in the form of long wave radiation to achieve an equilibrium (see Figures 3 and 4) [3].

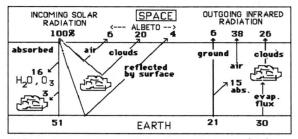

FIG 4 AVERAGE GLOBAL ENERGY BALANCE [2]

Figure 5 shows the development of the temperature profile of Earth's atmosphere. Figure 5a is the temperature profile of an atmosphere which does not absorb any incoming solar radiation. It cools exponentially with height until it reaches outer space temperatures. Figure 5b shows what would happen if there was a heat source at the 50 kilometer region. The ozone layer, which is a good absorber of a certain part of the solar spectrum, becomes the heat source. Figure 5c shows the temperature profile of today's atmosphere which absorbs heat in the outermost layers of the atmosphere and at the 50 kilometer ozone region. The reason this absorption is confined to bands, is because there is only so much energy available in the wavelengths being absorbed, or there is a limited number of absorbing molecules. By the time the sunlight hits the ground, it has been filtered in certain wavelengths.

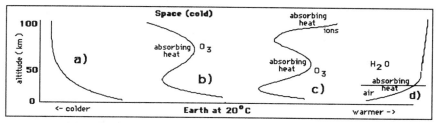

FIG 5 understanding Earth's temp. profile a) no sun   b) heat at 50km   c) heat at 50
& 100+ km (U.S. standard atmosphere)   d) water vapor canopy

MODEL SETUP

For the sake of completeness, it would be desirable to develop all pertinent equations required, but this is not possible in a report of this length. The equations are all basic to atmospheric physics and developed in detail in the references given.

The following simplifications are made:

- It is assumed that radiation is monochromatic (ie. same average or representative wavelength). This is of course not the case in a real atmosphere;ein spite of this, the model accurately predicts today's atmospheric temperature profile.

- There is only one species of molecule capable of absorbing radiation (this is essentially accurate for a water vapor canopy).

- The temperature profile is due to radiation transfer only. Convection and conduction are only a tiny part of the balance, and so can be ignored without significant loss in accuracy.

- The atmosphere can be treated as a number of thin layers which absorb and emit radiation.

- The first layer is deep enough to absorb approximately 60 percent of the long wave radiation from the Earth. This is about the same as in today's atmosphere. Some of the radiation not absorbed by the first layer will be absorbed by the base of the canopy as its absorption cross section is greater than the air layer below (see Figure 8). The remaining long wave radiation is lost to space through what is referred to as the atmospheric window.

Equations Required

$$n = n_0\, e^{-Z/H} \tag{1}$$

where:

n = number density of molecules.
no= number density at base of atmosphere (Z=0).
Z = height from ground.
H = scale height = RT/g.
R = gas constant.
T = temperature in degrees Kelvin.
g = local acceleration due to gravity
     For this model H can be assumed to be

145

8000 meters for air and 15000 meters for
water vapor.

$$\frac{di}{dz} = i\,c\,n \tag{2}$$

where:

di/dz = differential change in intensity with height.
i = intensity of radiation.
C = molecular cross sectional area (same hypothetical area on each molecule which is capable of absorbing energy).
n = number density of molecules (as above).

$$q = E\,sb\,T^4 \tag{3}$$

where:

q = energy absorbed (as above).
E = emissivity, the fraction of a body which can emit energy. When E=1 is referred to as blackbody radiation. E for polished foil is as low as .006. In the energy balance equation E is replaced by Cno.
T = absolute temperature in degrees Kelvin (deg.C + 273).
Sb= Stefan Boltzmann constant (5.67E-8).

Absorption Profile (Chapman Profile) [4]

The total number of absorbing molecules above a level Z, using equation (1), is given by:

$$n_o = \int_z^\infty n\,dZ = n_0\,H\,e^{-Z/H} \tag{4}$$

Integration of (2) substituting (1) for n gives:

$$i = i_\infty\,e^{[c\,n_0\,H\,e^{-Z/H}]} = i_\infty\,e^{-c\,n_t} \tag{5}$$

Introducing (1) and (5) into (2) gives a profile of absorption q as a function of height z as:

$$q = c\,n_0\,i_\infty\,e^{[-(Z/H + c\,n_0\,H\,e^{-Z/H})]} \tag{6}$$

This function is maximum when the exponent has a minimum absolute value. By differentiating it and equating to 0, this is found to occur when:

$$Z = Z_m = H\,\ln(c\,n_0\,H) \tag{7}$$

Equation (7) is a very useful formula because it gives the cross section times the number of absorption molecules as a function of the penetration depth and scale height (two predictable variables).

$$c\,n_0 = \frac{e^{z_*/H}}{H} \qquad (8)$$

Figure 6 shows this profile graphically. Some thought should bring meaning to the profile.

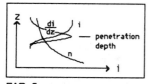

FIG 6 ABSORPTION PROFILE

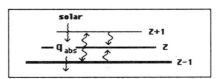

FIG 7 **RADIATION BALANCE** (FOR LAYER Z
ENERGY IN = ENERGY OUT)

Energy Balance

From Figure 7 we can write the following energy balance:

```
<----------------------- ENERGY IN -----------------------> = ENERGY OUT
absorbed          + # transmitting      # transmitting form  = up & down
short & longwave    molecules from above  Z-1 = # from Z       transmission
                                        (Kirchoff's Law)
```
(9)

$$q_a + c n_0 e^{-(z+1/H)}\, sb\, T_{z+1}^4 + c\, n_0\, e^{-z/H} sb\, T_{z-1}^4 = 2 c\, n_0 e^{-z/H} sb\, T_z^4$$

Figure 8 attempts to show graphically why layer Z can only absorb part of the energy transmitted from the layer below. The length of the lines represents the total absorbing cross section for that layer, and the thickness of the lines represents the relative number density of absorbing and emitting molecules.

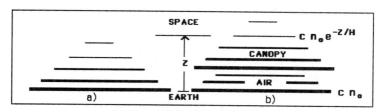

FIG 8 **GRAPHIC REPRESENTATION OF RADIATING AREAS**
a) todays atmosphere b) H₂O canopy atmosphere

Rearranging (9) gives the temperature of layer Z as a function of absorption and the temperatures from above and below.

$$\left[\frac{\dfrac{q_a}{Cn_0 sb} + e^{-(z+1/H)}T_{z-1}^4}{2\,e^{-z/h}}\right]^{1/4} = T_z \tag{10}$$

Equation 10 can now be solved on a computer to give the temperature profile using the finite-difference method [5].

Figure 9 shows the computer's output profile in today's atmosphere and in the pre-flood atmosphere. Table 1 shows typical computer printout.

Note: supersaturation levels of 8 to 1 are possible in pure water vapor [6].

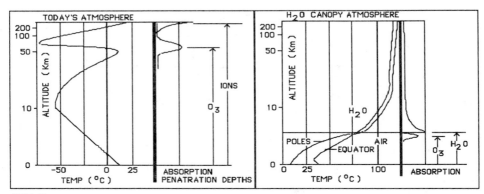

FIG 9 TEMPERATURE AND ABSORPTION PROFILES OF TODAY'S AND PRE-FLOOD ATMOSPHERES

TABLE 1 Typical output to 20000 meters (program works to a pressure of less than .5 millibars)

TEMPERATURE PROFILE FOR PRE-FLOOD CANOPY ATMOSPHERE

Solar flux=335 W/m2   ALBEDO= 15 %   PRESSURE= 2 ATM.
ZM= 6000 m   Base of canopy= 6371 Meters
Absorption of Insolation 22 % by canopy= 73 W/m2   top layer of air= 16.75 W/m2
Absorption of lw in canopy = 20 %   39 Wm2

ALT.[m]	PRES.[mb]	TEMP.[C]	L.R.[C/Km]	LAYER #	q [W/m2]	SUPERSAT		
0.0	1983	25						
2000	1735.06	21	-2.2	1	0	----		
4000	1518.48	35	7	2	0	----		
6000	1328.93	68	16.5	3	16.75	----		
8000	1163.05	88	10.4	4	38.97	1.76	10000	1017.87
84	-2.1	5	5.7	1.82				
12000	890.81	83	-.7	6	5.57	1.68		
14000	779.61	83	.3	7	5.36	1.43		
16000	682.3	85	1	8	5.1	1.16		
18000	597.13	88	1.5	9	4.8	.9		

CONCLUSIONS

The penetration depth of water vapor was never reached in the canopy, therefore, it continued to absorb increasing amounts of energy down to its base. The excess long wave radiation, which was not absorbed in the first air layer or emitted directly to space through the atmospheric window, would also be absorbed by the first canopy layer. This was due to the canopy's increased absorption cross section as shown in Figure 8. The base of the canopy would be warmed by short and long wavelength radiation. Ozone would, no doubt, have been produced in the air layer just below the canopy by the same photochemistry as in today's atmosphere. The ozone molecules in this layer would be of greater number density than today's ozone layer, because of the mass of the canopy above, and would therefore absorb the solar energy at the ozone's absorption wavelengths quickly. This in turn helped keep the canopy base warm enough not to precipitate.

As the water vapor began to diffuse down, it would heat up due to absorption of the long wave emission from the ground and rise back into the canopy. Remember that long wave emission occurs 24 hours per day and this would keep the base of the canopy warm at night.

Because of the temperature inversion, heated air at the ground could not rise and cool as it does today, therefore, there would have been no clouds under the canopy. However, hot gases from a volcano could rise against the inversion up into the canopy, providing precipitating nuclei. The supersaturated canopy would start to rain out and the entire planet would be engulfed in a thick cloud cover. This would greatly increase the albedo of the earth which would cause it to cool. The cloud cover would persist for many weeks and this would have caused the poles to freeze.

Further Studies:

- Broaden program to allow multiple penetration depths.
- Allow for selective absorption according to wavelength and temperature.
- Detailed look at diffusion.
- Detailed look at how volcanic ash rose up into the canopy.
- Details on the collapse and how long it would take the poles to freeze.
- Evidence to show Earth's near zero angle of declination before the flood.

REFERENCES

[1] NEW AMERICAN STANDARD BIBLE, 1977.
[2] CRC HANDBOOK, 19 Ed., 1971.
[3] Wallace & Hobbs, ATMOSPHERIC SCIENCE AN INTRODUCTORY SURVEY, Academic Press, New York, NY, 1977, Fig. 7.1 p. 321.
[4] Iribarne & Cho, ATMOSPHERIC PHYSICS, D. Reidel Publishing Co., Dordrecht, Holland, 1980, p. 56.
[5] Incropera & Dewitt, FUNDAMENTALS OF HEAT TRANSFER, John Wiley & Sons, New York, NY, 1981, sections 4.4 & 4.5.
[6] Miller & Thompson, ELEMENTS OF METEOROLOGY, 2nd Ed., Merrill, Columbus, OH, 1975, p. 34.

DISCUSSION

1) The "widely accepted theory" about a meteorite impact is that discussed with dinosaur extinctions. That meteorite was supposed to be only tens of kilometers wide, hardly large enough to tilt the earth. Do you have a reference for something larger, perhaps the size of the moon?

2a) Figure 2 discussion: The incremental surface areas on the sphere are indeed equal for equal h. They are also equal to the incremental surface area on a cylinder that is tangent to the equator. But the total solar energy intercepted by the polar regions is much less than that intercepted by the equator. The solar rays that are nearly an equatorial radius away from the rotation axis in the polar regions will miss the earth completely. The total intercepted energy, for equal h, varies with the cosine of the latitude. The poles will therefore intercept less energy and be cooler.

2b) The polar regions do not receive continuous sunlight. On an untilted earth all locations will have a 12 hour day except the exact points of the two poles themselves. For the tilted earth the continuous sunlight is only for a fraction of the year for regions poleward of the arctic and antarctic circles. The poles each have a six month day and a six month night.

3) Appendix comment on albedo. Albedo is the ratio of reflected to incident radiation. Most surfaces are assumed to be "Lambertian" in simple models like yours, meaning that the albedo is independent of incidence _angle_. This is not precisely true. When you fly in an airplane, the terrain is brighter close to the shadow of the airplane because direct backscatter is greater than scatter in other directions. Glass beads in signs, road paints, and on the moon have an even higher degree of direct backscatter and appear very bright when viewed from the direction of the light source. An increased albedo from low incidence angle would result from surfaces, like water, which are more mirror-like than uniform scatterers.

4) Water vapor is a good infrared black body at the canopy temperatures you produce. The top of the canopy should therefore radiate an abundance of energy into space, making the top of the canopy much cooler than the base. Such is shown in the Dillow model and the superior Rush and Vardiman model to be presented at this conference. Your lack of such a cold top makes your simple model highly suspect. You are probably getting nice results for wrong reasons.

Edmond W. Holroyd III, Ph.D.
Arvada, Colorado

Mr. Jorgensen has taken on the same project that a number of us have -- the reconstruction of the ancient earth's climate by means of the hypothesis of a vapor canopy. He has started with a simple model that allows room for expansion in the future. However, I have several points which I feel Mr. Jorgensen needs to address.

Mr. Jorgensen claims his model is valid because without a vapor canopy it accurately reconstructs today's atmospheric temperature profile, in Figure 9. However, since he does not consider convection, he should compare his model results with a pure radiational profile, not the actual profile. a pure radiational profile will have surface temperatures at 320-330 K, and a coolest temperature at about 10 Kilometers of 170-180 K. His model does not meet these criteria, and therefore further results are immediately suspect.

In canopy research reported elsewhere in this conference (Rush and Vardiman), we divided the longwave spectrum into as many as 350 separate intervals. Applied to a canopy of 1013 mb, each and every interval showed absorption by the canopy of 100.0% of incident terrestrial radiation. This disagrees sharply with the 20% figure reported by Mr. Jorgensen in Table 1. The effect of 100% absorption was the production of a very efficient "greenhouse," which raised surface temperatures above the boiling point of water.

Also concerning Mr. Jorgensen's Table 1, he lists the base of the canopy at 6371 meters; however, in the figures just below that, he lists a pressure of about 1300 mb at 6300 meters. This would give a canopy of about 1300 mb pressure and an atmosphere of only 700 mb, instead of 1013 mb for the canopy and 1013 mb for the atmosphere. His canopy also extends well into what is now space. At 180 kilometers, he shows a canopy pressure of nearly 600 mb. Even though our atmosphere and canopy were considerably hotter than his, and therefore would show a greater tendency to expand toward space, at a level of 100 km (the "top" of our canopy), we showed a pressure of only 2 mb. Also, our canopy showed a drop in temperature with increasing altitude as is typical with increase in temperature with altitude. It is not clear how a water vapor canopy would produce this unique effect.

David Rush, B.S.
San Diego, California

Mr. Jorgensen is to be commended on developing a relatively simple model of the pre-flood atmosphere and presenting a clear description of the workings of radiation in an atmosphere. However, I have two concerns which Mr. Jorgensen should address:

1. He makes the statement at the top of the second page of his paper that, "It is the 23.5 degree angle of declination (obliquity of the ecliptic) which is mostly responsible for today's cold polar regions." I believe this statement is in serious error and should be corrected so as not to mislead other researchers in this field. The 23 1/2 degree angle that the plane through the equator makes with the plane of the earth's orbit around the sun is the cause for the _seasons_ and its magnitude determines the contrast between the seasons. If the obliquity is large, winters will be cold and summers hot; if the obliquity is small, both summers and winters are mild. But, even if the obliquity is zero - the earth's equator lies in the same plane as the earth's orbit around the sun - the polar regions will be cold and the equatorial regions hot. Further discussion of these points may be found in Hess, S.L., 1959: *Introduction to Theoretical Meteorology*, Krieger Press, pp. 131-134, 155-160, Lorenz, E.N., 1967: *The Nature and Theory of the General Circulation of the Atmosphere*, World Meteorological Organization, pp. 54-55; Sellers, W.D., 1965: *Physical Climatology*, The University of Chicago Press, pp. 19-33, 225-227.

I have prepared a graph (below) of the solar radiation as a function of latitude at equinox. These observations shown in Sellers were extracted and shown for an obliquity of 0 degrees proposed by Mr. Jorgensen. It is evident from this graph that solar heating would be a maximum at the equator and a minimum at the poles for today's atmosphere. It is _not_ true that the 23 1/2 degree obliquity is responsible for today's cold polar regions.

I believe warm polar regions likely existed in the past under vapor canopy conditions. However, this could have been true whether the earth was tilted or not due to the trapping of infrared radiation by the canopy and heating of polar regions by atmospheric and oceanic circulations.

2. The temperature distribution shown in Figure 9 shows "cool" surface temperatures and "hot" temperatures aloft, exceeding 100° to 200 km and beyond. These results, although desirable, are in disagreement with those of a much more complex model reported by Rush and Vardiman in this conference. In our results we found an isothermal temperature distribution below an assumed vapor canopy which was too hot for human habitation, if the canopy had 50 mb or more of water content. We hope adding cloud layers to our model in the future will reduce the temperature problems.

Mr. Jorgensen does not describe his initial temperature conditions, the changes in the profile as the computer model runs, or boundary conditions. Because of this I am unable to determine why there is such a discrepancy between his result and ours.

Mr. Jorgensen refers to an "atmospheric window" for long-wave radiation in his conclusions. Vardiman and Rush have found that a canopy of the mass used in this paper has no "windows" left to radiate long-wave energy to space. This may explain the difference in our results. I would be pleased to learn of a "window" we may have overlooked.

Larry Vardiman, Ph.D.
Santee, California

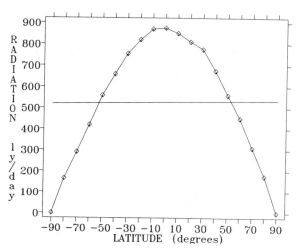

SOLAR RADIATION AS A FUNCTION OF LATITUDE AT EQUINOX

This paper begins by assuming the discredited Canopy Theory of the pre-Flood atmosphere, and builds an ingenious sophisticated mathematical and physical model on that basis.

Inasmuch as several in-depth analyses of the Canopy Theory (1) have shown it to be totally unwarranted by scripture as well as untenable by present natural laws, Mr. Jorgensen should have addressed this fact at the outset and given reasons for dismissing the strong case against the Canopy Theory in these earlier papers. Not having done so, this reviewer feels the paper is of purely academic value, regardless of its ingenuity. Furthermore, the author does not propose that the Creator operated the cosmos under a different set of natural laws before the Flood, yet the Canopy Theory clearly demands it!

(1) Whitelaw, R.L., THE FOUNTAINS OF THE GREAT DEEP AND THE WINDOWS OF HEAVEN, Science at the Crossroads, Proceedings of the National Creation Conference, Minneapolis, MN., 1983, pp. 95-104.

Robert L. Whitelaw, M.S.
Blacksburg, Virginia

CLOSURE

All comments were very helpful in revising my model. Fig.2 of the main paper states that "with no declination the pole receives the same solar energy as the equator". This statement is wrong. Even with a near zero inclination (declination is improper notation), the average energy received by the surface continually decreases to a value of zero at the poles (see Fig.2 below). The energy absorbed by the canopy was however, uniform over the entire globe or may even have increased at higher latitudes as shown in Fig.2. This enabled the canopy to remain intact.

The surface at the poles would have been frozen as shown in Fig. 1 below. This is quite contrary to the belief that at one time the entire planet was tropical. I believe now that there were ice caps at both poles under the canopy. This would answer the nagging questions about the origins of cold climate animals. They obviously did not adapt to cold climates after the flood because their physiology strongly indicates they were designed to live in cold climates. Some whales even have antifreeze in their bodies so they can survive in sub-zero salt water. The reason we see an ancient tropical climate at the poles is because of continental drift or the break-up of "Pangaea".

It has also come to my attention that the amount of water in the canopy was probably a lot less then previously reported. A careful reading of Genesis, Chapter One, verses 1 to 8 will reveal that the firmament was the oxygen and nitrogen atmosphere that God created on the second day. This means that before this, there was a water filled earth with only a water vapor atmosphere with a surface pressure dependent on the temperature of the water as shown in Table 1 below.

ANSWERS TO DISCUSSION:

Dr. Edmond W. Holroyd III

Comment 1) To my knowledge there is no direct evidence for an impact that would incline the earth to today's 23 1/2 deg., but I offer the following circumstantial evidence:

- A vapor canopy could not survive 6 months of darkness at the poles.

- A near 0 inclination would give the stable atmosphere required to keep the canopy from mixing and precipitating out.

- Many believe the year was created to be 360 days. Something massive must have hit the Earth to bring it to our present 365 days.

- A huge meteor impact would be an ideal trigger for breaking up the oceanic lithosphere required in Dr. Baumgardner's model.

- Uranus appears to have been "knocked over" 90 deg., and its core is still lagging behind. This would explain its strange magnetic field.

- Dr. Humphreys appears to need a mechanism to trigger strong convection in the Earth's core during the Deluge. Could this not have been a large meteor or even a large body passing close by the earth?

Comment 2) As stated above, Fig. 2 of the main paper is in error. Revised absorption curves are shown in Fig. 2 below.

Comment 3) Some of this backscatter at higher latitudes was absorbed by the canopy and was partly responsible for its maintenance.

Comment 4) It is true that water vapor is a good infrared black body, much higher than air. This is depicted graphically in Fig. 8 of the main paper. It is also true that water vapor is a better overall absorber of solar radiation than air. The canopy was warmer at higher altitudes for the same reasons ozone is warmer in today's atmosphere. The water vapor does take a dip in temperature at the 30,000 meter point. This is the point where the vapor may have become supersaturated and formed clouds.

Mr. David Rush

Comment 1) Does not match pure radiation curve.

I did not consider convection in my model. If there was a temperature inversion from the canopy to the ground, there would be little or no convection. This is why the canopy was so stable. In today's atmosphere, Fig.9 of the main paper, I hand fed some convection into the lower levels. When I plot a pure radiation curve and compare it to those provided by Mr. Rush, they are a close match, so I still have confidence in the equations. Now however, I believe that the canopy was high enough so that the inversion would not reach the ground. My model will have to be revised to include convection. The expected influence by convection is shown by the dashed line in Fig.1 below.

Comment 2) Errors pointed out in Table 1 as follows:

Twenty percent absorption of lw in canopy instead of 100%. Fig. 1 below is corrected to 100% absorption of lw radiation by the canopy. Base of canopy in Table 1 is in error: this is corrected in Fig.1. The 600 mb pressure is at 18 km not 180 km. My canopy now drops in temperature with height, but at 30,000 meters it starts to climb again due to solar absorption.

Dr. Larry Vardiman

Comment 1) I am in error in saying that the tilt of the earth's axis is responsible for today's cold poles.

Comment 2) The reason my model does not agree with yours is that I did not include convection. I feel however that the temperature does not have to be isothermal below the canopy because it was calm enough that the influence of convection heat transfer lagged behind the influence of radiation heat transfer. This is an area which needs some research.

- Initial conditions comment) My model gives the long-term equilibrium conditions only and is not designed to give the transient conditions to achieve this equilibrium.

- Atmospheric window comment) Fig. 1 below assumes no window.

Prof. Robert Whitelaw

Comment 1) Unwarranted by Scripture.

The Bible clearly teaches of the waters above and below the atmosphere. The created earth had no air, only water so would have had a water vapor atmosphere as described in my opening comments above.

Comment 2) Unable to exist by today's laws.

In his paper "THE FOUNTAINS OF THE GREAT DEEP AND THE WINDOWS OF HEAVEN", Prof. Whitelaw presents the following arguments as to why the canopy could not exist:

- It would diffuse to the ground in a matter of minutes) This is a common argument against the existence of the canopy, but it is simply not true. Most do not take the time to calculate it. Any fundamental book on transient mass transfer could be used to calculate it. Results show that after 2000 years little or no water vapor has diffused to the ground. These calculations ignore the gravitational field which would have helped buoy up the water vapor. Also ignored was the fact that as water molecules diffused down into the air below, they would have absorbed some long-wave radiation from below, warmed up, and rose back up into the canopy.

- Temperatures would not be high enough) It has been amply demonstrated that water vapor can be cooled, in the absence of precipitating nuclei, to -40 C.

I am confident that if we trust God's word and study the physics of a vapor canopy long enough we will come to the conclusion that it could and did exist by today's laws.

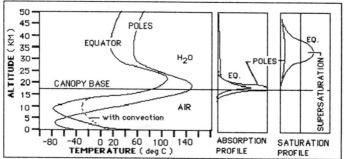

OCEAN TEMP.		CANOPY PRESSURE		
°C	°F	ft of watr	ATM	mb
100	212	34	1.00	1013
80	176	16	0.47	474
60	140	7	0.20	200
40	104	2.4	0.07	74
30	86	1.4	0.04	42
20	68	0.7	0.02	23

TABLE 1 Canopy pressure depends on Gen. 1 :1 ocean temp.

FIG 1 TEMPERATURE PROFILE FOR A 50 mb CANOPY ATMOSPHERE

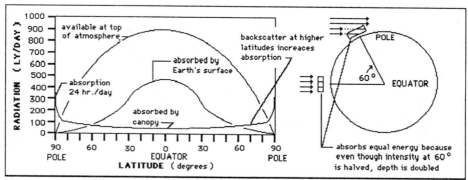

FIG 2 SOLAR ABSORPTION AS A FUNCTION OF LATITUDE FOR CANOPY & SURFACE (0° INCLINATION)

Greg S. Jorgensen, M.S.

THE PALUXY RIVER
FOOTPRINTS REVISITED

W. Fields, H. Miller, J. Whitmore,
D. Davis, G. Detwiler, J. Ditmars,
R. Whitelaw, G. Novaez

ABSTRACT

Field research by the authors at various times between 1982 and 1989 helped expose some of the elongate impressions imbedded in alleged 108 million year old Cretaceous ledges along the Paluxy River near Glen Rose, Texas. These human-like footprints were exposed in the same horizon with theropod dinosaur ichnites, as have prints in river itself over the decades, as reported by the local residents (1, 2).

In order to thoroughly document such significant discoveries, several excavations were initiated since the 1986 ICC proceedings in the search for pristine ichnites.

The results of these excavations plus the observable results of many previous excavations and the aspect ratio studies of many of the footprints strongly support the hypothesis that humans and dinosaurs coexisted. Furthermore, when radiocarbon dating results are combined with the paleoanthropological studies, the most logical conclusions are that: dinosaur extinction 65 million years ago is a myth; the long ages for sedimentary rock strata formation are non-existent; dinosaur extinction could have been caused by a major worldwide catastrophe happening perhaps only thousands of years ago.

INTRODUCTION

Field research by the authors et al. (2) at various times between 1982 and 1989 helped expose some of the 60 elongate impressions imbedded in alleged 108 million year old Cretaceous ledges along the Paluxy River near Glen Rose, Texas. They were exposed in the same horizon with distinct three toed bi-pedal dinosaur ichnites. The elongate impressions would often resemble human prints by virtue of one or more characteristics, i.e., toes or toe tips; aspect ratios equivalent to modern humans; more shallow than dinosaur prints; shorter and often more erratic stride than that of dinosaurs.

In order to thoroughly document such significant discoveries for this conference, several excavations were initiated since the 1986 ICC proceedings (3).

In October, 1986, a Creation Research Science Education Foundation (CRSEF) consultant with Carl Baugh followed badly eroded dinosaur and human-like trails under the "Kerr Island" top stratum. The last eroded elongate ichnite (40 cm long) had the front portion still protected by the top stratum; when excavated, five toes were visible in proper human-like alignment. No more ichnites of either species were uncovered when the excavation was continued another three meters by the Novaez-Davis team in April, 1988. This was considered a confirmed human trail.

The CRSEF team of 1988 excavated behind a good quality 28 cm elongate indicator print found in 1983. Two more human-like prints were excavated. Because of insufficient detail for the individual ichnites of the confirmed human-like trail of June, 1988, a more extensive excavation was carried out in August, 1989. In this instance, a trail of twelve 40 cm long elongate prints with a stride of 110 cm were revisited. This excavation was stopped in 1982; and, reportedly was protected by a 15-30 cm layer of fresh river bank sediment since the excavation. Unfortunately, a flood had torn away the protective sediment and obliterated the human-like but not the dinosaur ichnites which were deeper and more stable.

When the excavation was continued another 6 meters by the CRSEF team, the 40 cm elongate trail was discontinuous and a dinosaur trail was very shallow and barely visible in this same lithified area as where the human prints should have been. Happily, one human-like ichnite was uncovered going in the opposite direction; it was thought to have been made in a puddle of water that retarded local lithification.

We conclude that the large number of elongate impressions, combined by our own excavation experiences and aspect ratio data supports the hypothesis of human-dinosaur co-existence in time. But at what time period?

During the past 20 years, radiocarbon dates were obtained by independent teams at different laboratories. They were confirmed by this project at another laboratory in 1987. Carbonized wood for dating was excavated well back from the river between Cretaceous strata in the clay along with Coquinas in an excellent state of preservation. Measurable presence of C-14 in carbonized wood found in sedimentary rock strata cast serious doubts on the assumptions that such strata are 10's and 100's of millions of years old.

Thus, previous researchers and the good people of Glen Rose, Texas who brought these footprint discoveries to the attention of the scientific community have been vindicated. Also, the highly publicized myths of dinosaur extinction some amazing 65 million years ago along with the long ages for sedimentary rock strata, are laid to rest. Causes of recent extinctions and future research are discussed.

STRATIGRAPHY AND PALEONTOLOGY

The fossils described in this paper were found in the Glen Rose Formation along the Paluxy River at the McFall and Kerr sites. This formation is predominantely limestone bounded by sandstones: the Paluxy Formation on top and the Twin Mountains Formation on the bottom (4). These formations are part of the Cretaceous Trinity Group, which is part of the Comanchean Series. This locality consists of alternating layers of clay and limestone. The upper portion of the clay layer was shaley; the bottom marly. The study focuses on the three upper layers of rock at these sites: the top limestone layer P (30 cm thick), the middle layer of clay Q (15-20 cm thick), and the bottom layer of limestone R (Figure 1). Alternating layers of rock continue down to the river, about 2 meters below this site. P color is light brownish gray, (10 YR 6/12); Q color is olive; R color is white (10 YR 1/1).

The upper layer limestone contains 4 deep three-toed dinosaur footprints in a distinct trail. This layer does not easily erode away. The tracks have been exposed for years and have not been affected by high water levels.

During removal of the clay layer between limestone layers, several interesting fossils were found in the clay. Most common were bits and pieces of oyster Coquina and coalified vegetable material such as in Figure 1. The oysters, probably sub-family Ostreinae, were fragmented. The shells were cemented around a central core. Davis (4) mentioned an oyster reef facies in the Glen Rose limestone. These bits and pieces may be remnant parts of this facies. Vegetable remains are either coalified or carbonized plant remains. One piece, 15 cm long, 2.5 cm wide, and 0.5 cm thick, was spear shaped. This may have been a root tip of Lepidodendron. Another noted in Figure 1 and now being C-14 dated was identified as a Gymnosperm. A paleobotanist suggested either pine or spruce.

The surface of the lower limestone layer R was the main focus of this investigation. Many dinosaur tracks and trails have been found along with a significant number of human-like tracks and trails. In addition, a fish fossil and cat-like tracks have been found on this layer (displayed at the Creation Evidences Museum (CEM) in Glen Rose).

The tracks found in this layer vary in depth from deep to shallow (10 to 0.6 cm). Certainly the dinosaurs were fairly heavy and should have made deep tracks, but some of the dinosaur tracks in some trails were less distinct because of lack of depth. One explanation for shallowness could be the limestone hardened at different rates where prints were being made. One location that was setting up quickly would not have allowed deep impressions such as material that was setting up more slowly. This explains why some human trails become discontinuous in some areas where dinosaur prints become shallow.

One spurious fossil-like impression of a known configuration was exposed in very hard clay about 1 cm above layer R. When the print was later identified as truly being in the clay, it was allowed to bake several days in the hot sun; it cracked and was easily flaked away, whereas impressions in the rock neither crack nor flake away and are as hard as concrete until heavy rains or severe flooding cause erosion.

Dinosaur Fossil Ichnites

It seems odd that no one doubts that the three-toed impressions we see along the Paluxy River and elsewhere were made by these reptiles even though no one has studied the feet of a live one. However, when we view elongate impressions of the same configuration of our own feet with five toes and the same toe taper, we squeamishly call them human-like and quasihuman ichnofossils.

In 1989, the CRSEF team revisited the 1982 site where many witnesses, video tapes, press reports and documentation of several dinosaur trails and a human-like trail of an individual having a 40 cm long foot angled away from dinosaur trail B (Figure 1). These trails are examples of what is seen up and down the Paluxy on stratum R. A brief description is as follows: The B dinosaur trail tracks averaged 45 cm long, 32 cm wide, and 8 cm deep with a pace of 121 cm; there were 8.

The D dinosaur trail averaged 39 cm long, 32 cm wide, 8 cm deep and had a pace of 125 cm There were eight of these, also.

There were 13 M prints in a row with a pace of 132 cm with M-5,7,9,11 being only 0.5 to 3.5 cm deep; all were right footprints and nearer where a human-like trail should have been observed. Apparently, the rate of lithification was greater nearer the right foot of the dino and of course the expected human trail than the left foot of M. The left foot depth ranged from 2.5 to 10 cm deep except for M-12 (near M-11), which was only 1 cm deep. The average length of M was about 45 cm, and width 34 cm D and M were only 50 to 100 cm apart, but going in the opposite direction.

A Clark-size, human-like print was adjacent to the shallow M-11 dinosaur print. The Clark print, 1989-wm, was 34 cm long and about 13 cm wide at the ball, and 8 cm at the heel; and the dinosaur print M-11 was 49 cm long and about 35 cm wide. It was obvious that the human had come through first in this small patch of an area that had not yet lithified; it is interesting to note that the center toe of this dino print was relatively deep at 3.5 cm, compared to the print before and after that were 1 cm or less in depth.

One of the most important dinosaur trails was actually on the top ledge P, designated P-McF. There were 4 prints heading perpendicular from the river's edge to the river bank. What is important here is the fact that they were the only footprints of either kind on the top strata P. The average dimensions were 40 cm in length, 30 cm wide with a depth of 4 cm, and a pace of 128 cm. This rock strata has resisted six years of open weathering indicating a rock relatively free of illite clay and porosity, which cannot be said for layer R. Because of these prints, it can be said that any fossils in stratum P, Q or R were existing at the time of the dinosaurs. Such fossils include carbonized wood for C-14 dating, oyster shells, a possible human tooth and petrified human finger.

PALEOARCHEOLOGICAL MAPPING, EQUIPMENT, AND DISCUSSIONS (1989)

A team of ten investigators from Ohio, Michigan, Missouri, Texas, Oklahoma, and Kansas removed sections of a limestone layer along the Paluxy River bank near Glen Rose, Texas in August of 1989, hoping to uncover human-like fossil impressions along with the deeper dinosaur ones. We found a quality human-like footprint, and ten dinosaur ones, and exposed evidence of quickly laid, catastrophic deposits of Cretaceous sediments and clay.

The excavation was on the J.C. McFall ranch, about three miles west of Glen Rose, about a hundred yards north of the McFall house (Figure 1). The excavators used a jackhammer to break loose some sections of a hard 23 cm limestone layer P. This top layer had a distinct three-toed dinosaur trail but no human prints. The stone sections were lifted away by a backhoe. The clay was thoroughly examined for fossils; fossils were mapped and the last several centimeters of clay over layer R was removed carefully with sharpened ends of wooden instruments.

Beneath the upper limestone was a layer Q of marly and shaley clay 20 cm thick. In the clay, nearly a dozen specimens of tiny shells, oyster shells, Coquinas, carbonized wood, etc., were found. These suggest that the layer had been deposited by fast flowing watery mud that carried miscellaneous objects. Their excellent preservation suggests an unusual environment and/or short time deposition frame, which prevented complete petrification noted in layers P and R of Cretaceous limestone.

Beneath the clay layer Q was another limestone layer R which had been partially uncovered in 1982. It has at least four dinosaur trails nearby each other on its surface (B, M, D, WBB. Figure 1). This limestone contained a fish fossil (removed by Dr. Carl Baugh in 1982), suggesting a quick deposition of the material that hardened into limestone. The dinosaurs walked upon it before it lithified. A human-like trail of 40 cm prints headed downriver from dinosaur trail B. We tried to follow and confirm this trail, but it was discontinuous. Dinosaur prints, M-7, M-9, M-11, M-12, were extremely shallow, which explains why the human trail was discontinuous.

Paluxy River Excavations (1989 to 1983)

In August 1989, the lower limestone layer R, we found one dinosaur track (M-11) that had a 34 cm human-like right foot impression directly adjacent to the shallow dinosaur track. 1989-wm was 3 cm deep at the arch side and very shallow (0.6 cm) opposite; and its exact limits are not clearly visible. The dinosaur track mud up-push partly distorts one side of the man-like track. See M-11 and 1989-wm in Figure 1 photographs.

In June 1988, a team of seven investigators excavated the McFall site one meter behind fossil human-like footprint 1983-mb-2 and extending downriver about 4 meters. We could go no further into the embankment as a large shady tree impeded our progress (Figure 2).

It was predicted that one or maybe two more human ichnites could be discovered that would confirm this trail. When the excavation was completed, 1988-md-3 and 1988-md-4 were indeed identified. These discoveries fulfilled the criteria of three or more ichnites in a row required in paleontology to identify the species making said ichnites. Details will be discussed in the Anthropology section.

In April of 1988, 5 CRSEF investigators followed about 3 meters beyond an indicator 40 cm human-like impression but this trail proved discontinuous as has so many others. However, it was considered a human-like indicator trail thus justifying more research. An all terrain forklift was used at this almost river level Kerr site island across from McFall site 3 to remove the top rock.

In late October of 1986, the first independent efforts of CRSEF-led teams followed carefully mapped eroded human-like impressions. The big toe and four toe tips were observed in proper alignment on the freshly excavated anterior end of an eroded 40 cm long impression.

In 1983 and in 1984, individual CRSEF members or advisors participated in excavations in which 1983-mb-2, 1984-hb and 1984-db were discovered and documented.

ANTHROPOLOGICAL STUDIES

Aspect Ratios

In order to determine if the elongate impressions were indeed made by human beings walking through sedimentary mud, it was necessary to examine the modern human foot, both female and male, and compare them with the fossil ichnites. A podiatrist volunteered to gather the necessary data by measuring the length and widths of feet of 10 males and 10 females, as is shown in Table 1. Ratios were taken of the measurements, with deviations noted, in footnote (a) of Table 1. For females, the average R_1 aspect ratio was 2.47, and R_2 was 1.56. For males, the average R_1 aspect ratio was 2.51, and R_2 was 1.40. R_1 equals foot length divided by ball width and R_2 equals ball width divided by the heel width. There appears to be no other species with these ratios. For example, R_1 for bears ranges from 1.5 to 2.0 (Kodiak and Black bears respectively). Note that there is a significant difference between the human sexes and a relatively large deviation among females relative to males.

Now that the standards were set, the aspect ratios of the casts of the Paluxy River elongate impressions were calculated (Table 2). R_1, the length of each impression divided by the width at the ball (behind the toes), was in precise agreement with the ratios obtained by the podiatrist for modern man and woman. R_2, the width at the ball divided by the width at the heel was also in agreement.

The above comparative study confirms that these prints not only "look" human but that their aspect ratios also agree with the modern human foot.

Several of the footprints listed in Table 2 on aspect ratios had sufficient depths to offer further evidence of their obvious human source. For example, 1983-mb-2 was deepest at the ball (1.8 cm), as was 1989-wm (3.2 cm). Some prints were slide-ins or were made in mud that was almost completely lithified and therefore only permitted very shallow ichnites such as 1984-hb (0.6 cm). Even the cast of the controversial Caldwell print (1965-C) is deeper at the ball of the foot (3.2 cm) as one might expect.

158

TABLE 1:   RANDOM SAMPLING OF HUMAN FEET FOR ASPECT RATIO STUDIES (a)

	SEX	AGE, YEARS	FOOT LENGTH CM	HEEL WIDTH CM	BALL WIDTH CM
	M (10)	17 - 61	25.1 - 27.1	7.0 - 7.9	9.6 - 11.1
Average		40	26.3	7.5	10.5
	F (10)	14 - 79	21.6 - 24.3	5.2 - 7.4	8.3 - 10.8
Average		39	23.5	6.1	9.5

Aspect Ratio Formulas: R_1 = Foot length divided by ball width
R_2 = Ball width divided by heel width

(a) <u>AVERAGE</u> (R_1 and R_2)   <u>RANGE</u> (R_1 and R_2)

MALE	FEMALE	MALE	FEMALE
R_1 = 2.53	R_1 = 2.47	R_1 (2.41 - 2.5)	R_1 (2.19 - 2.84)
R_2 = 1.40	R_2 = 1.56	R_2 (1.36 - 1.45)	R_2 (1.35 - 1.86)

TABLE 2: MEASUREMENTS AND ASPECT RATIOS OF HUMAN-LIKE ICHNOFOSSILS

DATE	EXCAVATION & CASTING TEAM	FOOT (a) LENGTH CM	HEEL (a) WIDTH CM	BALL (a) WIDTH CM	OTHER HUMAN-LIKE CHARACTERISTICS
1983 -mb-2	Miller/Baugh (left foot)	27.3 R_1=2.53	7.0 R_2=1.55	10.8 R_3=2.1	5 toe tips; slight arch; toe taper and size (b)
1984 -hb	Hall/Baugh (left foot)	28.0 R_1=2.32	7.6 R_2=1.58	12.1 R_3=2.0	5 toe tips; arch; toe taper and size (c)
1965 -c	Caldwell (right foot)	38.1 R_1=2.5	10.2 R_2=1.5	15.2 R_3=2.3	5 distinct toes; good arch, toe taper and toe size (d)
1984 -db	Detwiler/Baugh (right foot)	40.0 R_1=2.5	13.5 R_2=1.19	15.9 R_3=1.9	5 toe tips; slight arch; toe taper, toe size (e)
1986 -gb	Geologist/Baugh (right foot)	40.0 R_1=2.6	12.7 R_2=1.2	15.2 R_3=NM	5 toe tips; toe taper; only toes were pristine (f)
1988 -md-3	Miller/Davis (right foot)	30.5 R_1=2.8	7.6 R_2=1.42	10.8 R_3=1.9	4 toe tips; toe tapers; tapers (g)
1988 -md-4	Miller/Davis (left foot)	30.5 R_1=4.0	7.6 R_2=NM	7.6 R_3=NM	Big toe; toe area tapers; no arch; slide-in (h)
1989 -wm	Wilson/Miller (right foot)	34.3 R_1=2.70	8.3 R_2=1.54	12.7 1.9	5 toe tips; distinct arch, toe taper and size (i)
1987 -cb	Clark/Baugh (left foot)	34.9 R_1=2.75	8.9 R_2=1.43	12.7 R_3=2.0	4 toe tips; distinct arch toe taper and size (j)
1984/ 1988 -bd	Baugh/Davis (left foot)	26.7 R_1=2.63	7.0 R_2=1.45	10.2 R_3=2.0	5 toe tips; distinct arch (k)
		R_1 Avg. =2.6	R_2 Avg. =1.45	R_3 Avg. =2.0	[1965-c & 1988-md-4 excluded]

Aspect Ratio Formulas: R_1 = Foot length divided by ball width
R_2 = Ball width divided by heel width
R_3 = Width of great toe divided by average width of other toes

<u>Footnotes to Table 2:</u>

(a) See above aspect ratio formulas. NM means not measurable.

(b) Exposed July 6, 1983 with four witnesses; location is in Figure 2. 1983-mb-2, which was 2 cm deep, was immediately cast and then recast several weeks later by a skeptic who was paid for his silicone rubber cast by one of the witnesses. In 1986, a mold of the original cast (plaster of Paris), was compared with the silicone rubber one's mold and they were identical, indicating the stability of pristine print; by 1985, the print had eroded but not beyond recognition; in the interim period, more erosion had occurred but toe taper and depth were still visible in 1988; no trace could be found due to a severe flood in 1989, which also wiped out many other human-like ichnites. The heel of 1983-mb-2 remained only 7 cm in front of the top stratum until 1988, when permission was granted to remove 1 meter more of the river bank Cretaceous stratum. A second human ichnite was discovered in front of 1983-mb-2 in 1983 and two more behind it in 1988 (md-3; md-4). This trail was perpendicular to the river and considered a confirmed human trail.

(c) This print was very shallow perhaps only 0.7 cm deep and was rather odd looking; however, the authors found a young man of 20 whose foot/toes fit into this one perfectly. Several other human-like ichnites were found near this one but all were discontinuous with no toes and were never mapped.

(d) This looks like a perfect human footprint with a mud suction uppull in the middle of arch area, but toes did not have a mud uppull which seems strange; unfortunately there appears to be little information as to its authenticity but for a geologist, Billy Caldwell, who saw and made a cast of the original after it had allegedly been cut out of the river at some undisclosed spot. It was about 2.5 cm deep at the ball.

(e) "Uncovered a 40 cm long human-like ichnite 1.3 cm deep in the same strata as dino prints 161 and 162; the sharpened end of a wooden paint brush was used as with the dino ichnites. I personally observed and participated in these discoveries. I later used my fingernails to dig at the bottom of the print to confirm to myself that it was genuine. Six casts of the print were made. During the casting, the surrounding Cretaceous limestone held up well; very little material stuck to the casts. I even put my foot into the ichnite; and, based on the toe spacing, toe taper, arch and general overall shape, I have no doubts about the print's authenticity and human characteristics (human #50)." Exposed August 4, 1984 by Detwiler/Baugh et al., as a pristine print.

(f) Six eroded human-like ichnites were observed and recorded in the river just a few feet south of the Kerr site in October, 1986. Although eroded, they had the aspect ratios of the modern human for R_1 and R_2 and ranged in length from 25 to 40 cm (one 25, three 30, two 40 cm - the same range noted for the McFall site human-like ichnites across the river and downstream). One of the 40 cm ones at what was thought to be the anterior end was unexposed. In the presence of a witness, the consulting geologist removed the remaining upper stratum and discovered five toe tips in the proper toe taper. This is considered confirmation of a trail, because toes were predicted to be found and they were indeed. Because this trail proved discontinuous when excavated another 3 meters in April of 1988, it was decided to try to confirm several other trails on the McFall site that had not been thoroughly authenticated. In this manner, two or more trails would help confirm the coexistence of dinosaur and humans; and in conjunction with the study of the aspect ratios of 5 or more individual fossil human-like ichnites, would provide statistical evidence for such a hypothesis.

(g) This print was excavated 10 cm to the rear and 45 cm downstream from 1983-mb-2. It was the fourth in a series of a right-left-right-left trail. The whole alleged trail gives the appearance of a human slipping and sliding in the mud as he or she fights to keep their balance or avoid something. Because the width of the four toes was the same as that for 1983-mb-2 we concluded it was made by the same individual.

(h) This print was excavated behind 1988-md-3's heel about 20 cm and to the right 20 cm. It might not have been a print but was considered so because the anterior had the correct toe taper and a possible great toe of a "left" foot. There is a small dinosaur print that appeared to have stepped into the "heel" area of this print. The crossover steps that this trail suggests is characteristic of the agility of human beings. A human-like impression only 1.4 cm deep and 40 cm long (no toes) was also excavated 4 meters away.

(i) 1989-wm was the only print found by our team this summer, even though we were allowed to remove 20 sq. m of layer P. It was an excellent human-like ichnite because of the distinct great toe, arch, heel and 4-toe tips in typical human-like taper. It was thought to have been made in a residual puddle of water which retarded lithification. It was adjacent to a much shallower (.64 cm) dinosaur impression which was made after the human-like print was made. Differing rates of lithification is the greatest problem researchers have at both the McFall and Kerr sites in discovering continuous trails. It is interesting to note that 1989-wm matches 1987-cb.

(j) 1987-cb was excavated across from the Kerr site, at McFall site 3, and appears to be a part of what is called the "Clark prints" as was 1989-wm. The aspect ratios seem to be very close as well as the lengths and width of each print. 1989-cb was a right foot and 1987-cb a left; both had very distinct big toes. A large, very distinct dinosaur footprint along with several human prints of other dimensions were found in a discontinuous pattern in this McFall site 3 some 100 meters upstream from site 1. 1987-cb is the only one that had toes at this site. The large dino impression had a mud uppull behind the center digit (like in the big toe of the 1987-cb human print). 1987-cb print was about 1.9 cm deep and the dinosaur print about 6.4 cm deep.

(k) This was a rediscovered print of the same size as 1983-mb-2 which was later ascertained to have been excavated in 1984 by CEM teams but was not recorded on the maps because it was discontinuous. It was eroded but had been protected by newly formed deposited sediment so toe impressions, arch and depth, were readily observed. Consequently, our casting manager made a cast. Later, it was totally eroded by the severe 1989 flooding that destroyed the 1982 trail of a 40 cm long human-like footprint sequence.

Other Aspect Ratios and Summary

Another interesting aspect ratio included in Table 2 was R-3: the ratio of the width of the great toe over the average width for the other toes. Ratio-4: the length from the tip of the big toe to the middle of the arch over the length from the mid-arch to the end of the heel is also discussed below.

In case of R-3, the ratio of the authors toes were 2.0 ± 0.1 and that of the Paluxy ichnites were easily the same, even though only the great toe and four toe tips were visible on most fossil ichnites.

In case of R-4, the ichnites containing quality arch impressions matched measurements for the modern human feet of about 1.3. The two Clark ichnites, 1987-cb and 1989-wm were prime examples of the investigators' ease in identifying these two ichnites as decidedly human in their origin and as prints made by the same individual. Differences existed between sexes.

Even 1983-mb-2 and 1988-md-3 could be shown to have been made by the same human individual, even though only the great toe and three toe tips were visible on 1988-md-3 as it slithered through a dinosaur tail balancing impression. We measured the width at the outer edge of the great toe to the outer edge of the fourth toe on each fossil ichnite and it was 8.8 cm. The toe tips were also close enough in width to identify the same person as having made this human-like trail.

This anthropological section can perhaps best be summarized by describing the eight pristine foot prints from Table 2 in the paleontological method of describing an alleged newly discovered species in the fossil record to see if it matches a known species. 1965-C is eliminated from consideration because of its lack of pristine or original data; 1988-md-4 is eliminated from consideration because it had only an elongate nature and proper toe taper at its anterior (but no confirmed toe tips). This description is as follows: elongate impressions in Cretaceous rock with the appearance of the modern human foot having as a rule a distinct great toe plus four smaller toe tips in the proper length, width and toe taper including a great toe pointing forward and not to the side as do the lower primates; the great toe almost always present in full extension with other toes as toe tips as would be expected for the human foot and weight distribution; the ball of the foot leaving a deeper impression than other areas when the species made a 2 cm deep impression; the presence of a human-like arch in some but not all impressions; a distinct heel in almost all ichnites, but the most eroded ichnite indicators (Kerr site); mathematical study using 4 aspect ratios in precise range of modern human foot whether using the techniques developed by the authors of this paper or that of Napier (8); trails left by these ichnites implies the source as having the same gait and directional agility for change as do modern humans.

The conclusion is inescapable. We have not found a new species. We have discovered homo sapiens making tracks with dinosaurs. For the details of each of the 10 ichnites, please refer to the extensive footnotes to Table 2.

Data from our measurements of man-like footprints up to 28 cm in length, fall within the minimum/maximum ranges of bare footprint measurements made by Dr. Louise Robbins (6). She sampled 514 subjects over 14 years old. Since some of our fossil ichnites exceed the 30.6 cm maximum length of Robbins' statistical group, we could not compare our data with hers beyond that point. Robbins is a professor of physical anthropology, a forensic footprint expert, and she has measured the Laetoli hominid footprints for Dr. Mary Leakey (Figure 2).

161

Our footprint ratios and ranges, based on our random sampling of human feet (Table 1), show sexual differentiation. This agrees with Robbins' finding that it is possible to project the probable sex of individuals making footprints.

We chose our reference points for measuring human and fossil footprints with the aim of establishing aspect ratios peculiar to man, like the indices by Napier (8) and Grieve and Gear (5). Other researchers (1, 2) have documented the Clark and Taylor trails using grid-contour gauges and computer graphics to enhance the accuracy of determining the identity of the footprint maker. Future research might employ the standardized human foot landmarks designated by Robbins (6), as well as her grid.

Sasquatch (Bigfoot)

It has been suggested, sometimes in jest, sometimes in all seriousness, that the often very large (12" - 16" long) elongate ichnites observed on the McFall sites along the Paluxy River could have been made by the illusive "Sasquatch." Grover Krantz, in his excellent study (7) of footprints made by this "new animal" has provided some very interesting casts made of such alleged creatures which roam the State of Washington and are reported in many other parts of the USA and the world. To see if this "Bigfoot" explanation for the Paluxy ichnites could be true, we compared the human footprint parameters of modern man with that of the human-like ichnites of the Paluxy River and that of the "Sasquatch" casts, as follows:

	Aspect Ratios	Modern Man	McFall Site Human-like Ichnites	Alleged Sasquatch Cast
I	(L/W at toes)	2.5	2.6	1.9 ± 0.1
II	(W at toes/W at heels)	1.47	1.45	2.0 ± 0.2
III	(W at great toe/ W at other toes	2.0	2.0	1.3 ± 0.2
	No. of Toes, size	Great toe plus 4 smaller ones	Same as modern man	Great toe plus 4 same size
	Dermal Ridges	Yes	None detected along Paluxy	Yes, in 0.01 mm sized loess
	Arch	Yes, varies flat to high	Yes, not always distinct	Distinct flat arch
	Toe angularity	Very angular	Same as modern man	Nearly straight

As seen from the available data above, the alleged Sasquatch or its progenitor evidently is not the maker of the human-like footprints at the McFall site.

RADIOCARBON DATING

As the Paluxy Project slowly matured and data was collected, the authors came across a report by Bierle and Fields, et al., (9) which discussed the discovery of an eight foot long tree limb imbedded in the Cretaceous limestone of the Paluxy River. Bierle had his specimen dated at 12,800 B.P. Morris, in his book (1), listed dates for other specimens collected from among the Paluxy rocks, all of which are listed in Table 3 as specimens no. 1, 2, and 3.

As a result of this fascinating information, we looked for an opportunity to radiocarbon date a suitable specimen ourselves. That time came in February 1987, in front of some 20 witnesses who had been invited to observe an excavation for human-like footprints at McFall site 3. As the clay between Cretaceous strata was being carefully removed and inspected for fossils, Dr. Baugh uncovered a 16 cm by 3 cm piece of carbonized wood, possibly a leaf or root of the Lepidodendron. Paluxy Project representatives asked for and Dr. Baugh generously gave us this wood. Several months later, other material was collected by our consulting geologist at the dinosaur burial site 5 km upriver, and both were radiocarbon dated, giving values of 37,480 B.P. and 45,920 B.P. (specimens 8 and 7 respectively), on

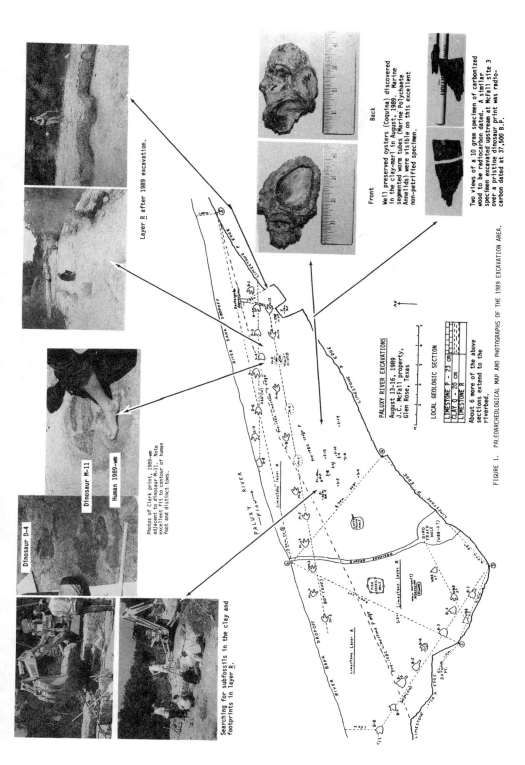

FIGURE 1. PALEOARCHEOLOGICAL MAP AND PHOTOGRAPHS OF THE 1989 EXCAVATION AREA.

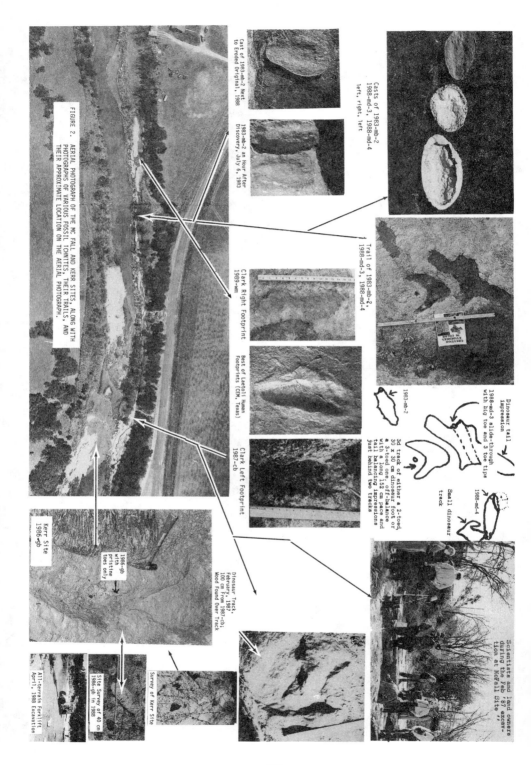

FIGURE 2. AERIAL PHOTOGRAPH OF THE MC FALL AND KERR SITES, ALONG WITH PHOTOGRAPHS OF VARIOUS FOSSIL ICHNITES, THEIR TRAILS, AND THEIR APPROXIMATE LOCATION ON THE AERIAL PHOTOGRAPH.

Casts of 1983-mb-2 Next to eroded Original, 1988
left, right, left

1988-md-3, 1988-md-4

1983-mb-2 an Hour After Discovery, July 6, 1983

Trail of 1983-mb-2, 1988-md-3, 1988-md-4

Clark Right Footprint 1989-wm

Best of Leetoli Human Footprints (CEM, Texas)

Clark Left Footprint 1987-cb

1988-md-3 slide-through with big toe and 3 toe tips

Dinosaur tail impression

1983-mb-2

3d track of either a 2-toed, 30 x 30 cm dinosaur foot or a 3-toed one, off-balance with a long 152 cm pace and tail dragging impression just behind two tracks

1988-md-4

Small dinosaur track

Kerr Site 1986-gb

1986-gb with pristine toes only

Dinosaur Track, February, 1985, From 1987-cb; 100 cm Wood Found Over Track

Survey of Kerr Site

Site Survey of 40 cm 1986-gb in 1988

All-terrain Forklift April, 1988 Excavation

Scientists and land owners during the Feb '87 excavation at McFall Site

164

TABLE 3: RADIOCARBON DATES FOR PALUXY RIVER STRATA AND PARALLEL PUBLISHED DATES OF INTEREST

	SPECIMEN/ REFERENCE (a)	WHERE FOUND	RADIOCARBON DATES YEARS. B.P.(b)	COMMENTS
1.	Carbonized wood	Taylor Site	38,000	1969
2.	Carbonized wood	Taylor Site	39,000	1969
3.	Charcoal	River bottom	12,800	1978
4.	Dinosaur coprolyte	Parker Ledge	39,500	1986
5.	Dinosaur bone	ditto	36,500+	1987
6.	Dinosaur pelvic bone fragments	ditto	32,400+ (c)	1989
7.	Coalified wood	ditto	45,920 +5550/-3250	1987
8.	Carbonized wood	McFall Ledge, clay	37,480 +2950/-2140	1987
9.	G-N - 1495, 2022 Neanderthal bones	Iraq, Libya, and Morocco	50,600; 40,700; 32,000+	Same age as most Paluxy dates
10.	UCLA-285, human and animal bones	Taban cave Phillipines	21,000	In between Paluxy specimens 3 and 4
11.	Y-103, skull	Florisbad, S. Africa	35,000+	Same age as most Paluxy dates
12.	UCLA-1292, Sabre tooth tiger femur	La Brea, CA tarpits	28,000	Roughly same as most Paluxy dates
13.	N-141-3, extinct fauna and flora fossils	Japan	29,300- 37,000	Same dates as extinct mammals and dinosaurs
14.	H-145, mammoth bone	Heidelberg, Germany	3,370	Supports post flood existence of mammoths
15.	Pi-75, calcareous petrified wood	Italy	10,090	Dating of some petrified wood possible
16.	L-228, fossil wood	Miocene sandstone, Washington State	27,000+	Wood in sandstone of 5 to 24 million B.P.
17.	C-580, carbonized wood	Moto, Angola	11,189	Carbonized - younger than Paluxy wood
18.	C-577, burned bone	France	11,109 ± 480	Example using bone to date stratum (d)
19.	Charcoal with bones of mammals	Texas, USA	37,000+	Elephants, horses, antelopes, etc.

(a) Specimens 11, 14, 16 in SCIENCE (1957-1962); Specimens 9, 10, 12, 13, 15, 17, 18, 19 in RADIOCARBON (vol. 1-10). Paluxy references 1 through 8 will be provided upon project completion.

(b) These dates are based on the assumption of $T_{\frac{1}{2}}$ = 5568 years and not corrected for difference between SPR and SDR (11). When corrected using difference between radiocarbon 14 production and decay rates (specific) as reported by Libby (10), as shown by Whitelaw (11), the dates over 10,000 B.P. can be corrected to alleged true dates ranging from 6,000 to 7,000 B.P.

(c) This specimen and perhaps another one will also be radiocarbon dated by the accelerated mass spectrometer.

(d) This is an example of using bone to date directly as has been done with CEM's dinosaur bones; this sample had "sufficient organic material obtained by acid dissolution."

equipment that had a sensitivity of 55,000 B.P. A similar carbonized wood specimen from McFall site 1 excavated 100 meters away will be radiocarbon dated also.

Dinosaur dung (coprolyte) and bone were radiocarbon dated at 39,500 plus and 36,500 plus B.P. (specimens 4 and 5). Dinosaur bone fragments (specimen 6) were dated by our team in 1989 at 32,400 plus B.P. The reliability of Paluxy area radiocarbon dates is considerably enhanced by dating four types of material: dinosaur coprolyte and pelvic bone fragments, and charcoal and carbonized wood. It has been suggested that the black to brown surface of the radiocarbon dated bones is due to the absorption of the dinosaur decay products. Indeed, when we scraped one gram from the bone surface, and analyzed quantitatively, significant carbon and hydrogen were discovered. The dark staining was limited to the limestone stratum encasing the dinosaur bones and the clay immediately above. Thus, it appears that the staining of the bones, etc., was due to the decomposition of dinosaur flesh.

The radiocarbon date of each specimen was then corrected by the Libby method as described in Table 3. This correction simply makes use of the fact, which Libby himself recorded (10), that the specific production rate of C-14 today in the earth's biosphere exceeds the specific decay rate so that ancient dead matter had a much lower specific activity (dis/min-gm) at the moment of death than it does today.

What then does all this mean? According to Whitelaw (11), assuming that the original carbon in these specimens had not been contaminated by alien carbon from more ancient dead vegetation, these dates signify wood, vegetation, or carbon-bearing animal matter that died a few centuries after creation and was already buried or otherwise preserved, when a catastrophe (noted in traditions of many civilizations), preserved it in sedimentary strata.

However, because radiocarbon dating is more difficult to interpret beyond 5,000 years, we truly cannot say exactly when the Glen Rose strata was deposited. All we can say is that human and dinosaurs were making tracks together during periodic and perhaps catastrophic deposition of thick, Cretaceous sediments. More research is required to determine whether the depositions resulted from catastrophic or non-catastrophic tidal flooding.

Table 3 also lists selected published radiocarbon dates that apply to the research that is being conducted along the Paluxy River. For example, Neanderthal skeletons have been dated from 32,000 up to 50,600 B.P., which are the same ages for the dinosaur and carbonized wood specimens from along the Paluxy. Calcareous petrified wood and carbonized wood specimens have both been radiocarbon dated. Fossil wood in Miocene strata shows a young date for ancient rock; and, coexistence of horses, elephants and antelope with dinosaurs and man is suggested by the date 37,000+ B.P. near Dallas, Texas.

FOSSIL ICHNITE DISCOVERIES AND THEIR CREDIBILITY

Texas, USA

This state seems to have more than its share of human-like fossil ichnites. The Paluxy River area provides the most sites which are scientifically discussed by Morris (1). Although most of these ichnites have been subject to erosion, and their credibility challenged by being confused with dinosaur ichnites, Morris has remained skeptical but extremely interested. He also recorded some very interesting C-14 dates from carbonized wood of the Paluxy River strata (1).

Baugh (2) has provided the main impetus in keeping alive the interest in the fossil ichnites along the Paluxy by concentrating on the strata well above the river and exposing pristine footprints. In his doctorate dissertation, he has documented 60 human-like fossil ichnites with over 200 dinosaur prints. One of his criteria for determining genuine human footprints is the aspect ratios of fossil ichnites, which is also used by others (6). He discusses the different trails he and his fellow workers have excavated under the top stratum as well as the famous Taylor and Ryals trails and other famous individual ichnites of alleged human origin. To the above he has added computer generated graphs of many fossil human ichnites that add even more credibility to an already overwhelming body of evidence supporting human-dinosaur coexistence. A human-like tooth and finger have also been thoroughly studied by Baugh, which were found in the clay-marl and limestone rock itself respectively. He also C-14 dated dinosaur fossils. It is fortunate for all interested in the study of origins that Dr. Carl Baugh decided to move to the Paluxy area to continue to study the phenomenon of possible Cretaceous human occupation since his initial major discoveries in 1982.

There have also been reports of fossil human ichnites in other locations in Texas including a serious one in the Trinity River in downtown Ft. Worth, Texas (12), and near a nuclear electric generator facility near Glen Rose, Texas.

Arizona, USA

In a two part paper (13) Rosnaw, Howe, et al., have begun a very serious study of surface impressions resembling dinosaur, human and mammals in Arizona. These are located in the Kayenta of Arizona and Tuba City. Although these researchers are not positive in their conclusions, they have established a set of seven criteria which are worthy of all serious researchers to follow. It would seem to us that the evidence which Baugh has provided in his dissertation has met all seven criteria for the human-like ichnofossils which are: size range, shape, many prints confirmed trails of three or more prints of normal human stride and gait, good internal detail (toes, etc.) prints bordered by mud (now rock) up-push and finally fossil human bones.

Connecticut, USA

In 1858, Hitchcock (14) mentions some interesting human-like fossil ichnites in the Connecticut Valley. In 1988, Whitmore (15) discussed these prints and those of dinosaurs in his masters thesis on the Hartford Basin. Hitchcock interpreted some of the dinosaur-like footprints as actually being birds, which if true, would be out of place fossils. Obviously, this is an area that requires more study also.

Turkmenia, USSR

We were very pleased to have been able to trace this rumor of human dinosaur coexistence through a fellow investigator of the Paluxy footprints from the Pittsburgh area. He had read about it in a brief abstract. A note to the author got us a copy of the original article (16), which stated that "Impressions resembling in shape a human footprint were discovered next to the tracks of the prehistoric animals." Some 1500 dinosaur prints had been observed on the surface rocks designated the "Mesozoic era or 150 million B.P."

The scientist involved responded to our Paluxy data two years later and if the current thaw in international relationships holds up we will invite this gentleman to our next excavation. Petrified dinosaur bones of two dinosaurs were excavated about three miles upstream from the major footprint sites along the Paluxy also indicating a catastrophe as in the Russian report, which also claims that "not far from the clearings with the dinosaur tracks we found heaps of stones, resembling dinosaur skeletons," etc. In another article, 86 horse-like footprints were observed in alleged 90 million year old strata but also not confirmed. We believe that a thorough mathematical study of modern mammalian feet as has been done by Baugh and the authors of this paper for human-like ichnofossils could be very productive in identifying hard to understand ichnofossils. There are more than enough fossil ichnites the world over to justify thorough investigations of their credibility, as this project has done.

CONCLUSIONS AND FUTURE RESEARCH

No one has disputed that the dinosaur tracks found at the Paluxy River sites are genuine. It is now time to recognize that the human-like ichnites, by virtue of meeting the most stringent of criteria, are indisputably human. Their credibility is significantly enhanced by repeated fresh discoveries in a pristine condition by many scientists as well as the stringent criteria of size, shape, aspect ratios, five toe configuration associated with the feet of living human beings. Evolutionary theorists might conclude that both species coexisted less than 3 million years ago; geologists conclude beyond 100 million years ago.

However, radiocarbon dates for coprolyte, wood, and bone discovered in and between rock layers containing dinosaur tracks demonstrate that dinosaurs were alive and plentiful only ten's of thousands of "radiocarbon" years B.P. Therefore, the most logical conclusions are that at least the Neanderthal and Cro-Magnon people coexisted with the dinosaurs; and, that the 100 million year old Cretaceous rock strata are only thousands of years old and did not take millions of years to form as the Mt. St. Helens experience and laboratory data attest.

The above underlined conclusions, along with massive Cretaceous and other sediments, conjures up the catastrophe noted frequently in many ancient civilizations - a worldwide flooding, perhaps coinciding with other catastrophes. Whether or not a flood was occurring at the time of the Paluxy sedimentation, the very fact of dinosaur coexistence with humans raises the possibility of recent asteroid and comet impaction with the earth. Asteroids could be an indirect cause of massive extinctions only thousands of years ago, not 65 million (17, 18, 19, 20, 21). Both scientists and news media are making much of an asteroid near miss in 1989, another one in 1937, and the famous Tunguska explosion in Siberia in 1908; all of which were undetected until after the fact. Therefore, we would be remiss if we failed to point out the compelling need for expanding asteroid monitoring projects in light of our conclusions. Perhaps technology now exists for attaching rockets to asteroids on a catastrophic collision course with the earth, thus altering their orbit.

Many thanks to all who have had the wisdom to support this project. Future research will include applying forensic, and two and three dimensional modeling techniques (22), to human and mammal ichnofossils; continued study of dinosaur bone fragments for radiometric dating; excavating seven strata during one major excavation; and determining rate of deposition of sedimentary layers and specific time periods.

REFERENCES

1. Morris, J.D., TRACKING THOSE INCREDIBLE DINOSAURS, AND THE PEOPLE WHO KNEW THEM, Master Books, 1984, Third Edition, 238 pp.

2. Baugh, Carl E., CRETACEOUS HUMAN OCCUPATION, Pacific College of Graduate Studies, Melbourne, Australia, 1989, 357 pp.

3. Miller, H., THE DISCOVERY OF QUASI-HUMAN ICHNOFOSSILS IN THE GLEN ROSE DOLOMITE, PALUXY RIVER, TEXAS, for Office for Research on Origins, Proceedings of the International Conference on Creationism, Vol. II, 1986, pp. 227-232.

4. Davis, Keith W., "Stratigraphy and Depositional Environments of the Glen Rose Formation, North Central Texas", BAYLOR GEOLOGICAL STUDIES, Bulletin No. 26, Baylor University, Waco, Texas, 1974, 27 pp.

5. Grieve, D.W., Gear, R.J., THE RELATIONSHIP BETWEEN LENGTH OF STRIDE, STEP FREQUENCY, TIME OF SWING AND SPEED OF WALKING FOR CHILDREN AND ADULTS, Ergonomics 5, 1985, pp. 379-399.

6. Robbins, Louise M., FOOTPRINTS, COLLECTION, ANALYSIS AND INTEGRATION, Charles C. Thomas Publisher, 1985, pp. 14-24.

7. Krantz, Grover S., ANATOMY AND DERMATOGLYPHICS OF THREE SASQUATCH FOOTPRINTS, Cryptozoology, Vol. 2, 1983, pp. 53-81.

8. Napier, J.R., BIGFOOT: THE YETI AND SASQUATCH IN MYTH AND REALITY, E.P. Dutton Publishers, 1973.

9. Beierle, Frederick P., et al., A NEW KIND OF EVIDENCE FROM THE PALUXY, Creation Research Society Quarterly, Vol. 16, 1979, pp. 87-88, 131.

10. Libby, Willard F., RADIOCARBON DATING, The University of Chicago Press, Second Edition, 1955, 175 pp.

11. Whitelaw, R.L., TIME, LIFE AND HISTORY IN THE LIGHT OF 15,000 RADIOCARBON DATES, Creation Research Society Quarterly, Vol. 7, 1970.

12. McConal, Jon, "Footprints Imbedded in Man's Memory" , Fort Worth Star, early 1980's.

13. Rosnau, Paul O. and Howe, George F., et al., ARE HUMAN AND MAMMAL TRACKS FOUND TOGETHER WITH THE TRACKS OF DINOSAURS IN THE KAYENTA OF ARIZONA, Creation Research Society Quarterly, Vol. 26, 1989, pp. 77-98

14. Hitchcock, Edward, ICHNOLOGY OF NEW ENGLAND, William White, Printer to the State, Boston, Massachusetts, 1858, 220 pp.

15. Whitmore, John H., THE HARTFORD BASIN OF CENTRAL CONNECTICUT: AN EVALUATION OF UNIFORMITARIAN AND CATASTROPHIC MODELS, Masters Thesis, Institute for Creation Research, Santee, California, 1988, pp. 58-100.

16. Romashko, Alexander, TRACKING DINOSAURS, Moscow News, No. 24, 1983, p. 10.

17. Austin, Steven A., CATASTROPHES IN EARTH HISTORY, ICR Technical Monograph 13, Institute for Creation Research, 1984, pp. 37-68.

18. Chapman, Clark R., AN ASTEROID OUT THERE MAY HAVE EARTH'S NAME ON IT, The Columbus Dispatch, January 7, 1990, p. 7H; TARGET EARTH: IT WILL HAPPEN, Sky and Telescope, March, 1990, pp. 261-265.

19. Randell, Teri, CRATER CALLED 'SMOKING GUN' OF DINOSAUR EXTINCTION, The Columbus Dispatch, July 30, 1989, p. 9B.

20. Holt, Henry, EARTH HAS 'CLOSE' ENCOUNTER, Columbus Dispatch, April 20, 1989.

21. Patten, Donald W., THE BIBLICAL FLOOD AND THE ICE AGE EPOCH, Pacific Meridian Publishing Co., Seattle, WA, 1966, 336 pp.

22. Walsh, R.E. and Brooks, C.L., TWO-DIMENSIONAL COMPUTER QUANTIFICATION OF FOOTPRINTS IN SEDIMENTARY LAYERS, Proceedings of the Modeling and Simulation Conference, University of Pittsburgh, Vol. 14, Part 1, pp. 41-45, 1983.

The radiocarbon ages from Paluxy samples reported in Table 3 are nearly all near the practical upper range of normal radiocarbon measurement apparatus. Such dates are very sensitive to contamination by modern carbon. The Paluxy site seems to be far from impervious to percolation by ground water bearing modern organic substances (e.g. humic acid) which could easily provide a source of modern contamination. Consequently, these dates should only be regarded as a lower limit on the radiocarbon age of the various samples. Thus, the only legitimate conclusion from the collective data set for the Paluxy samples is that it indicates an age for the associated strata greater than about 30,000 radiocarbon years Before Present. The conclusion that these radiocarbon dates demonstrate the youthfulness of the Paluxy strata is not warranted. In terms of a creationist model of the past, these radiocarbon results (when considered in isolation from their stratigraphic position) are only sufficient to conclude that the respective organisms died at some point in time prior to about five hundred years following the Flood (Aardsma, this conference).

Gerald E. Aardsma, Ph.D.
Santee, California

There are many flaws in this paper and I do not have space to detail all of them.

<u>The Tracks</u> Figure 1 shows a person's foot in an alleged human track. The map given below the photograph clearly shows that the alleged human track is the print of one toe of a three-toed dinosaur that is part of a long trackway. Close inspection of the photograph reveals the other two toe prints of the dinosaur track. The measurements given for the alleged human tracks are well within the range of dinosaur toes but match no humans known from any time. Where are the bones of humans that would make footprints 40 cm long? The aspect ratios prove nothing when measured on part of a track (a dinosaur toe print) instead of the entire track. Measuring just one toe print may yield numbers like those of humans, but they mean nothing. Furthermore, measuring a series of such toes will yield similar measurements, but they still do not indicate any affinity with humans. Also, note how the dinosaur tracks occur in trackways (right, left, right, left, . . .) but the "human" tracks do not.

Five toes does not a human footprint make. Farlow (1987, Figure 18) illustrates a number of sauropod dinosaur hand and foot skeletons that have five digits. Langston (1979; reproduced as Figure 9 in Farlow, 1987; see enclosures) has shown how a dinosaur footprint can come to superficially resemble a human footprint through loss of details in sediment layers above and below the actual track surface. Human-like tracks can also be made by the impression of the distal metatarsus of a dinosaur that normally kept that part off the substrate (Figure 39 of Farlow, 1987). Kuban (1989a, 1989b) has shown other ways in which man-like tracks could be produced by dinosaurs. None of the alleged human tracks shown in this article are convincing; even the one from Laetoli is such a poor photograph that the identity of its maker is questionable. How odd that the recent 454 page book on dinosaur footprints (Gillette and Lockley, 1989) is not cited even once. This shows either a lack of familiarity with the real scientific literature or a deliberate attempt to suppress information unfavorable to the Creationist view.

<u>Radiocarbon Dates</u> The wood that was radiocarbon dated came from <u>loose</u> clay, not from the rocks containing the footprints. To believe that they were contemporaneous demonstrates a lack of scientific skepticism. Shale layers between hard limestones can weather, disintegrate, and be washed away, leaving a space for more recent material to be washed in, especially near a river such as the Paluxy. No evidence was presented that the dated "dinosaur bone" and "dinosaur coprolite" were in fact from dinosaurs. Furthermore, the references of Table 3 are unacceptable vague, e.g., "SCIENCE 1957-1962" and "RADIOCARBON (vol. 1-10)". Specific dates must have specific references, giving author, year, volume and page. Without such references, the table is useless.

<u>Conclusion</u> Dinosaurs have been known scientifically since the 1820's. Their fossilized bones have been excavated from <u>hundreds</u> of sites <u>worldwide</u>. Scientists have collected <u>hundreds</u> of skeletons and <u>thousands</u> of bones of dinosaurs of many sizes from many different paleoenvironments. **No fossil human bones have every been found with dinosaur bones.** Furthermore, dinosaur bones have never been found with bones of horses, cows, sheep, goats, pigs, chickens, dogs, cats, or any other large vertebrate known to be contemporaneous with humans. These facts cannot be ignored, and it will take more than a few questionable interpretations of footprints to even suggest, much less prove, that humans were contemporaries of the dinosaurs. This kind of pseudoscience does nothing for the Creationist cause, and it is time that such efforts be directed into more productive areas of research. There are no human footprints in the Paluxy limestones.

REFERENCES:

Farlow, J.O., 1987. A Guide to Lower Cretaceous Dinosaur Footprints and Tracksites of the Paluxy River Valley, Somerville County, Texas. Field trip guidebook, South-Central Section, Geological Society of America. Baylor University, 50 pp.

Gillette, D.D., and Lockley, M.G. (eds.), 1989. Dinosaur Tracks and Traces. Cambridge University Press, N.Y., 454 pp.

Kuban, G.J., 1989a. Elongate Dinosaur Tracks in Gillette and Lockey, Dinosaur Tracks and Traces. Cambridge University Press, N.Y., pp. 57-72.

Kuban, G.J., 1989b. Color Distinctions and Other Curious Features of Dinosaur Tracks Near Glen Rose, Texas in Gillette and Lockley, Dinosaur Tracks and Traces. Cambridge University Press, N.Y., pp. 427-440.

Langston, W., Jr., 1979. Lower Cretaceous dinosaur tracks near Glen Rose, Texas. pp. 39-61 in B.F. Perkins and W. Langston, Jr., (eds.), Lower Cretaceous Shallow Marine Environments in the Glen Rose Formation: Dinosaur Tracks and Plants. Field Trip Guidebook, American Association of Stratigraphic Palynologists, Annual Meeting, Dallas (revised 1983).

Dale M. Gnidovec, Ph.D.
Columbus, Ohio

This paper has been master fully conceived and well executed. Glen Kuban left the impression with many people that the Taylor tracks, and by inference, all Paluxy tracks are simply dinosaur prints that within a few years will develop colored points at their tips. Would these authors be well advised to reference Kuban's paper(s) and tell the reader what relationship their work has to his?

Would it be wise to list where the authors had their C-14 dates done? I couldn't tell on table 3 or in the text who did the C-14 work.

Can the authors get an exact date for ref. #16?

George J. Howe, Ph.D.
Newhall, California

Since I am a specialist only in the fields of applied (toxicological/pharmacological) biochemistry and molecular biology, I have a possibility to evaluate only a few aspects of the paper by Dr. Fields, et.al., namely the aspects closed to analytical chemistry (correctness of the methods, calculations and techniques for chemical analyses of the samples studied).

I would like to note the following:

1) A review on radiocarbon dates has a representative list of references for well-known publications of the authors who have used adequate types of physical/chemical techniques for dating (both in respect of chemical treatment of the samples and mathematical treatment of the data).

2) The general conclusions of the paper look correct and well-argued in the physico-chemical aspects.

3) The forthcoming perspectives of this or similar research are interesting and very important.

Dmitri A. Kuznetsov, M.D., Ph.D., D.Sc.
Moscow, Soviet Union

It is doubtful that much of scientific merit can be extracted from this paper:

1)   The paper lacks a proper site description, as it lacks:

a) a formal description of the rocks involved.

b) a stratigraphic column of relationship for the rocks involved.

c) a proper map (with scale, orientation, etc.) of the location and orientation of all the prints alluded to.

2) The paper lacks a proper excavation description, as it lacks:

a) a complete list of the precise dates of excavation (e.g. for 1987-cb, 1984-hb, and 1984/88-bd).

b) a complete list of the excavators and witnesses.

c) descriptions of the various excavation procedures.

3) The paper lacks a proper description of the prints found, as it lacks:

a) a complete list of the prints located (e.g. the 'several human prints' found near 1987-cb of note j).

b) adequate photographic documentation of the prints located (e.g. the 'several human prints' near 1987-cb of note j, the impression 4 meters from 1988-mb-3 and -4 of note h, the five 'eroded human-like ichnites' near 1986-gb of note f, and 1984/1988-bd).

c) an adequate description of the method(s) employed to photograph and measure the prints.

d) orientation information on the prints.

e) complete depth information (e.g. 1983-mb-1, the prints excavated in 1986, the 'several' near 1987-cb of note j, 1988-md-3 and -4.

f) measurements on several of the prints (e.g. 1983-mb-1, the 'several' associated with 1987-cb in note j, the 5 eroded prints near 1986-gb of note f, and the impression 4 m. from 1988-md-3 and -4 of note h).

g) toe width measurements and R_4 aspect ratios.

4) It is extremely doubtful that the implied measurement errors are anywhere near being accurate, because:

a) according to table 2 and elsewhere, measurements were made to the tenth of a centimeter. The assumed measurement error of such a number would be ± 0.1 cm., and it is virtually impossible to make measurements on even the best of footprints to an accuracy of 0.1 cm.

b) I cannot measure even the most well-defined dimension of the cast of the Caldwell print in my possession (which the authors claim "looks like a perfect human footprint," and thus implicitly more defined than most of the others) to an accuracy of 0.1 cm. (length: ± 0.5 cm.; heel and ball widths: ± 0.2 cm.).

c) the photographs indicate that the prints involved are not well defined, especially compared to the Caldwell print, so the error is certainly much greater than even 0.2 cm.;

d) although the reported measurements imply an invariant measurement error, the photographs and the comments of the authors clearly indicate that the quality of the prints varies widely (e.g. the "exact limits are not clearly visible" in 1989-wm, whereas 1965-c "looks like a perfect human footprint").

5) The value of the print measurements themselves are suspect because:

a) the exaggerated measurement error heightens the possibility that the measurements were of imagined print outlines rather than actual features of the sediment surface.

b) my experience with pictures of the Taylor trail is that different viewers uninfluenced by others will trace different outlines for the same track. This means that reproducibility of measurements and casting by investigators uninfluenced by others should be a necessary part of Paluxy investigations, and such procedure is lacking here.

c) since a complete and precise description of the measurements taken is not provided, I am not convinced that comparable measurements were taken on different prints, or on different feet, or on feet vs. prints.

6)   **The paper lacks proper statistical procedure and measures:**

a) since the paper fails to establish the relationship between dimensions of print features and the dimensions of human feet, there is reason to doubt the true validity of the comparisons between the two.

b) although the reduced sample size of the ichnofossils cannot be helped, the sample size of human feet is too small for satisfactory statistical comparisons (10 male and 10 female measures for foot length, heel width, and ball width; and 8 authors for toe measurements).

c) means for human foot measurements are reported, but standard deviations are not, making proper statistical comparisons of the means impossible.

d) although the paper claims that there are significant differences between measurements of the feet of males and females and there is a lack of significant difference between the ichnites and the human feet, no statistical tests of confidence levels are reported; and

e) there are some anomalous claims in Table 2 (e.g. the mean male r_y 2.53, is outside the reported range of 2.41-2.5, and although both the heel width and ball width of 1988-md-4 are reported, R_z is listed as not measurable).

7)   **Used in the paper, though considered dubious by the authors, was the 'Caldwell Print' (1965-c). Excellent photos shown at the conference and a cross-section of this print make it very clear to me that the Caldwell print is <u>not</u> due to impression, but rather to mechanical erosion, and that probably due to human carving. The limestone in which the print is found is an algal limestone full of small algal stroms, apparently ripped up and deposited in a rather chaotic fashion. Qualitatively speaking, there seems to be a preferred orientation of the stroms which would indicate that the Caldwell print is on the *underside* of the slab. Furthermore, the laminae of the various stroms at the print-side surface of the slab are without exception cross-cut by the print itself. The laminae are not caused by the print, but cut into by the print. The print has clearly been cut into the rock after lithification.**

8)   **Unlike the authors claim, the paper fails to satisfactorily document even a single series of more than a single print. Three trails are referred to, implied, or claimed in the paper:**

a) 1989-wm and 1987-cb with other prints of the 'Clark trail', the 12 prints found in 1982, and possibly with 1986-gb and 5 other 'badly eroded' human-like trail(s) on the 'Kerr Island' site. The 'Clark trail' and the 'badly eroded' trail(s) were undescribed in the paper and their orientation and position relative to 1986-gb, 1987-cb, and 1989-wm were not indicated. 1989-wm, 1987-cb, and possibly 1986-gb were considered part of the same trail because of similar measurements (without a statistical defense) in spite of the fact that their relative orientation is not given and they appear to be spread along at least 100 meters of stream bed.

b) "a trail of twelve 40 cm long elongate prints" excavated in 1982 was not described in this paper. Attempts to follow the 'trail', which supposedly has been eroded away, met with no success.

c) 1983-mb-1, 1983-mb-2, 1988-md-3, and 1988-md-4. The dimensions and orientation of 1983-mb-1 was not discussed in the paper, and the nature of the remaining "slipping and sliding" prints is dubious:

    1) The 'stride' length and direction changes (1988-md-4 is 20 cm. behind and 20 cm. to the right of 1988-md-3, which in turn is 10 cm. behind and 45 cm. to the side of 1983-mb-2).

    2) the nature of 1988-md-4 is so distorted that "it might not have been a print" except for its position.

    3) the drawings of the prints in figure 2 are not human-like, and 4) the measurements of the prints change [1988-md-4 and 1988-md-3 to 1983-mb-2 in cms.: length (30.5 to 30.5 to 27.3); heel width (7.6 to 7.6 to 7.0); ball width (7.6 to 10.8 to 10.8); R_1 aspect ratio (4.0 to 2.8 to 2.53); R_2 aspect ratio (1 to 1.42 to 1.55), and R_3 aspect ratio (unmeasurable to 1.9 to 2.1)] and the relative orientation of the prints are not provided.

9) **The interpretation of the Carbon-14 data of the paluxy items is questionable:**

a) no procedure is mentioned in the paper whereby the effects of contamination were minimized or eliminated.

b) no references were provided.

c) age errors are not provided on most of the radiocarbon ages listed in Table 3.

10) **Many of the references made in this paper are dubious or absent:**

a) John Morris's book (Ref. 1) is considered by the authors as a 'scientific' discussion, containing apparently viable conclusions, and documentation of the Taylor and Clark trails with grid-contour gauges and computer graphics. In fact, the authors are wrong on all three counts: it was a lay publication which itself lacked substantial documentation, it was withdrawn from sale by the author because an unspecified number of its conclusions were no longer valid, and it 'documented' the Taylor and Clark trails only by photographs which lacked captions.

b) The conclusions of the paper rely substantially on the Carl Baugh's research (Ref. 2), which is claimed to be a 'doctorate dissertation'. A serious challenge to the validity of this degree and its issuing institution (Kuban, G.J., 1989, _NCSE Reports_, 9(6):15-18) raises serious questions about the conclusions and procedure involved in the production of this paper. furthermore, as far as I know, Baugh's paper has not been published -- either in full or abstract form -- so it is unavailable for critique.

c) a number of claims are not referenced (e.g. the identification of a piece of coalified or charcoalized wood as possibly a "root tip of Lepidodendron", the "requirement in paleontology" of three or more ichnites to identify species, the uniqueness of human aspect ratios, the aspect ratios of bears, the human prints near Glen Rose's electric generator facility, and how "Mt. St. Helens experience and laboratory data attest" to how the Glen Rose rock "did not take millions of years to form" -- an incorrect conclusion, by the way).

d) the reference for a 'serious' report of footprints in the Trinity River is from an imprecisely referenced newspaper account.

e) the Turkemia, USSR prints are undocumented except by a scientist without listed qualifications and a newspaper account.

11) **The conclusions of the entire paper are suspect when reference is made to other unconfirmed claims (e.g. cat-like tracks and a fossilized human finger in Glen Rose sediments) or even falsified claims (e.g. a "possible human tooth", which appears without much doubt at all to be a fish tooth: _Creat./Evo._, 21:38-39; _Creat./Evo. Newsl._, 7(4):15-16; 7(5):18-20; _NCSE Rept._, 9(3):14-15).**

Kurt P. Wise, Ph.D.
Dayton, Tennessee

CLOSURE

The authors thank each of the five respondents for taking the time to review this paper. Their questions and comments will be addressed within the ICC limitations of 1500 words. Because of these constraints the complete details including maps, photographs, etc., asked for by several reviewers will be made available as a supplement upon request from CRSEF, P.O. Box 292, Columbus, Ohio, 43216. We are indebted to the ICC Technical Review Committee for allowing us to include information on chemical analysis of dinosaur bones, part of which was presented as a poster session at the ICC by Dr. Lionel Dahmer. See Section 2, of this Volume for this analysis.

This is an ongoing project. It is subject to the delays and whims of both man and nature. Thus we ask the reader's patience and understanding as we ourselves try to sort out this controversial and complex subject. Many reviewers asked similar questions, one being "why haven't radiocarbon labs been identified?" These were not listed because one of our team members was denied lab time when he volunteered that his specimens were dinosaur bones. This caused a four year delay in getting these bones dated. Obviously we fear "stonewalling" of future requests for any of our dating. We have and can make available copies of our radiocarbon reports for this project. These reports will affirm the authenticity of the dates.

The question of recent carbon contamination was raised frequently. Such contamination has not been overlooked in the dating of our material. We feel if contamination has taken place it has been limited by the following factors. (1) The labs we worked with took great precaution in removing all humic acid (young carbon) while preparing the sample for dating. The specimens were treated with NaOH to remove humic material, rootlets, carbonates, all of which could add modern carbon. Contamination is unlikely according to the people with whom we worked. (2) There is no geological evidence that the clay (both hard and soft) at the Paluxy River in between the strata was washed out and then replaced as some have suggested. This phenomenon probably has happened in other areas, but there is no evidence for it here. If clay was ever washed out the strata would not be horizontal, but would be faulted in many places because there would be no material under the top limestone stratum to support it. (3) Clay layers are nearly impervious to water. The Paluxy strata has well compacted clay layers in between limestone layers which contained our wood specimens. This would have prevented new carbon getting in and old carbon getting out. The bone samples were taken directly from the limestone. Where the Acrocanthosaurus skeleton was found both the blackened rock and the surrounding dark clay above the dinosaur skeleton contained up to 0.5% carbon which suggests it was from the decay of the dinosaur. Only 30 cm above the skeleton the carbon percent had dropped to less than 0.1%, which suggests the carbon found was original carbon from the dinosaur, and it had not migrated far from the skeleton. Since the original carbon apparently had a hard time leaving the rock and clay wouldn't contamination from new carbon also be difficult? Other reasons against contamination will be found in our supplement.

We would like to thank Dr. Aardsma for his comments. We realize our dates should not be taken literally. But we do feel there is significance in them. It is incredible that something allegedly 100 million years old should give any radiocarbon dates at all. Because some radiocarbon was present, this shows our specimens to be much younger than conventional scientists allow. In several instances we went to labs who gave us plus and minus figures for our dates. Most reports in radiocarbon literature do not give plus and minus errors for older dates. We did send the same bone fragments to several labs and got similar dates with accuracies close to plus or minus 250 years (discussed in the supplement on chemical analysis of dinosaur bones).

We would like to thank Dr. Gnidovec for his comments. We did not get our wood from loose clay or float material as implied in his response. Our bones were identified by a competent paleontologist from a major Texas University. Three CRSEF members helped excavate the ten meter Acrocanthosaurus. Space limitations prevented us from giving full references for Table III. These references are available upon request.

We realize we have not yet found a good human-like trackway or a perfect footprint. But some of our fossil impressions are better in quality to Leakey's prints found in Africa which have hardly been disputed. However, what we have established is individual impressions are very human-like when compared to modern human feet. We also realize dinosaurs can make tracks which are close to human size (as in the eroded Taylor trail). They can be distinguished from one another by careful study. One new way we have employed is by anthropological studies using aspect ratios between modern humans and the fossils we have found. The newly excavated impressions agree well.

We would like to thank Dr. Howe for his complementary remarks. We agree there have been misinterpretations of eroded footprints (Taylor trail) as Kuban has done so well at pointing out. He has helped in the scientific study of these footprints and we appreciate his work.

With regard to reference 16, no additional information exists, however a copy of reference 16 is available upon request at the above address. Other information will be given in the supplement.

We would like to thank Dr. Kouznetsov for his response and comments.

Finally, we would like to thank Dr. Wise for his comments. They have helped us to critically evaluate our paper. Some of his questions have already been answered in the above paragraphs. Our site was north of Rte. 205 on the banks of the Paluxy River about five miles from Glen Rose, Texas. The site is located on the J.C. McFall property as noted in Figure 1 and the aerial view in Figure 2, the Glen Rose West Quadrangle.

Specific details about excavations were not included because of space limitations. Upon request details can be forwarded. We agree that footprint descriptions and photographs were inadequate, and we hope to present them in a more detailed paper focusing on these aspects when better footprints and a good trail have been excavated.

We agree with Dr. Wise's recommendations on measurements. We will use his suggestions for future publications. Our sample size of modern human feet needs to be larger, but our preliminary studies showed good correlation to reference 6.

Dr. Wise confuses the Caldwell print with the Burdick track; the photos at the ICC was the Burdick, not the Caldwell. Dr. Wise's comments will be forwarded to the Creation Evidences Museum (CEM) in Glen Rose, since they have been studying the Burdick impression.

We agree the Clark trail should have been the Clark prints. They are called Clark prints because they are similar in size. Perhaps they may be called a discontinuous trail. We have found no pristine trails, but the trail found in 1988, is considered a fair trail by us. Hopefully the supplement will demonstrate this. The Kerr tracks will also be discussed there.

We agree such things in the Paluxy such as the cat track, the finger, and the tooth are debatable. Some have claimed these to be the real things (not us). They are on display at the Creation Evidences Museum for study.

More careful work needs to be done on the fossils and the impressions found in the Paluxy River at Glen Rose, Texas. The reason for our paper was not to prove the tracks at Paluxy were of human origin, but to shed more light on this possibility. Our purpose was to show the book is still not closed on the Paluxy. Human-like footprint impressions, radiocarbon studies and pictographs of dinosaurs show the need for the university community to begin serious studies on the dinosaur and human coexistence hypothesis.

W. Fields, H. Miller, J. Whitmore, D. Davis,
G. Detwiler, J. Ditmars, R. Whitelaw, G.Novaez

DIAMICTITES: ICE-AGES OR GRAVITY FLOWS?

MATS MOLÉN, B. SC., B. SC.
BOX 82 S-913 00 HOLMSUND SWEDEN

ABSTRACT

A literature study directed mainly on sedimentological/erosional structures, combined with limited field work, give good grounds for rejecting the normal ice-age interpretation for relics from Pre-Pleistocene "ice-ages", in favour of an interpretation as (mainly) different kinds of gravity flows. The long ages held by uniformitarian geologists for the formation of these structures are therefore no longer necessary, and the data instead point to an interpretation favouring a short timescale.

Deposits from especially dense gravity flows can look very similar to till. Also, many structures formed in gravity flows can look very similar to structures formed or influenced by glaciers. Some examples are till fabric, the occurrence of erratics, polished and striated stones and bedrock, the occurence of dropstones and periglacial phenomena.

The following regularly occuring structures are features of Pre-Pleistocene "tillites" which are never or rarely formed by glaciers, but are usually formed by gravity flows: A) the small extension and great depth of the "tillites", B) the small size of erratics, C) stones pressed down in the underlying material, D-E) sorting of stones and erratics, F) channels eroded by water below the "tillites", G) layers of dolomite and coal in close connection with the "tillites", H) boulder pavements, I) no weathered till or soil profiles between different "tillite layers", and J) the geographical occurence and extension of late Precambrian "tillites".

All the above speaks against the interpretation of diamictites as glacial deposits, but favours gravity flows.

INTRODUCTION

Ever since the recognition of Pleistocene ice-ages, diamictites found in the geologic column have been interpreted as deposits from ancient ice-ages. Lately, however, it has been recognized that many supposed "ice-age remains" have been deposited by different kinds of gravity flows, for example turbidity currents and debris flows. Many geological structures show that one ought to question (or at least be less conclusive about) all interpretations which so far have been made in favour of Pre-Pleistocene ice-ages.

L. J. G. Schermerhorn is one of the foremost proponents for the gravity flow interpretation, shown in his classic work on late Precambrian diamictites (Schermerhorn 1974a, 1976a, 1976b, 1977). Many other researchers have shown the similarities between ice-age deposits and structures formed by different kinds of mass flows, especially more dense gravity flows (Crowell 1964, Mountjoy et al 1972, Derbyshire 1979).

SIMILARITIES BETWEEN GRAVITY FLOWS AND ICE-AGE DEPOSITS

The following is a short review of structures which are normally formed in connection with ice-ages, but which are also formed in connection with different kinds of gravity flows and other processes.

1) TILLITE STRUCTURE: Deposits from different kinds of gravity flows, and especially more dense gravity flows, often have a similar structure to till, with unsorted sharp-edged rock-material in a clayey matrix. Gravity flow deposits are sometimes indistinguishable from true tills (Lowe 1982, Visser 1983). A recent volcanic gravity flow has therefore been

misinterpreted as till (Schermerhorn 1974a).

In both tills and different kinds of gravity flows there is often a fabric. The long axes of pebbles in Pleistocene tills often show a 10-20 degree dip in the direction of the ice movement. In gravity flows the fabric can be similar to till fabric, but it can also display differences changing with the height in the sedimentary sequence, for example as in the "tillites" in Antarctica (Lindsay 1970). Therefore it is sometimes possible to decide whether a formation has been deposited as a gravity flow or not, but it can be more difficult to decide if the diamictite is a till (Lindsay 1968).

"Tillites" are often disturbed by gravity flows, or mainly deposited by "glacial marine sedimentation", and therefore it is difficult to distinguish them from normal gravity flows (Aalto 1971, Martin 1981, von Brunn & Stratten 1981, Gravenor et al 1984).

2) ERRATICS AND EXOTIC PEBBLES: Erratics can easily be transported by gravity flows. The largest known transported blocks are hundreds of square kilometers large and many blocks are more than one kilometer long. They have been moved many tens or hundreds of kilometers (Maxwell 1959, Wilson 1969, Mountjoy et al 1972, Schermerhorn 1975). Gravity flows contain more far-transported clasts than is contained in lodgement till (Visser 1983).

The largest known erratics in "ancient tills" are 40 and 320 meters long, and they can be shown to have been transported by gravity flows (Schermerhorn 1975).

Turbidity currents and other mass flows can transport debris many hundreds (Wilson 1969, Komar 1970) or thousands (Kuenen 1964) of kilometers, especially in a large catastrophe or if many gravity flows follow after each other (during a longer or shorter period of time). Far-transported clasts could become incorporated in sediments (Embley 1982), which after deposition once again became instable and took part in movement in a shorter and more dense gravity flow, which after deposition looked similar to a till. This would seem quite natural, because it always takes some time until a newly and quickly deposited sediment settles to stability. A similar interpretation was made for some exotic pebbles transported approximately 400 kilometers, which earlier were thought to have been ice-rafted (Jansa & Carozzi 1970).

The slope necessary for a gravity flow is less then 0,1 degrees, and sometimes less then 1 meter in height on 1000 meters in length (Kuenen 1964, Komar 1970, Embley 1982). If one compares with ancient "tillites", the slope in, for example, the Ordovician "tillites" in the Sahara is 1 degree (Fairbridge 1971), and in different places with "tillites" in South America the slope is 0.25-1 degree (Caputo & Crowell 1985).

3) POLISHED, FACETED AND STRIATED STONES: Polished, faceted and striated stones can form in different kinds of gravity flows, under water or on land, in overthrusts and even as a result of smaller movements in the bedrock, like uplifts or folding (Crowell 1957, Flint 1961, Schermerhorn & Stanton 1963, Winterer 1964, Leeder 1982, Hambrey 1983). Stones polished, faceted or striated in bedrock movements can later be transported with different kinds of gravity flows. Stones formed under these circumstances are often impossible to distinguish from stones polished, faceted and striated by the action of ice-movement.

In a recent gravity flow, one block of quartzite became striated (Schermerhorn 1974a). In a recent gravity flow in Australia almost half of the stones became striated (Winterer & von der Borsch 1968). The Australian gravity flow contained mostly sand. Only about 1 % of the grains were larger than sand-size, so one ought not to find many striated stones. In tills and "tillites", often not more than 10-20 % of the stones are striated and faceted (Schermerhorn 1974a).

The internal structure of some stones can give them an appearance of being striated, and mistakes have been made in the classification of "tillites" (Vellutini & Vicat 1983).

4) STRIATED, GROOVED AND POLISHED BEDROCK: Striated, grooved and polished bedrock can form as a result of different kinds of gravity flows - volcanic flows, avalanches, rock flows, earth slides and all kinds of underwater gravity flows (Wilson 1969, Harrington 1971, Daily et al 1973). The bedrock also can be grooved and polished by icebergs and overthrusts (Sandberg 1928, Flint 1961, Schermerhorn & Stanton 1963, Frakes et al 1969, Leeder 1982). Striations and grooves in underlying material have been formed in experimentally performed gravity flows (Evenson 1977). In at least some "tillites" there is a thin unit of sorted sediment in between the grooved pavement and the "tillite" - and there are grooved pavements only if there is a sorted sediment in between (Lindsay 1970).

If the gravity flow was denser, it would behave more plastically and similarly to glacier ice, and therefore striations, grooves and polishing would look similar to erosion made by glacier ice, at least on a local scale.

Many striations and grooves in sediments from "ancient ice-ages" have been formed in unconsolidated material (Lindsay 1970, Savage 1972).

On the island of Svalbard, in the Arctic Sea, 2-3 meter long striations and "ice-polished bedrock" (sandstone and shale) have been formed under the action of sea-ice and waves (Hoppe 1981). First these cliffs were thought to have been formed by action of glacier ice (Hoppe et al 1969).

5) DROPSTONES: Stones, gravel and sand can be transported together with floating roots from trees or floating algae. Especially if there would have been a large catastrophe much material would have been transported with up-rooted trees. In coal, boulders with weights up to 70 kg have been found. These boulders have been transported up to 100 kilometers or more, and one good explanation as to how they were transported is by floating entwined in roots (Price 1932).

Stones with diameters of 15 centimeters have been transported more than 400 kilometers, probably with the help of water and gravity flows. After deposition they have become incorporated in local gravity flows. Earlier these stones were thought to have been transported with icebergs (Jansa & Carozzi 1970).

Stones that are transported by gravity flows can be deposited high up in the sedimentary sequence, and therefore look like stones transported by icebergs - i. e. "left-overs" (Crowell 1964, Schermerhorn 1974a). One explanation to why "ice-transported" clasts are found in gravity flow deposits, is that they are just such "left-overs"; an explanation which can be proven by fabric analyses (Lindsay et al 1970). Clasts are often transported with gravity flows and found embedded in a clay matrix (Bouma 1964, Embley 1982).

Sand and chert can sometimes float directly on the surface of the sea (Hume 1963).

6) VARVED SEDIMENTS: "Varved sediments" (laminated beds) believed to have been deposited on a yearly basis, for example on the edge of a glacier, can form immediately by gravity flows (Kuenen 1964). Misinterpretations have been made, for example in the Gowganda formation (Miall 1983).

7) MARINE (AND LAKE) TILLITES: Till-material which is assumed to have been deposited in the sea, just outside a glacier, is often very disturbed by the action of water, streams, and gravity flows of different kinds. Therefore it may be very difficult, or impossible, to distinguish this material from deposits from gravity flows. Moreover, more and more of all known "tillites" are being reinterpreted as glaciomarine sediments, and the only evidence given for glaciation is dropstones (Frakes et al 1969, Binda & Eden 1972, McCann & Kennedy 1974).

8) PERIGLACIAL STRUCTURES: "Periglacial" structures can form by other processes than freeze and thaw, for example wetting and drying (Yehle 1954, Flint 1961, Wright & Moseley 1975, Black 1976, Walters 1978). "Ice wedges" from the Ordovician "glacial" of the Sahara were, in fact, sandstone dikes radiating from sand volcanoes (Fairbridge 1970).

DIFFERENCES BETWEEN GRAVITY FLOWS AND ICE-AGE DEPOSITS

Structures formed by the action of glaciers can, as shown above, also form from a lot of other different processes, mainly gravity flows. Although many processes have only been studied either locally or very seldom, we can not reject these explanations only on the basis of uniformitarian reasoning. What do we know of the past? Many kinds of catastrophes may have occurred, and the processes we have seen only on a local scale might on a number of occasions have been widespread, covering even continents (Ager 1981).

In addition to the argument that "ice-age structures" can be formed under different climates and with different processes, there are a lot of structures in deposits from "ancient ice-ages" which have very rarely or never been formed by Pleistocene ice-ages. Therefore these structures argue against the ice-age interpretation, but at the same time can give a good argument in favour of the gravity flow interpretation. Some of the structures which distinguish "ancient ice-ages" from the Pleistocene ice-ages are as follows:

A) The geographical extension of "tills" from "ancient ice-ages" is often comparatively small. The "tillites" are often dispersed as separate hills (Lindsay 1966, Finkl & Fairbridge 1979, Fairbridge & Finkl 1980). The "tillites" are also often many hundreds of meters to many kilometers thick (Volkheimer 1969, Schermerhorn 1974a), as are deposits from turbidity currents (Kuenen 1964).

In contrast to this, the last ice-age left extensive layers of tills, tens of thousands to hundreds of thousands of kilometers in extent. Separate till layers, with characteristic structure and mineral content, can be traced over thousands of kilometers and are often less than five meters thick. The thickest known till layer from the Pleistocene is only 400 meters thick. Most layers are less than 100 meters thick, and usually not more than 10 meters thick (in the county of Västerbotten, northern Sweden, the mean thickness of the till-layer is 8.2 meters; Rudberg 1954).

B) In all deposits from "ancient ice-ages" the erratics are mostly not larger than a few meters in diameter, and even erratics as large as one meter in diameter are rare (Kulling 1951, Flint 1961, Schwarzbach 1961). Very rarely have blocks larger than five meters in diameter been found.

The Pleistocene glaciers transported scores of large stones and boulders. Great areas are covered with thousands upon thousands of boulders with diameters larger than one meter. Erratics with diameters larger than 5-10 meters are not rare, and some erratics are hundreds of meter in diameter (Embleton & King 1968). The largest known block, which might have been transported with glacier ice measures 4000 x 2000 x 120 meters (Sugden & John 1982).

The above mentioned facts can be interpreted in favour of the gravity flow theory, especially gravity flows deposited under water. In water, the velocity and strength of the flow must be very large, before large stones can be transported (Komar 1970). The largest known transported boulders which have been found in the geological column, show many features that indicate catastrophic transportation by gravity flows in water. But, when gravity flows are less strong, when there is less water involved, and when the gravity flows are much denser, then the deposits ought to look more like tills. Here we can maybe find the explanation as to why deposits from "ancient ice-ages" do not contain many large erratics (Lowe 1982). They may have been formed by gravity flows, and, if this is correct, it seems that a size of 1-3 meters in diameter is most often the maximum size of the stones which can be transported by dense gravity flows (see Komar 1970, for further information on transportation of large stones by turbidity currents). When the stones are larger, stronger currents are necessary, and the sedimentary structures (for example, fluvial structures and different kinds of structures made by slides) more clearly indicate that there has been a gravity flow, and the difference between the deposit and a till is clear cut.

C) Stones in "tillites" from "ancient ice-ages" have been found pressed down into the underlying "bedrock" (Lindsay 1970, Hambrey 1983). This can easily be explained by a gravity flow over an unconsolidated sediment (but it does not rule out a glacial origin).

D) The largest boulders in "tillites" from "ancient ice-ages" are often found in the thickest sedimentary layer (Schermerhorn 1974a). This indicates transport by water and gravity flows (Dott 1963, Kuenen 1964, Derbyshire 1979, Lowe 1982). Transportation with ice gives a more random deposition.

E) "Tillites" which have been deposited in the sea or on land sometimes display graded bedding (Kulling 1951, Bowen 1969) - a clear indication of transportation by gravity flows approaching a turbidity flow.

F) The sedimentary layers below "ancient tillites" sometimes have erosional channels in their upper sections, formed by flowing water. These structures can indicate that the fastest flowing parts of a gravity flow first eroded the underlying sediments. Shortly afterwards, the more dense parts of the gravity flow arrived, and covered the erosional channels with sediments.

G) Layers of dolomite and coal are often found close to or in between deposits from "ancient ice-ages" (Coleman 1908, Engeln & Caster 1952, "Geophys. Disc." 1960, Plumstead 1964, Lindsay 1970, McKelvey et al 1972, Finkl & Fairbridge 1979, Gravenor et al 1984). Coal indicates a warm to subtropical climate and dolomite only forms in areas of high evaporation (Zenger 1980, Schermerhorn 1983). There is no indication that the Glossopteris flora is a cold climate flora, except the argument that the Dwyka formation and other Carboniferous/Permian deposits are formed from an ancient ice-age. It would seem as reasonable to argue that because there are a lot of warm climate fossils connected with the "tillites", the deposits cannot be tillites, and are therefore more probably gravity flow deposits. There are no similarities between ancient coal-forming processes and recent peat-forming processes. Coal seems to have been formed under catastrophic circumstances, from mats of floating trees (Austin 1979, Scheven 1986).

H) Many boulder pavements have been found in deposits from Pre-Pleistocene "tillites", in contrast to the deposits from the Pleistocene ice-ages (Derbyshire 1979, Martin 1981, von Brunn & Stratten 1981). They are often at the base of the "tillites" (Ghosh & Mitra 1969), and can sometimes be traced back to channel deposits (Lindsay 1970), similar to channel deposits from turbidity currents (Komar 1970). An origin by mudflow seems at least as possible as an origin beneath a glacier (Lowe 1982).

I) Weathered tills and soil profiles are not present in old "tillites", in contrast to deposits from Pleistocene ice-ages.

J) The late Precambrian "tillites" are spread over the whole world. Even if one takes continental drift and the many millions of years into account, it is difficult to avoid having ice-ages over large areas of the earth nearly simultaneously. In contrast, the dolomite layers argue for a warm climate. Deposits from most of the late Precambrian "ice-ages" are found in geosynclines, and very rarely are there any deposits on more stable bedrock. This can be taken as an indication that the deposits have been transported by gravity flows, from higher to lower areas. Deposits from all later ice-ages have been accumulated on stable bedrock (Schermerhorn 1974a).

K) There are also some general problems with the interpretation of "tillites". For example, climatic models and polar wander-paths give (at the very least) some opposing results (Schermerhorn 1971, McCann & Kennedy 1974, Caputo & Crowell 1985, Deynoux 1985, Crowley et al 1987).

AREAS WITH DEPOSITS FROM PRESUMED ICE AGES, SOME EXAMPLES AND INTERPRETATIONS

After this review of structures it can be interesting to see what kind of structures we find in so-called tillites. With a few examples, from some of the best known places, we can argue for deposition by gravity flows, with at least as much facts on hand as the uniformitarian ice-age theorists.

Except for the structures mentioned below, there are present a lot of structures, in all places, which can be found both in tills and in gravity flow deposits. I will not delve more into the structures that have equivocal interpretations, in this short review.

Dwyka, South Africa:

The Dwyka in South Africa is often put forth as one of the most well-documented ancient ice-ages on our planet.

The deposits contain in certain places sedimentary structures which have been demonstrated to be formed by gravity flows, containing boulders with a size of up to 30 meters in diameter (Martin 1981), traces of invertebrates and fishes, erosional channels and graded bedding (Gravenor et al 1984). Many boulder pavements have been found (Derbyshire 1979, Martin 1981, von Brunn & Stratten 1981). Many of the striations and grooves in the underlying "bedrock" are made in unconsolidated material (Savage 1972, Gravenor et al 1984). The "till" fabric seldom seems to show any preferred orientation (Bond 1981a). The thickness of the "tillite" varies between some tens of meters in the north to more than 1000 meters in the south (Flint 1975, John 1979). The largest erratics are about 5 meters in diameter (Du Toit 1926, von Brunn & Stratten 1981). Fossils of plants have been found between the "tillite" and the underlying "ice-polished bedrock" (Du Toit 1926, von Brunn & Stratten 1981). Coalified plant fragments and other fossils (Visser 1989) occur in some "tillite" layers, and layers of coal are situated on and between the "tillites" (Du Toit 1926, Sandberg 1928, Adie 1975, John 1979, Bond 1981a, 1981b, Gravenor et al 1984, Visser 1989). The plants are not typically cold-climate plants. They are more probably subtropical or tropical (Dott & Batten 1976), and they could probably not have grown close to a large continental glacier. Attempts to explain the history of the Dwyka "glaciation" seem to give opposing results from different areas (Truswell 1970, John 1979, Visser 1989).

There are researchers who have interpreted the Dwyka deposits as a volcanic flow (Sandberg 1928) or a mudflow ("Geophys. Disc." 1960). Most of the the Dwyka deposits have recently been interpreted as "glacial marine", mid-latitude (50-65 degrees) sedimentation, possibly in brackish water (Visser 1989), thus making it very difficult to distinguish the deposits from gravity flows.

The Sahara, Ordovician:

The Ordovician "glacial" of Sahara has only relatively recently been investigated more carefully (Biju-Duval et al 1981). Together with the Dwyka deposits, the Sahara deposits are considered to be one of the most well-documented ancient ice-ages.

At the bottom of the sedimentary sequence in the Sahara, on top of the Precambrian (layer I), there is a conglomerate followed by a layer of cross-bedded sandstone, 2 million square kilometers in area (layer II). The current direction is towards the north. After this follows a layer containing many twisted sedimentary structures formed by gravity flows and folds (layer III). In this layer "valleys" have been eroded, which are up to 300 meters deep. The valleys, together with the next layer in the sedimentary sequence (layer IV), contain, for example "till", "permafrost structures" and "eskers", and are regarded to have been formed by a large glacier.

Striations, grooves and other erosional structures have been formed on top of layer III when the sediment was still unconsolidated. Also, the striations are situated in many different layers, on top of each other, and there is an abundance of striations - in spite of the fact that there are very few clasts in the "tillite" - a highly unexplainable phenomenon for an "ice-age" deposit (Schermerhorn 1970, 1971). Also, at right angles to the striations there are sometimes minor ripples (Fairbridge 1971). These facts indicate a gravity flow origin.

The flow direction of the "ice" is the same as for the underlying crossbedded sandstone, which can be taken as an argument that the entire sequence may have been formed in one single great catastrophe, as the current direction has not changed. (Both the "tillite" and the underlying sediments are sandstones; Fairbridge 1970).

At the same time as all the sediments were unlithified, one has to believe that the hardest clasts of quartzite became heavily faceted and striated (Schermerhorn 1971). The findings would seem to indicate that the stones became striated and faceted earlier and far away, in any kind of abrasional process, and were transported to the present site with already intact structures.

At the top of layer IV there are many sedimentary structures which call for a catastrophic explanation, according to the scientists who have made the most complete research. For example, ripple-marks which are 25 centimeters high with a wave-lenght of 3 meter, and also water escape structures.

One published drawing which shows the "tillite" (layer IV), doesn't look very till-like, with long "stones" (?) that point in different directions (Allen 1975). A fabric analysis of a "till" similar to the drawing would probably show that it was a gravity flow. The largest diameter of an "erratic boulder" found in Sahara is about 2 meters.

Of all remains from "ancient ice-ages", it is (almost) only in the Sahara that researchers have found "eskers". However, these eskers can be explained as, for example, having been formed due to filling of water-eroded channels with more resistant material. When erosion and weathering processes started to break down the sedimentary sequences, the former channels, which had been filled with more resistant material, did not weather down as fast as the surrounding sediments (Biju-Duval et al 1981). Therefore they now stand up as esker-like formations. I have not seen any reports of glacial tectonic disturbances in these "eskers", similar to the disturbances shown in Pleistocene eskers, when the ice moved over them. Neither have I seen any reports of large erratics on top of or close to the top of the "eskers", which is very common on the Pleistocene eskers.

Fossils of trilobites and orthoceratites have also been found in parts of the "tillite". Complete marine fossils have never been found in Pleistocene till, for example fossils from shrimps and cuttlefish of different kinds (except in pebbles from already deposited and lithified rocks, which have been reworked). The "tillite" is also laminated in many places (Bryan 1983), as if it had been deposited by water. This is a good argument against the tillite interpretation and for the "gravity flow" interpretation.

To explain how this "ice-age" ended, researchers have suggested some kind of catastrophe, maybe connected with a rise of the sea-level by about 500 meters (Fairbridge 1981). This seems easier to explain by catastrophic flooding rather than by uniformitarian theories.

Researchers are urged to make more investigations in this area, to see if there really are any definitive arguments for an ice-age in the Sahara. Schermerhorn (1970, 1971) has earlier suggested an origin by mass-flow, and I have not seen that his arguments have been either falsified or explained in any way that is possible with a glacial origin.

Gowganda, Canada, Precambrian:

The "ice-age" which is thought to be best documented of all Precambrian "ice-ages" resulted in the Gowganda formation, situated north of the great lakes in Canada. The largest erratic found in these layers is 3.4 meters long (Lindsey 1969). A conglomerate below the "tillite" has superficial similarities to the "tillite", and it is not always made up of lithified stones (Frarey 1977) (it is very similar to a conglomerate below the "tillite" in the Varanger fjord, northern Norway; Bjorlykke 1967). There are lee side structures, connected to many stones which are thought to have been ice-rafted, but these structures show rather that the stones have been deposited in streaming water or by gravity flows. The fabric is different in different layers in the "tillite", which is a good argument for deposition by gravity flows (Lindsay 1968, Lindsey 1969).

It seems that at least some beds have an upper limit of clast size, which argues for a gravity flow (Frarey 1977).

Some researchers have at different times argued that the complete Gowganda formation (Crowell 1964, Miall 1983), or at least parts of it (Frarey 1977, Young 1981), has been deposited by gravity flows, or at least that the "tillite" has been resorted (Coleman 1908).

CONCLUSION

In conclusion, many formations which are thought to form only under a cold climate and by the action of ice, can also be shown to form under a lot of other different environments and due to different processes. Many structures which are not found in the Pleistocene glacial record are found in deposits from the Pre-Pleistocene "glacial" record, but these structures are easier explained with different kinds of gravity flows than with glacial/periglacial erosion and sedimentation. All "ancient ice-ages" might be mainly different kinds of gravity flows, instead of tillites or glaciofluvial material.

At least on one occasion a deposit has been interpreted as an ice-age, only until it was found that the deposit could not be in accordance with the geologic time scale for other areas (Schermerhorn 1974a, p. 809).

More and more researchers become aware of the gravity flow explanation, and that gravity flows form a large number of sedimentary deposits (Mountjoy et al 1972). Furthermore, many "ice-ages" have already been reinterpreted completely or in part as gravity flows or other phenomena (Crowell 1957, Newell 1957, Schermerhorn & Stanton 1963, Schwarzbach 1961, Winterer 1964, Lindsay 1966, Condie 1967 and others mentioned in this paper).

ACKNOWLEDGMENTS

I thank Mr. Gary W. Small and Mr. Bernt Ove Stenmark for correcting the language in this paper.

REFERENCES

Aalto, K. R. (1971) "Glacial Marine Sedimentation and Stratigraphy of the Toby Conglomerate (Upper Proterozoic), Southeastern British Columbia, Northwestern Idaho and Northeastern Washington", Canadian Journal of Earth Sciences, Vol. 8, pp. 753-787.
Adie, Raymond J. (1975) "Permo-Carboniferous Glaciation of the Southern Hemisphere" in Wright, A. E. & Moseley F. (Eds.), "Ice Ages: Ancient and Modern", Seal House Press, Liverpool, pp. 287-300.
Ager, Derek V. (1981) "The Nature of the Stratigraphical Record", 2nd ed., John Wiley, New York.
Allen, P. (1975) "Ordovician Glacials of Central Sahara" in Wright, A. E. & Moseley, F. (Eds.), "Ice Ages: Ancient and Modern", Seal House Press, Liverpool, pp. 275-286.
Austin, Steven A. (1979) "Depositional Environment of the Kentucky No. 12 Coal Bed (Middle Pennsylvanian) of Western Kentucky, With Special Reference to the Origin of Coal Lithotypes", State University of Pennsylvania (University Microfilms Int'l, Ann Arbor, MI, Order No. 8005972), 390 pp.
Biju-Duval, B., Deynoux, M. & Rognon, P. (1981) "Late Ordovician Tillites of the Central Sahara" in Hambrey, M. J. & Harland, W. B. (Eds.), "Earth's Pre-Pleistocene Glacial Record", Cambridge University Press, Cambridge, pp. 99-107.
Binda, P. L. & Van Eden, J. G. (1972) "Sedimentological Evidence on the Origin of the Precambrian Great Conglomerate (Kundelungu Tillite), Zambia", Palaeogeography, Palaeoclimatology, Palaeoecology, Vol. 12, pp. 151-168.
Bjorlykke, Knut (1967) "The Eocambrian 'Reusch Moraine' at Bigganjargga and the Geology around Varangerfjord; Northern Norway", Norges Geologiske Undersokelse, No. 251, Oslo, pp. 18-44.
Black, Robert F. (1976) "Periglacial Features Indicative of Permafrost: Ice and Soil Wedges", Quaternary Research, Vol. 6, pp. 3-26.
Bond, G. (1981a) "Late Paleozoic (Dwyka) Glaciation in the Middle Zambezi Region" in Hambrey, M. J. & Harland, W. B. (Eds.) "Earth's Pre-Pleistocene Glacial Record", Cambridge University Press, Cambridge, pp. 55-57.
Bond, G. (1981b) "Late Paleozoic (Dwyka) Glaciation in the Sabi-Limpopo Region, Zimbabwe" in Hambrey, M. J. & Harland, W. B. (Eds.) "Earth's Pre-Pleistocene Glacial Record", Cambridge University Press, Cambridge, pp. 58-60.

Bouma, A. H. (1964) "Turbidites" in Bouma, A. H. & Brouwer, A. (Eds.) "Turbidites", Elsevier Publ., Amsterdam 1964, p. 251.

Bowen, Richard L. (1969) "Late Paleozoic Glaciations - the Parana Basin of South America" in Amos, A. J. (Ed.) "Gondwana Stratigraphy", IUGS Symposium in Buenos Aires 1967, UNESCO, pp. 589-597.

Bryan, Martin (1983) review of Prof. P. Allens lecture "Ice Ages in the Central Sahara", OUGS Journal, Vol. 4 (2), pp. 51-53.

Caputo, Mário V. & Crowell, John C. (1985) "Migration of Glacial Centers Across Gondwana during Paleozoic Era", Geological Society of America Bulletin, Vol. 96, pp. 1020-1036.

Coleman, A. P. (1908) "Glacial Periods and Their Bearing on Geological Theories", Bulletin of the Geological Society of America, Vol. 19, p. 347-366.

Condie, Kent C. (1967) "Petrology of the Late Precambrian Tillite(?) Association in Northern Utah", Geological Society of America Bulletin, Vol. 78, pp. 1317-1343.

Crowell, John C. (1957) "Origin of Pebble Mudstones", Bulletin of the Geological Society of America, Vol. 68, pp. 993-1009.

Crowell, John C. (1964) "Climatic Significance of Sedimentary Deposits Containing Dispersed Megaclasts" in Nairn, A. E. M. (Ed.) "Problems in Palaeoclimatology", John Wiley & Sons, London, pp. 86-99.

Crowley, T. J., Mengel, J. G. & Short, D. A. (1987) "Gondwanaland's Seasonal Cycle", Nature, Vol. 329, pp. 803-807.

Daily, B., Gostin, V. A. & Nelson, C. A. (1973) "Tectonic Origin for an Assumed Glacial Pavement of Late Proterozoic Age, South Australia", Journal of the Geological Society of Australia, Vol. 20, March, pp. 75-78.

Derbyshire, Edward (1979) "Glaciers and Environment" in John, Brian S. (Ed.) "The Winters of the World", Davies & Charles, Newton Abbot, pp. 58-106.

Deynoux, M. (1985) "Les Glaciations du Sahara", La Recherche, No. 169, Vol. 16, pp. 986-997.

Dott, Robert H. (1963) "Dynamics of Subaqueous Gravity Depositional Processes", Bulletin of the American Association of Petroleum Geologists, Vol. 47, Jan., pp. 104-128.

Dott, Robert H. & Batten, Roger L. (1976) "Evolution of the Earth", 2nd ed., McGraw-Hill, New York, p. 285.

Du Toit, Alex L. (1926) "The Geology of South Africa", Oliver and Boyd, Edinburgh, pp. 205-215.

Embleton, C. & King, C. A. M. (1968) "Glacial and Periglacial Geomorphology", Edward Arnold, London, p. 304.

Embley, Robert W. (1982) "Anatomy of Some Atlantic Margin Sediment Slides and Some Comments on Ages and Mechanisms" in Saxov, Svend & Nieuwenhuis, J. K. (Ed.) "Marine Slides and Other Mass Movements" Plenum Press, New York, pp. 189-213.

Evenson, Edward B. (1977) "Subaquatic Flow Tills: A New Interpretation for the Genesis of Some Laminated Deposits", Boreas, Vol. 6, pp. 115-133.

Fairbridge, Rhodes W. (1970) "South Pole Reaches the Sahara", Science, Vol. 168, pp. 878-881.

Fairbridge, Rhodes W. (1971) "Upper Ordovician Glaciation in Northwest Africa? Reply", Geological Society of America Bulletin, Vol. 82, pp. 269-274.

Fairbridge, Rhodes W. (1979) "Traces From the Desert: Ordovician" in John, Brian S. (Ed.) "The Winters of the World", Davies & Charles, Newton Abbot, pp. 131-153.

Finkl, Charles W. Jr. & Fairbridge, Rhodes W. (1979) "Paleogeographic Evolution of a Rifted Cratonic Margin: S. W. Australia", Palaeogeography, Palaeoclimatology, Palaeoecology, Vol. 26, pp. 221-252.

Fairbridge, Rhodes W. & Finkl, Charles W. Jr. (1980) "Cratonic Erosional Unconformities and Peneplains", Journal of Geology, Vol. 88, p. 80.

Flint, Richard F. (1961) "Geological Evidence of Cold Climate" in Nairn, A. E. M. (Ed.), "Descriptive Palaeoclimatology", Interscience Publ., New York, p. 142.

Flint, R. F. (1975) "Features other than Diamicts as evidence of Ancient Glaciations" in Wright, A. E. & Moseley, F. (Eds.), "Ice Ages: Ancient and Modern", Seal House Press, Liverpool, pp. 121-136.

Frakes, L. A., Amos, A. A. & Crowell, J. C. (1969) "Origin and Stratigraphy of Late Paleozoic Diamictites in Argentina and Bolivia" in Amos, A. J. (Ed.) "Gondwana Stratigraphy", IUGS Symposium in Buenos Aires 1967, UNESCO, pp. 821-843.

Frarey, M. J. (1977) "Geology of the Huronian Belt Between Sault Ste. Marie and Blind River, Ontario", Geological Survey of Canada Memoir 383, pp. 38-49.

"Geophysical Discussion of the Royal Astronomical Society" (1960) Geophysical Journal of the Royal Astronomical Society (incorporating the Geophysical Supplement to the Monthly Notices of the R. A. S.), Vol. 3, pp. 127-132.

Ghosh, P. K. & Mitra, N. D. (1969) "Recent Studies on the Talchir Glaciation in India" in Amos, A. J. (Ed.) "Gondwana Stratigraphy", IUGS Symposium in Buenos Aires 1967, UNESCO, pp. 537-550.

Gravenor, C. P., von Brunn, V. & Dreimanis, A. (1984) "Nature and Classification of Waterlain Glaciogenic Sediments, Exemplified by Pleistocene, Late Paleozoic and Late Precambrian Deposits", Earth-Science Reviews, Vol. 20, March, pp. 105-166.

Hambrey, M. J. (1983) "Correlation of Late Proterozoic Tillites in the North Atlantic Region and Europe", Geological Magazine, Vol. 120, pp. 216-217.

184

Harrington, Horacio J. (1971) "Glacial-Like 'Striated Floor' Originated by Debris-Laden Torrential Water Flows", American Association of Petroleum Geologists Bulletin, Vol. 55, pp. 1344-1347.

Hoppe, G., Schytt, V. Häggblom, A. & Österholm, H. (1969) "Studies of the Glacial History of Hopen (Hopen Island), Svalbard", Geografiska Annaler, serie A, Vol. 51, No. 4, pp. 185-191.

Hoppe, Gunnar (1981) "Glacial Traces on the Island of Hopen, Svalbard: A Correction", Geografiska Annaler, Vol. 63, serie A, pp. 67-68.

Hume, James D. (1963) "Floating Sand and Pebbles near Barrow, Alaska", Geological Society of America Memoir 73, Abstracts for 1962, New York, p. 176.

Jansa, L. F. & Carozzi, A. V. (1970) "Exotic Pebbles in La Salle Limestone (Upper Pennsylvanian), La Salle, Illinois", Journal of Sedimentary Petrology, Vol. 40, June, pp. 688-694.

John, Brian S. (1979) "The Great Ice Age: Permo-Carboniferous" in John, Brian S. (Ed.) "The Winters of the World", Davies & Charles, Newton Abbot, pp. 154-172.

Komar, Paul D. (1970) "The Competence of Turbidity Current Flow", Geological Society of America Bulletin, Vol. 81, pp. 1555-1562.

Kuenen, Ph. H. (1964) "Deep Sea Sands and Ancient Turbidites" in Bouma, A. H. & Brouwer, A. (Eds.) "Turbidites", Elsevier Publ., Amsterdam, pp. 3-33.

Kulling, Oskar (1951) "Spår av Varangeristiden i Norrbotten", SGU, series C, No. 503, Stockholm, pp. 14, 24-25.

Leeder, M. R. (1982) "Sedimentology", George Allen & Unwin, London, p. 81.

Lindsay, John F. (1966) "Carboniferous Subaqueous Mass-Movement in the Manning-Macleay Basin, Kempsey, New South Wales", Journal of Sedimentary Petrology, Vol. 36, pp. 719-732.

Lindsay, John F. (1968) "The Development of Clast Fabric in Mudflows", Journal of Sedimentary Petrology, Vol. 38, pp. 1242-1253.

Lindsay, John F. (1970) "Depositional Environment of Paleozoic Glacial Rocks in the Central Transantarctic Mountains", Geological Society of America Bulletin, Vol. 81, pp. 1149-1171.

Lindsay, John F., Summerson, C. H. & Barrett, P. J. (1970) "A Long-Axis Clast Fabric Comparision of Squantum 'Tillite', Massachusetts and the Gowganda Formation, Ontario", Journal of Sedimentary Petrology, Vol. 40, pp. 475-479.

Lindsey, David A. (1969) "Glacial Sedimentology of the Precambrian Gowganda Formation, Ontario, Canada", Geological Society of America Bulletin, Vol. 80, pp. 1685-1701 & plate section, 8 figures.

Lowe, Donald R. "Sediment Gravity Flows: II. Depositional Models with Special Reference to the Deposits of High-Density Turbidity Currents", Journal of Sedimentary Petrology, Vol. 52, pp. 279-297.

Martin, H. (1981) "The Late Paleozoic Dwyka Group of the South Kalahari Basin in Namibia and Botswana, and the Subglacial Valleys of the Kaokoveld in Namibia" in Hambrey, M. J. & Harland, W. B. (Eds.) "Earth's Pre-Pleistocene Glacial Record", Cambridge University Press, Cambridge, pp. 61-66.

Maxwell, John C. (1959) "Turbidite, Tectonic and Gravity Transport, Northern Appenine Mountains, Italy", Bulletin of the American Association of Petroleum Geologists, Vol. 43, pp. 2701-2719.

McCann, A. M. & Kennedy, M. J. (1974) "A Probable Glacio-Marine Deposit of Late Ordovician - Early Silurian Age from the North Central Newfoundland Appalachian Belt", Geological Magazine, Vol. 111, pp. 549-563.

McKelvey, B. C., Webb, P. N., Gorton, M. P. & Kohn, B. P. (1972) "Stratigraphy of the Beacon Supergroup Between the Olympus and Boomerang Ranges, Victoria Land" in Adie, Raymond J. (Ed.), "Antarctic Geology and Geophysics", Universitetsforlaget, Oslo, pp. 345-352.

Miall, Andrew D. "Glaciomarine Sedimentation in the Gowganda Formation (Huronian), Northern Ontario", Journal of Sedimentary Petrology, Vol. 53, pp. 477-491.

Mountjoy, E. W., Cook, H. E., Pray, L. C. & McDaniel, P. N. (1972) "Allochthonous Carbonate Debris Flow - Worldwide Indicators of Reef Complexes, Banks or Shelf Margins" in McLaren, D. J. & Middleton, G. V. (Eds.) "Stratigraphy and Sedimentology" 24th International Geological Congress, Section 6, Montreal, pp. 172-189.

Newell, N. D. (1957) "Supposed Permian Tillites in Northern Mexico are Submarine Slide Deposits", Bulletin of the Geological Society of America, Vol. 68, pp. 1569-1576

Plumstead, Edna P. (1964) "Palaeobotany of Antarctica" in Adie, Raymond J. (Ed.), "Antarctic Geology", North-Holland Publ. Co., Amsterdam, pp. 643-652.

Price, Paul H. (1932) "Erratic Boulders in Sewell Coal of West Virginia", Journal of Geology, Vol. 40, pp. 62-73.

Rudberg, Sten (1954) "Västerbottens berggrundsmorfologi", Geographica, No. 2, Uppsala, p. 262.

Sandberg, C. G. S. (1928) "The Origin of the Dwyka Conglomerate of South Africa and Other 'Glacial' Deposits", Geological Magazine, Vol. 65, pp. 117-138.

Savage, Norman M. (1972) "Soft-Sediment Glacial Grooving of Dwyka Age in South Africa", Journal of Sedimentary Petrology, Vol. 42, pp. 307-308.

Schermerhorn, L. J. G. (1970) "Saharan Ice", Geotimes, Dec., pp. 7-8.

Schermerhorn, L. J. G. (1971) "Upper Ordovician Glaciation in Northwest Africa? Discussion", Geological Society of America Bulletin, Vol. 82, pp. 265-268.

Schermerhorn, L. J. G. (1974a) "Late Precambrian Mixtites: Glacial and/or Nonglacial?" American Journal of Science, Vol. 274, pp. 673-824.

Schermerhorn, L. J. G. (1974b) "No Evidence for Glacial Origin of Late Precambrian Tilloids in Angola", Nature, Vol. 252, pp 114-115.

Schermerhorn, L. J. G. (1975) "Tectonic Framework of Late Precambrian Supposed Glacials" in Wright, A. E. & Moseley, F. (Eds.), "Ice Ages: Ancient and Modern", Seal House Press, Liverpool, pp. 241-274.

Schermerhorn, L. J. G. (1976a) "Reply", American Journal of Science, Vol. 276, pp. 375-384.

Schermerhorn, L. J. G. (1976b) "Reply", American Journal of Science, Vol. 276, pp. 1315-1324.

Schermerhorn, L. J. G. (1977) "Late Precambrian Glacial Climate and the Earth's Obliquity - A Discussion", Geological Magazine, Vol. 114, pp. 57-64.

Schermerhorn, L. J. G. (1983) "Late Proterozoic Glaciation in the Light of CO_2 Depletion in the Atmosphere", Geological Society of America Memoir 161, pp. 309-315.

Schermerhorn, L. J. G. & Stanton, W. I. (1963) "Tilloids in the West Congo Geosyncline", Quarterly Journal of the Geological Society of London, Vol. 119, pp. 201-241.

Scheven, Joachim (1986) "Karbonstudien", Hänssler-Verlag, Neuhausen-Stuttgart.

Schwarzbach, M. (1961) "The Climatic History of Europe and North America" in Nairn, A. E. M. (Ed.), "Descriptive Palaeoclimatology", Interscience Publ. Inc., New York, pp. 255-291.

Sugden, David E. & John, Brian S. (1982) "Glaciers and Landscape", Edward Arnold, London, p. 161.

Truswell, J. F. (1970) "An Introduction to the Historical Geology of South Africa", Purnell & Sons, Cape Town, pp. 116-117.

Vellutini, Pierre & Vicat, Jean-Paul (1983) "Sur L'Origine Des Formation Conglomératiques de Base du Geosynclinal Ouest-Congolien (Gabon, Congo, Zaire, Angola)", Precambrian Research, Vol. 23, pp. 87-101.

Visser, J. N. J. (1983) "The Problems of Recognizing Ancient Subaqueous Debris Flow Deposits in Glacial Sequences", Transactions of the Geological Society of South Africa, Vol. 86, pp. 137-135.

Visser, J. N. J. (1989) "The Permo-Carboniferous Dwyka Formation of Southern Africa: Deposition by a Predominantly Subpolar Marine Ice Sheet", Palaeogeography, Palaeoclimatology, Palaeoecology, Vol. 70, pp. 377-391.

Volkheimer, Wolfgang (1969) "Palaeoclimatic Evolution in Argentina and Relations with Other Regions of Gondwana" in Amos, A. J. (Ed.) "Gondwana Stratigraphy", IUGS Symposium in Buenos Aires 1967, UNESCO, pp. 551-587.

von Brunn, V. & Stratten, T. (1981) "Late Paleozoic Tillites of the Karoo Basin of South Africa" in Hambrey, M. J. & Harland, W. B. (Eds.) "Earth's Pre-Pleistocene Glacial Record", Cambridge University Press, Cambridge, pp. 71-79.

von Engeln, O. D. & Caster, K. E. (1952) "Geology", McGraw-Hill Book Co., New York 1952, p. 537.

Walters, James C. (1978) "Polygonal Patterned Ground in Central New Jersey", Quaternary Research, Vol. 10, pp. 42-54.

Wilson, H. H. (1969) "Late Cretaceous Eugeosynclinal Sedimentation, Gravity Tectonics, and Ophiolite Emplacement in Oman Mountains, Southeast Arabia", American Association of Petroleum Geologists Bulletin, Vol. 53, pp. 626-671.

Winterer, Edward L. (1964) "Late Precambrian Pebbly Mudstone in Normandy, France: Tillite or Tilloid?" in Nairn, A. E. M. (Ed.) "Problems in Palaeoclimatology", John Wiley & Sons, London, pp. 159-178.

Winterer, Edward L. & von der Borch, C. C. (1968) "Striated Pebbles in a Mudflow Deposit, South Australia", Palaeogeography, Palaeoclimatology, Palaeoecology, Vol. 5, pp. 205-211.

Wright, A. E. & Moseley, F. (Eds.) (1975) "Ice Ages: Ancient and Modern", Seal House Press, Liverpool, p. 304.

Yehle, Lynn A. (1954) "Soil Tongues and Their Confusion with Certain Indicators of Periglacial Climate", American Journal of Science, Vol. 252, pp. 532-546.

Young, G. M. (1981) "The Early Proterozoic Gowganda Formation, Ontario, Canada" in Hambrey, M. J. & Harland, W. B. (Eds.) "Earth's Pre-Pleistocene Glacial Record", Cambridge University Press, Cambridge, pp. 807-812.

Zenger, D. H., Dunham, J. B. & Ethington, R. L. (Eds.) (1980) "Concepts and Models of Dolomitization" Society of Economic Paleontologists and Mineralogists, Spec. Publ. No. 28, Nov.

Mr. Molén has done a good job showing how gravity flows can mimic most glacial features, and how many features of diamictites are in more accord with gravity flows. I am confused on one point: If gravity flows and the Pleistocene ice sheets transported large erratics, Mr. Molén should clarify how erratics can be used to distinguish between the two mechanisms, especially since diamictites contain small erratics. Dropstone "varvites" are used to identify ancient ice ages, for instance the Gowanda tillite. How would the author explain this feature as a product of gravity flow? Many investigators admit that gravity flows are common in diamictite, but they counter by saying this is expected in ancient glaciomarine sediments (which most diamictites are claimed), and even in continental tillite as flow tills. What would be the author's response to these investigators? Some investigators realize that gravity flows can duplicate most glacial features. But then they say that when one feature occurs in abundance or when several different features are found in the same diamictite, it must be glaciogenic. How would Mr. Molen answer them?

Michael J. Oard, M.S.
Great Falls, Montana

Tillites of Precambrian and of Palaeozoic provenance can look remarkably similar. It is understandable that Precambrian diamictites have been declared to be of glacial origin. On the basis of a six days' creation - the first three days equalling the Precambrian - ice ages during this period are to be rejected. Mr. Molén's conclusion seems to be correct that gravity flows within synclines can be held responsible for the formation of these localized diamictites. --- The Permo-Carboniferous Dwyka of the Southern Hemisphere is of a different character. In the first place, it is extremely widespread. Its movements seem to follow a pattern consistent with an assumed center of glaciation. Polished and striated pavements bear a striking similarity to Pleistocene occurrences. Pebbles floating in sediment do indeed look like dropstones. But here the similarities end. Unlike a Pleistocene till the matrix of the Dwyka tillite is quite dense and resembles a volcanic rock in which the clastics are suspended. In South Africa the Dwyka may overlie coal no. 1 of the Ecca series. The matrix of dropstones is also indistinguishable from Ecca sediments. Therefore Glacial Dwyka and plant-bearing Ecca beds stand obviously in a close temporal relationship. Since the coals of Ecca are clearly pre-Flood vegetation gradually borne to rest after the Flood year it is conceivable that true glaciogenic processes on the Southern Hemisphere took place already immediately after the Flood. Such Permian glaciation may have required not more than a few decades and yet have left traces of a true ice age before being superseded by the Karoo succession. The reality of this pre-Pleistocene ice age cannot be ruled out.

Joachim Scheven, Ph.D.
Hagen, Germany

Mr. Molén's thorough literature review of published articles on diamictites nicely illustrates the manner in which mainstream scientists continually debate the merits of alternative hypotheses, subjecting each interpretation and the evidence offered in its support to questioning and peer review. The question as to whether any given diamictite is of glacial origin or of non-glacial subaerial or subaqueous origin is not, however, in any way relevant to the question of its geologic age. Evidence of rapid formation of a limited sedimentary sequence (or of a rock body of any origin) is not to be construed as necessarily being evidence of recent occurrence. Geologic ages of diamictites and all other sedimentary accumulations are established on entirely independent criteria, such as radiometric age determination. Mr. Molén's reference to evidence of catastrophic vis-a-vis non-catastrophic ("uniformitarian") processes and events is no longer relevant to the recent-creation/great age controversy because modern mainstream geology fully accommodates all possible natural catastrophic events of both extraterrestrial and terrestrial sources throughout the entire geologic record.

Arthur N. Strahler, Ph.D.
Santa Barbara, California

This paper provides a welcome review of an important class of geological evidences, arguing that gravity flows and related sedimentary processes can have some features similar to Pleistocene tillites, and that they also possess features which distinguish them from tillites. Several of the evidences discussed show that useful scientific work can be undertaken to test the conflicting hypotheses. Examples include the sorting effects of gravity flows, characteristics boulder sizes, the thicknesses of deposits, and the presence of internal sedimentary structures. This paper provides a good reference point for studies of this kind. There is always a potential danger of looking at evidences in isolation, whereas depositional interpretations generally require the investigator to assess the significance of several associated observations. The Saharan Ordovician deposits illustrate the point well: the reported mix of glacial and periglacial phenomena seems compelling, and although Mr. Molén has raised valid questions, the burden of proof still rests on those who challenge the conventional interpretation.

David J. Tyler, M.S.
Chesire, England

CLOSURE

I want to thank all reviewers for their comments to my paper, and I am glad that my paper has started up some discussions.

Mr. Michael J. Oard's comments:

Erratics: A glacier has high viscosity and can therefore lift up and transport very large erratics long distances with slow speed. A gravity flow, whether it is dense or not, can also transport large erratics, but it seems that there is an upper limit for the transporting power for dense gravity flows. If a large boulder is to be transported, strong currents are needed, and deposits produced by strong currents will show unmistakable evidence of this mechanism of transportation. Therefore, dense gravity flows, which result in the deposits that are the ones that look most like lodgement till, cannot transport boulders above a certain (usually not more than one meter in diameter); because if the current is too strong the flow will behave more like a turbidity flow, and the flow will not "freeze" as it stops, and the deposit will be more or less sorted and may have slide structures that are not present in lodgement till. It seems that the only gravity flows that can lift and transport very large boulders, with diameters larger than c. 3 meters, are the fastest/strongest ones, and therefore deposits made from such flows clearly reveal the mode of transport and are not labeled "tillites".

Dropstone "varvites": See my paper and combine points 3, 5 and 6. Many "varves" form almost simultaneously by any turbidity current; there is no reason to believe that they are yearly varves. Also, the "dropstones" usually are small, and in the Gowganda formation they are connected with lee side structures (see my paper).

Based on my own visit to parts of the Gowganda formation, August 1990, I will pass on the following observations: In the Gowganda formation "dropstones" usually break through the layers which encircle and cover them but not the ones below (the ones below are only compressed); thus giving evidence for erosion by currents on top of and at the side of the stones, and also quick deposition and compression of the sediments; but evidence is lacking for rapid fall down of stones from an iceberg. It seems improbable that all stones were frozen to small pieces of ice, so that they only slowly sunk to the bottom as the pieces of ice melted away. (But of course - the stones were not that big and maybe would not penetrate the layers at any rate. But, even in a gravity flow you would suspect that a few stones could penetrate the layers below.) One of the biggest stones observed (c. 5 cm in diameter) was lying in a thicker "varve" and the "varves" disappeared at both sides of the stone, which indicates that the stone and the "varves" were deposited simultaneously. That would only happen if the deposition was by a current (for example a turbidity flow) and the stone was a "left-over". Sometimes the "dropstones" form thin layers of sand and gravel between "varves", and this "dropped material" shows evidence of current levelling.

Glaciomarine sediments/flow tills: I know of no structure that can distinguish between glaciomarine sediments and different kinds of gravity flows; not when the "glaciomarine sediments" themselves are different kinds of gravity flows! (If there are glaciomarine sediments that do not contain gravity flows, then there are structures that can help to distinguish them from each other; see for example Schermerhorn & Stanton 1963, referred to in my paper.) At present, and maybe also for the future, I know of no other possibility than to look for other structures, for example lodgement "tillite". The same might be for many flow tills that actually are different kinds of gravity flows. It is necessary to find structures that are unique to glacial deposition if one is to prove that there has been an ice age.

Many features or one feature in abundance: You have to examine all features, as I have done in this paper (see also Schermerhorn & Stanton 1963). If all of the features can be formed by gravity flows, but all except one can be made by glacial action, then I would favor deposition by gravity flow (except in those cases where the gravity flow feature is only a minor part of a larger glacial feature). The other way around is of course also possible, and then I would favor glacial action.

Dr. Joachim Scheven's comments:

As briefly mentioned in my paper: 1) The movement can not be easily explained by an assumed center of glaciation (also, this does not matter very much; both gravity flows and glaciers would tend to slide from higher to lower elevation, thus giving a "pattern"). 2) "Polished and striated pavements" have often formed in soft material in the Dwyka formation, in contrast with the Pleistocene glaciation. 3) The dropstones can be explained as "left-overs"; and in one photo shown by Visser (1983, fig. 10 A) a vertically oriented "dropstone" actually shows a lee side structure. 4) There are coal deposits/plants both below, between and above the "tillites" (actually the Ecca overlies the Dwyka, by definition: von Brunn & Stratten 1981, referred to in my paper).

In addition I would like to mention the following: The Dwyka is about as widespread as the Ordovician "tillite" deposits in North Africa; both of them are in contrast with Precambrian "tillites". In the Dwyka formation there is also sometimes a layer of laminated sediment between the "glaciated pavement" and the "tillite" (Visser 1988, Visser & Loock 1988, see also point no. 4 in my paper).

Dr. Arthur N. Strahler's comments:

I would like to express my thanks to Dr. Strahler for the positive response, especially since he has written the most thorough book against "creationism" that has ever been written ("Science and Earth History - The Creation/Evolution Controversy", Promethius Books, Buffalo 1987, 552 pages). I believe that one can only work together, and learn from each other, when there is an atmosphere of mutual respect, in spite of having different philosophies. Then, also, the different philosophies and scientific interpretations can be weighed against each other, to see what will hold in the end.

Concerning the comments on radiometric dating etc, Dr. Strahler is correct. But, in my paper I did not write anything about absolute ages, only about how quick a special kind of lithology - diamictites - had formed (as I also stated in the abstract of my paper). His criticism of my paper on this point therefore is misplaced.

There is, however, one more point that is important. "Mainstream geology" has accommodated so many catastrophic events in the geologic column, that there is no longer millions of years left. More and more formations are believed to have been laid down in catastrophes, and the millions of years are in between the sedimentary strata - and are actually not there! My paper shows another instance where thousands or millions of years are diminished to almost no time at all. The question is, therefore: are radiometric dating methods giving true dates, or do they only give "model ages" that do not have any (or very little) absolute time significance? One only has to read one of the main works on this subject (Faure 1986) to get arguments against all time significance for radiometric dating. When one digs deeper in the subject, one finds a lot more ... (Molén 1988/1991).

Mr. David J. Tyler's comments:

As far as I can see Mr. Tyler is pleased with my paper. The only criticism he raises, if one can call an opinion a criticism, is that he thinks that the Ordovician deposits are best explained with a glacial interpretation. I can only refer to my paper, were I have gone through all the main evidences for a glaciation in the Ordovician of Sahara, in general in the first part of my paper and specifically in the later part. The main features are not in favor of an ice age, some features are equivocal, but none can be explained only by an ice age. To me the evidence speaks more of a gravity flow, even though every structure does not yet have a completely adequate explanation.

Until I know why Mr. Tyler favors a glacial interpretation I can not give him a better answer than this.

REFERENCES:

Faure, G. (1986) "Principles of Isotope Geology", 2nd ed., John Wiley & Sons, New York.
Molén, M. (1988/1991) "Vårt ursprung?", Salt & Ljus/Umeå FoU, Haninge/Umeå, pp. 96-110, 125-131, 135-141.
Visser, J. N. J. (1988) "A Permo-Carboniferous Tunnel Valley System East of Barkly West, Northern Cape Province", South African Journal of Geology, Vol. 91, pp. 350-357.
Visser, J. N. J. & Loock, J. C. (1988) "Sedimentary Facies of the Dwyka Formation Associated with the Nooitegedacht Glacial Pavements, Barkly West District", South African Journal of Geology, Vol. 91, pp. 38-48.

Mats Molén, B. Sc. B. Sc.

THE EVIDENCE FOR ONLY ONE ICE AGE

Michael J. Oard, M.S.
3600 7th. Ave. So.
Great Falls, Montana, 59405

ABSTRACT

Evolutionists believe in many Late Cenozoic ice ages, each lasting a long time. Previously, I showed that one ice age can occur very rapidly. Generally accepted evidence from history, climate simulations, paleontology, and the till deposits themselves indicate that one ice age is much more probable than many.

INTRODUCTION

Radiometric dating methods are not the only phenomenon that challenge the short time scale of Scripture. Many geophysical processes appear to need much more time than Scripture allows. One of these processes is the ice age.

Evolutionists believe that one Pleistocene ice age cycle or glacial/interglacial oscillation lasts 100,000 years, and that many such cycles repeated in succession during the Late Cenozoic Era of geological time. Ice ages are also claimed for other periods of geological time. These pre-Pleistocene ice ages are represented by rock layers within a sedimentary sequence that appear similar to lithified glacial till. However these till-like layers could just as well if not better be explained as the product of gigantic submarine mass flow during the Flood (as discussed by Mats Molen in this volume). The focus of this article will be on Late Cenozoic ice ages.

At the First International Conference on Creationism I discussed how one ice age can occur quickly - if different initial conditions are substituted for the uniformitarian principle (1). The initial conditions are extensive Flood and post-Flood volcanism that caused cooler summers, and a universally warm ocean which provided the copious moisture needed for an ice age. These conditions were triggered by the Genesis Flood. The duration of the ice age depends primarily upon the cooling time of the warm ocean. A reasonable estimate for the length of the ice age, based on the heat budgets of the ocean and atmosphere applied to post-Flood climatology, was about 600 years. Even using minimum and maximum estimates for the most important variables in the equations still resulted in a very short time. The amount of snow and ice during a post-Flood rapid ice age was estimated to be a little less than one-half uniformitarian estimates. The article ended with a brief summary of evidence for one Pleistocene ice age. In the present article I will expand this evidence. A detailed model of the ice age has been developed (2) and will be used as a backdrop for explaining several glacial features.

BRIEF HISTORICAL ANALYSIS

Before discussing the evidence for one ice age, I shall present a brief historical analysis of the multiple glaciation hypothesis. I believe the past is the key to the present in regard to this concept.

After the glacial theory as an explanation for the surface "drift" became popular in the mid 1800s, investigators at first believed in only one ice age. But because the glacial debris is complex and because multiple till layers are separated by non-glacial deposits in some areas, glacial geologists postulated multiple ice ages. Debate over the exact number ensued for many years, with those scientists who favored the astronomical theory preferring a large number of glaciations (3).

In the early twentieth century Albrecht Penck and Eduard Bruckner established what they thought was a method for determining the number of glaciations. By connecting gravel terraces along rivers in the northern foothills of the Alps upstream to end moraines, three glaciations were first proposed, but later four ice ages were claimed (4). Their method became known as the alpine model and was so influential that all data, worldwide was accommodated to it for the next sixty years. The four-ice-age model is now considered false and many reasons can be adduced to show why it is wrong.

The number of Late Cenozoic glaciations is now believed to range from fifteen to thirty, based on oxygen isotopes from foraminifera shells in deep-sea cores. There are a host of assumptions, problems, and unknowns associated with the interpretation of these cores (5-7). The connection to ice ages is inherently indirect and will not be discussed further. This article will focus on continental deposits, which in spite of glacial erosion, possess direct indications of the number of ice ages.

THE REINFORCEMENT SYNDROME

The alpine model teaches us a valuable lesson in self deception. Numerous research studies all "agreed," and the four-ice-age model was "confirmed" as the truth to laymen and scientists alike. This is an example of the reinforcement syndrome. Watkins states (8):
    Perhaps, the best known, or at least most significant, result of the "reinforcement syndrome" in the geological sciences is the very firmly established concept of four glacial periods during the last Ice Age. The initially defined system was confirmed by many different studies (quote his).
Verosub writes how the reinforcement syndrome works with the example of paleomagnetic excursions (9):
    The importance of the "reinforcement syndrome"...should not be underestimated. The initial report of a paleomagnetic excursion will encourage other workers to reexamine previously unexplained or disregarded "curious" results and to reinterpret sedimentation rates so that the anomalous behavior seen by them is contemporaneous with the paleomagnetic excursion. Subsequent work will also focus on sediments of the same age. Reported excursions will then tend to cluster around a single date, whereas negative results showing no anomalous behavior will tend to remain unpublished because they are "not interesting." Thus the initial reports exert considerable leverage on the direction of future research (quotes his).
Paleomagnetic excursions and the four-ice-age model are not the only concepts established by the reinforcement syndrome. It is "...an inherent weakness involved in experimental approaches and publication" (10). The reinforcement syndrome is a cancer in historical sciences. I believe the reinforcement syndrome is the reason why the geological column is "supported" by radioactive dating, and why many geological processes "agree" with each other.

The current belief in fifteen to thirty ice ages is basically a product of a reinforcement syndrome assuming the truth of the astronomical theory of the ice age. Continental deposits do not show anywhere near the number of ice ages deduced from the ocean sediments. In view of the reinforcement syndrome and the historical debate over the number of ice ages, I conclude that the number of glaciations is still an open question.

THE EVIDENCE FOR ONE ICE AGE

The evidence presented in this section will mostly be large-scale or general. Most glacial geologists would agree with the observational data. Small-scale data will be used sparingly because local data is usually complex and difficult to interpret within any framework. For example, a classical area for studying multiple glacial advances is the Scarborough Bluffs on the north shore of Lake Ontario near Toronto, Canada. Previous interpretation had divided three vertical lithologic units on the face of the cliff into three separate glacial advances. A more recent investigation placed the boundaries of lithological units at different heights on the bluffs because the lithological breaks pinched out or merged in the subsurface north of the cliffs (11). Moreover the sediments likely were not brought directly into place by an ice sheet at all but were deposited in a large lake by a floating ice shelf. If experts cannot agree whether a local succession was deposited directly below a glacier or dropped from an ice shelf in a large lake, glacial geology is in real trouble. I will avoid disputes of this nature by sticking mainly with large-scale data.

Perhaps the strongest evidence against ice ages repeating every 100,000 years is the uniformitarian principle itself. Williams showed, based on a reasonable climate simulation of the energy balance over a snow cover, that a summer temperature drop of at least 10 to 12 deg. C. with double the winter snowfall was required just to develop a perennial snow cover in northeast Canada (12). Presumably an ice age in northeast Canada could develop from this snow cover, although the atmosphere would tend to become drier than at present due to the colder air. If one ice age is this difficult to account for, what are the odds against two, three, or thirty ice ages in regular succession? Williams' experiment indicates a catastrophic mechanism is more likely for starting any ice age.

Ice age sediments, generally called till, also pose strong evidence against multiple ice ages. In the standard explanation for glaciation, each ice sheet developed in the far north and moved southward to the mid latitudes. During each advance the ice sheet picks up debris at its base and transports this debris farther and farther south. Thus we would expect to find a large amount of glacial till that has been transported long distances from the north. Is this what we observe? Other than a small number of "far-traveled" erratics, practically all the till is derived locally. Many investigators have commented on this observation. Feininger states (13):

Earlier in this report, the nearness of most glacial boulders to their source was cited as evidence that glacial transport is generally short. Even stronger evidence to support this view can be read from the tills themselves. Where the direction of movement carried a continental ice sheet from one terrain to another of markedly different rock type, the tills derived from each terrain are predominantly restricted to the area of their corresponding source rocks.

The local nature of most till is not what one expects even for one uniformitarian glacial/interglacial cycle. The claimed far-traveled erratics are rather enigmatic in view of the local nature of the remainder of the till and their occasional large size and angularity. The source for many erratics is unknown and may be buried nearby underneath till. Many erratics could have been transported long distances by icebergs. These icebergs could have traveled across large marine bays or extensive proglacial lakes, or been carried down large rivers swollen by meltwater. Regardless, the preponderance of the till favors one relatively thin ice sheet that did not move far. The ice sheet probably grew in situ and melted after a relatively short time.

One ice age is favored by the observation that practically all the till was deposited during the last advance of the last ice age (14). Glacial geologists commonly appeal to massive erosion and reworking by each successive ice sheet to explain this observation. Eroded and reworked till should at least be deposited at the periphery of the ice sheet. A great volume of till showing evidence of long distance transport should have accumulated at the periphery. However, there is little evidence of long distance transport or a huge thickness of till. A straightforward reading of the observed deposits, without resorting to additional hypotheses, better indicates the main volume of till is the result of just one ice age.

The character of glacial till observed in interior regions, like Canada and Scandinavia, points towards one ice age. Each successive ice sheet is believed to have built up to three thousand meters high in these areas. Thick deposits of till should be left over from the motion and melting of just the last thick ice sheet. The opposite is observed. The till is only two to ten meters thick on the average, and is found mainly in depressions and consists partly of stream and lake deposits (15). The till deposits seem too thin for all the postulated glacial activity. Furthermore the till is coarse grained, suggesting little transport and reworking.

A possible explanation for the above observation is that each successive ice sheet transported glacial debris from the Canadian shield to the periphery. If this was the case fifteen to thirty ice sheets should have deeply eroded the Canadian shield. However, the crystalline bedrock of Canada is still of moderate relief, and the relief is the same even under a cover of sedimentary rocks. Flint adds further (16):

Local evidence of slight depth of glacial erosion has been reported from many different districts...Indeed, the detailed adjustment of drainage to lithology, long antedating the glaciation and yet not destroyed by that event, is a feature that characterizes wide areas of the Canadian Shield.

Little erosion is also observed over Scandinavia. Eyles tries to explain this observation (17):

The absence of a thick drift cover on shield areas is not the result of enhanced glacial erosion as has been previously thought but rather is due to ineffective glacial deposition and the predominance of areal scouring rather than selective linear erosion...

In other words the thin till cover is due to both ineffective erosion and deposition. However ice sheet motion during development and melting throughout several million years should have considerably planed down the relief by now. Ineffective erosion and deposition and a thin till cover more directly support one thin short-lived ice sheet that probably was frozen to its bed and moved little.

Next we turn to the periphery where most of the till from the many postulated ice ages is supposed to collect. Even here the evidence better supports only one ice age. The average thickness of till at the periphery is not over thirty meters (18), and a significant proportion of this till is glaciofluvial and glaciolacustrine. Given the likelihood that the ice sheets incorporated unconsolidated pre-glacial surface deposits (19), the actual thickness of eroded bedrock is rather thin for all the purported ice ages.

How much time is required to deposit thirty meters of till? Under the right circumstances till can be eroded and deposited rapidly. Glacial erosion is enhanced if the glacier is warm-based, moves rapidly, is subject to surges, and the bedrock is soft. A wet-based glacier in the Alps moving at 250 meters/year has been observed to erode at a rate of about 36 millimeters/year (20). Assuming this constant erosion rate the glacier would erode thirty meters of rock in only 833 years. A glacier in Spitsbergen deposited a pile of till thirty meters high in only ten years (21). The ancient ice sheets over North America and Europe are now believed to have been relatively thin, moved rapidly over soft bedrock, and surged at the periphery (22,23). Thus thirty meters of till at the periphery is more in accord with one ice age and not multiple ice ages.

The direct evidence supporting multiple glaciation separated by interglacials comes from the periphery. This evidence consists mainly of soils and organic remains sandwiched between layers of till. Actually this evidence is rare: "Within the glaciated territory, interglacial horizons are rarely more than fragmentary" (24). The four-ice-age framework from the north central United States was based on soils overlying till. Since two soils are rarely found in a vertical sequence, the model was pieced together from different regions or type sites. It is now considered erroneous by most glacial geologists. Many problems are inherent in the interpretation of ice age soils, such as the recognition of a buried soil from a sediment layer that has undergone diagenesis, the general lack of the diagnostic A-horizon, and the likely formation of the typical clay soil of the ice age due to poor drainage or a high water table (25,26). So the physical evidence for interglacials from the glaciated territory that supports the multiple glaciation hypothesis is equivocal. The rare evidence for "interglacials" within glaciated terrain can be explained by one mild ice age that retreated, advanced, and surged at the periphery, similar to modern glaciers but on a larger scale.

Indirect evidence for multiple glaciation is postulated from the strongly eroded till south of the "last" glacial boundary in the north central United States, and alternating loess/soil layers south of the glaciated area in eastern Europe and China. However this indirect evidence can be explained with a post-Flood model if the ice sheet developed in situ in the north central United States at the beginning of the ice age. After a little climatic amelioration due to less volcanism, the ice sheet would melt back to a more stable position in the northern United States. Heavy precipitation on fresh glacial sediments would cause rapid erosion and an "old" appearance in a short time. The loess/soil alternations in eastern Europe and China could occur quickly at the end of a post-Flood ice age due to "dry" windy storms that would characterize this period. A classic area for a loess/soil stratigraphy is presented by Kukla along the west bank of the Svratka River in Czechoslovakia (27). About nine loess/soil cycles within various abandoned river terrace depressions putatively represent about one million years. The main basis for this length of time is simple curve matching to the oxygen isotope record in deep-sea cores. The depth of the sequence varies from ten to thirty meters. As discussed below, loess can be deposited rapidly in depressions. Ten to thirty meters can be deposited in a short time. The deposits along the west bank of the Svratka River show evidence of deposition by periodic strong winds, as indicated by frequent sandy interlayers and wind-moved rock fragments along the slopes. During periods of nondeposition, a soil (if they really are soils) could develop rapidly, especially in view of the fact modern soil formation rates are not known (28).

One final indication from the till for just one ice age can be garnered. At the periphery of the ancient glaciated area two relatively flat areas were not glaciated at all. These are the driftless areas in southwest Wisconsin (including small portions of southeast Minnesota and northeast Iowa) and a portion of the plains in northeast Montana (including a small section of south central Saskatchewan). These driftless areas should have been covered at least once by a thick ice sheet descending out of Canada. Driftless areas offer strong evidence for one thin ice sheet that missed a few areas along the periphery. How could many thick ice sheets all miss these areas, if indeed there were many thick ice sheets?

In addition to the till most loess (wind blown dust) was deposited during the later part of the last glaciation, at least in North America (29). Loess especially accumulated close to its source, in depressions, and against or in the lee side of wind breaks. Thus the thickness of loess is variable. In the central United States loess thickness occasionally exceeds sixty meters in favorable locations, but in general twenty to thirty meters is more typical (30). This much loess can be deposited quickly. During the dust bowl years in the midwestern United States, sand and dust storms rapidly covered fences and partially buried farms (31). During one storm that lasted two weeks, two meters of dust accumulated in places in southeast Colorado. The fact that cross bedding and fossils of large animals are sometimes found in loess is a strong indication of its rapid deposition at times (32). The missing loess from previous ice ages is usually explained by erosion. However, this does not make much sense since investigators cannot appeal to erosion and reworking by an ice sheet, and a soil cover would protect loess from erosion. Most of the loess from the last glaciation still remains, right before the next ice age is suppose to begin according to the astronomical theory of the ice age (unless of course the greenhouse effect takes over). Therefore, the observation that most of the loess,

194

especially from the central United States, was deposited at the end of the last glaciation and that loess can be deposited rapidly better supports one ice age.

Next we turn from the character of the till and loess to the paleontology of the ice age. Lack of evolutionary change in the plants and animals during each supposed glacial/interglacial oscillation better supports one ice age. Although the radical climatic changes should have provided abundant opportunities for evolutionary change, Flint states (33):
> Nevertheless, in Quaternary strata correlation by means of fossils encounters special difficulties. Rates of change of Quaternary environments were generally more rapid than rates of evolution in Quaternary organisms. The same faunas may appear repeatedly in successive strata, and their transgression of time is commonly evident.

Bowen adds with respect to the ice age flora: "The fact is that similar constellations of species were repeated several times in the Pleistocene, though not perhaps in the same relative abundance" (34). In other words, few fossil criteria are available to distinguish between each particular putative interglacial.

Another characteristic of the ice age plants and animals is that they are nearly all found in nonglaciated areas. Animals and plants would have repopulated glaciated areas after each ice sheet melted. The musk ox and reindeer would surely migrate back to the northland after the ice melted. We would expect to find some of their remains fossilized in protective hollows. However their near absence even along the periphery as well as from the interior is indeed mysterious within the multiple glaciation framework. The claim that the plants and animals simply did not become fossilized during each interglacial is hollow since the numerous fossils found in Alaska are attributed to an interglacial period (35).

A final paleontological argument in support of a single ice age is that nearly all of the regional and worldwide extinctions of large animals occurred after the last glaciation (36). Each ice age would have highly stressed the animals. How could they survive intact for fifteen to thirty ice ages over several million years, and then go extinct only after the last? Although scientists have been working on this puzzle for a long time, the evidence is more consistent with just one "mild" ice age which turned colder at the end.

A thick flow of ice would reduce irregularities in the landscape. But on Flowerpot Island in northern Lake Huron two rock pillars thirty and fifty feet high stand above the terrain along the eastern shore of the island (37). These pillars and other pinnacles in the area would have been planed down by even one thick ice sheet. This evidence suggests the ice sheet in this area was thin and moved very slow. One short ice age better fits this feature.

Ireland has an amazing record of ice age mammals - amazing from the point of view of the multiple glaciation hypothesis. The only record of ice age mammals comes from the very end of the last ice age (38,39). The giant deer or so-called Irish elk outnumbers all the other mammals, which includes only a few other species such as the mammoth, reindeer, and brown bear. Where is the record of previous glacials and interglacials in Ireland? Sutcliffe states the problem well (40):
> If Ireland was indeed previously uninhabited by mammals, then we are faced with the incredible prospect of a vast tract of land with ample rainfall and a luxuriant vegetation flourishing during the Last Interglacial (the Ipswichian of the British mainland, 120000 years ago) yet without any mammalian fauna to consume it; whilst a short distance away great herds of hippopotamus and other mammals competed for food.

Erosion of fossiliferous deposits from previous glacial or interglacial periods cannot be invoked since some of the fossils are found in caves. The Irish Sea would not have been a barrier for mammal migration to Ireland because the Irish Sea is shallow and England and Scotland are in close proximity. A passageway to Ireland would have been opened during each successive ice age if sea level lowered only forty-five meters below present sea level (41). The fact that animals arrived late in the last ice age indicates that they should have been able to make the crossing during other ice ages - if indeed there were any other ice ages.

SUMMARY

Table I summarizes the evidence for one ice age. Most of this evidence is directly from the glacial deposits themselves, so no further assumptions relating them to the ice age are required. The record from deep-sea cores needs many assumptions in order to connect the ocean sediments to glaciation. A straightforward reading of the evidence in Table I from the actual glacial deposits themselves better supports only one ice age.

TABLE I
Summary of evidence supporting a single post-Flood ice age

1)	One ice age meteorologically difficult
2)	Most till local
3)	Most till from the "last" ice age
4)	Interior till thin and coarse grained
5)	Bedrock eroded little interior areas
6)	Periphery till not that thick
7)	Driftless areas within the periphery
8)	Most loess U.S. from the "last" ice age
9)	Little change in ice age plants and animals
10)	Fossils rare in glaciated regions
11)	Most extinction after the "last" ice age
12)	Local survival of delicate landforms
13)	Irish mammals only from end of "last" ice age

REFERENCES

1.   Oard, M., "An Ice Age Within the Biblical Time Frame," Proceedings of The First International Conference on Creationism, Volume II, Creation Science Fellowship, Pittsburgh, 1987, p. 157-166.

2.   Oard, M., An Ice Age Caused by the Genesis Flood (in press).

3.   Charlesworth, J., The Quaternary Era, Volume II, Edward Arnold, London, 1957, p. 911.

4.   Bowen, D., Quaternary Geology A Stratigraphic Framework for Multidisciplinary Work, Pergamon Press, New York, 1976, p. 10,13.

5.   Oard, M., "Ice Ages: The Mystery Solved? Part I: The Inadequacy of a Uniformitarian Ice Age," Creation Research Society Quarterly, 21, 2, 1984, p. 66-76.

6.   Oard, M., "Ice Ages: The Mystery Solved? Part II: The Manipulation of Deep-Sea Cores," Creation Research Society Quarterly, 21, 3, 1984, p. 125-137.

7.   Oard, M., "Ice Ages: The Mystery Solved? Part III: Paleomagnetic Stratigraphy and Data Manipulation," Creation Research Society Quarterly, 21, 4, 1985, p. 170-181.

8.   Watkins, N., "Review of the Development of the Geomagnetic Polarity Time Scale and Discussion of Prospects for Its Finer Definition," Geological Society of America Bulletin, 83, 1972, p. 563.

9.   Verosub, K., "Paleomagnetic Excursions as Magnetostratigraphic Horizons: A Cautionary Note," Science, 190, 1975, p. 50.

10. Watkins, N., "Geomagnetic Polarity Events and the Problem of 'The Reinforcement Syndrome,'" Comments on Earth Sciences and Geophysics, 2, 1971, p. 38.

11. Eyles, C. and Eyles, N., "Sedimentation in a Large Lake: A Reinterpretation of the Late Pleistocene Stratigraphy at Scarborough Bluffs, Ontario, Canada," Geology, 11, 1983, p. 146-152.

12. Williams, L., "An Energy Balance Model of Potential Glacierization of Northern Canada," Arctic and Alpine Research, 11, 4, 1979, p. 443-456.

13. Feininger, T., "Chemical Weather and Glacial Erosion of Crystalline Rocks and the Origin of Till," U.S. Geological Survey Professional Paper 750-C, U.S. Government Printing Office, Washington, D.C., 1971, p. C79.

14. Sugden, D. and John, B., Glaciers and Landscape, Edward Arnold, London, 1976, p. 133,138.

15. Eyles, N., Dearman, W., and Douglas, T., "The Distribution of Glacial Landsystems in Britian and North America," Glacial Geology, N. Eyles, ed., Pergamon Press, New York, 1983, p. 227.

16. Flint, R., Glacial and Quaternary Geology, John Wiley and Sons, New York, 1971, p. 115.

17. Eyles, N., "Glacial Geology: A Landsystems Approach," Glacial Geology, N. Eyles, ed., Pergamon Press, New York, 1983, p. 4.

18. Flint, Op. Cit., p. 149-151.

19. Feininger, Op. Cit., p. C65-C81.

20. Drewry, D., Glacial Geological Processes, Edward Arnold, London, 1986, p. 84.

21. Flint, Op. Cit., p. 149.

22. Boulton, G., "A Paradigm Shift in Glaciology?" Nature, 322, 1986, p. 18.

23. Beget, J., "Modeling the Influence of Till Rheology on the Flow and Profile of the Lake Michigan Lobe, Southern Laurentide Ice Sheet, U.S.A.," Journal of Glaciology, 32, 111, 1986, p. 235-241.

24. Charlesworth, Op. Cit., p. 903.

25. Valentine, K. and Dalrymple, J., "Quaternary Buried Paleosols: A Critical Review," Quaternary Research, 6, 1976, p. 209-222.

26. Birkland, P., Soils and Geomorphology, Oxford University Press, New York, 1984.

27. Kukla, G., "Pleistocene Land-Sea Correlations 1. Europe," Earth Science Reviews, 13, 1977, p. 307-374.

28. Boardman, J., "Comparison of Soils in Midwestern United States and Western Europe with the Interglacial Record," Quaternary Research, 23, 1, 1985, p. 65.

29. Pye, K., Aeolian Dust and Dust Deposits, Academic Press, New York, 1987, p. 245.

30. Ibid., p. 204,207.

31. Landsberg, H., Physical Climatology, 2nd edition, Gray Printing Co., Dubois, Pennsylvania, 1958, p. 267,268.

32. Sutcliffe, A., On the Track of Ice Age Mammals, Harvard University Press, Cambridge, Massachusetts, 1985, p. 43.

33. Flint, Op. Cit., p. 376.

34. Bowen, Op. Cit., p. 38.

35. Flint, Op. Cit., p. 771.

36. Martin, P. and Klein, R., eds., Quaternary Extinctions: A Prehistoric Revolution, University of Arizona Press, Tuscon, 1984.

37. Cox, D., "Controversy About Ice Ages," Creation Research Society Quarterly, 16, 1, 1979, p. 23,24.

38. Sutcliffe, Op. Cit., p. 144-150.

39. Edwards, K. and Warren, W., eds., The Quaternary History of Ireland, Academic Press, New York, 1985.

40. Sutcliffe, Op. Cit., p. 147.

41. Flint, Op. Cit., p. 774.

DISCUSSION

Mr. Oard continues to excel in research on late Cenozoic glaciation. This paper provides detail not addressed in previous papers. It is an excellent summary of evidences supporting a single post-Flood ice age. Because of the abundance of Pleistocene strata and importance to creationist theory, further research is in order.

Steven Austin, Ph.D.
El Cajon, California

Mr. Oard has presented a commendable brief review of the physical evidence that calls for explanation as a consequence of continental glaciation. The twelve categories of evidence he cites from till, loess, erosion, and fossils within glaciated areas strongly call for explanation on the basis of only one glaciation. Combined with consideration of the severe unlikelihood of the meteorological conditions necessary for continental glaciation, this evidence forcibly constrains to a postulation of only one ice age, only one glaciation. The prevailing presumption of three ice ages over phanerozoic time is accordingly seen to be held because it meets the requirements of a speculative view concerning Earth history, and not as a logical consequence of the available directly-related evidence.

The data in the book of Genesis specifies an event (the Flood and its aftermath) which can be expected to provide meteorological conditions necessary for continental glaciation. In other publications which he cites Oard has shown that adequate time for one, but only one, continental glaciation cycle is provided by the chronological data in the Old Testament.

Robert H. Brown, Ph.D.
Loma Linda, California

Mr. Oard's model for a quick ice age is very interesting and probably the first and only that can explain an ice age. The evidences given for one ice age are compelling, but I believe that in such a catastrophic model the back and forth movement of large glaciers would give the appearance that there had been many ice ages.

The existence of wind-polished stones and bedrock below the Pleistocene till (Hillefors 1969, Rapp et al 1984) and peat between layers of till means that one would require sufficient time to get the peat growing and the bedrock polished. In northern Sweden, near the center of the glaciated areas, there are post-flood fossils and peat below the first till layer. Also, scientists have found hundreds of places, where the center of glaciation is thought to contain peat overlain with deformation till (Lagerback & Robertsson 1988).

The stone pillars (called "rauks") next to the Great Lakes might have been formed after the ice age by erosion from waves and lake ice. At least that is how similar stone pillars have been formed on the island of Gotland in Sweden.

Therefore, there needs to be some time for formation of peat deposits and other structures after the flood and before the ice age.

REFERENCES:
Hillefors, A. (1969), "Vastsveriges Glacia Historia och Geomorfologi", Meddelanden fran Lunds Universiets Geografiska Institution.

Lagerback, R. & Robertsson, M., (1988) "Kettle Holes - Stratigraphical Archives for Weichselian Geology and Palaeoenvironment in Northmost Sweden", Boreas, Vol. 17, pp. 439-468.

Rapp, A. et al (1984) "Nivationsnischerna vid Ugglerod, Rostanga", Svensk Geografisk Arsbok, Vol. 60, pp. 131-144.

Mats Molén, B.S., B.S.
Holmsund, Sweden

I am thankful that Mr. Oard is again addressing the Glacial Epoch, and that his observations and conclusions are of only one ice age. My observations agree with his. I, too, conclude that one ice age (with surges) adequately explains the data. I am also glad that he proposes that a catastrophic mechanism initiated the Glacial Epoch, i.e., the Flood. It would serve us well if Mr. Oard would elaborate on the causes and dynamics of the peripheral surges. Let me begin by proposing the following outline: As the continental ice sheets grew, the ice-source regions did not remain in the original locations, but the ice-source regions followed the terminal ice. Two factors apply:

1) Air beyond the terminal ice would be dry.

2) The advance of the glaciers could only be sustained by gravity gradients local to the terminal glaciers.

Therefore the sources and dynamics of the glaciers would reside in the terminal ice. And the atmospheric-ice interplay would produce periodic expansions and contractions of terminal glaciers.

Mr. Oard's comments concerning the peripheral surges would, I believe, also help address the major problem of varves, e.g., Antevs; 4300 varves along the Connecticut River Valley.

David P. Nelson, B.S.
Santa Barbara, California

I believe Mr. Oard has done an admirable job of arguing for a single ice age based on continental deposits. However, I would encourage him to address the same issue relative to deep-sea and ice cores in future work. Regarding this paper I have four questions:

1) How much does Mr. Oard believe the surging of the ice sheets contributes to the standard interpretation of multiple ice ages?

2) Does he have evidence that "dry" windy storms characterized the end of the post-flood ice age other than loess/soil alterations in eastern Europe and China?

3) I do not understand the author's reference to the greenhouse effect at the bottom of page 4. What does the greenhouse effect have to do with the removal of wind blown dust?

4) I assume Mr. Oard meant to say in Table I, that multiple ice ages are meteorologically difficult. Would he agree that we are in no immediate danger of entering a new ice age?

Larry Vardiman, Ph.D.
El Cajon, California

CLOSURE

I thank all those who commented on my article, and I hope my work is an encouragement to many.

From Mr. Mats Molén's comments, I may have to delete the stone pillars on Flowerpot Island as evidence for one ice age, since similar structures exist on the island of Gotland in the Baltic Sea. The pillars may have been formed by the vagaries of lake shore erosion, although I do not understand how this could happen. Still, there is the possibility that the pillars on Gotland, in the middle of the southern baltic Sea, survived one thin ice sheet of short duration. I would like to know if stone pillars exist along shorelines elsewhere within glaciated terrain. Other structures of sharp relief may still be evidence of one ice age, for instance the Niagara escarpment around the Great Lakes.

Further understanding of the details in my model may answer Mr. Molén's other comments. In my article, I stuck to mostly large-scale evidence because I knew that local areas can present complications that are difficult for even uniformitarian scientists to explain. Overall, there is very little fossil flora or fauna in surficial sediments from previously glaciated areas, especially interior areas. Nevertheless, I will attempt to explain the fossils and wind-polished stones (if that is what they are) that are found in Sweden.

There are at least three possible explanations. First, the fossils could have been left on or near the surface after the Genesis Flood. Second, glaciation in northwest Europe would have developed slower than over northeastern North America because of the onshore flow of air heated by the warm water of the sea (1). Snow and ice caps would develop first in the mountains of Scandinavia, coalesce, and gradually spread out into the lowlands. Due to the proximity of the warm ocean water, plants that could not tolerate the present climate likely would grow for awhile in the lowlands. Possibly, woolly mammoths could migrate up into the lowlands of Sweden and the deep mountain valleys of Norway before those areas glaciated. Plants and many animals would eventually be inundated by the growing ice sheet. Wind-polished stones could have formed during this pre-glacial period. Third, the fossils could be post-ice age. Since I have shown the ice sheets would melt rapidly, cold-tolerant plants may gain an early foothold. Woolly mammoths likely still survived awhile during deglaciation and could have migrated into Scandinavia. Any fossils found between till could result from entrapment by an oscillating ice margin, or by burial in flow till or mudflows after melting.

The third possibility very likely explains the data of Lagerbäck and Robertsson (2), who ar
bent on fitting data into the astronomical theory of multiple ice ages, which claims thre
stadials (ice age peaks) during the last ice age. In their article, they claim that organi
debris in kettle holes, associated with fresh, sharp-crested eskers, formed during a
interstadial after the first stadial. The delicate landforms subsequently survived the secon
and third stadials! The evidence more directly shows the organic debris followed immediatel
after total deglaciation of the area.

I believe Mr. David Nelson's idea on the dynamics of the ice sheet is correct, at least fo
North America. The greatest buildup of ice would occur along the southern and easter
periphery. Variable inputs of volcanic dust would fuel marginal oscillations. Thes
oscillations would be rapid because: 1) volcanic dust in the ice and mild temperature greatl
increase ice deformation, 2) basal water causes greater slip, 3) a steep terminal slope of th
ice sheet, and 4) a soft moist bedrock (3). Surges should be common and would be partl
responsible for multiple till sheets separated by glaciofluvial sand and gravel, interpreted a
multiple ice ages by uniformitarian geologists.

I do not believe that peripheral oscillations explain the varves in the Connecticut Rive
Valley, or in Scandinavia for that matter. From my calculations, the periphery of the ice shee
melts within one hundred years. This is, of course, contrary to the varve chronology from th
above areas. However, these chronologies are built on a number of assumptions. Two assumption
will be discussed.

The first assumption is that the varves are annual. Varves are complex and variable and can b
duplicated by turbidity currents, interflows, and overflows. A large number of rhythmites for
each year in brackish estuaries that drain glaciers. (4,5).

The second assumption is that short varve sections can be correlated by curve matching northwar
up the ancient lake bed. This is why Antevs claims the ice sheet took 4,300 years to melt u
the Connecticut Valley. I do not believe this procedure can be justified. One of the mai
reasons is that Antevs believed the varves were formed from south-flowing currents due t
draining of a slowly melting ice sheet. However, most of the sediment input to this thin, 40
km long lake came from the east and west by normal river sedimentation. How can varves then b
correlated northward up the river valley? Ashley (6), a recent investigator, states: "In m
opinion, the method of visually matching curves drawn from varve tapes, which was so successfu
in Sweden, is unreliable for the Connecticut Valley." The Swedish varves are another story wit
special problems and assumptions.

In reference to Dr. Vardiman's comments, there is other evidence, besides loess, of generall
dry, windy storms as the ice sheets melted. The mere presence of ice sheets and greater sea ic
would meteorologically result in a colder, drier climate at the mid and high latitudes of th
Northern Hemisphere. The temperature contrast from the ice sheets to the tropics, whic
determines strong strength, would be greater than at present. The Nebraska sand hills provide
further geological evidence for dry, windy storms.

Any ice age is meteorologically difficult. Special conditions are required that were fulfille
once by the unique climatic consequences of the Genesis Flood. We can rest assured that th
next ice age is not due next winter or soon thereafter, according to the astronomical theory o
the ice ages. Besides, the greenhouse effect, if real, will halt it (mostly an attempt a
humor).

In reference to Dr. Vardiman's comments, I am working on ice cores and deep-sea cores. Wit
respect to Dr. Brown's reference to Phanerozoic ice ages, I am now finishing up a monograph c
supposed pre-Pleistocene ice ages.

Michael J. Oard, M.S

CAVITATION: AN INTEGRAL AGENT OF
ENERGETIC GEOMORPHOLOGICAL PROCESSES

CLIFFORD A. PAIVA
2127 E.J. 8 AVE
LANCASTER, CA 93535

INTRODUCTION

Probably the gamut of geomorphological structures observed today were generated by the recession waters of the Genesis Flood. However geomorphology addresses only one aspect of structural geology. The etiological processes associated with sedimentary and igneous stratigraphy addresses yet an even more important study of Flood Geology. The general Flood model usually consists initially of a global fracture event occurring simultaneously with a global vapor canopy collapse, generating very energetic hydrodynamic processes — not the least of which is *cavitation* phenomena.(1) This explosive phenomenon (cavitation), resulting from exceedingly intense procession and recession of Flood waters, probably generated pressures well in excess of 200,000 psi(2) and is postulated to have occurred in the precession and the recession phases of the Flood. The paper is divided into two sections: 1. Cavitation Inception and 2. Cavitation Reduction.

The purpose of this investigation is to demonstrate the probability that cavitation existed as in *intrinsic* phenomenon of the Genesis Flood. There appears no way to obviate the necessity of cavitation processes, especially when considering calculations using Barnes' minimum cavitation velocity, as well as Ehrenberger's steep slope velocity. Further, the damage propensity presented in section two demonstrates that the Flood velocities are **not** required to be high in order for cavitation occur.(3) This will be demonstrated via interpretation of data obtained from the work conducted at the California Institute of Technology, using comparatively low flow velocities, is related to surface tensile strengths, including the granitic types. However, a brief mathematical approach using the Bernoulli formula for constant mass flow is in order.

CAVITATION INCEPTION

Barnes and Ehrenberger Velocities

A mathematical approach using the Bernoulli equation helps in appreciating the relationship between cavitation *inception*, and hardened surface damage — *cavitation reduction*. The former occurs in high dynamic fluid flow pressure zones (with corresponding low static pressures). The latter in low dynamic pressures and high hydrostatic pressures. It is important not to confuse cavitation *inception* with cavitation *reduction* since the fluid pressure environments are opposite. The mathematical formula used to predict both environments and the likelihood of cavitation is (4)

$$\frac{V_1{}^2}{2g} + \frac{P_1}{Y} = V_2{}^2 + \frac{P_2}{Y} \qquad \text{Bernoulli Formula} \qquad (1)$$

where

V_1 = initial stream velocity (ft per sec)
V_2 = velocity at cavitation inception (ft per sec)
g = acceleration of gravity (32.2 ft per sec^2)
P_1 = absolute pressure (14.7 lbs per in^2)
P_2 = fluid vapor pressure (0.36 lbs per in^2)
Y_1 = specific weight of water (62.42 lbs per ft^3)
Z_1 = stream depth (feet)
Z_2 = stream elevation = 0 (datum level assumed)

With the above boundary conditions V_1 may be calculated. V_1 is Barnes' estimate of velocity(5) required for cavitation inception. The following graph (Graph 1.1) is produced using Barnes' formula showing stream velocity versus Ehrenberger's steep slope velocity (as a function of stream bed angle).

$$V_1 = 4.6(33.1 + Z_1)^{.5} \tag{2}$$

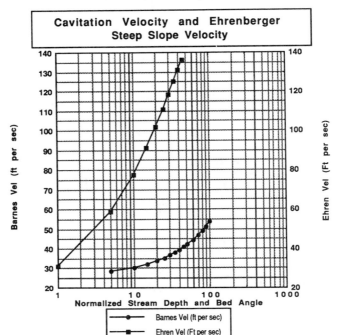

Note that the Ehrenberger steep slope velocity (as a function of stream bed angle) exceeds the Barnes' minimum velocity required for cavitation. Even at a stream depth of only five feet, with Barnes' required velocity for cavitation being 28 feet per second, the Ehrenberger velocity (32 feet per second) already exceeds the required cavitation velocity when assuming only one degree of bed angle! A closer look at the Ehrenberger Steep Slope Velocity will help to clarify its effect on cavitation inception. The Ehrenberger Steep Slope Velocity(6) is

$$V_E = 97R.52(\Sigma).^{40} \tag{3}$$

where Σ is the sine of the angle of the stream bed and R is the hydraulic radius (ratio of stream area to wetted perimeter of flow). Graph 1.2 shows the relationship of Ehrenberger velocity singularly as a function of stream angle. Hydraulic radius is assumed at 2.5:1. The highest flow velocity used by Cal Tech is 59.9 feet per second, which produced a supercavitated flow condition.(7) The term supercavitation is used to describe cavitation flows which exceed the length of the immersed object (pebbles, boulders, etc.) We conclude that since the majority of Flood recession stream bed angles probably exceeded ten degrees, most recession flows were supercavitated.

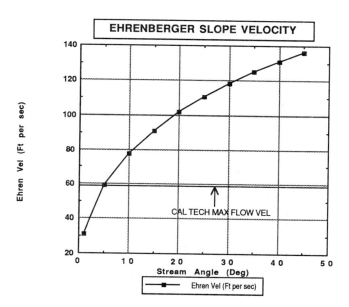

EHRENBERGER SLOPE VELOCITY

Ehren Vel (Ft per sec) vs Stream Angle (Deg)

CAL TECH MAX FLOW VEL

— ■ — Ehren Vel (Ft per sec)

CAVITATION REDUCTION

Comparative Tensile Strengths and Cavitation Losses

Table 1 shows a variety of physical parameters of interest to the study of cavitation loss. The losses are measured as functions of material composition, ambient temperature, tensile strength, yield point, and material hardness. Lower tensile strengths and hardness are included in the lower table. The objective of the use of these data is to depict the relatively low tensile strengths (with commensurate high loss susceptibility) of the granites. **If chrome steel is reduced by cavitation processes, then certainly granite (of much lower tensile strength) is significantly more affected.**

Table 6.03 and Table 6.04 reveal some of the information presented in Figure 6.05 and 6.06. Further, note that those types of materials which possess large amounts (greater than .47%) of silicon (Si) are significantly more affected by cavitation than those types with low concentrations of silicon. **Silicon (Si) based materials appear susceptible to cavitation.**

Graph 1.3 shows cavitation reduction as a function of percent silicon content. Included are tensile strength, Brinell hardness, and yield.

The alloy number refers to the different metal alloys depicted in Table 6.03. Note that those alloys strong in Si, particularly 11, 12 and 21 through 24 all exceed 100,000 psi tensile strength. Yet as Si content decreases as a function of alloy number, so does cavitation loss. The reason for this effect may be due to the resonance nature of silicon dioxide (SiO_2) coupled with piezoelectric type processes.

Another salient point to be considered is the *duration* of the tests which were conducted at the CIT. The maximum test duration is 16 *hours*. The Genesis Flood procession and recession phases are on the order of *years*! The energy which may be released in terms of cavitation processes over so long a period would be phenomenal.

Graph 1.4 shows cavitation singularly as a function of Si content (all alloys).

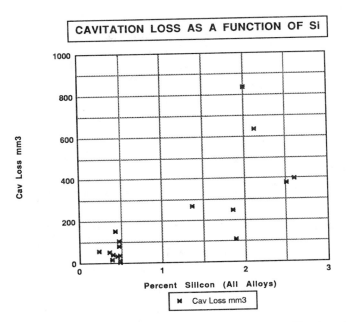

CAVITATION LOSS AS A FUNCTION OF Si

Graph 1.5 depicts the susceptibility of cavitation reduction to tensile strength of materials. It is this graph which correlates the high propensity of the granites to cavitation processes since their tensile strengths are much less than the harder surfaces indicated.

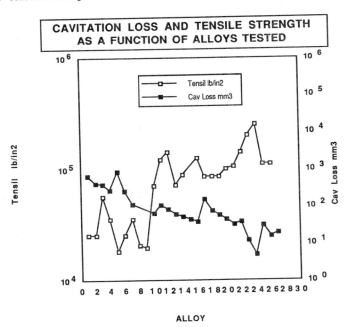

CAVITATION LOSS AND TENSILE STRENGTH AS A FUNCTION OF ALLOYS TESTED

Since the granites are on the order of 10^3 psi (see Table 6.04) it is difficult to imagine tha these materials would not be reduced by cavitation. Notice that cavitation loss is alread severe at 10^4 psi. Since granites contain significant amounts of SiO_2 we expect these types o stream bed surfaces to be rapidity eroded.

SUMMARY AND CONCLUSION

Cavitation should be considered an integral part of Flood Geology. There should be doubt stream velocities need not be excessively high, nor beds abnormally inclined, to attain prime cavitation conditions. If the Barnes' prediction for incipient cavitation is accurate to a first order; and if velocities as functions of stream bed slope are also first order correct, then cavitation inception should occur. Other variables would enhance the process. For example, and not mentioned in this paper, are(8)

- reduction of water tensile strength as a function of increased temperature
- decrease of ambient atmospheric pressure due to collapse of the vapor canopy with resultant lower cavitation number(9)
- resonance (acoustic) cavitation occurring as a function of shock impact against SiO_2.(10)
- disintegration of hardened surfaces, hydrodynamic plucking forces as a function of stream flow, with resultant angular bed surfaces inducing more cavitation

Although the physics behind an apparent susceptibility of SiO_2 type surfaces to cavitation is not understood, the general answer probably has to do with the resonance frequency of silicon dioxide crystal lattices and impacting shock frequencies. Further study is required to assess this correlation. Certainly the measurements made at the California Institute of Technology does confirm that cavitation reduction is directly proportional to tensile strength. Since the granites have tensile strengths on the order of 10^3 psi, we may expect these surfaces to be far more susceptible to cavitation than the 10^4 and 10^5 psi strengths of Table 6.03, although these stronger materials were also susceptible to cavitation over the 16 hour flow times.

REFERENCES

1. C.A. Paiva, *Cavitation in Macro-Fluvial Processes and the Implications for Geologic Time*, A Thesis, Institute for Creation Research, p. 1, 1988.

2. G.W. Sutton, *A Photoelastic Study of Strain Waves Caused by Cavitation*, Journal of Applied Mechanics, Vol. 24, pt. 3, pp. 340-348, 1957. Actually this number is often exceeded, for example when surface tension is increased as a function of decreased temperature, and cavitation occurs in high velocity flows. In any case it is due to the equivalence of the fluid static pressure to its vapor pressure, which results in minute cavities, hence the term cavitation.

3. F.R. Young, *Cavitation*, McGraw-Hill Book Company, London, 1989, pp. 198-199.

4. Ibid., 3, pp. 188-189.

5. H. Barnes, *Cavitation as a Geologic Agent*, American Journal of Science, Vol. 254, August 1956, pp. 493-505.

6. R. Ehrenberger, Zs. Osterreich Ischen Ing. und Arch. Heft 15/16, (1926).

7. Ibid. 3, p. 199. Fully extended (supercavitation) would be expected as the norm in Flood recession processes since theses v velocities would exceed 60 ft sec^{-1}.

8. Ibid. 1, pp. 37-40.

9. This number is commonly designated as $\Sigma = \dfrac{P\,[(ambient) - P\,(vapor)]}{.5\,\partial\,v^2}$ where ∂ and v are the fluid density and velocity respectively. The lower the cavitation number the higher the probability of cavitation.

10. Ibid. 3. This process takes up more than 180 pages of Young's text. Basically if the ambient pressure of the fluid drops below the fluid's vapor pressure (as in hydrodynamic cavitation) due to rapidly expanding shock fronts (from bubble implosion), the induced rarefaction regions behind the front may also cavitate with a net result of amplification of the phenomenon.

DISCUSSION

Mr. Paiva has not clearly demonstrated in his first part that cavitation can be achieved at low stream velocities. His referenced works and equations may indeed support such an assertion, but the author does not present a logical argument. Ignoring the steel-to-granite extrapolation as well, there is little of substance left to salvage. I had hoped that this paper would be more polished because creationist literature needs more contributions on the subject of cavitation, but the quality of papers needs to be as high as that required by all reputable scientific journals.

The author should, however, be encouraged to continue his research into this important area. Perhaps Mr. Paiva could document the durability of various rock species under cavitation. We need those numbers. We also need laboratory measurements of cavitation as water flows over recently laid basalt barriers, because hot water cavitates better than cold. He should carefully document his threshold speeds for cavitation if indeed they need not be large.

Edmond W. Holroyd, Ph.D.
Arvada, Colorado

Mr. Paiva's paper distills the findings from the first large scale study of cavitation from a creation-science or flood geology perspective. It should be read along with the two other papers on cavitation and the Clark and Voss paper, "Resonance and Sedimentary Layering in the Context of a Global Flood." All were given at the 1990 International Conference on Creationism.

Most people might agree that cavitation occurring in moving fluids would be globally significant if a combination of high velocity, rough surface, weak materials and long time frames were operative, but Mr. Paiva shows that significant if a combination of high velocity, rough surface, weak materials and long time frames were operative, but the author shows that significant cavitation reduction needs not even one of these factors. Much of this paper is based on actual lab tests of cavitation acting on very strong materials. Given the abundance of silicon in the crust of the earth, it is significant that cavitation influence goes up with and increase in silicon content. The possibility that silicon content increases the vulnerability to resonant influences calls for investigation of this factor.

Mr. Paiva's paper helps provide the needed explanation of a process that can reduce the pre-flood crust to all the sediment needed to form the sedimentary layer, and in a short time.

Paul M. MacKinney
Carlsbad, California

While it is true that if the post flood streams had bed angles greater than 1 degree, cavitation would be a widespread phenomena, it is quite unlikely that any stream could have had the required gradient. The Mississippi River falls about 1,000 feet from the source to the mouth over a straight line distance of about 1,225 miles. This yields an average bed angle of .008 degrees: a value that is much smaller than the value of 1 to 10 degrees assumed by Dr. Slusher and Mr. Paiva.

Even if one were to assume a 10 degree gradient for the river beds, this would require an impossible and unrealistic source elevation for any moderately long stream. A 10 degree slope on the Mississippi River requires a source elevation of 212 miles. Even a 1 degree slope requires a 21 mile elevation.

What needs to be explained is why are we to expect the immediate post-flood topology to be so steep?

Glenn R. Morton, M.S.
Dallas, Texas

CLOSURE

Mr. Paiva did not respond to his reviewers.

DISCONTINUITY SYSTEMATICS:
A NEW METHODOLOGY OF BIOSYSTEMATICS
RELEVANT TO THE CREATION MODEL

Walter J. ReMine
783 Iglehart Avenue
Saint Paul, MN 55104

ABSTRACT

According to the creation model, an important feature of life is discontinuity -- the discontinuity between the originally created life forms. Yet, all existing methods of biosystematics are inherently incapable of recognizing, or even describing, the discontinuities of life. To meet these needs, a new method of biosystematics is proposed, called Discontinuity Systematics. Four new terms are introduced -- holobaramin, monobaramin, polybaramin, and apobaramin -- these terms allow for the identification, description, and evaluation, necessary in the new systematics. The special inter-relationship of the terms allows biosystematic knowledge to be constructed in a methodical way. Lineage, reproductive viability, biological experimentation, and similarity are discussed, showing how they assist the identification of groups in the new systematics. Discontinuity Systematics will aid discussion of a significant biological system pattern, and begin the accumulation of evidence relevant to the creation model.

INTRODUCTION

The difference between the modern views of creationists and evolutionists is discontinuity. In the creationist's view, many groups of organisms are separate and distinct -- disconnected from other groups. In contrast to the predictions of evolutionary theory, creationists feel that life displays an important pattern of discontinuity. Yet, currently there is no method of biosystematics which is capable of identifying and studying discontinuity.

All traditional methods of biosystematics are insensitive to discontinuity, and are inherently incapable of identifying it -- they are "blind" to discontinuity. Phylogenetic systematics and evolutionary taxonomy explicitly assume continuity, and thus always conclude that continuity is a characteristic of life. The methods of phenetics and transformed cladistics produce data structures such as phenograms and cladograms. These data structures locate life forms at the tips of the branches of a tree-like diagram. Many people erroneously identify such diagrams with an evolutionary tree (phylogeny), and thus prematurely presume the evolutionary continuity of life. Nonetheless, these systematic methods do not try to determine whether or not discontinuity actually exists.

A new biosystematic method for identifying discontinuity would help scientists study this important aspect of life's pattern. This would also enable creationists and evolutionists to more clearly communicate information and viewpoints. This paper proposes such a method for the study and description of the earth's biota. The method is called Discontinuity Systematics because it focuses on discontinuity as a pattern of life. Discontinuity Systematics seeks to identify the boundaries of common descent.

KINDS

Many creationists have used the term "kind" for their biosystematic unit. However, this is an inadequate term for Discontinuity Systematics. Many anti-creationists have cogently argued that 'kind' is an ill-defined and ambiguous term (1:278-284, 2:164-9, 4:115-9, 5:187, 6:71, 7:208-9, 8:151-5, 13:74,361-3,430).

First, confusion arises from the history of the words 'species' and 'kind.' At one time the two words were synonymous. In fact, 'species' was merely the Latin word for 'kind.' Before Darwin, some scientists used the term 'species' with virtually the same meaning that creationists use 'kind' today. For example, von Baer, in 1828 (9:257) defined a species as "the sum of the individuals that are united by common descent." Even today some people equate 'kind' with 'species.' However, the term species has been redefined in many new ways by modern scientists. There are now a wide variety of species definitions, and significant disagreement exists about which of those definitions are most appropriate (9,10,11). The modern term 'species' carries much unwanted baggage of semantic ambiguity and confusion. Therefore, equating 'kind' with 'species' only results in further confusion.

Second, there are several colloquial, non-biosystematic definitions of 'kind', which lead to ambiguity. Third, 'kind' has several conflicting biosystematic definitions, once again leading to ambiguity. Fourth, a single term, like 'kind', is insufficient for doing serious work in biosystematics. Several interrelated terms are necessary for precisely conveying the results of biosystematic research.

THE NEW TERMINOLOGY

Frank Marsh (1947) coined the term baramin to mean "created kind." Marsh constructed the term as a compound of two Hebrew roots: bara meaning created, and min meaning kinds. This unique word serves as a root for the new terminology of Discontinuity Systematics.

Discontinuity Systematics classifies only real, known organisms, not hypothetical, imaginary or undiscovered organisms. Discontinuity Systematics classifies known organisms into groups. These groups are defined relative to all known life forms, fossil or living. Each group includes only known life forms, and excludes only known life forms. Thus, these groups can neither include nor exclude organisms that remain undiscovered. Therefore, as new organisms are discovered, some specific groupings would need to be adjusted accordingly. For example, if a certain group is said to contain "all" its ancestors, then this refers only to known data. As new ancestors are discovered, they would need to be added to the group.

There are four types of groups, defined as follows:

<u>Holobaramin</u> -- A complete set of organisms related by common descent. A group containing all and only those organisms related by common descent. (This may be taken to represent a set of organisms directly originated as a single reproductive unit, together with all their descendants.)

<u>Monobaramin</u> -- A group containing only organisms related by common descent, but not necessarily all of them. (i.e. A group comprising an entire holobaramin or a portion thereof.)

<u>Apobaramin</u> -- A group of organisms which contains all the ancestors and descendants of any of its members, but which may contain subgroupings that are unrelated to each other. A group of organisms not sharing an ancestor or descendant with any organism outside the group. (i.e. A group containing one or more holobaramins.)

<u>Polybaramin</u> -- A group of organisms which does not share a common ancestor. (i.e. A group containing members of more than one holobaramin.)

Remember that these are specialized terms, defined for use within Discontinuity Systematics -- they are defined as referring only to known organisms, that is, they include and exclude only known organisms.

Each of the above four terms was followed immediately by its definition. These definitions are used by the Discontinuity Systematist to identify groups of organisms. Along with each definition, a secondary meaning is provided within parentheses as a comment. The secondary meaning shows how the terms are interconnected, and ultimately how they may relate to creation theory. The special interconnection of the terms allows biosystematic knowledge of life's pattern to be constructed in a methodical way.

The plural form of each term is constructed by adding -s (e.g. holobaramins). The adjective form is constructed by adding -ic (e.g. mammals are apobaraminic; dogs and wolves are monobaraminic).

When a group is identified, it can be communicated to other researchers as a list of recognized organisms. Or, the group can be given a specific name according to the organisms it contains, just as current taxa are named according to contained subtaxa. For example, the placental dogs, coyotes, wolves, foxes, and jackals can be called the canid monobaramin. If existing formal taxonomic names (e.g. Canidae) are used, then they should be used cautiously. This is because existing formal taxonomic names have been defined by means of another biosystematic method, and can vary somewhat arbitrarily as that biosystematic method develops.

Time modifiers can be used with the terminology to more precisely identify groups of interest (e.g. the Devonian shark apobaramin; the living canid monobaramin). This basic terminology is sufficiently versatile to identify, describe, revise, and discuss taxonomic groups within Discontinuity Systematics.

Discontinuities should interest evolutionists, since these might represent punctuational or saltational events of rapid undocumented evolution. Discontinuities would require special attention and explanation from evolutionists, and the precise identification of discontinuities would be the first step in their understanding. Thus, the new systematics should interest those evolutionists who boldly seek to test their theory or understand it further.

Moreover, Discontinuity Systematics has a clear impact on the origins debate. Evolutionists claim that all life arose from one common ancestor -- thus, they would claim that ultimately there is only one holobaramin. Modern creationists claim that numerous life forms were separately created, varying somewhat thereafter. This suggests that we should find many separate holobaramins. Therefore, the discovery of a clear and consistent pattern of numerous separate holobaramins would be a major evidence for creation and against evolution.

The new biosystematic terminology interfaces with creation theory in an uncomplicated way, as discussed next. Baramin is a term sometimes used in creation theory, meaning a group of organisms directly created as a reproductive unit and all their descendants. Creation theorists use this term in their theories to explain: 1) the originally created pattern of life, and 2) how that pattern has varied since creation.

Yet baramins have been difficult to study scientifically. One difficulty has been identifying and delineating the baramins. Another difficulty is that most individual organisms are undiscovered. (They either perish without a trace or their traces have yet to be found.) Thus, most organisms from a baramin remain undiscovered and cannot be known. These factors have hampered scientific study of baramins.

However, a holobaramin is comprised solely of known organisms and therefore it lends itself to scientific investigation. Moreover, a relationship between holobaramin and baramin tentatively suggests itself. A holobaramin tentatively may be taken to represent those members of a baramin who have been discovered. Thus, the term holobaramin (from an empirical science of biosystematics) has a suggested connection with the term baramin (from creation theory).

THE NEW METHODOLOGY

Discontinuity Systematics seeks to collect organisms into identifiable groups. It seeks to eliminate all polybaraminic groups, and instead identify groups that are monobaraminic, apobaraminic, or better still, holobaraminic.

Our knowledge of monobaramins is improved by additively combining them together into a larger monobaramin. On the other hand, our knowledge of apobaramins is improved by subdividing them into smaller apobaramins.

The ultimate goal of Discontinuity Systematics is the identification and description of all holobaramins. Holobaramins are identified through a process of successive refinement. Since every monobaramin is a subset of a holobaramin, a holobaramin is approached as a monobaramin is successively increased in membership. For example, as more members are added to the canid monobaramin (the placental dogs, coyotes, foxes, wolves, and jackals) the holobaramin in which they are found is gradually approached. On the other hand, since every holobaramin is a subset of an apobaramin, the holobaramin is also approached as an apobaramin is subdivided into smaller apobaramins. For example, as the mammal apobaramin is successively subdivided into smaller apobaramins, the holobaramin containing placental dogs is approached. In this way the successive increase of the placental dog monobaramin and the successive subdivision of the mammal apobaramin will converge on the holobaramin that includes dogs. Thus, holobaramins are identified by successively refining our knowledge of monobaramins and apobaramins.

THE MEMBERSHIP CRITERIA

An important aspect of Discontinuity Systematics is the membership criteria -- the criteria that determine when an organism is (or is not) a member of a certain group. Group membership is based on continuity through common descent, therefore the membership criteria seek to identify continuity and its boundaries.

Continuity and discontinuity are related observations. You cannot see the one without having "eyes" to see the other. Thus, to see discontinuity you must have a way to see continuity, and the membership criteria supply this capability. The membership criteria are intended as a consistent set of tools for recognizing continuity and discontinuity.

Discontinuity Systematics seeks to identify the boundaries between common descent and discontinuity. It views all available scientific evidences as legitimate, with two explicit clarifications.

First, Discontinuity Systematics is independent of creation theories, that is, the methodology uses no outside knowledge of the biotic pattern originally created (or intended) by life's designer. Rather, the methodology attempts to discern life's pattern as seen by a neutral scientific observer.

Second, Discontinuity Systematics holds that cladograms and phenograms are inconclusive as evidence of evolutionary continuity. These diagrams have the appearance of an evolutionary tree (a phylogeny), yet they are not. In fact, they fail to identify any real ancestor-descendant relationships in the data. The specification that cladograms and phenograms are inconclusive merely formalizes a view already widely held by many scientists. This specification can be further justified. Several adequate methods already exist for studying the phenogram and cladogram patterns in nature. Discontinuity Systematics acknowledges the existence of these patterns, and formally sets them aside so the remaining pattern may be clearly examined. Thus, Discontinuity Systematics studies a pattern that is unstudied by any other existing systematic method.

In short, the methodology tries to identify the boundaries of evolutionary continuity by emulating a neutral scientist who 1) has no detailed knowledge of creation theory, and 2) views phenograms and cladograms skeptically or agnostically.

Discontinuity Systematics has a strong bearing on the evidence for creation and evolution, yet it gives special privilege to neither theory. Discontinuity Systematics is a methodology for neutrally examining an important pattern of nature and communicating the results. This new biosystematics is an empirical science that uses only data observable with the senses. Groups are identified in a tentative manner, and these may be challenged, debated, and revised based on the available data. The membership criteria provide the means by which groups are tentatively identified.

The membership criteria are crucially important to Discontinuity Systematics. A few of these criteria are discussed below.

The Lineage Criterion

Virtually all "lineages" (and "phylogenies") offered by evolutionists are not lineages, rather they are cladograms and phenograms having an appearance (falsely) of an evolutionary tree. These fail to identify real ancestor-descendant relationships in the data, therefore they are not lineages.

Organisms may be viewed as data points within a multidimensional morphology space. Lineages must curve their way through morphology space with ancestors and descendants in succession. A nondescript "cloud" of data points in morphology space is not a lineage. Rather, a lineage must have a special pattern. A lineage must be a trail of data points, long and narrow, with an absence of data points in the regions adjacent to the lineage. If two organisms are connected by a clear-cut lineage in morphology space, then this qualifies as sound empirical evidence that they are in the same monobaramin. If a lineage is sufficiently clear-cut, then it can unite organisms into a monobaramin, even if there are large morphological distances between the data points in the record of life. This criterion only requires that the data have a special type of pattern -- a lineage. This criterion is quite powerful, and in principle could span large "gaps" in the record of life.

Nonetheless, I suggest that life generally fails to be joined together by clear-cut lineages. Lineages do not span life on a large scale. In most cases evolutionists cannot even agree among themselves about the ancestors of a given group. Moreover, life lacks clear-cut lineages especially at those places where they are most desired by evolutionists -- at the origin of major new biotic designs. I suggest that large-scale lineages are systematically lacking from the record of life. Discontinuity Systematics seeks to precisely document this situation by identifying the boundaries of continuity. This is one of the major challenges of the new biosystematics.

Reproductive Viability Criteria

Reproductive viability is the ability of two organisms to interbreed. Reproductive viability is a membership criterion that is already widely used by creationists. This criterion also plays a crucial role in the definition of most traditional biosystematic units.

Reproductive viability is often complete: yielding viable, fertile offspring. Such a circumstance is sound evidence that the two organisms are in the same monobaramin. Although this criterion is a good one for identifying monobaramins, there are some difficulties to be discussed. Reproductive viability is sometimes incomplete or partial. For example, hybrid offspring may be viable but infertile. This occurs when horses and donkeys mate to yield a mule. The mule is a healthy, viable organism, but it is sterile. Nonetheless, most creationists feel that this case has sufficient evidence to place the horse, donkey and mule in the same monobaramin.

Partial reproductive viability is sometimes difficult to assess. For example, when a mating between two species yields inviable "offspring" that do not survive even to birth. These cases need more research.

Even more difficult to assess are cases were man has artificially forced the genome of one species into another species to form a "hybrid." For example, man has used gene recombination techniques to place human genes into bacteria. Likewise, viruses can sometimes transfer small pieces of genetic material from one species into another quite different species. Such "hybridization" is very fragmentary and partial, for it is the mixture of minor parts of genomes from different organisms. Presently, most creationists feel that such severely fragmentary and artificial hybridization fails to unite two species into a monobaramin.

Thus, reproductive viability spans a range of outcomes, from complete to fragmentary to incomplete. More research must be done to further develop this membership criterion.

Using reproductive viability as a criterion; the horses, mules, asses, zebras, and onagers are united into a monobaramin. Lions and tigers are placed into a monobaramin; as are cattle, buffalo, yaks and bison. Mallards and pintail ducks are united into their own monobaramin; as are placental dogs, wolves, coyotes, jackals, and foxes united into their own. One of the first tasks for Discontinuity Systematics should be the documentation of all such monobaramins.

Overall Similarity

Presently, the measurement of overall similarity seems to be an interesting, though often unreliable criterion for determining common descent. Even at the level of DNA, measurements of overall similarity can give results that are difficult to interpret. For example, there are two Drosophila species that are morphologically quite similar. Yet the DNA of these two species are thirty times more dissimilar than the DNA differences between chimpanzee and human, which are morphologically more distinct (3:246, 9:241, 12:129- 130). Thus, overall similarity of DNA does not necessarily correlate well with overall morphological similarity. Moreover, there does not appear to be a clear threshold of overall DNA similarity that would consistently indicate the presence or lack of common descent. The measurement of DNA similarity is yet in its infancy, and its role at this time is unclear.

Several types of overall similarity measurements might be helpful as membership criteria, but much research needs to be done to determine how to use them.

The Experimentation Criteria

Experimentation is strong evidence for demonstrating the likelihood of common descent. When a breeding experiment produces a range of new morphologies, then this range becomes a standard by which we can measure the morphological differences between comparable organisms. For example, if interbreeding two organisms creates a diversity of morphology which reasonably overlaps that of a third organism, then there is reasonable evidence that the third organism belongs in the monobaramin of the first two.

By analogy this criterion can be cautiously applied to fossil organisms. Suppose two living organisms are comparable to two fossil organisms. If interbreeding the two living organisms produces a range of morphology greater than the difference between the two fossil organisms, then there is evidence that the two fossil organisms belong together in a monobaramin.

If the members of a monobaramin define a region of multidimensional morphological space within which a test organism falls, then there is evidence that the test organism should be included in that monobaramin.

Other membership criteria will undoubtedly be developed, and these will be an active area of discussion and research. Creationists should pursue the identification and refinement of such criteria.

The Identification of Apobaramins

So far, this paper has discussed the criteria used for joining organisms together into one evolutionarily unified group -- a monobaramin. This same consistent set of criteria are also used to identify an apobaramin. In particular, an apobaramin is identified because it fails all the membership criteria that would connect it with any other group. An apobaramin is a separate, distinct group that is unrelated to any other group. If a group fails to demonstrate reproductive viability with any non-member, and if there is no clear-cut lineage linking the group with non-members, and if biological experimentation fails to span the gap between the group and non-members, then there is sound empirical evidence that the group is an apobaramin. In short, an apobaramin is a group which empirically fails to be evolutionary united with any known organism outside the group.

I suggest that life is comprised of numerous apobaramins. Discontinuity Systematics seeks to study this situation and communicate the results. This matter should be of interest to all scientists concerned with the origins debate.

CONCLUSION

Discontinuity Systematics provides the only systematic method for identifying and studying the discontinuities of life. Discontinuity Systematics is a methodology for studying this pattern from a neutral point of view. Yet as this pattern is systematically documented, it can provide substantial evidence for the creation model. In addition, the new biosystematics provides creationists and evolutionists with the terminology necessary for convenient discussion of their viewpoints.

Discontinuity Systematics introduces only four new terms. The interrelationship among these terms allows for the knowledge within the field to be built in a methodical way. Holobaramins are identified by successive refinement, through the convergence of monobaramins (by addition) and apobaramins (by subdivision).

As more researchers study Discontinuity Systematics, the membership criteria will be improved and overall subjectivity will decrease. The terminology of Discontinuity Systematics is versatile enough to allow for that kind of perpetual improvement.

Discontinuity Systematics stimulates several types of research. One important research project would be the identification of monobaraminic groups based on a criterion of reproductive viability. Another research project could evaluate partial reproductive viability as a criterion for identifying monobaramins. Yet another research project could begin a preliminary identification of apobaramins by looking at higher taxonomic levels and recognizing the largest (and most certain) discontinuities. For example, whales and bats each seem to be a coarse, yet defensible, apobaramin.

Another project could review comparative DNA studies and evaluate their significance to Discontinuity Systematics. Can overall DNA similarity be systematically used to identify monobaramins and/or apobaramins? Another project would be the evaluation of phenotypic similarity studies, and their impact on Discontinuity Systematics.

The accumulation and comparison of all this data will give scientists their first chance to see the living world through a systematic method that bears on the modern creation model. I encourage creationists to embrace this new biosystematics and begin the laborious task of resystematizing the life on earth.

ACKNOWLEDGEMENTS

I wish to specially thank Dr. Kurt Wise for his many constructive comments, suggestions and reviews of this material.

REFERENCES

1.   Awbrey, F. T., 1983, Defining 'kinds' -- Do creationists apply a double standard?, pp. 278-284 In Zetterberg, J. P. (ed.), Evolution Versus Creationism: The Public Education Controversy, Oryx Press, Phoenix, AZ, 528 pp.

2.   Cracraft, J., 1983, Systematics, comparative biology, and the case against creationism, pp. 163-191 In Godfrey, L. R. (ed.), Scientists Confront Creationism, Norton, New York, NY, 352 pp.

3.   Dover, G. A., 1980, Problems in the use of DNA for the study of species relationships and the evolutionary significance of genomic differences,, pp. 241-268 In Bisby, F. A., J. G. Vaughan, and C. A. Wright (eds.), Chemosystematics: Principles and Practice (The Systematics Association Special Volume No. 16), Proceedings of an international symposium held at the University of Southampton, Academic Press, San Diego, CA.

4.   Eldredge, N., 1982, The Monkey Business: A Scientist Looks at Creationism, Washington Square Press, New York, NY, 157 pp.

5.   Futuyma, D., 1983, Science On Trial: The Case for Evolution, Pantheon, New York, NY, 251 pp.

6. Gepner, I., 1982, The fallacy of kinds, pp. 69-72 In Paster, S., and W. Haviland (eds.), Confronting the Creationists, Northeastern Anthropological Association Occasional Proceedings No. 1, Am. Anthrop. Ass'n., Washington, DC.

7. Godfrey, L. R., 1983, Creationism and gaps in the fossil record, pp. 193-218 In Godfrey, L. R. (ed.), Scientists Confront Creationism, Norton, New York, NY, 351 pp.

8. Kitcher, P., 1982, Abusing Science: The Case Against Creationism, MIT Press, Cambridge, MA, 224 pp.

9. Mayr, E., 1982, The Growth of Biological Thought: Diversity, Evolution, and Inheritance, Belknap Press, Cambridge, MA, 974 pp.

10. Merrell, D. J., 1981, Ecological Genetics, Univ. of Minnesota Press, Minneapolis, MN, 512 pp.

11. Rosenberg, A., 1985, The Structure of Biological Science, Cambridge Univ. Press, Cambridge, England, 352 pp.

12. Stebbins, G. L., 1982, Darwin to DNA: Molecules to Humanity, Freeman, New York, NY, 491 pp.

13. Strahler, A. N., 1987, Science and Earth History -- The Creation/Evolution Controversy, Prometheus, Buffalo, NY, 552 pp.

To say the least this paper by Mr. ReMine is an exciting one. The term discontinuity systematics appears to be and to contain ideal terminology for methodology that creationists heretofore generally vaguely have been grasping to obtain. We have talked about gaps between the groups, but discontinuity (a word which to some extent has been used by others, including Frank L. Marsh) is a somewhat more elegant term, since we readily can distinguish it from continuity (or common descent).

To my knowledge the term baramin was first published privately in Lincoln, Nebraska by Frank L. Marsh in his book, Fundamental Biology. The term baramin has enjoyed a considerable measure of popularity among creationists, but more commonly the term "kind" is used because of its association with the biblical word "kind" in chapter one of Genesis. To my knowledge this paper for the first time has expanded kinds (baramins) into a number of real categories which should have considerable utility for systematists.

Hopefully, with this new terminology, a specialist working with particular organisms will be able to see more clearly what direction he is going. According to Mr. ReMine, the ideal is to add to monobaramins and subdivide apobaramins in order to elucidate the holobaramins.

The challenge before discontinuity systematics is how to identify the groups. Of course reproductive viability is the main criterion. Also, I like the experimentation criteria expressed here regarding morphological ranges which could include fossils. The author makes a good point about DNA, because at this stage of our understanding, DNA in many cases is not a reliable indicator of presence or lack of relationship among organisms. So at the present time discontinuity systematics will be obliged to work primarily with phenotypes of organisms, until the chemistry can be better understood.

Even as a student at universities, I was frequently disturbed by being forced to play the "biological game" of figuring out what the hypothetical ancestors for particular groups could have been. To my way of thinking, discontinuity is basically more realistic, and in one sense it can relieve investigators of the tension of having to determine how the gaps between groups could have been bridged. Now we can go as far as the evidence is compelling and not feel obliged to jump from one group to another by way of hypothetical ancestors.

Currently, mainline evolutionists tend to ignore the writings of creation scientists, and they often look at "scientists" who reject a macroevolutionary viewpoint as doing pseudoscience or actually religion under the pretense of science. So at this time I do not anticipate their jumping on the bandwagon of this "new" systematics. Its being a "neutral" approach, however, should make the view somewhat more attractive for their consideration. Active creation scientists probably will feel comfortable with the discontinuity model, and hopefully they will start using and refining it.

I sense that there is an increased momentum for obtaining an improved systematic methodology for dealing with living and fossil forms. More than one hundred years of research has substantiated that "gaps" exist between types of organisms. Now systematists need to be encouraged seriously to elucidate characteristics which will make it possible to distinguish the monobaramins and holobaramins. I applaud this paper as something we have been awaiting for decades and hopefully now will see implemented.

Wayne Frair, Ph.D.
Briarcliff Manor, NY

Here W.J. ReMine commissions us to preserve a scientific taxonomy, gives us a workable vocabulary, and outlines a possible research program. Earlier he co-authored a definitive reply to those who assert that a "human tail" is a tribute to evolution; see Bible-Science Newsletter 20(8):p.8.

The only addenda I might profitably make are historical and bibliographic. Since our current taxonomy originated from a creationist (Linnaeus), it would be proper for creation scientists to revise it. Their search for boundaries of the baramin will enable us to identify the limits beyond which the Creator has not caused speciation to occur. Genera, families, and other higher categories can still be seen as Linnaeus saw them: part of the Creator's outline and not as phylogenetic remnants.

The word "baramin" seems to have been used first by the scientist Frank Marsh in 1941 - his later book is available from C.R.S. Books. An article by Marsh about the baramin is in the Creation Research Society Quarterly 1969 6(1):13-25. Later the zoologist A.J. Jones analyzed the limits of "kinds" as related to how many animals would have entered Noah's ark' C.R.S.Q. 9(1):53-77; 9(2):114-123; and 9(3):102-108. The reader may examine my own thesis that in some cases the boundaries of the plant baramins may lie at the genus level - C.R.S.Q. 16(1):38-43. There are many others who have published on the need for a creationist taxonomic revision and a few of these are J.J. Dutrene deWit, W.E. Lammerts, W. Frair, J.W. Klotz, L.P. Lester, and E.N. Smith. May new workers arise to heed ReMine's cry for a scientifically based taxonomy.

George F. Howe, Ph.D.
Newhall, California

Walter ReMine has made significant, positive, and truly original contributions to creation biosystematics -- in perspective, in purpose, and in methodology.

In perspective: Myopically focusing on *within*-kind relationship, creation biologists have heretofore failed to produce a reproducible definition of a "Biblical created kind." ReMine's perspective shift to the *between*-kind discontinuities is what we have needed all along for us to "see" that which has been obvious to us all along. This contribution in perspective is what I believe will be remembered as ReMine's most brilliant and significant contribution.

In purpose: ReMine has stubbornly (and justifiably) insisted on producing a systematics method which is scientifically respectable. This purpose has, in turn, led to other significant and positive contributions:
1. *The abandonment of previous systematics methods and terms* allows for the creation of a precise terminology.
2. *The creation of a model-neutral systematics*
   a. allows it to be used by virtually any biologist,
   b. may permit its acceptance into some quarters of conventional biology, and
   c. may eventually facilitate learned and profitable communication between creationists and non-creationists.
3. *The creation of a modifiable classification method* allows for
   a. the improvement of the methodology through time, and
   b. the falsification and modification of hypotheses with new data.
4. *The definition of terms (holobaramin, etc.) based upon known organisms*
   a. extracts much unnecessary speculation from the method, and
   b. allows for reproducibility.

In methodology: The methodology of discontinuity systematics is disturbingly simple and brilliantly efficient: to approach the holobaramin and above and below by successive division of larger groups and the successive building of subgroups. Difficulty will prevent no biologist from using the method, and will encourage much profitable improvement.

I would strongly recommend that creation biologists everywhere heartily endorse discontinuity systematics as the foundation for the creation of biosystematics methods of their own (e.g. baraminology, Wise, this volume).

Kurt P. Wise, Ph.D.
Dayton, Tennessee

CLOSURE

I am pleased and encouraged by the positive response from each of the reviewers. Dr. Wise's four-point outline, especially, is a cogent and concise illumination of elements left unemphasized in my paper.

Dr. Frair, who has studied the biosystematics of turtles, recognizes that overall DNA similarity is presently not a reliable indicator of relationships. I agree with him that more research must be done on DNA before it can be a dependable systematic tool.

Dr. Howe draws our attention to our current hierarchical system of taxonomy which originated with the creationist, Karl Linneaus. That system has been enormously successful at making life's diversity more comprehensible, and as a biological information "storage and retrieval system." We should not abandon it.

Discontinuity Systematics, however, does not focus on hierarchical patterns (whether phenetic or cladistic), rather it focuses on a pattern ignored by all other methods. Phenetics, cladistics, and Discontinuity Systematics are entirely independent methods. There is no overlap in the patterns they study.

While species will remain as an important concept of biosystematics, the holobaramin concept may well have some impact on the international conventions of nomenclature that are used by hierarchical (i.e. Linnean) taxonomists. This remains to be seen.

However, when discussing specific organisms, I do expect that in many cases the holobaramins will correspond to stable taxonomic groupings that already have a widely recognized name. Therefore, I expect that new names will typically not be needed. In this respect I think the impact on Linnean taxonomy will be minimal.

Though Discontinuity Systematics is a neutral scientific methodology for studying nature, I think Dr. Frair may well be correct that mainline evolutionists will not be in a hurry to "jump on the bandwagon." The method brings into focus (and thus into doubt) matters that many evolutionists would rather leave unquestioned. Creationists will probably have to lead the way on this methodology.

I believe there are many evolutionists of integrity and curiosity, who will find the method interesting, useful, and a convenient medium for communicating research. Yet before they commit to the method, they may perhaps need to see that it results in a fruitful body of research. Again, this initial task may be for creationists.

Fortunately, since the method is neutral and scientific, it is a suitable recipient of government grants for research projects of merit. I encourage creation researchers not to forego this avenue of funding.

I mentioned that some evolutionists may desire to use Discontinuity Systematics. For example, those interested in punctuated equilibria may find the method useful for identifying "discontinuities" alleged to occur at punctuation events. This use is legitimate because the method seeks to identify discontinuities, not explain them. (The business of explanation is left to scientific theories.) Once the pattern of discontinuities is identified then it may spark considerable discussion and debate, but identification is the first step in our empiric scientific enterprise.

Discontinuity Systematics will be discussed at length in a book to be released later this year.

I thank Doctors Wise, Frair, and Howe for their kind reviews ... and for their "kinds" review -- (pardon the pun) -- they review the etymological history of the terms "kinds" and baramins. They have also tracked down the first occurrence of the term "baramin," something I had not been able to locate.

Walter J. ReMine

DETACHMENT FAULTS IN THE SOUTHWESTERN UNITED STATES - EVIDENCE FOR A SHORT AND CATASTROPHIC TERTIARY PERIOD

Scott H. Rugg M.S.
Engineering Science Applications
8534 Commerce Avenue, Suite B
San Diego, CA 92121

ABSTRACT

Low-angle mid-Tertiary detachment faults (gravity slides) within the southwestern United States are best understood as developing very rapidly (<100 years) within a catastrophic framework. This is supported by the example of modern and ancient gravity slides which occur very rapidly (within seconds, minutes, or days) and are usually initiated by catastrophic events such as earthquakes. Evolutionists believe that detachment faulting and related geologic events occurred over a period of 10 to 20 million years. However, the basic principles of rock mechanics reveal that upper-plate movement is impossible under docile uniformitarian conditions. Movement was assisted by large and frequent earthquakes which provided both lateral and horizontal forces to overcome the restraining forces against movement due to friction and cohesion. Studies indicate that rapid basement warping, extensive dike emplacement, volcanism, and hydrothermal mineralization occurred contemporaneous with detachment faulting due to a high heat flow rate within the earth's crust. Thick deposits of coarse grained sediments and megabreccias also indicate rapid uplift, erosion, and deposition. This reveals that an unparalleled amount of seismic energy was released at this time. The rapid development of detachment terrane indicates that the Tertiary period was similar to the latter stages of Noah's Flood as the "mountains rose" and "valleys sank down" and was significantly shorter than the millions of years assigned under the uniformitarian model.

INTRODUCTION

Thousands of gravity induced landslides occur each year around the world. They range in size from several thousand square meters to several square kilometers and are most often initiated during other catastrophic events such as torrential rain storms, earthquakes or volcanic eruptions. Movement is nearly always rapid; occurring within several seconds, minutes, or days.

Ancient landslides have also been identified throughout the world. These "old" landslides are usually several orders of magnitude larger than modern landslides. The conventional uniformitarian view concerning ancient landslides, is that movement occurred slowly (several centimeters per year) over a period of several millions of years. This view is a contradiction of the uniformitarian doctrine that "the present is the key to the past," since it is clear from experience that landslides occur rapidly and not slowly.

Not all have swallowed the "slow slide" pill. William G. Pierce has eloquently argued that the Heart Mountain Detachment (ancient Tertiary gravity slide) in Wyoming was a cataclysmic event. This interpretation displeases his fellow uniformitarian geologists because other synchronous (coeval) geologic events associated with movement, such as erosion, sedimentation, and accumulation of several hundred meters of volcanic deposits, would have occurred during the same time frame as the cataclysmic sliding.

Many of these ancient landslides (Tertiary detachment faults) have been identified in western North America, in a region west of the Rockies, stretching from the Canadian border of the United States into Sonora, Mexico (Figure 1). Recent intensive study has been focused within the region surrounding the Colorado River which includes southeastern California, southwestern Arizona, and southern Nevada. Nearly every mountain range within this region has been affected by detachment faulting (Figure 2).

In this paper, we intend to show that the most tenable explanation for detachment faulting in the southwestern United States is that it occurred rapidly (within minutes, days, or years) in response to other catastrophic events, under conditions similar to those which would have been present during Noah's flood. It will be shown that other synchronous geologic events such as erosion, sedimentation, hydrothermal mineralization, and basement warping also occurred rapidly during development of detachment terrane. This catastrophic scenario is also supported by historic and ancient examples of landsliding which were clearly catastrophic and by the basic principles of rock mechanics.

GENERAL DESCRIPTION OF DETACHMENT FAULTED TERRANE

A detachment fault (low-angle normal fault, denudational fault, decollement, or gravity fault) is a nearly horizontal surface which separates a detached and displaced upper-plate allochthon from a lower-plate authochthon. Peter Misch (1960), who first closely studied these faults within the Great Basin region of the western United States, attributed upper-plate movement to compressional forces (thrusting). However, it was soon determined that the upper-plate had actually been distended, which made it clear that movement was accomplished by tensional forces and not compression (Anderson, 1971). The total amount of upper-plate distention ranges up to 50 to 100 percent (Spencer, 1985) and possibly as high as 400 percent in some areas (Lister et al., 1986).

Nearly every mountain range within the region extending west of the Colorado Plateau to the San Andreas fault, from Death Valley and southern Nevada to Sonora, Mexico (Colorado River borderland) has been affected by detachment faulting. It is believed that this event initiated at the beginning of the late Oligocene and continued through mid-Miocene time (10 to 20 million years). The detachment surface is a regional feature with lateral upper-plate displacement ranging from a few kilometers to as much as 50 to 80 kilometers (Reynolds and Spencer, 1985; Stewart, 1983). The direction of transport has generally been toward the northeast, but a few areas exhibit westward directed upper-plate transport. The fault has been deformed into a sinuous configuration of antiforms and synforms by lower-plate warping which occurred during detachment faulting. Present slopes on the detachment surface range from horizontal to 60# (Berg et al., 1982). Prior to warping, the surface was a gently sloping feature of probably less than 5#.

The upper-plate consists of a combination of Tertiary volcanic and sedimentary rocks and Mesozoic and Precambrian crystalline rocks. In many mountain ranges, the upper-plate consists almost exclusively of the Tertiary rocks. The structure of the upper-plate is characterized by high-angle curved normal faults (listric faults) which flatten at depth and merge into the basal detachment surface (refer to Figure 3). This has resulted in the formation of an imbricated system of parallel half-graben blocks. During distention, the half-graben blocks underwent rotation, resulting in bedding structure which dips in a direction opposite the transport direction of the upper-plate.

The lower-plate is composed of Mesozoic and Precambrian metamorphic and crystalline rocks. The lower-plate is generally arched upward which has caused deformation of the detachment surface. In some ranges, the lower-plate has a foliation (mylonization) which is truncated by the detachment surface.

In a few mountain ranges, several stacked series of detachment faults have been identified (John and Howard, 1982). Other ranges however, do not exhibit any signs of the regional detachment surface (Dahm, 1983).

Several mechanisms have been proposed to account for wide-scale distention exhibited in the upper-plate. Some have attributed distention to a pure shear model related to a crustal spreading at depth, which has caused decoupling of the upper-plate with little or no gravity sliding occurring. However, widespread displacement of the upper-plate can only be accommodated by large-scale transport (Reynolds and Spencer, 1985) of which gravity sliding had to play a primary role (Seager, 1970; Shackelford, 1975; Davis et al., 1979).

GEOLOGIC EVENTS COEVAL WITH DETACHMENT FAULTING

Sedimentation/Erosion

The upper-plate is composed of a high percentage of Tertiary volcanic and sedimentary rocks. The sedimentary rocks are characterized by high energy deposits including fanglomerates, volcaniclastic rocks, conglomerates, arkosic sandstones, siltstones, boulder breccias, and megabreccias with clasts as large as 6 meters in diameter (Pike and Hansen, 1982). They are over one kilometer thick in some areas and are often interbedded or intertongued with volcanic flows (Teel and Frost, 1982). In the Trigo Mountains, volcaniclastic beds up to 20 meters thick are interbedded with volcanic flows within the lower section of the upper-plate and exhibit sharp bedding contacts (Rugg, 1986). The interbedding of the coarse grain sedimentary rocks and volcanic flows reveals that deposition was extremely rapid and continuous, with no time for erosion, and took place in hot water several hundreds of meters deep.

Within the Whipple, Chemehuevi, Copper, and Kofa Mountains, the sedimentary bedding has a consistent increase in dip down-section within the rotated upper-plate half-graben blocks. This structural configuration, known as growth faulting (see right side of Figure 3), demonstrates that upper-plate movement occurred contemporaneous with deposition of the sedimentary rocks (Frost, 1979).

Most of the sedimentary clasts have been derived from the area that they have been deposited. Within the Chemehuevi Mountains, the composition of the clasts change up-section in conformance with progressive unroofing of different zones of lower-plate basement rock lithology (Miller and John, 1988). This pattern is additional confirmation of coeval sedimentation, erosion, and detachment faulting. Surely, this would have required a tremendous amount of rapidly moving water to transport and lay down all the thick deposits of coarse grained sediments.

Hydrothermal Mineralization

Identifying detachment terrane has taken on economic significance because of the relationship between the detachment fault and a variety of hydrothermally mineralized deposits. Faulting has resulted in the development of a breccia zone up to a hundred meters thick. This fractured zone has provided an excellent conduit for the transport of hot mineralizing fluids and the deposition of large ore bodies along the detachment fault and within thinner breccia zones associated with the upper-plate listric faults.

Spencer and Welty (1986) have shown that hydrothermal mineralization in the Buckskin-Rawhide-Whipple Mountains area was continuous with detachment faulting. They found several generations of mineralized deposits at different depths within the upper-plate. These deposits could only have been formed by movement passed a mineralizing interface. Bartley and Glazner (1985) also confer that mineralization was synchronous with upper-plate movement. They believe that the hydrothermal fluids may have played a key role in accommodating upper-plate movement due to the buoyant effects of inferred high fluid pressures within the detachment zone.

Lower-Plate Warping

The borderland region of the Colorado River has been deformed into a system of roughly parallel arches and basins aligned with their major axis in a northeast-southwest direction (Otton and Dokka, 1981). The amplitudes of these features range up to 2 kilometers with axial lengths on the order of 20 kilometers or more. In several areas, a superimposed set of nearly perpendicular northwest trending folds have further deformed the northeast trending folds into dome shaped features (Cameron and Frost, 1981).

It appears that folding is related to warping of the metamorphic and crystalline basement rocks during a highly ductile phase of the lower-plate. Cameron and Frost (1981) indicate that the regional antiformal/synformal character of the detachment surface developed in response to this large scale basement folding and occurred simultaneously with detachment faulting. Spencer (1984) suggests that uplifting of the lower-plate resulted from isostatic rebound due to upper-plate movement which unroofed and exposed vast areas of basement rock. He believes that the warping occurred rapidly during a period of very low flexural rigidity of the basement rocks, which suggests a high heat flow rate during this time. Spencer and Welty (1986) indicate that the geothermal gradient at this time was greater than 100# C/km. Undoubtedly, there would have been a tremendous amount of seismic energy release during uplifting of the basement rock material. Little consideration has been given to the effects of this seismic energy release and the development of detachment terrane.

Dike Emplacement

Dike swarms are extensive and occur within many of the mountain ranges of the Colorado River borderland, particularly in the northern region of this area in the Homer, Sacramento, and Newberry Mountains (Spencer, 1985). In some regions, the dikes are so numerous that they compose over 40% of the total surface outcrops. The dikes typically dip very steeply and are oriented in a northwest-southeast configuration, however, east-west and north-south trending swarms have also been identified. The composition of the dikes (rhyolite to andesite) is similar to the composition of the Tertiary volcanic flows within this region, indicating that dike fissure flow may have been the source for many of the volcanic flow deposits. The Castle Dome Mountains, where some of the most remarkable dike swarms within the United States are found (Logan and Hirsch, 1982), have also been identified by Gutmann (1981) as an ancient caldera from which exuded much of the volcanic rocks for this region.

The dike swarms are primarily concentrated within lower-plate crystalline rocks. However, dikes have also been observed penetrating the detachment surface in a few isolated areas (Spencer 1985). This pattern reveals that the majority of dike emplacement occurred just prior to movement of the upper-plate and continued at a lesser amount during and after upper-plate movement. It appears that dike emplacement was facilitated by concave upward flexure (warping) of the lower-plate (Spencer, 1985). This relationship also establishes a genetic link between dike emplacement, lower-plate warping, and a high heat flow rate.

Additional Geologic Observations

The Tertiary period was unparalleled in the amount of volcanic activity which occurred. This activity indicates that the vast amount of water which also occupied this region was significantly warmer than present day oceans. Nutting (1984) demonstrated that sedimentary red beds indicate a hydrothermal depositional environment. A thick sequence of chaotic Tertiary red beds occur directly below and in conformable contact with volcanic deposits within the Trigo Peaks and Dome Rock Mountains region (Dahm, 1983), indicating the presence of hydrothermal waters in this region during deposition. This "hot" water could have also been the source for the mineralizing fluids which were present during detachment faulting.

The majority of the basalt flows in this region are nearly flat-lying which indicates that detachment faulting had nearly ceased by the time basaltic volcanism initiated. Basaltic volcanism is not as energetic as the rhyolitic/andesitic volcanism associated with detachment faulting. Rhyolitic/andesitic volcanism is associated with explosive eruptions like that of Mount Saint Helens. The close link between the cessation of detachment faulting at the close of explosive rhyolitic/andesitic volcanism would indicate that movement of the upper-plate was facilitated by tremendous energy release during volcanism.

PROBLEMS RELATED TO LOW-ANGLE GRAVITY SLIDING

Before a landslide can occur, the sum of the driving forces, which act with movement, must exceed the sum of the restraining forces, which act against movement. The primary driving force for landsliding is gravity. This force decreases from a maximum in a vertical orientation to zero along a horizontal plane. The restraining forces are those resulting from the internal friction and cohesive strength of the rock material. Most rock and soil material have an internal friction angle of approximately 33#. This means that under cohesionless conditions, gravity sliding can only occur on surfaces greater than 33# (called the angle of repose). This is why dry beach sand, which is cohesionless, cannot form slope faces of in excess of 33#. However, all rock and most soil have significant cohesion which is why slope faces greater than the angle of repose can develop.

These basic principles of rock mechanics have caused considerable controversy among geologists for decades because most ancient detachment surfaces slope significantly less (<5#) than the angle of repose. Therefore, it would be impossible for the small lateral component of gravitational forces acting along the slide plane to overcome the forces acting against movement due to friction and cohesion. This indicates that there had to be another type of driving force. However, little consideration has been given to what this force was, because of the imposition of uniformitarian philosophy.

In attempting to resolve this problem, Hubbert and Rubey (1959) asserted that high pore-fluid pressures developed within the detachment zone which caused the upper-plate to float, thus voiding the forces due to friction and allowing sliding to occur on any surface over 0#. Their model is based on two assumptions: 1) the cohesion factor was equal to zero; and 2) high pore-fluid pressures could be maintained for millions of years. Hsu (1969) has pointed out that the cohesion value would be a significant factor, requiring tremendous forces to overcome. Therefore, there would have to have been a significant lateral force to initiate a detachment surface. Here again however, gravity alone could not account for that total force.

Hubbert's and Rubey's second assumption is also highly questionable. The main detachment surface as well as faults and fractures which would develop within the upper-plate would provide excellent conduits for the rapid release of pore pressure. Guth (1982) has also shown that the phenomena of rock hydrofracture would cause a rapid reduction of high pore pressure within confining layers. This shows that the assumption of high pore-fluid pressures being maintained over periods of millions of years is unlikely.

EFFECTS OF HIGH GROUND ACCELERATIONS

The effects of high ground accelerations from catastrophic seismic events has been given little consideration in the role of detachment faulting. Large earthquakes can generate both horizontal and vertical ground accelerations significantly greater than 1g. These seismic forces would have several effects: 1) they would cause fracturing of the rock material, thus reducing the restraining forces due to cohesion in the upper-plate; 2) they would assist upper-plate movement by providing laterally directed seismic forces; and 3) they would reduce the frictional forces by providing vertically directed components of seismic ground accelerations that would act in opposition to gravity. Under these conditions upper-plate movement would occur very rapidly.

To initiate detachment faulting the earthquakes would have to have been much larger and frequent than modern earthquakes. Earthquake generated upper-plate movement would be similar to the movement of objects that vibrate down a very slightly sloping board surface when it is smoothed with a vibratory sander.

It is clear that during Tertiary detachment faulting, an unparalleled amount of seismic energy was released due to volcanism, rapid basement warping and other forms of faulting. In fact, we have seen that cessation of detachment faulting occurred during a transition to a much lower seismically active period. This shows the clear relationship between detachment faulting and intense periods of seismic activity.

It is also interesting to note that in many ranges, the detachment surface occurs only at the contact between Tertiary rocks and the crystalline basement material. This suggests a plane of low shear strength at the contact, which indicates that movement probably occurred directly after deposition of the upper-plate, before cohesion to the lower-plate could occur and not after millions of years had passed.

EXAMPLES OF CATASTROPHIC DETACHMENT FAULTING

Heart Mountain Detachment

Heart Mountain is located in the northwest corner of the state of Wyoming. Dake (1918) was the first to recognize a low-angle (as low as 2#) fault at the base of Heart Mountain, which he identified as an overthrust. William G. Pierce, who has worked in the Heart Mountain region since the mid 1930's, reinterpreted this fault in 1957 as a "detachment thrust" which had broken loose along a basal shear plane and moved over long distances probably by gravity gliding. The area of sliding encompasses over 3400 square kilometers with a break-away zone of 105 kilometers in length. The upper-plate broke up into over 50 blocks which moved southeast over distances ranging up to 50 kilometers. The largest upper-plate block is over 8 kilometers wide. Extensive study in this area later led Pierce (1979) to conclude that movement was a rapid event related to "cataclysmic" phenomena. Cataclysmic implies that movement would have occurred within a time frame of several days or hours, or possibly as short as several minutes.

Pierce proposed that upper-plate movement was initiated by a catastrophic earthquake with vertical ground accelerations approaching 1g, which caused separation and gravity assisted downslope sliding of the upper-plate carbonate material. Rapid movement is supported by the presence of slide generated carbonate breccia (calcibreccia) injected as clastic dikes into the base of several of the detachment blocks. The injection of the dikes could only occur as a result of rapid lithostatic loading of the thick volcanic cover (Wapiti Formation) which encases many of the detached blocks. The calcibreccia material also occurs along the surface of the detachment ramp below the detached blocks and below the Wapiti Formation where it was deposited directly on unroofed sections of the detachment ramp. This clearly indicates rapid deposition of the Wapiti Formation soon after upper-plate movement, before erosion of the exposed calcibreccia on the detachment ramp could take place.

This author asserts that the initiation of volcanism and the earthqauke that iduced upper-plate movement were related events. This implies that the entire sequence of events probably occurred within several days. Field relationships also indicate that a conglomerate deposit developed in the time frame between movement and accumulation of the Wapiti Formation. This indicates that very rapid erosional and depositional processes were in operation during these events.

Turnagain Heights Landslide

On March 27, 1964, an earthquake estimated as high as 8.75 Richter magnitude rocked northern Alaska. Over 50,000 square miles of Alaska was tilted at new attitudes as a result of dynamically induced subsidence (Hansen, 1975; Hansen et al., 1966). The quake caused thousands of avalanches and rock slides. The most disastrous effects were in the upscale residential development of Turnagain Heights. The damages were caused by two landslides which merged and engulfed a total area of 130 acres within a period of less than 2 minutes. The slide moved seaward with a maximum lateral slippage estimated at two-thirds of a kilometer down a failure slope of 2.2# (Voight, 1973). The slide took place retrogressively starting at an unrestrained bluff face and failed landward with a headward regression of approximately 400 meters. The landslide was broken into numerous half-graben blocks which exhibited both rotational and translational movement. Separation occurred along a low shear strength clay layer.

Many of the upper-plate features observed at Turnagain Heights are identical to features observed in Tertiary detachment terrane. The most obvious are the development of rotated half-graben blocks, curved upper-plate fault surfaces which merge into the basal detachment surface, and upper-plate distention. The Turnagain Heights landslide is one of many examples of large catastrophic failures initiated by seismic activity. Most importantly, this landslide has established a connection between catastrophic seismic events and gravity sliding down very low sloping detachment surfaces, similar to those observed in the southwest United States.

The example of Heart Mountain has also shown the connection between ancient detachment faulting, volcanism, and earthquake activity. A dramatic increase in the rates of erosional and depositional processes has also been demonstrated by this example.

CONCLUSIONS

The resolution of the movement problem along low-angle detachment faults lies in the consideration of the strong and frequent seismic events which were occurring contemporaneous with upper-plate movement. The effects of the seismic energy release would provide an additional driving force to overcome the restraining forces against movement due to friction and cohesion and would lessen the effects of friction by countering vertical components of gravitational acceleration with vertical components of seismic ground acceleration. Earthquake induced landslides are common events which occur almost daily and on a significantly larger scale during ancient past. This has been demonstrated by the examples of Heart Mountain and Turnagain Heights.

The Tertiary period within the southwestern United States was a time of colossal release of tectonic and seismic energy. This was caused by a very high heat flow rate which resulted in basement warping, explosive volcanism, and rapid erosion and sedimentation as the mountains rose out of the water. Basement warping and volcanism would also have been accompanied by large and frequent earthquakes. This allowed for an immense amount of geologic work to be accomplished over a very short period of time. The character of the sedimentary rocks within this region is also clear testimony to the cataclysmic events which occurred during the Tertiary period. The existence of interbedded sediments and volcanic rocks is evidence for rapid continuous deposition in a hot deep body of water. This indicates hydrothermal mineraliztion was also ongoing at this time.

Under uniformitarian conditions, the energy released during the Tertiary period is spread out over millions of years with geologic events separated by large gaps of time. This geologic environment is relatively docile and innocuous and is not much different from what we see today. Sufficient geologic power is not available to accomplish the work needed to account for the highly energetic geologic events of the Tertiary period. However, if the Tertiary period were only a few hundred or thousands of years long, the geologic power to do work would have been dramatically greater. Under these condition, the geologic events are closely spaced in time and have a direct cause and effect relationship with one another, being individual interrelated parts of one overall geologic phenomena. Also, the power available to do work is at a level necessary to accomplish detachment faulting and related catastrophic events.

Rapid mountain building and vast quantities of turbulent hot water were the primary agents in the geologic development of this region. This is clearly indicative of the latter stages of Noah's flood when the land surface emerged from the flood waters. This event would have required tremendous amounts of energy to accomplish and would have been accompanied been explosive volcanism and violent earthquakes beyond modern day comparison. The seismic generated forces from this event would have been sufficient to cause sliding on the scale of Heart Mountain and the detachment terrane within the southwestern United States.

REFERENCES

Anderson, R.E., 1971, Thin-skin distension in Tertiary rocks of southeastern Nevada: Geological Society of America Bulletin, v. 82, p. 43-58.

Bartley, J.M., and Glazner, A.F., 1985, Hydrothermal systems and Tertiary low-angle normal faulting in the southwestern United States: Geology, v. 13, p. 562-564.

Berg, L., Leveille,G., and Geis, P., 1982, Mid-Tertiary detachment faulting and manganese mineralization in the Midway Mountains, Imperial County, California: in Anderson-Hamilton volume, Mesozoic-Cenozoic Tectonic Evolution of the Colorado River Region, California, Arizona, and Nevada: Eric Frost and Donna Martin (eds.), p. 298-311.

Cameron, T., and Frost, E., 1981, Regional development of major antiforms and synforms coincident with detachment faulting in California, Arizona, Nevada, and Sonora: Geological Society of America Abstracts with Programs, v. 13, n. 7, p. 421-422.

Dahm, J.B., 1983, Geometry and Timing of Tertiary Deformation of the Dome Rock Mountains, Yuma County, Arizona: unpublished Master's thesis, San Diego State University, 176 p.

Dake, C.L., 1918, The Hart Mountain Overthrust and associated structures in Park County, Wyoming: Journal of Geology, v. 26, p. 45-55.

Davis, G.A., Anderson, J.L., and Frost, E.G., 1979, A regional gravity slide complex of Tertiary age, eastern San Bernardino County, California, and Western Arizona: Geological Society of America Abstracts with Programs, v. 11, n. 7, p. 410.

Davis, G.A., Anderson, L.J., Frost, E.G., Shackelford, T.J., 1980, Mylonitization and detachment faulting in the Whipple-Buckskin-Rawhide Mountains terrane, southeastern California and western Arizona: Geological Society of America Memoir 153, p. 79-129.

Frost, E.G., 1979, Growth fault character of Tertiary detachment faulting, Whipple Mountains, San Bernardino County, California, and Buckskin Mountains, Yuma County, Arizona: Geological Society of America Abstracts with Programs, v. 11, n. 7, p. 429.

Guth, P.L., Hodges, K.V., and Willemin, G.H., 1982, Limitations on the role of pore pressure in gravity gliding: Geological Society of America Bulletin, v. 93, p. 606-612.

Gutmann, J.T., 1981, Geologic framework and hot dry rock geothermal potential of the Castle Dome area, Yuma County, Arizona: Los Alamos Scientific Laboratory in house report, LA-8723-HDR, UC-66b, 23 p.

Hansen, W.R., 1965, Effects of the earthquake of March 27, 1964 at Anchorage, Alaska: United States Geological Survey Prof. Paper 542-A, 68 p.

Hansen, W.R., Eckel, G.B., Schaem, W.E., Lyle, R.E., George, W., and Chance, G., 1966, The Alaska Earthquake March 27, 1964: Field investigations and reconstruction effort: United States Geological Survey Prof. Paper 541, 111 p.

Hsu, K.J., 1969, Role of cohesive strength in the mechanics of overthrust faulting and of landsliding: Geological Society of America bulletin, v. 80, p. 927-952.

Hubbert, M.K., and Rubey, W.W., 1959, Role of fluid pressure in mechanics of overthrust faulting: Geological Society of America Bulletin, v. 70, p. 115-205.

John, B.E., and Howard, K.A., 1982, Multiple low-angle Tertiary faults in the Chemehuevi and Mohave mountains, California and Arizona: Geological Society of America Abstracts with Programs, v. 14, p. 175.

Lister, G.S., Etheridge, M.A., and Symonds, P.A., 1986, Detachment faulting and the evolution of passive continental margins: Geology, v. 14, p. 246-250.

Logan, R.E., and Hirsch, D.D., 1982, Geometry of detachment faulting and dike emplacement in the southwestern Castle Dome Mountains, Yuma County, California; in Anderson-Hamilton volume, Mesozoic-Cenozoic Tectonic Evolution of the Colorado River Region, California, Arizona, and Nevada: Eric Frost and Donna Martin (eds.), p. 598-607.

Lyle, J.H., 1982, Interrelationship of late Mesozoic thrust faulting and mid-Tertiary detachment faulting in the Riverside Mountains, southeastern California: in Anderson-Hamilton Volume, Mesozoic-Cenozoic Tectonic Evolution of the Colorado River Region, California, Arizona, and Nevada: Eric Frost and Donna Martin (eds.), p. 470-491.

Miller, J.M., and John, B.J., 1988, Detached strata in a Tertiary low-angle normal fault terrane, southeastern California: A sedimentary record of unroofing, breaching, and continued slip: Geology, v. 16, p. 645-648.

Misch, P., 1960, Regional structural reconnaissance in central-northeast Nevada and some adjacent areas: Observations and interpretations: in Guidebook to Geology of East Central Nevada, Intermountain Association of Petroleum Geologists, v. 11, p. 17-42.

Nutting, D.E., 1984, Origin of bedded salt deposits: A critique of evaporite models and defense of a hydrothermal model: unpublished master's thesis on file at the Institute for Creation Research, Santee, California.

Otton, James K., and Dokka, Roy K., 1981, The role of stretch folding in crustal extension in the Mojave and Sonoran Deserts: A low strain rate mode: Geological Society of America Abstracts with Programs, v. 13, n. 7, p. 524.

Pierce, W.G., 1957, Heart Mountain and South Fork detachment thrusts of Wyoming: Bulletin of the American Association of Petroleum Geologists, v. 41, p. 591-626.

Pierce, W.G., 1979, Clastic dikes of Heart Mountain fault breccia, northwestern Wyoming and their significance: United States Geological Survey Prof. Paper 1133, 25 p.

Pike, J.E., and Hansen, V.L., 1982, Complex Tertiary stratigraphy and structure, Mohave Mountains, Arizona: A prliminary report: in Anderson-Hamilton volume, Mesozoic-Cenozoic Tectonic Evolution of the Colorado River Region, California, Arizona, and Nevada: Eric Frost and Donna Martin (eds.), p. 91-96.

Reynolds, S.J., and Spencer, J.E., 1985, Evidence for large-scale transport on the Bullard detachment fault, west- central Arizona: Geology, v. 13, p. 353-356.

Rugg, S.H., 1986, Detachment Faulting in the northern Trigo Mountains, Arizona: A Catastrophic Interpretation of Tertiary Geologic Processes: unpublished master's thesis on file at the Institute for Creation Research, Santee, California p. 154.

Seager, W.R., 1970, Low-angle gravity glide structures in the northern Virgin Mountains, Nevada and Arizona: Geological Society of America Bulletin, v. 81, p. 1517-1538.

Shackelford, T.J., 1975, Late Tertiary gravity sliding in the Rawhide Mountains, western Arizona: Geological Society of America Abstracts with Programs, v. 7, p. 372-373.

Spencer, J.E., 1984, Role of tectonic denudation in warping and uplift of low-angle normal faults, Geology, v. 12, p. 95-98.

Spencer, J.E., 1985, Miocene low-angle faulting and dike emplacement, Homer Mountain and surrounding areas, southeastern California and southernmost Nevada, Geological Society of America Bulletin, v. 96, p. 1140-1155.

Spencer, J.E., and Welty, J.W., 1986, Possible control of base- and precious-metal mineralization associated with Tertiary detachment faults in the lower Colorado River trough, Arizona and California: Geology, v. 14, p. 195-198.

Stewart, J.H., 1983, Extentional tectonics in the Death Valley area, California: Transport of the Panamint Range structural block 80 kilometers northwestward: Geology, v. 11, p. 153-157.

Teel, D.B., and Frost, E.G., 1982, Synorogenic evolution of the Copper Basin Formation in the eastern Whipple Mountains, San Bernardino County, California: in Anderson-Hamilton volume, Mesozoic-Cenozoic Tectonic Evolution of the Colorado River Region, California, Arizona, and Nevada: Eric Frost and Donna Martin (eds.), p. 275-285.

Voight, B., 1973, The mechanics of retrogressive block gliding, with emphasis on the evolution of the Turnagain Heights Landslide, Anchorage, Alaska: in Gravity and Tectonics, DeJong, K.A., and Scholten, R., (eds.), p. 97-121.

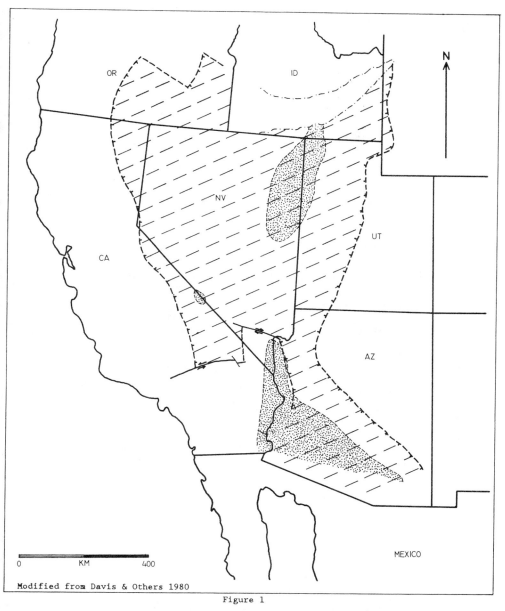

Figure 1

Map of Western United States Showing Region of Tertiary Extensional Tectonism
(indicated by diagonal pattern). Stippled pattern indicates areas affected by
detachment faulting.

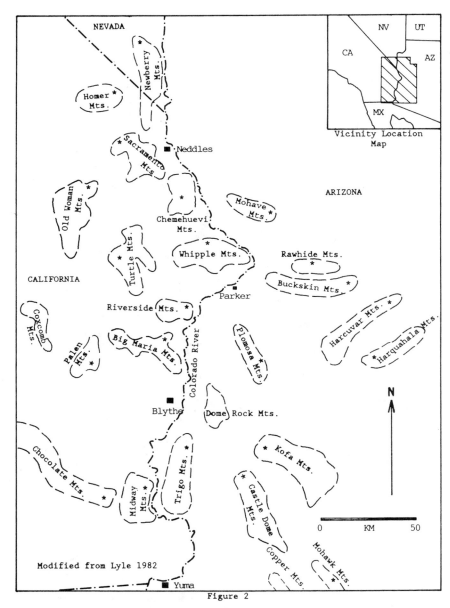

Figure 2

Index Map of Mountain Ranges in Detachment Terrane of the Colorado River
Borderland. (* - indicates those ranges where a detachment fault has been
recognized)

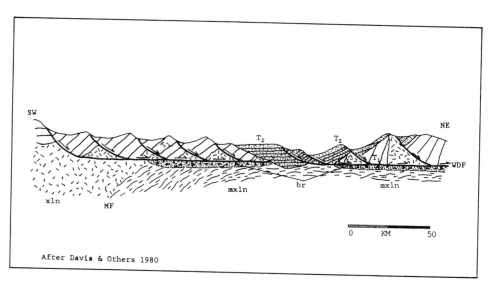

Figure 3

Diagrammatic Cross-section Showing Two Phases of Rotational (listric) Normal
Faulting Associated with Low-angle Detachment Faulting Along the Whipple
Detachment Fault (WDF), Whipple Mountains, Arizona. Upper-plate movement was
toward the northeast. Inclined bedding has resulted from northeast rotation of
the upper-plate half-graben blocks. Note the growth nature of the faults at the
northeast side of the section indicating that upper-plate movement and deposition
were contemporaneous. T_1 = Gene Canyon sedimentary and volcanic rocks; T_2 =
Copper Basin sedimentary and volcanic rocks; MF = mylonitic front; xln =
intrusive rocks; mxln = mylonitic equivalents of xln; br = tectonic breccia.

DISCUSSION

The geologic evidence for detachment faults is compelling and needs to be explained by current tectonic models. Mr. Rugg has shown why uniformitarian tectonic models fail to explain detachment-faulted terranes. Catastrophic tectonic models are needed. The enormous size of the detachment terranes of southeastern California and western Arizona argue for a regional catastrophic cause. The analogy of detachment faults to the Turnagain Heights Landslide (Alaska, 1964) makes catastrophic detachment faulting very believable. We need small-scale modern examples to help us reason in the colossal scale required by the evidence. The author is to be commended for his valuable addition to creationist research.

Steven A. Austin, Ph.D.
Santee, California

The arguments provided by Mr. Rugg do not adequately support his conclusions. The main conclusion is that the detachment faults in the southwestern U.S. are evidence for a short and catastrophic Tertiary period which characterized the latter stages of Noah's Flood.

The author reasons that these detachment faults resulted from frequent earthquakes (of a magnitude larger than we observe today) which were associated with explosive volcanos composed of rhyolite and andesite. Repeated tremors would cause large blocks of earth to slide along a fault plane.

Here are some difficulties with such reasoning:

1. In the Tertiary strata of S.W. United States there are numerous examples of non-explosive, quiet lava flows composed of rhyolite and andesite which are far from any volcano, while in the same region there are many examples of highly explosive volcanos composed of basalt.

2. Most earthquakes, and the largest earthquakes in the world today, are related to fault movement, not volcanos.

3. Detachment faults come in many sizes and shapes and are the result of numerous factors, only one of which is earthquakes.

4. Much of the Tertiary strata found throughout the world is characterized bb a quiet, non-catastrophic environment. This is much different than the author's Tertiary model for S.W. United States.

5. To cause such large detachment faults, the author postulates much larger volcano-related earthquakes than seismologists have recorded in recent history.

Uniformitarianism says that the present is a key to the past. Its principles set the guidelines for geologic research. Mr. Rugg seems to waiver between uniformitarian principles and his own guidelines, whichever suit his purpose. Claiming that "explosive volcanism and violent earthquakes beyond modern day comparison" isn't playing by the rules and most geologists won't accept that kind of speculation as convincing evidence.

Kirk W. McCabe, M.S.
Pittsburgh, Pennsylvania

Mr. Rugg has presented an interesting hypothesis concerning the origin of detachment faulting. However, he seems to bump the two very different types of detachment faulting into the same category. The extensional type of detachment faulting shown in figure 3, as a relatively newly identified phenomenon. In this type of detachment faulting, older rocks are not moved on top of younger strata. In the previously identified style, compressive forces are required to explain the crustal shortening observed, since the rocks are piled upon top of each other rather than being spread out.

It would also be nice if Mr. Rugg had presented detailed calculations that reasonable seismic energy released could provide the mechanical energy necessary to initiate movement.

Glenn R. Morton, M.S.
Dallas, Texas

Mr. McCabe has erroneously characterized the scope of my model for detachment faulting in the southwestern United States by implying that the sole seismic energy source for initiating upper-plate movement is volcanism. A proper reading of the paper clearly indicates that seismicity from volcanism is only one component of an intensely energetic tectonic phase. Other events occurring at this time were extensive dike emplacement, high heat flow and several thousands of feet of basement warping. The sum of these events would have undoubtedly been accompanied by an immense release of seismic energy by both magma displacement and faulting. I would also like to point out that this region is cut by a multitude of high-angle Tertiary faults.

Although "much" of the worldwide Tertiary strata may apparently indicate a "quiet, non-catastrophic environment", much of the strata is also clearly indicative of a catastrophic environment. Although I cannot take the space here to expound on this, I will say that the rock record in the southwestern United States, of which my paper was limited, is clearly indicative of highly energetic catastrophic processes.

I hope I made no misrepresentations; my paper was not intended to be a standard uniformitarian exegesis. Therefore, I thought I was not required to follow its rules. Mr. McCabe seems to believe that uniformitarianism is a scientific fact as indicated by his statement that "Its principles set the guidelines for geologic research". Uniformitarianism is only one _theory_ used to interpret the body of geologic data. Catastrophism is another _theory_ used to do the same. I wasn't there to see it happen and neither was Mr. McCabe.

It is correct that detachment terrane in the southwestern United States is of extensional origin which is dissimilar to the compressional origin of overthrust faults. However, many detachment faults were previously identified as overthrust faults because of their location and similar fault configuration. This was the case for the Heart Mountain detachment which William G. Pierce has shown to have been a cataclysmic gravity slide unrelated to compressional tectonics.

It should be noted that due to the similarity in fault configuration (nearly horizontal fault surface) between extensional detachment faults and overthrusts, the mechanical problems associated with upper-plate movement in both cases is nearly identical. The difference being the type forces required to initiate and maintain movement.

Scott H. Rugg, M.S.

PRE-FLOOD VAPOR CANOPY
RADIATIVE TEMPERATURE PROFILES

David E. Rush, M.S., and Larry Vardiman, Ph.D.
Institute for Creation Research
San Diego, California

ABSTRACT

Using a widely accepted radiance program, temperature profiles for various pre-Flood vapor canopies are calculated. The profiles are for pure radiative equilibrium, with no clouds or convective adjustments. This is the first step in answering the question, "Could a vapor canopy have provided a world-wide climate suitable for human habitation?" It is found that water vapor canopies ranging in size from 10 to 1013 mb produce temperatures at the canopy base hot enough to maintain water in the vapor phase, and hence ensure a stable canopy. However, canopies in the range from 50 to 1013 mb, and perhaps even canopies from 10 to 50 mb, also produce inhospitably high surface temperatures. The addition of clouds in future work would appear to hold promise of modifying these conclusions greatly.

INTRODUCTION

The idea that the atmosphere of the ancient earth may have been overlain by water in one phase or another was apparently first thought of, at least in modern times, by Isaac Vail (1905), a uniformitarian. For Vail, the canopy that collapsed to contribute to the biblical flood of Noah's time was merely the last of many canopies that had existed throughout earth's long history. They had formed from outgassing of the earth's interior, and their collapse over geologic time had formed the oceans. But the idea of a vapor canopy in Noah's time appealed to creationists, where it took root and began to be incorporated by them in models of earth history. The modern day revival of creationism is usually dated to 1961, with the publication of *The Genesis Flood* by Whitcomb and Morris. A water vapor canopy played an important part in their model. It continues to have a major role in many creationist models of the ancient earth.

There is no direct support from science for the existence of a water vapor canopy surrounding the earth in the past. However, a survey of the solar system reveals that five of the nine planets, including the one closest to us in distance and size, Venus, have thick cloud canopies. Direct support from Scripture for a canopy comes from Day Two of Creation Week. "And God made the firmament (atmosphere), and divided the waters which were under the firmament from the waters which were above the firmament: and it was so" *(Genesis 1:7)*.

An important effect of canopies in the solar system today is to moderate temperatures beneath them. Planets that do not have canopies show a much wider variance in temperature — diurnally, yearly, and latitudinally. Earth is characterized by a fairly large and permanent temperature gradient between its equator and poles. This temperature gradient produces a pressure gradient, which becomes the driving force behind weather systems of the planet. But nearly all creationists and uniformitarians agree that at some time in the past the planet enjoyed a warmer, more uniform climate from pole to pole. Concerning the Cretaceous for example, uniformitarians Barron et al. (1981) say,

> The contrast between the climate of the Cretaceous period (65 million to 140 million years ago) and that of the present epoch is the largest in the history of the earth that has been fairly well documented. A fundamental problem in paleoclimatology is how a globally ice-free climate could be maintained ... The Cretaceous climate has

been classically described as warm and equable on the basis of 'climate sensitive' sedimentary indicators, characteristics of fossil floras and faunas, and oxygen isotope data ... The Cretaceous was the acme of exothermic reptiles. As yet, unequivocal evidence of permanent ice is unknown ... Cretaceous polar temperatures have been estimated by various observers to be between 5 and 19°C.

Scripture also offers some evidence that the pre-Flood climate worldwide may have been dramatically different than today's. *Genesis 2:5,6* raise the possibility that there was no rain on the earth from Adam to Noah. During this time vegetation was watered by a mist rather than rain. *Genesis 2:25* implies that climatic conditions were warm everywhere on earth because Adam and Eve and their descendants were to populate the earth and be comfortable all year around without clothing. *Genesis 8:22* first mentions hot and cold, summer and winter, in connection with seasons. *Genesis 9:12-16* establishes the Noahic Covenant, with its sign, the rainbow. This is the first time that a rainbow or a cloud is mentioned in Scripture. Clouds are of course necessary for rain, and a rainbow is simply an optical phenomena caused by sunlight on rain drops. As before, however, the Bible does not explicitly state they did not exist before the Flood. For amplification of biblical arguments for a warm pre-Flood climate, see Dillow (1982).

These tantalizing hints from the Bible are certainly compatible with the idea that earth's climate has been very different. Taken together, they are consistent with a warm climate worldwide. A warm, equable climate year-round would be less likely to have any of the atmospheric "natural disasters" that periodically afflict today's world, such as hurricanes, floods, tornadoes, blizzards, hailstorms, etc.

So we see that evidence from geology and the Bible seem to point to a very different global climate in the past. In addition, elements of many ancient legends also tend to support this conclusion (Dillow, 1982, ch.4).

This paper addresses one traditional tenet of the Creation Model. A water canopy in some form has been proposed by many creationists to explain Biblical and scientific evidence for climatic conditions before the Flood. This paper is a status report of ongoing research to solidify the physical basis for the vapor canopy model.

POSSIBLE CAUSES OF A WARM CLIMATE

To warm the earth significantly, at least one of two things must happen: either the earth must receive more radiant energy from the sun, or it must retain more of the heat it does get. We may label the first possibility as processes that affect primarily the incident solar, or shortwave, radiation absorbed at the earth's surface. We may call the second option processes that primarily affect the infrared, or longwave, radiation the earth emits. The first possibility, that of increased shortwave radiation, may be met by a hotter sun, a decreased earth-sun distance, lower albedo (reflectivity) of the atmosphere or the surface, or any other process that increases the net absorbed solar radiation at the surface. Most creationists and uniformitarians say that shortwave factors may indeed have been contributing causes, but they look to the longwave for the primary cause of ancient warmth. A longwave factor means that the earth somehow retained more of the solar radiation it received. The only way this could be done is with a different atmosphere.

Of key importance to us on earth are only three constituents of the atmosphere: CO_2, H_2O, and O_3. These three species account for about 99% of radiative interplay. The three major components of the atmosphere, nitrogen, oxygen, and argon, are practically transparent to both shortwave and longwave radiation (except for one narrow solar absorption band of oxygen). Today's atmosphere is not primarily heated from above, by the sun, but from below, by the earth. This is because the atmosphere is more transparent to shortwave radiation than longwave. Increasing mixing ratios (concentrations) of those molecules that absorb more longwave than shortwave (as both water vapor and carbon dioxide do) has the net effect of *warming* the atmosphere, which in turn emits more longwave. This warms the surface further — resulting in the so-called "greenhouse effect."

In modeling the ancient climate, uniformitarians usually assume that the total amount of water vapor in the atmosphere has not changed significantly in the past. That is, even though the water vapor concentration (mixing ratio) today varies widely with location and time, the assumption is that the total amount of water vapor in the atmosphere has been essentially unchanging over very long periods of time. Uniformitarians also assume the amount of ozone, which has a fairly minor effect overall compared to the others, has also been constant. So, they normally introduce large amounts of carbon dioxide into their models (e.g. Hunt, 1984; Budyko, 1988, p.3; Berner et al. , 1983). Carbon dioxide is uniformly mixed throughout the atmosphere (unlike water vapor and ozone), and is assumed to have had a much higher concentration in the past. The excess carbon dioxide is now thought to be tied up in rocks of the crust.

The Bible, however, hints at another cause for a worldwide equable climate — "the waters which were above the firmament." The Bible never says the original atmosphere was different than today's (indeed, it can't be much different and support the life it does). What it does say is that the atmosphere ("firmament") was standing between waters beneath it (the oceans) and waters above it. At present there are of course no waters above the atmosphere; but at the beginning of the Flood, God "opened the windows of heaven" and perhaps emptied onto the earth all the waters that had been there. Some creationists have proposed that the antediluvian "waters above" would have been stable (at least for thousands of years) if the water was in its vapor phase. This would have the effect of covering the present atmosphere with a water vapor blanket, or canopy. From the time of creation until the Flood, a canopy of water in vapor form surrounded and rested upon an atmosphere similar to today's. This canopy, a longwave forcing mechanism, provided an equable worldwide climate until the beginning of the Flood, when its collapse produced 40 days and nights of rain.

A successful vapor canopy will meet two criteria:

- The canopy must be stable. Once in place, it must be kept in place by the laws of physics. (Arguments that appeal to a continuing miracle to maintain the canopy, such as Johnson's (1986) and Udd's (1975), are by this criterion rejected.)

- The surface temperature must be hospitable to human beings.

A one-dimensional radiation balance between the earth-atmosphere-canopy system is the necessary starting point in meeting these criteria. This is so because exchange of radiant energy is the dominant mode of energy exchange in the atmosphere. Dillow (1982) attempted this, but freely admitted (p.247) that his work was a "*progress report*" rather than a complete solution." His handicap was the lack of a sophisticated radiance program with detailed spectral data. Such a program is now available and may be used to construct vertical temperature profiles from radiation balances with a high degree of confidence. Such profiles may not in themselves provide definitive solutions to the two primary criteria of stability and surface temperature, but they are a necessary starting point. The goal of this work therefore is construction of one-dimensional, pure radiative equilibrium temperature profiles of the earth-atmosphere-canopy system.

DEVELOPMENT OF THE METHOD

A number of simplifying assumptions have been made:

- The problem is addressed in one dimension only. Two and three dimensional analyses, which involve meridional heat and mass transfer, in the atmosphere and preferably the oceans also, are much too complex for the first phase of this study. Such routines require expensive main-frame time, and in any case rely ultimately on a one-dimensional analysis.

- Radiation only will be considered. Other processes active in today's atmosphere are convection, diffusion, conduction, and latent heat release/gain. Of these, only convection and latent heat processes (besides radiation) noticeably modify the temperature profile in the stratosphere and below. However, the radiation calculation must be done first, and its shape will determine whether or not convection can take place. If convection is active, knowledge of water vapor content as a function of altitude may then be used to figure latent heat effects, which will further modify the temperature profile. The addition of these two effects is relatively simple, and could readily be added onto this work if necessary.

• Calculations will be done in a clear sky, with no clouds and no aerosols.

The goal is to obtain one-dimensional, pure radiative temperature profiles for various water vapor canopies covering today's atmosphere. The key element in this whole process is determining radiances. For nearly 20 years scientists at the U.S. Air Force Geophysical Laboratories (AFGL) have worked on a public domain atmospheric radiance (and transmission) program called LOWTRAN. The present version, LOWTRAN 7, is dated 1989, and contains 18,000 source lines of Fortran code (Kneizys, 1988). The spectral data used is from the Laboratories and is generally considered the finest available anywhere. The program is capable of calculating atmospheric absorption and radiance for a wide range of absorber concentrations, pressures, and temperatures. Its primary purpose is not for climate modeling as such, but since it gives radiances it may be used to calculate fluxes, and hence temperature profiles. A number of programs, totaling some 2200 Fortran lines, were written for this research to manage LOWTRAN 7 for the task.

LOWTRAN 7 has significant improvements over earlier versions. Foremost among these are the addition of multiple scattering, updated water vapor continuum absorption values that now include the region from 0-350 cm^{-1} (∞-28.6μm^{-1}), and an improved solar source function. For further details, see Kneizys et al. (1988) or Kneizys et al. (1983). LOWTRAN 7 is used to compute the integrated radiances at given levels in the atmosphere. Five separate calculations are made: (1) shortwave directly-transmitted solar radiation, (2) shortwave multiple-scattered downward solar radiation, (3) shortwave multiple-scattered upward solar radiation, (4) longwave upward emitted radiation, and (5) longwave downward emitted radiation. Once the integrated radiance over the desired wavelength interval is obtained from LOWTRAN 7, net fluxes are calculated. The total flux leaving a layer is subtracted from that entering, and the result, ΔF, is used to figure the heating.

The atmosphere is divided into twenty or more "atmospheric levels" of specified altitude, pressure, temperature, and absorber concentration. Pressure and absorber concentrations at each level are constant, altitudes and temperatures vary with time. All radiance calculations are taken at constant pressure "flux levels", chosen so that each atmospheric level is exactly halfway between two flux levels. The region between two flux levels is called a layer. The cooling rate of a given layer is then:

$$\frac{dT}{dt} = \frac{g\Delta F}{C_P \Delta P} \tag{1}$$

where dT/dt is the rate of change in temperature of the layer, g is the acceleration due to gravity, C_P is heat capacity at constant pressure, and ΔP is the pressure change across the layer. The heating (cooling) rate is then converted to a new atmospheric level temperature by the equation,

$$T_{n+1} = T_n + \frac{dT}{dt}\Delta t \tag{2}$$

where T_n is the temperature at the nth iteration, and Δt is the time interval. The process is then repeated as often as needed until pre-set criteria for equilibrium are met.

TESTING OF THE MODEL

As stated earlier, the goal of this study is to construct several one-dimensional pure radiative equilibrium temperature profiles through today's atmosphere with various water vapor canopies overlying. LOWTRAN 7 has been compared with other radiation models, according to AFGL, and is in wide use. But to our knowledge it has not been used in its entirety in this type of theoretical study, though parts of it have been used by others (e.g., Thompson and Warren, 1982; Chou, 1986). Professor Pallmann of St. Louis University is in the process of incorporating LOWTRAN 7 into a radiation program (Pallmann, 1989). Accordingly, it was mandatory that our method be compared to known results for today's atmosphere. Manabe and Strickler (1964, hereinafter MS) constructed a widely accepted pure radiation profile for today's atmosphere (see e.g., Liou, 1980, pp.336-338). This was based on research by Manabe and Möller (1961). Even though the last 25 years have seen much work on the radiation problem, and many new results on individual aspects of it, the net effect has been simply to confirm the MS profile. Their curve is still widely honored as a calibration curve, with the exception that their surface temperature is too high, which will be discussed later.

The MS procedure was followed as closely as possible. To ensure an overall energy balance, two conditions are monitored: (1) The earth's surface is assumed to have zero heat storage capacity; therefore all incoming shortwave and longwave radiation absorbed by the ground is returned upward as longwave radiation. This ensures a surface net flux of zero at all times. (2) As a criterion for equilibrium, the planetary heat balance (the net incoming shortwave less the outgoing longwave, measured at the top of the atmosphere) is expected to approach zero. Other conditions of the MS modeling are also met. The time interval chosen is eight hours, except that shorter intervals are used as equilibrium is approached. Air temperature of the lowest layer is assumed to be the same as the ground temperature. Variable absorber concentrations (H_2O and O_3) are taken from MS figures, both for April at 35°N. Constant pressure levels are set the same as theirs. Surface albedo is assumed to be 0.10. MS do not say how scattering was handled except that Rayleigh scattering was assumed to contribute 7% to the planetary albedo. This assumption was not used. Instead, scattering fluxes (up and down) were obtained by integrating radiances over a hemisphere.

Fig 1 shows the warming of an initially cold isothermal atmosphere. The top of each line represents the "top" of the atmosphere at 2.3 mb. It slowly rises as the atmosphere beneath it warms up. It is apparent from Fig 1 that a pure radiative equilibrium profile does not accurately describe the actual temperature profile in today's atmosphere. The surface is too warm and the upper troposphere too cold. The reason is that convection is not taken into account. When MS added a convective adjustment, their results were a much better approximation to the actual temperature profile. However, for this study we are interested only in a radiative profile.

Two deviations from Manabe and Strickler's equilibrium are evident. Their surface temperature is 332 K, and ours only 320 K (The original Manabe and Möller (1961) value was 313 K). However, 332 K is above that of most modeling programs currently in use, which give temperatures in the 320's (Briegleb, 1989; Pallmann, 1989). Both Briegleb and Pallmann say a value of 320 K is acceptable. The precise value depends on exact absorber profiles, absorption coefficients, and a host of minor parameters. The other deviation is in the stratosphere, but this could be caused by slight differences in absorber concentrations. Manabe and Strickler note that "The upper stratospheric equilibrium temperature depends very much on the distribution of water vapor" (though the overall heating of the stratosphere is caused of course by ozone). Also, efforts over the years at AFGL and elsewhere have provided more precise absorption coefficients for all absorbers. In any case, MS say that the stratospheric temperature profile "...affects the temperature of the earth's surface and troposphere very little (less than 1 deg) judging from the present results." Therefore, the deviation between their results and ours in the stratosphere is not judged important for this work. We may conclude that our model compares favorably with an accepted standard for today's atmosphere.

In addition to the MS comparison, a set of flux values were calculated for an atmosphere used by the National Center for Atmospheric Research to test radiance programs (Kiehl et al, 1987). Comparison with their results was also favorable (Briegleb, 1989).

INITIAL CANOPY CONDITIONS

Four different canopies were carried to completion. Water vapor amounts in the canopies were 10, 50, 125, and 1013 millibars. Unless otherwise noted, characteristics of the atmosphere and other assumptions were the same as in the MS calibration test. The MS atmosphere was geared to April, 35°N, and differed only slightly from the U.S. Standard Atmosphere. The solar zenith angle was set at 60°, and day fraction at 0.5. This approximates average conditions on the earth. A surface albedo of 0.13 was used (Barron et al., 1981), a value midway between today's values of 0.08-0.20 in humid regions (Laval and Picon, 1986). It happens that the ocean albedo at a solar zenith angle of 60° is also 0.13 (Ramanathan et al., 1989). This is somewhat less than today's average surface albedo for the earth (including polar regions) of 0.14-0.18 (Ramanathan and Coakley, 1978). The day of the year is 109, a day in mid-April, a time of average earth-sun distance. This gives an average value for the solar constant. Spectral intervals used unless otherwise noted: Solar direct: 3500-40000 cm^{-1} (2.86-0.25μm^{-1}) $d\nu$ = 20 cm^{-1}. Scattering:

8000-40000 cm^{-1} (1.25-0.25μm^{-1}) $d\nu$ = 1000 cm^{-1}. Longwave: 20-3500 cm^{-1} (500-2.86μm^{-1}) $d\nu$ = 20 cm^{-1}. Longwave fluxes were calculated by the formula $F = \pi I$. Shortwave scattering fluxes were calculated by numerical integration of radiances over the hemisphere. Shortwave directly transmitted flux is obtained straight from LOWTRAN 7. It was not necessary to calculate each of the solar fluxes at every iteration, as they are only slightly temperature dependent. New solar fluxes were obtained only once every thirty iterations, or less often as equilibrium was approached, saving much computer time.

DISCUSSION OF 50MB CANOPY RESULTS

The 50 mb canopy will be described in some detail and the other results summarized. 50 mb of water vapor is equivalent to 20 inches of precipitable water. Fig 2 shows radiative equilibrium approached from a cold isothermal beginning point. The top of each line represents the "top" of the canopy. Thus at Day 0, the atmosphere-canopy is cold and low. By Day 10, the surface is already heated to 296 K, and lower layers of the atmosphere are also rapidly heating. This is due to the intense solar radiation that has been absorbed by the ground and reemitted as infrared, where it is readily absorbed by the relatively high water content of the lower layers. The middle layers are relatively low in water vapor and ozone (carbon dioxide has the same mixing ratio everywhere) and so they tend to be transparent to both shortwave and longwave. The upper layers constitute the stratosphere in today's atmosphere and therefore are low in water vapor and high in ozone. They are heated by absorption of solar ultraviolet.

The discontinuity at about 18 km in Day 10 represents the top of the atmosphere and base of the canopy. Note that the great majority of the mass of the atmosphere-canopy is below 18 km. The lower portion of the canopy is heated primarily by absorption of longwave from the ground, but also somewhat by solar absorption. From 18 km (pressure = 50 mb) to about 52 km (pressure = 1.00 mb) the canopy cools as longwave radiation is emitted to space. The top cools so well that it is several months before it again attains its starting point of 170 K. However, additional months of heating do not have much effect, and it ends up at only 189 K, or -84°C. Since the water vapor pressure at the top of the canopy (1.279 mb; changed from 1.00 during the model run) is much higher than the saturation vapor pressure at 189 K (2×10^{-5}mb), the vapor will turn to ice. At the next level, this is also true. The vapor pressure is 4.615 mb, the saturation pressure (at 246 K) only 0.27 mb, and the vapor will also tend to become ice. At the next level down however, the vapor pressure is 11.597 mb, the saturation pressure (at 284 K) is 13 mb, and the vapor will remain in the vapor form. At all lower levels of the canopy the vapor pressure is lower than the saturation pressure and the water will be in the vapor phase. A temperature of 387 K at the base of the canopy (50 mb) guarantees the vapor phase. In the final profile, the canopy base has risen to 35 km and the top (1.279 mb) to 83 km.

The critical lapse rate for water vapor, if we assume no phase change, is the adiabatic one, which is 5.3 deg/km. If the observed lapse rate exceeds this, convection will occur as hotter, less dense gas tends to rise and colder, more dense gas tends to sink. If the observed lapse rate is less than the critical one, there is no tendency to overturn and the canopy is stable. The lapse rate in the lowest canopy layer between 50 and 48 mb is 9.6 deg/km. Therefore, convection will begin. The next layer also shows a tendency to convect. Beyond this, all higher layers have a lapse rate below 5.3 deg/km, and will be stable. The situation is similar to that of the atmosphere today, where unstable lower layers often send mass and heat up into higher, stable layers. The topmost layers of the canopy involve a phase change, so their critical lapse rate will be different from the adiabatic one. The atmosphere itself is nearly isothermal down to the lower layers, which show slightly higher temperatures. Only in the lowest two (thin) layers is the critical (adiabatic) lapse rate of 10 deg/km exceeded. There will be a slight convective transport of heat from the surface into the first several hundred meters. This will lower the surface temperature by a degree or two, and raise the temperature just above by a corresponding amount. Overall, the atmosphere will be quite stable. At the surface, the initial rapid heating has slowed so much that the final six months see a rise of only one degree, to 409 K, or 35° above the boiling point of water at 1063 mb.

Fig 3 shows the heat balance of the earth at equilibrium and transmission values for the infrared, all for the 50 mb canopy. Of 100 units of incoming solar, 19 units are absorbed by water vapor in the canopy. (All absorption values include a small amount due to absorption of reflected (outgoing) solar). 8 additional units (of the 100) are absorbed by the atmosphere, and 5 units reflected by the atmosphere-canopy to space. That leaves 68 units that make it to the surface, most transmitted directly but some scattered. 8 units are reflected at the surface, contributing to the total planetary albedo of 13 units, and leaving 60 units absorbed by the earth. These 60 units are then reemitted as longwave radiaton. Actually, because of the very high surface temperature 478 units total are emitted by the surface, but 418 of these have been received as longwave from the canopy and atmosphere, for a net infrared loss of 60. This balances the net solar gain of 60.

An infrared energy balance of the atmosphere shows 478 units of terrestrial radiation, 349 units of infrared from the canopy entering, 418 units leaving to the ground, and 417 leaving for the canopy, for a net infrared cooling of 8 units. This balances the solar absorption of 8 units. A balance on the canopy shows it receiving 417 units from below, losing 349 units downward, and 87 upward to space. This is a net infrared cooling of 19 units, which balances the solar absorption of 19 units.

Overall, the 87 longwave units emitted to space plus the 13 shortwave units reflected to space account for the original 100 units received from the sun. It is readily apparent that the canopy is very effective at trapping the earth's radiation. Without the windows to space that exist today, temperatures build until the canopy's emission to space finally equals the net incoming solar. To be more precise, the windows are not totally closed with the 50 mb canopy. Also shown in Fig 3 are transmission data. These percentages show the amount of surface longwave radiation that arrives unimpeded at the canopy base (27%) and at the canopy top (11%). Without the canopy, 27% of the terrestrial radiation would escape straight to space, but with it only 11% does so. This difference may at first seem small, but it means that the entire earth-atmosphere-canopy system must heat up to the point where it radiates enough extra energy to space to make up the difference.

In conclusion, only 50 mb of water vapor added above the present atmosphere would raise the surface temperature as determined by a radiation balance from 320 K to 409 K. A better comparison is to include convection effects. Convection lowered the MS ground temperature in today's atmosphere (less clouds) from a pure radiational 332 K to 300 K (MS, 1964), much closer to the observed 288 K. As mentioned in discussion earlier, convection in the atmosphere under the 50 mb canopy would probably lower the surface temperature only a degree or two. So it seems that addition of only 50 mb of water vapor above the present atmosphere would raise the surface temperature more than 100 degrees.

Kasting and Ackerman (1986) added 10 $bars$ of CO_2 and got a surface temperature of only 400 K, including convection effects, at present solar luminosity. Truly, the water molecule has an amazing ability to absorb radiation. The contrast with CO_2 is all the more marked when it is seen that a large part of the Kasting and Ackerman "CO_2 caused" temperature increase is actually caused by water vapor from increased oceanic and lake evaporation. In the 50 mb canopy, there would certainly be increased tropospheric water content from evaporation, but it has not been considered.

DISCUSSION OF OTHER CANOPY RESULTS

Vertical temperature profiles for canopies with 10, 125, and 1013 mb of water vapor show similar distributions as the 50 mb canopy but hotter for thicker canopies and cooler for the thinner canopy. Fig 4 shows the surface temperature as a function of the mass of the canopy. As the mass of the canopy is slowly increased from zero, the surface temperature rapidly increases. At a canopy mass of 125 mb, the longwave windows to space are nearly closed, and additional water vapor has little marginal effect. At 1013 mb (1 atm), the windows are totally closed. No longwave terrestrial radiation escapes straight to space.

Surface temperatures are directly related to the mass of the canopy and produce too warm a surface temperature to be hospitable for life under pure radiative equilibrium for all canopies studied. However, for the 10 mb case inclusion of convection would noticeably decrease the surface temperature, perhaps into the suitable 300-310 K range. In each case the temperature at the top of the canopy is below freezing. The cold temperature causes the saturation vapor pressure to fall below the ambient pressure, producing a cirrus cloud layer. Near the surface of the earth and at the base of the canopy thin layers are convectively unstable, based on the temperature lapse rate.

CONCLUSIONS

It was stated earlier in this paper that two criteria for the vapor canopy would need to be met: 1) Stability, and 2) A surface temperature suitable for habitation. The first criterion was met. For any size canopy considered, at least from radiation analyses of pure water vapor canopies, it was shown that the temperature is always high enough throughout most of the canopy, particularly at the base, to easily ensure the vapor phase. The second criterion is not as straightforward to evaluate. Radiation considerations strongly suggest surface temperatures are not suitable for the 1013, 125, and 50 mb canopies. The canopy blanket is simply so effective that the surface temperature becomes inhospitable. This could also be true for the 10 mb canopy, though convection considerations may alter this conclusion. Inclusion of convection in the denser canopies would not change this verdict.

It does seem reasonable to suppose that somewhere between 0 and 50 mb there exists a value that would lead to a successful canopy. Remarkably, this is the same conclusion reached by Kofahl (1977) with his "sliderule estimates." He suggested a total water vapor content in the atmosphere-canopy of six inches, or five inches (12 mb) more than the atmosphere alone. The chief drawback to a thin canopy is that it would not significantly contribute to the 40 days and nights of rain for the Flood.

Morton (1979) was apparently the first to conclude that the canopy would have made the earth's surface too hot for human habitation (Kofahl did not calculate surface temperatures). Morton made a number of assumptions that greatly simplified the problem, and his surface temperatures are much higher than ours, but the general conclusion is the same: Life as we know it would not have been possible under a canopy of 1013 mb (1 atm), nor even with a canopy of only 50 mb. When other features such as clouds are added to the model, this conclusion could be modified greatly, however. Preliminary explorations with cloud layers at the top of the 50 mb canopy have shown significant radiation effects which lower the surface temperature drastically. Unfortunately, while the surface temperature decreases when clouds are added, so does the temperature of the canopy, reducing its stability.

RECOMMENDATIONS

Recommendations for future work are shown in Table 1. The features which should be added to the canopy model to make it more realistic are arranged in descending order of probable impact, first for cooling, then for heating. The most important feature is the addition of clouds. Clouds in the upper canopy would provide a dramatic increase in the planet's albedo, thereby lowering the net influx of solar radiation to the canopy-atmosphere-earth system. Temperatures at the top of the canopy are cool enough to freeze vapor, even without nuclei. Therefore, we may expect that thin cirrus clouds would form. They could not exist everywhere all the time, as stars need to be visible at night to satisfy biblical criteria. Today such clouds actually heat the

Table 1. Recommended features which should be added to the canopy model in future work and the likely effects.

Recommended Features to be Added	Likely Effects at the Earth's Surface
Clouds	Cooling
Aerosols	Cooling or Heating
Convection	Cooling
Latitudinal Transport of Heat	Cooling
Ozone	Cooling
Vertical Conduction	Cooling
Constant Rel. Humidity	Heating
Minor Absorbers	Heating

earth (Liou and Ou, 1983), because they are more effective at trapping outgoing radiation than reflecting incoming solar. But under canopy conditions they should cool it since the longwave spectrum is already saturated. Although not expected to be as significant as cloud layers, the other suggested features in Table 1 could produce important effects on cooling or heating, particularly in certain regions of the atmosphere. The other features are discussed in detail in Rush (1990).

Incorporating clouds and constant relative humidity below the canopy should give us a good idea of the temperature profile at an average spot on earth. By running the model at different latitudes, an idea of temperature profiles at various points on earth could be obtained. The difference between these profiles will give an indication of the driving force that will set up circulation patterns.

Beyond this however, different methods exist for constructing what are called general circulation models (GCMs). Different groups around the world have built their own GCMs. The Canadians call theirs the "Canadian Climate Centre Spectral Atmospheric General Circulation Model." Its elements are described by Boer et al. (1984). Ramanathan et al. (1983) describe modification to a U. S. National Center for Atmospheric Research GCM. Semtner (1984) considers an atmospheric model coupled to three different ocean models. With the interest in possible climate warming caused by increased CO_2, much research has gone into this area.

Future creationist research could perhaps modify a public domain GCM, or build a new creationist one. Although it would take a great amount of computing power, a GCM could give us exciting glimpses into worldwide climate under a vapor canopy.

REFERENCES

Barron, E.J., Thompson, S.L., and Schneider, S.H., "An Ice Free Cretaceous? Results from Climate Model Simulations", SCIENCE, 212:501, 1981.

Berner, R.A., Lasaga, A.C., and Garrals, R.M., "The Carbonate-silicate Geochemical Cycle and its Effect on Atmospheric Carbon Dioxide over the past 100 Million Years", AMERICAN JOURNAL OF SCIENCE, 283:641, 1983.

Boer, G.J., McFarlane, N.A., Laprise, R., Henderson, J.D., and Blanchet, J.-P.,"The Canadian Climate Centre Spectral Atmospheric General Circulation Model", ATMOSPHERE-OCEAN, 22:397, 1984.

Briegleb, B., personal communication, 1989. Mr. Briegleb is a climate modeler with the National Center for Atmospheric Research, Boulder, Colorado.

Budyko, M.I., Golitsyn, G.S., and Izrael, Y.A., GLOBAL CLIMATE CATASTROPHES, Springer-Verlag, Berlin, 1988.

Chou, M.-D., "Atmospheric Solar Heating Rate in the Water Vapor Bands", JOURNAL OF CLIMATE AND APPLIED METEOROLOGY, 25:1532, 1986.

Dillow, J.C., THE WATERS ABOVE: EARTH'S PRE-FLOOD VAPOR CANOPY, revised ed., Moody Press, Chicago, 1982.

Hunt, B.G., "Polar glaciation and the genesis of ice ages", (a letter to) NATURE, 308:48, 1984.

Johnson, G.L., "Global Heat Balance with a Liquid Water and Ice Canopy", CREATION RESEARCH SOCIETY QUARTERLY 23:54, 1986.

Kasting, J.F., and Ackerman, T.P., "Climatic Consequences of Very High Carbon Dioxide Levels in the Earth's Early Atmosphere", SCIENCE 234:1383, 1986.

Kiehl, J.T., Wolski, R.J., Briegleb, B.P., Ramanathan, V., "Documentation of Radiation and Cloud Routines in the NCAR Community Climate Model (CCM1)", National Center for Atmospheric Research, Boulder, Colorado, 1987.

Kneizys, F.X., Shettle, E.P., Abreu, L.W., Chetwynd, J.H., Fenn, R.W., Gallery, W.O., Selby, J.E.A., and Clough, S.A., ATMOSPHERIC TRANSMITTANCE/RADIANCE: COMPUTER CODE LOWTRAN 6, AFGL-TR-83-0187, Air Force Geophysics Laboratory, Hanscom AFB, Massachusetts, 1983.

Kneizys, F.X., Shettle, E.P., Abreu, L.W., Chetwynd, J.H., Anderson, G.P., Gallery, W.O., Selby, J.E.A., and Clough, S.A., USERS GUIDE TO LOWTRAN 7, AFGL-TR-88-0177, Environmental

Research Papers, No.1010, Air Force Geophysics Laboratory, Hanscom AFB, Massachusetts, 1988. This report cites many of the research papers used in construction of Lowtran 7. The more complete description of Lowtran 7 is entitled, Atmospheric Transmittance/Radiance: The Lowtran 7 Model (currently in preparation).

Kofahl, R.E., "Could the Flood Waters Have Come from a Canopy or Extraterrestrial Source?", CREATION RESEARCH SOCIETY QUARTERLY, 13:202, 1977.

Laval, K., and Picon, L., "Effect of a Change of the Surface Albedo of the Sahel on Climate", JOURNAL OF THE ATMOSPHERIC SCIENCES, 43:2418, 1986.

Liou, K.-N., AN INTRODUCTION TO ATMOSPHERIC RADIATION, Academic Press, New York, 1980.

Liou, K.-N., and Ou, S.-C., "Theory of Equilibrium Temperatures in Radiative-Turbulent Atmospheres", JOURNAL OF THE ATMOSPHERIC SCIENCES, 40:214, 1983.

Manabe, S., and Strickler, R.F., "Thermal Equilibrium of the Atmosphere with a Convective Adjustment", JOURNAL OF THE ATMOSPHERIC SCIENCES, 21:361, 1964.

Manabe, S., and Moller, F., "On the Radiative Equilibrium and Heat Balance of the Atmosphere", MONTHLY WEATHER REVIEW, 89:503, 1961.

Morton, G.R., "Can the Canopy Hold Water?", CREATION RESEARCH SOCIETY QUARTERLY, 16:164, 1979.

Pallmann, A.J., personal communication, 1989.

Ramanathan, V., and Coakley, J.A., "Climate Modeling Through Radiative-Convective Models", REVIEWS OF GEOPHYSICS AND SPACE PHYSICS, 16(4):465, 1978.

Ramanathan, V., Pitcher E.J., Malone, R.C., and Blackmon, M.L., "The Response of a Spectral General Circulation Model to Refinements in Radiative Processes", JOURNAL OF THE ATMOSPHERIC SCIENCES, 40:605, 1983.

Ramanathan, V., Cess, R.D., Harrison, E.F., Minnis, P., Barkstrom, B.R., Ahmad, E., Hartmann, D., "Cloud-Radiative Forcing and Climate: Results from the Earth Radiation Budget Experiment", SCIENCE, 243:57, 1989.

Rush, D.E., RADIATIVE EQUILIBRIUM TEMPERATURE PROFILES UNDER A VAPOR CANOPY, (M.S. Thesis) Institute for Creation Research, San Diego, 1990.

Semtner, A.J., "Development of Efficient, Dynamical Ocean-Atmosphere Models for Climatic Studies", JOURNAL OF CLIMATE AND APPLIED METEOROLOGY 23(3):353, 1984.

Thompson, S.L., and Warren, S.G., "Parameterization of Outgoing Infrared Radiation Derived from Detailed Radiative Calculations", JOURNAL OF THE ATMOSPHERIC SCIENCES, 39:2667, 1982.

Udd, S.V., "The Canopy and Genesis 1:6-8", CREATION RESEARCH SOCIETY QUARTERLY, 12:90, 1975.

Vail, I.N., THE DELUGE AND ITS CAUSE, Suggestion Publishing Co., Chicago, 1905.

Whitcomb, J.C., and Morris, H.M., THE GENESIS FLOOD, Presbyterian and Reformed Publishing.

TODAY'S ATMOSPHERE

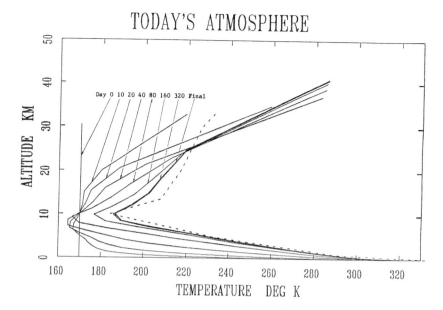

Fig. 1. Vertical temperature profile for today's atmosphere starting from an isothermal 170° condition approaching the Manabe and Strickler (1964) result. Solid profiles are model results at indicated days after day 0 and dashed line is MS profile.

CANOPY – 50 MB

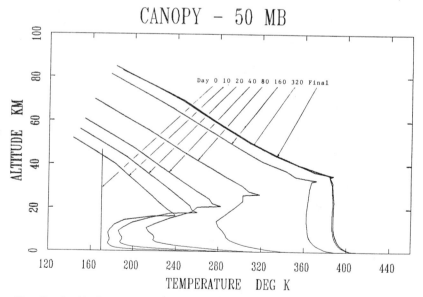

Fig. 2. Vertical temperature profiles of a 50mb canopy above today's atmosphere starting from an isothermal 170° condition approaching equilibrium.

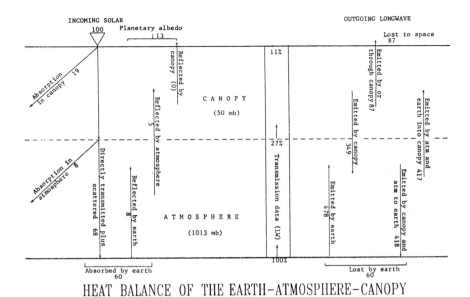

HEAT BALANCE OF THE EARTH–ATMOSPHERE–CANOPY

Fig. 3. The heat balance of the earth-atmosphere-canopy system for a 50mb canopy over today's atmosphere. The left portion of the diagram shows the flux of short-wave radiation, the right portion the flux of long-wave radiation, and the middle portion the transmission of long-wave radiation upward to space. The canopy is above the dashed line and the atmosphere is below the dashed line.

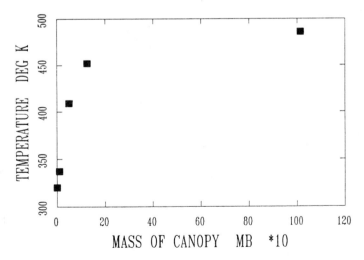

Fig. 4. Radiative equilibrium surface temperature as a function of mass of the overlying canopy.

It is highly encouraging to derive a canopy model with a temperature profile that allows the vapor to be hot enough to keep from condensing, at least for part of the canopy. Most of Dillow's simulations were too cold everywhere. It is therefore worthwhile to proceed with model refinements.

Adding clouds is the best place to start. Dillow's model kept the earth cool with a stratus cloud below the inversion. Investigating an ice cloud at the top of the canopy appears necessary for both models because the radiative temperature is too cold there. Perhaps there would have been dissociation of water molecules into hydrogen and oxygen at the top of the canopy and then the formation of ozone which could keep the top of the canopy hot enough to prevent cloud formation.

Figure 2 could have had the water vapor pressure curve plotted for reference so that the readers might know where the canopy appears cool enough for your canopy and for that of Dillow (1983) and Baumgardner. It was necessary to make a few reasonable assumptions in converting pressures to altitudes.

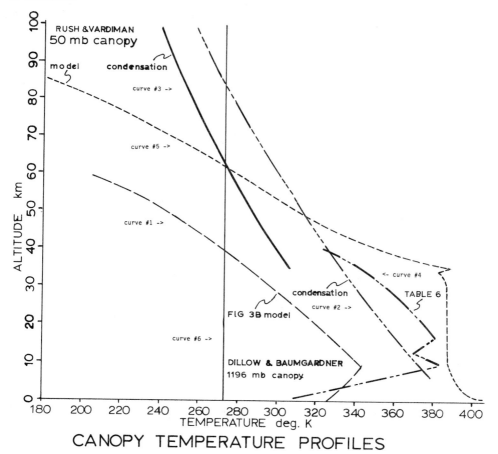

CANOPY TEMPERATURE PROFILES

The Rush and Vardiman model profile (curve #5) for 50 mb of vapor in the canopy crosses the condensation curve (curve #2) just a couple of degrees above the melting point (curve #6). They are therefore correct in pointing out that their canopy would have an ice cloud at the top.

The profile presented in Dillow's Figure 3, curve B (curve #1) is typical of most of their simulations. Their special equatorial simulation from their Table 6 is shown (curve #4) for comparison. The condensation profile that applies to their canopy (curve #3) is between the two in the lower canopy and warmer than both simulations for the top of their canopy.

REFERENCE:

Dillow, J.C., 1983. THE VERTICAL TEMPERATURE STRUCTURE OF THE PRE-FLOOD VAPOR CANOPY, Creation Research Society Quarterly, Vol. 20, pp. 7-14.

Edmond W. Holroyd III, Ph.D.
Arvada, Colorado

I applaud Mr. Rush and Dr. Vardiman for a detailed, scientific analysis of the vapor canopy. Their approach is standard in climate modeling. Unfortunately, for those who believe in a vapor canopy, the article poses some grave challenges. Although the results are only the first step, it seems that two problems are apparent: either the surface is too hot or there isn't enough moisture in the canopy for 40 days and nights of rain. A three-dimensional climate model with convection and clouds would help, but I have my doubts that it will solve the problems, because of the magnitude of the heating. I have several questions: How is the lapse rate in pure water vapor determined? What would relative humidity mean? In convection, clouds form when the relative humidity reaches 100%. When would clouds form? Seems to me the release of latent heat in convection would catastrophically rain out the canopy in the calculated temperature profile. Why wouldn't this happen? One possibility to solve the heat problem are the cirrus clouds at the top. In the canopy model, they would likely be so thick that they may reflect more sunlight than cirrus (especially thin cirrus) in today's climate. Wouldn't this be true, and would it partially solve the problems? The only aerosols that would reach the canopy are extra-terrestrial. Are these CCW? Assuming extra-terrestrial particles are poor CCW, what effect would a lack of CCW have on canopy cloud formation?

Michael J. Oard, M.S.
Great Falls, Montana

CLOSURE

We wish to thank Dr. Holroyd for the extra effort he took in plotting condensation curves for the different models. We certainly agree that the next step in canopy research should be the addition of high-level cirrus clouds.

In reply to Mr. Oard's comments, the lapse rate of pure water vapor is given by the formula (g/C_{pv}, were g is the acceleration due to gravity and C_{pv} is the heat capacity at constant pressure of pure water vapor. For water vapor, this is only 5.3 deg/km, as opposed to 9.8 deg/km for dry air.

Relative humidity may be defined as the ratio of the amount of water vapor a parcel of air holds to the amount it would hold at saturation. In the canopy therefore, with nothing but water vapor, the term would technically be meaningless. Instead, if we compare the actual pressure at a given level due to the weight of the overlying vapor to the saturation water vapor pressure at the temperature of the same level, we can determine if the vapor will condense. If the saturation vapor pressure of the canopy is less than the actual pressure, then (given the presence of condensation nuclei) additional vapor will condense out as either liquid droplets or ice crystals, depending on temperature, and form clouds. If condensation nuclei were absent before the Flood, the saturation vapor pressure could have been effectively doubled or tripled, allowing more water to be stored in the canopy without condensation.

We have not quantitatively considered convection effects in this work, nor have we considered latent heat effects. Its our feeling that convection would have no significant effect on the final temperature profile. Only a small fraction (less than 1'0%) of the canopy base, and would slightly lower the base temperature and slightly raise the temperature just above the base. As pointed out in the discussion of the 50 mb results, we would not expect this temperature correction to be more than a degree or two. The temperature at the base is so high (409 °K) and the pressure so low (50 mb) that the vapor phase -- and stability -- would be easily assured.

At the top of the canopy, the release of latent heat by condensation and freezing would indeed alter the temperature profile, but again, not significantly. The topmost layer is at a low enough temperature (189 °K) and pressure (1 mb) to easily ensure the ice phase, and hence cirrus-type clouds.

The chief reason why we cannot allow thick clouds is a Biblical one: heavenly objects need to be visible, at least during part of the diurnal cycle.

As Mr. Oard correctly notes, our 50 mb canopy (20 inches of precipitable water) would hardly provide 40 days and nights of heavy rainfall. The collapse of the canopy may not have contributed much water to the Flood, but the canopy in place before the Flood would certainly have had a dramatic effect on climate.

David Rush, M.S.
Larry Vardiman, Ph.D.

THE FLOOD/POST-FLOOD BOUNDARY
IN THE FOSSIL RECORD

Jöachim Scheven
Museum "LEBENDIGE VORWELT"
Unterm Hagen 22
D-5800 Hagen 5, West Germany

ABSTRACT

Fossil assemblages through most of the Phanerozoic are evaluated for the presence or absence of in situ life communities. It is shown that most of the water-laid deposits of Palaeozoic "age" must have been formed during approximately the first five months of the Biblical Flood year. From the appearance of emergence surfaces and briefly inhabited sediments and hardgrounds after the Carboniferous (Pennsylvanian) it is deduced that the transition from Flood-laid to post-Flood rocks took place at the turn from the late Palaeozoic era to the Permian "period" of the conventional time scale.

INTRODUCTION

Adherents of Flood geology have been baffled how index fossils of the various geological systems seem to point to evolutionary changes of life on earth rather than to a cataclysmic mêlange of drowned creatures. Claimed instances of fossils "out of place" or strata laid down in the "wrong order" have been of no help in resolving this mystery. Moreover, the preservation of temporary surfaces and sea floors, particularly in the upper parts of the geological column, defy all attempts to accommodate the entire sequence of fossil-bearing strata within the one year of the Flood. However, does the Bible teach this? Are not major geological events connected with the division of the earth in the days of Peleg, during the second and third century after the Flood? Does not plain reason dictate that a literal worldwide Flood resulted in a literal devastation of the entire earth? Could a natural re-colonization have occurred other than through worldwide ecological successions? In the following paragraphs we will highlight some fundamental distinctions between the pre-Permian and the post-Carboniferous fossil record. Although all true fossils owe their existence to a temporary setting aside of natural processes by the Flood events, a boundary can be drawn between those formed during the Flood year proper and those that came progressively into being during the following 2-3 centuries.

I. DEFICIENCIES OF THE CONVENTIONAL INDEX FOSSIL CONCEPT IN THE LOWER PALAEOZOIC

1. Erroneous Evolutionary Lineages

Members of many animal species vary morphologically in time and space. The species contained in rocks of the Lower Palaeozoic are no exception in this respect. Proponents of historical geology have stressed the time factor and have ascribed the observed alterations of shape in fossils to evolutionary processes operating during long periods of time. If, on the other hand, a rapid deposition of these sediments is envisaged, the observable morphological differences between the superimposed fossil organisms must necessarily stem from variations within different contemporaneous populations that lived in separate areas. The black Upper Cambrian alum shales of Sweden are perfectly uniform and must have been accumulated from an equally uniform environment. The frequently interspersed bituminous limestone lenses contain distinguishable trilobite assemblages that have been used for defining chronostratigraphical units. Thus, the 8 metres section of Råbäck in Västergötland yields, in ascending order, the olenid trilobite genera Olenus, Parabolina, Leptoplastus, Eurycare, Ctenopyge, and Peltura (Figure 1). These are said to represent an evolutionary period of about 18 million years. In actual fact, many of the described species are grading into one another. According to Henningsmoen (1), "within a phylogentic trend the number of thoracic segments may increase or decrease ... Features that may seem to be lost in a phylogenetic lineage ... may reappear later in the lineage." In other words, these lineages, proposed solely on the successions of designated index species, cannot be regarded as established. Thus, a convincing case for the elapse of millions of years during

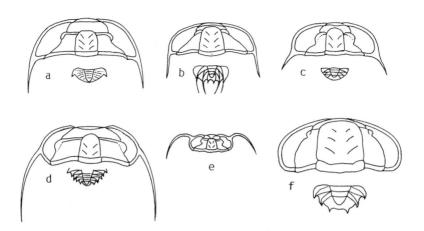

Figure 1. Heads and pygidia of some olenid trilobites that are used for defining stratigraphic horizons in the Upper Cambrian of Scandinavia: Olenus (a), Parabolina (b), Leptoplastus (c), Eurycare (d), Ctenopyge (e), and Peltura (f). Many olenid "species" are connected through intermediate forms and seem to represent different populations rather than members of successive evolutionary stages. Adapted from Henningsmoen (1).

this part of the Palaeozoic cannot be built.

Graptolites are similarly inept for this purpose. The evolutionary dendrogram of this group given by Elles (2) rests on the assumption that an originally "pendent" Didymograptus type gradually evolved via "declined", "deflexed", "horizontal", "reflexed" and "reclined" stages eventually to the "scandent" type seen in Diplograptus and Monograptus (Figure 2). A "rapid" evolution is suggested even by this author since the horizontal, reclined and scandent types of graptolites are already present in the Arenigian stage, i.e. rather shortly after their first appearance (Figure 3). Equating the banded sequence in the 1600 metres Bannisdale slates with a deposition time of roughly 700,000 years, Marr (3) calculated at about 350,000 years the duration of a single graptolite zone, and the duration of both the Ordovician and the Silurian "periods" together at 9.5 million years. If, on the other hand, the graptolite zones are viewed as deposited assemblages of spatially different communities, the time factor for producing these formations becomes evanescent.

Every student of conodonts is struck by the similarities of many differently named elements between their rise in the Ordovician and their decline in the Triassic. Lindström (4) remarks on the so-called platform elements: "The third, or lateral, process is reduced in many stocks but turns up again and again in the course of later evolution. This is the homeomorphy which is a recurrent feature of conodont evolution. The basic pattern appears in the Lower Ordovician and recurs until the Upper Triassic, and this indicates a strong correlation between shape and function." Whilst this is true, a more immediate conclusion is that the conodont-bearing animal lived in a water body that was circulating through "Palaeozoic" as well as "Triassic" life communities. The disintegrated parts of these presumably pelagic creatures were then added to the respective fossil assemblages where they signify the true contemporaneity of those supposedly vastly distant "ages".

2. Index Graptolites Unreliable as Time Markers

Graptolite shales have been generally regarded as old floors beneath abyssal seas, whereas fossiliferous Palaeozoic limestones are thought to represent formerly shallow near-shore communities composed of corals, crinoids, brachiopods and various trilobites. Usually, one of these faunal types occurs to the exclusion of the other. Since sediments are derived materials the same must be postulated of their fossils. The coarse reefal debris must have necessarily been subject to currents of higher energy than the muds that settled as shale. Index graptolites in relation to Palaeozoic limestones may be therefore quite misleading as time markers. A puzzling problem are the "Silurian" Monograptus shales separating "Ordovician" limestones

248

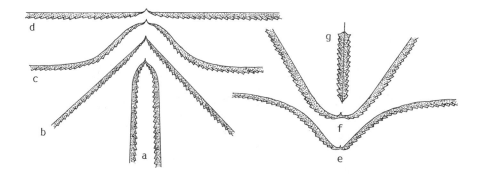

Figure 2. The supposed evolution of graptolite types from the originally "pendent" condition (a) through the "declined", the "deflexed", the "horizontal", the "reflexed", the "reclined" to the eventual "scandent" one (b-g). Adapted from Elles (2).

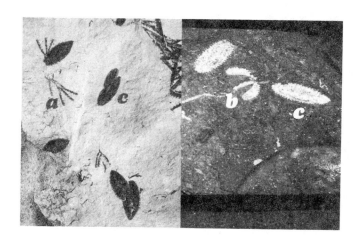

Figure 3. Ordovician graptolite assemblages with mixtures of "declined" (a), "reclined" (b), and "scandent" (c) stages of the assumed evolution of graptolites. Left: Bendigo, Australia; right: Trail Creek Pass, Idaho. About natural size.

in the Kallholn quarry of Dalarna, Sweden. Ingenious explanations such as fissure fillings have been put forward. However, the clearly stratified graptolite shales within the supposedly much older limestone calls for a more convincing explanation, namely that shale and limestone arrived at about the same time.

Figure 4. Tails (pygidia) of the trilobite Eobronteus as an example of a supposedly "advanced" type appearing already during the Ordovician. The external similarity of species from the Ordovician and the Devonian points to similar ecological
conditions rather than to an "evolutionary progress". About natural size.

3. Ecologically Similar Trilobites from the Ordovician to the Devonian

The assumption that the occurrence of index fossils has anything to do with evolutionary progress must be doubted on yet another ground. The pygidium of the Devonian trilobite genus
Scutellum (Bronteus) used to be regarded as the more highly evolved version of "older" pygidia composed of originally movable segments. The Ordovician Eobronteus, however, shows the
same "advanced" specialization and must have corresponded to very similar, if not identical,
ecological conditions (Figure 4). A number of other distinctive trilobite genera make their
first appearance in the Ordovician (or Silurian) and continue right into the Devonian, eg
"Harpes", "Calymene", "Phacops". This suggests life in ecologically similar habitats rather
than during widely separated "ages".

4. Specifically Identical Forms from the Ordovician to the Devonian

The whole of the marine Palaeozoic may be regarded as an originally coherent aquatic ecosystem
composed of a number of different habitats. These, upon their deposition in the course of the
Flood, gave rise to the Cambrian through the Permo-Carboniferous and (in part) Triassic systems. Each of these are more or less distinguished by their characteristic assemblages of index fossils. The above view is confirmed by the existence of indisputably identical fossil species ranging from the Ordovician to the Devonian. The tabulate corals Heliolites, Favosites,
and Alveolites and a number of stromatoporoid species are common to all three of these systems.
The tabulate coral Halysites reaches from the Ordovician to the lowermost Devonian (or Upper
Silurian - according to definition). The bivalve Goniophora volvens is recorded from the Ordovician and reappears under the name G. gallica in the Devonian (5,6). The genus Conocardium has
an even greater vertical range. It is known from the Ordovician to the Permian (and, possibly,
Triassic) (Figure 5). The most natural explanation for these cases of persistence is that the

marine Palaeozoic does not represent an era of geological time but on the remains of various parts of one aquatic pre-Flood ecosystem that came to the surface when the "fountains of the deep" erupted.

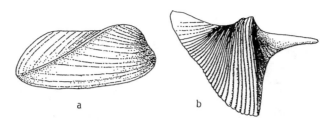

Figure 5. Representatives of two bivalve genera, Goniophora (a) and Conocardium (b), as examples of forms that persist through most of the Palaeozoic. Such distinct types may be interpreted as local members of an aquatic pre-Flood ecosystem inhabiting the sub-terranean part of the antediluvian water cycle.

II. CLAIMED INSTANCES OF AUTHENTIC SEA FLOORS IN THE LOWER PALAEOZOIC

1. Mistaken Autochthony

The above cases have been adduced in order to corroborate the contention that a demarkation line can be fixed between rocks deposited during the 370 days of the Flood events, and those that formed afterwards. Of the almost innumerable cases of autochthony in lower Palaeozoic rocks described in the geological literature only the most typical ones can be dealt with here. Nearly any layer exhibiting bioturbation has been automatically regarded as an ancient sea floor, and substantial times for the existence of each have been set apart. The very preserv-ation of a surface with trace fossils, however, betrays its practically instantaneous forma-tion and this the more so as the producers of the tracks etc are regularly absent, i.e. swept away with the same current that transported the sediment. Whole series of trace fossil hori-zons within one rock unit only strengthen this view. The most obvious proof for the transient nature of these alleged sea floors are the "escape shafts", i.e. sediment-filled tunnels with-in the sediment that terminate at the surface. In this form typical of Lower Palaeozoic sand-stones, they are usually ascribed to the activity of some trilobite (Figure 6).

An even more ponderous claim of autochthony is based upon the thick sheets of Palaeozoic lime-stones. Most of them have been declared to be "reefs" built from stromatoporoids, tabulate and/or rugose corals, bryozoa, calcareous algae, etc. Widely known are the Silurian (Niagaran) "reefs" of Gotland in the Baltic Sea. Lumps of coherent reef frames (the "ballstones" of Brit-ain) may indeed reach enormous proportions, but it is quite certain that even the largest of these lumps (the "reef cores" of authors) have been dumped into their present position and not grown in place during hundreds of thousands of tranquil years. The fact of their water-borne transport may be gathered from the way they impress into the underlying marls, best seen along the NW coast of Gotland (Figure 7), and beautifully exposed by the sea as the famous "Philip structures" (7). Their allochthony may also be deduced from the sometimes "wrong" orientation of the original reef fabric. A pile of "ballstones" at Hoburgen, the southern tip of Gotland, demonstrates this most convincingly (Figure 8). These lumps are often draped with sediment layers which may be continuous over several "reef cores". Observations like this preclude the possibility that such sediment sheets can have originated as true reef talus.

The voids between individual pieces of coral etc in limestones are frequently filled with lin-ings of fibrous calcite (Figure 9). They are known under the name Stromatactis and have been erroneously interpreted as of organic origin. In the literature they are quoted as algal coat-ings which cement loose fragments to a reef fabric. As such they would make a strong case for autochthony. However, the few cases of organic remains incorporated in Stromatactis that have been described in the literature seem to be merely accidental. Stromatactis is of a plainly inorganic nature and is known from "reefal" limestones as widely distinct as the Ordovician of Dalarna in Sweden, the Silurian of the Carnian Alps, the Devonian of the "Lahn marble" in West Germany, the Carboniferous limestone of Derbyshire, the alpine Triassic, and others. Pressurized water seems to have played a vital part in the formation of these linings with fibrous calcite since Stromatactis occurs only in limestones associated with tectonic stress. The time factor involved is obviously quite negligible.

251

Figure 6. Underside of a sandstone layer with "escape shaft" of a trilobite. The animal has dug itself upwards after being overwhelmed by sand. Preserved bioturbation layers of this kind cannot be interpreted as true sea floors. Silurian, Gotland (Sweden).

Figure 7. A "ballstone" in the Silurian of Gotland. These structures are erroneously regarded as reefs that have grown in place. Ballstones are made up of dislodged and transported reef fabric. After deposition and very rapid lithification, the calcitic ballstone resisted compaction and caused the underlying marl to be pressed downwards. Snäckgärdsbaden, Gotland.

ca 25 m

ca 40 m

Figure 8. A pile of huge Silurian "ballstones" in a cliff face at the southern tip of the Isle of Gotland. The crescent-shaped lines indicate the orientation of hat-like stromatoporoids that are the main constituents of the original reef fabric. Hoburgen.

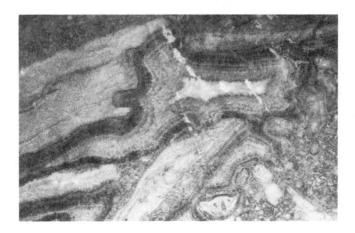

Figure 9. Vertical section through an alleged reef fabric known as Stromatactis in a Devonian limestone. What appears to be an in situ cementation of organic frame builders consists in reality of inorganic fibrous calcite that lines the voids of loosely packed stromatoporoid crusts etc. Lahn marble, Wirbelau (Westerwald, West Germany).

253

2. Inconclusive Cases

A debate of long standing concerns the Permian "reefs" of the Guadalupe Mountains in New Mexico and Texas. Both the advocates of authochthony and of allochthony can list points in favour of their views. Large colonies of highly aberrant productid brachiopods suggest at least some autochthonous growth, while the adherents of allochthony tend to emphasise the haphazardly floating character of such colonies within a stratified matrix (8,9). A certain analogy may be seen in the Upper Permian Zechstein reefs of Germany where an undoubtedly allochthonous carpet of Productus shells is variously associated with heaps of bryozoa etc that in turn are fixed by a stromatolitic algal growth known as Stromaria. Such mixtures of dead allochthonous and living autochthonous components are here termed "inhabited dumps" ("Belebte Deponien"). Inhabited dumps are a feature of many marine deposits of post-Carboniferous origin.

Johnson & Baarli (10) have drawn attention to a site in Manitoba, Canada, where Silurian limestone is in contact with the Precambrian basement. They report instances where colonies of the tabulate coral Favosites are still attached to the Precambrian rock surface which is said to have formed an ancient shore line. If the observation is correct it would confirm that the Silurian as part of a pre-Flood ecosystem does indeed rest on an unfossiliferous, i.e. on a created surface of the earth. However, since the fossiliferous limestone does not differ from other Silurian occurrences the evidence for a genuine in situ growth of Favosites is not convincing.

3. Platform Autochthony

Apart from the unsettled cases like the one just mentioned, the intervention of a certain amount of time must be granted for certain other rocks of the Palaeozoic. Lower Cambrian "reefs" or "bioherms" in Labrador are on record that are made up of archaeocyathids. Their autochthonous growth is deduced from the presence of algal borings, as one type of bioerosion. The borings are said to occur on the upper side of the archaeocyathid colonies and would indicate a brief period of undisturbed growth (11). Similar borings have been reported from a number of other Palaeozoic skeletal organisms, but the Manitoba site seems to be the only instance of an in situ growth in the Lower Cambrian.

Another sure indication of briefly stable conditions found in Palaeozoic rocks are the algal coatings formed around the shells of brachiopods, etc, in the Upper Silurian of Gotland. The resulting sphaerules, known as Sphaerocodium, are especially interesting in that they appear in as widely different geological systems as the Silurian, the Triassic, and the Tertiary (Figure 10). The explanation for this occurrence of Sphaerocodium in Palaeozoic rocks is to be sought in the exceptionally shallow situation of the Silurian platform of Gotland where the terminal surface seems to have lain exposed for some months or so after the Flood.

Such platform situations lead to an understanding of emergence surfaces as "low" as the early Palaeozoic. The Cambrian salt pseudomorphs of the Salt Range in Pakistan as well as all other mudcracks, raindrop impressions, etc, below the Permian, eg the Old Red, are likely to find their explanation in this way.

III. THE EARLIEST KNOWN AUTOCHTHONOUS SEA FLOORS

1. Stromaria Reefs of the German Zechstein

The palaeo-geographical relations between the type locality of the Permian on the Russian platform and the occurrences of this system in Central Europe are not well understood. This much can be said, however: The former bears distinct marks of rapid deposition whereas the latter shows some evidence of a formation lingering on through, perhaps, a few years. This is particularly so where the Upper Permian (Zechstein, Magnesian Limestone) is developed in its reefal facies. Although the original fabric of these "reefs" is difficult to ascertain, the massive debris of bryozoa and small bivalves is usually fixed within large cupular stromatolitic structures named Stromaria that are ascribed to the growth activity of algae (Figure 11). Perhaps the best known example of such Stromaria reefs are the famous "Westersteine" at the W foot of the Hartz Mts. in West Germany. The reefs of the Zechstein seem to be the geologically earliest structures that can be classified as true temporary sea bottoms. For a brief period of settlement rather than for being brought in from a foreign source argues also the very much impoverished fauna of these deposits.

2. Placunopsis Crusts of the German Muschelkalk

Another expansion of epeiric seas comparable to the Zechstein transgression is the German Muschelkalk of the Middle Triassic. Genuine hardgrounds are among the distinguishing features of

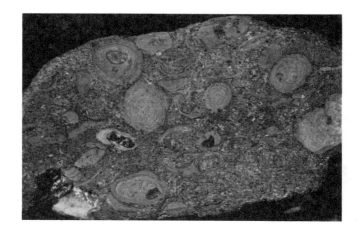

Figure 10. Algal coating around shell fragments in section known as _Sphaerocodium_. Occurrences in rocks of the Lower Palaeozoic indicate that the original sediments remained exposed on shallow platforms for some time after the Flood year. The above specimen is from the Upper Muschelkalk, Triassic, of Germany. Slightly enlarged.

Figure 11. Stromatolitic reef fabric known as _Stromaria_ in the Zechstein (Magnesian Limestone) of the Permian of Europe. The cupular layers are ascribed to the activity of an encrusting type of algae. Permian reefs are the first temporary sea floors developing after the Flood. Westersteine, W. Germany.

Figure 12. A crust of the tiny oyster-like bivalve _Placunopsis_ in the German Muschelkalk. The Muschelkalk sea existed approximately 50 years after the Flood and may have lasted for hardly more than 20 years. Specimen from Schwäbisch Hall, Germany. The size of the coin is 16 mm.

this limestone sheet that is spread across much of the Middle of Europe. Certain areas of the floor of the shallow Muschelkalk sea must have been overgrown with meadows of sea lilies (_Encrinus_) as witnessed by the enormous accumulations of stem ossicles, the "Trochitenkalk", that are derived from them. For this type of shifting sea basins the term "dynamic seas" seems appropriate. The tiny oyster-like bivalve _Placunopsis_ was able to colonize some of the temporary hardgrounds before this living veneer itself was buried under a new blanket of sediment. The sessile clams provided their own hardgrounds on which to settle (Figure 12). Layers of _Placunopsis_ growing upon each other are locally known to have reached up to 60 cm in thickness. In grossly over-estimating the individual lifetime of these exceptionally small bivalves, durations of many thousands of years for such hardgrounds have been proposed. More realistic values that take into account the short life of the tiny _Placunopsis_ lie within the range of weeks or months. An additional proof for an error in calculating the duration of the Upper Muschelkalk sea in connection with _Placunopsis_ will be given in a later paragraph. Space forbids to link the facies of the German Triassic to the different types of the "alpine" Triassic elsewhere. Suffice it here to state that the erratic blocks or massifs of the "Hallstatt facies" that are floating in other types of sediments cannot be included among the other post-Flood deposits of temporary dynamic seas. It is probable that they consist of pre-Flood sediments and their included faunal remains.

IV. THE TRANSIENT MUDFLATS AND DESERTS OF THE PERMO-TRIASSIC

The epeiric seas of the early post-Flood geography were bordered by immense alluvial plains, mudflats, and deserts of redbed character. Redbeds set in universally with the Permo-Triassic and signal an important turning point of the sedimentary régime. The "Rotliegendes" of the Lower Permian of Central Europe is the lowermost deposit in which mudcracks, impressions of raindrops and tracks of vertebrates are a constant accompanying feature. In Britain, where the marine Triassic is missing, there is no ascertainable boundary between the terrestrial Permian and the Triassic. Both are, consequently, united as the "New Red".

The sedimentological evidences for the brief duration of the New Red episode are so overwhelming that the proponents of long ages have resorted to accommodating the missing "geological time" within the bedding planes of stratified formations. The uniform petrology of superimposed layers betrays the fallacy of such procedure. Large scale cross-bedding and thick pebble beds can only be interpreted in terms of regional catastrophes. As might be expected, claims of

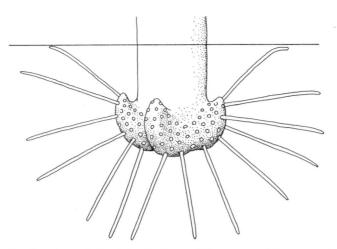

Figure 13. Stem base of the Triassic lycopod <u>Pleuromeia</u> with some roots restored. The peculiar arrangement of the root scars, analogous to that of the Carboniferous scale trees, suggests an aquatic mode of life. This renders claims of a prolonged <u>in situ</u> growth of <u>Pleuromeia</u> in redbeds meaningless. Adapted from Mägdefrau (12).

prolonged persistence have been raised for some of the Permo-Triassic redbeds. So-called "purple horizons" have been interpreted as temporary soils. These often quoted palaeosols are poorly stratified purplish rock layers within the redbeds that seem to signify short interruptions of aggradation. It is certainly possible that during such intervals a scant vegetation could have developed. A variety of horsetails, ferns, cycads, etc are known especially from Triassic redbeds while the general aspect of the flora remains unchanged up to the Lower Cretaceous. The famous <u>Pleuromeia</u>, far from being a late descendant of the Carboniferous scale trees, was an aquatic herb that seems to have formed floating carpets on water. This can be gathered from the peculiar shape of the stem bases that are preserved as <u>steinkerns</u> (Figure 13). The diversity of created animals and plants was obviously much greater than today, and many of them did not outlive the time during which they fulfilled an indispensable function as inhabitants of the transient mudflats and seas of early post-Flood years and decades. Most of those creatures became extinct. Notable exceptions are the Permo-Triassic crustaceans "<u>Estheria</u>" and the more conspicuous <u>Triops cancriformis</u> (Figure 14). Their living representatives are indistinguishable from their Mesozoic predecessors.

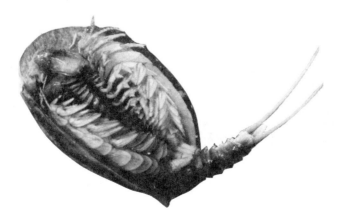

Figure 14. <u>Triops cancriformis</u>, a crustacean living in temporary ditches in the cooler parts of the Northern Hemisphere. The same organism populated shallow ponds of the early post-Flood redbeds during the Permo-Triassic of Europe. Twice natural size.

V. MEGA-SUCCESSIONS: STAGES IN RE-COLONISATION OF THE EARTH

1. Mass Propagations of Single Species

Present day life communities are usually composed of a great variety of species. A striking feature of fossil life communities preserved in post-Carboniferous rocks is their relatively monotonous composition of a few species only, but these in great numbers. Mass propagations always indicate disturbed ecosystems. Under natural conditions such impaired ecosystems tend to revert to normal by themselves. The different stages on the way are termed "successions". The final state resembles the original one and is called "climax".

After its devastation by the Flood the earth must have passed through many such stages of re-colonization. Since whole seas and land masses were involved we speak of "mega-successions". Ecological processes of this kind explain the worldwide occurrence of post-Carboniferous index fossils without having to resort to auxiliary hypotheses of evolution. The mega-successions proceeded in step with the geological changes that developed after the Flood. (These will be briefly dealt with in a later paragraph.) It is indeed unusual to discover that fossils of vastly separated localities, particularly in the Mesozoic, turn out to be specifically the same. Thus, the Cretaceous ammonite Pulchellia is found from Germany to Colombia in South America; the bivalve Gervillela in Europe and South Africa; other bivalves like Pterotrigonia in Europe, S.Africa and S.America, or Neithea in Europe and N.America. None of these genera can be traced back to some hypothetical "more primitive stock". It is therefore evident that we have to do with organisms that survived the Flood in small numbers but became detectable only after special conditions had arisen which provided for population explosions on this scale.

One of the incipient stages of marine successions is the German Muschelkalk. The deposits of this early epicontinental sea are confined to Europe and the Near East. Of the almost innumerable ammonite genera of the Triassic that have been described from the Hallstatt facies, hardly more than one or two (Beneckeia, Ceratites) found their way into the shallow Muschelkalk basin where they multiplied and gave rise to a much more limited variety of populations. These represent genuine, infra-specific, evolutionary lineages from several originally polymorphic stocks. Anyone conversant with Mesozoic marine fossils is able to add examples of such mass propagations and will readily confirm the enormous genetic diversity of many species.

2. Mass Propagations in Rock-Forming Quantities

Another aspect of these post-Flood mass propagations is the occurrence of fossils in sometimes rock-forming quantities. Perhaps the most striking of all is the ordinary chalk. If viewed under the SE microscope chalk reveals its entirely organic composition from platelets of coccolithophorids and tests of foraminifera (Figure 15). Both types of organisms are abundant in present day seas but never accumulate on the sea floor to form any quantity of chalk. Instead, their limey skeletons are dissolved by the sea water during their slow descent to the bottom. The fact that these remains are preserved as chalk is proof that the Cretaceous seas were so shallow that the dissolving of those skeletal parts could not take place. The very conspicuous banding of many vertical chalk exposures suggests that the bottom sediments of the chalk seas were first carried away when these epicontinental basins suddenly drained off just before the "Tertiary". The superposition of those sediments then led to the banding now observable. The great faunal break with its mass extinctions of very many Mesozoic organisms can be linked with the commencement of the "Tertiary catastrophe" that is alluded to, by revelation, in Genesis 10:25. Ammonites, dinosaurs, and many Mesozoic plants of the semi-deserts suddenly lost their habitats and made room for the Tertiary stage of the post-Flood mega-successions.

Among all the systems of earth history the Tertiary is the one most complicated and most difficult to comprehend. Fault-bounded subsidence, movements of whole continental plates, mountain-building, volcanism and impacts from space led to immediate processes of erosion and deposition of great violence. These events occurred after the earth had already been largely re-populated with the greatest possible variety of organisms. Such was certainly the case at the end of the second or the beginning of the third century after the Flood. The orderly progression of post-Flood mega-successions had reached its climax.

3. The Climax Communities of the Tertiary

That such climax stage existed after the Flood can be easily demonstrated. Very many of the tree genera and species that are now confined to limited parts on the continents of the Northern Hemisphere had a vast distribution through the Old and the New World before the ice age. For example, fossil leaves of the maidenhair tree (Ginkgo biloba) are known from North Dakota, Scotland, Germany and Italy whereas the wild occurrence of Ginkgo now is in a remote part of

Figure 15. Detached skeletal parts of coccolithophorid algae made visible under SEM in chalk of the Cretaceous. The mass propagation of these algae and their preservation without being dissolved in sea water bespeaks the extraordinary productivity of the Cretaceous stage of the post-Flood mega-successions.

China. Similarly, Ailanthus, Pterocarya, and Koelreuteria are known in the fossil state from Wyoming and Colorado as well as from Europe; their living representatives survive only in the Far East, apart from Pterocarya which has also one species in the Caucasus. Conversely, fossil leaves of Sassafras and Comptonia, Liriodendron and Liquidambar are known from Europe while their closest relatives now live in N.America. Further species of these genera, extinct in Europe, reappear in China or Taiwan. This list could considerably be increased. From this former wealth of plant life across the Northern Hemisphere in the Tertiary it can be deduced that the culminating point of re-colonisation has long since been surpassed. The geological revolutions during the Tertiary changed large parts of the earth to barren mountain ranges and deserts, and the ensuing ice age did its part to wipe out much of this luxuriant plant and animal life. All this occurred before post-Flood man could rise into prominence.

VI. TESTING THE CONCEPT

1. The Bible as Standard of Comparison

a. The lack of pre-Flood land communities in the fossil record -. From a number of evidences it is possible to fix the Flood/post-Flood boundary within the fossil record at the turn from the Carboniferous to the Permian. This coincides with the commencement of discernible mega-successions. All earlier fossil life communities, including the Carboniferous coal forests, are associated with water. If land communities from pre-Flood times were known, a distinction between Flood-laid and post-Flood rocks would become impossible. However, no such land-living communities exist. The reason for the total absence of fossils associated with ante-diluvian man is found in the Bible. God says in Genesis 6:7, "I will destroy man". In this place a Hebrew verb is used that actually means erase or put out of sight. The reason for this must be sought in God's purpose to save only those who believe Him by their free will. If God's judgement upon mankind in the past had remained visible we would be unable to believe Him, i.e. to take Him at His Word also regarding the impending future judgement. Ezekiel 31: 18 intimates that the inhabitants of the pre-Flood world were brought down "unto the nether parts of the earth". This revealed fact is fully borne out by the existence of Palaeozoic hydrocarbons (petroleum) derived from organisms whose organic compounds have not passed through the natural pathways of decay but were processed to energy-rich substances with complete loss of their shapes.

b. The formation of synclinal troughs after the onset of the Flood -. By far the thickest stacks of sediment belong to the Palaeozoic era. The Ordovician greywacke complex of Wales, for instance, amounts to many kilometres. The Devonian deposits of the Rhenanian Slate Mountains of Germany have been estimated at 12 - 15 kilometres thickness. Similar values are obtained in the troughs of the Millard and Magog Belts bordering the N.American continent. Subsidence and migration of synclinal troughs do occur after the Palaeozoic, but they are clearly on a smaller scale. The general trend is in line with the Biblical order of events. The eruption of the subterranean waters belonging to the pre-Flood water cycle must have resulted in the sudden collapse of entire continental plates. Thus', the Flood account of the Bible provides the background for appreciating the true speed of geological events during the Palaeozoic.

c. Early post-Flood conditions reflected by deserts and epeiric seas -. The striking change of the sedimentary régime from synclinal basins to epeiric seas after the Palaeozoic is in perfect accord with developments that are to be expected in the wake of a worldwide Flood. The barrenness of sands without topsoil and the ever shifting sea beds that were burying incipient marine life communities beneath them are abundantly demonstrable in rocks of this age. Attention must also be drawn to the enormous amounts of carbonate fixation by marine organisms in Permian, Triassic, Jurassic, and later deposits. This can only have been caused by an imbalance in the carbon cycle. After the destruction of the entire biosphere, such imbalances in the atmospheric turnover of carbon should be expected.

d. Continental drift and mountain-building in the days of Peleg -. From geological evidence it appears that the earth emerging from the Flood waters was initially one coherent land mass. Many horizontal movements, no doubt, went on from the beginning of the Flood, but the real drift commenced probably not before the end of the Cretaceous. Since the birth of Peleg is fixed at 101 years after the Flood, the Cretaceous stage of mega-successions may have lasted well into the second century after the Flood. The period of post-Flood mountain-building, the most marked feature of the Tertiary, is likely to have continued into the third century. Only after the hot crust burst and came into contact with water could sufficient evaporation occur to generate a sudden precipitation of ice, resulting in an ice age. If we reduce the Tertiary from its conventional 63 million years to a more reasonable period of little more than one century, the development of a sudden ice age through catastrophic evaporation would be a natural consequence fully within the limits of known physical laws.

2. Was There Geological Time?

a. Uninterrupted sedimentation during the Lower Palaeozoic -. Many examples of alleged sea floors during the Palaeozoic era are listed in the geological literature. These cases cannot be reviewed here. As has been pointed out under a previous paragraph, they are either mistaken, inconclusive, or refer to platform autochthony. From field evidence it can be regarded as certain that the whole of the marine Lower Palaeozoic may be accommodated within less than the 370 days of the Flood year.

b. Coal seams from mats of aquatic forests -. All Carboniferous coals of the Euro-American coal fields were primarily composed of scale trees. Their roots formed densely interwoven mats that included large amounts of air in plant tissues and enabled these ecosystems to float on water. The now superimposed coal seams (sometimes more than 200) must have originally grown on one and the same surface before they were swept away and deposited in subsiding synclines. It follows that these forests were all of the same age before burial. A "coal age" lasting 40 million years has evidently never existed.

c. Lessons from Placunopsis -. Minute sessile clams were able to colonize temporary floors in the Triassic Muschelkalk sea of Central Europe. Layered "reefs" of Placunopsis may reach more than 2 metres in thickness. The densely packed shells were successively cemented upon each other during their consecutive lifetimes. One centimetre contains about 25 shell layers. By fixing the unknown average lifespan of the individual clams at five years, a one centimetre increment of the Muschelkalk sea floor has been estimated to have required 125 years. This would bring a "reef" of 2 metres to a lifetime of 25,000 years. Such quantitative calculations of geological time from field evidence have been naturally valued as the most accurate. The flaw in this neat looking example is that, in actual fact, nothing is known about the true speed of development of Placunopsis. It has been overlooked that spat of recent clams in tropical seas may attain about the same size within days of weeks. An even more devastating fact is the disclosure that particularly the largest of these "reefs" are lenticular or globular in shape with shells overgrowing the entire upper and lower surface! (Figure 16). During life, these aggregates stayed more or less suspended in water as water-borne reefs, as it were. In the situations where they are found now they were obviously set aground together with the sed-

Figure 16. A globular reef composed of the minute sessile clam <u>Placunopsis ostracina</u> in the Upper Muschelkalk (Middle Triassic). During life, these aggregates stayed more or less suspended above the sea floor as evidenced by <u>Placunopsis</u> shells overgrowing the entire surface, including the one at the bottom. Such reefs have obviously not grown in one place but were dumped into their terminal position together with the sediment. Langensteinach, W. Germany. Reproduced from Scheven (13).

iment. The Muschelkalk sea is likely to have existed for about 20 to 30 years which may seem, at the first glance, very little. However, certain is that the burial of suspended reefs with 2 metres of sediment can be accomplished within a matter of minutes.

d. The natural breakdown of mass propagations -. Was there "geological time"? A strong denial comes also from a biological consideration. Index fossils as supposed markers of geological time qualify as such only if they are reasonably common. As a rule, they are very common indeed. Mass propagations as expressions of disturbed ecological conditions cannot have gone on longer than for a few years. Far from forming stable communities they would only lead to the next stage within a succession. Even granting that many fossil concentrations have come about through water sorting, the great and often truly incredible numbers of individuals found in fossil-bearing rocks were caused by biological conditions. The concept of geological time marked out by successive index fossils is, on biological grounds, untenable.

3. Some Applications to Regional Geology

a. The relationship of the "Old Red" to the "New Red" -. A Flood/post-Flood boundary at roughly the beginning of the Permian "New Red" is seemingly contradicted by the existence of emergence surfaces as early as in the Devonian "Old Red". Both systems are separated by the Carboniferous limestone and the coal measures. Basing our argument on Biblical revelation, the first temporary flats with mudcracks may have already appeared soon after the Flood waters had begun to recede, i.e. during the 6th or 7th month of the Flood year. Certain Old Red exposures in Britain are indistinguishable from those of the New Red. The only significant difference between the two red sandstones appear to be the lack of tetrapod tracks in the former and the lack of shock-induced convolute bedding in the latter. The highly idealized and horizontally condensed N-S section through Britain of Figure 17 may serve to illustrate the relationship of the two geological systems on a regional scale.

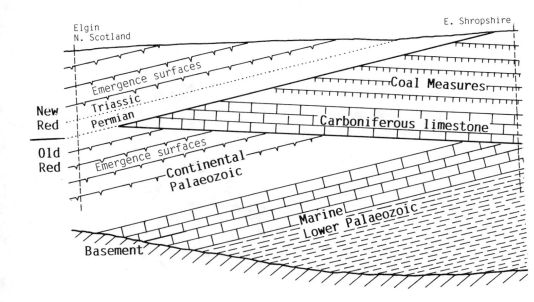

Figure 17. Highly idealised and horizontally shortened N-S section through a part of Britain. The separation of the Old Red from the New Red by the rocks of the Carboniferous is due to tilting movements of the basement during the Flood year.

b. The burial of floating coal forests marks the end of the Flood year-. The previously mentioned coal forests of the Northern Hemisphere stood on water and covered very extensive areas of the pre-Flood earth. Their actual location was probably within and perhaps beyond the north polar circle. The floating mode of life of this type of vegetation is well established. All Euro-American coal fields have in common that several, up to very many, coal seams lie superimposed upon each other. The deposition of these floating forests in coal troughs can obviously not have taken place as long as the Flood waters were still rising, i.e. during the first 150 days. Likewise, the deposition cannot have taken place after the waters had completely drained off, i.e. after 370 days. This leaves us with about 7 months of a "coal age" within the Flood year. The Carboniferous, as the most accurately datable geological system, thus serves as the most important marker on the time scale of Biblical earth history (Figure 18).

c. The worldwide identity of Palaeozoic marine faunas points to their pre-Flood origin -. The various epeiric seas, from the Magnesian limestone to the Tertiary, have covered the earth only locally. Their fossil faunas are restricted accordingly. The distribution of Palaeozoic fossils, however, follows quite a different pattern. Almost all genera of coral, trilobites, crinoids, conodonts, graptolites, etc occur worldwide. Included into the Palaeozoic here are the Triassic limestones of the Hallstatt facies whose fossil contents remains perfectly the same from the European Alps to the Island of Timor. The Hallstatt harbours typically "Palaeozoic" fossils like orthoceratids and conodonts and is linked to the other Palaeozoic rocks on this account. The difference between worldwide occurring and more locally appearing marine fossil assemblages enables us to distinguish between sediments derived from the partly subterranean and interconnected habitats of the pre-Flood water cycle and those of entirely subaerial marine habitats of post-Flood times. The former were ejected at the breaking up of the fountains of the great deep; the latter had to pass through mega-successions that slowly led to a variety of local faunas, the familiar condition that obtains today.

Figure 18 (opposite page). Synoptic chart of Biblical earth history from Creation to about 1000 years before Christ. The end of the Flood coincides with the Carboniferous (Pennsylvanian). The division of the earth in the days of Peleg commences with the late Jurassic and reaches its culminating point during the Tertiary. The ice age is interpreted as the natural outcome of heated magmatic rocks brought into contact with shallow seas during the "Tertiary Catastrophe". Bold ellipses signify some of the post-Flood mega-successions known from their fossil assemblages. All assemblages that do not reach the right hand margin are extinct.

262

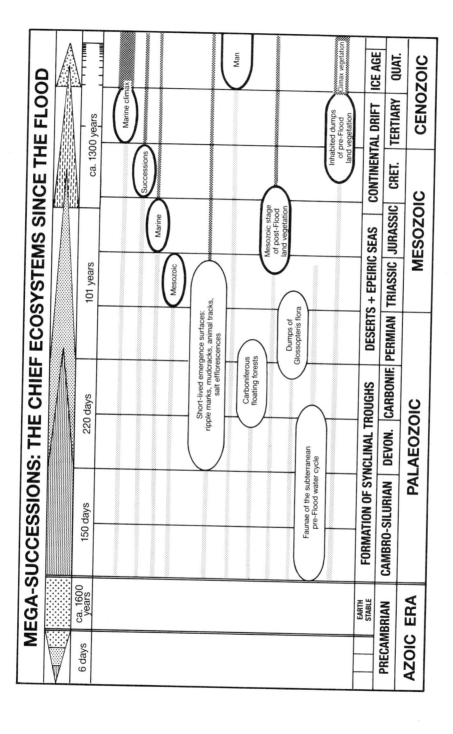

MEGA-SUCCESSIONS: THE CHIEF ECOSYSTEMS SINCE THE FLOOD

		AZOIC ERA	PALAEOZOIC					MESOZOIC			CENOZOIC		
	EARTH STABLE	PRECAMBRIAN	FORMATION OF SYNCLINAL TROUGHS				DESERTS + EPEIRIC SEAS			CONTINENTAL DRIFT		ICE AGE
			CAMBRO-SILURIAN	DEVON.	CARBONIF.	PERMIAN	TRIASSIC	JURASSIC	CRET.	TERTIARY	QUAT.

ca. 1600 years · 6 days · 150 days · 220 days · 101 years · ca. 1300 years

- Faunae of the subterranean pre-Flood water cycle
- Short-lived emergence surfaces: ripple marks, mudcracks, animal tracks, salt efflorescences
- Carboniferous floating forests
- Dumps of Glossopteris flora
- Mesozoic stage of post-Flood land vegetation
- Inhabited dumps of pre-Flood land vegetation
- Climax vegetation
- Mesozoic
- Marine
- Successions
- Marine climax
- Man

263

REFERENCES

1. Henningsmoen, G., THE TRILOBITE FAMILY OLENIDAE, 304 pp, 31 pl., Oslo, 1957

2. Elles, G.L., "The graptolite faunas of the British Isles". Proceedings of the Geologist's Association, 33, pp.168 - 200, 1 table, London, 1922

3. Marr, J.E., "A possible chronometric scale for the graptolite-bearing strata". Palaeontologica, 1, pp.161 - 162, Vienna, Leipzig, 1928

4. Lindström, M., "The conodont apparatus as a food-gathering mechanism". Palaeontology, 17, 4, pp. 729 - 744, 1974

5. Isberg, O., STUDIEN ÜBER DIE LAMELLIBRANCHIATEN DES LEPTAENAKALKES IN DALARNA. 428 pp., 32 pl., Lund, 1934

6. Babin, C., MOLLUSQUES BIVALVES ET CEPHALOPODES DU PALAEOZOIQUE ARMORICAIN. Dissertation University of Brest, 1966

7. Eriksson, C.O. and Laufeld, S., "Philip structures in the submarine Silurian of Gotland". Geolog. Surv. of Sweden, Stockholm, 1978

8. Achauer, C.W.. "Origin of Capitan Formation, Guadalupe Mountains, New Mexico and Texas". The American Association of Petroleum Geologists Bulletin, 53, 11 (Nov. 1969), pp. 2314 - 2323.

9. Cys, J.M., "Origin of Capitan Formation, Guadalupe Mountains, New Mexico and Texas: Discussion". The American Association of Petroleum Geologists Bulletin, 55, 2 (Feb.1971) pp. 310 - 315.

10. Johnson, M.E. and Baarli, B.G., "Encrusting corals on a latest Ordovician to earliest Silurian rocky shore, southwest Hudson Bay, Manitoba, Canada". Geology, 15, pp. 15 - 17, Jan. 1987.

11. James, N.P. and Kobluk, D.R., "Lower Cambrian patch reefs and associated sediments: southern Labrador, Canada". Sedimentology, 25, pp. 1 - 35, 1978

12. Mägdefrau, K., PALÄOBIOLOGIE DER PFLANZEN. 549 pp., Stuttgart, 1968.

13. Scheven, J., MEGA-SUKZESSIONEN UND KLIMAX IM TERTIÄR. 223 pp., Stuttgart, 1988.

Appendix: The geological changes recorded in Flood-laid and post-Flood rocks:

geological changes	Flood period	post-Flood period
changes of régime	sedimentation in deep synclinal troughs	sedimentation progressively more in shallow basins
	emergence surfaces are rare	emergence surfaces are common
	no mountain-building activities	increase of mountain-building with culmination during the Tertiary
changes of lithology	greywacke and derivatives prominent	progressively more organogenic sediments, eg chalk
changes of ecology	aquatic assemblages	aquatic and non-aquatic assemblages
	no authentic sea beds, no autochthonously grown reefs	true fossilised sea floors and autochthonous reefs
	no faunal provinces	faunal and floral provinces exist

DISCUSSION

This paper attempts to solve one of the most difficult stratigraphic problems as it relates to the Flood—the boundary between the Flood and Post-Flood. The primary evidence brought to bear on the boundary question is the presence or absence of in situ fossil assemblages. Several field examples are cited and a few literature references are included. The paper, however, lacks sufficient documentation for the conclusions presented, and does not make reference to the variety of geologic evidences which are needed to adequately establish the Flood/Post-Flood boundary (welded tuff beds, hardgrounds, paleomagnetic stratigraphy, interregional versus basinal deposits). How do we know that the Upper Permian Zechstien reefs indeed represent the earliest post-Flood autochthonous sea floors? The evidence presented is far from adequate. How do we know that Permo-Triassic Sandstones represent desert dune deposits on transient mudflats after the Flood? The geologic evidence presented is far from compelling. Those who know the equivalent strata on the North American continent would have great difficulty accepting the Flood/Post-Flood boundary near the Permo-Triassic boundary. We need a variety of geologic and paleontologic evidences applied to solve the Flood/Post-Flood boundary problem.

Steven A. Austin, Ph.D.
San Diego, California

The existence of distinctive index fossils and characteristic assemblages has long provided a challenge for flood geology interpretations. Dr. Scheven's paper accepts that they have a chronological significance and proposes a model from within the diluvialist paradigm. It provides a panorama of events, and leaves the details to be filled in subsequently. Thus, statements like: "graptolite zones are viewed as deposited assemblages of spatially different communities" are actually hypotheses yet to be tested. The reader will be able to note numerous similar examples.

Geological and palaeontological data are suggested to favor the following general scheme: Palaeozoic rocks are the main diluvial deposits; Mesozoic and Cenozoic rocks are the remains of post-Flood catastrophes affecting temporary ecosystems. This model is powerful and deserves to be tested further by specific investigations of field evidences. Serious consideration needs to be given to the Old Red Sandstone facies with their evidence of emergent surfaces. Dr. Scheven recognizes the problem (Section VI.3a), but does not do justice to these rocks by referring to "temporary flats with mudcracks".

The term "continental drift" (Section VI.1d) is so closely linked with mantle convection mechanisms and long timescales that this reviewer favors the use of an alternative word by diluvialists. The term "continental separation" has no association with specific mechanism and retains all the essentials.

David J. Tyler, M.S.
Chesire, England

[Review: of Part I] Since Dr. Scheven has not systematically considered all Lower Paleozoic index fossils, he is not justified in concluding that the conventional index fossil concept is invalid. Furthermore, since he has not considered post-Lower paleozoic index fossils at all, he has not demonstrated that the lower Paleozoic is substantially different from the remainder of the column. For an example, most taxa have stratigraphic ranges which run continuously through the Carboniferous and Permian. There is not a good faunal break between the Carboriferous and Permian. At the end of the Permian, YES; at the beginning of the Permian, NO.

[Review: of Parts II & III] Dr. Scheven provides insufficient documentation and discussion to conclude either that claims of pre-Permian autochthony are invalid or that claims of post-Carboniferous autochthony are valid. What if the Permo-Triassic sediments are buried and/or redeposited pre-flood soils (Ariel Roth, personal communication) - perhaps representing the beginning of the inundation of the land?

[Review: of Part IV] As Dr. Scheven claims, the Permo-Triassic sediments represent a change in lithology over the Paleozoic. These and other Mesozoic sediments, however, also seem to be distributed globally (like the Paleozoic, but unlike the Cenozoic) and deposited catastrophical- ly. This would imply that the Mesozoic is part of the same global event which deposited the Paleozoic. Why couldn't the Paleozoic represent submarine deposition in the early Flood and the permo-Mesozoic represent the transgression over the land in the later Flood? The Permo-Triassic exposure features could then be pre-flood in origin.

[Review: of Part V] Even though modern life communities have a high diversity of species, species abundance follows the a pattern of a hollow curve. Only a few species are abundant; most species are very rare. A less than perfect fossil record of even climax communities will tend to be composed of just a few species with high abundance. Unlike the claim of Dr. Scheven, monotypic fossil communities do not represent disturbed ecosystems. Although Dr. Scheven claims that post-Carboniferous fossil communities tend to be monotypic (or nearly so), he does not show that this is not true of the pre-Permian. It is my impression that low diversity "communities' are quite common in the Paleozoic (e.g. Mississippian Crinoid Conglomerates, Carboniferous Coals, Carboniferous Lingula Beds, Cambrian Ollenelus Shales, Ordovician Graptolite Shales, etc.).

References:

1. Sepkoski, J., John, Jr., 1981, "A Factor Analytic Description of the Phanerozoic Marine Fossil Record", Paleobiology, 7 (1): 36-53.

2. For continuity of Lingula and Coelacanth ranges: Wise, K. P., 1989, The Estimation of True Taxonomic Durations from Fossil Occurrence Data, Ph.D. Dissertation, Harvard University, 550 pages.

Kurt P. Wise, Ph.D.
Dayton, Tennessee

CLOSURE

Dr. Scheven was unable to respond at this time, but wishes to thank his reviewers for their comments and criticism.

THE LIFETIME AND RENEWAL OF COMETS

WILLIAM E. STILLMAN, PH.D.
415 CRESTRIDGE DRIVE
GREENSBURG, PA 15601

ABSTRACT

A brief review is conducted of some of the more well-known comets detected in the solar system. The measured attrition rates of Halley's and other comets are used to project a rigorous calculation of their anticipated lifetimes. Some backward projections are made to provide estimates of reasonable upper limits on their current ages.

Some postulated theories for the replenishment of the comet inventory from the assumed "Oort Cloud" are assessed together with proposed schemes for solar capture of their orbits. Orbital mechanics is used to evaluate the probability of the validity of these theories.

INTRODUCTION

In addition to the sun and the planets our solar system contains many other objects such as asteroids and comets. Comets have the property of orbit elongation such that they make periodic approaches to the sun, during which the loss of material to solar pressure leaves one or more tails to impress and awe mankind. Some of these orbits are so elongated (eccentric) as to make their return a thing only to be predicted on the basis of a single solar passage. Others have returned repeatedly and established a schedule so rigorous as to be very beneficial in the development of the science of orbital mechanics.

Comets are normally divided into two categories according to period. The division between short and long periods is somewhere between 100 and 200 years[1]. The short period comets are the ones found most interesting since their returns have been observed in modern times and can usually be predicted precisely. Furthermore, observation can reveal much more information about the material properties of the body.

It has been found that a comet cannot be treated simply as a particle in the solution of the two-body problem. Several factors contribute from the variation from an exact elliptical orbit about the sun. First the interaction with other relatively large planets produces perturbations on the standard orbit. Then the comet itself has variations in configuration (not perfectly spherical), mass density, and behavior, since it appears that some of them are spinning and/or ejecting matter in different directions[2]. Nevertheless it can be shown that the two-body solution can predict orbits within a very close tolerance, enough to satisfy the purpose of this paper, which is to assess their expected lifetimes.

Most of our specific information about comets comes from the study of the famous Halley's comet. From it we deduce that this and others are composed primarily of frozen water and gases, such as methane and ammonia. The latest measurements indicate that the Halley mass is presently about $(10)11$ tons and that its mass loss at or near perihelion is about 20 tons per second[3]. Extrapolation of these figures and application to the orbits of other short period comets is used to give a predicted lifetime for these objects.

TWO BODY PROBLEM

Six parameters are required to provide a complete description of the solar orbit of a body[4]. Three of these numbers describe the orientation and location of the orbit with respect to the plane of the ecliptic and are unnecessary for this study. The other three factors are normally expressed as the period, P, eccentricity, e, and semi-major axis, a. See Figure 1. From this one develops that the perihelion is

$$q = a(1-e)$$

(1)

Assessment of a comet's mass loss requires a knowledge of its distance from the sun (the focus of the orbit), since mass loss rate is considered inverse to the squared distance. This is obtained by relating the eccentric anomaly, E, to the mean anomaly, M (Figure 2). The mean anomaly is simply the position on the enclosing circular orbit and is some given fraction of the total orbit expressed in radians. i.e. $P=2\pi$. This relationship is given by the well-known Kepler equation:

$$E - e \sin E = M \qquad (2)$$

This nonlinear equation cannot be solved directly. Various approximation and iteration schemes have been suggested. Here we use the method of successive approximations:

$$E_0 = M$$

$$E_1 = M - e \sin E_0$$

$$E_2 = m - e \sin E_1$$

etc.

Having obtained a value for E, we say finally that the distance is

$$r = a \ (\ 1 - e \cos E \ ) \qquad (3)$$

MASS LOSS

The computation of mass loss is based on the assumption that this loss is caused primarily by solar pressure. A postulate that the energy so provided does not attenuate with distance leads to the conclusion that this pressure varies inversely with the square of the distance from the sun. Thus,

$$p = k \ r^{-2} \qquad (4)$$

If the mass loss rate is proportional to pressure then

$$\frac{dm}{dt} = c \, p \qquad (5)$$

so that

$$dm = c \, p \, dt$$

$$dm = k \ r^{-2} \, dt \qquad (6)$$

The maximum mass loss rate occurs at the point of minimum distance, or perihelion. Here M = E = 0 and

$$r = a(1-e) \qquad (7)$$

Therefore

$$k = a^2 \ (1-e) \ \frac{dm}{dt} \text{max} \qquad (8)$$

The mass loss in a single orbit is

$$\Delta m = \int_0^\tau \frac{k}{r^2} dt \qquad (9)$$

Now since M = θ = nt, we have dθ = n dt. Substitute to get

$$\Delta m = \frac{2k}{n} \int_0^n \frac{d\theta}{r^2}$$

(10)

where symmetry has been used to consider only half an orbit. With numerical quadrature we get, finally

$$\Delta m = \frac{2k}{n} \sum \frac{\Delta\theta}{r_{av}^2}$$

(11)

NUMERICAL SOLUTION

Recent measurements on Halley's comet lead to the assertion that its mass loss rate in the vicinity of perihelion was about 20 tons/second. This is assumed to be the maximum magnitude of dm/dt and is used in the equation above for the computation of k. In the absence of much other meaningful data this value is used for all short period comets to be considered here. The average radius in the summation above is the arithmetic mean of the beginning and ending values in a given segment of orbit.

A Fortran77 program was written to compute the mass loss for a single orbit based on that summation. The first assessment was made with respect to Halley's comet. The first segment in the computation starts at the perihelion. Different numbers of segments were considered, with the number increased until the point was reached at which no significant change in the computed result was realized. This is known as convergence of the numerical solution. In this case a converged result was with 10,000 segments. This does not mean, however, that 10,000 steps are required in the solution. In actuality increases in segment size are made when the incremental ratio Δm/m falls below a certain tolerance and an absolute tolerance is set at which all calculation is terminated since further increments of mass loss are trivial at such large distances from the sun.

For a single orbit a certain mass loss is computed. Indications are that the typical comet size is 0.5 to 2 km. With a specific gravity of 1 to 2 (composition is indicated to be frozen water, methane, or ammonia) one deduces a mass of about $(10)11$ tons, the accepted value of the nucleus of Halley's comet. This value is used for all short period comets to be considered. The single orbit mass loss is divided into the assumed initial mass to yield an estimated lifetime in number of orbits and, therefore, a life in years. The program was developed on an Apollo DN3500 engineering work station. Actual computations were completed on a Cray X/MP computer.

Predicted lifetime of Halley's comet is 214 orbits or 16272 years. This compares favorably with the projection given by F. Whipple(5). A complete listing of comets considered(6) is given in Table 1. Note the conclusion that all short comets will be extinct in some 20,000 years and nearly all will have disappeared in about 3,000 years.

COMET REPLENISHMENT

Since the maximum predicted lifetime of the current solar system inventory of comets is limited to 20,000 years some interesting conclusions can be drawn. First, if one assumes that the average comet has lost half of its mass since appearing as a short period comet one can say that the solar system as we know it is only 20,000 years old. An assumption that 5/6 of the average mass has already been lost still leads to a limit of 100,000 years. This becomes additionally significant in view of the fact that assertions are often made that comets contain some of the original material of the solar system. Clearly this conclusion is untenable to most modern astronomers.

The primary explanation advanced to deal with the obvious "youth" of the current comets is that they are continuously being replenished from the "Oort cloud", a collection of millions of similar objects orbiting at a radius of 0.5 to 2 light years, or halfway to the nearest star. So large a number of masses spread out over so large a volume of space is subject to the occasional near miss of some other object (a passing star?). An approach of this type propels the mass into an orbit with a relatively small perihelion, thus making it a long period comet. Now some of these comets are, in turn, transformed into short period comets by passage close to some heavy mass such as Jupiter or Saturn. Hence it is usually argued that the evident low age of the present system of short period comets is no argument against conventional astronomical dating of the solar system at 4-6 billion years. In the discussion to follow an assessment will be made of the mathematical requirements to produce a short period comet in two stages from the hypothetical Oort cloud.

LONG PERIOD COMETS

Assume the radius of the postulated Oort cloud to be one-half year or 34000 AU (astronomical units). The optimum disturbance to a circular orbit of this size would yield a new orbit with aphelion of 34000 AU and perihelion of, say 5 AU, the orbital radius of Jupiter. Clearly the semi-major axis, being the average of the two, is 17000 AU. It should be noted that this would in itself be a very restricted case, since the vast majority of perturbation effects would produce a radial as well as tangential component of velocity change. Whether inward or outward would be inconsequential, since the effect would be to elongate the orbit beyond the postulated size.

Note also that

$$n = (\mu/a^3)^{1/2}$$

The period $P = 2\pi/n$. For a solar orbit $m = 4\pi^2$ and $P = a^{3/2}$. For the given value of a this gives a period of 2.2 million years. Recall that this is a very conservative minimum value.

SHORT PERIOD TRANSITION

A short period comet has a much smaller size orbit than one produced by ejection from an Oort cloud. Note from Eq. (7) that

$$a = q / (1 - e) \tag{12}$$

where q is the radius of perihelion. A brief review of the results in Table 1 leads to the observation that the maximum a of this collection of comets is 28.9. Let us say conservatively that a short period comet must have a semi-major axis no greater than 100. The investigation is made to determine how this value can be achieved from a starting point of 17000.

The basis of any transition is that a relatively large third body exerts a force such that close passage can significantly alter the orbital parameters of a long period comet. It was demonstrated a century ago by Tisserand(7) that within a nearly spherical volume of space about a third body that body has an influence greater than that of the primary body, even in a heliocentric system. The resulting expression is

$$r_e/r_p = (m/M)^{2/5} \tag{13}$$

The mass ratio of Jupiter to the sun is .00095. With Jupiter's orbit at 5.2 AU we have that

$$r_a = (.00095)^{2/5} \tag{14}$$

$$= .32 \ AU$$

This means that a passage within .32 AU of Jupiter will produce effects large enough to modify perceptibly the orbital parameters of the comet.

Roy(6) presents the equations of orbital perturbation in a three- body system. For our purposes we have

$$\frac{da}{dt} = \frac{2}{n\sqrt{1-e^2}} \left[S_e + \frac{p}{r} T \right] \tag{15}$$

270

$$\frac{de}{dt} = \frac{\sqrt{1-e^2}}{na}\left[S + T\cos E\right] \tag{16}$$

where S and T are the radial (with respect to the disturbing body, in this case Jupiter) and tangential (in the plane of the comet's orbit) components of the disturbing acceleration experienced by the comet. Also $p = a\,(1-e^2)$.

Now a body passing by a third body would experience the maximum effect when this passage occurs at a right angle to the principal axis of the orbit (Figure 3). In this configuration $p = r$. The disturbing acceleration is

$$F = -G\,m_1/r = -\mu/r \tag{17}$$

the negative sign indicating that the effect is directed inward.

The minimum distance between the comet orbit and the third body is called d. Then from Figure 4 follows that

$$S = -\frac{\mu}{r}\frac{d}{r}; \quad T = \frac{\mu}{r}\frac{\sqrt{r^2-d^2}}{r} \tag{18}$$

Since

$$\frac{d}{r} = \cos\alpha; \quad r = \frac{d}{\cos\alpha} \tag{19}$$

$$\frac{\sqrt{r^2-d^2}}{r} = \sin\alpha$$

then

$$S = -\mu\frac{\cos^2\alpha}{d}; \quad T = \mu\frac{\sin\alpha\cos\alpha}{d} \tag{20}$$

Also a segment of orbit, considered rectilinear in this relatively small region, is

$$dx = vdt = rd\alpha,$$

or

$$dt = rd\alpha\,/\,v. \tag{21}$$

If v is assumed constant during passage through the sphere of influence one obtains, finally

$$da = \frac{2\mu}{vn\sqrt{1-e^2}}\,(-e\cos\alpha + \sin\alpha)\,d\alpha \tag{22}$$

$$de = \mu \frac{\sqrt{1-e^2}}{nav} \left(-\cos\alpha + \sin\alpha \cos E\right) da \qquad (23)$$

For the earth-sun system

$$\mu = G(M + m_1) = 4\pi^2 \frac{a_1^3}{T_1^2} \qquad (24)$$

$$= 4\pi^2$$

Therefore, approximately,

$$GM = 4\pi^2 \qquad (25)$$

For a planet we have

$$\mu = GM_1 = 4\pi^2 \, (m/M) \qquad (26)$$

In the case of Jupiter

$$\mu = 4\pi^2 \, (.00095) \qquad (27)$$

$$= .0375$$

Energy conservation gives the velocity in a solar orbit as

$$v^2 = \mu \, [(2/v) - (1/a)] \qquad (28)$$

At Jupiter's radius, r = 5.2. With $\mu = 4\pi^2$ we get

$$v = 3.9 \ AU/yr \qquad (29)$$

The largest effect occurs when Jupiter is oriented so that f = π/2. solution for E is gained from,

$$\tan\frac{f}{2} = \left[\frac{1+e}{1-e}\right]^{1/2} \tan\frac{E}{2} \qquad (30)$$

Also

$$r = \frac{a(1-e^2)}{1 + e\cos f} \qquad (31)$$

When f = π/2, then

$$r = a(1 - e^2)$$

With r = 5.2, we obtain

$$e = .99985. \qquad (32)$$

Solving eqn.(30) gives E = .01782 and

$$\cos E = .99985. \qquad (33)$$

Integration of eq. (22) yields

$$\Delta a = \frac{2\mu_1}{nv\sqrt{1-e^2}} \, (-2e \sin\alpha_1)$$

(34)

$$= \frac{-4\mu_1 e}{nv\sqrt{1-e^2}} \, \frac{\sqrt{R^2 - d^2}}{R}$$

Now d indicates the closest passage distance. In the limit (though clearly impossible) d = 0 and

$$\Delta a = 770,000.$$

Likewise eq (23) is integrated to get

$$\Delta e = \frac{\sqrt{1-e^2} \; \mu_1}{nav} \, (-2 \sin\alpha_1)$$

(35)

The limiting value is e = .07.

These integrations were based on the assumption that a and e were modified trivially on their passage through the sphere of influence. Obviously this is not the case and a more complex integration process is required for a rigorous answer. The point of this study is demonstrate that the parameters can be modified sufficiently by close approach to a massive body (in this case Jupiter) to modify the orbit from long period to short period.

TRANSITION PROBABILITY

Having demonstrated that the conversion of a long period comet to short period is theoretically possible it remains to be seen just how likely such a phenomenon would be. Consider the geometrical intersection of the allowable volumes of a comet orbit and the orbit of Jupiter. Since the Oort cloud is assumed spherical a long period orbit can have any inclination and the potential space affected would be an annular spherical shell while the corresponding volume swept out by the planet would be a torus. Both the annular thickness and the toroidal diameter would be the diameter of the sphere of influence. The major radius of the torus would be the radius of Jupiter's orbit.

If we denote the orbital radius of the planet as r1 and the radius of influence as r2 then the annular volume is

$$V_c = (4/3) \, \pi \, [(r_1 + r_2)^3 - (r_1 - r_2)^3]$$

(36)

while the toroidal volume is,

$$V_j = 2\pi^2 \, r_1 \, r_2^2$$

(37)

Now the ratio of V_j / V_c would be that fraction of the comet's trajectory likely to be in the affected zone produced by Jupiter. However this alone would be inadequate to produce the effect in question, since the planet would not necessarily be in the vicinity of the comet when it comes through the torus. Rather it is required to find the intersection of the sphere of influence

273

$$V_s = (4/3) \pi r_2^3$$

with the annular volume.

Therefore the probability of being affected is

$$\frac{V_s}{V_c} = \frac{r_2^3}{\left[(r_1 - r_2)^3 - (r_1 - r_2)^3 \right]} = \frac{r_2^2}{2(2r_1^2 + r_2^2)} \tag{38}$$

$$= .000945$$

This indicates a one in 1000 likelihood of a comet passing within the distance of a planet adequate to produce the change to short period. With a period previously developed to be 2.2 million years this means that on the average two billion years would be required for an individual comet. It is conceded that perhaps only a minute fraction of long period comets would need to experience this transition to replenish the current supply of short period comets. Nevertheless it should be noted that the time available for a complete turnover is only on the order of 100,000 years based on presently observed data. Furthermore many conservatisms were used in these calculations.

CONCLUSIONS

The preseetly obserred hort period comett are being dissipateddaa a relatively rapid rate. All of them will vanish within 100,000 years. A backward extrapolation brings the conclusion that those with which we are presently have been in their present orbits for no longer than the same magnitude of time period - 100,000 years.

A close passage of a long period comet by a massive planetary body - most probably Jupiter - can produce changes in orbital characteristics enough to convert the comet into a short period comet. Note that on the other hand the axis a could be increased by passing on the inside rather than the outside of the third body's orbit.

The probability of a flyby close enough to affect the comet's orbit significantly is no more than one in 1000. Without mention of the many conservative assumptions made this seems insufficient to produce the current supply of short period comets.

There has never been any but the most tenuous of deductions - no evidence - that the Oort cloud actually exists. It is a necessary postulate for the widely accepted long age (about two billion years) of the solar system.

REFERENCES

1. Sagan, C. and Druyan, A., Comets, Random House, New York, 1985.

2. Whipple, F. L., "The Spin of Comets," Scientific American, 1980.

3. Balsiger, H., Fechtig, H., and Geiss, J., "A Close Look at Halley's Comet," Scientific American, 1988.

4. Roy, A. E., The Fundamentals of Astrodynamics, Macmillan, Mew York, 1965.

5. Whipple, F. L., The Telescope.

6. Brown, P. L., Comets, Meteorites and Men, Taplinger, New York, 1973.

7. Tisserand, F. Traite de Mecanique, Gauthier-Villars, Paris, 1889.

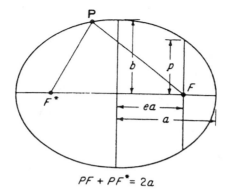

$$PF + PF^* = 2a$$

FIGURE 1. Ellipse

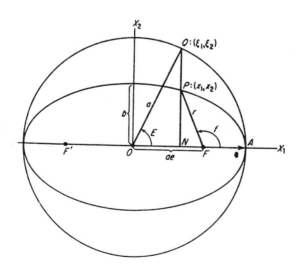

FIGURE 2. Elliptic Anomalies

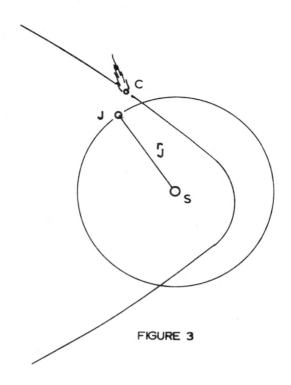

FIGURE 3

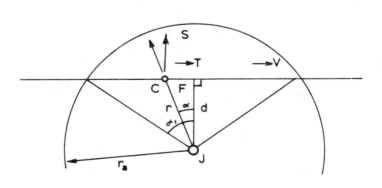

FIGURE 4

Other calculations for Comet Halley based on its dust trail give a history of 23,000 years (1) and a future of at least 100,000 years (2). Can you explain this discrepancy with your shorter time results?

The probability argument for the long period to short period transition leaves out the large number of comets assumed in the Oort cloud, perhaps trillions. Factored in, this gives dozens of possible new short period comets each year. Perhaps the main question is the existence of the Oort cloud, not probabilities.

The study depends heavily on the 1980s Halley mass loss, 20 tons/second. This loss is highly variable among comets, and also greatly decreases with each perihelion passage. The Halley figure is therefore of questionable significance.

REFERENCES:

1) Maddox, J. 1989. Halley's Comet is quite young. Nature 339:95.

2) Snow, T. 1988. The Dynamic Universe. West Pub. Co., NY., pg. 306.

Don B. DeYoung, Ph.D.
Winona Lake, Indiana

This is an excellent paper. I strongly recommend it.

Harold S. Slusher, Ph.D.
El Paso, Texas

Dr. Stillman re-investigates the implications of short cometary lifetimes for the age of the solar system. Unfortunately, his mass loss analysis is flawed by the assumption that it is inversely proportional to the square of the distance from the sun because it is dependent upon solar pressure. It appears rather that mass loss occurs in jets whose existence depends upon temperature, which may be stochastic in nature, and which do not occur beyond a certain distance from the sun. His estimates, however, are probably close enough to be illustrative. In his dynamic analysis, he neglects the theoretical "inner Oort cloud" which was postulated to overcome the difficulties of transition from long-period to short-period comets. The ultimate conclusions are not significantly changed by these oversights, but an analysis which included them would be more convincing.

Paul Steidl, M.S.
Snohomish, Washington

CLOSURE

Dr. DeYoung refers to a short review by Maddux in Nature (vol.339,1989). This article discusses a recent Canadian study which relied on a chain of inferences and some radar-obtained dust measurements to deduce that Halley's comet has been present in the inner solar system for no more than 23,000 years. The number and magnitude of uncertainties present in that study hardly say anything about the interpretations one could draw from the computations presented in this paper which, after all, is primarily devoted to a forward look based on some scanty information now available. The inferred future of at least 100,000 years is at variance with much of the scientific literature, as well as the reported extrapolation here.

The Halley's comet mass loss figure is a weak reed on which to lean, but essentially it's all we've got at this time. Acknowledging that the constant mass loss rate (for a given radius) assumption is somewhat dubious I extended the scope of the numerical integration program to consider loss rate proportional to the surface area of the comet nucleus. With a variable loss rate it became necessary to integrate over the entire projected life of the comet, rather than the half-orbit examined in the body of the paper. After running the Apollo computer much longer we obtain the revised prediction of Halley's comet life of 25,169 years, compared to the more simplistic value of 16,273 years presented earlier. An increase in life of approximately 50% hardly affects the thrust of this paper.

The presence of ejecta in comet nuclei is well known. There are also observed variations in dynamic behavior (jumps) which can probably be attributed to unobserved jetting. As measurement capabilities are enhanced and more data are accumulated it is expected that much more rigorous (and satisfying) studies of comet durability can be conducted. Nevertheless it is safe to say that the basic conclusion of the study - namely the extinction of short-period comets in a very few thousand years - will in all likelihood remain little affected.

The Oort cloud is at present little more than a myth, although a very necessary myth, as indicated by the amount of space devoted to the concept by Sagan and Druyan. Even more dubious is a so-called inner Oort cloud mentioned by Mr. Steidl. The whole point of the exercise was to play some games with this idea, should it be granted any substance, which I doubt. Yes there are postulated to be perhaps trillions of comet nuclei in this entity, generally positioned at incredible distances from the sun. We did not examine the first half of the scenario, which is the generation of long period comets passing close enough to the sun to be affected by one of the larger planets. A subsequent study, it is hoped, will indicate that the number of potential long period comets is quite limited. Clearly the second portion, which I briefly addressed, is also worthy of much more attention.

William E. Stillman, Ph.D.

THE ULTIMATE HOAX: ARCHAEOPTERYX LITHOGRAPHICA

Ian Taylor
President of TFE Publishing
P.O. Box 1344, Stn. F
Toronto, Ontario M4Y 2T1
Canada

ABSTRACT

The recent claims that the London specimen of the Archaeopteryx is a hoax have been clarified and there would seem to be grounds for suspicion. The published work on the Berlin specimen shows that it has every indication of being a hoax of the same kind, that is, a modified, genuine fossil of the Compsognathus. All four of the more recent "discoveries" are shown to be nothing more than reclassifications of genuine fossils of the same small dinosaur.

INTRODUCTION

To many people the very word 'fossil' causes about as much excitement as watching grass grow. However, when we lift the veil which shrouds the world's most famous fossil, we find a labyrinth of intrigue and deception making it all somehow far more palatable. The fossil of the Archaeopteryx is said to be the paleontologist's "Rosetta Stone" providing irrefutable evidence that evolution of the species actually occurred. It has taken pride of place in every biology textbook for over a century and has recently been wreathed in controversy following the claims that one of the principal specimens is a fake. We will first trace out the history of the discovery of the various specimens, then examine the claims that the London specimen is fraudulent. Following this, we will determine if the more famous Berlin specimen can withstand the harsh light of scrutiny. It will be shown that the weight of evidence from both human activity and technical detail for all the known specimens points overwhelmingly to both the London and Berlin specimens of the Archaeopteryx being nothing more than a clever hoax.

THE DISCOVERY OF THE SPECIMENS

When it came to evidence for his theory, Charles Darwin lamented that none had yet been discovered. Writing in 1859 he said:

> ...as this process of extermination [survival of the fittest] has acted on an enormous scale, so must the number of intermediate varieties, which have formerly existed on the earth, be truly enormous. Why then is not every geological formation and every stratum full of such intermediate links? Geology assuredly does not reveal any such finely graduated organic chain; and this, perhaps, is the most obvious and gravest objection which can be urged against my theory. The explanation lies, as I believe, in the extreme imperfection of the geological record. [1].

And to this day this is still the tidy explanation offered to the public. An unintended side-effect of the publication of Darwin's Origin was that by bewailing the absence of "intermediate varieties"; i.e., fossils of creatures in transition from one species to another, a charter was provided for fossil forgers. As early as 1833 French paleontologist Geoffroy Saint-Hilaire had proposed that the birds had evolved from the reptiles [2] and later Darwinian enthusiasts began to speculate on what some of these transitions should have looked like; the alleged transition between the reptiles and the birds was based upon the fact that the bone structure of certain extinct dinosaurs and that of the birds have some similar features.

Within a matter of months after the publication of the German edition of the Origin, paleontologist Hermann von Meyer came into possession of the fossil of a single feather impression. The two halves of the small limestone slab containing the impression were supposed to have been found at the Solnhofen Quarry (Southern Germany) but details of its background never were given adequately. Meyer named the specimen Archaeopteryx lithographica [3]; the genus name meant "ancient wing" while the species name reflected the fact that the particular limestone at the quarry was used for the production of lithographic plates in the printing industry. The specimen made news, because, although the feather looked perfectly modern, it was supposed to have been found in strata of the Jurassic period and therefore 150 million years old. This meant that birds had evolved far earlier than anyone had expected, and, at the time, this was a severe blow to Cuvier's then popular theory of multiple floods. One further detail worth noting was the fact that in a very unusual move the two halves of the slab were sold separately to the Berlin and the Munich museums respectively; normally, the slab and counter-slab are kept together. The agent for the sale of this extremely rare fossil was Dr. Karl Haberlein, medical officer for the district of Pappenheim.

Less than two months later, in 1861, Haberlein had another specimen for sale, but this time it was of the entire creature except for its head. About as big as a pigeon, it was said to have been discovered in the strata of the Jurassic period at the Solnhofen quarry while this time the two halves, slab and counter-slab, were kept together. Haberlein invited museum representatives to see it, but they were not permitted to make notes or drawings; further, by refusing each offer he effectively drove up the price. One observer, M. Witte of Hanover, gave a very complete verbal description to professor Andreas Wagner who had discovered and named a small dinosaur Compsognathus. Wagner recognized from the description what seemed to him to be his Compsognathus but with feathers! He was extremely suspicious, and, in his paper in which he called the new discovery Griphosaurus, added the following warning:

> ....I must add a few words to ward off Darwinian misinterpretations of our new Saurian. At first glance of Griphosaurus we might certainly form a notion that we had before us an intermediate creature, engaged in a transition from the Saurian to the bird. Darwin and his adherents will probably employ the new discovery as an exceedingly welcome occurrence for the justification of their strange views upon the transformation of the animals. But they will be wrong.[4]

And, of course, Wagner was absolutely right; the Darwinians made it their Rosetta Stone. Haberlein's reaction to Wagner's paper can well be imagined and he resolved to unload the fossil at the next offer. He did not have to wait long, and, while the Germans argued among themselves, "real or forgery", an offer came from England.

Richard Owen, in charge of the British Natural History Museum, read Wagner's description and immediately sent the geologist, George Waterhouse, to Pappenheim where the specimen changed hands for 600 pounds. The dispute now shifted to England. Owen published his description and an accurate engraving of just the slab, not the counter-slab, in 1864 [5]. The fact that it had fully developed feathers classified it as a bird and there were speculations as to whether the head would have had teeth or not; having teeth would place it more centrally between the reptile and the bird and thus be a more perfect confirmation of Darwin's theory. Sure enough, sixteen years later, another Archaeopteryx turned up complete with head and it did have teeth! In the meantime, neither Darwin nor Thomas Huxley could be convinced that the London specimen was a transition. Darwin mentioned it in the 1866 (fourth) edition of his Origin as merely "a strange bird" [6] while Huxley expressed a similar opinion to the Royal Society in 1868 [7]. However, in his classic 1867 paper on the classification of birds [8], Huxley proposed the new taxonomic order Sauropsida for both reptiles and birds thus relating them on paper if not in fact.

The second Archaeopteryx discovery in 1877 was again claimed to have been made at the Solnhofen site and passed through the hands of Karl Haberlein's son, Ernst [9]; this time the enormous sum of thirty-six thousand gold marks was demanded for the prize. Far more than any museum could afford and after four years of negotiations, it was eventually bought by the industrial magnate, Werner Seimens. Seimens then sold it to the Prussian ministry so that it ended up in the Humbolt Museum in 1881. The formal description by professor Dames did not appear until 1884 [10]. The patriotic gesture by Seimens to ensure that the prize did not leave German soil was later rewarded by naming the creature Archaeopteryx siemensii. Later still, the classification name was changed to Archaeopteryx lithographica or, more usually, the Berlin Specimen. Because it is the most complete, photographs of this specimen are shown in practically every school biology textbook as definitive evidence of a transition from one major group to another.

Textbooks sometimes speak of "many other examples" and by this is meant: A poorly preserved specimen discovered in 1956 assigned by Heller as an Archaeopteryx and known as the Maxberg Specimen [11]; it remains in a private collection. A specimen discovered in 1855 and classified as a pterosaur by the Teyer Museum until 1970 when it was re-classified as an Archaeopteryx by Ostrom; it is referred to as the Haarlem Specimen [12]. A specimen discovered in 1951 and classified as a Compsognathus longipes re-classified by Mayr in 1973 as an Archaeopteryx and known today as the Eichstatt Specimen [13]. The most recent specimen was "discovered" in a private collection and classified by Wellnhofer in 1988 as an Archaeopteryx; it is referred to as the Solnhofen Specimen [14]. It is to be emphasized that none of these last four specimens show feather impressions. More will be said of this later. The great bird expert, Professor Ostrom, writing before the 1988 specimen was assigned said of these latest specimens:

...these specimens are not particularly like modern birds at all. If feather impressions had not been preserved in the London and Berlin specimens, they [the Maxberg, Haarlem and Eichstatt specimens] would never have been identified as birds...notice [they] were all misidentified at first, and the Eichstatt Specimen for 20 years was thought to be a small specimen of the dinosaur Compsognathus. [15].

The six specimens of Archaeopteryx lithographica together with the feather reported by Herman von Meyer, are summarized in Table 1. The first column gives the date on which disclosure was made.

TABLE 1
Archaeopteryx lithographica

1860	Single feather referred to as von Meyer's.
1861	London Specimen found at Solnhofen.
1877	Berlin Specimen found at Solnhofen.
1956	Maxberg Specimen assigned as Archaeopteryx.
1970	1855 Haarlem Specimen (pterosaur) re-assigned.
1973	1951 Eichstadt Compsognathus re-assigned.
1988	Solnhofen Specimen assigned as Archaeopteryx.

THE CHARGE OF FRAUD

Dr. Lee Spetner of the Weizman Institute, Israel, long suspected that the London specimen was a fake and eventually persuaded the British Natural History Museum authorities to let him examine the actual specimen. Museum specimens of the calibre of the Archaeopteryx are securely squirreled away in vaults only accessible to the eye of certified believers; the public sees a mere plaster copy. British scientist, Sir Fred Hoyle had also expressed reservations about the London specimen's authenticity and Dr. Spetner invited him to co-operate in the examination of this fossil. Just before Christmas 1984 the precious artifact was exposed, perhaps for the first time in this century, to the skeptical eye of unbelievers. To forestall charges of fraud, an International Archaeopteryx Conference had been held at Eichstatt just three months earlier where 80 of the faithful had gathered but they were denied the chance to see either the London or the Berlin specimens; the London Specimen was claimed to be "too fragile to travel" and the Berlin Specimen was said to be "in Japan" [16].

During Spetner and Hoyle's examination physical contact was not permitted but a great many photographs were taken using techniques intended to highlight the contours. This was important because the surface upon which the fossil impression lies is three-dimensional; published photographs leave the viewer with the impression that the fossil lies on a two-dimensional plane. The results were most revealing but when it came to publication the ranks and minds of the scientific press were solidly closed! In the end, Hoyle and Spetner and their associates published their findings in a series of photographic articles in The British Journal of Photography [17-20]. The charges led to counter-charges by Alan Charig and others of the British Museum [21]. In the meantime, the public press reminded of the Piltdown affair at the same museum in 1953, smelled the makings of another scandal and eagerly fanned the flames of contention. Sir Fred Hoyle quickly published a little book containing some very interesting photographs and documentation of the charges and counter-charges [22]. Finally, in late 1987, the museum put their most famous fossil on display with a list of rebuttals to the charges of hoax in an attempt to regain the public confidence. From that day to this the public had heard nothing more of the debacle.

Hoyle and Spetner concluded that the London Specimen was actually a genuine fossil of the Compsognathus, an extinct reptile, to which had been added the impressions of modern feathers. Hoyle suggested that the forgers had spread a mixture of finely ground limestone and gum arabic thinly across the wing and tail areas then pressed modern feathers into this mixture. The feathers were removed after the cement had completely hardened [23]. They also suggested that the first discovery, the von Meyer specimen, had been produced in the same way and pointed out that the texture of the slab and counter-slab were not the same as would be expected from a genuine fossil. It would seem that this would provide a very good reason for the forgers to have sold the two halves to separate museums [24]. Fossil forgery was not a new thing to the enterprising quarry owners of Solnhofen; Wendt shows for example that a fossil forgery business had flourished at Ohningen just 120 miles from Solnhofen for over a century [25].

The London Specimen is unique in having an oversized furcula or wish-bone which is found in birds but not usually in reptiles. Indeed, it is the feather impressions and the furcula which give this fossil its avian status. However, in a paper communicated to the Royal Society in 1868, T.H. Huxley not only doubted that it was a furcula but declared it to be "conspicuous" and "bouleversement" or up-side-down. He then gleefully showed how this had completely confused his rival, the great Richard Owen in his description of the fossil [26]. In the same paper Huxley concluded:

> In fact, in its form, and strength relatively to the shoulder girdle, the so-called "furculum" appears to me to be the greatest osteological difficulty presented by Archaeopteryx. [27]

Hoyle's suspicions regarding the furcula centered upon the corresponding cavity in the counter-slap which appears to be insufficient to contain the prominent furcula. He suggested that the forgers had added a crude furcula then attempted to excavate a cavity in the counter-slab to get it to fit [28]. However, a recent profile analysis has shown that there is, in fact, a perfect fit but detailed discussion of the feathers, furcula and other bones from all specimens will follow later. At this point a list of the principal evidences for hoax and the museum rebuttals will be given:

a)The tail lies at the bottom of a depression in the surface of the slab and there is no corresponding raised area in the counter-slab. Hoyle maintained that when originally split the tail lay beneath the surface of the slab but the forgers excavated around the tail bone, back-filled part of the way with a cement of finely ground limestone and gum arabic, then set feathers in place so as to leave the impressions. Hoyle mistakenly refers to the tail area as "the tail feather" but of course the impressions consist of a number of feathers, two to each bone in the vertebrae. The museum maintains that it was scientists at the museum who removed some rock from the slab to reveal the tail feathers. However, if this was the case then it must have been carried out by Richard Owen's staff prior to his 1864 publication [5]. This contains an excellent engraving of the slab complete with every tail feather as it is today but Owen mentioned nothing of any excavation work.

b)The feather impressions mostly appear on the slab and not on the counter-slab except for one tiny piece described by Hoyle as 'gum-like'; when analysed it showed traces of foreign substances. Hoyle's photograph of this piece showed that it has feather impressions, but the museum's explanation fails to mention this and simply says that the foreign substances probably came from mould-making or the sealer which has been applied to the surface. Neither explanation would account for the feather impressions. Hoyle's supposition that the thin layer of 'cement' spread on the counter-slab by the forgers did not 'take' but fell off except for the one isolated 'gum-like' piece appears to be the more probable explanation [29].

c)The museum granted Spetner two very small samples of the fossil surface; one from the "wing" area and the other as a control remote from the "wing" area. A scanning electron microscope analysis carried out at the Weizman Institute showed that the control sample was clean crystalline limestone as one would expect but that from the "wing" area was amorphous; X-ray luminescence analysis revealed that it had a strange composition. Suspicions that it was indeed the glue and limestone mixture which had been suggested, were close to being confirmed. Yet another sample was necessary to be sure the first sample was truly representative and not an artifact. The museum refused all further testing [30].

d)Hoyle and his associates (but not Spetner) suggested that Richard Owen knew that the fossil was a forgery when he purchased it [20]. Hoyle argued that Owen was a creationist (untrue) and his intention was to expose it as a fraud after Darwin had accepted it and thus discredit Darwin and especially Huxley and the theory of evolution. However, this was an unfortunate piece of speculation which Gould has taken great delight in showing to be totally untrue [31].

The museum's prime evidences for the fossil being genuine are:

e) There are hairline cracks in the feathered areas which match exactly on the slab and the counter-slab. These cracks are filled with natural crystals and so must have been in the slab before it was split open. Spetner and others have pointed out that when cracks in a wall are plastered over they re-appear as the house settles. The London specimen has indeed received much pounding by the hammer during the past century and removing of the "brain-case" was only one instance when cracks had ample opportunity to propagate through the thin layer of forger's cement.

f) Dendritic patterns, some of which match exactly on the slab and counter-slab, appear to overlie the feather impressions. Dendrites are tree-like growths of dark mineral crystals and take centuries to form. Dr. Spetner shows from his photographs that the dendritic pattern is genuine but does not overlie the feathered area [30] while in private correspondence he more forcefully states that "the matching dendrite claim is simply fraudulent" [31].

So much for the London specimen and the observations of those who have actually examined it in contrast to those defenders of the faith, such as Gould [32], who write from a more distant ivory tower.

THE BERLIN SPECIMEN

The Berlin Archaeopteryx, discovered in 1877, is the most perfect of all the specimens since it not only has feathers on the wings and tail but is complete with the head having teeth and has both legs and both feet. The public was first made aware of this specimen in an engraving prepared from a drawing by Professors Steinmann and Doderlein and appeared in Karl Zittel's prestigious Handbuch der Palaeontologie for 1887 [33]. The engraving was labeled "nach dem Berliner skelet..." (after the Berlin skeleton...) and consisted of an imaginary composite of the London and Berlin specimens including the up-side-down furcula. The illustration appeared in countless textbooks and led the public to believe the evidence to be more convincing than was actually the case. The complete engraving is shown in Figure 1 and the furcula ('U'-shaped object top, center) is labeled 'Cl' for clavicle which is believed to be the reptile counterpart of the bird's furcula. Figure 2 is a recent photograph of the same specimen and there is no sign of a furcula. Yet, as we shall see, there is worse to come and the discerning reader may suspect that this, most famous of all fossils, is another forgery.

Professor C.H. Hurst personally examined and photographed the Berlin Specimen in 1893 and observed that there were serious discrepancies between the engraving and the actual specimen [34]. The furcula has already been mentioned. The principal discrepancy occurred in the wing area, and the engraving and his photograph of the left-wing are reproduced in Figures 3 and 4. Hurst's photograph of the wing area was genuine and identical to the corresponding part of a photograph of the entire specimen published by Carl Vogt sometime shortly after its discovery in 1877. Hurst claimed that the original drawing was deliberately falsified to make it appear that the primary quill feathers originated in the 'arm' and not in the 'hand'. He invited his readers to place a straight edge on the photograph and observe that the fourth primary feather is straight. Incredibly, modern photographs now show the wing feathers to be 'bent' exactly as in the engraving. Comparison between an early and a modern photograph may be made between Figures 2 and 4 but Figures 3 and 4 show the difference more clearly. The first three distal feathers curve very slightly backwards towards the base of the fourth and the remaining primary feathers curve slightly forwards towards the same point; all these primary feathers thus originate in the manus or hand. In contrast, the engraving shows that all seven primary quills are bent backwards, some almost 40 degrees which has increased their length and doubled it in the case of the third quill.

Professor Hurst also pointed out that not only was the engraving unfaithful to the facts but argued that strongly curved feathers are useless for flight. Hurst also showed that in his detailed description of the specimen, Dames [10, p.138], states that the primary quills were attached to the longest finger [35]. The publication of Dr. Hurst's criticism of the Berlin Specimen led to a lengthy rebuttal paper read to the British Association by Dr. W.P. Pycraft of the British Museum [36]. Pycraft defended the fossil on the basis of Hurst's photograph rather than the engraving and rightly pointed out that straight primary feathers could be expected to originate from the fingers. This is true of most modern birds but the engraving and every modern photograph of the Berlin wing, including Heilmann's dated 1923 [37], now show that the primary feathers are bent and originate in the ulna or fore-arm region. The change from straight to bent feathers in the photographs evidently took place sometime between 1893 and 1923.

In the same paper Professor Hurst made another observation that "these fingers lie not in the wing at all, but upon its feather-clad surface" (his emphasis) [38]. He concluded that the Archaeopteryx was a winged quadruped which used its fingers for climbing. While few claim it to be a quadruped there has been much speculation as to whether the creature could fly or was it simply a climber? Recalling that the surface of the slab is actually in three dimensions and not two, then since the bones are exposed, there is little option but for the feather impressions to appear to lie beneath them. Without removing the bones there can be no proof that they do but it is self-evident that if the situation were reversed with the bones beneath the feather impressions then the bones would not be seen at all. Any forger with his wits about him would be aware of this and arrange for the wing to appear to lay beneath the arm bones in the following way: The wing area adjacent to the 'arm' and 'hand' was masked off with wax and the surface gently etched away with acid to remove perhaps 2 mm. This was then partially back-filled with the comminuted limestone/gum arabic mixture and modern feathers pressed in place. No clumsy hammering and risk of damage would be involved.

It is now almost a century since Professor Hurst published his criticisms based upon personal observations of both the London [39] and Berlin specimens. It may be wondered why this information is not more widely known. The scientific establishment has been virtually dominated by biologists ever since Darwin's day and a kind of censorship of any work critical of evolution has been in effect throughout this time. Hurst had published his work in a scholarly journal offering a balanced airing of contrary opinions; the journal was short-lived (from 1892 to 1899) and is seldom found in library collections today. Similarly, because of the nature of Hoyle and Spetner's findings, these were not found acceptable to the mainline biological journals and they were obliged to report them in The British Journal of Photography.

IS THE ARCHAEOPTERYX REALLY A BIRD?

Having seen some of the short-comings of both the London and Berlin specimens we will now briefly survey the various features of all the specimens bearing in mind Spetner and Hoyle's contention that the London Specimen is a fraudulently modified Compsognathus. First, we will examine the two features which give the creature its status as a bird i.e. the feathers and the furcula.

THE FEATHERS. Impressions of modern feathers only appear on the London and Berlin specimens and only on the tail and in the wing areas. Hurst had remarked on the marvelous state of preservation of the feather impressions saying, "even the barbules of some of the quills are recognizable" [40]. It may be added that there are no other examples of feathers having been preserved in such detail in the fossil record. One very recent case reported in 1988 from Spain [41] is of a single, half-inch long feather but this had been carbonized. That the preservation of such microscopic detail should occur in the two specimens already shrouded in suspicion is simply what one might expect from a forgery where the forgers had little choice but to use modern feathers. It raises an interesting question concerning the kind of detail present in the wing areas of the Berlin Specimen after its apparent modification about a century ago? As far as specimens assigned more recently to the status of Archaeopteryx are concerned, the popular accounts typically say that "feather impressions are distinct" [42] but, in fact, the investigator's statements say, "These features are interpreted as imprints of feather shafts" [43]. Quite a different thing where for example the "feather shaft impressions" may have been produced by quills and not feathers. Moreover, there is not a hint of a feather or feather shaft impression near any of the tails of the Maxberg, Haarlem, or Solnhofen specimens; Wellnhofer [14] claims there are feather impressions in the tail area of the Eichstatt specimen but Ostrom denies this.

THE FURCULA. While no one is quite sure of the function of the furcula, most evolutionary biologists believe that it came about by the fusion of the clavicles or collar-bones in the ancestor of the bird. This has led to much speculation among armchair scientists who may never have examined the actual specimens and it would seem better to accept with caution the arguments of those who have. John Ostrom is probably the world's greatest expert on birds and has personally examined every one of the Archaeopteryx specimens. We will be referring to his 1975/6 papers [15,44] which can probably be regarded as the definitive work. Ostrom describes the furcula of the London specimen as a "boomerang" [45] while even to the untutored eye it is nothing like the delicate wish-bone found in any chicken; this should be cause for question but, so far, it has seemingly been accepted on faith alone. Ostrom maintains that the Berlin Specimen has fragments of bone which many claim as the furcula "although it cannot be proved" and expresses surprise that there is no trace of a furcula in the otherwise well-preserved Eichstatt Specimen [46]. Ostrom also maintains that "a similar bone is partially preserved in the two slabs of the Maxberg Specimen" [47]. This specimen is in the hands of a private collector and photographs of the furcula have not been published; in private correspondence with the author, professor Ostrom has provided a photograph of the alleged furcula but it is far from convincing while he admits that Heller [11] failed to even mention this vital detail. Finally, Ostrom points out that the presence of a furcula seems paradoxical together with the apparent absence of a sternum in every one of the Archaeopteryx specimens [48]. Moreover, there are many little avian details which are entirely absent in all these specimens such as the hypocleideum on the furcula or the external cnemial (shin) crest on the tibia [49].

EVIDENCES FOR THE COMPSOGNATHUS

Over the years opinions have shifted back and forth between the Archaeopteryx being a feathered reptile to it being a bird with reptile features; the latter view prevails today. Among the claims for avian status has been "the perching feet" and "the orientation of the pubis" (the pubis bone of the birds faces backwards, that of the dinosaurians face forwards). Interestingly, and perhaps uniquely among dinosaurs, the Compsognathus is said to have had a backward facing pubis like that of a bird [50]. Ostrom refers to the classic work of Heilmann [37] who in 1926 gave an impressive list of the similarities between the Archaeopteryx on the one hand and the coelurosaurian theropods on the other. However, Heilmann then dismissed the theropod connection because it was believed that this branch of reptiles did not possess a clavicle; Ostrom cites more recent work to show that some theropods do have a clavicle thus removing this negative evidence. After spending half a lifetime studying the Archaeopteryx Ostrom concludes his 1976 paper with:

> Were it not for those remarkable feather imprints...both specimens [the London and Berlin] would be identified unquestionably as coelurosaurian theropods...there is only one skeletal feature that is not currently known in any theropod specimen. This single feature is the fusion of the clavicles into a furcula" [51].

And in his 1975 paper, Ostrom is more specific:

> The presumed bird-like orientation of the pubis in the Berlin Specimen is probably not correct, but due to post-mortem displacement. The bird-like feet and hind-legs are equally theropodous and all of the other so-called bird-like features (hands, arms, pelvis, and skull) are actually more like those of theropod dinosaurs than they are bird-like" [52].

The list of similarities is impressive there being for example, nine major points of similarity between the head of the Archaeopteryx and that of the Compsognathus alone [53]. But then this is precisely what would be expected if the Archaeopteryx is nothing more than a modified Compsognathus. Heilmann's restoration of the Compsognathus is shown in Figure 5.

CONCLUSION

In this paper we have not been concerned with the unlikely possibility that the Archaeopteryx was a strange mosaic creature like Australia's duck-billed platypus. The concern has been with fraud: its motive seems to have been monetary gain, the result has been to provide evidence for a theory. When all the published facts regarding the Archaeopteryx are brought forward, any unbiased jury would find it extremely difficult not to conclude that both the London and Berlin specimens were fraudulent. The more recent "discoveries" are seemingly an attempt to restore confidence in an oft-told myth and have been carried out by mere re-classification of the same kind of fossil used for the hoax; the feather evidence, like Percival Lowell's 700 canals on Mars, is more in the eye of faith than it is in fact. Professor Ostrom, who has examined every specimen confesses that only the London and Berlin specimens contain clear feather impressions while the Eichstatt tail has a "plume" but no evidence of feathers. The London specimen is the only one having a clearly defined feature said to be a furcula and, while Ostrom claims the Maxberg specimen has a furcula, this is not at all convincing. Even if an undoubted furcula were discovered in another specimen, this would only tend to confirm that the furcula in the London specimen was genuine. However, it would not remove the suspicion of fraud because it seems likely that the Compsognathus itself may have had fused clavicles. Finally, it is surely incumbent upon the paleontologist to provide convincing explanations for: a) the change from straight feather impressions to the unlikely bent feather impressions in the Berlin specimen and b) why primary feathers, which are modern in every respect, attach to the ulna instead of the manus as in modern birds? Until such explanations are forthcoming the suspicion of fraud will remain.

REFERENCES

1. Darwin, Charles. The Origin of Species
   London: John Murray, 1859, p.280.

2. Saint-Hilaire, Geoffroy E. La degre d'influence du monde...
   Memoires de l'Academie Royale des Sciences.. (Paris) 1833, Vol.12, p.80.

3. Meyer, Herman von. Vogel-Federn und Palpipes priscus von Solnhofen
   Neuess Jahrbuch fur Mineralogie, Geologie und Paleontologie
   (Stuttgart) 1861, p.561.

4. Wagner, J.A. (Translation by W.S. Dallas). On a New Fossil Reptile Supposed to be
   Furnished with Feathers.
   Annual Magazine of Natural History (London) Series 3.
   April 1862, Vol.9, p.266.

5. Owen, Richard. On the Archaeopteryx of von Meyer...
   Royal Society of London: Phil. trans. 1

6. Darwin, Origin 1866, (Fourth ed.) p.367.

7. Huxley, Thomas H. Remarks upon Archaeopteryx lithographica.
   Proceedings of the Royal Society of London 1868, Vol.16, p.248.

8. Huxley, Thomas H. On the Classification of Birds...
   Proceedings of the Zoological Society of London 1867, Vol.15, p.415-472.

9. Haberlein, Ernst. (edited by C.Giebel). Neueste Entdeckung einer zweiten
   Archaeopteryx lithographica.
   Zeitschrift fur die Gesamte Naturwissenshaften (Berlin) 1877,
   Vol.49, p.326-327.

10. Dames, Wilhelm B. Ueber Archaeopteryx.
    Paleontologische Abhandlungen (Berlin) 1884, Bd.2, Hft.3, p.119-198.

11. Heller, F. Ein dritter Archaeopteryx Fund aus des Solnhofen...
    Erlanger Geologische Abhandlungen (Erlangen) 1959, Vol.31, p.1-25.

12. Ostrom, John H. Archaeopteryx: Notice of a "New" Specimen.
    Science October 30, 1970, Vol.170, p.537-538.

13. Mayr, F.X. Ein neuer Archaeopteryx Fund.
    Palaeontologische Zeitschrift (Stuttgart) 1973, Vol.47, p.17-24.

14. Wellnhofer, Peter. A New Specimen of Archaeopteryx.
    Science June 24, 1988, Vol.240, p.1790-92.

15. Ostrom, John H. The Origin of Birds.
    Annual Review of Earth and Planetary Sciences (Palo Alto) 1975, Vol.3, p.61.

16. Howgate, Michael E. Back to the Trees for Archaeopteryx ...
    Nature (London) February 7, 1985, Vol.313, p.435-436.

17. Watkins, R.S.; F. Hoyle et al. Archaeopteryx: A Photographic Study
    The British Journal of Photography (London) March 8, 1985, Vol.132, p.264-266.

18. Idem. March 29, 1985, Vol.132, p.358-359.

19. Idem. April 26, 1985, Vol.132, p.468-470.

20. Idem. June 21, 1985, Vol.132, p.693-695.

21. Charig, Alan J. et al. Archaeopteryx is not a forgery.
    Science May 2, 1986, Vol.232, p.622-625.

22. Hoyle, F. and C. Wickramasinghe. Archaeopteryx: The Primodrial Bird.
    Swansea, U.K.: Christopher Davies 1986.

23. Ibid. p.67.

24. Ibid. p.41.

25. Wendt, Herbert. Before the Deluge. New York: Doubleday 1968.

26. Huxley, Thomas H. Remarks upon Archaeopteryx lithographica. Proceedings of the Royal Society of London 1868, Vol.16, p.246.

27. Ibid. p.247.

28. See reference 22, p.92, plate XVII.

29. Ibid. p.63, plate IX.

30. Spetner, L.M., F.Hoyle et al. Archaeopteryx: More evidence for a forgery. The British Journal of Photography (London) January 7, 1988, Vol.135, p.14-17.

31. Spetner, L.M. to I.Taylor August 30, 1989 private correspondence.

32. Gould, Stephen J. The Archaeopteryx Flap. Natural History (New York) September 1986, Vol.95, p.16-25.

33. Zittel, Karl A. Handbuch der Palaeontolgie. Muchen: R.Oldenbourg 1887-1890 (3 volumes) Vol.3, p.820.

34. Hurst, C.H. Biological theories: The Digits on a Birds Wing. Natural Science (London) October 1893, Vol.3, p.275-281.

35. Ibid. p.276.

36. Pyecraft, W.P. The Wing of Archaeopteryx. Natural Science (London) November 1894, Vol.5, p.350-60.

37. Heilmann, Gerhard. The Origin of Birds. London: Witherby 1926, p.32.

38. See reference 34, p.276.

39. Hurst, C.H. The Structure and Habits of Archaeopteryx. Natural Science (London) February 1895, Vol.6, p.112-122.

40. See reference 34, p.275.

41. Sanz, J.L., J.F. Bonapart et al. Unusual Early Cretaceous Birds from Spain. Nature (London) February 4, 1988, Vol.331, p.433-435.

42. Shipman, Pat. Sixth Find is a Feathered Friend. Discover (New York) January 1989, p.63.

43. See reference 14, p.1792.

44. Ostrom, John H. Archaeopteryx and the Origin of Birds. Biological Journal of the Linnean Soc. (London), June 1976, Vol.8, p.91-182.

45. Ibid p.138.

46. Ibid p.139.

47. Ibid p.138.

48. See reference 15, p.73.

49. See reference 44, p.123, and p.138.

50. See reference 15, p.60.

51. See reference 44, p.109 and ref.15, p.59-62.

52. See reference 15, p.73.

53. See reference 44, p.132.

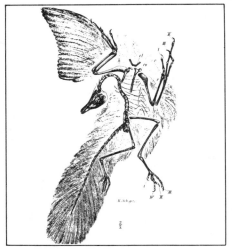

FIGURE 1.
Engraving after the Steinmann-Doderlein
drawing which appeared about 1884.
The right-wing was omitted. Cl=furcula.

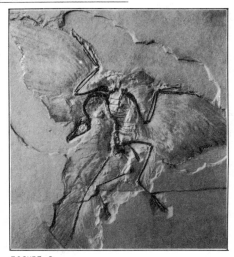

FIGURE 2.
Photograph of a plaster-cast of the
specimen as it is today and as it
appears in text-books.

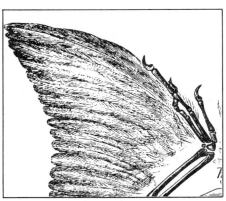

FIGURE 3.
Detail of the 1884 engraving showing
the Left-wing. h = humerus. Radius and
ulna = 'forearm'. Claws = the 'hand'.

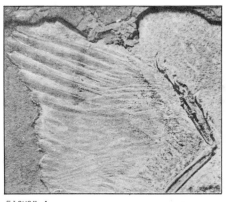

FIGURE 4.
Professor Hurst's 1893 photograph of
the left-wing. Note the primary feathers
at the top/left are virtually straight.

FIGURE 5.
Restoration of Compsognathus longipes
by Gerhard Heilmann [37] p.167.
About the size of a domestic cat.

Based mainly on the research of Hoyle and Spetner and the 1975/1976 opinion of J. H. Ostrom, Mr. Taylor concludes that the specimens of Archaeopteryx are hoaxes, and actually are specimens of Compsognathus. The argument, however, fails in many instances, for example the following:

As organisms turn into fossils, the minerals exactly around and inside the fossil usually become harder than the surroundings, because of the organic content in the buried animal or plant. That actually is one of the main reasons why we can find fossils - that the minerals in and close by the organisms get another structure than the surrounding material. Therefore, it is very possible that the minerals in the feather imprints have an another structure and composition than the surroundings. It would be mire peculiar if it was not so.

Furthermore, scientists have prepared this fossil for more than 100 years, and it would not be surprising if pieces of the slabs have been scraped away.

Moreover, there is no reason why the slab and counter slab need to have the same texture (as seen from the work of fossiliferous limestone). Also the 1884 picture does not necessarily have to look exactly the 1893 photograph, since scientists in working those days sometimes did not or could not make drawings/engravings that looked exactly as the original.

If Mr. Taylor examine the recent research surrounding this fossil, he will find that there is no reason to classify Archaeopteryx as Compsognathus (Hecht, et al, 1985; Haubitz, et al, 1988). Archaeopteryx has been carefully described as a diving bird using it's wings as the propelling agent, thus offering evidence as to why Archaeopteryx has been so carefully preserved in the sediments (Duffet, 1983). Archaeopteryx, does not fit in with evolutionary theory and the descriptions become more and more bird-like (Hecht, et al, 1985; Haubitz, et al, 1988).

REFERENCES:

Duffet, G., Archaeopteryx Lithographica Reconsidered, Biblical Creation Society, 1983.

Haubitz, et al, Computed Tomography of Archaeopteryx, Paleobiology, Vol. 14, 1988, pp. 206-213.

Hecht, et al, The Beginnings of Birds, Eichstatt, 1985, pp. 16-17, 26-28, 75-79, 149-160, 177-183, 211-215.

Mats Molen, M.S.
Umea, Sweden

Mr. Taylor has done a good job researching the status of the fossil Archaeopteryx. In particular, I commend him on his original findings regarding the Berlin specimen, which were unknown to me until he wrote me about it. He has written a good expository paper. Except for a few minor points of presentation, which I omit for lack of space, I offer the following remark:

Mr. Taylor said that the "claims that the specimen is a hoax have been examined and substantiated." As one who has been in the center of this controversy from the beginning, I can only say that I wish this statement were true, but unfortunately it is not. Upon examining about a milligram of material from a feathered area in the fossil and comparing it to a similar amount off the feathered area, we have found evidence pointing to a forgery. Had our findings been repeated on several more samples from the feathered and nonfeathered areas, the suspicion of a hoax would have been clearly established. As it is, however, the museum contends that the amorphous nature of feathered material is an artifact explainable by preservatives that they have put on the fossil. The clean appearance of the control sample could perhaps be explained by saying that the preservative did not get to the region from which that material was taken. An unequivocal substantiation of the suspicious of a hoax can only be arrived at with a similar examination of several samples from different places in the fossil. The British Museum, however, refuses to grant us any more material and refuses to make any tests themselves. Their attitude is frustrating and is cause for further suspicion, but it prevents us from coming to a unequivocal conclusion.

L.M. Spetner, Ph.D.
Trenton, New Jersey

This paper does not do justice to the efforts of the British Museum (Natural History) to respond to the charges of forgery. The definitive paper by Charig et al, (1986) receives only a brief mention, but it deserves to be repeatedly consulted in assessing the various claims. For example, the museum's prime evidences for the fossil being genuine are said to be twofold:

1) Matching hairline cracks containing natural crystals. The response to Spetner, cited by Mr. taylor misses the point here. The presence of natural crystalline material in the cracks shows that no surface covering has been deposited by a forger.

2) Matching dendritic patterns overlie the feather impressions. Charig et al (1986) have published photographs)Figure 3) showing a specific example. Hard evidence like this deserves more serious attention than that given by the author.

Mr. Taylor concludes that the skeletons are those of Compsognathus. there are a number of research papers which show that this is not the case, but their significance is not explored by the author. Palaeontological evidence must be addressed if the charge of forgery is to be seriously considered. The interpretations of Duffet, in his monograph Archaeopteryx Lithographica Reconsidered (Biblical Creation Society, 1983), is strongly recommended as an alternative to Mr. Taylor's approach.

The charge of forgery requires that the von Meyer feather be a case of "testing the market". Judging from the comments in this paper, substantial evidence to support this idea appears to be lacking.

David J. Tyler, M.S.
Chesire, England

Mr. Taylor's paper lacks both original research and a convincing argument for the artificiality of Archaeopteryx feathers. By my count, the author provides 15 evidences of forgery. Most of them can be adequately explained by the more parsimonious theory of authenticity as follows:

I.   Mr. Taylor's primary claim is that an 1877 photograph of the Berlin specimen differs from all subsequent photographs, thus documenting a distinct (artificial) change in the feather direction. In point of fact, the photographs the author showed at the conference demonstrate that his claim is incorrect. All the features of later photographs can be found in the photograph of 1877.
II.   2 of Mr. Taylor's evidences fail to cast any true suspicion on the specimens at all: (2) In spite of their age, the Archaeopteryx feathers happen to be some of the best-preserved feathers in the fossil record. This would not surprise a paleontologist who learns that all the specimens were from the Sohlenhofen limestone. The Sohlenhofen is one of the most famous "lagerstatten" in the world, containing some of the best fossils of a wide variety of organisms; and (3) Andreas Wagner, publishing in 1862, expressed serious doubts about the specimen. Wagner had done this without seeing the fossil. His objections seem to be entirely motivated by ideology, not observation.
III. 3 'evidences' are very common practices in 19th century paleontology, and lead us to be suspicious only from the perspective of the practices of 20th century paleontology: (4) Haberlein's desire to receive top dollar for his specimens; (5) Haberlein sold the Von Meyer slab and counterslab separately (for another example of how slabs and counterslabs were viewed in the past see S.J. Gould's Wonderful Life); and (6) Zittel's figure drawing alters (in fact, 'improves') the specimen.
IV.   3 can be adequately answered by a hypothesis of authenticity: (7) The London specimen's tail being in a low area on the slab without the corresponding raised area on the counterslab could simply be due to excavation of rock in the process of fossil preparation; (8) The feather-impressed, non-pure, gum-like piece on the counterslab of the London specimen might be the remnant of a cast taken of the specimen sometime in the past 130 years or so; and (9) The non-pure nature of the slab in the area of the wing might also be a result of impregnating chemicals from casting processes carried out over the last century or so.
V.   4 are claims given without sufficient data to evaluate their veracity: (10) The London specimen's furcula is 'strange'; (11) (Huxley's argument) The London specimen's furcula is 'up-side-down' and too large; (12) the Von Meyer slab is of a different texture than its counterslab; and (13) Darwin and Huxley both rejected the transitional nature of Archaeopteryx.
VI.   2 would be unexplained coincidences if the specimens were authentic, but are weak evidences because of their circumstantial nature: (14) the timing of the discoveries with the creation of the theories which needed them as proof; and (15) in the region where the fossils were found at the time of their discovery, fossil forgery is known to have been a common industry.

On the other hand, the two evidences for the authenticity of the London specimen given by the British Museum appear to have substantial merit: A) Unlike Mr. Taylor claims, in the photograph the author himself showed at the conference, dendrites do appear to overlie both the wing area and the adjacent slab and B) although, as Mr. Taylor claims, cracks can propagate through a specimen and overlying plaster as the specimen is being prepared, the British Museum claims that 'natural crystals' can be found in the crack. In my experience, 'natural crystals' do not form in cracks <u>after</u> excavation.

Mr. Taylor's paper not only lacks compelling evidence to demonstrate the artificiality of Archaeopteryx feather impressions, but presents sufficient evidence to argue for their authenticity.

Kurt P. Wise, Ph.D.
Dayton, Tennessee

CLOSURE

I would like to express thanks to Mr. Mats Molen, Dr. Lee Spetner, Mr. David Tyler, and especially Dr. Kurt Wise for taking the time to respond to my paper. While none of us, including Dr. Wise, will ever have the opportunity to carry out original research work on the precious specimens, my thesis is based upon those who have and quotes by chapter and verse have been given. With the single exception of Dr. Spetner, who has examined the London specimen and has left convinced that it is a hoax, the remarks of the other respondents fall into the category of arm-chair speculation. In answer to Mr. Molen objections, firstly, we would expect both genuine fossil and a fake to have different textures from their matrix so this is not definitive. However, the fact that "shrinkage cracks" occur only in the London and Berlin specimens and then only in those areas which it is believed have been tampered with and not, for example, around the head, set these specimens apart for suspicion. Secondly, Heilmann (Ref. 37) who did examine the specimens, gives an exhaustive list of characteristics which identifies the Archaeopteryx with the Compsognathus and makes the claims of Hecht et al that it was a diving bird look like a poor attempt to explain away a creature having modern feathers but no sternum. Duffet mentioned Heilmann's work but he seems to have missed the significance of:

  a) The unusual number of similarities with the Compsognathus.

  b) The reclassifications of more recent specimens including that of the Eichstadt Compsognathus.

Mr. Tyler focussed upon the matching hairline cracks and the matching dendrites in slab and counter-slab of the London specimen and it can only be assumed that my treatment of these objections given in points (e) and (f) was insufficient. That hair-line cracks perpendicular to the cleavage plane undoubtedly existed for centuries during which time mineral crystals formed within them. After cleavage to expose the fossil, it is proposed that a thin layer of cement spread over the surface would initially cover the cracks like snow over a crevasse. Elementary rules of fracture mechanics tell us that the cracks would act as stress raisers and with time and tensile stresses, these cracks would propagate through the thin layer of cement. This is exactly what happens with re-plastered walls. As far as the dendrite claim is concerned, I suggest we accept the observations of Dr. Spetner who points out that the claims of the British Museum are "simply fraudulent". It should be borne in mind that we shall never see, nor has the public ever seen, the slab counter-slab on display together.

Dr. Wise has diligently counted 15 evidences of forgery in my paper without evidence of having actually read it! This is not only cause for suspicion regarding the authenticity of the two specimens but also suggests that this reader may be blinded by commitment to another faith. Furthermore, Dr. Wise has missed entirely the most serious claim. Does he know the attachment point of primary feathers in the modern bird? They attach to the manus or hand whereas in today's photographs of the Berlin specimen they are bent, some 40 degrees, and attach to the ulna. Apart from seriously bent feathers being useless for flight, both the engraving of 1884 and modern photographs show these features very clearly. In contrast, the photographs of Hurst (1893) and another taken a few years earlier by Carl Vogt, show the primary feathers are straight and originate in the manus area. And this is not my opinion but that of Professor Dames who described the specimen in 1884. Then again, in 1894, Dr. Pyecraft of the British Museum built a case based upon the straight primary feathers of the Berlin specimen originating from the manus and provided detailed drawings showing how modern feathers attach to the same area. All this was carefully documented in my paper and every relevant illustration reproduced during the lecture. Dr. Wise's claim (b), that the london and Berlin specimens have the best preserved feathers because they originated in the Solnhofen limestone utterly fails to explain why the Maxberg specimen, found at the London specimen site, or the Eichstadt and Solnhofen specimens, found at the Berlin specimen site do not contain even the vestige of a feather. The argument simply heaps more suspicion upon the already suspect specimens. I trust discerning readers will see through the remaining equally tendentious arguments without space having to be taken to so in this reply.

Ian Taylor, B.S.

A TECTONICALLY-CONTROLLED ROCK CYCLE

David J. Tyler, M.S.

ABSTRACT

A rock cycle is proposed, in which geological processes of erosion, deposition and metamorphism are primarily controlled by vertical movements of crustal blocks. This rock cycle is considered to provide a framework for the scientific study of catastrophic episodes of Earth history.

INTRODUCTION

Geological texts on sedimentary petrology generally reveal a strong preference for adopting 'modern analogues'. Most will give detailed descriptions of a wide range of modern sedimentary environments. Fluvial deposits include those laid down by meandering and braided rivers and by alluvial fans. Sedimentation in other terrestrial environments involve erosion and deposition in deserts and in glacial areas. On the continental margins are found more varied sites of deposition: deltas, coasts, shorelines, siliclastic shelf seas and carbonate shelf seas. Deep sea environments have abyssal plain sedimentation and the input of clastics via submarine fans. These categories are familiar to all sedimentologists, the majority of whom would say they are directly applicable to most ancient environments. The underlying philosophy here is that 'the present is the key to the past'. The approach of most textbooks and working sedimentologists is governed by a deeply held commitment to a philosophy known as Lyellian Uniformitarianism.

It should be noted that the textbooks mirror the teaching practice in almost all university courses on sedimentary geology. One must ask whether it is right for students to be steered so early in their studies towards a wholesale adoption of modern analogues for the interpretation of ancient rocks? The contemporary trend in geology is away from Lyellian Uniformitarianism, and there is a growing recognition that the present-day norms are not the key to the past. Thus, Ager (1) writes:

> In other words, we have allowed ourselves to be brainwashed into avoiding any interpretation of the past that involves extreme and what may be termed 'catastrophic' processes. However, it seems to me that the stratigraphical record is full of examples of processes that are far from 'normal' in the usual sense of the word. In particular we must conclude that SEDIMENTATION IN THE PAST HAS OFTEN BEEN VERY RAPID INDEED AND VERY SPASMODIC. This may be called the Phenomenon of the Catastrophic Nature of much of the Stratigraphical Record (pp.46-47).

> In other words, the history of any one part of the earth, like the life of a soldier, consists of long periods of boredom and short periods of terror (pp.106--107).

The problem that must be addressed by all sedimentary geologists is that of organising ideas into a coherent whole. A framework for study is required - and this is all too conveniently provided by contemporary patterns of erosion and deposition. The picture is encapsulated in the conventional 'rock cycle' which was first developed by James Hutton, sometimes referred to as the 'Father of Geology'. The influence of his particular contribution to the study of historical geology is difficult to overestimate. It appears to have dominated the thinking of all the Nineteenth Century geologists, including catastrophists like Cuvier, Buckland and Miller, and it is the unquestioned orthodoxy of Twentieth Century geology. Yet Hutton's thinking was rooted in a marriage of Empiricist philosophy and Deism and, contrary to popular opinion, was not a product of extensive field study (2,3,4).

Since the Huttonian rock cycle invokes present-day processes, it is foundational to Lyellian Uniformitarianism. It is suggested here that the continuing dominance of Lyellian geology is because no real challenge has ever been made to the Huttonian rock cycle. Geology students are introduced to this cycle at the outset of their studies, so that their mindset is established. Since few question the foundations of their chosen subject, this early exposure to uniformitarian concepts ensures that all subsequent views are coloured by it.

In recent years, the role of tectonic processes in the formation of sediments has been recognised and given more prominence. To take one example: few students of English geology will be unaware of the Alston and Askrigg blocks in the Pennines. Tectonic movements of these blocks are invoked to explain observed patterns of sedimentation. In some instances, evidences for synsedimentary faulting are present, showing even more clearly that tectonic activity and sedimentary processes are linked. Tectonic features and catastrophic events are now quite widely recognised, but are still fitted into the framework dictated by the Huttonian rock cycle (5).

This paper is an attempt to describe a rock cycle that is dominated by tectonically-controlled processes. This new model provides for the "short periods of terror" as described by Ager, but has little provision for the "long periods of boredom". These long ages of geological time are essential for evolutionary theories but are not necessarily required by the rock record. Figure 1 provides an overview of the proposed rock cycle. In the interests of brevity, the processes are outlined below without extensive elaboration.

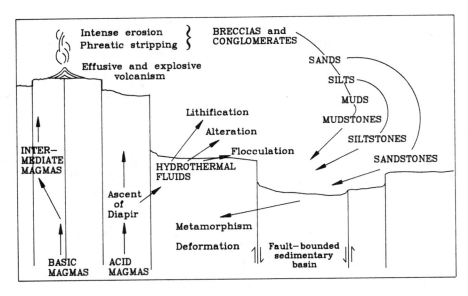

Figure 1. A tectonically-controlled rock cycle.

IGNEOUS PROCESSES

Basic and Intermediate Rocks

In this model, basic magmas originate by partial melting of upper mantle ultra-basic rocks. Since these magmas have low viscosity, they are able to move rapidly through faults and other conduits in the Earth's crust towards the surface. Fractional crystallisation of basic magma leads to the formation of magma of intermediate composition. If conditions are suitable, magmas emerge on the Earth's surface to form volcanoes, lava flows and lava sheets.

Acid Rocks

Acid rocks are considered here to have a source separate from that of basic and intermediate rocks. In this model, they derive from the partial melting of pre-existent continental crust. The magmas are highly viscous and are not able to move easily up conduits by convective flow. Consequently, these magmas form large diapirs at depth. Their vertical movements are described by Stokes Law:

$$V = \frac{2\,r^2\,g\,\Delta\rho}{9\,\eta} \qquad\qquad (1)$$

V = velocity of rise of diapir (ms^{-1})
r = radius of diapir (m)
g = acceleration due to gravity (ms^{-2})
$\Delta\rho$ = density difference between diapir and crustal rocks (kgm^{-3})
η = dynamic viscosity (Pas)

Using g = 10ms^{-2}, $\Delta\rho$ = 300kgm^{-3}, η = 10^{12}Pas, and a diapir radius of 2 km, a molten granite mass will pass through the whole of the Earth's crust in less than half a year. Larger diapirs are even faster. The situation is certainly complicated by the loss of heat energy by contact with the country rock, although this cooling effect is likely to reduce the size of a diapir rather than its temperature. Consequently, it is possible for a magma body to reach the surface soon after it is formed. Since many granitic diapirs appear to have had considerable amounts of water dissolved in them, solidification before reaching the surface is anticipated. However, in a typical case, upward forces would still act on the body so that it would continue to rise, resulting in the elevation of a tectonic block and the generation of innumerable fissures. These fissures have an important role to play in the subsequent convective cooling of the pluton, as is explained in the following sub-section. If the pluton is near the surface when it solidifies, it may continue to rise tectonically and introduce much faulting, fracturing and folding in the overlying strata. Granitic diapirs that actually reach the surface produce large volumes of ash fall and ash flow tuffs and also rhyolite flows. Magmatic fluids expelled from solidifying magmas are responsible for the formation of pegmatites and hydrothermal vein deposits. The escaping fraction of these liquids may provide chemicals which influence contemporaneous sedimentation and diagenetic processes.

Convective Cooling of Large Magma Bodies

Most calculations of cooling rates for large magma bodies assume that conductive energy heat loss predominates. The country rocks are considered to be dry, with gentle temperature gradients, so that cooling timescales extend over hundreds of thousands or millions of years. However, recent observations at the mid-ocean ridges indicate that, under certain conditions, convective heat loss is of major importance.

Exploration of the ocean floor in the vicinity of the mid-oceanic ridges has revealed the presence of hydrothermal vents and dependent ecological systems (6). Hot rocks under the mid-ocean ridges are being cooled extremely efficiently by the large-scale movements of sea-water through the basaltic ocean crust. At an East Pacific Rise location, some black smoker vents had water temperatures of about 350 degrees centigrade and discharge velocities of 2-3 metres per second. Macdonald et al. (7) demonstrate that the convective energy loss from one small black smoker is approximately the same as that from conduction through a 60 kilometre square of the Earth's surface. The vents are short-lived because they are so efficient: convective heat flow slows when the source rocks are cooled. Further useful discussion is provided by Cann and Stiens (8).

It would appear realistic to infer large-scale convective cooling for all magma bodies in contact with groundwaters where the country rocks permit circulation. It is necessary to investigate whether convective cooling has played a significant part in the cooling of continental plutonic rocks. Parmentier and Schedl (9) have considered the thermal aureoles of the Mull intrusive complex, the Skye Cuillin gabbro, and the El Salvador porphry copper deposits. The shapes of the metamorphic aureoles are inconsistent with purely conductive heat loss but can be explained by invoking convective activity. Recent reports from the Soviet Union deep drilling project (10) have revealed the presence of considerable volumes of water at depths previously thought impossible because of the high pressures exerted by overlying rocks. With water existing at depths of up to 12 kilometres, the opportunities for invoking convective cooling are greatly extended. In the tectonically-controlled rock cycle, the magma bodies themselves are considered to produce fractures in the country rock, thus permitting a freer circulation of waters at depth.

Crystal Growth in Magmatic Liquids

It is widely believed that coarse-grained granites and gabbros have had a very slow cooling history. This sub-section suggests that this belief is inferred and is not warranted by experimental and theoretical research programmes into the topic.

Most of the information on the petrology of igneous rocks is in the form of phase diagrams applicable to magmas in an equilibrium state. Before 1975, experiments on the rates of crystal growth were exceedingly few. An excellent summary of relevant work is provided by Dowty (11). Two factors are of major importance: rates of nucleation and rates of crystal growth.

Experimental work to determine nucleation rates is extremely difficult. Most of the relevant studies have reported nucleation densities to provide a basis for comparing minerals measured by the same investigator. Lofgren (12) has concluded that nucleation behaviour is more important than crystal growth rates in producing various mineral features and rock textures.

Crystal growth rates have been measured, mostly for single-component melts. Maximum growth rates for common minerals are of the order of 1×10^{-5} centimetres per second. Water in the melt tends to decrease growth rates; multiple-component melts tend to have smaller crystal growth rates than single-component melts. More realistic figures appear to be of the order of 1×10^{-7} centimetres per second, obtained in studies of wet granitic melts.

Whilst maximum cooling times may not be inferred from studies of this kind, it is possible to comment on minimum cooling times. The number of seconds in one year is 3.15×10^{7}, which should be compared with the crystal growth rates of wet granitic melts. Timescales of 1 - 10 years might be considered realistic minimum cooling times. A comment by Luth (13) provides a fitting conclusion:
> It is frequently assumed that the presence of large crystals in these phases implies slow growth over long periods of time. Although this may be the case, the intent here is to demonstrate that it does not necessarily hold (p. 405).

EROSION AND DEPOSITION PROCESSES

Both volcanic and plutonic activity lead to intense weathering of surface rocks. Elevation of crustal blocks because of igneous activity at depth increases precipitation and erosion. Volcanic dust introduced to the atmosphere provides nuclei for condensation and seeds torrential rainfall and flash flooding. In a situation where vast quantities of heat energy are released, evaporation of water occurs readily and the hydrological cycle is intensified. Since the uplifted ground is full of joints, cracks and faults because of tectonic movements, it can be weathered swiftly and the debris transported to lower altitudes. Extensive deposits of alluvial fan breccias and conglomerates around mountainous regions testify of such abnormally erosive processes operating in the past. Examples include the fanglomerates around the Troodos Mountains of Cyprus and the Molasse deposits of the Alps.

Continuing transport of materials by rivers and oceanic waters leads to the winnowing and sorting of sediments into sands, silts and muds. Weathering of minerals is both physical and chemical, and both may be intense. Chemical weathering may be further promoted by the presence of fluids of volcanic origin. A considerable proportion of clay minerals may be derived from volcanic ash (14).

An additional catastrophic mechanism for erosion is provided by phreatic stripping. Hot igneous bodies emplaced at depth initiate the circulation of groundwaters. The water temperatures will generally exceed 100 degrees Centigrade because of the pressure exerted by the overburden. So, around a magma body, a shroud of superheated water develops. A sudden release in pressure may lead to remarkable effects. Initially, some super-heated water changes into steam which instantly seeks to occupy a much greater volume. The resultant high pressure physically lifts the overburden and forms fractures through which steam can escape. However, this is but the start of an avalanche process, as continuing vapourisation of superheated water leads to a violent explosion. The overburden, together with all the sediments containing the superheated water, is erupted into the atmosphere. In this way, large volumes of water-permeated materials may be stripped away from above a hot pluton.

Probably the best examples of the phreatic stripping mechanism are found in Yellowstone National Park in the USA. At least ten craters in the Park, ranging in diameter from a few tens of metres to about 170 metres, were identified as hydrothermal explosion craters by Muffler et al (15). Subsequently, Mary Bay in Yellowstone Lake, with a diameter in excess of 2.5 kilometres, was added to the list by Wold et al (16). Explosions have been associated with the waning stages of a glacial period and the following mechanism has been suggested. It is thought that an ice-dammed lake existed over a hydrothermal system. The waters permeating the unconsolidated sediments were superheated, but the situation was stable because of the confining pressure. When the dam broke because of the ablating ice-field, the lake was drained rapidly, reducing the pressure on the hydrothermal system. At a critical moment, some of the superheated water flashed to steam, violently disrupting the water-logged sediments, further reducing the pressure and initiating a run-away explosion. The debris ejected from Mary Bay may be inspected readily in sections created by road cuttings. Additional examples of hydrothermal explosion craters have been reported from California, Nevada, New Zealand and Italy (15).

In the Global Flood cataclysm, all the ingredients of hydrothermal explosions are present, but on a much grander scale. Wet sediments overlying hot magma bodies may be removed catastrophically when tectonic movements reduce the confining pressures exerted by floodwaters.

Tectonic processes not only influence patterns of erosion, but also patterns of deposition. Sedimentary basins are formed by the lowering of tectonic blocks. These basins may develop as graben-like structures, with fault movements linked to igneous activity. A further mechanism is provided by the collapse of the Fountains of the Great Deep during the Global Flood (17). Movements of sediment into these fault-bounded basins are not normally considered seriously by the advocates of Lyellian uniformitarianism. However, this model of catastrophic sedimentation provides a framework for interpreting such distinctive features as good lateral persistence of beds, abrupt transitions between beds, regular and thick bed thicknesses, constant orientation of bedding planes, and planar unconformities.

The features described above are well displayed in the classic Grand Canyon sections. The difficulty for the Huttonian rock cycle approach to interpretation is that present day processes fail to do justice to these evidences. Modern environments do not lead to these large-scale distinctive features. Ample scope exists for non-uniformitarian depositional models for Grand Canyon rocks. Catastrophic mechanisms will need to be adopted in order to transport sedimentary material on a different scale to that occurring in the present day. This is not to imply that it is of little value to study modern-day environments, but it does mean that they should no longer be regarded as the key to the past. Rather, interests should be developed in different modern analogues, as are found in catastrophic events, and in what they can achieve (18). It means looking at scaling factors, so that catastrophic processes can be brought within the orbit of scientific analysis.

The widespread occurrence of cyclicity in sedimentary rock units has provided many puzzles for traditional gradualistic models of sedimentation. To account for the field evidences, sedimentologists have found it necessary to propose quite complex, and often contrived, patterns of erosion, deposition and base-level changes. A vigorous challenge to this approach has been made by Goodwin and Anderson (19), who have cast aside overtly the old paradigm and have boldly proposed an alternative. Their hypothesis of punctuated aggradational cycles (PAC) focuses attention, not on a localised area of deposition, but on the sedimentary basin considered as a whole. Base-level changes affecting the basin affect all the sedimentary processes taking place within the basin. This model is one which has considerable explanatory power and deserves extensive discussion. Of the mechanisms considered by Goodwin and Anderson, one is particularly relevant to the tectonically-controlled rock cycle: episodic crustal movements. Catastrophic events in the history of the Earth provide a framework for further developing the PAC hypothesis.

Other features of the rock record which seem particularly suited to catastrophic interpretations include the mixing of sediments of different character (eg sandstones and limestones), syndepositional faulting, and turbidic sedimentation (20).

Within the tectonically-controlled rock cycle model, sedimentation occurs relatively fast. Even muds may be rapidly deposited, as flocculation rates increase with the density of clay particles and also with the presence of salt.

Disturbed ecosystems must ensue from these catastrophic processes. The depositional environments envisaged provide ideal sites for the preservation of body fossils, trace fossils and sedimentary structures. Rupke's (21) discussion of ephemeral markings provides a useful starting point for studies of these transient features and their implications for cataclysmal deposition. There is no doubt that a great variety of organisms have left behind them evidences of moving and feeding behaviour which are often beautifully preserved for scientific investigation. Whereas most studies of trace fossils attempt to use modern analogues to interpret past environments and ecosystems, there seems to be ample scope for innovative investigation. For example, Brand (22) has used evidence from vertebrate footprints to challenge the conventional view that the Coconino Sandstone exposed in the Grand Canyon was formed by aeolian deposition. The writer (23) has studied limulid trace fossils in the Bude Formation of south-west England and concluded that a catastrophic scenario is far more appropriate than the previously-held consensus that the assemblage represents a "sea-level lake community".

DIAGENETIC AND POST-DEPOSITIONAL PROCESSES

If sedimentation is rapid, compaction and dewatering of sediments must take place much faster than is customarily thought. Contemporaneous igneous activity releases volcanic fluids, particularly siliceous fluids, which help to cement the particles together. Other waters carrying calcium carbonate in solution are circulated by convection currents associated with hot intrusions, and these waters provide cementation with calcite. In some cases, such cementation can be proved to have taken place rapidly - as in coal balls. Similar reasoning leads to the conclusion that iron-carrying solutions were able to produce ironstones of varying kinds soon after sediment deposition. Rapid cementation and preservation of fish tissues in a phosphate-rich matrix is reported for Brazilian fishes (24).

Post-depositional deformation may occur while the sediments are still only partially lithified. It is quite possible that soft-sediment deformation over short timescales rather than consolidated rock deformation over long timescales (creep) is the norm in mountain belts.

This tectonically-controlled rock cycle opens the door for a fresh look at metamorphic processes. These are traditionally viewed as taking place over vast ages of time, primarily because of the Huttonian constraints on temperature and pressure changes. However, tectonic blocks may be dropped deep down into the Earth's crust, allowing deformation under high pressures, contact with hot rocks, and convective movements of superheated water (carried down with the tectonic block). Since water facilitates most geochemical changes, there are many possibilities here for reinterpreting metamorphic episodes. The timescales in metamorphic petrology are not determined primarily by rates of reactions, which can be studied over short periods in petrology laboratories. Rather, the timescales are associated with interpretations of slow changes of pressure and temperature, which are not part of this new rock cycle.

This view of rapid vertical movements of crustal blocks also provides a framework for reinterpreting both the processes of mountain-building and the formation of extensive overthrusts. The role of crustal block movements in the creation of mountain belts warrants serious investigation.

Many nappes are devoid of roots and their formation is a mystery within geology dominated by Lyellian uniformitarianism. A catastrophist geology, incorporating rapid vertical movements of tectonic blocks, does not have these problems. Gravity sliding of nappes, with water lubrication to explain the undisturbed nature of the thrust planes (25), seems to provide a feasible explanation of their origin.

Butler's review (26) of the subject area acknowledges major problems with conventional views, but points out important evidence that nappes are tectonically emplaced, and were not deposited in their current positions. Much diluvialist thinking has neglected this evidence, concentrating on the character of the contact planes at the expense of the evidence taken as a whole. The writer's view is that nappes do exist and are best explained using catastrophic mechanisms.

SUMMARY

A new rock cycle is proposed, in which tectonic processes control the formation, erosion, deposition and alteration of crustal materials. This rock cycle is inherently catastrophic, demanding short time-scales for geologic activity. Many of the concepts employed (tectonic blocks, fault-bounded sedimentary basins, synsedimentary faulting, diapiric rise of acid rocks, etc) are familiar to geologists today, but here they are given a more prominent role. Other concepts are incorporated which are not recognised by contemporary geologists (rapid rise of diapirs, phreatic stripping, cyclicity as an evidence of tectonic control, rapid metamorphic episodes, catastrophic overthrusting, etc). Nevertheless, within the tectonic framework that has been described, these concepts show coherence and possess considerable explanatory power.

If catastrophic geology is to develop as a science, it must show evidence of being able to handle field data in an orderly and systematic way. It is hoped that the tectonically--controlled rock cycle will assist this development.

REFERENCES

1. Ager, D.V., THE NATURE OF THE STRATIGRAPHICAL RECORD, 2nd ed., Macmillan Press Ltd., 1981.
2. O'Rourke, J.E., "A comparison of James Hutton's Principles of Knowledge and Theory of the Earth", ISIS, 69(246), 1978, 5-20.
3. Gould, S.J., TIME'S ARROW, TIME'S CYCLE, Harvard University Press, 1987.
4. Tyler, D.J., "Religious presuppositions in historical science", ORIGINS, 3(7), 1989, 13-16.

5. Gould, S.J., "Toward the vindication of punctuational change", In: Berggren, W.A. and Van Couvering, J.A. (Eds), CATASTROPHES AND EARTH HISTORY, New Jersey: Princeton University Press, 1984, 9-34.

6. Macdonald, K.C. and Luyendyk, B.P., "The crest of the East Pacific Rise", SCIENTIFIC AMERICAN, 244(5), 1981, 86-99.

7. Macdonald, K.C., Becker, K., Spiess, F.N. and Ballard, R.D., "Hydrothermal heat flux of the "Black Smoker" vents on the East Pacific Rise", EARTH AND PLANETARY SCIENCE LETTERS, 48, 1980, 1-7.

8. Cann, J.R. and Stiens, M.R., "Black smokers fuelled by freezing magma", NATURE, 298(8 July), 1982, 147-149.

9. Parmentier, E.M. and Schedl, A., "Thermal aureoles of igneous intrusions: some possible indications of hydrothermal convective cooling", JOURNAL OF GEOLOGY, 89, 1981, 1-22.

10. Yardley, B.W.D., "Is there water in the deep continental crust?", NATURE, 323(11 September), 1986, 111.

11. Dowty, E., "Crystal growth and nucleation theory and the numerical simulation of igneous crystallisation", In: Hargreaves, R.B. (Ed), PHYSICS OF MAGMATIC PROCESSES, New Jersey: Princeton University Press, 1980, 419-485.

12. Lofgren, G., "Experimental studies on the dynamic crystallization of silicate melts", In: Hargreaves, R.B. (Ed), PHYSICS OF MAGMATIC PROCESSES, New Jersey: Princeton University Press, 1980, 487-551.

13. Luth, W.C., "Granitic rocks", In: Bailey, D.K. and Macdonald, R. (Eds), THE EVOLUTION OF THE CRYSTALLINE ROCKS, London: Academic Press, 1976, 333-417.

14. Snelling, A. and Mackay, J., "Coal, volcanism and Noah's Flood", EN TECH.J., 1, 1984, 11-29.

15. Muffler, L.J.P., White, D.E. and Truesdell, A.H., "Hydrothermal explosion craters in Yellowstone National Park", GEOLOGICAL SOCIETY OF AMERICA BULLETIN, 82(March), 1971, 723-740.

16. Wold, R.J., Mayhew, M.A. and Smith, R.B., "Bathymetric and geophysical evidence for a hydrothermal explosion crater in Mary Bay, Yellowstone Lake, Wyoming", JOURNAL OF GEOPHYSICAL RESEARCH, 82(26), 1977, 3733-3738.

17. Scheven, J., "The interpretation of fossils and the Principle of Actualism", BIBLICAL CREATION, 7(18), 1984, 5-19.

18. Baker, V.R. and Costa, J.E., "Flood power", In: Mayer, L. and Nash, D. (Eds), CATASTROPHIC FLOODING, Boston: Allen & Unwin, 1987, 1-21.

19. Goodwin, P.W. and Anderson, E.J., "Punctuated aggradational cycles: a general hypothesis of episodic stratigraphic accumulation", JOURNAL OF GEOLOGY, 93(5), 1985, 515-533.

20. Tyler, D.J., "Flood Geology and the formation of turbidites", In: SCIENCE AT THE CROSSROADS: OBSERVATION OR SPECULATION?, Onesimus Publishing, 1985, 79-81.

21. Rupke, N.A., "Prolegomena to a study of cataclysmal sedimentation", In: Lammerts, W.E (Ed), WHY NOT CREATION?, Nutley: Presbyterian and Reformed Publishing Co., 1970, 141-179.

22. Brand, L., "Field and laboratory studies on the Coconino Sandstone (Permian) vertebrate footprints and their paleoecological implications", PALAEOGEOGRAPHY, PALAEOCLIMATOLOGY, PALAEOECOLOGY, 28, 1979, 25-38.

23. Tyler, D.J., "Evidence and significance of limulid instars from trackways in the Bude Formation (Westphalian), south-west England", PROCEEDINGS OF THE USSHER SOCIETY, 7(1), 1988, 77-80.

24. Martill, D.M., "Preservation of fish in the cretaceous Santana Formation of Brazil", PALAEONTOLOGY, 31(1), 1988, 1-18.

25. Gretener, P.E., "On the character of thrust faults with particular reference to basal tongues", BULLETIN OF CANADIAN PETROLEUM GEOLOGY, 25(1), 1977, 110-122.

26. Butler, R.W.H., "Thrust tectonics: A personal view", GEOLOGICAL MAGAZINE, 122(3), 1985, 223-232.

Mr. Tyler takes an innovative approach to the "rock cycle" explaining it in terms of cata-strophic tectonics and processes which can be understood to proceed from catastrophic tectonics. This pioneering study will no doubt stimulate interest in exploring the implications for plutonism, metamorphism, erosion, sedimentation and lithification. The author displays his wide experience with the subjects being discussed. The notion of convective cooling of plutons is central to tectonically induced diapiric processes. It would merit a separate paper. The concept of catastrophic erosion by phreatic stripping is a valuable addition to catastrophist theory. It should be investigated in a later study. Perhaps the best way to test the theory of the rock cycle suggested by Mr. Tyler would be with specific application to a region of the earth's crust. I look forward to application of the theory presented in this paper.

Steven A. Austin, Ph.D.
Santee, California

This paper by Mr. Tyler includes many interesting and important discussions and observations. My questions regarding the author's paper are:

1) Does the equation on diapirism (Stoke's Law) really work for melted lava or solid rocks in the earth's crust?

2) What about the possibility that the equation is only valid for small scale experiments, in the laboratory, in liquid media?

Mats Molen, M.S.
Umea, Sweden

A delusion of almost two centuries' standing is struck here at its roots. The enormity of the Huttonian error is just beginning to dawn on contemporary geologists. This is witnessed by allusions to "event" or "spasmodic" occurrences in geology scattered through the more recent literature although all the while interspersed with vitriolic remarks for those who are committed to the construction of a scientific framework of biblical earth history. In "organizing ideas into a coherent whole" the author has built his case on the revealed facts about the former conditions on our planet and the changes triggered off by the Flood. He has thus succeeded in an area of model-building where many luminaries of geology have failed. The evidence for the rapid cementation of sediments can be amplified by referring to fossils, and the ensuing problem for uniformitarian geology may be even more acute than creationists are aware of. The lithification of buried organisms, i.e. the change from organic to inorganic compounds without loss of form, has so far withstood all attempts at experimental repetition and is likely to continue outside the realm of phenomena that are scientifically explicable.

Joachim Scheven, Ph.D.
Hagen, Germany

Mr. Tyler's paper is an exciting and valuable contribution to flood geology. Hutton's rock cycle with its explicit requirements of "deep time" has persisted in geology for over two hundred years — virtually without challenge. The author's tectonically-controlled rock cycle may well be the needed challenge to Huttonian geology from catastrophist geology.

Upper mantle viscosity seems to be too high to allow deformation or motion to occur on the time scales necessary (month/days) for this model (isostatic rebound is thought to take 1000's to 10's of thousands of years.) How does Mr. Tyler explain the necessary motions at depth?

If basic/intermediate rocks & acidic rocks have distinct origins, how does one account for the continuous range of igneous rock composition? Would not this model predict a rarity (if not an absence) of rocks between intermediate & acidic composition? Are the predictions borne out be evidence?

Why did such a cycle only occur during one episode in earth history? What causes are necessary and sufficient to initiate it? (i.e. what would have initiated the partial melting of the mantle and crustal rocks?) What caused the cycle to stop? (i.e. what terminated the partial melting?)

Kurt P. Wise, Ph.D.
Bryan, Tennessee

Dr. Austin is thanked for his comments. The tectonically-controlled rock cycle is intended to provide a framework for interpreting field evidences and, if it does not lead to further papers on the subjects of convective cooling of plutons, phreatic stripping and regional case studies, I will not have achieved my objectives. In geological circles, one often hears people speaking of the impact of new ways of thinking: "We didn't see it because we were not looking for it — but now we're thinking in this new way, we have no difficulty finding examples of it in the field!" This my own experience with the tectonically-controlled rock cycle, and it is my hope that many others will find it useful.

Mr. Molen's specific questions relate to my use of Stokes' Law to describe the flow of magmas though the solid crust of the Earth. Insofar as the crustal rocks have a measurable viscosity, the equation can be applied. The main doubts concern (a) the magnitude of the dynamic viscosity of the crustal rocks, and (b) the onset of brittle fracture and fault movements as the diapir approaches the Earth's surface. The value of viscosity I have used is non-controversial among the geological community, so the case for catastrophism cannot be lightly dismissed. The second question is one which must be considered at quite a different level. It concerns the application of a physical law to a situation where it has not been proved in laboratory experiments. The sciences of Physics and Chemistry have developed with the assumption that laws which are discovered may be applied generally to physical and chemical phenomena. It is wise to be open to the possibility that physical laws may be inapplicable outside the context of their proven validity but, in any particular case, experimental evidence should be sought to provide some test of the theory.

I am grateful for Dr. Scheven's remarks. We live at an exciting time when catastrophic ideas are making headway in the geological literature. However, most thinking continues to be locked into traditional timescales and catastrophic events are perceived as intermittent and fragmentary punctuations of the general calm. Consequently, there is little opportunity for catastrophism to provide a unifying framework for geological interpretations. This is one intellectual reason why resistance to flood geology concepts continues to be so strong even among neo-catastrophists. Only by discarding the rigid timescale for the formation of the different strata can justice be done to the field evidences, and only by anchoring our thinking to the biblical framework of history can we avoid floundering about in a sea of chaotic scenarios.

Dr. Wise's comments on the significance of this challenge to Huttonian geology are encouraging. So much of geological thinking is paradigm-dependent, and yet this is rarely appreciated without the advantages of viable alternative frameworks for theoretical ideas. I am sure this is true of upper mantle viscosity estimates, where the values associated with the various parameters do not appear to be independent of conventional timescales. There are various ways of responding to the point that upper mantle viscosities seem to be too high. The vertical movements of crustal plates, proposed in the tectonically-controlled rock cycle commits itself to any mechanisms of mountain building and plutonic activity. The tectonic framework is one which has been inferred from the field evidences: mapping of major vertical movements, analysis of sediments adjacent to the fault boundaries produced during movement of the tectonic blocks, the character of inter-block sediments, seismic reflection data, etc. Nevertheless, it has been argued that one mechanism for the rapid vertical movements of crustal rocks is diapirism, and this mechanism has no requirement for unusual mantle viscosities.

Regarding the prediction that rocks of intermediate composition are less prevalent than basic and acidic rocks, this is a fair reflection of the field data with which I am familiar.

The remaining questions are concerned with the causes of catastrophism, which are undoubtedly of great interest. However, it is my argument that it is not necessary to identify specific causes in order to work on a science of catastrophic processes. I am confident that Biblical history gives us the framework within which we can make progress, but there would appear to be considerable scope for alternative ideas on the technical details of cause and effect in global catastrophes.

David J. Tyler, M.S.

THE MECHANISM OF ICE CRYSTAL GROWTH
AND THE THEORY OF EVOLUTION

Larry Vardiman, Ph.D.
Institute for Creation Research
San Diego, California

ABSTRACT

Ice crystal growth has been cited as an example of how evolution creates greater order. The modern explanation of ice crystal shape is described. The *second law of thermodynamics* is developed in terms of entropy change and applied to ice crystal growth. The difference between the *operation* of thermodynamic systems and their *origin* is discussed. It is concluded that ice crystal growth is similar to the *operation* of life processes but does not support the *origin* of life as described by the theory of evolution.

INTRODUCTION

Johannes Kepler, the yet-to-be famous astronomer, presented a unique New Year's gift to his patron in the winter of 1611. The scientist gave his benefactor a witty, reasoned discussion on why snowflakes (more precisely, ice crystals) have six corners. Since microscopes and diffraction instruments had not yet been invented, no one really knew why crystals took the shapes they did. Kepler [1] argued for the development of external shapes in crystals by the filling of three-dimensional space with atoms in various packing arrangements. He used analogies such as stacked cannon balls, bee hives, and packing of other geometric shapes. Since he was unable to convince himself that the internal structure produced the external shapes, Kepler concluded that there is a *formative faculty* which maintains six-cornered shapes. For his efforts to understand the cause of crystal shapes and his arguments which almost resulted in an explanation of crystalline shapes, he has been called by some "the father of crystallography".

Ice crystals are still being studied today. It is not completely clear, even now, why crystals grow into some of the beautiful shapes like that shown in Figure 1. Since the growth of ice crystals results in greater order, or a decrease in entropy, some have attempted to justify the theory of evolution by an analogy to crystal growth. This paper will discuss ice crystal growth, the *second law of thermodynamics*, and why neither support the theory of evolution. This work is supportive of the creation model because it refutes the concept that there is a self-organizing principle in matter which moves from molecules to man. Rather, the organization in form and process we observe all around us is due to the design of the Creator and the operation of the *second law of thermodynamics* instituted by the Creator.

THE MODERN EXPLANATION OF CRYSTAL SHAPE

The hexagonal symmetry of an ice crystal is an outward manifestation of an internal arrangement of the atoms in the ice. Each water molecule is V-shaped with an oxygen atom at the vertex and a hydrogen atom at the two extremities. An angle of 105 degrees separates the legs. Ice molecules are bound together in an open lattice and form puckered layers with hexagonal symmetry, as seen in Figure 2 and described by Fletcher [2]. Each molecule is surrounded by four nearest neighbors, so that each group has one molecule at the center and the other four at the corners of a tetrahedron, all the same distance away. The molecules are held in place mainly by electrostatic attraction between the positive charge of the hydrogen atom and the negative electrons of the neighboring oxygen atom. This is called a hydrogen bond.

Ice crystals grow as thin hexagonal plates or long hexagonal columns, depending on temperature. Two faces can be defined for ice crystals - the basal face and the prism face. The basal face is typically the surface which shows hexagonal symmetry. For example, the basal face in Figure 1 is the surface facing the reader. Both the upper and lower surfaces are basal faces. The prism face is perpendicular to the basal face. It faces outward from an arm or portion of an arm. This face does not exhibit hexagonal symmetry. For some temperatures, the basal face grows faster than the prism face, resulting in long hexagonal columns or needles. At other temperatures, the prism face grows faster, resulting in thin hexagonal plates, starlike stellar crystals, and fern-like dendrites. The shape(habit) of ice crystals as a function of temperature found by Magono and Lee [3] is shown in Figure 3. The fern-like dendritic nature of crystals is caused by the humidity. The greater the humidity, the more feathery the crystals will appear.

Hallet and Mason [4] have explored the reasons the basal and prism faces grow at different rates as a function of temperature. They have discovered that water vapor molecules collect on the ice and migrate across the surface to their final lattice positions. The rate at which the molecules migrate across the surface varies with temperature, and is different for the basal and prism faces. For some temperature ranges there is a net surface migration from the basal to the prism faces, resulting in a plate-like shape or habit. For other temperature ranges the situation is reversed, resulting in a net flux of molecules from the prism to the basal faces and the formation of columns or needles.

Figure 4 is a result of the work of Mason et. al. [5] which shows the mean migration distance of water molecules on the basal surface of ice as a function of temperature. It shows a complex relationship with two maxima at 0°C and -10°C. If a similar relationship is assumed for the prism face but shifted about 5°C to warmer temperatures, the ice crystal habits in Figure 3 can be explained.

THERMODYNAMICS AND ENTROPY

The *second law of thermodynamics* states that for all real processes the entropy of the universe always increases. The change in entropy can be defined in terms such as heat flow, volume change, pressure change, energy available to do work, or order and disorder. All but the last of these quantities are called macroscopic variables, i.e., they are large-scale quantities representing large numbers of molecules. For example, the differential change in entropy may be defined as:

$$dS = \frac{dQ}{T} \tag{1}$$

where dS is the change in entropy, dQ is the quantity of heat removed from or added to a system, and T is the absolute temperature. We can demonstrate how entropy changes according to the second law by considering a simple, everyday experience. Assume two blocks of equal mass, initially at 20°C and 0°C, are placed in thermal contact and allowed to come to thermal equilibrium. The blocks, shown in Figure 5, will come to a final temperature of 10°C. If the total system is expressed as a subsystem (1,2), a medium (3), and the rest of the universe (4); then equation 1 becomes:

$$dS = \frac{dQ_1}{T_1} + \frac{dQ_2}{T_2} + \frac{dQ_3}{T_3} + \frac{dQ_4}{T_4} \tag{2}$$

Assuming in this case the heat transfer only occurs from the hot block to the cold block within the subsystem, not to the medium ($dQ_3 = 0$) and the rest of the universe surrounding the two blocks ($dQ_4 = 0$), then:

$$dQ_1 = m_1 c_1 dT_1 \tag{3}$$

and:

$$dQ_2 = m_2 c_2 dT_2 \tag{4}$$

where m_1 and m_2 are the masses of the hot and cold blocks, respectively, c_1 and c_2 are the specific heats, and dT_1 and dT_2 are the changes in temperature. Substituting dQ_1, dQ_2, dQ_3, and dQ_4 back into equation 2:

$$dS = m_1 c_1 \frac{dT_1}{T_1} + m_2 c_2 \frac{dT_2}{T_2} \tag{5}$$

Integrating both sides of equation 5 results in:

$$\Delta S = \int_{S_o}^{S_f} dS = \int_{T_1}^{T_f} m_1 c_1 \frac{dT_1}{T_1} + \int_{T_2}^{T_f} m_2 c_2 \frac{dT_2}{T_2} \tag{6}$$

where ΔS is the total change in entropy; S_o and S_f are the initial and final entropy states, respectively; T_1 and T_2 are the initial temperatures of the hot and cold blocks, respectively; and T_f is the final temperature of the two blocks in contact.

Then:

$$\Delta S = m_1 c_1 \ln \frac{T_f}{T_1} + m_2 c_2 \ln \frac{T_f}{T_2} \tag{7}$$

For the purpose of this exercise, we have assumed that the masses of the two blocks are equal to 1 kg each and the specific heat is 1000 J/kgK. This is not necessary to demonstrate the general result, but permits a simpler illustration. Substituting the assumed values for mass, specific heat, and temperature results in:

$$\Delta S = (1kg)(1000\frac{J}{kgK}) \ln \frac{283K}{293K} + (1kg)(1000\frac{J}{kgK}) \ln \frac{283K}{273K} \tag{8}$$

or:

$$\Delta S = -34.73\frac{J}{K} + 35.98\frac{J}{K} \tag{9}$$

or:

$$\Delta S = +1.25\frac{J}{K} \tag{10}$$

The entropy change for this simple illustration is positive, in agreement with the *second law of thermodynamics*. However, it is important to note that the entropy of a portion of the system, the hot block in this case, actually decreased. Because heat was removed from the hot block, dQ_1 was negative, and its entropy decreased. When this heat was transferred to the cold block, dQ_2 was positive and the entropy increased for this block. Since the change in entropy is defined as the heat transferred divided by the temperature of the block, the same quantity of heat transferred from the hot block will result in a smaller change of entropy than for the cold block. Consequently, the net change in entropy for the universe was positive. This will always be the case for all real processes for heat transfer or any other real process no matter how entropy is defined.

ORDER AND ENTROPY

We have seen how a change in entropy can be calculated from macroscale quantities like heat flow. However, we have yet to understand what entropy actually is. It turns out that entropy is a measure of how mass and energy are distributed in the universe. The more heterogeneous the distribution of mass in space and the greater the difference in levels of energy, the more ordered the universe. Part of the difficulty with understanding entropy is that it actually measures the *disorder* of things. When we say that the entropy of the universe always increases, we are actually saying that total mass and energy of the universe tend in the direction of less order. This does not mean that mass and energy can not become more ordered at some location in the universe, but only that the total universe becomes less ordered with time.

The basic concept of the *second law of thermodynamics* is in agreement with the Biblical statements of the creation account and the subsequent initiation of death and decay. During the six days of creation God ordered the universe by creating mass, space, and time; energizing the mass; and arranging the mass and energy in specific ways. On the seventh day God rested. The *second law of thermodynamics* was probably instituted at the time of Adam's sin in the garden of Eden. It is in operation today and will be so until God intervenes at the end of the ages. He also intervenes intermittently in the form of miracles from time to time. The disorder of the universe normally increases with time under God's oversight. A reasonable analog to the action of the second law is the winding down of a clock. The mass and energy of a clock is ordered by design and its initial winding. When released, the clock slowly winds down, decreasing its order with time. The clock will always wind down - never wind up by itself.

For us to reach a better understanding of entropy, we will need to study a second illustration, this time on the microscale. Consider a box with a barrier in the middle, as seen in Figure 6. On one side are black marbles and on the other side white marbles. Now we take out the barrier and let them mix. How has the entropy changed? Is the trend toward an increase or a decrease in entropy? To more easily quantify this example, we will assume originally 3 black marbles on one side of the partition, 2 white marbles on the other side, and 6 possible energy states available to the marbles on each side. The marbles are allowed to move around and randomly assume six possible energy states. Only one marble can occupy a given energy state at a time. Although the marbles are in random motion, the total number of possible configurations is determined by the original design of the system. We will define Ω to be the number of possible energy configurations in which the system may be arranged. This variable is called the thermodynamic probability by Zemansky and Dittman [6]. Considering the black side first, the number of possible energy configurations is given by:

$$\Omega_B = \frac{6!}{(6-3)!3!} = \frac{6 \cdot 5 \cdot 4 \cdot 3 \cdot 2 \cdot 1}{(3 \cdot 2 \cdot 1)(3 \cdot 2 \cdot 1)} = 20 \tag{11}$$

where Ω_B is the number of energy configurations on the black side of the partition. This result is due to the number of possible combinations and permutations of 6 energy states taken 3 at a time. Since the 3 marbles are indistinguishable, the result must be corrected by 3! in the denominator, resulting in 20 possible ways the 3 black marbles may be arranged with the partition in place. Considering next the white side, we find the number of possible energy configurations to be:

$$\Omega_W = \frac{6!}{(6-2)!(2!)} = \frac{6 \cdot 5 \cdot 4 \cdot 3 \cdot 2 \cdot 1}{(4 \cdot 3 \cdot 2 \cdot 1)(2 \cdot 1)} = 15 \tag{12}$$

where Ω_W is the number of energy configurations on the white side of the partition. Here 6 energy states were taken 2 at a time. The result was corrected by 2! to account for the 2 marbles being indistinguishable.

A definition of entropy in terms of microscale quantities is:

$$S = k \ln \Omega \tag{13}$$

where S is the entropy of a given system, k is the Boltzman constant equal to 1.38×10^{-23} J/Kg, and Ω is the number of possible energy configurations of the system. With this definition, the entropy, S_P, of the box of black and white marbles in the box with the partition is:

$$S_P = S_B + S_W \tag{14}$$

where S_P is the total entropy of the box of black and white marbles, S_B is the entropy of the black side and S_W is the entropy of the white side. Substituting equation 11 and equation 12 into equation 13 separately and then both into equation 14 results in:

$$S_P = k \ln \Omega_B + k \ln \Omega_W \tag{15}$$

or:

$$S_P = k \ln(\Omega_B \Omega_W) \tag{16}$$

When values for the variables are substituted:

$$S_P = (1.38 \times 10^{-23} \frac{J}{K}) \ln(20 \cdot 15) \tag{17}$$

or:

$$S_P = 7.87 \times 10^{-23} \frac{J}{K} \tag{18}$$

This is the configurational entropy of the box of marbles with a partition dividing the black marbles from the white marbles. If the partition is now removed, the total number of available energy states is 12. The 5 marbles are free to arrange themselves throughout the entire box, not just to the original 6 energy states on one side of the partition. The number of possible configurations of energy with no partition, Ω_{NP}, is:

$$\Omega_{NP} = \frac{12!}{(12-5)!2!3!} = \frac{12 \cdot 11 \cdot 10 \cdot 9 \cdot 8 \cdot 7 \cdot 6 \cdot 5 \cdot 4 \cdot 3 \cdot 2 \cdot 1}{(7 \cdot 6 \cdot 5 \cdot 4 \cdot 3 \cdot 2 \cdot 1)(2 \cdot 1)(3 \cdot 2 \cdot 1)} \tag{19}$$

or:

$$\Omega_{NP} = 7,920 \tag{20}$$

The entropy of the box without the partition, S_{NP}, is:

$$S_{NP} = k \ln \Omega_{NP} = 12.39 \times 10^{-23} \frac{J}{K} \tag{21}$$

The change in entropy by removing the partition is then:

$$\Delta S = S_{NP} - S_P = +4.52 \times 10^{-23} \frac{J}{K} \tag{22}$$

By removing the partition we have caused the entropy to increase. The reason for this increase is the greater number of ways in which the marbles can be distributed. Feynman [7] in discussing this example concludes that entropy is greater when the marbles have fewer restrictions on their distribution. He goes on to show that a box originally containing all black marbles on one end and white marbles on the other will become mixed with time such that the black and white marbles will become evenly distributed throughout the box. The probability is so low that an original mixture of a large number of black and white marbles will separate with time into all black marbles at one end and white marbles at the other, that one never observes such an event. The diffusion of smoke from a source throughout a room is always the normal sequence of events, never the concentration of smoke into a small volume from an original wide dispersion.

Entropy is then a measure of how energy and mass are distributed in the universe. It can be calculated from macroscopic quantities like heat transfer, but is also quantifiable at the molecular scale by knowing the distribution of individual molecules. In fact, entropy calculated from macroscale quantities should be identical to the summation of the contributions of the entropy from molecular-scale configurations. Unfortunately, it is often difficult to account for all the degrees of freedom and sources of order when considering large numbers of molecules and possible energy states. Approximations are often made which need to be validated. Fortunately, the macroscopic-scale entropy should be an upper limit to entropy calculations. Therefore, if we are dealing with a change in configurational entropy on the microscale, like the formation of an ice crystal, we can measure the upper limit of entropy change on the macroscale by the amount of latent heat removed because of the phase change.

ICE CRYSTAL GROWTH AND ENTROPY

Let's take these principles we've reviewed and apply them to the growth of an ice crystal. We will first calculate the macroscale entropy change in growing an ice crystal and then find the equivalent microscale entropy change. Assume a subsystem contains 1 m^3 of air saturated with water vapor at 0°C and a pressure of 1 atmosphere, as shown in Figure 7. This volume will contain approximately 2.67×10^{25} air molecules and about 1.62×10^{23} water vapor molecules. If heat is now removed from this subsystem, the air and water vapor will cool, the air will become supersaturated, and cloud droplets will form, if normal concentrations of condensation nuclei are present. These cloud droplets will release latent heat of condensation as they form. As more heat is removed the temperature of the air, water vapor, and cloud droplets will cool until ice crystals are nucleated and begin to grow by vapor-to-solid deposition. Latent heat of deposition is also released by the growing ice crystals. By the removal of heat, water vapor molecules originally in completely random motion of the vapor state, are incorporated into more ordered liquid and solid states of cloud droplets and ice crystals. The removal of heat from the subsystem is defined as a negative quantity, so the macroscopic change in entropy of the subsystem is negative. This decrease in entropy is what would be expected for an increasingly ordered arrangement of molecules on the microscale.

The heat extracted from the subsystem must be accounted for somewhere else, however. We will assume that the heat will be distributed into the medium surrounding the subsystem, as shown in Figure 7. Furthermore, we will assume that the medium is sufficiently massive that the quantity of heat removed from the subsystem will not change its temperature nor affect the rest of the universe. These assumptions are common practice both theoretically and experimentally. For example, it is typical to immerse an experimental apparatus in a water bath to maintain a constant temperature. The water bath absorbs or gives up small quantities of heat but maintains isothermal conditions if it is sufficiently massive. This is convenient theoretically because entropy changes are easy to calculate under isothermal conditions and the entropy changes can be restricted to a limited volume in space. One important feature of such a system is that the boundary between the subsystem and the medium allows heat but not mass to flow through, permitting the subsystem to be defined as a "closed system". On the other hand, since we have contained all the heat changes to the subsystem and the medium, the boundary between the medium and the universe will not permit heat to flow through. This boundary defines the total medium and subsystem as an "isolated system". A third type of boundary often referred to in thermodynamic discussions is the "open system". A boundary enclosing such a system will permit both mass and heat to flow. Such boundaries and definitions may be conveniently placed as desired around a system or process but care must be taken to properly treat where the sources and sinks of mass and heat occur.

Going back to the water vapor being cooled and converted into ice, let's assume that we only remove the heat necessary for one ice crystal to form at 0°C. This would require slow extraction of heat so that cloud droplets would not form and the suspension of an ice embryo in the volume of the subsystem at 0°C. Although these conditions are uncommon for clouds, it would be possible to do this experimentally if care were taken. Theoretically, this has the benefit of ignoring all other sources of heat such as latent heat of condensation and the heat capacity of air and cloud droplets. This is no different than partitioning the energy by type of process - in this case the latent heat of deposition. The amount of heat released by forming a single hexagonal plate 1 millimeter in diameter and 100 micrometers thick is:

$$dQ = -mL = -\rho V L \qquad (23)$$

or:

$$dQ = -(.9164\frac{gm}{cm^3})(6.50 \times 10^{-5}cm^3)(2834\frac{J}{gm}) \qquad (24)$$

or:

$$dQ = -1.69 \times 10^{-1}J \qquad (25)$$

where dQ is the amount of latent heat released by deposition, m is the mass of the crystal, ρ is the density of ice, and L is the latent heat of deposition (sublimation), and V is the volume of a 1-millimeter diameter, hexagonal plate 100 micrometers thick. During the growth of the ice crystal its temperature will remain at 0°C, as observed during phase changes at a pressure of 1 atmosphere. The temperature of the air and water vapor will also remain at 0°C if the heat is removed slowly enough. The change of entropy by the removal of the latent heat of deposition for the mass of this ice crystal at 0°C is then:

$$\Delta S = \frac{dQ}{T} = \frac{-1.69 \times 10^{-1}J}{273K} \qquad (26)$$

$$\Delta S = -6.18 \times 10^{-4}\frac{J}{K} \qquad (27)$$

This change in entropy on the macroscale should be the upper limit to estimates of entropy change on the microscale.

Now, let's consider the entropy change on the microscale by the reconfiguration of the molecules from the vapor state to the solid state of a hexagonal plate. First, we need to know the entropy of the water vapor in its initial state. A mixture of air and water vapor obeys the ideal gas law very closely, even when near the condensation point for water vapor. Consequently, the derivation for the entropy of an ideal gas will be followed. The full treatment of the ideal gas statistics may be found in Goodstein [8]. The final result of this derivation for the entropy of an ideal gas is:

$$S = -Nk\ln\frac{N}{V} + \frac{3}{2}Nk\ln kT + Nk(\frac{5}{2} + \frac{3}{2}\ln\frac{2\pi m}{h^2}) \qquad (28)$$

where S is entropy, N is the number of molecules in the gas, V is the volume, k is the Boltzman constant, m is the mass of a molecule of water vapor, and h is the Planck constant. Since only the water vapor molecules change phase, we will ignore the entropy of the air molecules. They have the same entropy before and after the formation of an ice crystal because the volume and temperature are held constant. The air molecules are present to facilitate the transfer of latent heat released at the crystal to the boundary of the subsystem. Substituting the values of N, V, and T specified earlier into equation 28 results in:

$$S = +49.89501\frac{J}{K} \qquad (29)$$

where S_N is the entropy of the water vapor in the gaseous state before the ice crystal has been grown. Of the 1.62×10^{23} molecules in the initial volume, 1.98×10^{18} of these molecules will be incorporated into the lattice of the ice crystal. The entropy of the water molecules in the volume remaining after the ice crystal is grown may be found by substituting the same V and T but a new N (equal to $1.62 \times 10^{23} - 1.98 \times 10^{18}$ molecules) into 28, giving:

$$S_{N-\Delta N} = +49.89441\frac{J}{K} \qquad (30)$$

309

where $S_{N-\Delta N}$ is the entropy of the water vapor after the crystal is grown. The original entropy of the ΔN molecules which are incorporated into the ice crystal is then:

$$S_{\Delta N} = S_N - S_{N-\Delta N} = +6.03 \times 10^{-4} \frac{J}{K} \tag{31}$$

This procedure for finding the entropy of the water molecules which are incorporated into the ice crystal is a close approximation. It did not consider the affect of the air molecules on entropy. Because the number of molecules is so large, however, the error is small. Now, let the number of water molecules incorporated into the ice crystal, in general, be given by n and the number of positions available to these molecules in the crystal be given by n'. In the case where a perfect crystal is formed with no vacancies and no dislocations, the number of positions, n', will be the same as the number of molecules, n. Since all n molecules are indistinguishable, the number of ways in which the molecules may be arranged must be corrected by a factor, $n!$ Therefore, the number of configurations in an ice crystal, Ω_s, is given by:

$$\Omega_s = \frac{n!}{(n-n)!n!} = 1 \tag{32}$$

This results in the configurational entropy of an ice crystal, S_s, being:

$$S_s = k \ln \Omega_s = 0 \tag{33}$$

The change in entropy of water vapor molecules in the subsystem, ΔS_{Sub}, in going from the vapor state to the solid state is then:

$$\Delta S_{Sub} = S_s - S_{\Delta N} = -6.03 \times 10^{-4} \frac{J}{K} \tag{34}$$

This agrees within about 3% of the result from the macroscopic calculation of entropy change in equation 27. This slight difference is due to the lack of consideration of other sources of entropy change, such as the orientation of the water molecules in space, the vibrational contributions, and the electronic contributions. A water molecule is not simply a spherical ping-pong ball-like object in the vapor which is stacked like cannon balls in the lattice, but rather, has smaller-scale features which contribute to energy and entropy calculations. In calculating the latent heat removed, all these characteristics were integrated into the latent heat, but were not considered in the microscale calculations of configurational entropy change. If they had been, the microscale entropy change would be identical to the macroscale value of entropy change. The fact that the microscale entropy change is close to and slightly smaller than the macroscale entropy change, validates the fact that our procedures are correct. Further consideration of the other sources of entropy change would likely bring the microscale calculations into full agreement with the macroscale.

In order to decrease the entropy in the subsystem by growing an ice crystal heat had to be pumped from the subsystem into the medium, which has the same temperature as the subsystem. The heat pumped into the medium is positive and equal to $1.69 \times 10^{-1}J$ from equation 25. If no other sources of heat were involved, the change in entropy for the medium, ΔS_{Med} would be:

$$\Delta S_{Med} = \frac{dQ}{T} = \frac{+1.69 \times 10^{-1}J}{273K} = +6.18 \times 10^{-4} \frac{J}{K} \tag{35}$$

This means that the net change in entropy, ΔS, considering only the subsystem and medium, will be zero.

$$\Delta S = \Delta S_{Sub} + \Delta S_{Med} = 0 \tag{36}$$

However, the work necessary to pump the heat from the subsystem to the medium was generated at the expense of an increase in entropy somewhere else in the universe. The total change in entropy, ΔS, for all components of this process over the entire universe will be greater than zero, once more agreeing with the *second law of thermodynamics*.

The extraction of heat from the vapor results in more order in the subsystem as the water molecules form hexagonal patterns and collapse into lower energy states. The hexagonal structure the molecules assume and the manner in which they migrate to assume these patterns is circumscribed by the original design imposed on the water molecules. If the environmental conditions are slightly different, e.g. the temperature varies slightly, the shape of the crystals will change somewhat but always in a pre-determined response to the environmental conditions. If we were working with the vapor of some other chemical material, the crystals could form shapes according to cubic, monoclinic, or other crystal systems. The shapes and patterns will form according to the design built into the molecules of the material. We could continue to explore to deeper and deeper levels as to why the atoms combine into molecules as they do, why the protons, neutrons, and electrons combine into atoms as they do, etc. However, we will continue to come to the same conclusion as that of Kepler [1] at his level of observation when he stated that a *formative faculty* exists in nature which causes the six-sided shape of snowflakes. He attributed this *formative faculty* to the Creator's design which is preserved from the origin of the universe until now. Such design could not have originated by chance because the order of the universe as a whole does not increase, but decreases. Ice crystal growth then is in full agreement with the *second law of thermodynamics* and exhibits original design by the Creator.

EVOLUTION AND THE SNOWFLAKE

It is my belief that biological life processes *operate* in a very similar manner to ice crystals. Work is extracted from higher energy states to drive the metabolism and other processes of plants and animals. Order can be increased in a local subsystem by a decrease in order of the universe as a whole. These complex processes are proscribed by the original design built into them which does not change with time. See Thaxton et. al. [9] for a discussion of the difference between order and complexity. Like ice crystals, design is evident in the operation of biological processes.

Evolutionists would extrapolate this description of the *operation* of biological systems to the *origin* of life processes. The generation of order is given free reign and not restricted by design constraints. The earth's biosphere is visualized to be an "open system" which energizes biochemical processes to organize simple inorganic molecules into complex macromolecules. However, we have shown that the growth of ice crystals is a result of extracting heat from water vapor. It completely obeys the second law of thermodynamics. The shapes ice crystals assume is proscribed by the environmental conditions and the original design of water molecules by the Creator. Ice crystal shapes have not "evolved" over time as evolutionists would suggest for life processes. The same ice crystal shapes are observed today as reported by Han Ying [10] over two thousand years ago.

Even if plants and animals were not bound by original design and could evolve, the information necessary for life processes to operate today would have taken longer to develop than the 20 billion years or so our universe has assumed to have existed by evolutionists. Even Crick [11] and Hoyle [12] have recently recognized this problem. Crick [11] has resorted to *panspermia* to explain the formation of life on the earth. *Panspermia* is the concept that life did not succeed in starting on earth by itself, but was seeded by microorganisms wafted in from space. This is a tacit admission that life is so complex that random processes could not possibly have formed macromolecules containing this information without design. The basic error that evolutionists have made is to explain the *origin* of life in terms of processes by which life *operates*. The information evident in the existence and complexity of life demands a Creator. Even the growth of an ice crystal demands a Creator.

This paper is intended to be expanded in future research to show how entropy changes in biologic processes and how much information content macromolecules contain. It is intended that the calculations of Hoyle [12] will be repeated and used to quantify the statements made about biological processes in this paper.

CONCLUSIONS

Ice crystal growth is consistent with the *second law of thermodynamics*. It is a consequence of the removal of heat from water vapor and the inherent design of water molecules to form an orderly crystal lattice. The growth of ice crystals is similar to the *operation* of life processes, but does not support the *origin* of life as described by the theory of evolution. Even the growth of an ice crystal demands a Creator.

REFERENCES

[1] Kepler, Johannes, THE SIX-CORNERED SNOWFLAKE, edited by Colin Hardie, Oxford at the Clarendon Press, London, England, 1966, 74 pp.

[2] Fletcher, N. H., THE CHEMICAL PHYSICS OF ICE, Cambridge Univ. Press, Cambridge, England, 1970, 271 pp.

[3] Magono, Choji and Lee, Chung Woo, "Meteorological Classification of Natural Snow Crystals", JOURNAL OF THE FACULTY OF SCIENCE, Hokkaido University, Hokkaido, Japan, Series VII, Vol. 2, No. 4., 1966, pp. 321-335, 27 Plates.

[4] Hallett, J. and Mason, B.J., "The influence of temperature and supersaturation on the habit of ice crystals grown from the vapour", PROC. OF THE ROY. SOC., London, England, A247, 1958, p. 440.

[5] Mason, B.J., Bryant, G.W., and Van den Heuval, A.P., "The growth habits and surface structure of ice crystals, PHIL. MAG., 8, 1963, pp. 505-526.

[6] Zemansky, M.W. and Dittman, R.H., HEAT AND THERMODYNAMICS, McGraw-Hill, New York, N.Y., 1981.

[7] Feynman, R.P., Leighton, R.B., and Sands, M., THE FEYNMAN LECTURES ON PHYSICS, Addison-Wesley Publishing Company, Inc., 1963, Chap. 46, pp. 1-9.

[8] Goodstein, David L., STATES OF MATTER, Dover Publications, Inc., New York, N.Y., 1985, pp. 98-102.

[9] Thaxton, Charles B., Bradley, Walter L., and Olsen, Roger L., THE MYSTERY OF LIFE'S ORIGIN: REASSESSING CURRENT THEORIES, Philosophical Library, New York, N.Y., 1984.

[10] Ying, Han, HAN SHIH WAI CHUAN (Moral Discourses Illustrating the Han Text of the Book of Odes), China, 135 B.C.

[11] Crick, Francis, LIFE ITSELF, ITS ORIGIN AND NATURE, Simon and Schuster, New York, 1981.

[12] Hoyle, Fred, THE INTELLIGENT UNIVERSE, Holt, Rhinehart and Winston, New York, 1983.

Figure 1. A plane dendritic ice crystal
approximately 5mm in diameter.

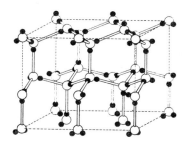

Figure 2. A three-dimensional lattice of
water molecules in an ice crystal. The white
balls are oxygen atoms and the black balls
are hydrogen. After Fletcher [2].

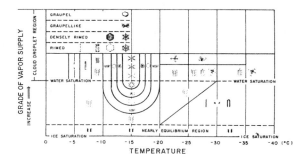

Figure 3. Temperature and humidity conditions
for the growth of ice crystals. After Magono and Lee [3].

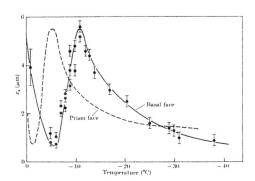

Figure 4. The mean surface migration distance x_s,
as a function of temperature. After Mason et. al. [5].

313

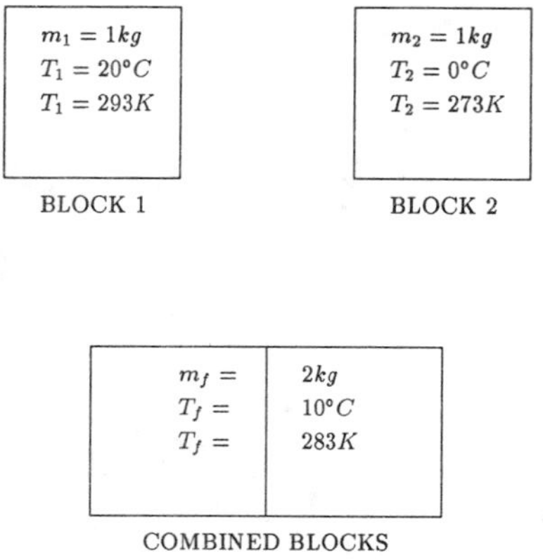

$$m_1 = 1kg$$
$$T_1 = 20°C$$
$$T_1 = 293K$$

BLOCK 1

$$m_2 = 1kg$$
$$T_2 = 0°C$$
$$T_2 = 273K$$

BLOCK 2

$m_f =$	$2kg$
$T_f =$	$10°C$
$T_f =$	$283K$

COMBINED BLOCKS

Figure 5. Two blocks originally separated at
different temperatures, then placed in contact and
allowed to come to thermal equilibrium.

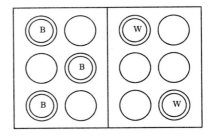

Figure 6. Black and white marbles in a partitioned box.
B are black marbles, W are white marbles, and
blank circles are empty positions.

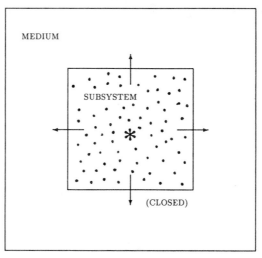

REST OF UNIVERSE

MEDIUM

SUBSYSTEM

(CLOSED)

(ISOLATED)

Figure 7. Ice crystal and vapor in a closed subsystem
which is free to exchange heat with the surrounding medium.
The subsystem and medium constitute an isolated system which
can not exchange either mass or heat with the rest of the universe.

314

Entropy can be a hard concept to grasp. This paper is useful in providing several simple illustrations by which to calculate entropy change. A "simple" water vapor-to-ice phase change is a good place to begin before tackling the more complicated organics.

On page 2, paragraph 5, the two blocks of equal mass must be assumed to be of the same specific heat as well. "Of the same substance" would satisfy the requirement.

Edmond W. Holroyd III, Ph.D.
Arvada, Colorado

This paper highlights one of the more serious flaws in the atheistic views on the creation of the universe, namely the absence of reason and understanding in basic physics, for when the reasoning process operates and fundamental laws of physics are considered the conclusions do not support the "chance" theory of creation of matter and life. Such unreasoned approaches to explaining the universe actually take more "belief" or "faith" than does accepting the existence of a Creator! Consider, for instance, the probability of the molecules arranging themselves in the shape of the ice crystals shown in Figure 1 or in the very precise structure of the lattice in Figure 2. Its kind of like the probability that a book could be reformed into its original form after running it through a paper shredder, then thoroughly stirring up the millions of pieces of paper with their fragments of ink on them! This paper underscores the importance in the education process of teaching children (and older students, too) how to think (judging from the abstract, Hedtke's paper addresses this issue).

I do have two questions, however. Regarding the microscale entropy change discussed following Eq. 34,1 is it possible to calculate the contributions of orientation, and of the vibrational and electronic states? And, is it possible that when these are considered the difference between the macroscale and microscale could be larger than 3%, i.e. that the entropy change could be even larger than the macroscale? In the same paragraph, you state in one place that the microscale entropy change "would be identical to the macroscale" if these other factors were considered, then later on (in the last sentence) you state the change "would likely" be the same as the macroscale. Which do you mean and if it is the former, on what basis can you be so definite that the results on the two scales would be identical?

The second general question deals with your statement in the section on "Order and Entropy" where you state that the second law was probably instituted at the time of Adam's sin in the garden. Please elaborate. Why couldn't the second law have been instituted on the fourth day of the creation when the starts were created, or on the sixth day after everything was created?

Laurence D. Mendenhall, Ph.D.
Placentia, California

CLOSURE

Response to Dr. Holroyd:

In the example of entropy change when two blocks come to thermal equilibrium, I did not specify "of the same substance" or "of the same mass" until equation (8). At this point, I made these assumptions to show that entropy increases, without complicating the example. However, entropy will increase even if both the masses and specific heats are assumed to be different for the two blocks.

Reponse to Dr. Mendenhall:

I believe it is possible to calculate the entropy explicitly considering the contribution of orientation, vibrational, and electronic states of the water molecules. In fact, to accomplish my long-term goal of entropy calculations on the DNA molecule, this must be done. I would not expect this contribution to be larger than the 3% because the total entropy change is bounded by the macroscopic changes.

The use of the phrase "would be identical to the macroscale" incorporates qualifying clauses from the previous sentences. If "smaller-scale features which contribute to energy and entropy" had been fully considered in the microscale calculations of configurational entropy change, the microscale and macroscale would be "identical". The phrase "would likely" later in the paragraph following equation (34) refers to the expectation to when this is actually attempted.

The macroscale entropy change is simply the summation of microscale entropy change. If we are aware of all microscale effects and adequately treat them, they should add up to the macroscale estimate of entropy change calculated by energy flow and temperature effects.

The time at which the second law was instituted is a controversial issue. Some have stated that the curse upon creation after Adam's sin was actually the institution of the second law because "death" is the essence of the second law. However, others have questioned how the creation could have operated from creation to Adam's sin without the second law. It is a fundamental law which is basic to all physical and biological processes such as heat exchange or digestion. My preference for institution of the second law after Adam's sin is to explain the operation of physical processes before Adam's sin by a different set of basic laws.

We are told this will also be true in the New Heavens and New Earth after the end of time. God apparently causes the world to operate in accordance with different principles in different ages.

Larry Vardiman, Ph.D.

THE HARTFORD BASIN OF CENTRAL CONNECTICUT:
MULTIPLE EVIDENCES OF CATASTROPHISM

John H. Whitmore, M.S.
811 W. Spruce, B
Ravenna, Ohio 44266

ABSTRACT

The Hartford basin consists of a long band of clastic sediments and basalts outcropping in Central Connecticut and Massachusetts. Geologists have long considered these sediments to be deposited by uniformitarian processes. Evidence will be presented in support of catastrophic deposition of these sediments over a short period of time. A possible Flood model for the formation of the basin shall be proposed.

INTRODUCTION

The Hartford Basin is a classic area geologically. It has been visited by many prominent geologists including Sir Charles Lyell, Edward Hitchcock, William Morris Davis, and Paul D. Krynine. These and others have used the outcrops in the basin to support their uniformitarian models. Hubert et al. (1) proposed the basin took up to 24 million years to form. During this time, caliche horizons, multiple layers of mudcracks, dinosaur footprints, and black shales allegedly formed. All of these features indicate long periods of time from a uniformitarian viewpoint. Therefore this area is important for those who hold to a Creation/Flood model for earth history.

The Hartford basin is about 140 km long and 30 km at its widest point. It is part of the Newark Supergroup, a group of about 20 sedimentary basins which range in age from Triassic to Jurassic, along the east coast of the United States. In Connecticut, the area of this study, the basin consists of four sedimentary and three basalt formations. In general, the units dip about 10 to 15 degrees to the east. The basin is bordered on the east by a large border fault.

There are features of the basin which some would look at and immediately assume the basin took millions of years to be deposited. Some of these features include black shales, mudcracks, dolomite nodules, caliche horizons, skeletal halites, multiple layers of dinosaur footprints, and redbeds. The scope and length of this paper prevent a discussion of these problems in detail. Alternate explanations and interpretations have been given in the author's masters thesis that do not require millions of years for formation (2). For example, it was shown "mudcracks" did not form by exposure and drying to the sun, but were formed substratally, after burial. It was shown the paleosol caliche zones present in the New Haven Arkose did not have the necessary features to be interpreted as such.

The purpose of this paper is to show that the long held uniformitarian interpretations are not valid for the Hartford basin. Evidence will be presented in support of catastrophic sedimentation. A brief discussion of how the Flood may have played a part in the development of the basin will conclude this paper.

STRATIGRAPHY AND PALEONTOLOGY

The important features of the stratigraphy of the Hartford basin have been summarized in Figure 1. Where sandstones and siltstones are found they are generally poorly sorted and red in color. Sand grains tend to be angular and subangular. In places where sedimentary units outcrop near the eastern border fault, a large breccia facies is found. Clasts of over one meter in diameter have been seen in this area. Conglomerate lenses occur throughout the rocks of the basin, but are most notable in the New Haven Arkose. Plant fragments and fish remains are well known from the black shales of the upper three clastic units of the basin. Partial dinosaur skeletons and abundant footprints have also been found in these formations. Very few fossils of any kind have been found in the New Haven beds.

STRATIGRAPHY OF THE HARTFORD BASIN

Formation	Thickness	Description
Portland	1250m	coarse siltstones and fine grained sandstones sediments are poorly sorted and angular conglomerates and breccias near border fault black shales contain fish dinosaur tracks and rare skeletons
Hampden Basalt	15-50m	consists of eight different flows
East Berlin	150-300m	red mudstones, siltstones, and sandstones all sediments are angular and poorly sorted shrinkage cracks and dinosaur footprints common fish preservation excellent in black shales
Holyoke Basalt	100-200m	forms prominent ridges throughout Connecticut consists of two different flows
Shuttle Meadow	100-300m	red mudstones, siltstones and sandstones climbing ripples and mudchip breccias common black shales with fish dinosaur footprints in red siltstones
Talcott Basalt	30-75m	no single flows are extensive complex stratigraphy, extensive pillows
New Haven Arkose	2500-3000m	mostly sandstones, very few siltstones, shale poorly sorted, subangular to angular sediments no fossils, calcite rich zones, lenses of gravel quartz boulders up to 1 meter at base

Figure 1. Stratigraphy of the Hartford Basin.

PROBLEMS WITH DATING THE BASIN

Geologists have relied upon paleontological means to determine the age of the rocks in the basin. Because there are so few fossils in the basin, this has proven difficult. Even modern radiometric dating methods have not been able to resolve the problem. After doing a paleomagnetic study of the three basalts in the basin, deBoer (3) came to the conclusion that absolute dating methods cannot provide enough resolution to differentiate between their ages. Since this is the case, how can one tell what period of time these rocks were deposited without using paleontological methods?   These methods may be inaccurate not only because of the scarcity of fossils in the basin, but also because of circular reasoning and the assumption of the evolutionary theory to arrive at a date.   (For an explanation of this circular reasoning process see Morris (4)).

No one has satisfactorily demonstrated that the Hartford basin was deposited over millions of years. It has yet to be shown that the basin was deposited in a short amount of time. Austin and Morris (5) have argued that a large thickness of strata in California was folded plastically not long after deposition. Tight folds occur throughout the section which supposedly took millions of years to deposit.   In a uniformitarian model the oldest beds should have been lithified by the time of deformation and should have behaved in a brittle manner, not a plastic one. Their arguments show it is unreasonable to believe rocks in this area remained unlithified for millions of years until deformation took place (which the uniformitarian model demands) and therefore deposition and deformation must have occurred within a short time of each other. Unfortunately, large sedimentary outcrops are few and far apart in the Hartford basin, and those which do occur do not contain structures appropriate for applying the studies Austin and Morris. However, there is no evidence which prevents a short depositional time span for the basin. Evidence of catastrophism will now be examined.

EVIDENCES OF CATASTROPHISM

Black Shales and Fossil Fish

The black shales of the Hartford basin have been interpreted as forming from organic rich sediments deposited in oxygen-poor waters at the bottom of a relatively large lake. The lake bottom was supposedly free of scavengers and bacteria which could have decomposed the numerous fish that are now found as well preserved fossils in the black shales (6). It has been common for most authors to attribute black shale formation to oxygen-poor, deep sea environments. The shales were thought to accumulate by simple settling processes over long periods of time.

Black shales are contained within the Shuttle Meadow, East Berlin, and Portland Formations. The shales range in thickness from about 0.1 to 4 meters. The shales are often very dark and rich in kerogenous organic material. Often fish scales, whole fish, fish coprolites, and plant material can be found within the finely laminated shales. The fine lamination of the shales is an indication to many sedimentologists that these shales were deposited below wave base in an oxygen-poor environment where bioturbating organisms could not survive. The black shales are sometimes interbedded with coarser gray siltstones rich in micaceous material.

Even though a shale is black, that does not automatically indicate it was deposited in deep, quiet, toxic bottom water. Ruedemann (7) discussed some conclusions made by Richter regarding the black Hunsruchschiefer shale. This shale was generally inferred to have been deposited under "standard black shale conditions" but Richter found evidence that this was not the case. He found "small ripples, cross-bedding, sandstone lenses, and the drifted positions of starfish arms that [proved] the water was in motion." Also the presence of branching worm burrows showed life was able to exist in this black shale environment. Another study by Zangerl and Richardson (8) suggests movement of bottom water from the evidence of oriented plant and fish remains in the black shales they studied. No studies are known on the orientation of fossils in black shales of the Hartford basin. A study of this nature for the Hartford basin would be beneficial.

Fissile shales have been interpreted (and rightly so) as shales which were deposited in environments with no bioturbation and therefore no (or very few) animals were present in the environment at the time of deposition (9). Azoic environments are those which are also anoxic or extremely deep. Therefore, most sedimentologists would conclude any fissile shale with no bioturbation (especially a black shale) would accumulate either in deep or anoxic environments. However, another possibility exists.

Piper (10) reported how a variety of different laminated mudstone beds were formed by turbidites. Whittington (11) also reported that the well preserved invertebrate organisms from the famous Burgess Shale were quickly buried. Could lack of bioturbation in the finely laminated black shales of the Hartford basin be due to the rapid deposition of these sediments? From the papers by Piper and Whittington it is apparent that fine-grained sediments can accumulate rather quickly. J. H. Bretz (12) described how thick sequences of silt beds were formed quickly due to backflooding during the Lake Missoula floods. Lambert and Hsu (13) described how silt and clay layers formed rapidly by catastrophic, turbid water underflows. These are just a few of the papers which describe how fine grained sediments can accumulate quickly. This is contrary to the commonly held view that shales accumulate slowly due to simple settling processes.

The black shales of the Hartford basin contain evidence for rapid deposition. The shales contain numerous fish fossils. Cornet et al. (14) reported over 450 fish in a 2 cubic meter excavation of shale. It is apparent, in order for a fish to be preserved, it must be rapidly buried. When fish die, some float on the surface of the water. Here they most likely would be eaten by scavengers or by bacterial decay. If a dead fish sinks to the bottom of a body of water for burial, it seems reasonable that the fish would decay to the point of disarticulation before it could be buried by the slow processes of sediment accumulation envisioned for shales (tens or hundreds of years depending on the size of the fish). Brett and Baird (15) claimed disarticulation of fish occurred in short periods of time (days to a few weeks) in anaerobic experimental conditions. They went on to argue anaerobic conditions alone are insufficient to preserve intact skeletons and deposits which contained these skeletons were formed by rapid burial.

Of the thousands of sediment cores recorded from various lakes, Vallentyne (16) reported only one known case on record of fish remains being found. He goes on to describe fish remains (mostly scales) which he found in some deep water lake sediments. His study shows whole fish were not found, only parts and pieces such as scales, vertebrae, neural and hemal arches, ribs, skulls, and opercular bones. This report is significant because we find whole, perfectly preserved fishes in the black shales of Connecticut. Vallentyne's study shows that present lake processes are dissimilar to the processes which deposited the black shales of the Hartford basin. Since perfectly preserved fish have been found, one must come to the conclusion that they were buried catastrophically. Therefore, the black shales of the basin must have been deposited in a different way than black sediments forming today.

The shales did not necessarily have to be deposited laminae by laminae. A slurry of organic material, similar to a turbidite flow, could have taken place as a hyperpycnal flow. This slurry conceivably would have buried many organisms, including fish. Shale fissility could have developed post-depositionally. White (17) has shown experimentally how fissility can develop post-depositionally in certain types of clays. Lambert and Hsu (18) have seen up to five graded laminae deposited in a single year in Lake Walensee in Switzerland. Previously geologists thought the laminae in this lake and others like it were deposited as varves-- two layers each year. The "varves" in this lake were formed rapidly by turbidity underflows. A French geologist (19) has shown how lamination can develop rapidly in slurries of fine-grained suspensions.

There are many ways, besides simple settling, in which fine grained sediments with laminations can develop. These possibilities should be considered when examining the black shales of the Hartford basin, especially when the catastrophic evidence of the fish is present. Any other conclusion besides catastrophic burial is hardly reasonable.

Dinosaur Tracks

Coombs (20) reported what he called swimming dinosaur tracks which were found at Dinosaur State Park in Rocky Hill, Connecticut. Coombs was not the first to recognize such features. Bird (21) reported swimming Brontosaurus tracks found near Glen Rose, Texas. The tracks from Connecticut show there was a moderate amount of water in which an animal had to swim. Also significant, is the fact that in order to eventually be preserved, these tracks had to be buried soon after formation. These dinosaur tracks show swimming animals, in relatively deep water, in which burial of the tracks occurred soon after formation. If burial did not happen quickly, it is reasonable they would have eroded soon after formation.

Bioturbation

The general absence of widespread bioturbation throughout the rocks of the Hartford basin and other rocks throughout the world, is an indication these sediments were deposited quickly enough that bioturbation did not have time to take place. Another possibility is that the sediments were deposited slowly and there was no animal or plant life to cause bioturbation. The former interpretation is favored because animals and plants were present during deposition of the basin sediments, demonstrated by their fossil remains. Hitchcock (22) and Lull (23) recognized up to 27 different track, trail and burrow genera made by invertebrates throughout the basin. These fossil remains were supposedly made by larval and adult insects, crustaceans, myriapods, annelids, mollusks, and other forms. Tracks, trails, and burrows are present throughout the basin, but they are only found in abundance locally.

In recent marine environments, bedded sediments are destroyed by burrowing organisms. Dott (24) reported bedded sediments deposited by Hurricane Carla in 1961 were completely homogenized when they were investigated in 1981. Rhoads (25) studied rates of sediment reworking in Buzzard Bay, Massachusetts and Long Island Sound. He determined that bottom fauna is capable of reworking the annual sediment accumulation several times over. If marine organisms are capable of reworking sediment so quickly, and sediments were deposited at uniformitarian rates in the past, why are bedded marine sediments preserved in the fossil record? Any marine sediments which are bedded, and contained organisms which were capable of bioturbation, must have been deposited in thick sequences (catastrophically), or else the organisms would have had time to destroy bedding through bioturbation.

The rocks contained in the Hartford basin are not of marine origin, but the same principle can be applied. Organisms and plants were obviously present in the basin. In fact, abundant plant life must have been present to support the dinosaur population. Although only scarce remains of the invertebrates have been found, there are scattered tracks and trails which prove their presence. If the basin was deposited over 24 million years, would this not be sufficient time for small burrowing organisms to destroy bedding in the finer grained red sediments of, for example, the East Berlin Formation? This was supposed to be deposited in shallow, quiet lakes. Plants on supposed floodplains of the basin would have destroyed any finely laminated floodplain sediment.

In conclusion, the general absence of abundant bioturbation in the basin supports catastrophic sedimentation and does not support the uniformitarian model for basin deposition. Bioturbation takes place only if organisms or plants are present to do work. They apparently were present during basin deposition, for we have evidence of their presence, but deposition occurred so quickly they did not have time to re-root and cause any significant bioturbation.

Basalts

One of the most impressive evidences of catastrophism in the basin are the basalts: The Talcott, the Holyoke, and the Hampden. Almost everyone would agree that each flow of these basalts was laid down within a short period of time. It is very impressive that these basalts contain pillows, vesicles, amygdules, and other features at their contacts, which indicate the basalt flows occurred shortly after clastic deposition, while the sediments were still wet.

Only the lower most basalt, the Talcott, is extensively pillowed. In Meriden, the pillows range from 0.5 to 1.0 meters in diameter. Gray (26) reported pillows up to 2.0 meters in diameter. It is generally agreed that lava must be spewed out in a subaqueous environment for pillows to be formed. Snyder and Fraser (27) who have done extensive review on the literature of pillow formation have come to the conclusion that the only way for pillows to form is the contact of hot magma with water or mud. Authors such as Krynine (28), Hubert et al. (29), and Gray (30) also support the idea that the pillows were formed in a wet environment.

Due to the extensive pillowed nature of the Talcott Basalt at most localities, it seems reasonable the Talcott was deposited under water, on muddy, water saturated sediments, or both. This is very obvious at the New Haven Arkose/Talcott Basalt contact in the Farmington River Gorge at Tariffville, Connecticut. Gray (31) described the pillows at the base of the contact as "intimately intermixed with the underlying sediment." At this contact pillows of basalt can be seen one meter below the main contact completely surrounded by the New Haven sediments. Either the characteristics of this outcrop indicate the deposition of the sediments and the basalt was contemporaneous; or, when the basalt was deposited, the underlying sediments were so soft and muddy they actually "swallowed up" some of the pillows. Whatever the case, it is obvious water was present when this particular flow took place. Since these sediments were soft and unconsolidated when the flow occurred, not much time passed by between clastic sedimentation and the basalt flow. The universality of pillows in the Talcott indicates that the New Haven Arkose was totally covered with water at the time of the Talcott flows or at least was extremely water saturated. The shales of the New Haven remain fissile right up to the contact with the Talcott Basalt. This is remarkable considering the uniformitarian viewpoint. Why haven't the shales been bioturbated by plant or animal life? Why isn't there a soil here? This is evidence that the Talcott flow occurred soon after clastic deposition.

The lowest of the three basalts in Connecticut is extensively pillowed. The Holyoke and the Hampden contain rare pillows. A few pillows about a meter in diameter were observed in the Hampden Basalt by the author near Branford. It seems these basalts were deposited under different conditions, because pillows are scarcely found in the upper basalts. However, it seems water was present because of the wide occurrence of vesicles and amygdules in these basalts. These features occur widely at the base of the first Hampden flow and at the base of some of the other Hampden flows (32). Large pipe amygdules occur near Trinity College in Hartford. Chapman argued these formed by steam rising from the moist sediments below.

If in fact the Hartford basin was deposited over millions of years, there should be a paleosol below the basalt contact. Bedding should have been obliterated by plants and trees that grew in this soil. Why aren't plant roots preserved here? Would not this be the ideal place? The contacts were carefully observed and the literature was searched for such features at the basalt/clastic boundaries. As far as the literature shows, no evidence of paleosols exist at these contacts. It appears as though the East Berlin sediments were deposited before any kind of plant life could be established. The Hampden flows occurred while the sediments were still water saturated from depositional processes.

The contact between the East Berlin and the Hampden Basalt is very sharp and regular. As just mentioned, there is no organic debris or soil horizon present at or below the contact. Between the eight Hampden flows, no clastic sediment has been reported. This contact is also sharp and usually defined by a layer of amygdules or vesicles. This is evidence that the flows were deposited immediately after the previous one occurred. If these flows occurred hundreds or thousands of years apart one would expect to find a hummocky, erosional surface between the flows and some type of sedimentary material. Instead, one finds sharp contacts, indicating rapid succession of each flow.

The upper contact of the Hampden with the Portland Formation is interesting because there are small pockets of red sediment in the basalt just below the upper contact. This shows that red sediment was being deposited contemporaneously with the basalt. How else could the sediment have gotten into the small pockets? The contacts with the red sediment are sharp. At its upper surface the basalt is very sharp and angular. There was no erosion of the basalt before the Portland was deposited.

The Holyoke consists of two flows. Gray (33) noted that the upper surface of the lower flow suffered little erosional relief and sediment accumulation before the second flow was deposited. This evidence indicates that the second flow occurred soon after the first. Again, this is evidence for rapid succession of events for deposition of rocks in the Hartford basin.

Sedimentology

The sediments of the Hartford basin support the idea that the basin was deposited in a short period of time. The sedimentary features which indicate rapid deposition include conglomerates, breccias, the Great Unconformity found in Southington, soft-sediment deformation, cross-bedding, flaser bedding, mud-chip breccias and angular sediments. Paul D. Krynine (34) is credited for the most thoroughly documented study of the sediments of the Hartford basin. He recognized the angularity of the basin sediments throughout many parts of his classic work. He emphasizes the idea that erosion was rapid and violent without much weathering.

Krynine believed the basin was deposited over millions of years. A current estimate by Hubert et al. (35) is that deposition took 24 million years. Because the basin is about 5 km thick, the average rate of sediment deposition would be .0002 m/yr or 2 cm per 100 years. Would not this rate be slow enough to allow rounding of sediments and weathering of minerals? No references could be found concerning how fast rounding and weathering could take place (on an absolute time scale). It is expected at these sedimentary rates much more evidence of rounding and weathering should be present. Therefore, it is concluded from the evidence of angularity of the sediments, the basin must have been deposited in a shorter time span than authors such as Hubert would suggest. Angularity does not show exactly how fast the basin was deposited (nor will any known method), but it does indicate it was deposited quickly and not over millions of years.

Only one place in the Hartford basin shows sediments found in contact with the underlying crystalline bedrock. On the western edge of Southington, Connecticut, 1/2 km upstream from where Roaring Brook crosses Mt. Vernon Rd., this contact is exposed. It has been described and observed by William M. Davis (36), Rice and Gregory (37), Krynine (38) and other authors. This has been named the "Great Unconformity" (39) because 200 million years of time is unaccounted for, and unrepresented by rock. The erosional contact occurs between the Devonian Southington Mountain Member of the Straits Schist and the Upper Triassic New Haven Arkose. Of course, the present author does not agree with the geological ages of millions of years placed on these rocks, nor does he agree there are 200 million years of missing time. However, he does concur that there is an unconformity at this locality which is extremely significant.

The contact occurs about 100 meters along the north side of Roaring Brook. The most significant part of the outcrop is found furthest upstream where the topography begins to steepen. This is the area where one can go from the easily erodible New Haven Arkose to the more resistant metamorphic rocks of the Western Highlands. Although difficult to find the contact downstream, it can be found by close inspection. The New Haven Arkose fills deep channels in the schist below. It is difficult to determine how deep the largest channels are. The channels' upper contacts are lost in vegetation as they are traced up the ravine wall. The channels within the larger channels are from 1 to 3 meters deep. All channels are carved along strike of the foliation of the schist (approximately N-S).

The New Haven Arkose which fills the channels is brown to tan in color. It mostly consists of a very coarse to granular sandstone, which is poorly sorted and subangular. Many metamorphic clasts are contained within the arkose. They originated from the metamorphic rocks surrounding the Hartford basin. Clasts found in the immediate vicinity of the unconformity range from granules to cobbles about 150 mm in diameter. Bedding is indistinguishable near the contact but becomes more apparent higher in the ravine wall. If observed from a distance, a hint of trough cross-bedding can be observed in the outcrop. The contact between the New Haven and the Straits Schist is very sharp.

Downstream from the main contact, large quartz boulders, at least a meter in diameter (possibly up to 2 meters), are found resting on the unconformity. These boulders were probably transported from the Western Metamorphic highlands, not too far from where they are now found. They might have come from the east which would make their transport even more phenomenal. It is interesting to note that large boulders such as this have been observed on the Precambrian/Cambrian contact at many places around the world. It is significant they are also found here. Their significance will be discussed in the next section.

The features of this outcrop (its angularity, sorting, sediment size, and channels) indicated it was deposited under catastrophic conditions. The matrix supported, poorly sorted, angular nature of the sediments near the contact probably indicates these sediments were being transported by suspension processes such as a mud flow. However, the bedded nature of the sediments a meter or so above the contact indicates that transportation may have been occurring by processes closer to traction. Whatever the method of transport and deposition that occurred here, one thing is evident-- it required catastrophic processes to carve the large channels and deposit the sediment at this locality.

Cross-bedding by itself is not an indication of catastrophism. Cross-bedding forms under normal fluvial and marine conditions today. Extraordinarily large cross-beds are not present in the Hartford basin. The largest cross-beds observed are in an outcrop along the North Branch of the Park River at the University of Hartford campus. These large cross-beds were in 1-2 meter sets. Cross-beds elsewhere in the basin were commonly present, often found as trough cross-stratification. Although cross-bedding doesn't necessarily indicate catastrophic deposition, it does indicate moving water, active deposition, and erosional processes. Larger cross-beds (which are occasionally present) do indicate large amounts of moving water. Mud chip breccias and climbing ripples indicate erosional and depositional processes were actively occurring and not stagnant. These two features are very common throughout the basin, especially in the Shuttle Meadow, East Berlin, and western Portland Formations.

FLOOD MODEL

Now that the evidence for catastrophism has been discussed, it is appropriate to apply this evidence and the features of the basin within a possible Flood model. Based upon field work and research the best possible model will be presented and is subject to change upon further research and new data.

Crystalline rocks exist below the sediments of the Hartford basin, as they are assumed to exist under all sediments on the earth. As discussed previously, schist lies below the New Haven Arkose. At this contact, large, angular quartz boulders up to and exceeding one meter in diameter can be found. Similar contacts and boulders exist in the Grand Canyon between the Shinumo Quartzite and the Tapeats Sandstone: the contact between the Cambrian and the Precambrian. The boulders in the Canyon were found up to 40 meters in diameter! Angular quartz boulders can also be observed between the Cambrian and Precambrian in the Black Hills of South Dakota. In fact, this unconformity is worldwide and sometimes referred to as the Great Unconformity. Ager (40) refers to this as the basal Cambrian quartzite and recognizes this as a worldwide contact. It seems reasonable this worldwide basal conglomerate, which represents the beginning of fossilized remains, marks the beginning of the Flood. The author would like to tentatively suggest the unconformity between the basin floor and the New Haven correlates to the world wide basal unconformity.

It is assumed that a great catastrophe such as the Flood would produce deposits which show evidence of rapid erosion and deposition. As previously discussed, there is solid evidence for this in the Hartford basin. After initial erosion and deposition of the basal conglomerate and New Haven Arkose, a fissure developed which allowed the basalt flows of the Talcott to form. The Talcott was deposited in rising Flood waters or on water saturated sediments. The formation of the rift not only allowed basalt flows, but also an influx of sediments to fill the basin. The sediments found in the basin can be traced to surrounding igneous and metamorphic rocks around the basin. Basalt flows are not exclusive to the Hartford basin, but can be found in some of the other basins along the east coast.

As Flood waters rose, dinosaurs left tracks in the newly laid mud while trying to escape to higher ground. Fish and large amounts of plant material were quickly buried to form large organic deposits (coal in some Newark basins), later turning into black shales. Today there is little evidence of marine sediments covering the Hartford basin. However they do cover some other Newark basins along the east coast. Presumably, they also covered the Hartford. These sediments probably eroded away after the Flood due to the action of receding waters, glaciers, and melt wash streams.

CONCLUSION

There are many evidences within the Hartford basin which suggest that it was not deposited in a conventional manner, but catastrophically. When considering depositional models for the basin, its black shales, fossils (especially fish), basalts, and sediments cannot be overlooked. These features point towards catastrophic deposition. Currently, there is no known evidence to suggest the basin has taken millions of years to deposit as those with uniformitarian biases would like to believe. Even radiometric dating techniques have proven unsuccessful in distinguishing the ages between basalt flows in the basin. In considering a possible model for deposition, the catastrophic Flood model agrees with the evidence better than the conventional uniformitarian view does.

This study has bearing on other Newark basins which are found along the east coast of the United States. All of the basins are strikingly similar in structure and sedimentology to each other (41). Even the northwestern Triassic sediments of Europe are similar to the Newark (42). Because of the similarities to the Hartford basin, conclusions reached here may also be applicable to these other areas.

ACKNOWLEDGMENTS

Thanks to everyone, far too many to mention by name, who have contributed to this study over the past five years. Teachers, advisors, friends, and family have all added to this study, many without even realizing the role they have played. Extra special appreciation goes to my wife who has encouraged and helped me more than any one else. Thank you Jamie.

REFERENCES

1. Hubert, J. F., Reed, A. A., Dowdall, W. L., and Gilchrist, J. M., GUIDE TO THE MESOZOIC REDBEDS OF CENTRAL CONNECTICUT, State Geological and Natural History Survey of Connecticut Guidebook, No. 4, 1978, p. 36.

2. Whitmore, John H., THE HARTFORD BASIN OF CENTRAL CONNECTICUT: AN EVALUATION OF UNIFORMITARIAN AND CATASTROPHIC MODELS, Masters Thesis, Institute for Creation Research, Santee, California, 1988, pp. 58-100.

3. deBoer, J., "Paleomagnetic Differentiation and Correlation of the Late Triassic Volcanic Rocks in the Central Appalachians (with Special Reference to the Connecticut Valley)", GEOLOGICAL SOCIETY OF AMERICA, BULLETIN, Vol. 79, 1968, p. 624.

4. Morris, H. M., "Circular Reasoning in Evolutionary Geology", IMPACT SERIES, No. 48, Institute for Creation Research, El Cajon, California, 1977, pp. 1-4.

5. Austin, S. A. and Morris, J. M., "Tight Folds and Clastic Dikes as Evidence for Rapid Deposition and Deformation of Two Very Thick Stratigraphic Sequences", PROCEEDINGS OF THE FIRST INTERNATIONAL CONFERENCE ON CREATIONISM, Vol. 2, Pittsburgh, Pennsylvania, Creation Science Fellowship, 1986, pp. 3-15.

6. McDonald, N. G., "Paleontology of the Mesozoic Rocks of the Connecticut Valley", GUIDEBOOK FOR FIELDTRIPS IN CONNECTICUT AND SOUTH CENTRAL MASSACHUSETTS, NEW ENGLAND INTERCOLLEGIATE GEOLOGICAL CONFERENCE, Guidebook No. 5, State Geological and Natural History Survey of Connecticut, 1982, p. 147.

7. Ruedemann, R., "Ecology of Black Mud Shales of Eastern New York", JOURNAL OF PALEONTOLOGY, Vol. 9, No. 1, 1935, p. 81.

8. Zangerl, R. and Richardson, E. S., "The Paleoecological History of Two Pennsylvanian Black Shales", FIELDIANA-- GEOLOGY MEM., Vol. 4, 352pp.

9. Byers, C. W., "Shale Fissility: Relation to Bioturbation", SEDIMENTOLOGY, Vol. 21, 1974, p. 479.

10. Piper, D. J. W., "Turbidite Origin of Some Laminated Mudstones", GEOLOGY MAGAZINE, Vol. 109, No. 2, 1972, pp. 115-126.

11. Whittington, H. B., THE BURGESS SHALE, Yale University Press, New Haven, Connecticut, 1985, pp. 33-35.

12. Bretz, J. H., "The Lake Missoula Floods and the Channeled Scabland", JOURNAL OF GEOLOGY, Vol. 77, 1969, pp. 505-543.

13. Lambert, A. and Hsu, K. J., "Non-annual Cycles of Varve-like Sedimentation in Walensee, Switzerland, SEDIMENTOLOGY, Vol. 26, 1979, pp. 453-461.

14. Cornet, B., Traverse, A. and McDonald, N. G., "Fossil Spores, Pollen, and Fishes from Connecticut Indicate Early Jurassic Age for part of the Newark Group, SCIENCE, Vol. 182, 1973, p. 1245.

15. Brett, C. E. and Baird, G. C., "Comparative Taphonomy: A Key to Paleoenvironmental Interpretation Based on Fossil Preservation", PALAIOS, Vol. 1, 1986, p. 212.

16. Vallentyne, J. R., "On Fish Remains in Lacustrine Sediments", AMERICAN JOURNAL OF SCIENCE, Vol. 258-A, 1960, p. 344.

17. White, W. A., "Colloid Phenomena in Sedimentation of Argillaceous Rocks", JOURNAL OF SEDIMENTARY PETROLOGY, Vol. 31, No. 4, 1961, pp. 560-570.

18. Lambert and Hsu, op. cit., p. 453.

19. Berthalt, G., "Experiences Sur la Lamination des Sediments par Granoclassement Periodique Posterier au Deopt. Contribution a L'explication de la Lamination Dans Nombre de Sediments et de Roches Sedimentaires", C. R. ACAD. SC. PARIS, t. 303, Serie II, No. 17, 1986, pp. 1569-1574.

20. Coombs, W. P., Jr., "Swimming Ability of Carnivorous Dinosaurs", SCIENCE, Vol. 207, 1980, pp. 1198-1200.

21. Bird, R. T., "Did Brontosaurus Ever Walk on Land?", NATURAL HISTORY, Vol. 53, No. 2, 1944, pp. 60-67.

22. Hitchcock, Edward, ICHNOLOGY OF NEW ENGLAND, William White, printer to the State, Boston, Massachusetts, 1858, 220pp.

23. Lull, R. S., TRIASSIC LIFE OF THE CONNECTICUT VALLEY, State of Connecticut Geological and Natural History Survey, Bulletin No. 81, 1953, 336pp.

24. Dott, R. H., "1982 SEPM Presidential Address: Episodic Sedimentation-- How Normal is Average? How Rare is Rare? Does it Matter?", JOURNAL OF SEDIMENTARY PETROLOGY, Vol. 53, No. 1, 1983, p. 12.

25. Rhoads, D. C., "Rates of Sediment Reworking by Yolia limatula in Buzzard's Bay, Massachusetts, and Long Island Sound", JOURNAL OF SEDIMENTARY PETROLOGY, Vol. 33, No. 3, 1963, p. 727.

26. Gray, N. H., "Mesozoic Volcanism in North-Central Connecticut", GUIDEBOOK FOR FIELDTRIPS IN CONNECTICUT AND SOUTH CENTRAL MASSACHUSETTS, Guidebook No. 5, State Geological and Natural History Survey of Connecticut, 1982, p. 173.

27. Snyder, G. L. and Fraser, G. D., "Pillowed Lavas, II: A Review of Selected Recent Literature", United States Geological Survey Professional Paper 454-C, pp. C1-C7.

28. Krynine, Paul D., PETROLOGY, STRATIGRAPHY AND ORIGIN OF THE TRIASSIC SEDIMENTARY ROCKS OF CONNECTICUT, State Geological and Natural History Survey of Connecticut, Bulletin No. 73, 1950, p. 169.

29. Hubert et al., op. cit., p. 49.

30. Gray, op. cit., p. 185.

31. Gray, op. cit., p. 180.

32. Chapman, R. W., "Stratigraphy and Petrology of the Hampden Basalt in Central Connecticut", State Geological and Natural History Survey of Connecticut, Report of Investigations, No. 3, 1965, p. 5.

33. Gray, op. cit., p. 36.

34. Krynine, op. cit., pp. 79, 80, 92, 93, 94, 157.

35. Hubert et al., op. cit., p. 36.

36. Davis, W. M., "The Triassic Formation of Connecticut", EIGHTEENTH ANNUAL REPORT OF THE UNITED STATES GEOLOGICAL SURVEY, 1896-1897, PART II, 1898, pp. 19-23.

37. Rice, W. N. and Gregory, H. E., MANUAL OF THE GEOLOGY OF CONNECTICUT, State Geological and Natural History Survey of Connecticut, Bulletin No. 6, 1906, p. 81.

38. Krynine, op. cit., p. 49.

39. Bell, M., THE FACE OF CONNECTICUT, State Geological and Natural History Survey of Connecticut, Bulletin No. 110, 1985, p. 117.

40. Ager, D. V., THE NATURE OF THE STRATIGRAPHICAL RECORD, Macmillan Press, London, second edition, 1981, p. 11.

41. Whitmore, op. cit., p. 160-168.

42. Ager, op. cit., p. 6.

DISCUSSION

Let me commend Mr. Whitmore on a fine paper. However, there are a few comments or questions I would like to raise.

Under the section "Problems with dating the basin," I was unconvinced by the author's proposed logical flaw, and his citing of Dr. Austin's and my paper. It would be better to attempt to demonstrate that each layer was most likely laid down rapidly, and that there is no evidence of long time passage between the layers. If so, the likelihood of a short time is established.

Regarding black shales, Mr. Whitmore says there are many intact fish fossils. Earlier he had claimed a very few fish had been found. Which is correct? Did he make a study of the fish, bioturbation, etc., and find evidence supporting rapid deposition and short time? It is not enough to list the various mechanisms for rapid deposition of shale, what does *this* shale indicate? If the study has not yet been made, what suggestions can the author offer?

Mr. Whitmore made a good point regarding "swimming dinosaur prints." This was no mud flat. Also, the intermingling of basalts with soft, recently deposited sediments is a good point, rightly arguing for a rapid sequence of events.

Mr. Whitmore mentioned "conglomerate lenses throughout the rocks of the basin, but described them only along the basal unconformity. Are there others, and if so what is their character? Good Job!

John D. Morris, Ph.D.
Santee, California

Mr. Whitmore excels as a field geologist, and this paper show his work well. While others may be content in sitting in their arm chair and citing the literature, the author is at the outcrop examining the strata. His empirical approach to stratigraphy should be an example for both uniformitarian and catastrophist geologists. The evidences for catastrophic depositional processes in Hartford Basin are obvious in black shales, fish fossils, dinosaur tracks, bioturbation, basalt flows and arkosic sandstones. Catastrophism is alive and well in Connecticut Valley!

Mr. Whitmore's paper does not mention very significant observations made concerning shrinkage cracks in shaley sediments of Hartford Basin. Although shrinkages are usually supposed to form by drying in a subaerial environment, field studies in the Hartford Basin indicate that these have formed after burial in a substratal environment. This could be the subject for a future paper.

Steve Austin, Ph.D.
Santee, California

CLOSURE

I would like to thank Dr. Morris for taking the time to review my paper and offering his favorable comments.

It would be tremendous if large folded outcrops of sedimentary rock could be found in Connecticut. There are a few large outcrops (for example, interstate road cuts east of Hartford), but these contain relatively horizontal strata. The point I was trying to make was if there were folds, this might be an additional argument for short time spans as Dr. Morris argued in California and Colorado (5).

I did not claim very few fish fossils had been found. Possibly Dr. Morris is referring to the section when I was discussing modern lake sediments. In modern lake sediments, fish remains are very rare (16). I have not made in depth studies on black shales and their mechanism for deposition. A good study would be to examine modern black shale environments and bioturbation within them. A comparison then could be made to fossil shales with inferences to how or how not they were deposited. I believe black shales have much to offer creationists and catastrophists. Some of the arguments I have used in Connecticut would be good starting points.

Yes, there are many areas conglomerate lenses are found throughout the basin besides the basal unconformity. Notably, they also occur along the eastern margin of the basin, clasts being angular and occasionally exceeding a meter in diameter. Smaller areas of subangular to subrounded conglomerates can be found as lenses throughout the central and western part of the basin.

I would like to thank Dr. Austin, for the time spent with me in the field and the classroom. I appreciate his kind comments.

Unfortunately, the length of this paper was too short to include my studies of shrinkage cracks in Connecticut. Because of their natural likeness to mudcracks, they have been interpreted as such by many authors. I have only begun to look into this subject, but initial studies show, at least at one location, cracks were formed substratally after deposition. See my thesis (2) pages 63-71 for more information. More than likely this will be a forthcoming paper.

John Whitmore, M.S.

GEOLOGIC SETTING OF POLONIUM RADIOHALOS

RICHARD WAKEFIELD
385 MAIN STREET,
BEAVERTON, ONTARIO
CANADA LOK 1A0

GREGG WILKERSON, PHD
6008 LISA CT.
BAKERSFIELD, CA 93304

INTRODUCTION

The existence of radiation-damage halos, also known as Radiation-Induced Colour Halos, or RICHes (Odom & Rink, 1989), in minerals has been known since 1907 (Joly, 1907, 1917). Histories of the study of these halos is given by Gentry (1988), Wise (1989), and Wilkerson (1990 in press). Interest in radiohalos and in particular certain varieties of Po halos has been revived by Gentry and others (Gentry, 1966a,b, 1968, 1970, 1971, 1973, 1974, 1978, 1979, 1986b, 1988; Gentry et. al 1973, 1974, 1976,1978).

The existence of Polonium halos in Precambrian "granites" has been interpreted as proof of the instant creation of the earth (Gentry, 1988). Due to the very short half life of one of the isotopes, Po-218, the length of time of this creation is interpreted to have been "less than three minutes (Gentry, 1986, p.34)". Po halos, according to this model, would be expected to be found in the oldest rocks of the earth's crust. Absent from almost all of these investigations is a documentation of the geology of sites from which Po halos have been described. There are no precisely-described specimen localities except for two --the Silver Crater Mine and the Faraday Mine near Bancroft, Ontario, Canada.

Wakefield (1988a,b) described the geology of these sites which shows clear incompatibility with this particular creation model. Here we present a synthesis of what is now known of the regional and local geologic setting of this and other Po halo sites. The geological complexity of the Po halo localities, specifically the Canadian Precambrian ones, the fact that the Po hosting pegmatites are definitely intrusive, and that sedimentary and volcanic successions pre-date Po halos are evidence against this creation model.

GEOLOGY OF POLONIUM HALOS

A) The Canadian Shield:

Two of Gentry's published locations --Faraday Mine and Silver Crater Mine--and one unpublished location --Fission Mine-- (Wakefield 1988) are located in the late Proterozoic Grenville Supergroup of the Precambrian Canadian Shield. The Precambrian is divided into two main eras: the Archean and the Proterozoic based on specific geological criteria. Each of these eras is subdivided into reconstructible events such as large scale metamorphic activity or sedimentary and volcanic deposition.

A great deal of work has been carried out on the Precambrian Canadian Shield. The Shield is made up of seven distinct geological "Provinces" --west to east from the Northwest Territories to Quebec and in an arc around Hudson's Bay: the Bear, the Slave, the Churchill, the Superior, the Southern, the Grenville, and the Nain. Ontario, where Gentry's samples came from, includes three of these provinces. The Superior, situated in northern Ontario, is the oldest (all isotopic ages are greater than 2,500 Ma and hence is Archean) both radiometrically and structurally. It consists of many types of metasediments and several types of metavolcanics intruded by a variety of igneous bodies. The Southern Province, which rests unconformably (with fossil soil, Robertson (1968)) on the Superior, is mostly folded metasediments intruded by some granites and is middle to early Proterozoic (all isotopic ages are between 2,500 to 1,800 Ma) in age. The Grenville, located in southern Ontario, is the youngest Province and is late Proterozoic (all isotopic ages are 1,500 to 900 Ma). It consists mostly of deformed metasediments in the north, a large metamorphosed intrusive gneiss complex (called the Algonquin Batholith) in the middle, and the Grenville Supergroup in the south.

The Grenville Supergroup, which contains Gentry's locations, is a very complex succession of metasediments, metavolcanics, alkalic intrusive rocks, mafic intrusive rocks and granitic intrusive rocks. It is located in a region of low- to very high-grade metamorphism that has altered many of the igneous, sedimentary and volcanic rocks into gneisses. Many original igneous, sedimentary and volcanic features are preserved. Hydrothermally altered rocks and metasomatic rocks (wall-rocks that have been included within and altered by intrusive melts) are common. The metavolcanics, called the Tudor Formation, (the lowermost rock units in the Supergroup) consist of pillow lavas (indicative of underwater extrusion), breccias (fragmented lavas), tuffs and pyroclastics (similar to what came out of Mt. St. Helens), all altered to varying degrees by metamorphism. The intrusive rocks consist of varying types like gabbros (a dense rock high in the mafic minerals which contain iron and magnesium), granites (light-coloured rocks low in mafic minerals but high in potassium and sodium silicates like feldspar and quartz), diorites (intermediate in composition between the former two), syenites (poor in quartz), nepheline syenite (like syenite but higher in alkali metals and lower in silica), and pegmatites (any of the above in small dikes with large to very-large crystals). Many, but not all, of these intrusive rocks have been altered by low-grade metamorphism.

Many of the metasedimentary rocks, called the Hastings Formation, show clear and unambiguous sedimentary features like clastic grains, cobbles, ripple marks, mudcracks, bedding plains and, most important, stromatolites --fossil blue-green algal mats and domes.

Discussions defending the Po halo creation interpretation have denied the authenticity of the stromatolite fossils found in this area (Gentry, 1988, p.326). One reference, Hofmann (1971), has been taken out of context to show that there is no consensus on that interpretation. Hofmann specifically noted:

"A reconsideration of the evidence for a stromatolite hypothesis is in order. The gross morphology, internal structure, distribution pattern, marker laminae, and bulk lithology are very much like a great many stromatolite occurrences in undeformed Proterozoic carbonate sequences. What distinguishes those at L'Amable is the coarse grain size, the non-regularity and large spacing of the darker laminae, and the deformed (squeezed) nature, all of which could be attributed to the effects of high-grade metamorphism. The notion that a relatively little deformed remnant of marble should be preserved in a more severely squeezed, plastically deformed belt need not invalidate the stromatolite interpretation,...

In addition, there are abundant outcrops showing well-preserved primary bedding (Hewitt and James, 1956, pp.19,21), so it is possible to have a favourably situated block containing remnants of primary sedimentary features. ...

Although a stromatolite origin for the original structures at L'Amable is reasonable, it is not considered proven (Hofmann, 1971)."

We must not get confused here. Hofmann is describing only one stromatolite occurrence --the one at L'Amable a few kilometers south of Bancroft. There are many other locations, mostly in the much less deformed areas south of Bancroft, which have well defined stromatolites. The stromatolites from Belmont Lake island (Figure 1) are undeniable. The L'Amable ones are not as good due to the higher metamorphic grade of the area.

A more recent publication describing stromatolites in all the localities noted:

"Biosedimentary structures preserved in the rocks of the map area and other parts of the Central Metasedimentary Belt [of which the Supergroup is part of] are stromatolites, ...

Stromatolites in the Burleigh Falls-Bancroft-Madoc area comprise five main types, distinguished by variations in morphology. In ascending order of morphologic complexity these are: (1) algal laminates (mats); (2) domal stromatolites; (3) columnar stromatolites; (4)conophyton forms; and (5) jacutonphyton forms. ...

In general, mid-amphibolite facies recrystalization is not, without moderate to strong deformation, sufficient to prohibit recognition of stromatolitic structures. ...

The ubiquity of stromatolites in the map area provides well constrained evidence that the prevailing depositional setting consists of one or more relatively extensive carbonate platforms. [Bartlett and DeKemp (1987)]"

They note that the setting for these stromatolites in dolomitic marble would indicate a "shallow marine environment" with some of the sedimentary rocks showing turbidite series. The pegmatites and vein-dikes which contain the Po halos are STRUCTURALLY YOUNGER than these depositional rocks.

Stromatolite fossils differ slightly from other fossils in that it is not the actual organisms which are preserved as rock, it is the structures of detritus these organisms form into their mounds which are preserved. However, this does not detract from the inference derived by comparison with living versions. Hofmann (1987) describes many other Precambrian fossils which also predate Po localities.

The Fission (also known as the Richardson) Mine is located 2 km east of Wilberforce on lot 4, concession XXI, Cardiff Township (Lat. 45o3'15"N; Long. 78o11'40"W, Figure 2) and consists of a single abandoned adit driven into a hill. This site is a common mineral-collecting locality for apatite, biotite, radioactive minerals, and fluorite.

From the description in Hogarth et al (1972) it is clear that this is a small calcite vein-dike (a rock containing mostly large crystals of calcium carbonate and other minerals like mica) body. The biotite grew outward, replacing the calcite, from the syentized wall-rock as a result of reactions between the wall-rock, calcite core and volatile fluids (Moyd, Personal Communication, Aug. 1987). This vein-dike is small in length and width, it cuts metasedimentary rocks which still retain bedding planes, and radioactive minerals abound. In another mineral collecting guidebook it was noted that at this site "Uraninite was found in cavities in pegmatites with magnetite, mica or calcite-fluorite intergrowths." (Sabina, 1986, p.79). Clearly radioactive minerals occur in this locality.

The Silver Crater (Basin) Mine is located 12 km west of Bancroft on lot 31, concession XV, Faraday Township (Lat. 45o01'50"N; Long. 78o00'30"W) 3 km north of the settlement of Monck Road (Figure 2). This abandoned mine consists of an adit with some drifting and a raise. The calcite vein-dike body here was mined for its biotite content. This is the locality of the mica that contains Gentry's 'spectacle' halo which "...exhibits true radiohalo characteristics.". This site is similar to the Fission site and the calcite vein-dike is part of the same group of calcite vein-dikes dotting the country side near Bancroft. A full description of the relative geological setting of this site can be found in Hewitt, (1957).

Contrary to Gentry's general claims, the rock types at the Silver Crater and the Fission Mines are not granites. The composition and mode of origin is totally wrong for a granite. Recent research about the origin of the calcite vein-dike material, due to the presence of rounded calcite in the biotite and other large minerals in the dikes, indicates that the biotite grew as a replacement within the solid calcite vein-dike matrix. This process occurs when the solid calcite vein-dike (which was hydrothermally deposited, or injected as a molten liquid) is reheated enough to cause the evenly distributed minerals of biotite, hornblende, betafite, apatite, etc. in the wall-rock and calcite vein-dike to start to migrate and form larger crystals in the calcite vein-dike (Moyd 1989).

The Faraday (now called the Madawaska) Mine is located 5 km west of Bancroft on Highway #28 on the north-east end of Bow Lake (Lat. 77o55'30"N; Long. 45o00'15"W, Figure 2). The mine workings consisted of several adits, drifting and several levels. Figure 3 shows the surface geology at this site. The mine was opened for the uranium in a granite pegmatite, which cuts a gabbro/metagabbro intrusive body 10 km long and 1.25 km wide, which itself cuts metasedimentary rocks, mostly marble.

The history of events recorded in the rock record witness material eroded from some preexisting rock, deposited as a sedimentary rock (probably a volcanic arc island setting (Easton, 1986b)), then deformed and recrystallized by high-grade metamorphism (referred to as the Grenville Orogeny (Lumbers, 1982)) which changed this rock to paragneisses. This in turn was intruded by the gabbro, which later underwent another metamorphic episode during the latter stages of the orogeny. Finally, these rocks were intruded by the granite pegmatite. The biotite which hosts some of these Po halos came from this pegmatite. The pegmatites are 91.5 to 915 meters long, 3 to 46 meters wide and some extend down dip more than 300 meters. (Masson and Gordon, 1981, p.60). This entire sequence was then altered by fluid migration called fenitization, introducing calcium altering the chemistry of the rocks in the area (Lumbers, 1988 personal communication).

A.R. Bullis writing on the geology of the Faraday mine notes the structure of the pegmatites: "...in other places [the pegmatites] are discordant and show cross-cutting relationship to all of the wall-rocks. The contacts are sharp and clear cut and others are in the nature of irregular, gradational zones that show a change, or alteration, from paragneiss to granitic pegmatite over widths of up to 24 inches. It is obvious that both injection and metasomatic processes have taken place during the intrusion of the pegmatites. Chilled edges are rare or non-existent. Magmatic stopping, or the engulfing of the country rock has taken place on a large scale; there are many blocks of paragneiss and pyroxenite within the pegmatite [xenoliths]. Most of the inclusions are fresh looking, but many are highly altered and ghost-like in appearance (Bullis, 1965, p.717)."

All three Bancroft sites, and many others, are uranium localities. Some, including the Faraday pegmatite, were mined for uranium. Four million tons of ore was mined from the Faraday for 3.3 million kg of uranium oxide until it closed in 1984. The average concentration consisted of 0.1074% uranium oxide. The most common radioactive mineral is uranothorite, hence plenty of uranium and thorium were present. These minerals are very small (less than .1 mm) and scattered throughout the pegmatite becoming ore grade in the quartz and magnetite regions of the pegmatite.

The Silver Crater and Fission mines are lithologically different, but they too contain abundant radioactive minerals --especially betafite (a radioactive variety of the mineral pyrochlore, which is a complex calcium-sodium-(uranium)-niobate- tantalate-hydroxide). It was noted by Satterly that "Betafite [at the Silver Crater] is often found in close association with clusters of mica books and apatite crystals. Small crystals of betafite have been found within the books of mica. (Satterly, 1957, p.130)"

Figure 5 diagrammatically shows the geological relationships of part of the Shield and the location, in relation to the geology, of Gentry's Faraday samples. These relationships are not based primarily on the "uniformitarian principle" but on hard-won field observations over almost 100 years of work by thousands of geologists. At the bottom-left of the figure is a block diagram of Figure 3. The pegmatite dikes cut a gabbro (shown at the bottom right), which cuts different types of metasedimentary rocks. These metasedimentary rocks can be shown, in the field, to rest in a complex way on metavolcanics around the Madoc area south of Bancroft (middle block). This, in turn, rests unconformably on the metamorphosed Algonquin Batholith, which intrudes the deep- and shallow-water metasediments to the north (top block), which abuts (by a major fault) and partly rests on the metasedimentary column of the Southern Province, which rests unconformably on the "greenstone" metasediments and metavolcanics intruded by granites, which abuts the metasedimentary and gneissic belts to the north in the Superior Province. So if Gentry's claim of created granite is valid, then this entire sequence also must have been instantly created--in "just three brief minutes". Since these Po halo dikes are demonstrably the last rocks to form in the Shield then, by his reasoning, the entire Shield must have been "instantly created".

It would help now to understand what geologists define as a pegmatite: "Pegmatites represent the final water-rich, siliceous melts of intermediate to silicic igneous magmas, and can generally be thought of as final residual melts... Although pegmatites can be found in almost any shape, they are most commonly dike-like or lensoid. Most pegmatites are small, but dimensions can vary from a few meters to hundreds of meters in the longest dimension and from 1 cm to as much as 200 meters in width. ... Since igneous pegmatites characteristically solidify late in igneous activity, they tend to be associated with plutonic or hypabyssal intrusions from which the volatile fractions could not readily escape. The great majority of pegmatites developed in deep-seated high-pressure environments (Guilbert and Park, 1986, p. 488)."

There are 4 basic types of pegmatites: simple zoned, complex zoned, simple unzoned and complex unzoned (most U/Th mineralization in the Bancroft area is in this type). The simple types are original and unaffected after emplacement. The complex type show various stages of alteration after solidification. The zoned pegmatite dikes show clear mineralogical zoning from the edges to the core of the dike due to the inability of the fluid to lose volatile components. On a highway rock cut just north of Buckhorn, west of Bancroft, a small zoned pegmatite, with 4 to 8 inch sized biotite and uranium mineralization, contains polonium halos (Collins, 1989, personal communication.) Zoned pegmatites are common in the Supergroup. The unzoned pegmatites cool much more quickly due to the loss of volatile components during crystallization of the melt. The grain size of zoned is generally greater than the unzoned.

The Faraday Mine pegmatites are considered a complex unzoned type (Masson & Gordon, 1981) where the pegmatite has undergone post-magmatic alteration involving deformation, hydrothermal activity and metasomatic reactions with the wall-rock. The uranium enrichment in the pegmatites is a two-stage process of a primary magmatic concentration and a secondary, later, concentration due to fluids picking up U and Th from both the pegmatites and the wall-rocks (mostly the syenites). Subsequently the U and Th minerals are precipitates. Masson and Gordon (1981) note that there are 5 principle controls for U deposits in the Bancroft area. 1) Premetamorphic concentration of U in the sedimentary deposits of the Supergroup. 2) High-rank regional metamorphism (the Grenville Orogeny). 3) Regional deformation of the country rocks causing fractures and openings for the emplacement of the pegmatites. 4) The proper geochemistry of the country rocks for mobilization of uranium, such as syenite and marble. 5) Large granitic bodies near by for the remelting and production of the magma, during the latter stages of regional metamorpism, for the pegmatites.

There are many types of dikes, other than pegmatites, that cut the other rock units of the Shield. In northern Ontario the most common of these are diabase dikes, which are found in very large clusters called dike swarms. Diabase dikes are narrow (from centimeters to many tens of meters) and very long (kilometers to hundreds of kilometers). Some dikes are fine-grained at the contact with the wall-rock and grade to course-grained in the centre. In the Sudbury area some of these dikes are known to cut through over 30 other rock units (Pye, et al, 1984) In the Archean area of the Shield at least 4 different sets of different-aged diabase dikes cross-cut each other (Fahrig & West 1986).

Some dikes have a clear-cut, or chilled, contact with the wall-rock, while others have a gradational contact because the heat of the intrusive dike partly melted the wall-rock. This occurs in the pegmatite at the Faraday Mine. And some of the dikes are vein-dikes deposited in cracks or cavities by fluids. This is the case with the Fission and Silver Crater sites. Just about all reports where pegmatites and other intrusives are described, there exists xenoliths. Xenoliths are pieces of wall rock which have broken off and caught up in the melt. Many of these exist in the Faraday mine pegmatite.

Based on the physical relationships of the rock sequences, it seems unreasonable to consider that polonium halos show instant creation of the earth. There is just too much pre-existing rock with clear evidence for a complex series of depositional, intrusive and metamorphic events to accept Gentry's "creation model."

B) Grain size and creation:

The grain size of minerals is also supposed to be an indicator of created rocks. According to Gentry, large crystals cannot form naturally (Gentry, 1986, p.131, 301). However, evidence from the geological record reveals this is not the case. It is not uncommon for dikes and plutons to show a gradation in crystal sizes from microscopic at the contacts, to pegmatitic in the core. Also intrusive rocks known as porphories, which contain very large crystals in a fine-grained matrix, contradict this model (Wilkerson, 1990 in press). Igneous rocks with both large and small grain sizes both predate and postdate the Po-halo bearing (e.g. "created") rocks.

C) Geologic Setting of other Po Halo Occurrences:

A listing of Po halo localities has been given by Wise (1989) and Wilkerson (1990 in press). Po haloes are known from Canada, Scandinavia, Japan, Madagascar, United States and Germany. The halos occur in rocks from Precambrian to Tertiary age. All are related to uranium/thorium mineralization. Some occur within the mica of pegmatites while others are found within accessory minerals in vein deposits. Several Po-containing mineral deposits cut across (and hence are younger than) fossiliferous host sediments.

MICROSCOPIC OBSERVATIONS

Thin section analysis of Po halos show that they are concentrated along fractures and cleavage planes (York, 1979). Photographs of Po halos often show the same diameter, indicating that all are within the same plane (Wilkerson, 1990 in press).

Several Po halo deposits show mineralogic replacement textures both in the mineralized zones (Wakefield, 1988a,b) and in the host rocks. At one of the Polonium halo sites, the Silver Crater Mine in Ontario, the biotite exhibits mineralogic and stratigraphic relationships that indicate a secondary origin. These vein-dike deposits show evidence of crystal growth by replacement of pre-existing vein-dike material. Such crystals contain within them relics of the original rock. The country rock also show clear signs of alteration. The alteration is probably due to circulating fluids simultaneously dissolving some minerals and replacing them with others.

The "Spectacle Halo" (Gentry et al, 1974) gives clear evidence for migration of Po-210 radiocenter along fractures and around spherical dislocations in a biotite crystal lattice (Wilkerson, 1990 in press).

In some specimens, there is an overlapping of Po and U halos (Gentry et al., 1986, fig. 1). In order to account for this observation and still maintain a young-earth interpretation, the ad hoc assumption must be made that decay rates varied many orders of magnitude in the past (Gentry 1988 p. 316, 317). If radioactive decay rates have been constant, as all existing experimental evidence suggests, then very long periods of time must be required for both Po and U halo formation (Brown, 1986).

Some Po halos are deformed (Gentry et al., 1976). Elliptical (deformed) and spherical (undeformed) are known from the same Po inclusion (Gentry et al, 1976, fig. 3). These observations indicate that Po halo generation is an on-going process that both pre-dates and post-dates deformation of their host rocks. Their formation involves a non-instantaneous series of events.

ISOTOPIC OBSERVATIONS

The other line of evidence in support of a natural origin for the Polonium halos is in the fact that every location were these halos are found, there exists abnormally high uranium and/or thorium concentrations. The Po halo sites in Ontario were mined for uranium (Wakefield, 1988a,b). The Conway granite, a Po-halo source, has been proposed as a commercial source of thorium (Richardson, 1964; Richardson and Adams, 1964).

A secondary origin of Po halos is suggested by the fact that selenium (Brown, 1986, Gentry, 1986, 1988 p.318) and uranium (Gentry, 1971, Wilkerson, 1990 in press) exist in some Po radiocenters. Since selenium has no radioactive origin, it must have been precipitated (and formed with) the Po through chemical reaction.

CONCLUSIONS

Summarizing the geology of the Po halo sites: 1) The samples of biotite that contain Po halos come from pegmatite dikes and calcite vein-dikes that cross-cut metamorphosed volcanic, sedimentary and igneous rock units --the dikes are clearly the last to form, not the first. 2) These dikes are not the vast extensive granite gneisses Gentry claims are the backbone of the mountains and continents --they are relatively small features. 3) Two of the sites are not even granites but calcite vein-dikes, most likely of hydrothermal origin. The biotite was formed in the solid matrix by metamorphism and metasomatism. 4) Crystal size variation in igneous, vein and metamorphic rocks is primarily due to cooling rates and crystal growth, and cannot be used to identify "created" rocks.

The sequence of rock units in the Bancroft/Madoc area is summarized in Figure 4. Formation of Po halos was one of the last events to occur in this area since the pegmatites are last. If the Po halo creation model were true, then a creation of rock with features known to have natural explanations would be required. Such a creation of apparent history would be so extensive as to make Phillip Gosse meek in comparison.

The available geologic data from other Po halo sites also indicates that they are components of relatively young mineral deposits within older host rocks. Rocks with Po halos are NOT the oldest (e.g. created) rocks of the earth's crust.

The origin of Po halos must involve a mechanism whereby Po is segregated from its U and Th precursors. This mechanism must result in concentration of Po haloes along fractures and cleavage planes. It must explain the simultaneous formation of Se with the Po.

One such mechanism is isolation or "orphanage" of uranium/thorium daughter products from U/Th precursors through radon accumulation and migration. Inclusions of radon at flaws in a mineral's crystal lattice would result in Po halos without the rings diagnostic of uranium or thorium precursors. There are several lines of evidence supporting a U-rich fluid migration precipitating the Po (probably via radon) which then produces the halos. 1) Po halos apparently occur in areas of unusually high uranium mineralization and metamorphism. 2) There are no halos for the thorium decay chain, even though the Th to U ratio is over 5:1 in the Faraday pegmatite, due to the insolubility of Th compounds (Brown, 1987). 3) No halos have been found in lunar rocks. 4) The geology of the mine sites listed above have different origins (magmatic -Faraday pegmatites- and hydrothermal -Silver Crater/Fission) suggesting that the halos can form in a variety of geologic environments, but that common to all of them is secondary migration of U/Th daughter products through fluid migration which has been shown to have occurred extensively in the area (Lumbers personal communication 1988, Lorence Collins personal communication 1990). 5) The U mineralization is primarily a precipitation (mainly in mafic minerals like biotite) in a reducing environment near the contact of the wall-rock and in fractures and cleavages in the case of the Faraday pegmatite (Masson & Gordon, 1981). 6) Oxygenated fluids rich in fluorine, phosphorus, and carbon dioxide readily dissolve uranium and increase the fluid's mobility (Masson & Gordon, 1981). And 7) polonium found in soil samples, migrated via radon, is used in prospecting to discover underlying uranium mineralization (Card & Bell, 1980).

We conclude, therefore, that Polonium halos are not some kind of "mystery" to science at all. The complex geological features the Po halo are hosted in indicates that it is unreasonable to invoke supernaturalism to explain Po halos. The available evidence strongly suggests a secondary origin.

REFERENCES:

Bartlett, J.R., and DeKemp, E.A., 1987, Lithofacies, Stromatolite Localities, Metallic Mineral Occurrences and Geochemical Anomalies Associated with Carbonate Metasediments of the Burleigh Falls-Bancroft-Madoc Area, Southern Ontario: Preliminary Map P.3079, Geological Series, Scale 1:126,720.

Bedell, R.L. and Schwerdtner, W.M., 1981, Structural Controles of U-Ore Bearing Pegmatite Dikes at Madawaska (Faraday) Mine, Bancroft, Ontario, in Geoscience Research Grant Program, 1981-1982: edited by E.G. Pye, Ontario Geological Survey, Miscellaneous Paper 103, pp.1-11

Bourque, M.S., 1981, Stratigraphy and Sedimentation of Carbonate Metasediments Within the Grenville Supergroup; pp.77-79 in Summary of Field Work, 1981: Ontario Geological Survey, edited by J. Wood, O.L. White, R.B. Barlow, and A.C. Colvine, Miscellaneous Paper 100, 255p.

Brock, B.S. and Moore, J.M., 1983, Chronology, Chemistry and Tectonics of Igneous Rocks in Terranes of the Grenville Province, Canada; Geological Society of America: Program with Abstracts, v. 15, 533p.

Brown, R.H., 1986, Radiometric Dating from the Perspective of Biblical Chronology, First International Conference on Creationism, p.31-57.

Brown, R.H., 1987, Radiohalos: unpublished. Available from the author at Geoscience Research Institute, Loma Linda University, Loma Linda, CA, 92350

Brown, R.H., Coffin, H.G., Gibson, L.J., Roth, A.A. and Webster, C.L. 1988 Examining Radiohalos, Origins, Geoscience Research Institute, Loma Linda University.

Bullis, A.R., 1965, Geology of Metal Mines Limited (Bancroft Division), Canadian Institute of Mining and Metallurgy Bulletin: v. 58, no. 639,pp.713-720

Chaudhuri, N.K. and Iyer, R.H., 1980, Origin of Unusual Radioactive Haloes: Radiation Effects, v.53, pp.1-6

Card, J.W. and Bell, K, 1980 Further Investigation of the Radon Decay Product Collector Method of Uranium Exploration, Grant 38,P.24-38 in Geoscience Research Grant Program, Summary of Research, 1979-1980, edited by E.G. Pye, Ontario Geological Survey, Misc. Paper 93, 262p.

Damon, P.E with replies by Gentry, R.V. and Kazmann, R.G., 1979, Time: Measured Responses, EOS, v.60, no.22, p.474

Easton, R.M., 1986a, Geochronology Compilation Series, Ontario Geological Survey, Open File Report 5592, with maps P2840-2844, Compilation Series-Preliminary Map, scale 1:1,013,760

Easton, R.M., 1986b, Paleoenvironment and Facies of the Apsley Formation, Peterborough County, pp.141-151 in Summary of Field Work, 1986: Ontario Geological Survey, edited by P.C. Thurston, O.L. White, R.B. Barlow, M.E. Cherry and A.C. Colvine, Miscellaneous Paper 132, 435p.

Easton, R.M., 1986c, Geochronology of the Grenville Province, The Grenville Province: edited by J.M. Moore, A Davidson, and A.J. Baer, Geological Association of Canada, Special Paper 31

Evans, A.M., 1964, Geology of Ashby and Benbigh Townships, Ontario: Ontario Geological Survey, Report 26. Accompanied by maps 2032 & 2049

Fahrig, W.F. and West, T.D. 1986, Diabase Dyke Swams of the Canadian Shield; Geological Survey of Canada, Map 1627A

Gentry, R.V., 1966a, Alpha radioactivity of unknown origin and the discovery of a new pleochroic halo, Earth Planet. Sci. Letters, v.1, p.453-454.

Gentry, R.V., 1966b, Abnormally long a-particle tracks in biotite (mica)., Appl. Phys. Lett. v.8, p. 65-67.

Gentry, R.V., 1968, Fossil alpha-recoil analysis of certain variant   radioactive halos, Science: v. 160, pp.1228-1230

Gentry, R.V. 1970, Giant Radioactive Halos: Indicators of Unknown Radioactivity?, Science, v.169, pp.670-673

Gentry, R.V., 1971, Radiohalos: Some Unique Lead Isotope Ratios and Unknown Alpha Radioactivity, Science: v. 173, pp.727-731

Gentry, R.V., 1973, Radioactive Halos, Annual Review of Nuclear and Particle Science, v.23, pp.347-362.

Gentry, R.V., 1972, Radioactive Halos, Annual Review of Nuclear and Particle Physics: v. 23, pp.347-362

Gentry, R.V., 1974, Radiohalos in a Radiochronological and Cosmological Perspective, Science: v. 184, pp.62-66

Gentry, R.V., 1978, Are Any Unusual Radiohalos Evidence for SHE?, in International Symposium on Superheavy Elements, Lubbock, Tx, edited by M.A.K. Lodhi, Pergamon Press, New York 228p.

Gentry, R.V., 1980, Polonium Halos, EOS, v.61, no.27, p.514

Gentry, R.V., 1986a, Radioactive Halos: Implications for Creation. First International Conference on Creationism, pp.89-112.

Gentry, R.V., 1986b, Creation's Tiny Mystery, Earth Science Associates, Knotsville, TN.

Gentry, R.V., 1988, Creation's Tiny Mystery, 2nd Edition, Earth Science Associates, Knotsville, TN.

Gentry, R.V., 1990 in press, Polonium Halos: Unrefuted Evidence for Creation, Origins Research

Gentry, R.V., Cristy, S.S., McLaughlin, J.F., and McHugh, J.A., 1973, Ion Microprobe Confirmation of Pb Isotope Ratios and Search for Isomer Precursors in Polonium Radiohaloes, Nature: v. 244, pp.282-283

Gentry, R.V., Hulett, L.D., Cristy, S.S., McLaughlin, J.F., McHugh, J.A.,and Bayard, M., 1974, 'Spectacle' Array of Po 210 Halo Radiocentres in Biotite: A Nuclear Geophysical Enigma, Nature: v. 252, pp.564-566

Gentry, R.V., L.D. Hulett, D.H. Smith, J.F. Emery, S.A. Reynolds, R. Walker, S.S. Cristy and P.A. Gentry, 1976, Radiohalos in coalified wood: New evidence relating to the time of uranium introduction and coalification, Science, v.194, p.315-318.

Gentry, R.V., T.A. Cahill, N.R. Fletcher, H.C. Kaufman, L.R. Medsker, J.W. Nelson, and R.G. Floochini, 1977, Phys. Today, v.30, p.17.

Gentry, R.V., W.H. Christie, D.H. Smith, J.W. Boyle, S.S.Cristy, and J.F. McLaughlin, 1978, Nature, v.274, p.457.

Guilbert, J.M. & Park Jr., C.F., 1986, The Geology of Ore Deposits: W.H. Freeman and Co., New York, 985p.

Hashemi-Nezhad, S.R., Fremlin, J.H. & Durrani, S.A., 1979, Polonium Haloes in Mica, Nature: v. 278, pp. 333-335

Henderson, G.H., 1939, A Quantitative study of pleochroic haloes, V. The genesis of haloes, Proceedings, Royal Society of London: pp.250-264

Hewitt, D.F., 1956, Geology of Dungannon and Mayo Townships, Hastings County: Ontario Department of Mines, Annual Report for 1955, v. 64, part 8

Hewitt, D.F., 1957, Geology of the Cardiff and Faraday Townships: Ontario Dept. of Mines, v. 66, part 3

Hewitt, D.F., 1968, Geology of Madoc Township: Ontario Geological Survey, Report 73, 45p. Accompanied by Map 2154, scale 1 inch to 1/2 mile.

Hofmann, H.J. 1971 Precambrian fossils, Pseudofossils, and Problematica in Canada, Geological Survey of Canada, Bulletin 189, Dept. of Energy, Mines and Resources, Canada.

Hofmann, H.J. 1987, Paleocene #7. Precambrian Biostratigraphy, Geoscience Canada, v.14, no.3, pp.135-154

Hogarth, D.D., Moyd, L., Rose, E.R. and Steacy, H.R., 1972, Classic Mineral Collecting Localities in Ontario and Quebec: edited by D.J. Glass, XXIV International Geological Congress, Montreal, Quebec, 79p.

Joly, J., 1907, On the origin of pleochroic halos, Phil.Mag., v.13, p.381-383.

Joly, J., 1917, Radio-active halos, Phil. Trans. Roy. Soc. London, Ser. A. v.217, p.5.

Laakso, R.K. 1968, Geology of Lake Township, Ontario, Ontario Geological Survey, Report 54, Accompanied by Map 2106.

Lumbers, S.B. 1968, Geology of Cashel Township, Ontario, Ontario Geological Survey, Report 71, Accompanied by Map 2142.

Lumbers, S.B., 1982, Summary of Metallogeny, Renfrew County Area, Ontario Geological Survey, Report 212. Accompanied by maps 2459-2462.

Masson, S.L., 1982, Geology and Mineral Deposits of the Bancroft Area, Western Part, Southern Ontario: Ontario Geological Survey, Map P. 2523, Geological Series -Preliminary Map, Scale 1:10,000

Masson, S.L. and Gordon, J.B., 1981, Radioactive Mineral Deposits of the Pembroke-Renfrew Area: Ontario Geological Survey, Mineral Deposits Circular 23, 155p. Accompanied by Preliminary Map P.2210, scale 1:126,720

Meier, H. and Hecker, W., 1976, Radioactive halos as possible indicators for geochemical processes in magmatites: Geochemical Journal, v. 10, pp.185-195

Moazed, C., Spector, R.M. & Ward, R.F., 1973, Polonium Radiohalos: An Alternate Interpretation, Science: v. 180, pp.1272-1274

Moyd, L., 1989 In press, Large Nepheline, Biotite and Albite-Antiperthite Crystals in Calcite-Cored Vien-dikes in Nephelinized Gneiss at Davis Hill Near Bancroft, Ontario, Mineralogical Record.

Odom, A.L., Rink, W.J., 1989, Giant Radiation-Induced Color Halos in Quartz: Solution to a Riddle, Science, v. 246 , pp.107-109

Ontario Geological Survey, Geological Compilation Series, Maps 2161 (1968), 2166 (1969), 2202 (1971), 2205 (1973), 2220 (1972), 2232 (1973), 2361 (1977), & 2419 (1979), scale 1:253,440 and Maps 2392 (1978), 2393 (1978) & 2391 (1978), scale 1:1,013,760

Richardson, K.A., 1964, Thorium, uranium, and potassium in the Conway Granite, New Hampshire, U.S.A., in The Natural Radiation Environment, J.A.S. Adams and W.M. Lowder, editors, University of Chicago Press, p. 39-50.

Richardson, K.A. and J.A.S. Adams, 1964, Effect of Weathering on Radioactive Elements in the Conway Granite of New Hampshire, Geol. Soc. Am., Special. Paper #76, p. 137.

Robertson, J.A., 1968, Geology of Townships 149 and 150: Ontario Geological Survey, Report 57, 162p. Accompanied by Maps 2113 and 2114, scale 1 inch to 1/4 mile, and charts.

Sabina, Ann P., 1986, Rocks and Minerals for the Collector: Bancroft - Parry Sound and Southern Ontario: Geological Survey of Canada, Miscellaneous Report 39, 182p.

Satterly, J., 1957, Radioactive Mineral Occurrences in the Bancroft Area: Ontario Dept. of Mines, Annual Report 1956, v. 65, part 6, pp.108-116

Shaw, D.M. & Hewitt, D.F., 1962, Geology of Chandos and Wollaston Townships, Peterborough and Hastings Counties: Ontario Geological Survey, Report 11, Accompanied by Maps 2019 & 2020, scale 1:31,360

Wakefield, J.R., 1988a, Gentry's Tiny Mystery --Unsupported by geology, Creation/Evolution, Issue XXII, v.7, no.3, Buffalo, New York

Wakefield, R., 1988b, The geology of Gentry's "tiny mystery", Journal of Geological Education, v.36, p.161-175.

Wilkerson, G., 1990 in press, Po Radiohalos Do Not Provide Evidence for Fiat Creation, Origins Research

Wise, K.P., 1989, Gentry's Mystery considered: Theological and scientific considerations, Creation Research Society Quarterly, January, 1989

York, D. 1979, Polonium halos and geochronology, EOS, v.60, pp.617-618.

Figure 1. Stromatolites on an island in Belmont Lake, Ontario. These are in sedimentary rock structurally older that the Po containing pegmatites some 35 kilometers to the north.

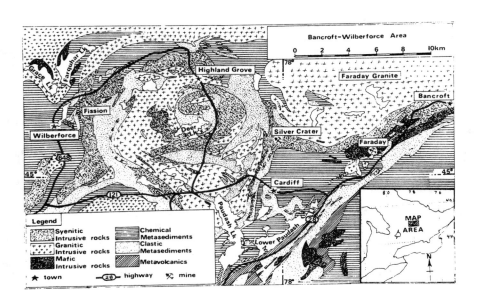

Figure 2. Basic geology of the Bancroft area showing the three mine sites where Po halos were observed.

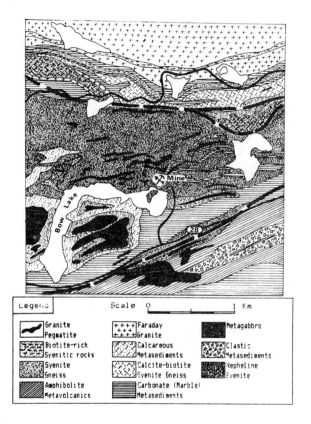

Figure 3. Detailed geology of the Faraday Mine. The Po halo containing pegmatites are long thin features crosscutting a series of rock units including marble.

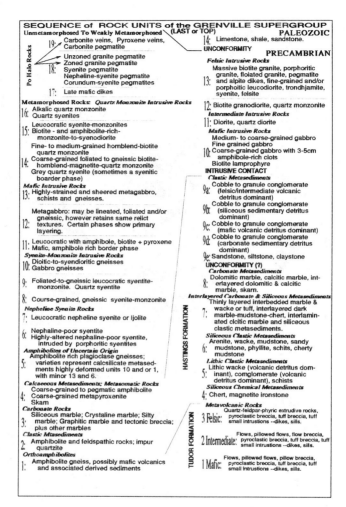

Figure 4. Stratigraphic succession of rock units of the Bancroft (left) and Madoc (right) area, from OGS Preliminary Maps P.2524 (1984) and P.2488 (1982)

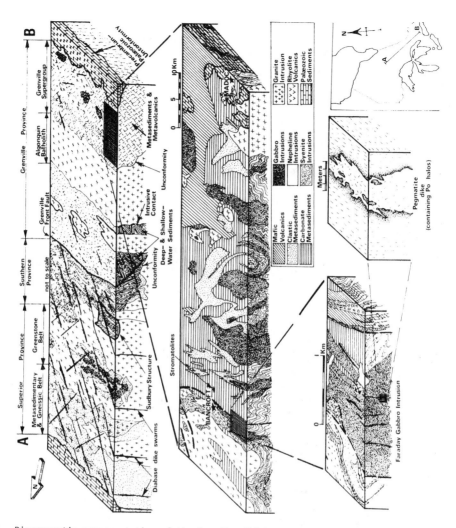

Figure 5. Diagrammatic representation of the Canadian Shield through the Bancroft area. The upper block is a cross section through the three provinces which make up this portion of the Shield. In succession the oldest rock unit is the Greenstone Belt area of the Superior Province. The Greenstones are successive volcanic and sedimentary units intruded by granites, which in turn intruded by diabase dikes. The Southern Province rests uncomformably on the Superior. This province consists of a large sequence of sedimentary rock units intruded by various intrusive rocks. The Sudbury Structure is a very complex entity (evidence supports an astrobleme) consisting of fall-back breccia, varved sedimentary sequence, grading intrusion and surrounding rock fracturing including shatter cones. This whole structure cuts both the Superior and Southern, but is itself deformed, and then cut by the diabase dikes. Separating the Southern from the Grenville is a major fault complex. The Grenville Province is a series of sedimentary rocks, with many intrusive bodies, some quite large like the Algonquin Intrusive Complex. The Grenville Supergroup is one of many complex substructures within the Grenville. The middle block represents a section through the Madoc/Bancroft area. The succession of rock units of this sequence is in Figure 4. The left lower block is of Figure 3, while the right lower block shows the relationship and structure of the pegmatites with the gabbro. The gabbro is an intrusive body into marble and other metasedimentary rocks.

If the Po halos creation model were true, then the entire Shield sequence of complex volcanic, sedimentary and intrusive rocks were created, in a three minute span, in a sequence which appears to be a long complex succession of deposition, erosion and intrusion.

341

DISCUSSION

The authors provide valuable data on the geologic conditions in which radiohalos occur. The authors correctly conclude that in many cases radiohalos occur in rocks which have formed by geologic processes and have been altered by geologic processes. This work will be a valuable addition to the literature responding to the conclusion of Dr. Gentry. Radiohalos do occur in rocks formed by igneous processes.

Steven A. Austin, Ph.D.
San Diego, California

The authors' comprehensive description of some of the halo sites is much appreciated. Although they claim it, their evidence for a secondary origin is in concert with uniformitarians of the past, and can only be justified by their strong dependence on the uniformitarian model. A creation model does indeed require massive short-time rock formation. The eyewitness account reports the world inhabited by the sixth day.

The halo circumstances are accurate - high local radioactivity, a gaseous immediate precursor, natural cleavage in mica, solubility ow Uranium and Polonium - all understood by Dr. Gentry when he started his unsuccessful search for a viable mechanism for secondary Precambrian ^{218}Po halos. The authors fail, however, to recognize that the unmistakable secondary halos which Dr. Gentry, happily, found in coal have distinct differences from the Precambrian halos, so that the mechanism cannot be rationally transplanted. The Selenium is indeed in these secondary halos. I suggest that the authors be more careful to delineate between ^{218}Po and ^{214}Po for which neither they nor anyone else has modeled secondary halos, and ^{210}Po, for which they have been observed.

William M. Overn, BSEE
Minneapolis, Minnesota

To establish that the Polonium (Po) halos are in rocks younger than those containing fossils (e.g. bacteria), would invalidate Gentry's model for the primordial (creation) origin of radiohalos. In spite of requirements to the contrary, however, (Gentry, 1988, 1989), Mr. Wakefield and Dr. Wilkerson have established neither the biogenic nature of the stromatolites, nor a continuous, unbroken contact between the Po-containing rocks and the fossils.

Though Mr. Wakefield and Dr. Wilkerson make much of the Precambrian history written in the rock, Gentry (1988, 1989) has made it clear that such history means little to him, as God can create it that way with little "difficulty". It has not been demonstrated that Gentry is wrong on this point.

The natural origin of Po halos is suggested by the evidence - it is not as firmly established as Mr. Wakefield and Dr. wilkerson seem to indicate. Po halos in crystalline rocks have not been produced naturally in experiment and no viable hypothesis has surfaced for the precise process.

Mr. Wakefield and Dr. Wilkerson's argument for the natural hydrothermal origin of radiohalos is not as powerful as it could be (1). Besides the fact that Po halos are found along fractures and cleavage planes (noting that any position in a biotite crystal is close to a cleavage plane), evidences include: Po halos are found only in minerals which can be produced hydrothermally; the only Po isotopes known as halos are only those Po isotopes known from the decay series of Uranium (U) and Thorium (Th); the concentration of Po halos may be related to the concentration of Uranium in the rock; Po may not be found within the crystalline matrix as is U and TH (Meier and Hecker: 1976:188).

Mr. Wakefield and Dr. Wilkerson's paper provides very little increase in information over previously published papers (e.g. Wakefield, 1988 a,b), and seems to ignore some pertinent works (1 [incorrectly referenced], 2) and fails to pursue many possible fruitful lines of inquiry on the subject, such as verifying the claims of the previous paragraph.

1.   Wise, Kurt, P., 1989, "Radioactive Halos: Geological Concerns", <u>Creation Research Society Quarterly</u> 25 (4):171-176.

2.   Gentry, Robert, V., 1989, "Response to Wise", <u>Creation Research Society Quarterly</u>, 25 (4):176-180.

Kurt P. Wise, Ph.D.
Dayton, Tennessee

Response to Dr. Steven Austin:

Dr. Austin and one of us (Wilkerson) participated in a debate about the age of the earth at the 1990 ICC Conference. As geologists we understand and apply the basic principles of superposition, original horizontality, and cross-cutting relationships to our work. On the basis of these principles we concluded that Po radiohaloes are the last things to form in the uranium deposits that host them. This is a very simple deduction based on logical principles and stands on its own merits apart from assumptions about process rates or the age of the earth. Young-earth creationists will do well to abandon Gentry's arguments for a young earth and for instantaneous creation of Po haloes.

Response to Mr. William Overn:

The Silver Crater, Fission and Faraday uranium deposits we investigated contain Po-210, Po-214 and Po-218 halos. Our conclusions apply to all of these Po halo types, since all of them are known to exist in these deposits. The halos are younger than the fractures along which they form. The fractures in the biotite are younger than the biotite. The biotite is younger than the calcite which it replaces. The calcite vein-dike is younger than the wall rocks which host them. Our deduction of a *sequence of events* for all Po haloes takes into consideration data which we feel Gentry has marginalized or ignored.

It is not necessary (as Mr. Overn suggests) to have experimental evidence or even a model for Po halo formation to demonstrate that Po halos are not primordial. Our argument is based on the logic of cross-cutting relationships, not on uniformitarianism. We object to the habit that young-earth creationists have of discounting contrary opinion only on the philosophical grounds of anti-uniformitarianism. We are not uniformitarians, we are actualists and insist only that geologic observations be interpreted in the light of known physical laws.

Mr. Overn's phrase "The eyewitness account reports the world inhabited by the sixth day" shows that he, as a young-earth creationist, objects to our actualistic interpretation mainly because of a pre-conceived theological mind-set. No amount of empirical data will ever change the mind of persons committed to such a religious belief.

Response to Dr. Kurt Wise:

We believe that the stratigraphic record of the Precambrian in the Bancroft area is sufficiently well known to demonstrate a continuous series of geologic events between stromatolite localities and the Po halo-containing uranium deposits. The stromatolites nearest the uranium deposits we investigated are in the Hastings Formation and are deformed. Because of this deformation the identification of them as biogenic has been questioned. In our presentation we showed photographs and gave descriptions of undeformed stromatolites from the Hastings Formation 20 km south of Bancroft at Belmont Lake. Dr. Wise makes the assertion that the stromatolites we cite are not of biologic origin despite their oval shape, attenuated layering and carbon content-- precisely what would be expected if they were metamorphosed algal colonies. He objects to our interpretation, yet he offers no non-biologic explanation for their origin. We know of no non-biologic mechanism that could produce these structures that resemble so closely unaltered algal colonies.

Dr. Gentry's ad hoc attempts to fit his theory into the known geologic and mineralogic details of the uranium deposits we studied lead to several illogical conclusions (Wilkerson, 1991 in press). The trouble with Dr. Gentry and other young-earth creationists is that, regardless of the evidence for a sequence of events, one can always say "God made it that way". So Gentry will, of course, find "little difficulty" in incorporating our data into some variation of his "model". That's O.K. for a believer, but for the skeptic it just won't wash.

Our work summarized data for the first time--and from a variety of sources--data which indicate that Po radiohaloes must have formed as orphaned isotopes, separated permanently from their radioactive parents. Wise's contention that a hydrothermal origin for Po halos be questioned because "Po halos in crystalline rocks have not been produced naturally in experiment..." is flawed. The argument is a common creationist tact and implies that experimental duplication is the only way to deduce scientific truth. Such a narrow view of scientific truth is not held by us. The argument also ignores the thermal requirements of uranium deposit, metamorphic and igneous rock formation which require lots more time than young-earth "creation models" can afford.

In our paper we do not advance a model for Po halo formation. We only show that there are very tight mineralogical and geological constraints that all models must incorporate. It seems more reasonable to us that Po was separated (orphaned) from U and Th parents by the migration Po precursors (Ra, Rn, Bi) than that they were created with an appearance of age. In order to accommodate our data and also keep a young-earth view, creationists will have to erect additional ad-hoc hypotheses such as variations in radioactive decay rates.

Richard Wakefield
Gregg Wilkerson, Ph.D.

Kurt P. Wise
Assistant Professor of Science
Director of Origins Research
Bryan College, Box 7585
Box 7000
Dayton, TN 37321-7000

ABSTRACT

Walter ReMine's (1) discontinuity systematics can be used as a basis for a biological classification system either within creation or evolution theory. Such a model-neutral methodology can be more efficiently utilized within any given theory of life by supplementing it with model-dependent membership criteria. Discontinuity systematics supplemented with young-earth creation model-dependent membership criteria is here called baraminology. Four young-earth creation model-dependent membership criteria are here suggested -- one based on Scripture, another based upon molecular similarity studies, a third based on cladistically-defined frequency of homoplasy, and a fourth based on flood-generated diversity bottlenecks.

This paper also attempts to relate the empirically-defined holobaramins, monobaramins, apobaramins, and polybaramins of baraminology and discontinuity systematics to Biblical, creationist, and evolutionist thought. The original, created group of individuals capable of reproduction is a theoretical construct, here called an archaebaramin. Frank Marsh's term baramin is considered the created 'kind' (or 'Biblical kind'), and is here redefined as the archaebaramin and all its descendants. Baramins are apobaraminic groups, and may be holobaraminic in most, if not all, cases. Microevolutionary processes, including speciation occur within the baramin. Extra- and interbaraminic evolution is considered impossible.

Baraminology is an easily employed and extremely powerful biosystematic method. Baraminology is the most efficient method of classifying life available to the young-earth creation biologist. It will allow the collection of an abundance of heretofore unrecognizable data in favor of a creation model, and serve as an empirical foundation upon which to construct a creationist reclassification of life.

INTRODUCTION

Eighteenth century creation theory viewed life as both invariant and typological -- both unchanging and polyphyletic. This view can be described as a "Creationist Lawn" view of life (see figure 1A). In this metaphor, each species in the earth's biota is represented by a distinct blade of grass in a newly cut lawn. Each blade has its own separate root (or origin) and continues upward (through time) unchanged, as one sprig of grass among many thousands. Darwin challenged the Creationist Lawn metaphor with a metaphor of his own: the "Evolutionary Tree" (see figure 1B). In this metaphor life is monophyletic -- i.e. there is one common ancestor at the base of the tree of life. As one follows the trunk upward it branches repeatedly to produce the many thousands of terminal twigs we recognize as species today. Evolutionary theory thus views life as monophyletic, variant, and relatively unconstrained. By the beginning of this century Darwin's Evolutionary Tree had largely displaced the previous metaphor of the Creationist Lawn.

Some modern creationists are suggesting a metaphor of their own -- a metaphor which is planted somewhere between the Evolutionary Tree and the Creationist Lawn. The new metaphor may be described as the "Neo-creationist Orchard" (see figure 1C). In this metaphor, life is specially created (as fruit trees are specially planted) and polyphyletic (i.e. each tree has a separate trunk and root system). There are also discontinuities between the major groups (trees are spaced so that branches do not overlap and could not and never did anastomose) and there are constraints to change (a given tree is limited to a particular size and branching style according to its type). In these ways the Neo-creationist Orchard is similar to the Creationist Lawn. They differ, though, in that the Neo-creationist Orchard allows change, including speciation, within each created group (each tree branches off of the main stem). Permitting this kind of change (variously called by creationists 'diversification', 'variation', 'horizontal evolution', and 'microevolution') in different amounts in different groups allows the creation model to accommodate microevolutionary evidences (e.g. changing allelic ratios, genetic recombination, speciation, etc.).

According to the creation model, genetic and morphological discontinuities are not only extant, but they are a common and important characteristic of life. To be consistent with their own model of earth history, creationists will need to identify the discontinuities among life-forms and then use them to classify those life-forms. Unfortunately, all of the traditional biosystematic methods are incapable of either recognizing or utilizing any such discontinuities even if they were a common characteristic of life. Phylogenetic systematics and evolutionary taxonomy explicitly assume continuity, and thus always conclude that continuity is a characteristic of life. The methods of phenetics and transformed cladistics are also blind to discontinuity for three reasons. First, each method orders organisms only according to similarities. Differences are employed only in the sense of dissimilar similarities (e.g. 'synapomorphies', or 'shared differences'). Since similarities can be identified between any two items in the universe, it is impossible to identify any discontinuity using these methods. Second, the products of these methods are data structures such as phenograms and cladograms. These structures locate life forms at the tips of the branches of tree-like diagrams. By their very nature such diagrams connect all organisms considered, so it is not only impossible to identify discontinuity, but it is also impossible to graphically display it. Third, phenograms and cladograms are so similar to representations of evolutionary trees that many people wrongly conclude that they do represent evolutionary phylogenies. The very appearance of these data structures persuasively, but subtly, argues for the inherent continuity of life and against discontinuity. All traditional biosystematic methods, because they are insensitive (completely blind) to discontinuity, are thus inappropriate classification methods for creationists who are seeking to find the discontinuities they believe to characterize life.

Walter ReMine's (1) recent introduction of "Discontinuity Systematics" should be very encouraging to creation biologists. Discontinuity systematics can be used to identify the discontinuities of life which creation theory predicts, and then use that information to classify life. It is also very simple conceptually, and is easily modified to the creation model. After briefly familiarizing the reader with discontinuity systematics, this paper will introduce a modification for use in young-earth creation theory.

DISCONTINUITY SYSTEMATICS

Justification

Two organisms or organismal groups which appear to lack a common ancestor can be said to be separated by what might be called a 'phyletic discontinuity'. A group of organisms which contains creatures related to one another but unrelated to organisms outside the group makes up a truly natural group. Since biosystematics methods search for natural groups and classify organisms accordingly, phyletic discontinuities can be used as a basis for classification. ReMine's (1) 'discontinuity systematics' does just that. It focuses on searching for and identifying phyletic discontinuities and then using them to classify organisms.

One of the strengths of discontinuity systematics is that the phyletic discontinuities do not necessarily have to be real for the classification method to work. Since our knowledge of the world is partial, identified phyletic discontinuities can be either real or apparent. Some, many, or all of the phyletic discontinuities we identify may be separating organisms which really do share a common ancestor. It is still possible, for example, that different mechanisms of genetic change separate different organismal groups. If so, these thresholds of change can still be used to classify organisms into natural groups. Another strength of discontinuity systematics is that as current research changes the nature and position of phyletic discontinuities, discontinuity systematics can accommodate those changes. A third strength is that discontinuity systematics is easily adapted to different theories of life. Macroevolutionary biologists, for example, assume that all phyletic discontinuities are apparent, until it is demonstrated that they are real. Currently recognized discontinuities may well reveal the existence of a mechanism of change yet not characterized (e.g. macromutation, regulatory gene mutation, etc.). To conclude that a phyletic discontinuity was real would be the last choice of a macroevolutionary biologist. Creation biologists, on the other hand, believe that life is polyphyletic. They would assume that phyletic discontinuities are real until they are demonstrated otherwise. In some small way, therefore, the creationist would tend to interpret the phyletic data more literally than the evolutionist.

Terminology

Discontinuity systematics involves the identification and classification of organismal groups completely bounded by phyletic discontinuity. ReMine (1) felt that most of the biosystematic terms in current usage are inappropriate to describe this kind of biological group. Since 'species' is derived from the Latin word for 'kind' -- the divinely-created kind -- it would seem to be appropriate for this unit. Yet, even though etymologically 'species' is used to describe a group of organisms completely bounded by phyletic discontinuity, nowhere in current usage does the word species carry that meaning. It is unreasonable to think that a new meaning could be added to the word 'species' without causing undue confusion. A second word is often used by creationists: 'kind'. This has reference to the created unit. However, 'kind' also has too many colloquial meanings to avoid the inevitable confusion which would come about with the use of this word. As a result, ReMine (1) turned to the word 'baramin', created by Frank Marsh (2). A combined form of two Hebrew words meaning 'created kind', Marsh envisioned the baramin as being both the created biological unit and the reproductive unit. ReMine used this word as a root word for the creation of the terminology of discontinuity systematics. Wisely, ReMine did not use baramin itself to mean anything in his system. This allows the terminology of discontinuity systematics to be model-neutral. Clark's baramin can continue to refer to the created biological unit, and still allow ReMine's terms to exist independently without a creation model-dependent meaning.

Four terms were introduced by ReMine to create the necessary terminology for discontinuity systematics: holobaramin, apobaramin, polybaramin, and monobaramin. Each of these terms is used to describe a set of known organisms. Since this is a method of classification, it is only used to describe and classify organisms which are known to exist or to have existed. It does not include any imaginary creatures. The **holobaramin** is the desired basic unit. This is a group of organisms which is surrounded by a phyletic discontinuity and yet is not completely divided by one. Once all the holobaramins and phyletic discontinuities have been identified and characterized, the primary goals of discontinuity systematics will have been achieved. The **monobaramin** is a group of organisms which is not completely divided by a phyletic discontinuity, but may or may not be separated from all other organisms by phyletic discontinuities. In other words the monobaramin is a subset of the holobaramin. The **polybaramin** is a group of organisms divided by at least one phyletic discontinuity. The polybaramin may or may not be completely separated from all other organisms by phyletic discontinuities. Thus the polybaramin contains at least parts of at least two holobaramins. The **apobaramin** is separated from all other organisms by phyletic discontinuity, but may or may not be divided by at least one phyletic discontinuity. The apobaramin thus contains one or more complete holobaramins. ReMine's (1) actual definitions are included in Appendix A. These terms are pluralized by the addition of an 's' (e.g. five apobaramins and six polybaramins), and are made into an adjective form by adding 'ic' (e.g. reptiles are polybaraminic, and may be apobaraminic).

Methodology

The methodology of discontinuity systematics simply involves identifying holobaramins through a method of successive approximations from what might be termed above and below -- by successive subtraction and addition respectively. Holobaramins are approached by addition by identifying monobaramins and increasing their membership. In this way the holobaramin is approached from 'below'. Holobaramins are approached by subtraction by identifying apobaramins and dividing them into smaller apobaramins along identified phyletic discontinuities. In this way the holobaramin is approached from 'above'. Approaching the holobaramin simultaneously from above and below by successive subtraction and addition allows the systematist to identify the holobaramin most quickly.

Membership Criteria

The challenge to the Discontinuity Systematist is in defining what are called 'membership criteria' -- those criteria used to include organisms in monobaramins and exclude other organisms from apobaramins. The membership criteria are the methods used to determine whether or not a phyletic discontinuity exists between two organisms. ReMine (1) offered only a very few membership criteria, leaving most of the task of finding such criteria up the biosystematists of the future.

Similarity - Because discontinuity systematics searches for and studies phyletic discontinuities, it must reject similarity as sufficient evidence to demonstrate relatedness. This is in contrast to common practice in biology, but not without justification. Macroevolutionary theory maintains that, lacking any evidence to the contrary, similarities between two organisms are most judiciously interpreted as due to inheritance from a common ancestor with that same characteristic. In other words, when lacking evidence to the contrary, macroevolutionary theorists assume similarity indicates phyletic continuity between two organisms. They automatically interpret similarity as homology -- i.e. as similarity which is due to common descent. There are at least three major difficulties with this particular claim. First, similarities can be identified between any two objects in the universe. In fact, the very fact that two objects are in this universe means that they share a number of features which identify them as part of this universe. The very fact that two organisms are living means they share a number of additional features which are used to identify both as living. If similarity means genetic relatedness, then stars are genetically related to muons, etc. Even if the similarities among organisms are restricted to heritable traits, most traits are still included, since nearly every characteristic of an organism is determined or at least influenced by its DNA -- information which it passes on to the next generation. It seems impossible to ever conclude that any two objects -- living or not -- are completely dissimilar. Second, as ReMine (1) indicated, degree of relatedness is not always directly tied to degree of similarity. Third, an increasing number of similarities which were formerly interpreted as homologies (i.e. due to common descent) are now being reinterpreted as homoplasies (i.e. independently derived; not due

347

to common descent) (see Nelson, this volume). Because an increasing percentage of similarities are being reinterpreted as homoplasies, the traditional evolutionary assumption of homology is becoming increasingly dubious. For these reasons, similarity alone is acknowledged as insufficient evidence to establish relatedness.

Successful Hybridization -- ReMine (1) suggests three additive membership criteria, or what he calls *continuity criteria*. One of these is the criterion of successful hybridization. It is expected that many of the descendants of a given ancestor remain capable of successfully mating with contemporaneous descendants of the same ancestor. It also seems unlikely that the ancestral lineages of two organisms which can now successfully mate could possibly have avoided trading genetic material throughout their entire history. It therefore seems reasonable to posit that two organisms which can mate and produce viable offspring are descendants of a common ancestor and are thus not separated by a phyletic discontinuity. They are then to be considered members of the same monobaramin. If an organism can mate and produce viable offspring with even one organism from a monobaramin, then that organism should be included within that monobaramin.

The first challenge which will be encountered in using the criterion of successful hybridization will be in defining what is a successful cross. Two organisms which produce reproductively viable offspring clearly demonstrate hybrid viability. However, there are cases where organisms produce reproductively non-viable offspring (e.g. mules from donkeys and horses), and other cases where organisms produce offspring which do not survive to reproductive age. Furthermore, with modern recombinatory techniques, portions of one organism's DNA can be incorporated into the DNA of another organism in what might be called partial hybridization. If genetic incompatibility as well as partial and complete barriers to gene flow can be produced in the course of time, then successful hybridization can include a number of these categories as well. It is ReMine's (1) contention, and my own, that reproductive isolation is a common enough phenomenon of life for the successful hybridization of an entire genome to be sufficient evidence for phyletic continuity. Therefore, if the entire genomes of two organisms can be hybridized, regardless of whether the cross was natural or artificial, and regardless of whether or not their offspring were reproductively viable or even survived, those two organisms are to be considered part of the same monobaramin. Partial hybridization is not accepted by ReMine or myself to be sufficient evidence for phyletic continuity.

Known Variation -- Another of ReMine's (1) continuity criteria is that of observed and experimentally determined variation. Regardless of whether an organism has been tested for successful hybridization, it may be included into a monobaramin with other organisms according to sufficient similarity. It seems reasonable to assume that sufficiently similar morphologies are the result of sufficiently similar genetics to allow successful hybridization. Sufficient similarity can thus proxy for successful hybridization. When a morphology falls within the range of variation of organisms which are capable of successful hybridization, this is taken as sufficient evidence of phyletic continuity. This known variation can be observed under either natural or artificial breeding conditions. At this time morphology which is less similar than this is not accepted as sufficient evidence of phyletic continuity.

Unambiguous Lineage -- ReMine's remaining continuity criterion is that of an unambiguous lineage. An unambiguous lineage would be a series of geographically and temporally closely-spaced populations (membership two or more) where each population occupies a restricted region of morphology space typical of monobaramins of similar organisms, and where adjacent populations define overlapping regions of morphology space. It is assumed that such a restricted morphology spread combined with an apparently unbroken lineage is best explained by phyletic continuity, even if successful hybridization has not been demonstrated among any members of the group. At this time a lineage which is less complete than this will not be accepted as sufficient evidence of phyletic continuity.

Discontinuity Criteria -- In addition to continuity criteria (or what might also be called additive criteria), discontinuity systematics also requires *discontinuity* (or subtractive) *criteria* to divide apobaramins into smaller apobaramins -- in other words to identify phyletic discontinuities. ReMine's (1) suggestion was to say that a severe failure to demonstrate phyletic continuity is sufficient evidence to claim a phyletic discontinuity exists. Thus if an organism cannot be successfully hybridized with any member of a particular monobaramin, and it is well outside the known natural and experimentally-determined morphological variation of a monobaramin's members, and it is not connected with that monobaramin through a clear-cut lineage, then it can be postulated that the organism is separated from that monobaramin by a phyletic discontinuity.

BARAMINOLOGY

Justification

Although discontinuity systematics is useful because of its adaptability, it is not the most efficient method of identifying phyletic discontinuities and classifying organisms. Depending upon a researcher's view of life and its history, membership criteria can be added to those of discontinuity systematics to make the resultant biosystematics method more efficient. Since, however, this method will be dependent upon a particular model for the history of life, this biosystematics method will be model-dependent. To maximize the efficiency of their biological classification, researchers employing any particular model of life's history should adapt discontinuity systematics to their particular model. The author is here modifying discontinuity systematics by adding membership criteria which are young-earth creation model-dependent. The resultant biosystematics method is here called baraminology.

Terminology and Methodology

Baraminology utilizes all the terminology and methodology of discontinuity systematics. However, since it is based upon a specific model of the history of life, baraminology often claims a particular interpretation of discontinuity systematics terms. Because young-earth creationism maintains that many different groups of organisms were separately created, it posits that life is polyphyletic and full of actual phyletic discontinuities. Whereas discontinuity systematics studies discontinuity, it makes no attempt to determine whether the phyletic discontinuities are real or apparent -- to determine why they exist. Baraminology, on the other hand, claims that phyletic discontinuities are real and due to the polyphyletic origin of life at the hand of a Creator.

Membership Criteria

Criteria of Discontinuity Systematics -- Baraminology accepts all the continuity (additive) membership criteria thus far proposed for discontinuity systematics and the rationale for those criteria. Baraminology supplements those criteria with criteria based upon the young-earth creation model.

Although the proposed discontinuity criterion of discontinuity systematics (substantial failure to show phyletic continuity) is also accepted, it is suggested that whenever possible, it not be used alone. If additive and subtractive approaches to holobaramins are to be the most effective and error-free, the continuity and discontinuity criteria would be best defined independently of one another. If it is at all possible, neither should be defined simply as the negative of the other, particularly when one is defined as the failure to get positive results using the other. Such negative evidence, if it is all the evidence you have is adequate for the moment, but systematists should be encouraged to find stronger, positive ways to define a discontinuity. The discontinuity criterion of discontinuity systematics, though such a negative criterion, is the only one so-far defined. Baraminologists are encouraged to adopt positive discontinuity criteria to strengthen their argument for discontinuity. Several such criteria are suggested below.

Biblical Criteria -- Since most advocates of the young-earth creation model accept the authority of the Scriptures, it is here suggested that baraminology should include, or at least consider, Biblical criteria for the definition of holobaramins and apobaramins. In actual fact, the Scripture offers only a very few suggestions, but they may turn out to be very important in the early development of baraminology's membership criteria. They can be used in some cases as a check on the reliability and/or adequacy of other membership criteria.

Since man is separately created (Genesis 1:26-7; 2:7, etc.) and all people have descended from Adam (Genesis 2:21-3; 3:20), humans are holobaraminic. Similarly on Scriptural grounds, the 'tree of knowledge of good and evil' (Genesis 2:9, 17) and the 'tree of life' (Genesis 2:9; 3:24) each constituted its own holobaramin -- each presumably having gone extinct after having been represented by only a single individual. The serpent also (Genesis 3:1) and whatever it became (Genesis 3:14) constitutes its own holobaramin. It is not impossible that it, too, became extinct with the death of a single member.

Scripture also strongly implies that the 'raven' (Genesis 8:7) and the 'dove' (Genesis 8:8-12) must be separated by a real phyletic discontinuity, and reside in separate holobaramins. Since two (or seven) of each land baramin were taken onto the ark, their separate mention indicates that the dove and raven are from different holobaramins, and in turn must be separated by a real phyletic discontinuity. We can also infer that the land plants, the sea and winged creatures, and the land animals are three separate apobaramins, since each were created on separate days of the creation week (Genesis 1:11-13, 20-23, 24-31). The land plant and the land animal apobaramins are in turn divisible into 3 apobaramins each (Genesis 1:11-12, 20-22), and the sea creatures and winged creatures are similarly separated by a phyletic discontinuity (Genesis 1:20-21). We might also infer that the thorn-bearing plants make up yet another apobaramin within the land plant apobaramin (Genesis 3:18). The organisms listed elsewhere in Scripture, especially those listed in the dietary laws, may further aid us in establishing groups according to Biblical criteria (e.g. cud-eating mammals as a separate apobaramin).

Much work can still be done in the original languages of the Scriptures to give us further clues about the higher classification of life. It must be cautioned, however, that Scripture provides only a very few clues about the definitions of baramins. It remains for creation systematists to do much research to fill in the many gaps. Another caution is that most of these designations are themselves somewhat tentative. For example, we often do not know for sure to which organism a particular Hebrew word is actually referring. As a further example, there is uncertainty over exactly how the three groups of plants and the three groups of land animals of Genesis one are defined. We can use the Scripture as an initial springboard, but it is probably only rarely that it will provide us with any definitive answers.

Once defined and clarified, however, these Biblical criteria may be very important in evaluating the other criteria of baraminology. For example, the knowledge that humans are holobaraminic makes it clear that morphological and genetic similarity is insufficient evidence for phyletic continuity, for humans and chimpanzees are very similar in morphology and structural DNA. Furthermore, until a criterion is located (in addition to the failure to bridge the morphological gap) which can distinguish humans and chimpanzees, then we know that other criteria are still to be identified.

Molecular Typology -- Comparative DNA studies have recently yielded some very interesting results. In these measures of similarity, the similarity between a given organism and a number of others seems to assume various high values for a certain small set of other organisms, whereas the similarity with any other member of the earth's biota seems to assume a somewhat invariable non-zero value. This is true, for example, when archaebacteria are compared with other organisms (3). The similarity among species of archaebacteria examined is in a range of high positive values, but the similarity between any archaebacterium species examined and any given non-archaebacterium species examined is virtually the same. This may be due to the fact that archaebacteria form an apobaramin. Similar sorts of molecular typology examples can be seen in Denton (4). It is suggested that using ANOVA and related statistics on molecular similarity matrixes can be used to define coherent apobaraminic groups. It can be postulated that the group which has significantly similar similarity values which are also equally dissimilar from another organism is separated from that organism by a phyletic discontinuity.

It is suggested that baraminology provisionally accept the statistically-determined discontinuities of molecular similarity as evidence of phyletic discontinuity. Baraminology also welcomes the different divisions made by different molecules as a way to maximize the efficiency of apobaramin construction. What one molecule divides into two apobaramins, for example, another molecule might divide into two different apobaramins. Using both molecules it may then be possible to create three or four apobaramins. Using many molecules on many different organisms, the efficiency of baraminology should increase.

Frequency of Homoplasy -- If Biblical claims are correct, then organisms can be divided into a number of separately created organismal groups (baramins). All genetic and morphological similarities shared between organisms of different baramins would then be homoplasous (i.e. non-inherited) similarities. Homoplasous similarities, then, would be a common feature of life. In fact, creationists have insisted for some time that the common hand of the Creator would produce many similarities among unrelated organisms (e.g. Agassiz, 1879 (5)). Since there are most probably many baramins and many more interbaraminic similarities per baramin than are currently known, young-earth creation theory predicts that homoplasy is an extremely common phenomenon of life.

Unlike the source of intrabaraminic diversity, diversity *within* a holobaramin is due to natural biological processes, including evolution. In general, natural biological processes more easily produce similarity by common descent than by independent evolution. Therefore, within genetically related organisms, most of the similarities should be homologous in nature (i.e. inherited from a common ancestor). Whereas between holobaramins the frequency of homoplasies should abound, within holobaramins the frequency of homologies should abound. If, then, there were ways of differentiating homoplasous and homologous similarity, then holobaramins could be defined by the frequency of homologous or homoplasous similarity. When most of the similarities between two organisms are homoplasous similarities, then they are separated by a phyletic discontinuity. When a vast majority of the similarities between two organisms are homologies, then they can be considered part of the same monobaramin.

Distinguishing homoplasous and homologous similarities, however, is not an easy task. In macroevolutionary theory, homoplasies are thought to be the result of independent (convergent) evolution. Convergent evolution is considered an unlikely phenomenon, especially if the feature is not strongly adaptive. Therefore, in contrast to creation theory, macroevolutionary theory claims that homoplasous similarity should be an uncommon feature of the biological world. For the purpose of minimizing error, then, conventional biologists automatically declare any similarities between two organisms to be homologous in nature, until suspected or proven otherwise. To make things worse, evolutionary systematics, which until the last couple decades was the conventional biosystematics method of the last century and a half, has prevented the recognition of much homoplasous similarity. Evolutionary systematics seeks to classify organisms in a way which reflects their phylogeny. By definition, homoplasous similarity does not indicate relationship, so homoplasies are simply ignored by the evolutionary systematists. Homoplasous similarities were thought for many years to be non-data, and were consistently unreported. Under the reign of evolutionary systematics, the impression was gained that homoplasous similarity is a very rare feature of life, just as macroevolutionary theory predicted. Yet, since homoplasous similarity would have been systematically ignored even if it were present and common, is the rarity of homoplasy a real characteristic of life or merely an artifact of the biosystematic method?

In the mid-twentieth century, cladistics was developed. Although not so intended, cladistics, for the first time, allowed the systematic identification of homoplasous similarity. Whereas the evolutionary systematists considered only homologous characters, cladists consider any shared, derived characters, even if those characters are homoplasies. A byproduct of the popularity of cladistics is that an increasing number of similarities formerly assumed to be homologous have been reinterpreted as homoplasous similarities.

It is suggested that cladistic methods can be used by the baraminologist to locate homoplasies and determine their frequency. When no cladogram can be constructed for a group of organisms which eliminates homoplasy, then it can be concluded that homoplasous similarity exists. When a large number of characters is examined cladistically in a polybaraminic group of organisms, a young-earth creationist would expect that homoplasies would be unavoidable and frequent between organisms of different holobaramins. Conversely, for the organisms in the group which are part of the same holobaramin, it should be possible to construct a cladogram with few or no homoplasies.

Cladists rarely find it possible to construct their cladograms without the use of the computer. They have designed a number of computer programs which take the data from a character matrix and construct cladograms from them. Baraminologists should design their own computer programs which take the data from that same character matrix and construct "baraminograms" from them. The program would be designed to identify phyletic discontinuities according to the frequency of homoplasy. It would thus group organisms according to apobaraminic groups. The larger the number of characters, the closer the apobaramins should be to monobaramins. The output of the program (the so-called 'baraminogram') would include traditional cladograms for members of each identified apobaramin, as well as a list of the minimum number of homoplasies which justify each phyletic discontinuity identified.

Flood-Generated Diversity Bottlenecks -- According to the young-earth creation model the history of life's diversity has encountered at least one significant mass extinction -- namely at the time of the Flood. The diversity and abundance of the bios at the creation is unknown, but it is reasonable to assume that in the sixteen centuries or so after the creation and before the flood, organismal abundance may have increased at a more or less consistent rate. It is most likely that the abundance increased logarithmically. It may have increased and leveled off as does bacterial abundance within a petri dish containing limited resources. If intrabaraminic speciation was a common phenomenon, then diversity also increased through the antediluvian period and may also have done so geometrically. The flood, however, introduced a major extinction into the history of life. Post-flood land animal diversity dropped down to the number of baramins. The diversity decimation in the marine realm may have been comparable. Since God purposed to save all the land baramins through the flood it is reasonable to assume that he also intended all the aquatic baramins to survive the flood as well. It is likely that most of the intrabaraminic diversity was decimated by the flood, just as it was on the land. Land animal abundance dropped to two or seven per species. Although the abundance decimation in the marine realm was probably not nearly so severe, the number of marine fossils indicates that it was nevertheless extensive.

After the flood organismal abundance once again increased -- probably in a logarithmic fashion. With a different, perhaps more varied, post-flood climate and topography organismal diversity may have also increased rapidly. However, it is likely that the organisms seen after the flood were rather different than those known before the flood. The abundance bottleneck of the flood would allow for rapid allelic fixation (genetic drift) in the small post-flood populations. This, and the fact that the population which survived the flood may have carried less than the complete pre-flood gene pool (i.e. the founder effect), would cause post-flood populations to differ from the same baramin's populations before the flood. The different climate and topography after the flood may well have encouraged a different type of intrabaraminic diversity (through natural selection) than that which characterized the pre-flood world. Thus the post-flood intrabaraminic morphotypes (species, etc.) are likely to be different than those of the pre-flood period. This means that the flood-deposited fossil species would be expected to differ from the species of the present.

If this is true, then all or nearly all species in flood sediments are likely to be different than modern species. At some higher taxonomic level, however, the modern group will be recognizable in the fossil record. The taxonomic level where the groups go from non-modern to modern, should approximate the holobaramins of land animals and birds. Depending upon how extensive the decimation of sea creatures were, the same reasoning could be used to approximate many of life's holobaramins.

DISCUSSION

For baraminology to adequately function as an arm of the young-earth creation model, it is necessary that it be incorporated into the larger framework of the model. This means that it will be necessary to associate the terminology of baraminology with both the terminology of evolutionary biology, conventional creation biology, and the Scripture. An initial attempt at this is included here. It seems necessary to introduce or reintroduce two terms in order to adequately bridge the gap and reduce potential confusion -- the archaebaramin and the baramin.

The Archaebaramin -- For each biological 'kind' (Hebrew: min), the originally created individuals comprise that kind's **archaebaramin**. The monobaramins, holobaramins, polybaramins, and apobaramins of discontinuity systematics and baraminology are made up <u>only</u> of organisms for which we have physical evidence -- either living or fossil. In contrast, it is possible that we have very little (if any) non-literary physical evidence of any archaebaramin member. It is very unlikely that any archaebaramin member survived to the present, and relatively few may have survived to the time of the flood to be buried in its sediments. Evidences would include fossils made before the flood and not redeposited by the flood (e.g. Pre-Vendian fossils?), fossils made before the flood but redeposited during the flood (e.g. reef core organisms and peat plant debris), and archaebaramin members still alive at the time of the flood but buried in the flood sediments (e.g. some long-lived conifers similar to bristlecone pines). The nature of the archaebaramin as a concept is thus fundamentally different than that of the mono-, holo-, poly-, and apobaramins. Rather than being restricted entirely to known organisms united on the basis of reproducible criteria (those indicating common ancestry), the membership and the nature of the archaebaramins is a theoretical construct, must be largely inferred, and may never be reconstructed with certainty.

Simplifying assumptions which are made about archaebaramins are listed as follows:

1) <u>The archaebaramin was completely bounded by genetic constraints.</u> Since the archaebaramins of Genesis were constrained by divine command to thereafter always breed true, it is assumed that they were provided with some sort of internally-defined genetic constraints which bounded them from morphological change in any direction. They were thus prevented from crossing with non-members and, presumably, from assuming any morphology outside those bounds.

2) <u>Although genetic constraints may have made particular intra-archaebaraminic hybridizations impossible, no genetic constraints completely divided any archaebaramin.</u> If they existed, intra-archaebaraminic genetic barriers only partially divided archaebaramins. Thus it would have been possible to find some particular series of matings which could make gene flow possible between any given archaebaramin member and any other. Each of these matings might have produced reproductively viable offspring as well.

3) <u>Although gene flow was theoretically possible among all members of an archaebaramin, intra-archaebaraminic gene flow may have actually been incomplete.</u> If archaebaramin membership was at all large, it is unreasonable to assume that all members bred with all other members of the archaebaramin!

4) <u>The archaebaramin represented only a very small fraction of the morphological space defined by its genetic constraints.</u> Because even a small region of multidimensional morphological space has a theoretically infinite variety of possible morphologies, an earth with limited resources seems to make it unlikely that the full complement of morphologies were present in the archaebaramin. It also seems reasonable that divine providence would provide the descendants of these organisms with the ability to adapt to conditions not yet realized.

5) <u>The genetic constraints of the archaebaramin defined a region of morphological space which did not overlap the morphological space of any other archaebaramin.</u>

The Baramin -- Baraminology accepts the **baramin** as the created 'kind' (Hebrew: min) repeatedly referred to in Genesis chapter one. Baraminology's reintroduction of Frank Marsh's term is with a slightly different meaning than that understood by Marsh. The baramin is here defined as the archaebaramin and all its descendants. As with the archaebaramin, the baramin is a theoretical construct, for it is not restricted to known organisms united by reproducible criteria of common ancestry. The baramin includes its own archaebaramin (which is itself a theoretical concept), all known descendants of the archaebaramin, and all unknown archaebaramin descendants. Just as with the archaebaramin, the full characterization of the baramin is known only by inference, without complete certainty. There are some things that can be known about the baramin, and they are each a consequence of features of the archaebaramin. They are as follows and numbered according to the numbered features of the archaebaramin listed above upon which they are based:

1) <u>The baramin is completely bounded by genetic constraints (i.e. baramins are apobaraminic).</u> Since the genetic constraints bounding an archaebaramin are thought to be internally defined and heritable, the baramin is considered to be completely bounded by the same constraints. Thus inter- or extra- baraminic evolution is not possible.

2) <u>Complete intrabaraminic genetic barriers can develop over time.</u> It seems possible for genetic constraints to both increase in magnitude and even arise where there were none before. It is also possible that intrabaraminic extinction might prevent gene flow between two parts of the same baramin. Scripture does not indicate that baramin members were always required to be able to successfully hybridize with all other members. It is thus conceivable that genetic and other constraints might arise to completely and permanently divide a baramin into two or more gene pools. Thus whereas successful hybridization with reproductively viable offspring might be possible among all members of the archaebaramin, it will become increasingly less likely through time. Because of this, we are required to broaden the definition of successful hybridization to mean complete hybridization regardless of the physical or reproductive fitness of the offspring.

3) <u>The baramin might contain more than one holobaramin (i.e. baramins are not necessarily holobaraminic).</u> Since gene flow within the archaebaramin was incomplete and relatively little time has elapsed since the creation, it is conceivable that different portions of the same archaebaramin and their descendants remained genetically separate through time. This would be a true phyletic discontinuity which is historically and not genetically constrained. Such baramins would not be holobaraminic. Under these circumstances the assumptions behind the hybridization and variation criteria of discontinuity systematics would be invalid, and would risk incorrectly identifying polybaraminic groups as holobaramins. Further additive similarity criteria will be needed to minimize this difficulty. It will also be useful to acknowledge that the groups more likely to be incorrectly classified would be those with reduced gene flow. Holobaraminic classification can remain more tentative for those groups. All in all, however, this kind of error would have little detrimental effect upon creationist classification, because the resultant holobaramins will actually be closer to baramins. If better means can be found for identifying true monobaraminic relationship, then the criteria we already have can be used to unite holobaramins into baramins. Because it has little negative effect on creationist taxonomy, and we lack criteria to say otherwise, and its effects were minimized in the population bottleneck of the flood, it is reasonable for baraminology to assume that all phyletic discontinuities are due to genetic barriers and not historical (etc.) constraints.

4) <u>Within a baramin there is considerable room for microevolutionary change, including speciation.</u> Change of allelic frequencies (by genetic drift, founder effect, natural selection, etc.), allelic recombination (including of entire organ or species packages as well as of unexpressed genetic material), mutations, chromosomal aberrations, and speciation are observed, real phenomena. Each of these operates completely within the confines of a baramin. With the exception of mutations and chromosomal aberrations, each of these is non-creative -- that is, they produce no new genetic material -- they simply combine genetic material in novel ways. In the case of mutations and chromosomal aberrations, there is no known case of unadulterated benefit to the organism. It is likely that all such errors in replication and division are either neutral or deleterious to the organism.

5) <u>The genetic constraints to the baramin define a region of morphological space which does not overlap with any other baramin's potential morphological space.</u> A consequence of this same feature of the archaebaramin, a baramin is here assumed to be morphologically distinguishable from other baramins by a interbaraminic morphological gap.

Baraminology focuses on identifying holobaramins. By focusing on organisms that are known, and not on hypothetical organisms, this process avoids the kind of disagreements and confusion that have classically plagued creationists as they discussed the concept of the 'Biblical kind'. Once holobaramins are identified, then separate discussion can follow about methods of intra- and inter-baraminic classification and taxonomy. Simultaneously, an increased understanding of holobaramins will augment our understanding of the baramins. This will allow another distinct series of discussions about the nature of the archaebaramin, the baramin, and the baraminic constraints. It is thought that baraminology will extract the creationist from the traditional mire of confusing terminology and allow him to more properly reclassify organisms, speculate about genetic constraints to change, and generally, to understand better the biological creation.

CONCLUSION

Creation theory maintains that there are many real phyletic discontinuities among the earth's biota. Current taxonomic methods do not reflect this claim because they lack any means of recognizing or identifying such discontinuities, let alone characterizing them. In order to make this evidence of creation available, there is a serious need for creation biologists to create, adopt, and employ a reproducible method of flagging phyletic discontinuities. With such discontinuities identified, the classification of the earth's biota will then be in need of serious reconsideration. Although the classification within phyletically continuous groups need not change, the classification of such groups into larger groups is in desperate need of revision.

It is suggested that baraminology provides the tool necessary for the identification of true phyletic discontinuities, and thus the basis for a creationist taxonomic revision. With all the criteria of discontinuity systematics (the continuity criteria of successful hybridization, known natural and experimental variation, and unambiguous lineage, and the discontinuity criterion of the radical failure of continuity criteria), and further young-earth creation model-dependent membership criteria (cladistically-determined homoplasy frequency, flood-generated diversity bottlenecks, and molecular typology studies aided by Biblical criteria), baraminology is the most efficient means available of identifying and characterizing true phyletic discontinuities.

There is still much work that needs to be done in fleshing out the criteria already presented. Young-earth creation biologists are encouraged to critique, refine, and if necessary, reject, the proposed criteria. Even more importantly, they are encouraged to introduce new and better criteria. The more valid criteria that are employed the more successful and rapid will be the accumulation of phyletic discontinuity evidence of creation. It will also be necessary to decide upon the best method of naming holobaramins, and then for classifying holobaramins into successively higher groups. It is hoped that baraminology can be improved to where it will be effective in meeting the classification needs of the young-earth creation biologist.

APPENDIX A

Walter ReMine's (1) definitions for the discontinuity systematics terminology (his emphasis included):

Holobaramin -- A complete set of organisms related by common descent. A group containing all and only those organisms related by common descent.

Monobaramin -- A group containing only organisms related by common descent, but not necessarily all of them.

Polybaramin -- A group of organisms which does not share a common ancestor.

Apobaramin -- A group of organisms which contains all the ancestors and descendants of any of it members, but which may contain subgroupings that are unrelated to each other. A group of organisms not sharing an ancestor or descendant with any organism outside the group.

APPENDIX B

Membership criteria (with numbers) and assumptions (with letters) involved in each:

Continuity (Additive) Criteria of Discontinuity Systematics

1. *Hybridization which results in reproductively viable offspring under natural conditions* is sufficient evidence of phyletic continuity (i.e. parents and offspring are part of the same monobaramin). ASSUMPTIONS:

   A. A large percentage of the descendants of a given ancestor remain capable of successfully mating with a large number of contemporaneous descendants of the same ancestor; and

   B. The ancestral line of two organisms which can now successfully mate are very unlikely to have avoided trading genetic material throughout their entire history.

2. *Hybridization which results in reproductively viable offspring under artificial conditions* is sufficient evidence of phyletic continuity (i.e. parents and offspring are part of the same monobaramin). ASSUMPTIONS: A and B and

   C. Geographic isolation of some descendants of a given ancestor from those of other descendants of the same ancestor is a common event; and/or

   D. Differential change in sexual behavior (e.g. timing of reproduction, sexual preference, etc.) in two descendant lineages from a common ancestor may result in those lineages not hybridizing under natural conditions; and/or

E. Differential mechanical and biochemical change in two descendant lineages from a common ancestor may result in those lineages not being able to hybridize under natural conditions.

3. *Hybridization which results in reproductively non-viable offspring which survive to reproductive age is sufficient evidence of phyletic continuity* (i.e. parents and offspring are part of the same monobaramin). ASSUMPTIONS: A and B and
   F. Differential change in sexual development in two descendant lineages from a common ancestor may result in inter-lineage crosses with unsuccessful reproductive system development.

4. *Hybridization which results in successful gametic fusion but unsuccessful offspring survival to reproductive age is sufficient evidence of phyletic continuity* (i.e. parents and offspring are part of the same monobaramin). ASSUMPTIONS: A and B and
   G. Differential genetic change in two descendant lineages from a common ancestor may result in inter-lineage crosses with non-fit developmental patterns.

5. *Unsuccessful gametic fusion, but successful partial hybridization* (i.e. portions of the DNA from one organism can be successfully incorporated into the DNA of another organism) is <u>in</u>sufficient evidence of phyletic continuity (i.e. the two organisms cannot necessarily be considered part of the same monobaramin). ASSUMPTION:
   H. DNA segments can be transferred across phyletic discontinuities, either 'naturally' by viruses, or artificially by man's biotechnology.

6. *When one organism's total morphology falls within the known morphological natural variation of related organisms there is sufficient evidence to claim phyletic continuity* between the organism and the group of related organisms (i.e. an organism which has a morphology which falls within the natural morphological range of a monobaramin's members is part of that monobaramin). ASSUMPTIONS: A and B and
   I. A morphology which is found within the range of morphological variation of related organisms is very likely to have been produced as a result of DNA which is sufficiently similar to allow successful hybridization between the organism and the group of related organisms.

7. *When one organism's total morphology falls within the experimentally-determined morphological variation of related organisms there is sufficient evidence to claim phyletic continuity between the organism and the group of related organisms* (i.e. an organism which has a morphology which falls within the experimentally-determined morphological range of a monobaramin's members is part of that monobaramin). ASSUMPTIONS: A through G and I.

8. *When a series of populations of membership two or more are located with all of the following characteristics:*
   a. *geographically close-spaced;*
   b. *temporally close-spaced;*
   b. *each population occupies a restricted region of morphology space typical of monobaramins of similar organisms; and*
   c. *adjacent populations define overlapping regions of morphology space,*
   then there is sufficient evidence to claim phyletic continuity among all populations and all members thereof (i.e. organisms which are part of an unambiguous lineage are part of the same monobaramin). ASSUMPTIONS: I and
   J. A restricted morphology spread combined with what is for all practical purposes an unbroken lineage is most easily explained by phyletic continuity.

Continuity (Additive) Criteria of Baraminology

9. *When the Scripture indicates that two organisms had a common ancestor, there is sufficient evidence to claim that they are part of the same monobaramin.* ASSUMPTIONS:
   K. A literal interpretation of Scripture is Truth.

10. *When a complete cladistic analysis between organisms indicates that many, most, or all their similarities are due to homology, then there is sufficient evidence to claim that they may be part of the same monobaramin.*
    NOTE: Since conclusion of homology is the failure to conclude homoplasy, this criterion is a weak one. The reliability of this criterion is directly related to the state of understanding of the organisms' morphology and genetics. ASSUMPTIONS:
    L. Similarity is very difficult to achieve by independent (i.e. convergent) evolution from separate ancestors. Homoplasous similarity should therefore be uncommon among related organisms. Nearly all to all similarity among related organisms should be homology, not homoplasy.
    M. Cladistics is an efficient method of distinguishing homologous and homoplasous

similarity when an understanding of organismal morphology is extensive.

Discontinuity (Subtractive) Criteria of Discontinuity Systematics

11. *When the genetic gap between two organisms is substantially larger than that which can be crossed by successful hybridization, and the morphological gap between two organisms is substantially larger than that traversable by artificially-produced variation and that observed in natural variation, and when the two organisms are not part of an unambiguous lineage, then there is sufficient evidence to claim that those two organisms are separated by a phyletic discontinuity.* ASSUMPTIONS: A through G, I, J, and

N.   Phyletic discontinuities are coincident with substantial morphological and genetic gaps. In other words, the actual and potential morphological space of a group of genetically related organisms does not overlap with that of any other genetically unrelated group.

Discontinuity (Subtractive) Criteria of Baraminology

12. *When the Scripture indicates that two organisms were separately created, there is sufficient evidence to claim that they are separated by a phyletic discontinuity.* ASSUMPTION: K.

13. *When a molecular similarity matrix relates organisms within one group at a particular invariant level of similarity which is significantly different than the similarities each of these members have with the remainder of the bios, then there is sufficient evidence to claim that that group is separated from all other organisms by a phyletic discontinuity.* NOTE: Organisms with the same molecular similarity may have different ancestors, so these phyletic discontinuities define apobaramins, not holobaramins. ASSUMPTIONS:

O.   Beneficial, rapid changes in biomolecules are extremely rare to non-existent events in the history of life. Phylogenies should then show either slow or no change in biomolecules through time. Discontinuities in molecular similarities are understood to indicate a lack of a phyletic continuum.

P.   Similarity among genetically unrelated organisms is a likely consequence of a common Creator, just as common elements of writing style characterize different novels by the same novelist and common elements of brush style can identify common artists. Similarity (namely homoplasous similarity) should therefore be common between created groups. It should therefore be possible, on a molecule to molecule basis, to get non-zero identical molecular similarity values between unrelated organisms.

14. *When a complete cladistic analysis between two organisms indicates that many of their similarities are due to homoplasy, then there is sufficient evidence to claim that they are separated by a phyletic discontinuity.* ASSUMPTIONS: L, M and P.

15. *The taxonomic group from the Flood sediments which is identical to the taxonomic group of the present, but where no Flood sediment subtaxa are identical to the present subtaxa, should be a close approximation to the holobaramin.* NOTE: This is valid reasoning for the land animals and birds, since they were decimated to two (or seven) representatives of each baramin. The validity of this claim for the remainder of the biota is directly related to the degree of their Flood-generated intrabaraminic decimation. NOTE ALSO: The accuracy of this approximation is directly related to the accuracy and fineness of the classification system used. The more unnatural the groups and the greater the number of subtaxa, the less accurate is the approximation. ASSUMPTIONS:

Q.   The high intrabaraminic abundance and divergence just before the Flood was decimated during the Flood. For example, Land animals and birds were decimated to 2 to 7 specimens per baramin. Much of this pre-Flood biota was buried in Flood sediments.

R.   Because of the founder effect, genetic drift, and natural selection in new post-Flood environments, the extensive post-Flood intrabaraminic divergence created very morphotypes (including species) from the pre-Flood world. Thus although the same baramins exist in Flood sediments and the present, present intrabaraminic taxa would differ from the intrabaraminic taxa found in Flood sediments.

REFERENCES

1. ReMine, W., 1991, Discontinuity systematics: a new biosystematics relevant to the creation model, this volume.

2. Marsh, F. L., 1941, <u>Fundamental Biology</u>, Self-published, Lincoln, NB.

3. Woese, C. R., 1981, Archaebacteria, <u>Sci. Am.</u>, 244(6):98-122.

4. Denton, M., 1985, <u>Evolution: A Theory in Crisis</u>, Adler & Adler, Bethesda, MD, 368 pp.

5. Agassiz, Louis, 1894, <u>Evolution and Permanence of Type: A Refutation of the Darwinian Theory of Evolution</u>, Christian Book Club of America, Hawthorne, CA.

(A)

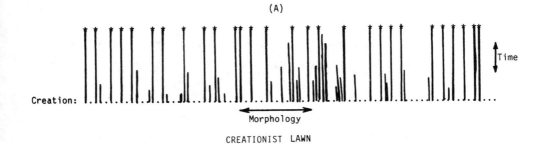

Time

Creation:

Morphology

CREATIONIST LAWN

(B)

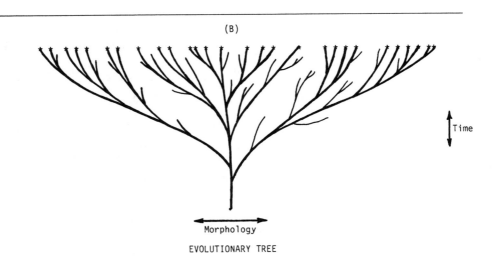

Time

Morphology

EVOLUTIONARY TREE

(C)

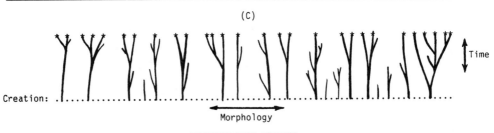

Time

Creation:

Morphology

NEOCREATIONIST ORCHARD

FIGURE 1: Three different analogies for the history of life. A: The analogy of the "Linnaean Lawn", consistent with the invariant typology which was popular in the eighteenth and early nineteenth centuries. B: The analogy of the "Evolutionary Tree", introduced by Charles Darwin and popular in evolutionary literature since that time. C: The analogy of the "Creationist Orchard", consistent with a creation model.

DISCUSSION

During the 1981 Little Rock, Arkansas creation/evolution trial concerning the teaching of creation in public schools, ACLU attorneys consistently attempted to show, while cross-examining creation witnesses, the vagueness of the creation concept of "Genesis Kind". They hoped thus to show the unscientific nature of the creation theory of origins. The evolutionary scenario for the development of the great variety of living organisms sees the species as one transitory step in the continuing evolutionary process. This understanding makes the defining of a species difficult because it becomes less stable and nebulous. Thus evolutionists as well as creationists have definition difficulties.

Dr. Wise's paper is a most helpful discussion of the "Genesis Kind" problem. He has not solved the problem, but he has clarified it and suggested solutions. However, the avenues he outlines toward defining the "Genesis Kind" will neither be easily followed nor quickly achieved.

Harold G. Coffin, Ph.D.
Loma Linda, California

The importance of good classification has been emphasized by R.A. Crowson who said, "Classifying things is perhaps the most fundamental and characteristic activity of the human mind, and underlies all forms of science."(1) Systematics deals with <u>principles</u> of classification and naming. These principles are an expression of our basic philosophy which for the christian in science includes not only observation and research in the natural world, but also biblical revelation. A big difference between discontinuity systematics and baraminology is the inclusion in the latter of biblical information along with observational data collected from nature. Personally, I feel that this approach is requisite for a christian systematist who must understand the interlocking of the "Word and the world."

Whereas discontinuity systematics is neutral, the baraminology described by Dr. Wise incorporates a young earth position and the Noachian Flood. He defines a new term "archaebaramin" as the original created group which I assume, using Marsh's terminology, could be the monotypic (as man with one type) or polytypic (as dog with three types) baramin.(2) Dr. Wise's paper serves to strengthen the contention that a "baraminologist" creationist would interpret available phyletic data more literally than a macroevolutionist would, for the creationist is not compelled to jump gaps with hypothetical ancestors. I like the author's references to baraminograms, which would be like dendrograms or cladograms, but based on criteria set forth in this paper.

It is important that we have some theoretical constructs for the systematist as he tackles the difficult problems with classification of his organisms. I would like to think that there will be a ready acceptance ow Dr. Wise's model by christians within the scientific community. Even if there may be some delay, the viewpoint certainly is a step in the right direction. I would like to see many young people who are embarking on their scientific careers become excited about taxonomy. In this field they can:

1) Contribute to the scientific enterprise.

2) Aid the christian church in understanding God's revelation.

This paper by Dr. Wise can serve as a tool for procedural tactics which can fulfill both of these goals.

REFERENCES:

1. Crowson, R., A. <u>Classification and Biology</u>, Atherton Press, N.Y., 1970, p. 1.

2. Marsh, Frank, L., <u>Evolution, Creation, and Science</u>, Review and Herald, Washington D.C., 1947, pp. 179-180.

Wayne Frair, Ph.D.
Briarcliff Manor, NY

Dr. Wise cogently and concisely presents the contraindications of the current phylogenic systematic paradigm to creationist-compatible biosystematics. At that point, his review clearly identifies a defect of logic inherent to the traditional biosystematic methodology. Evolutionary systematics, predicted on similarities, is but one more painful tautology in a philosophical argument rife with circular arguments. That is, a classification predicated on similarities will inevitably demonstrate them in support of preconceived phylogenetic affinities! Discontinuity systematics, on the otherhand, can be, conceptually, model independent, though in its application can be geared to either evolutionary or creationist concepts of life, as we have it in cladistics and baraminology, respectively. A focus on dissimilarities is not merely a reciprocal approach to the conventional classification scheme, though some may at first reading misconstrue it as such. Baramin systematics appropriately identifies homoplasies, while accommodating real (vs. assumed or imagined) homologies. Among other utilitarian virtues, such clarifies the position (and significance) of many parasitic groups, in particular , whose phylogeny has clearly been forced, yet by the evolutionary systematic concept remains distressingly obscure. Most importantly, to the scientific credibility of a creationist model, baraminology accommodates with the creationist polyphyletic concept of life the undeniable reality of genetically based diversification in time - to the extent of "microevolutionary speciation".

Richard D. Lumsden, Ph.D.
Santee, California

CLOSURE

I would like to thank Drs. Coffin, Frair, and Lumsden for their encouraging remarks, and I am looking forward to the continuing research in Baraminology.

Kurt P. Wise, Ph.D.

CAUSES FOR THE BIOGEOGRAPHIC DISTRIBUTION
OF LAND VERTEBRATES AFTER THE FLOOD

JOHN WOODMORAPPE
M. S. GEOLOGY; B.S. BIOLOGY

ABSTRACT

This study evaluates patterns in the global spread of land animals after their release from the Ark, and shows that: 1) most families have a heterogeneous biogeographic distribution; 2) causes for this include sweepstakes routes caused by the Ice Age and selective anthropogenic introductions. The distribution of problematic groups (e. g. Australian marsupials) appears to be explicable in a Creationist context.

INTRODUCTION

The (imagined) inability of the Creation model to explain the biogeographic distribution of living things was a major factor in its 19th century rejection in favor of organic evolution (Laferriere 1989). Although, as pointed out by the anti-Creationist Jeffery (1983), it is untrue that modern Creationists have ignored biogeography, the global distribution of animals has never been systematically studied from a modern Creationist perspective. This work is a pilot study designed to investigate some of these factors. It is of direct relevance to the young-earth concept in showing that millions of years of organic evolution (i. e. in isolated populations) are not necessary to explain the peculiar biogeographic distribution of certain land vertebrates.

As is the case with most sciences, biogeography as a discipline was largely founded by scientific Creationists (Browne 1983):

> The idea of an Ark in which pairs of animals were preserved during the Deluge had been a concept of far-reaching significance, as had the disembarkation on Mount Ararat and the subsequent dispersal of animals over the unoccupied globe. The biblical story, in fact, had done a great deal to stimulate investigations into the natural world and, among other things, provided the first systematic explanation for the phenomena of biogeography. Far from being the intellectual impediment ridiculed by Darwin and his circle,.. the idea of an Ark focused scholarly attention on the topographic arrangements of species, as well as encouraging naturalists to build up a repertoire of theoretical commitments and practical expertise in the analysis of organic distribution.

METHODOLOGY

This work is limited to animals released from the Ark. It does not consider the biogeography of living things before the Flood (a subject considered elsewhere (Woodmorappe 1983) as part of the explanation for the stratigraphic separation of fossils). Only land vertebrates are recognized as having been on the Ark for the reasons given in Jones(1973). Non-volant vertebrates are emphasized, since the birds and the bats have fossil records too fragmentary (see Carroll 1988) for a meaningful paleobiogeographic analysis of their extant families. At the same time, it should be remembered that most extant avian families are not endemic to particular continents (see Fig. 31 in Rich and Van Tets 1984), while some avian families have near-hemispheric distributions (see Table 1 in Keast 1984).

Throughout this work I assume only naturalistic causes for biogeographic patterns and reject the notion, advocated by some, that post-Flood vertebrates were guided back supernaturally to their former locations on the antediluvian earth. Only Late Tertiary rock contains faunas similar to extant life, but this is not evidence for such a return. Miocene/Pliocene rock is qualitatively different (in terms of thickness, areal distribution, and other features: see Ronov 1982) from earlier rock, so there is ample reason for concluding that Late Tertiary rock and its fauna are mostly post-Flood).

Most biogeographic studies to date have been at the specific level, yet it is almost universally recognized by Creationists that the original Created kind is broader than this. There are numerous instances of interbreeding between species, including those throughout large portions of families (for example, species within Anatidae: Scherer 1986), to say nothing of interbreeding between members of different genera (see Van Gelder 1977 for mammalian examples). Of course, many types of living things must have lost the capability of interbreeding at some time since the Creation. Jones (1972), using Biblical and scientific evidence, has concluded that the original Created kind most closely corresponds to the family level of current taxonomy. This is accepted here. Since biogeographic distributions within kinds (i. e. usually within families) must have resulted from "microevolution" since the Flood (see Lester and Bohlin 1984 for examples of rapid speciation), they are not considered further.

This work approaches biogeography on an intercontinental, not subcontinental, scale. It should be noted, however, that biogeographic differentiation of families on a subcontinental scale is not great. Raup(1982), using computer-based randomly-chosen points on earth (as centers of circular areas of specified radius), has shown that a randomlychosen hemisphere encompasses, on average, all living individuals of only 12% (and maximum of 25%) of terrestrial families.

The paleontological record shows that many if not most living things have had a more widespread distribution than they do today (for example, consider tortoises: Auffenberg 1974). A comprehensive source for the biogeography of extant families as seen from both extant and fossil distributions (Carroll 1988) was therefore used as the primary source throughout this work. Since we cannot know which families have gone extinct only since their disembarkation from the Ark, no extinct families (except for extinct Australian marsupials) are considered here. It should be added that biogeographic differentiation at all levels (but especially lower taxa) has been overstated because of "chauvinotypy" (Rosen 1988): the tendency to generate synonyms by naming taxa from one's nation, biogeographic unit, etc., as unique.

This work assumes that continents have always been fixed. However, if continental drift took place during the Flood, it is irrelevant to post-Flood biogeographic distributions. If it took place at the time of Peleg (Gen 10:25), then all the factors discussed here remain valid. Only their sequence and timing would change.

ANALYSIS

The biogeography of extant (Nowak & Paradiso 1982) and extinct(Carroll 1988) mammalian families, as well as that of reptiles (Carroll 1988), has been examined for biogeographic heterogeneity. Large areas of high endemicity (e. g. Australia, Madagascar) are considered separately below, while the initial focus is on the families native (or once native) to Eurasia/Africa versus North/South America

The table gives the number of families particular to a given group of continents. Of the 40 families common to both blocs of continents, 4 are families presently restricted to one bloc but once living also on the other (as seen from the Miocene/Pliocene: hence post-Flood sediments). We see that 81 of the 112 families occur in at least one of the continents proximate to Ararat, whereas the remaining 31 occur only in North and/or South America. This latter group demands an explanation.

TABLE 1

	Eurasia/Africa	N. & S. America	All 5 Continents
REPTILIAN ORDERS			
Chelonia	0	0	1
Squamata	6	6	14
MAMMALIAN ORDERS			
Rodentia	10	12	6
Carnivora	2	0	5
Insectivora	4	2	3
Primates	11	3	0
Edentata	0	5	1
Artiodactyla	4	1	4
SUM of Families	41	31	40

FACTORS IN POST-FLOOD DISTRIBUTION OF LAND VERTEBRATES

Since animals left the Ark after their kinds (Jones 1973), there was ample opportunity for vicariance (splitting) of faunas in the Middle East, even to some extent without sweepstakes routes. Yet the key to the dispersal of animals from Noah's Ark are the many sweepstakes situations in existence. The Ararat region is mountainous, generating nonrandom routes for migrating animals. The geography includes the Caspian and Black seas as barriers. The fauna, already separated by these local and regional sweepstakes routes, was in a position to be separated on an intercontinental scale.

Ice Age and Climate

The ice age after the Flood (Oard 1986) must have closed off large portions of the northern hemisphere to the animals originally spreading from the Ararat region. But an ice cover is not even necessary. If Oard's hypothesis is correct, volcanic dust caused a reduction in surface land temperatures. By analogy with nuclear winter models (Covey et. al. 1984), interior portions of continents (especially Eurasia) would have been too cold to support life for some time after the Flood.

Consider the situation depicted in top, left. Except for coastal regions, where oceanic warming is a factor, Eurasia and North America are inhospitably cold (i. e. the dark region). The inhabitants disembarking from the Ark are introduced to this situation. After the Middle East is populated, the animals effectively have only 2 sweepstakes routes to take-- southwestward to Africa or southeastward to southeast Asia and Australia. This causes an immediate bifurcation of faunas and, among other things, explains why the tropical faunas of Africa, southeast Asia, and (later) South America have little in common.

Subsequently, (top, left) mountainous regions (such as the Urals) warm up. This is caused by the temperature inversion engendered by the atmospheric dust. A new sweepstakes route now opens up, allowing animals to migrate northward from the Middle East. Since a polar ice cap does not yet exist, the Asian Arctic is at first hospitable to these animals. Many of these continue to expand their distributions along this coast, eventually reaching North America via the Bering land bridge. Eventually the Gulf Stream becomes dominant, warming Europe and western Asia (as predicted in a nuclear winter situation: Covey et. al. 1984). This creates yet another sweepstakes route--from the Middle East to Europe. Some of the fauna that has by now populated the Asian Arctic (and North America) also moves to Europe. This explains the faunas that occur only in Europe and North America.

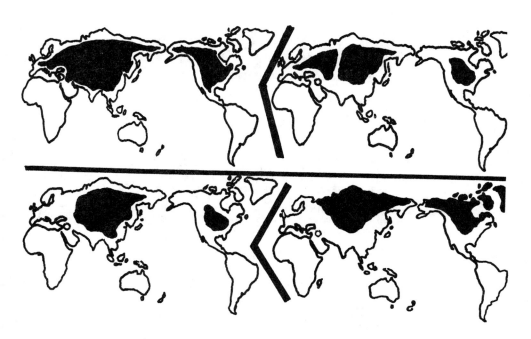

Since the earlier movement of faunas between Eurasia and North America had been disjointed and subject to sweepstakes routes, it is not surprising that the faunas are so different. The ice age seals this situation (bottom, right). Life along the Asian and North American Arctic coasts is snuffed out, and there is no further possibility of interchange between the faunas of Eurasia and North America.

The scenario described above is an oversimplification. In reality, sweepstakes routes must have opened and re-closed repeatedly as regions of inhospitable cold changed over a time span ranging from days to decades. This caused a further vicariance of migrating animals.

Anthropogenic Introductions

A major factor, heretofore neglected in the understanding of the spread of exotic faunas throughout remote parts of the world (i e. relative to Ararat), is the fact that humans began a large-scale dispersal from the Middle East region only after the Tower of Babel incident (Gen 11:78). Prior to this time, they must have been tending many of the animals that had been rapidly multiplying following their release from the Ark. As humans were forced to leave their habitations around Babel, they undoubtedly took animals with them for husbandry, game, and as a reminder of their former area of living. (For a summary of the numerous and diverse reasons for historically recent anthropogenic introductions of animals, see Table 4 in Myers 1986).

These recent examples can offer only a very limited analogy to what must have taken place after the Flood. Post-Babel humans were actually in a position to bring along with them (and introduce to other continents) a much greater diversity of living things than would later be the case (when, for example, only European faunas could be brought by the post 15th century colonists to the New World). First of all, introductions into barren continents had a much greater effect on biogeography than the later introductions of living things into already-populated continents. Also, the diversity of living things in the Middle East was very great soon after the Flood. After all, first the Ark itself and then the whole Middle East region was a microcosm of the full diversity of land vertebrates that would eventually populate the entire globe. Most every group of animals initially taken from the Middle East had a good chance of being a unique faunal assemblage when introduced to distant continents.

It is important to note that introduced animals spread much more rapidly as a result of repeated anthropogenic introductions than they do through their own biological capabilities (Myers 1986). This means that, even if normal spreading tends to make faunas more homogeneous over geographic areas, anthropogenic introductions will make faunal distributions more heterogeneous at a faster rate. Also, consider the rate of population increase among Ark-released animals. If, soon after the Tower of Babel incident, the inhabitants of the Middle East knew (i. e. from advance parties) that remote areas of the earth lacked vertebrates, they had that much more motivation to take many animals with them as "they scattered all over the globe.

LAND VERTEBRATES WITH PECULIAR BIOGEOGRAPHIC DISTRIBUTIONS

There are a number of animals groups that provide classic examples of endemic distribution. Many of these, at first, seem difficult to explain in terms of an origin from the Ark at Ararat. This work offers some novel solutions, with anthropogenic introductions being the main factor.

We have modern examples of entire faunas whose original biogeographic distributions have been completely inverted by anthropogenic introductions combined with geographically-selective extinctions. For instance, wild camels, native to north Africa and the Middle East, are now extinct there, whereas camels introduced to Australia form the largest free-living herd in the world (Myers 1986). The Middle East, originally crowded with the entire diversity of animals released from the Ark, could permanently support only a fraction of these. The rest were doomed to local extinction (or global extinction if they had no representatives beyond the Middle East). For example, the Australian marsupials are a group which was introduced there (see below) but has been long extinct in the Middle East.

Australian Marsupials

These creatures are not only highly endemic and far removed from Ararat, but also comprise a closely related group (as opposed to random assortment of unrelated exotic faunas). However, it must be remembered that the diversity of marsupials (and especially Australian ones) is exceedingly low in comparison to placentals. Only 15 of 53 principal ecological niches exploited by placentals are used by any marsupial (Lee and Cockburn 1985). Furthermore, there are only 17 families (including 4 extinct) of Australian marsupials in contrast to over 250 living and extinct placental families worldwide (Carroll 1988). It would have been no great difficulty for a post-Babel adventurer to have brought with himself 17 pairs of marsupial kinds from the Middle East to Australia. Having a reminder of one's homeland is a powerful motivator for the introduction of animals (Baker 1986) and, if some of the descendants of Noah's family had grown accustomed to marsupials near their respective homes in the Middle East region, they would thus have the motivation to take marsupials with them.

I now consider possible deterministic factors in the exclusive introduction of certain marsupials to Australia. There are a number of features which nearly all Australian marsupials have in common that may have made them especially appealing for the knowledgeable traveler to have taken them along (and at the expense of placentals). Their low rates of postnatal growth (Lee and Cockburn 1985) and lesser food requirements would have made them especially suitable for long voyages, as would the near-lack of diurnal marsupials.

There is some suggestive evidence that Australian marsupials are not a naturally-occurring group but an introduced one. The thylacine, or marsupial wolf, shows close dental and pelvic resemblance to the South American borhyaenids, and evolutionists must invoke "a remarkable amount of convergent or parallel evolution" (Thomas et. al. 1989) to reconcile this with DNA-based evidence that the thylacine is closer to other Australian, and not South American, marsupials. Once it is accepted that marsupials were specially Created and eventually subject to anthropogenic dispersal, it is not surprising that there are astounding similarities between marsupials found on continents occurring at opposite parts of the globe. Thus, the South American Dromiciops stands out in close similarity to Australian, not South American, marsupials (Szalay 1982). Such an oddity makes sense in the light of anthropogenic dispersals of fauna: some marsupials now found only in Australia were also introduced to South America, possibly by the same crew. Indeed, the crew may have largely pre-traced the route taken by later explorers (i. e. James Cook) which would have taken them first to South America and then Australia.

It is also interesting that there are very few truly carnivorous Australian marsupials (Lee and Cockburn 1985), in contrast to the large group of carnivorous South American marsupials. It is the dingo that (apart from bats and rodents) is the only "native" Australian placental. In conventional evolutionary thought, it is claimed that the Australian marsupial fauna evolved over millions of years whereas the dingo was introduced by humans only a few thousand years ago. Accepting both the dingo and the entire Australian marsupial fauna as having been recently introduced provides us with a simple unified explanation: the ancient postdiluvian colonists evidently had preferred to bring along with them the familiar eutherian dog instead of a large group of carnivorous marsupials.

The flip side of anthropogenic introductions as a cause of the Australian marsupial fauna is that there is an explanation for otherwise surprising absences. For instance, the South American freshwater fish are completely unknown to Australia (Briggs 1987). It is not difficult to imagine why if the distributions of faunas was largely governed by the vicissitudes of anthropogenic introduction.

The Fauna of Madagascar

Next to Australia, the island of Madagascar is a striking example of a highly endemic fauna. Occurring off the east coast of Africa on a southerly maritime route from the Middle East, it is not difficult to understand why. The island was a major stopping point for colonists from the Ararat region. This not only explains the endemism of the Madagascaran biota, but also its great diversity (Mittermeier 1988). At the same time, the uniqueness of the Madagascaran fauna finds a partial explanation through African extinctions (as demonstrated, for example, by the faunas found in Madagascar and South America but not Africa: Briggs 1987).

The South American Fauna

The South American fauna contains unique groups, such as the caviomorph rodents. Its avifauna is quite endemic, involving 31 unique families (Rich and van Tets 1984).

Part of the South American fauna, of course, came from Eurasia via North American. This can be illustrated by those elements of the South American fauna which occur only as fossils in North America or Eurasia. Other South American forms were undoubtedly introduced by voyagers from the Middle East. Since South America is relatively close across the Atlantic on a southwesterly route from the Straits of Gibraltar, it is not surprising that it was repeatedly colonized soon after the Tower of Babel incident.

The Fauna of Mid-oceanic Islands

For the colonization of Pacific islands, it has been found that animals are much more capable of colonizing islands even hundreds of km's from a mainland than had been earlier supposed (Diamond 1987). At the same time, oceanic islands vary considerably in terms of diversity of vertebrate life and its similarity to that of the nearest continent. This can be explained by the varying successes of colonization as well as the uneven anthropogenic introductions of vertebrates. Flightless birds occur on certain islands. They do not form a taxonomic group themselves, as they are individual counterparts to volant varieties. Flightless birds can arise from volant ancestors in a few generations (Olson 1973, Worthy 1988), making it possible for islands to have been colonized by volant birds whose recent ancestors had been released from the Ark. (This rapid "devolution" via mutations that cause loss of function and/or structure also solves the apparent problem of vestigial wings. We need not suppose that God created birds with nonfunctional wings).

CONCLUSIONS

The Creation model not only explains the distribution of living things on earth, but is also scientifically superior to the evolution model. This is because the Creation model is more parsimonious. For example, it is much simpler to explain the similarities between the Australian and certain South American marsupials in terms of anthropogenic introductions after the Flood than it is to accept their evolution, over millions of years, while the continents drifted.

Biogeographic studies can either be approached in terms of testable hypotheses or cumulative inductive evidence (Rosen 1988). This pilot study must be followed up by more detailed research into factors relevant to the spread of animals following their release from the Ark: 1) Climatic factors (i. e., the Ice Age) as a cause of sweepstakes routes operable on a transcontinental scale; 2) Anthropogenic introductions involving entire faunas of closely-related forms of life; 3) Identifiable features in Australian marsupials and Madagascaran lemurs leading to their onetime collective introductions by post-Babel humans; 4) the immediate post A-Flood period and the Ararat region with its constantly-changing sweepstakes routes.

REFERENCES

1. Archer M. & G. Clayton (eds). 1984. Vertebrate Zoogeography and Evolution in Australasia. Hesperion Press, Australia, 1203pp..

2. Auffenberg W. 1974. Checklist of Fossil Land Tortoises (Testudinae). Bulletin of the Florida State Museum 18(3)121-251.

3. Baker S. J. 1986. Irresponsible introductions and reintroductions of animals into Europe with particular reference to Britain. International Zoo Yearbook 24/25:200-5.

4. Briggs J. C. 1987. Biogeography and Plate Tectonics. Elsevier, Amsterdam,204pp.

5. Browne J. 1983. The Secular Ark. Yale University Press, 273pp.

6. Carroll R. L. 1988. Vertebrate Paleontology and Evolution. Freeman and Company, New York, 698p.

7. Covey, C., Schneider, S. H. & S. Thompson. 1984. Global atmospheric effects of massive smoke injections from a nuclear war. Nature 308:21-5.

8. Diamond J. M. 1987. How do flightless mammals colonize oceanic islands?, Nature 327: 374.

9. Jeffery D. E. 1983. Dealing with Creationism. Evolution 37(5)1097-1100.

10. Jones A. J. 1972. Boundaries of the Min: An analysis of the Mosaic lists of clean and unclean animals. Creation Research Society Quarterly 9(2)114-23.

11. Jones A. J. 1973. How many animals in the Ark? Creation Research Society Quarterly 10(2)102-8.

12. Keast A. 1984. Contemporary ornithogeography: the Australian avifauna, its relationships and evolution. (pp. 457-69) In Archer & Clayton (eds) op. cit.

13. Laferriere J. E. 1989. Certainty and proof in Creationist thought. Skeptical Inquirer 13(2) 185-8.

14. Lee A. K. & A. Cockburn. 1985. _Evolutionary ecology of marsupials_. Cambridge University Press, Cambridge, London, 274pp.

15. Lester L. P. & R. G. Bohlin. 1984. _The Natural Limits to Biological Change_. Zondervan, Grand Rapids, Michigan, 207pp.

16. Mittermeier R. A. 1988. Primate diversity and the tropical forest: case studies from Brazil and Madagascar and the importance of the megadiversity countries (pp. 145-57) In Wilson E. O. (ed). _Biodiversity_, National Academy Press, Washington, D. C., 521pp.

17. Myers K. 1986. Introduced vertebrates in Australia, with emphasis on the mammals (pp. 121-136) In Groves R. H., and J. J. Burden. (eds). _Ecology of Biological Invasions_, Cambridge University Press, London, New York, 166pp.

18. Nowak R. M. & J. L. Paradiso. 1983. _Walker's Mammals of the World. 4th Ed._, John Hopkins University Press, Baltimore, Vol. 1, pp. xxi-xliv.

19. Oard M. J. 1987. An ice age within the Biblical time frame. (pp. 157-66) In Walsh R., Brooks C. L., & R. S. Crowell. (eds). _Proceedings of the First International Conference on Creationism_, Creation Science Fellowship, Pittsburgh, PA, Vol. II, 254pp.

20. Olson S. L. 1973. Evolution of the rails of the south Atlantic islands (Aves:Rallidae). _Smithsonian Contributions to Zoology_ 152:1-53.

21. Raup D. M. 1982. Biogeographic extinction: a feasibility test (pp. 277-81) In Silver L. T. & P. H. Schultz (eds). Geological implications of impacts of large asteroids and comets on the earth. _Geological Society of America Special Paper 190_, 528pp.

22. Rich P. & G. Van Tets. 1984. What fossil birds contribute towards an understanding of origin and development of the Australian avifauna. (pp. 421-47). In Archer & Clayton (eds) op. cit.

23. Ronov A. B. 1982. The earth's sedimentary shell. _International Geology Review_ 24(2)1365-1388.

24. Rosen B. R. 1988. From fossils to earth history: applied historical biogeography. (pp.437-81) In Myers A. A. & P. S. Giller (eds). _Analytical Biogeography_. Chapman & Hall, London, New York, 578pp.

25. Savage D. E. and D. E. Russell. 1983. _Mammalian Paleofaunas of the World_. Addition-Wesley, London, Amsterdam, 432p.

26. Scherer, S. 1986. On the limits of variability (pp. 219-241) In Andrews E. H., Gitt W. Gi H., & W. J. Ouweneel (eds). _Concepts in Creationism._, 266pp.

27. Szalay F. S. 1982. A new appraisal of marsupial phylogeny and classification (pp. 621-40) In Archer M. (ed). _Carnivorous Marsupials._, Royal Zoological Society of New South Wales, Sydney, Vol. 2, 804pp.

28. Thomas R. T., Schaffner W., Wilson A. C., & S. Paabo. 1989. DNA Phylogeny of the extinct marsupial wolf. _Nature_ 340:465-7.

29. Van Gelder R. G. 1977. Mammalian hybrids and generic limits. _American Museum Novitates No. 2635_, 25pp.

30. Woodmorappe J. 1983. A diluviological treatise on the stratigraphic separation of fossils. _Creation Research Society Quarterly_ 20(3).

31. Worthy T. H. 1988. Loss of flight ability in the extinct New Zealand duck Euryanas finschi. _Journal of Zoology (London)_ 215:619-28.

DISCUSSION

First Mr. Woodmorappe states that some animals were carried into South America by repeated colonizations of peoples from the Middle East. If this is so, why do South American Indians more closely resemble Asians rather than their Middle Eastern progenitors?

Secondly, within the author's views, why are living kangaroos only found on Australia *and* why are the only fossil kangaroos found on Australia? Some evolutionists have criticized creationist biogeography on this point. How does Mr. Woodmorappe address this problem?

Glenn R. Morton, M.S.
Dallas, Texas

Mr. Woodmorappe is to be congratulated for tackling a problem - large scale biogeographic distribution - that many evolutionists regard as completely unsolvable on any young earth model. While I enjoyed the paper, and found it highly suggestive for further avenues of research, I have two criticisms:

1) The paper says nothing about the shortcomings of various evolutionary biogeographic models (e.g., dispersal or vicariance hypotheses). While these shortcomings may be well known to Mr. Woodmorappe, and to many evolutionists, they are, in my estimation, unknown to most of the creation community. It is vitally important that we learn from the failures of others, so we do not repeat them.

2) In that vein, Mr. Woodmorappe provides few if any constraints to his hypothesis of anthropogenic introductions. However, the unconstrained use in explanation of merely possible hypotheses has led many evolutionists to reject earlier theories of dispersal biogeography.

Can Mr. Woodmorappe suggest constraints (perhaps by way of <u>tests</u>) on his interesting hypothesis of anthropogenic introductions?

Paul A. Nelson
Chicago, Illinois

Commendation: Mr. Woodmorappe's simultaneous consideration of Mid-Eastern geography post-flood climatology, and anthropogenic introductions is a valuable contribution to creationist biogeography.

A Caution: There is too much uncertainty on such things as the stratigraphic location of the flood/post-flood boundary and the identification of created kinds for the author to be as certain as he is about the former being the Oligocene/Miocene boundary, and the latter being families. He needs to exhibit much more caution and qualification on these points.

Corrections: Mr. Woodmorappe claims that he cannot know which baramins [sic] went extinct after the flood. It seems that can be known. According to Scripture, all land baramins were represented on the ark. If so, then all land baramins survived the flood, so any extinct land baramins went extinct *after* the flood.

If the Flood/Post-Flood boundary turns out to be significantly earlier than the Oligocene/ Miocene boundary, then plate tectonics will have to be considered as another factor in post-flood biogeography. Tectonics allows for (e.g. Africa-to-Sough America) migrations to occurs easily that are very difficult without it.

Critiques: Mr. Woodmorappe's table needs recalculating. Extinct families need to be considered. Amphibians need to be considered, and *all* orders need to be listed. All continents and Madagascar need to be listed separately. The current table seriously understated the biogeographical import of South America, Australia and Madagascar.

The author does not explain why Europe is not initially a third "sweepstakes" route. It looks like it should be in his figure, and I see no reason why the coast could not be a migration route.

The *extremely* important South American endemism is not dealt with properly. How do post-Babel peoples communicate with one another via advanced parties when their languages have been disrupted?

Conclusion: Mr. Woodmorappe's biogeographic "explanations" are nothing more than scenarios — untested, non-&-all-explanatory just-so stories which are inadequate biogeographic explanations.

Kurt P. Wise, Ph.D
Dayton, Tennessee

CLOSURE

This is a response to both the written questions above as well as to those given orally after the speaker's presentation.

Mr. Mats Molen is correct in pointing out that the maps do not show glaciated and nonglaciated areas with total accuracy. However, this is because the maps are intended only for schematic and illustrative purposes. The absence (or near-absence) of humans in the Miocene can be explained by the fact that human population growth after the Flood was much slower than that of the animals released from the Ark. Consequently, there may not have been a large enough population of humans to contribute to the Miocene faunas. Moreover, humans probably lived primarily in upland regions and were therefore unlikely to be fossilized during post-Flood catastrophic depositional events.

Mr. Paul Nelson is correct in noting that I did not discuss the difficulties which conventional evolutionary theory encounters in attempting to explain biogeographic distributions. This is because the focus of this work is the positive explanatory power of the Creationist-Diluvialist paradigm. However, I did mention that the Creationist view is more parsimonious in that, for example, it is much simpler to explain the amazing similarity of some Australian and South American marsupials in terms of anthropogenic introductions than in the evolutionary view of common ancestors and drifting continents. I am well aware of the difficulties of evolutionary theory in the explanation of biogeography. Even without a Creationist explanation, evolutionary theory does not ipso facto encounter fewer difficulties in explaining biogeographic distribution.

Mr. Glen Morton's remark about the distribution of kangaroos seems odd in the light of my discussion of Australian marsupials. Perhaps Mr. Morton has not read my entire paper. Likewise, the similarity of fossils to their extant distribution has been discussed. It is true only for the uppermost strata — hence post-Flood rocks (thus fossil kangaroos in Australia). As to the similarity between south American Indians and east Asiatic peoples, this can be easily explained by the differences between successive waves of immigrants. The Indians, coming from eastern Asia, could have easily supplanted the original settlers from the Babel region just as the Indians were in turn overshadowed by the European settlers who now form the bulk of the population of the Americas.

Here are some replies to Dr. Wise's comments:

Both the family unit as the closest Linnean equivalent to the Created kind, and the Oligocene/ Miocene boundary as Flood-post-Flood boundary seem to be supported by strong independent evidence. This is not to say that all Miocene-Recent rocks are post-Flood nor that there are no post-Flood pre-Miocene rocks. Consequently, while I agree that all land vertebrates, fossil and extant, were on the Ark, I maintain that we cannot know for certain which Miocene/Pliocene extinct land faunas with their biogeographic distributions were governed by post-Flood factors. I could easily expand my Table to include all extinct faunas as Dr. Wise suggests, but I doubt if it would significantly alter any of the positions and conclusions of this work. I disagree that amphibians need to be considered, for the simple reason that they were not taken on the Ark (see Jones 1973). I can see how Europe could have served as a sweepstakes route, but that would have depended on the degree of its connection with North America.

I would fully agree with Mr. Nelson and Dr. Wise that it is difficult to test fully the biogeographic theories advanced by my paper, but it must be remembered that this is only a pilot study. The theories advanced here are not ad hoc for the following reasons:

1) We know that anthropogenic factors are very significant in biogeography. How much more so if terrestrial vertebrate biogeography had to start "from scratch" from the Ararat region!

2) The climatic sweepstakes routes are not ad hoc because we know of the reality of glaciation from independent evidence.

3) The areas with the most exotic faunas (Madagascar, Australia, and South America) are not randomly distributed on earth: their geographic placement (especially Madagascar) is one that would intercept ships carrying passengers from the Ararat region.

4) The views advanced here do __not__ explain "any and every" possible biogeographic distribution.

For example, the theories are falsifiable at least to the extent that we could conceive of biogeographic situations which would be very difficult if not impossible to explain by an origin from Ararat combined with anthropogenic introductions. For example, the Australian marsupial fauna could have consisted of hundreds of endemic families (not 17, as is the case) in which case anthropogenic introduction would have been a nonviable explanation. Also, if the diversity of terrestrial vertebrate families in the Americas had been much greater than that in Eurasia/Africa, it would be very difficult to explain this in terms of a single origin from the Ararat region. If Madagascar, South America, and Australia were found very close to Ararat (say, in the Mediterranean Sea), it would be difficult to even imagine how they could have such exotic faunas in the light of anthropogenic introduction.

As a matter of fact, the theories in this work suggest many areas for further study as well as testable hypotheses (some of which have been suggested by the audience). Some examples: possible (pagan) religious factors leading to humans having been attracted towards marsupials as a group (Oard), the utility of South American endemics as pets, and the use of certain reptiles for medicinal purposes.

For a truly comprehensive scientific test of my hypothesis of anthropogenic introduction, we need a much more thorough understanding of it, as examples in the scientific literature are basically limited to the relatively few modern examples. Of course, there is no strong conceptual driving force in the evolutionary paradigm to study it in great detail. We especially need to know the factors that may have motivated humans to introduce specific groups of animals (such as the Australian marsupials). The discovery of such factors would support my hypothesis, while the failure to discover any would tend to falsify it.

John Woodmorappe, M.S.

Section 3

Additional Topics

Section 3

Additional Topics

REPORT ON CHEMICAL ANALYSIS AND FURTHER DATING OF DINOSAUR BONES AND DINOSAUR PETROGLYPTHS

L. Dahmer, D. Kouznetsov, A. Ivenov, J. Hall,
J. Whitmore, G. Detwiler, H. Miller

ABSTRACT

Much of the material in this report was presented at the 1990 ICC poster sessions. Our radiocarbon dates of dinosaur bones and the other information in this report should be alarming to the evolutionary community and should be given serious study considering our preliminary results.

INTRODUCTION

The hypothesis that blackened dinosaur bones may be the result of absorption by the bones of decaying flesh of the dinosaur itself was suggested by members of two teams excavating an Acrocanthosaurus skeleton in August of 1984, near Glen Rose, Texas. The blackened bones were found covered by up to three feet of clay and imbedded in limestone. A sandstone stratum was above the clay stratum. The two teams consisted of members from the Creation Evidences Museum (CEM) of Glen Rose, Texas and the Creation Research Science Education Foundation (CRSEF) of Columbus, Ohio. The location was approximately three miles upstream from the Paluxy River footprint site, on the Parker Ranch. We are particularly indebted to G. Detwiler, Robbi and Bill Roberson all of CRSEF for their persistence in bringing the details of the Acrocanthosaurus excavation to our attention. Thanks also to Carl Baugh and Don Patton of CEM for their valuable assistance.

In 1986, James Hall of Liberty University, Lynchburg, Virginia, proposed independently that his black Allosaurus bones may have similarly been carbonized, later confirmed by two other labs. Hugh Miller confirmed the Acrocanthosaurus bones were carbonized when the chemical firm by whom he was employed had the scrapings from the bones analyzed for carbon in 1989.

CHEMICAL AND METALLOGRAPHIC ANALYSIS OF THE BONES

After learning that the Texas dinosaur bone surfaces contained 3.5% carbon, CRSEF member Hugh Miller, and Lionel Dahmer surveyed the contents of a large dinosaur bone storage room of a major U.S. museum and estimated that about 80% of the bones ranged from dark gray to black in color. We were fortunate to obtain eight bone samples from this museum along with documentation of genus, location, and collector. Analysis of the surface scrapings from these bones are given in Table I. The scrapings ranged from 1.9% to 7.4% carbon.

The carbon values were obtained on scrapings after the bone fragments were first ultrasonically cleaned with methanol, 10% acetic acid, and water. The purpose of cleaning with methanol and dilute acetic acid is to remove surficial preservatives and carbonates respectively. Several final washings with Milli Q high purity water is, of course, necessary to remove residual methanol or acetic acid before drying and sampling for carbon determination. Cleaned bone surfaces were then scraped with a serrated knife and the powder was analyzed in a Leco high temperature induction furnace or in a Carlo-Erba elemental analyzer.

Metallographic studies of an Acrocanthosaurus bone fragment indicated that the surface cracks and pores of the bone fragments contained dark material which could have contributed to the carbon already in the bones. Pores in other bones contained light colored material although the surfaces were indeed black and carbonized, e.g. sample No. 10, Table I. Some of the bone fragments were very brittle and could be broken by pressure which might be attributed to carbon embrittlement.

Thanks to Roy Holt and others, we were able to obtain some information that some dinosaur bones contain carbonaceous materials such as collagen and noncollagen amino acids. These 1988 discoveries show that the idea that there is nothing left of the original bone material is not always correct. That is, the idea that fossil formation always involves a faithful atom by atom replacement of the original anatomy by silicate and carbonate is not always valid. From a conventional point of view, it is amazing that these organic materials are still existent 145 million years after the dinosaur's demise. Perhaps the reason they contain carbon compounds is that they are millions of years younger than previously thought. Analysis of the bones for 30 elements revealed no differences from modern bones with the exception of uranium and fluoride which are well known to be extremely mobile in ground water. Whether this specific data will be presented in book form or in technical journals remains to be decided, we were told. On the same note, Tony Raines has published some notes confirming the above communication (see *Maps Digest*, "Collection and Preservation of Large Vertebrates Including Dinosaurs," Vol. 13:6, Summer 1990).

RADIOCARBON AND LASER MASS SPECTROMETER ANALYSIS DATING

Carbonized bone, wood, and charcoal wood samples were dated by various Paluxy teams as noted in Figure 3 of the "The Paluxy Footprints Revisited" (specimens 1-8). Since then Acrocanthosaurus crushed bone fragment gases collected from sample 6 (Table 3 of Paluxy Footprints paper) and scrapings from another bone fragment were radiocarbon dated at an AMS lab (see Table II, this paper). Note that the scrapings which would most certainly have been more free of contamination by young carbon were actually about 2,000 radiocarbon years younger than the crushed bone sample date. This suggests older carbon may have contaminated the bones instead of younger as many have suspected of our studies.

Two other samples from Table I of this paper were dated by conventional radiocarbon dating systems and were found to be relatively young compared to the Acrocanthosaurus. It was felt there was no need to date these on the much more expensive, but accurate, AMS because of the younger dates. A lack of funds has prevented radiocarbon dating of our other dinosaur bone samples. The AMS costs $500 per analysis. Contributions (both large and small) would be appreciated towards this vital project.

A second piece of carbonized wood was radiocarbon dated at no younger than 37,420 ± 6120-3430 years before present using the conventional technique. A photo of this sample appeared in Figure 1 of our Paluxy paper and was very close in age to specimen 8 in Table 3. Both were 3-4 meters back from the river under the top Cretaceous strata and imbedded in the very compacted intermediate clay stratum some 100 meters apart.

It has always been the aim of this project to find a second dating technique that might enable the team to falsify or confirm the radiocarbon dates. Potassium-argon was considered and ruled out. It wasn't until our communication with Dr. D. Kouznetsov and Mr. A. Ivenov, M.S. (a laser mass spectromitrist), that such a system became available. They first analyzed bone fragments of the Acrocanthosaurus and obtained a quick 22 element analysis and a rough estimate of its age between 30,000 and 100,000 years. The ratio indices between C, N, O, P, and Cl were used to calculate the above approximate age. Significantly, their carbon value on an entirely different fragment was 3.4% which agreed very closely with the two other samples of 3.3 and 3.5% carbon at two other labs. They are currently completing an in depth report on all the other dinosaur specimens which shows them to lie between 20,000 and 40,000 B.P. Most assuredly another paper will be published regarding these matters. In any science, when a team of scientists is able to confirm one set of data by an entirely different technique, the chance of both being correct is better. From these dating systems alone it can be concluded that both dinosaurs and the sedimentary rocks in which they are deposited are of the same age. Therefore, the rocks must be the same age as the fossils, and the fossils must be the same age of the rocks.

PETROGLYPH OF THE HAVA SUPAI CANYON

Note that the two specimens in Table I of this report were collected by Charles W. Gilmore. Gilmore was a scientist of national repute in the 1920's, being Curator of Vertebrate Paleontolotgy at the U.S. National Museum. He was also a member of the Doheny scientific expedition in October, 1924 to the Hava Supai Canyon in Northern Arizona, to investigate a petroglyph of an apparent Diplodocus dinosaur on a canyon wall. With the help of Bert Thomas, a book by author A. Hyatt Verill and by a chance discovery at the Oakland, California museum, Lionel Dahmer obtained the report. Dr. Robert Whitelaw (one of the "Paluxy River Footprints Revisited" authors) visited the Smithsonian and found the original notes of Dr. Gilmore from the expedition. There in the original notes were the drawings of animals he saw, including Diplodocus. The Drawing of Diplodocus add additional evidence that man and dinosaurs once coexisted. Anyone desiring the Doheny expedition report (38 pages) or the supplement report to the "Paluxy Footprints Revisited" for research, may obtain it through the CRSEF, P.O. Box 292, Columbus, Ohio, 43216, for a contribution (allow several weeks).

The hypothesis of dinosaur and human coexistence has not been conclusively proved. In fact, much more work has to be done. From the chemical analyses of dinosaur bones, the radiocarbon dates that have been obtained, dinosaur petroglyphs, and human like impressions found with dinosaur footprints, it is apparent the hypothesis is far from being disproved. The work on these particular subjects in the past has not been the best (ours is not an exception), but it is being improved. The creationist community must pool its efforts and resources to investigate these very important findings. Let us work together to find the answers.

FUTURE RESEARCH

Some of our plans include radiocarbon dating of more dinosaur bones; dating of blackened mammalian bones (including carbon analysis of surface scrappings); dating of Eurasian dinosaur and mammalian bones and carbonized wood; excavation for mammalian bones with dinosaur bones (we need possible localities for such bone sites); core sampling for carbonized wood in ancient strata; excavation for a "good human-like track way along Paluxy" and at other locations. We need between $30,000 and $100,000 to begin to accomplish these goals. Foundations have been a big help to date; any help from our readers would be appreciated. Our research is geared towards showing the young age of the earth and the probability of dinosaur and human coexistence.

Table I. Analyses of Dinosaur Bone Surface Scrapings for Carbon

#	GENUS	LOCATION	COLLECTOR	%CARBON
1.	Acrocanthosaurus	Glen Rose, TX	Baugh	3.28
2.	Allosaurus	Grand Junction, CO	Hall	2.70
3.	Diplodocus	Albany Co., WY	Gilmore	2.54
4.	Barosaurus	Uintah Co., UT	Douglass	2.29
5.	Camarasaurus	Johnson Co., WY	Utterback	5.13
6.	Stegosaurus	Albany Co., WY	Wortman	6.92
7.	Camarasaurus	Carbon Co., WY	Gilmore	7.43
8.	Apatosaurus	Carbon Co., WY	Wortman	3.23
9.	Camarasaurus	Johnson Co., WY	Utterback	4.32
10.	Unidentified	Wyoming	Unknown	1.90

Table II. Radiocarbon Dating of Dinosaur Bones and Carbon Analysis of Clay and Rock Samples.

Specimen	Location	Radiocarbon Dates/ Lab (a) years B.P.	% Carbon
Acrocanthosaurus #1 in above table #6 in Table 3, Paluxy Footprint paper	Parker Ranch Glen Rose, TX	23,760 ± 270 USA bone scrappings	3.5 3.4 3.3
Acrocanthosaurus #1 in above table #6 in Table 3, Paluxy Footprint paper	Parker Ranch Glen Rose, TX	25,750 ± 280 Overseas crushed bone	3.5 3.4 3.3
Allosaurus #2 in above table	Grand Junction, CO	16,120 ± 220 USA	2.7
Unidentified dinosaur bone fragment, #10 in above table	Wyoming according to museum curator	9,890 ± 60	1.9
Clay from bone stratum, #6, Table 3, Paluxy Footprints Paper	Parker Ranch, Glen Rose, TX		0.5 (b)
Clay from 30 cm above bone stratum, #6, Table 3, Paluxy Footprints Paper	Parker Ranch, Glen Rose, TX		0.1 (b)
Rock from Allosaurus, #2 in above table	Grand Junction, CO		2.0 (b)

(a)   Our reports on radiocarbon dating are extant. A future paper will contain these report sources, however we must protect our sources at this early stage of research.

(b)   Note that there was very little migration of carbon into the clay from the remains of the dinosaur skeleton. A higher percentage of carbon was found in the rock containing the Allosaurus. More research will be needed to establish all of the migration parameters and other factors to give a reasonable interpretation. However, since the bones had a higher percentage of carbon in them than the surrounding rock or clay, the hypothesis is that the carbon came from the dinosaur and did not migrate into the area. Instead, these results show the carbon is migrating away from the area.

THE EVOLUTIONARY WORLDVIEW AND AMERICAN LAW

DR. JOHN EIDSMOE

Evolution is the nineteenth century's number one contribution to Western thought.

By this I do not mean evolution merely as a scientific model. In a broader sense I refer to evolution as a philosophy, an ideology, a religion, or a comprehensive world view. In this sense, evolution has transformed Western thought. As Richard Hofstadter says in Social Darwinism in American Thought,

> Many scientific discoveries affect ways of living more profoundly than evolution did; but none have had a greater impact on ways of thinking and believing. In this respect, the space age does not promise even remotely to match it.(1)

To be sure, evolution did not transform Western thought overnight. Evolution did not originate with Charles Darwin's *Origin of Species* in 1859. Darwin's grandfather, Erasmus Darwin (1739-1802) had formulated theories of evolution, as had the French naturalist Jean Lamarck (1744-1829); and in fact, evolutionary thought can be found in ancient Rome, Greece, and Babylon. Darwin's contribution was to systematize evolutionary thought into a scientific model and to popularize it for the Western world.

And Darwin did not overwhelm an unwilling world with the brilliance of his reasoning or the weight of his evidence. Louis Agassiz of Harvard, the leading geologist, biologist, and zoologist of the time, lectured extensively refuting Darwin's theories, and other leading scientists of the day such as Louis Pasteur similarly opposed Darwin(2); but their arguments were ignored as the Western world eagerly jumped on Darwin's evolutionary bandwagon. As John Hallowell says,

> The popularity of Darwin's theory is to be accounted for, at least in part, by the fact that it suited the times in which it was formulated, it confirmed many individuals in believing what they already wanted to believe.(3)

Darwinism was the capstone of a gradual intellectual shift from the God-centered worldview of the Middle Ages and the Reformation to the man-centered worldview of today. Europe in the days of Luther and Calvin, Protestant and Catholic alike, would have turned a cold shoulder to evolutionary thought. The Pilgrims and Puritans who settled New England would have been repelled by Darwin. But the Enlightenment, while not totally unchristian, provided avenues for humanistic thought. And the Enlightenment had an influence in America, although that influence was considerably less than in Europe and was greatly tempered by two great religious revivals; the First Great Awakening of the 1740s and the Second Great Awakening around 1800. But during the 1800s the rise of Unitarianism, Transcendentalism, and other movements in American thought cooled the biblical Christianity of an earlier era, so that by 1853 America was ready for a major intellectual shift.

For thousands of years, Western thought had regarded truth as objective, absolute, and unchanging. But Georg Wilhelm Freidrich Hegel (1770-1831) undercut this view by treating truth as a changing process. According to the Hegelian dialectic, in each age there is a central idea, called the thesis. In opposition to the thesis there arises a contrary thought, called the antithesis. In the conflict between thesis and antithesis, the best of both emerge and combine as the synthesis. This becomes the thesis of the next age, another antithesis arises in opposition to it, another synthesis, and so on. Truth is an ever-changing, ever-upward process. After Hegel's death, his followers splintered into various camps, including the "left Hegelians" who went beyond Hegel into various forms of radicalism including Marxism, and the "Right Hegelians" who tried to reconcile the Hegelian dialectic with Christianity.(4)

As a whole, though, Hegelian thought constituted a frontal attack upon Christianity by regarding truth as a changing, evolving process.

The work of August Comte (1798-1857) was another influential force. Comte is sometimes called the father of modern science and the father of modern sociology, though others compete for these titles, but he is the undisputed father of positivism. Positivism is the belief that the only really meaningful or knowable truth is that which can be empirically verified, that is, that which can be verified through the five senses. Positivism does not necessarily reject God; rather, it relegates God to the limbo of unverifiable and therefore meaningless propositions. Such values as liberty, justice, equality, and the like are likewise regarded as unverifiable and meaningless.(5)

Combine Hegel's concept of truth as an evolving process with Comte's view of truth as only that which can be empirically verified, and we have come a long way from the classical Christian view of truth as absolute and unchanging and understood through divine revelation aided by the God-given facility of human reason. Add to this the "great chain of being" idea popular in America in the early 1800s that views man and nature as part of one great chain of being, the transcendentalist view that sees the spark of divinity within each human being, and the general American faith in upward mobility or human progress, and we find that by the middle of the nineteenth century, America -- at least, the American intellectual community -- was ready for a major paradigm shift from a God-centered worldview to a man-centered worldview. One thing held men back: the fact that man was created by God. How can a creature be greater than his Creator? This sobering realization forced men, intellectually at least, to kneel before the throne of God.

Darwin gave the Western world a way of explaining origins that did not have to involve God -- not a satisfactory explanation in my opinion, but an explanation nevertheless. In this way evolution was Western man's declaration of independence from God.

It is questionable whether Darwin ever imagined that his work would have such far-reaching implications. Possibly he himself never fully comprehended the extent to which evolution would become a central tenet of the humanistic worldview. But another man realized it quickly, and he immediately went to work. As Huntington Cairns explains,

> Herbert Spencer, in his autobiography, has related how, in the last days of 1857, at about the age of 37, when he was collecting, revising and publishing a number of essays, he was impressed with the kinship and connections between the ideas of his various articles. Suddenly there came to him the thought that the concrete sciences at large -- astronomy, geology, biology, psychology and sociology -- should have their various classes of facts presented in subordination to the universal principle of evolution. Clearly, it seemed to him, these sciences form a connected and unified aggregate of phenomena; and clearly, therefore, they should be arranged into a coherent body of doctrine. Thereafter, he set himself to the formidable task of composing the volumes which would relate all departments of knowledge, which he believed were separated only by conventions, to the theory of evolution . . . . For the next forty-odd years Spencer carried out his plan of demonstrating the universal application of this formula.(6)

While Spencer's name is not very well known today, he was a major force in the latter half of the nineteenth century, and he influenced many who in turn have influenced our thinking today. Hofstadter says, "In the three decades after the Civil War it was impossible to be active in any field of intellectual work without mastering Spencer . . . The generation that acclaimed Grant as its hero took Spencer as its thinker."(7) According to Henry Holt,

> Probably no other philosopher . . . ever had such a vogue as Spencer had from about 1870 to 1890. Most preceding philosophers had presumably been mainly restricted to readers habitually given to the study of philosophy, but not only was Spencer considerably read and generally talked about by the whole intelligent world in England and America, but that world was wider than any that preceded it.(8)

As a result, according to Huntington Cairns, "Nineteenth-century social thought, after the formula of the theory of biological evolution, was dominated by a theory of cultural evolution."(9)

ECONOMICS

Spencer (1820-1903) is best known today for his economic theories, described as laissez faire capitalism and often called Social Darwinism. Unlike Biblical capitalism, which stresses initiative, industry, and private property, but which also stresses compassion and moral responsibility, Social Darwinism taught that the marketplace is a tooth-and-claw struggle in which survival of the fittest is the governing principle. It is the duty of a businessmen to drive his weaker competitors out of business, because in so doing he improves the quality of american business and advances the human race.

During that era of big business, many captains of industry shared Spencer's vision. Andrew Carnegie, the steel industrialist, describes in his autobiography how he had become despondent upon losing his faith in Christianity and the Bible, until he read Darwin and Spencer:

> I remember that light came as in a flood and all was clear. Not only had I got rid of theology and the supernatural, but I had found the truth of evolution. "All is well since all grows better," became my motto, my true source of comfort. Man was not created with an instinct for his own degradation, but from the lower he had risen to the higher forms. Nor is there any conceivable end to his march to perfection. His face is turned to the light; he stands in the sun and looks upward.(10)

Railroad magnate James J. Hill echoed a similar thought: "The fortunes of railroad companies are determined by the law of the survival of the fittest."(11) And John D. Rockefeller added, "The growth of a large business is merely a survival of the fittest . . . The American Beauty rose can be produced in the splendor and fragrance which bring cheer to its beholder only by sacrificing the early buds which grow up around it."(12)

It is largely because of this tooth-and-claw distorted version of capitalism that free enterprise is looked upon with some disfavor in many circles today.

THEOLOGY

Of all academic disciplines, theology might seem the most likely to be insulated from evolutionary thought. Yet the influence of evolution upon the study of the Bible is as clear as in any other field.

Jews and Christians have traditionally believed that the first five books of the Old Testament, Genesis through Deuteronomy, were written by Moses under divine inspiration. They have regarded God's law as given to Moses on Mt. Sinai, and they have viewed Israel's history as the struggle of the faithful to maintain the purity of God's revelation against the apostate and pagan forces that warred against it.

During the nineteenth century an alternative view arose. It is often called the documentary hypothesis, the Graf-Wellhausen theory (after its two principle architects), or, more commonly, the JEDP theory. The view holds that the Pentateuch was the work of four different authors whose names are unknown but who are identified by the letters J, E, D and P: "J", who always referred to God as Jehovah or Yahweh; "E", who always referred to God as Elohim; "D", who wrote the initial version of Deuteronomy; and "P", a priest who lived sometime after the Babylonian exile (605-539 B.C.) and who edited and redacted the works of J, E, and D and put the Pentateuch in substantially its present form.

The evidence for this theory is sadly lacking, and it is probably less popular today than it was fifty years ago. It does not seem to occur to these people that Moses, writing under the inspiration of the Holy Spirit over a long period of time and in different places and with different themes and purposes in mind, might have used more than one name for God. In fact, there are good reasons for the different usages: "Jehovah" is God's name; "Elohim" is the plural form of a generic word for god. One might use the word "elohim" for pagan gods, but one would never call a pagan god Jehovah.

Herbert F. Hahn, who shares the views of the liberal critics, forthrightly acknowledges that the JEDP theory is based upon evolutionary thought. He writes,

> . . . this conception did not grow merely from an objective reading of the sources. In a larger sense, it was a reflection of the intellectual temper of the times. The genetic conception of Old Testament history fitted in with the evolutionary principle of interpretation prevailing in contemporary science and philosophy. In the natural sciences, the influence of Darwin had made the theory of evolution the predominant hypothesis affecting research. In the historical sciences and in the areas of religious and philosophical thought, the influence after Hegel had substituted the notion of "becoming" for the idea of "being" . . . In every department of historical investigation the conception of development was being used to explain the history of man's thought, his institutions, and even his religious faith. It was not strange that the same principle should be applied to the explanation of Old Testament history.(13)

Concerning Julius Wellhausen, one of the principle architects of the Graf-Wellhausen theory, Hahn says,

He consciously based his exposition on the evolutionary view of history. . . . From the evolutionary point of view, which assumed that development invariably took place from lower to higher forms, it was inconceivable that the nomadic ancestors of the Israelites could have held the lofty, monotheistic conceptions ascribed to Abraham.(14)

Translation: Abraham could not have believed in the one Jehovah as Genesis describes him as believing, because Abraham was still too much of a cave-man! He hadn't evolved to the point of monotheism, so he simply believed in a large pantheon of gods as the other pagans of the time believed. By the time of Moses and the exodus from Egypt, Abraham's descendants had evolved to the point where they could believe in their God as greater than all the others but still one among many. Only when we get to the Babylonian exile do the children of Israel truly become monotheistic.

This view depends not on evidence but on evolutionary faith. As Hahn says,

. . . the history of Israel's religion no longer appeared as a continual struggle to maintain an ideal system established at the beginning; instead, it took on the character of gradual growth from the simple to the complex, with the Levitical institutions as the climax of the whole development. . . . The evolutionary conception proved of great value in ordering and explaining various phenomena of this sort which had puzzled earlier scholars. Now the characteristic ideas and institutions of each age could be understood as parts of the continuous process of development through which Israel's religion had gone.(15)

It is not surprising that evolution would influence such wide and diverse areas of human thought. One's beliefs about the nature of physical reality will affect one's beliefs about spiritual reality. One's beliefs about the nature and origin of the universe affects one's beliefs about the nature and origin of man. These in turn affect one's beliefs about God, His laws, His actions in history, His relationships with man, His provisions for man, His demands upon man, and His plan for the future. It is impossible, or at least intellectually unsound, to neatly separate thought into categories of the "religious" and "secular," for each has a profound effect upon the other.

LAW

For thousands of years, Jewish, Christian, and classical pagan thinkers had regarded law as the outworking of the will of God. Jews and Christians alike believed that God had spoken on Mt. Sinai and that Moses had recorded His laws. Classical Greek and Roman thinkers such as Sophocles, Plutarch, and Cicero spoke of the law of God. Theologians from Augustine to Aquinas to Luther and Calvin spoke of the law of God as revealed in Scripture and in the law of nature. English thinkers such as Blackstone and Locke expressed essentially the same view; and when Jefferson wrote in the Declaration of Independence of the "Laws of Nature and of Nature's God," he used language that all Americans from the sternest Puritan to the most radical Deist could accept. At the time this nation was founded, a consensus existed that human law is or should be man's attempt to follow the will of God as revealed by God through Scripture or through nature. And since God does not change, His law does not change either, although the application of His law may vary from one circumstances to another.(16)

Just as the evolutionary worldview has challenged the Christian worldview in every other field of academic discipline, so it has arisen to challenge the Christian view of law. The alternative view is generally known as legal positivism. It made its debut at the Harvard Law School in the 1870s under Harvard's dean, Christopher Columbus Langdell, and it reigns virtually unchallenged in most law schools today. Combining elements of the Hegelian dialectic (truth is a changing process), Comte's positivism (the only meaningful truth is that which can be empirically verified), Darwin and Spencer (the evolutionary view of man and the world), legal positivism can be summarized in five basic tenets:

(1) There is no higher law of God; or, if there is, it is irrelevant for the legal system today.

(2) Man is the source of law; law is law because the highest human authority, the state, has said it is law and has the power to enforce it.

(3) Since man is the source of law and man is an evolving animal, the law which man creates must evolve as well.

(4) Somebody must guide the evolution of law, since God isn't guiding it, and the persons best qualified to guide the law through their written decisions guide the evolution of law.

(5) The best and most "scientific" way to study law is to read the decisions of judges. After all, the true source of law is the mind of the judge, and the best way to study the mind of the

judge is to read the decisions he has written. Hence the study of law at most law schools today consists primarily of the reading of cases. This is called the case-law method of legal study, and it was pioneered by Dean Langdell of Harvard in the 1870s. Prior to that time the study of law consisted primarily of reading of statutes and classical and modern works of jurisprudence such as Blackstone's Commentaries, and apprenticing oneself to a successful lawyer and learning his ways. Some of America's greatest lawyers, including Clarence Darrow, Abraham Lincoln, and Chief Justice John Marshall, studied law the "old" way without ever going to law school, and their careers and reputations do not appear to have suffered too much as a result.

Oliver Wendell Holmes, Jr., a Harvard law graduate and Harvard law professor and an Associate Justice of the Supreme Court from 1902 to 1932, was probably the best-known exponent of legal positivism. Several of his statements clearly show the nature of legal positivism:

> For my own part I often doubt whether it would not be a gain if every word of moral significance could be banished from the law altogether, and other words adopted which should convey legal ideas uncolored by anything outside the law. . . .

> . . . for legal purposes a right is only the hypostasis of a prophecy -- the imagination of a substance supporting the fact that the public force will be brought to bear upon those who do things said to contravene it -- just as we talk of the force of gravitation accounting for the conduct of bodies in space. . . .

> No society has ever admitted that it could not sacrifice individual welfare to its own existence. . . .

> The prophecies of what the courts will do in fact and nothing more pretentious, are what I mean by the law. . . .(17)

Legal principles, Holmes believed, were not based upon divine principles or upon God-given human rights; rather, they are based on "deep-seated preferences."(18) Man is simply a complex animal, more complex than any ape but not of any greater intrinsic value than an animal.

Jerome Frank, a noted judge and law professor, summarized the view of legal positivism well:

> There is no rule by which you can force a judge to follow an old rule or by which you can predict when he will verbalize his conclusion in the form of a new rule, or by; which he can determine when to consider a case an exception to an old rule, or by which he can make up his mind to accept one or another old rule to explain or guide his judgment. His decision is primary, the rules he may happen to refer to are incidental.

> The law, therefore, consists of decisions, not of rules. If so, then whenever a judge decides a case he is making law.(19)

This evolving view of law, in which the judge controls the evolutionary process in the name of humanity, is rooted squarely in evolutionary thought. Holmes wrote to Sir Frederick Pollock in 1894 that no writer in English except Charles Darwin had done so much as Herbert Spencer to affect our whole way of thinking.(20) It is not surprising, then, that this evolutionary worldview affects our way of looking at law and even the Constitution as well.

President Woodrow Wilson argued for an evolutionary interpretation of the Constitution in his book The New Freedom. He noted, first, that the Constitution was framed in terms of a Newtonian worldview:

> . . . in every generation all sorts of speculation and thinking tend to fall under the formula of the dominant thought of the age. For example, after the Newtonian Theory of the Universe had been developed, almost all thinking tended to express itself in the analogies of the Newtonian Theory and since the Darwinian Theory has reigned amongst us, everybody is likely to express whatever he wishes to expound in terms of development and accommodation to environment.(21)

By the Newtonian Theory, he means the worldview of Sir Isaac Newton, which saw the universe in terms of unchanging, absolute, God-ordained laws: the laws of mathematics, the laws of motion, of physics, chemistry, and the like, and also the moral laws that govern mankind. Wilson continued:

> . . . the Constitution of the United States had been made under the dominion of the Newtonian theory. You have only to read the papers of The Federalist to see that fact written on every page. They speak of the "checks and balances" of the Constitution, and use to express their idea the simile of the organization of the universe, and particularly of the solar system, how by the attraction of gravitation the various parts are held in

their orbits; and then they proceed to represent Congress, the Judiciary, and the President as a sort of imitation of the solar system.

They were only following the English Whigs, who gave Great Britain its modern Constitution. Not that those Englishmen analyzed the matter, or had any theory about it; Englishmen care little for theories. It was a Frenchman, Montesquieu, who pointed out to them how faithfully they had copied Newton's description of the heavens.

The makers of our Federal Constitution read Montesquieu with true scientific enthusiasm. They were scientists in their way -- the best way of their age -- those fathers of the nation. Jefferson wrote "the laws of Nature" -- and then by the way of afterthought -- "and of Nature's God." And they constructed a government as they would have constructed an orrery -- to display the laws of Nature. Politics in their thought was a variety of mechanics. The Constitution was founded on the law of gravitation. The government was to exist and move by virtue of the efficacy of "checks and balances."

Except for his reference to Jefferson's phrase as an "afterthought" (it was a direct quote from Blackstone), Wilson has stated the Framers' views correctly. They viewed the world in Newtonian terms of fixed, absolute laws, and in so doing their views were fully compatible with those of biblical Christianity. As I have demonstrated in my book Christianity and the Constitution (Grand Rapids: Baker, 1987, 1990), the vast majority of the Founding Fathers were professing orthodox Christians. Even those few who probably were not Christians, like Jefferson and Franklin, strongly believed in a God who governs the universe according to His laws.

And the Founding Fathers fully intended that the Constitution should be interpreted according to the unchanging principles that were in effect when it was written. The recent call for jurisprudence of original intent, issued so forthrightly by Attorney General Edwin Meese at the meeting of the American Bar Association in 1985, , would have found the Framers nodding in strong agreement. In fact, not knowing of the rise of evolutionary humanism and legal positivism over the intervening two centuries, they would have wondered why it is even necessary to articulate points that are so self-evidently true.

The Founding Fathers clearly believed in jurisprudence of original intent. James Madison, whom many call the father of the Constitution, wrote:

[If] the sense in which the Constitution was accepted and ratified by the Nation . . . be not the guide in expounding it, there can be no security for a faithful exercise of its powers.

His views were echoed by Thomas Jefferson:

The Constitution on which our Union rests, shall be administered by me according to the safe and honest meaning contemplated by the plain understanding of the people of the United States, at the time of its adoption.

And George Washington, Chairman of the Convention and first President thereafter, warned,

If, in the opinion of the people, the distribution or modification of the Constitutional powers be at any particular wrong, let it be corrected by an amendment in the way the Constitution designates. But let there be no change by usurpation; though this may in one instance be the instrument of good, it is the customary weapon by which free governments are destroyed.

But while Wilson correctly understood the views of the Founding Fathers, he concluded that they were wrong in their Newtonian view of the Constitution:

The trouble with the theory is that government is not a machine, but a living thing. It falls, not under the theory of the universe, but under the theory of organic life. It is accountable to Darwin, not to Newton. . . . No living thing can have its organs offset against each other, as checks, and live. On the contrary, its life is dependent upon their quick co-operation, their ready response to the commands of instinct or intelligence, their amicable community of purpose. . . . Living political constitutions must be Darwinian in structure and in practice. Society is a living organism and must obey the laws of Life, not of mechanics; it must develop.

All that progressives ask or desire is permission -- in an era when "development," "evolution," is the scientific word -- to interpret the Constitution according to the Darwinian principle; all they ask is recognition of the fact that a nation is a living thing and not a machine.

When Attorney General Meese delivered his call for a return to jurisprudence of original intent at the ABA meeting in 1985, he touched off a storm of protest. Among the sharpest and most visible was the reply of Associate Justice William Brennan, the most eloquent member of the Court's liberal bloc. Speaking at a symposium at Georgetown University later in 1985, Justice Brennan declared that "the genius of the Constitution rests not in any static meaning it might have had in a world that is dead and gone." Rather, each generation must reinterpret the Constitution for itself "through an evolutionary process [that] is inevitable and, indeed, it is the true interpretive genius of the text."

This was not the first time Justice Brennan had used the evolutionary concept for constitutional interpretation. In Furman v. Georgia, 408 U.S. 238 at 299 (1972), the Court considered a capital punishment case. Nine separate opinions were written in the case, five of which concluded that capital punishment, as applied in that situation, was unconstitutional. The various justices gave differing opinions for reaching their conclusions, but Justices Brennan and Marshall concluded that capital punishment today violates the Eighth Amendment prohibition against "cruel and unusual punishment." How could this be when the authors of the Eighth Amendment clearly believed in capital punishment and stated their belief in concurrently passing the Fifth Amendment? Borrowing a phrase from former Chief Justice Earl Warren, Brennan and Marshall wrote "that the words of the Amendment are not precise, and that their scope is not static. The Amendment must draw its meaning from the evolving standards of decency that mark the progress of a maturing society." Brennan added, "The evolution of this punishment evidences, not that it is an inevitable part of the American scene, but that it has proved progressively more troublesome to the national conscience." In other words, even though capital punishment was not cruel and unusual by the primitive and barbaric standard of 1789, it is cruel and unusual by the enlightened and human standard of today!

This evolutionary interpretation is not limited to the liberal bloc. Four ears later, in 1976, the Supreme Court considered another capital punishment case in Gregg v. Georgia, 428 U.S. 153. By a 5-4 vote, the majority upheld capital punishment. Brennan and Marshall dissented, again arguing the evolving standard of decency. But the majority, noting the number of states that had adopted capital punishment laws, concluded that society had not yet evolved to the point at which capital punishment could be said to be cruel and unusual. Note that the basic evolutionary interpretation is not disputed by the majority or the minority; the argument is over how far we have progressed on the evolutionary scale!

The evolutionary model of constitutional interpretation rests upon American faith and hope that change is progress, and the evolution of American law will always be in an upward direction toward greater recognition of human rights and human dignity. The abortion battle is a case in point. While resting the case for abortion "rights" on an ephemeral right of privacy that supposedly hovers somewhere around the due process clause of the Fourteenth Amendment or, even more vaguely, somewhere in the "penumbra" of the Constitution, the more honest of abortion advocates forthrightly admit that the so-called right to an abortion rests upon a very strained interpretation of the Constitution -- especially if original intent makes any difference. But the evolutionary approach gives the Constitution breathing room to expand and encompass more and more rights as time goes on (except, of course, the rights of unborn children).

But what if this evolutionary faith in upward progress is wrong? What if the world isn't inevitably getting better? What if history moves in cycles, sometimes upward and sometimes downward? What if the Bible is correct in teaching that man was created in an ideal state and that he has degenerated since the Fall? What if, as premillennial Christians believe, the world is getting worse and will continue to get worse until and through he Tribulation? Don't the signs of the times -- the savagery of modern weaponry, the crime rate, the rise of Satanism, acid rock, violence in our movies and television, the increase of child abuse, etc. -- indicate that we are moving toward a new age of barbarism?

In such an age, an "evolving standard of decency" is no firm basis on which to rest human rights. The same court that can use an evolving standard to abolish capital punishment, can also use an evolving standard to approve death by torture and other atrocities as acceptable under the "evolving standard of decency" that marks the progress of a mature, broad-minded, tolerant and decadent society. And the same court that can read into the Constitution new rights that aren't really there (such as the right to an abortion or the right to engage in homosexual conduct) can also read out of the Constitution rights that are there (such as the right to own firearms, or to own property, or to freely exercise one's religion). No, the only firm basis for protecting human rights is the timeless standard of the Constitution as interpreted according to the original intent of the Founding Fathers, men who drafted the Constitution according to the timeless principles of the Word of God.

God's Word provides a firm basis for believing in human rights and human equality, for it teaches that man is created in the image of God (Genesis 1:27). Evolutionary theory undermines that belief and opens the door to totalitarianism and racism -- not that evolutionists are inevitably totalitarian or racist, most of them are not; but evolution undermines the basis for believing in human equality and human rights. If man is the result of a naturalistic evolutionary process, what is the basis for believing in human rights? Did ape-men have rights? If so, where did those rights come from? What basis does the evolutionist have for believing that man has any more rights than an ape, or an amphibian, or an amoeba?

And if man is the result of a natural evolutionary process, how can we be sure that some races haven't evolved further than others? In fact, in the famous Scopes trial of 1925, the textbook John Scopes used to teach evolution to his students contained blatant racism! H.L. Mencken didn't see fit to tell the American public about this, nor did the American Civil Liberties Union which financed Clarence Darrow's defense of Scopes. But on page 196 of Hunter's A Civic Biology, the text Scopes used, the following language appears:

> The Races of Man. -- At the present time there exist upon the earth five races or varieties of man, each very different from the other in instincts, social customs, and, to an extent, in structure. These are the Ethiopian or negro type, originating in Africa; the Malay or brown race, from the islands of the Pacific; the American Indian; the Mongolian or yellow race, including the natives of China, Japan, and the Eskimos; and finally, the highest type of all, the Caucasians, represented by the civilized white inhabitants of Europe and America.

Nor can evolutionists escape the plain language of Adolph Hitler in Mein Kampf:

> If nature does not wish that weaker individuals should mate with stronger, she wishes even less that a superior race should intermingle with an inferior one. Why? Because in such a case her efforts, throughout hundreds of thousands of years, to establish an evolutionary higher stage of life, may thus be rendered futile.

Lon L. Fuller correctly notes that "It is no wonder that for the seventy-five years prior to Hitler's rise in power the positivist philosophy of law achieved a standing in Germany that it had achieved nowhere else. The German scholars considered it scientific, and thought that, in contrast, Anglo-Saxon law was a mess."

It is reassuring to remember that Jefferson and the Founders of this nation rested their faith in human equality and human rights squarely upon the biblical doctrine of creation:

> We hold these truths to be self-evident, that all men are created equal, that they are endowed by their Creator with certain unalienable Rights, that among these are Life, Liberty, and the pursuit of Happiness.

The positivist view of law leads to judicial tyranny, not only in Nazi Germany but also in the United States. For if judges are not bound by the plain wording of the Constitution, interpreted according to the intent of those who wrote and ratified it, their judicial power knows no bounds. As Attorney General Meese warned the ABA,

> It was not long ago when constitutional interpretation was understood to move between the poles of "strict construction" and "loose construction." Today, it is argued that constitutional interpretation moves between "interpretive review" and "non-interpretive review." As one observer has pointed out, under the old system the question was how to read the Constitution; under the new approach, the question is whether to read the Constitution. . . .

> The result is that some judges and academics feel free (to borrow the language of the great New York jurist, Chancellor James Kent) to "roam at large in the trackless fields of their own imaginations."

The further result is that these same judges and justices wield enormous and virtually unchecked power. Far from being the "least dangerous branch" of government, as Alexander Hamilton described the judiciary, the federal judiciary has become the most powerful and important branch of government, having a virtual veto over anything any other branch or level of government may do. The result is government by the majority vote of a nine-person committee of lawyers, unelected and holding office in effect for life.

Some liberal scholars have forthrightly argued that judges and justices should wield such power. The late Alexander Bickel, Professor of Constitutional Law at Yale, wrote:

> The function of Justices . . . is to immerse themselves in the tradition of our society and of kindred societies that have gone before, in history and in the sediment of history which is law, and . . . in the thought and the vision of the philosophers and the poets. The Justices will then be fit to extract "fundamental presuppositions" from their deepest selves, but in fact from the evolving morality of our tradition.

So judges are to study tradition, history, the philosophers, and the poets. Not the Constitution? Not the _Federalist_? Not Blackstone's _Commentaries_? Not the Bible?

And why should judges wield such power? Why not mechanics, or farmers, or businessmen, or legislators, or clergymen? Here is Professor Bickel's answer:

> Courts have certain capacities for dealing with matters of principle that legislatures and executives do not possess. Judges have, or should have, the leisure, the training, and the insulation to follow the ways of the scholar in pursuing the ends of government.

s to following the "ways off the scholar" in pursuing the ends of government, I am tempted to reply with William F. Buckley, Jr., that I would rather be governed by the first one hundred names in the Boston telephone book than by the Harvard faculty. But I will content myself with the words of Robert Bork, who served as the Alexander Bickel Professor of Law at Yale as well as serving as a federal judge:

> Other than to heave a wistful sigh, I will pass by this vision of a judge's life without comment.

RECLAIMING OUR CONSTITUTION

What can be done to return our nation to the rule of law under the Constitution? Of all of the branches of government, the judiciary is probably the hardest to influence. To some extent the Founders intended it that way. They wanted the judiciary to be somewhat independent of the political process, so the judges would make their decisions based upon principles of right and wrong rather than political popularity or expediency. Governor Morris, who drafted most of the final wording of the Constitution, strongly favored life tenure for appellate judges because "Those who are charged with the important duties of administering justice should, if possible, depend only on God." The problem is, too many judges today do not depend on God. In fact, it could be said that many judges think they are gods!

Nevertheless, there are steps we can take:

(1)   We can support law schools with a Christian mission, such as Regent University in Virginia, Simon Greenleaf School of Law in California, and Cumberland School of Law and Jones School of Law both of Alabama, as they seek to train a new generation of lawyers with a distinctive vision of law.

(2)   We can support Christian groups on secular law school campuses, such as the Christian Legal Society and the Rutherford Institute, and the conservative Federalist Society, as they work within the secular law school community for Christian and/or conservative constitutional values.

(3)   We can support groups like the Rutherford Institute, the Christian Legal Society, the National Legal Foundation, the Home School Legal Defense Association, Concerned Women for America, Eagle Forum, the American Family Association, Focus on the Family, the National Center for Constitutional Studies, and many others as they work to influence our nation for conservative Biblical values.

(4)   We can work for the appointment or election of judges who believe in jurisprudence of original intent. Again, it is much more difficult to evaluate the philosophy or ideology of judges than it is for candidates for other offices. Many conservative and liberal groups rate candidates for legislative offices according to how they vote on key issues; a group might take ten key issues, list how each legislative offices according to how they vote on key issues; a group might take ten key issues, list how each legislator voted, and rate each legislator 80% liberal, or 40% conservative, or however he stacks up. It is much more difficult to rate judges, because no two judges vote on the same issues; each judge has his own caseload. To help people vote intelligently on the election or retention of judges, it is essential that people start examining the general record of judges and let the public know the judges' record. Again, no two judges vote on the same issues; but the fact that Judge Hanson convicted 76% of the drunk driving defendants in his courtroom last ear while Judge Smith convicted only 38% of the drunk driving defendants in his courtroom, says something about their performance in office

(5)   A constitutional amendment providing that "This Constitution shall be interpreted strictly according to the intent of those who framed and ratified it" might help to restore jurisprudence of original intent. The problem is that this amendment would be interpreted by the same judges who have used the evolving standard in the past, but it might cause some judges to temper their activism.

(6)   Article III, Section 2, Clause (2) of the Constitution provides that, except for a few cases involving original jurisdiction, the Supreme Court shall have appellate jurisdiction "with such Exceptions, and under such Regulations as the Congress shall make." Many are unaware that Congress has the authority to limit the appellate jurisdiction of the Supreme Court. This does not violate the constitutional separation of powers; it is one of the checks and balances the Framers of the Constitution wisely placed upon the Supreme Court. In the early decades of our constitutional history Congress limited the Court's appellate jurisdiction with some frequency, but Congress has not done so since Reconstruction. The Framers intended this check to be used, and the current flag-burning controversy might provide an appropriate occasion to use it.

These remedies may help curb the power of the Supreme Court, but they will not avert the danger of tyranny in general. For only God's law can limit the authority of man's law. Unless there exist a higher authority by which the law of man must be judged, man is his own judge, and the state (the highest expression of humanity in the pagan view) can do no wrong.

As Hallowell says,

> It is a short step from the conception of law as the product of the will of the state, whether the state be conceived as an instrument for the satisfaction of human desires (utilitarianism) or whether conceived as the personification of the good life (idealism) o the notion that law is the command of the stronger . . . Since the will of the state has no reality apart from the will of individuals who act in the name of the state the identification of the law with the will of the state amounts in practice to the identification of the law with the will of those who act in the name of the state. . .
>
> From this point of view every decision is a correct one. There can be no such thing as an incorrect decision or an unjust one. It is not the content of a decision that makes it law but the source from which it emanates. . . Ultimately the basis of law is fear and force rather than consent and justice. . .
>
> As an augury of things to come realistic jurisprudence certainly suggests that tyranny is an inevitability. For the only way out of the intellectual and moral anarchy underlying the realist's conception of the law is tyranny. If force alone, as Justice Holmes believed, is the only possible arbiter of our "deep-seated preferences", if moral judgments are nothing more than expressions of individual taste or preference, and if law, as Jerome Frank declares, is simply what men arbitrarily declare it to be, then we have no choice but to submit our differences to the arena of force. In that arena it is not the best reason that will prevail but the mightiest fist.

Liberty within the constraints of God's law, or tyranny under the oppression of man's law: That, ultimately, is the choice God gives to us. Which we choose depends largely upon whether we accept a creationist or evolutionary worldview.

REFERENCES:

1.   Richard Hofstadter, <u>Social Darwinism in American Thought</u> (New York: George Braziller, Inc., 1944, 1955), p. 3.

2.   Wendell Bird, <u>The Origin of Species Revisited</u> (New York: Philosophical Library, 1987), I:22-23, 35-37, 84-85; II:201, 219, 312, 319-322.

3.   John H. Hallowell, <u>Main Currents in Modern Political Thought</u> (New York: Holt, Rinehart and Winston, 1950, 1960), p. 303.

4.   <u>The World Book Encyclopedia</u>, s.v., "Hegel."

5.   Hallowell, pp. 33-34.

6.   Huntington Cairns, <u>Law and the Social Sciences</u> (New York: Augustus M. Kelly, 1935, 1969), pp. 136-137.

7.   Hofstadter, pp. 33-34.

8.   Henry Holt, quoted by Hofstadter, p. 34.

9.   Cairns. p. 161.

10.   Andrew Carnegie, <u>Autobiography</u> (Boston, 1920), p. 339, quoted by Hofstadter, p. 45.

11.   James J. Hill, <u>Highways of Progress</u> (New York, 1910), p. 126; quoted by Hofstadter, p. 45.

12. John D. Rockefeller, quoted by Hofstadter, p. 45.

13. Herbert F. Hahn, The Old Testament in Modern Research (Philadelphia: Fortress Press, 1954, 1966), pp. 9-10.

14. Ibid., p. 12.

15. Ibid., p. 8.

16. For a general discussion of a biblical view of law, see John Eidsmoe, The Christian Legal Advisor (Grand Rapids: Baker Book house, 1984, 1987), Chapters One through Six.

17. Oliver Wendell Holmes, Jr., quoted by Hallowell, pp. 359-367.

18. Holmes, quoted by Hallowell, p. 359.

19. Jerome Frank, Law and the Modern Mind (New York: Coward-McAnn, Inc., 1935), p. 128. It should be noted that Frank apparently moved away from positivism and toward natural law theory shortly before he died.

20. Merle Curti, The Growth of American Thought (New York: Harper & Row, 1943, 1951, 1964), p. 552.

21. Woodrow Wilson, The New Freedom (New York, 1914), pp. 44-48.

22. Ibid.

23. Edwin Meese, III, Address to the American Bar Association, Washington, D.C., July 9, 1985; adapted in "Toward a Jurisprudence of Original Intention," Benchmark, Vol II., No. 1, January-February 1986, pp. 1-10, at 6.

24. James Madison, The Writing of James Madison, ed. G. Hunt (1899-1910), p. 191; quoted by William d. Graves, Brief of Defendants, Bell and McCord v. The Little Axe Independent School District No. 70 of Cleveland County, in the U.S. District Court for the Western District of Oklahoma, filed May 13, 1982, p. 17.

25. Thomas Jefferson, quoted in Thomas Jefferson (Salt Lake City, Utah: Freeman Institute, American Classic Series, 1981), p. 65.

26. George Washington, American Historical Documents (New York: Barnes and Nobel, Inc. 1960), p. 144.

27. Woodrow Wilson, op. cit.

28. William Brennan, Jr. "The Constitution of the United States: Contemporary Ratification," Teaching Symposium, Georgetown University, Washington, D.C., October 12, 1985, p. 39.

29. George William Hunter, A Civic Biology: Presented in Problems (Chicago: American Book Company, 1914), p. 196; reprinted in Monkey Trial: State of Tennessee v. John Thomas Scopes, ed. Sheldon Grebstein (Boston: Houghton Mifflin, 1960), p. 30.

30. Adolph Hitler, Mein Kampf.

31. Lon L. Fuller, "Positivism and Fidelity in Law -- A Reply to Professor Hart," Harvard Law Review, Vol. 71, No. 4, February 1958, pp. 630-672; cited by Herbert Schlossberg, Idols for Destruction (Nashville: Thomas Nelson, 1983), p. 207.

32. Declaration of Independence.

33. Meese, op. cit.

34. Lino Graglia, Professor of Constitutional Law, University of Texas, "Judicial Review on the Basis of 'Regime Principles': A Prescription for Government by Judges," South Texas Law Journal, Vol. 26, No. 3 (Fall 1985), pp. 435-452, at 446.

35. Alexander Bickel, The Least Dangerous Branch (1962), p. 236.

36. Ibid., pp. 25-26.

37. Robert H. Bork, "Styles in Constitutional Theory," South Texas Law Journal, Vol. 26, No. 3 (Fall 1985), pp. 383-396, at 389.

38. Gouverneur Morris, Speech Prepared for the King of France, reprinted in Jared Sparks, _The Life of Gouverneur Morris, with Selections from His Correspondence and Miscellaneous Papers_ (Boston: Gray and Bowen, 1832), II: 506.

39. Hallowell, pp. 343, 363-364, 367.